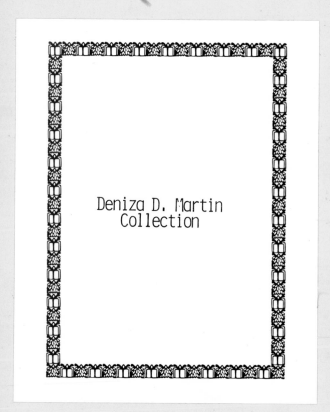

LORD ROSEBERY

Lord Rosebery, about 1869

Lord Rosebery

by

THE MARQUESS OF CREWE, K.G.

ILLUSTRATED

Harper & Brothers Publishers

NEW YORK AND LONDON

1931

LORD ROSEBERY

Copyright, 1931, by Robert Offley Ashburton Crewe-Milnes

Printed in the United States

—————

FIRST EDITION

L-F.

TO

MY WIFE

THIS ATTEMPT TO TELL THE STORY OF

ONE WE BOTH LOVED

July, 1931

CONTENTS

[vii]

[viii]

ILLUSTRATIONS

PREFACE

Soon after Lord Rosebery died his family asked me to write his Life. I had seen more of him than most could. There was a long-standing family friendship; I had known him for fifty years and been his near relation for thirty. But I did not disguise from myself the difficulty of the task. There was a great mass of material, of which some important elements were separately sorted, while others were indiscriminately dotted about at his different homes. He seldom destroyed even a trivial letter, so the work of selection was arduous. And the multiplicity of his interests made it imperative to include some illustration of each. But the labour was lightened by the ungrudging help rendered by the surviving members of Rosebery's family, by his secretary Mr. Stanley Brown, and by some of his old servants.

The material used in writing this book—apart from official documents and the correspondence of which acknowledgement is made in the Preface—may be summarized under three heads. First from the time he grew up, until his serious illness, Lord Rosebery made entries in a Lett's Diary. Often he only mentioned the weather and his own movements, but he sometimes included short notes of great interest. Next, when travelling abroad he generally kept a tolerably copious journal, using a students' notebook. Lastly, especially in his later years, he jotted down impressions and appreciations, of persons or situations, on script sheets of letter-paper. Lady Rosebery's brief diaries have also been helpful.

It will be observed that I have not attempted to give in detail a political history, even of the few years during which Lord Rosebery held high office. Such notable books as John Morley's *Life of Gladstone*, Lord Fitzmaurice's *Lord Granville*, Mr. A. G. Gardiner's *Sir William Harcourt*, and Mr. J. A. Spender's *Sir Henry Campbell-Bannerman* cover much of the same ground, and I am greatly indebted to these, to say nothing of such histories as are concerned with the years from 1880 to 1910.

I have purposely placed the Racing chapters at the end of either volume. Though the turf filled an important part in Rosebery's life, it seemed better not to break the continuity of the ordinary narrative by frequent interpolations of detail on a subject not of universal interest.

In the first place, I must offer my grateful duty to His Majesty the King, who graciously allowed me access to all relevant papers in the Windsor archives. It will be seen how greatly the book has gained from this permission.

Next I must respectfully thank those friends of Lord Rosebery and myself who have responded generously to my appeal for his letters. If I specially mention a few names, it is because their contributions have been large in bulk, and therefore frequently serviceable; but some single letters have proved to be of great value. The Trustees of Mr. Gladstone's papers were good enough to send me all the Rosebery letters, and I have also been favoured with his correspondence with Mrs. Drew (Mary Gladstone). The late Lord Esher was equally prompt, and Sir Robert Perks made an invaluable contribution. I have to thank Lord Spencer for a series of letters to his father and his uncle; Miss Haldane for those to her brother; and the sons of Sir George Trevelyan and Mr. Frederic Harrison for copious correspondence with their distinguished parents.

Outside the inner circle of the family, Sir George Murray and Lord Novar knew Rosebery better than anybody, and I cannot thank either sufficiently for his assistance. Sir George was also one of the executors of Rosebery's will; his colleague, Mr. C. Edmunds, long agent at Mentmore, has also helped me greatly.

Mr. John Buchan edited in 1921 two volumes of *Miscellanies* in which most of Rosebery's non-political addresses and some of his shorter writings are included. I have found these volumes indispensable for reference, and Mr. Buchan has been kind enough to read the proofs of the Scottish portions of the book.

Rosebery's brother, Everard Primrose, contemplated writing a history of the family. This was never done, but Mr. J. Macbeth Forbes of Edinburgh embarked on the enterprise. The work shows signs of research, its author evidently being specially attracted by the legal transactions and personal affairs of the earlier Primroses, while sufficiently narrating their public doings. It seems never to have been published, and it is questionable whether any copy exists besides the proof which was sent to Dalmeny. Apparently the notices of recent family doings, though harmless enough, were not approved there.

In 1900 Miss Jane T. Stoddart, a Scottish lady, brought out a popular sketch of Lord Rosebery in one volume adorned by a number of illustrations. It is a lively and good-natured chronicle of its hero's public and private life, evidently inspired by much respect and admiration.

I launch this barque on the waves of public opinion with some words which Lord Davidson of Lambeth wrote to me when a biography was being talked of:

"I have certainly known no public man's life so difficult to depict in its odd combinations and perplexing variety of facets.

"But there was never to me any doubt as to the sterling quality of the underlying metal."

CREWE

London
September, 1931

CHAPTER I

The Primrose Family—Boyhood—Eton

THE old Royal Burgh of Culross, on the northern shore of the Firth of Forth, some seven miles from Dunfermline, is described by a Scottish author as "a nook of Fife, difficult to get at, and still harder to get away from." The family of Colville, whose title is attached to the Burgh, became its principal lairds, but at the close of the fifteenth century the town and its neighbourhood knew many inhabitants of the name of Primrose, written in half a dozen various forms, as was usual in that age. There were lands styled Primrose near Dunfermline, the property of its ancient abbey, but there is no reason to claim that the Primroses in or near Culross could describe themselves as "of that ilk." They were small landowners and "portioners" in Culross district, and, like many of their kind, brought up their sons to the liberal professions—the Church, the Law, and Medicine. The exact inter-relationships of many of this busy family during the sixteenth century, and the earlier years of the seventeenth when the Scottish and English crowns were united, remain obscure. One Archibald "Prymrois" was a collector of the King's taxes in 1588, and became the chief adviser of King James VI for the Scottish Inland Revenue. Gilbert Primrose was Sergeant Chirurgeon to the same sovereign both in Edinburgh and afterwards in London, dying in 1616. A younger physician, James Primrose, endeavoured, with misplaced ardour, to refute Harvey's demonstration of the circulation of the blood,[1] but also published a work[2] exposing the folly of various popular medical theories, such as that forbidding the linen of the sick to be changed; another Gilbert, a man of real distinction, became Pastor of the Reformed Church at Bordeaux, and later of the French Church founded by King Edward VI in London, ending as a Canon of Windsor; and a third Gilbert

---

[1] *Exercitationes et Animadversiones in Librum de Motu Cordis et Circulatione Sanguinis.* (London, 1630.)
[2] *De Vulgi Erroibus in Medicina.* (London, 1638.)

was assistant to his father James Primrose as Clerk to the Privy Council.

This James Primrose, who was born about 1570, became a notable figure in Scotland, and as the instrument of the purely personal rule of King James VI in his northern kingdom, exercised powers that were almost despotic. He can be regarded as the Great Elector, so to speak, of the Primrose line. His son Archibald Primrose proceeded to establish the dynasty on a solid foundation. Born in 1616, he succeeded his father as Clerk of the Privy Council when only twenty-five years old, and became the confidential agent of Charles I. He fought under Montrose, was convicted of high treason, and was fortunate in escaping with his life. In 1651 he followed Charles II on the march that ended at Worcester, and was created a Baronet of Nova Scotia a month before that crowning disaster. His estates were confiscated, but he does not seem to have been personally molested. When the tide turned in 1660 he at once rose to the surface as Lord Clerk Register of Scotland, and soon afterwards became a Lord of Session, with the title of Lord Carrington. The Lord Clerk Register was one of the eight great officers of state who sat *ex officio* in the Scottish Parliament, and Sir Archibald was the principal draughtsman of the startling Rescissory Act, which annulled all the proceedings of Parliament during the past twenty-eight years, and of the series of Acts declaring the royal prerogative. His critical friend, Bishop Burnet, later noted: "He often confessed to me that he thought he was as one bewitched while he drew them; for not considering the ill use which might be made of them afterwards, he drew them with preambles full of extravagant rhetoric reflecting severely on the proceedings of the late times, and swelled them up with the highest phrases and fullest clauses that he could invent." This would be impossible nowadays, but even in these less spacious times we have known briefer and less ornate preambles that have brought trouble upon their authors.

There has been no period in British or in any other history when intrigue flourished more rankly than in the reign of Charles II, and even a man of Sir Archibald Primrose's adroitness was bound sooner or later to become its victim. He could not steer a permanent course between the rivalries of the Earl of Middleton and the Duke of Lauderdale, and he was first deprived of his office of Lord Clerk Register and given the lower appointment of Justice-General. Two years later he was again retired, and in 1679 he died at the age of sixty-three. He had bought, in 1662, the Castle of Barnbougle, with

its surrounding estate of Dalmeny, from the 4th Earl of Hadding-
ton, and had also acquired various other properties in the Lothians.
His portrait hangs at Dalmeny—a sidelong, furtive figure, but by
no means devoid of strength of character.

Bishop Burnet's summary of his character has often been quoted:

"The subtilest of all Lord Middletoun's friends was Sir Archibald
Primrose; a man of long and great practice in affairs; for he and his
father had served the crown successively a hundred years all but one,
when he was turned out of employment. He was a dexterous man of
business: he always had expedients ready at any difficulty. He had an
art of speaking to all men according to their sense of things: and so
drew out their secrets, while he concealed his own: for words went for
nothing with him. He said everything that was necessary to persuade
those he spoke to, that he was of their mind; and did it in so genuine
a way, that he seemed to speak his heart. He was always for soft
counsels and slow methods; and thought that the chief thing that a
great man ought to do was to raise his family and his kindred, who
naturally stick to him; for he had seen so much of the world, that he did
not depend much on friends, and so took no care in making any."[3]

Sir Archibald was twice married, first to Elizabeth Keith, an
offshoot of the great family of the Earls Marischal; and secondly
to Agnes, daughter of Sir William Gray of Pittendrum, and widow
of Sir James Dundas of Newliston. By the first marriage he had
five sons and three daughters, by the second he had one son and two
daughters.

The early constitutional history of Scotland is dark and confused
from the absence of such continuous documentary evidence as is
available to students in England; but it is established that peerages,
of the English pattern, did not exist there till late in the sixteenth
century, and that they were not legalised in the strict sense till 1689.
The great territorial earldoms dating from the twelfth century,
mainly held by families of Norman origin, the powerful lords who
guarded the English border, owning lands in the south and east, and
the chiefs of the most powerful Highland septs, made up a feudal
nobility as turbulent and masterful as the Orsini and Savelli of
mediæval Rome. It was in no sense parliamentary. The great Baron
had his seat in the Estates, but so had the small freeholder who was
a tenant-in-chief. And as the representation of shires and burghs
became systematised there grew up alongside the feudal baronage a

[3] *History of His Own Time*, Burnet (*History of the Reign of King Charles II*,
1660). (Oxford Clarendon Press, 1823, vol. i, p. 178.)

[3]

noblesse de robe, which has no exact parallel in England, but bears some resemblance to the French order so described. The French Parliaments became in the end purely legal bodies because the Kings of France were usually able to stave off all popular government in a way seldom open to the Kings of Scotland. At the same time the Three Estates of the Scottish Parliament, while struggling inter- mittently to play their part in legislation, regularly carried on their judicial functions. The College of Justice was a Committee of the Estates dating in its original form from the fourteenth century, and its members bore, as they still bear, the title of "Lord." But there was also a preponderating legal element in what we should now call the Civil Service. Writers and advocates, many of them cadets of landowning families, became secretaries and auditors in the service of the Crown, and from time to time were ennobled. From such origins sprang the northern *noblesse de robe*, which included names as distinguished as those of Rollo and Hope, Napier and Nairne.

However, neither Sir Archibald Primrose's services, nor those of his father, quite raised him to the peerage, and his eldest surviving son, Sir William Primrose, who had been jobbed into a high legal office in his seventeenth year, neglected his duties, was dismissed, became paralysed, and died young.

His wife was Mary Scot of Thirlestane, and by her he had seven children, of whom the eldest surviving son, James, succeeded as a child to the baronetcy and the estate of Carrington. He was elected Member of Parliament for the County of Edinburgh in Queen Anne's first Parliament in 1703, and in November of the same year was created Viscount Primrose, with the addition of two baronies. This elevation of a man of twenty-four may perhaps have been partly due to the services of his forbears to earlier Stuart sovereigns, and partly to the fact that his half-uncle, Archibald, representing the younger line, had already been made a peer in 1700. James, Lord Primrose, married Mary Campbell, daughter of the 2nd Earl of Loudoun, by whom he had four children, and, though he took part in one of Marlborough's campaigns, is remembered only as a matri- monial misdemeanant. The story goes that Lady Primrose, following a practice as old as King Saul and as modern as the advertisement columns of to-day's newspaper, went to consult a fashionable pro- fessor of the occult, having for a long time had no news of her absent husband. Looking into a magic mirror, she witnessed a marriage ceremony in a foreign church, which was suddenly inter- rupted by the arrival of armed intruders. Later, she heard from her

[4]

brother that, on that very day, he had chanced to be in Holland, and had forcibly interfered to prevent Lord Primrose's marriage to an innocent Dutch girl of great fortune. The tale is told in Dr. Robert Chamber's *Traditions of Edinburgh*, and by Sir Walter Scott, under fictitious names, in the story *My Aunt Margaret's Mirror*.[4]

The scapegrace returned to Scotland, and died there when only twenty-seven. His two sons succeeded in turn to his title, the elder, Archibald, dying as a boy of sixteen, the younger, Hugh, distinguishing himself in the Army under Prince Eugène, and dying as a Colonel, in 1741, before he was forty. He married the daughter of Dean Drelincourt, but was childless, so that his baronetcy, and possibly his peerages, passed to his cousin, the 2nd Earl of Rosebery.

Archibald Primrose, the eldest son of Sir Archibald, Lord Carrington, by his second marriage, was born in 1664. He served against the Turks in the Imperial Army in Hungary, got into some trouble with James II's Scottish officials just before the Revolution, and after it joined the Household of Prince George of Denmark. Member for Edinburgh in 1695, he was created Viscount Rosebery five years later, and advanced to an earldom after the accession of Queen Anne. He was one of the Commissioners for the Treaty of Union, and after its acceptance was chosen to be a representative peer. His wife was Dorothea Cressy, an attractive Yorkshire girl of ancient family, and he died in 1723. The records show him to have been a man of some ability, and not without taste. Some satirical verses are ascribed to him, but they were not printed. His eldest son, James, succeeded as second Earl. He had been imprisoned in the Old Tolbooth for debt in his father's lifetime, and seems to have been in money difficulties all his life, less from any picturesque habits of extravagance (though he was debauched enough), than from being on the border-line of insanity and a practitioner of unsuccessful litigation, especially with his nearest relatives. He enjoyed the entailed estates of Dalmeny, but his father took care to leave all his personal property to his younger children. He married Mary Campbell, sister of the 4th Duke of Argyll, and thus became brother-in-law to Simon, Lord Lovat, who actually succeeded in borrowing money from him. One of his three sisters married her cousin, Sir Archibald Primrose, who had assumed his mother's name in place of that of

---

[4] *My Aunt Margaret's Mirror*, not considered worthy of a place in the first series of *Chronicles of the Canongate* (1827), appeared in Charles Heath's *Keepsake* in 1828. Lockhart says (*Life*, vol. vii, p. 108) : "Sir Walter regretted having meddled in any way with the toy-shop of literature, and would never do so again, though repeatedly offered very large sums."

his father, Sir John Foulis, and was executed for his part in the rebellion of 1745. Lord Rosebery died in 1755, leaving two sons and two daughters.

The elder of the sons, who died as Lord Dalmeny a few months before his father, was of very different metal—cultivated, high-minded, and the main support of his mother and sisters during the prolonged family squabbles. His own marriage was a romance with a strange ending. He met in London Catherine Canham, the daughter of a rich Essex yeoman. It was a misalliance, so the marriage was private, and the couple went abroad as Mr. and Mrs. Williams, living mainly in northern Italy. After four years she died at Verona, and in her last hours wrote in pencil the confession that she was the wife of the Rev. Alexander Gough, Vicar of Thorpe-le-Soken, where she begged that she might be buried. Her embalmed body was taken home, and by a strange sequence of events, her two husbands met, first in anger, then with sympathy; and they walked side by side at the pompous obsequies in Thorpe churchyard.[5]

The death of Lord Dalmeny left his brother Neil, some four years younger, the only male representative of the Primroses, two other brothers having died in childhood. Following the sensible practice of many Scottish younger sons, he had gone into a merchant's business in London, and this training helped him to repair the rather dilapidated family fortunes. He first married a Norfolk heiress, daughter of Sir Edward Ward of Bixley, and secondly the daughter of Sir Francis Vincent of Stoke D'Abernon, having six children by this last marriage. He was a Representative Peer, a Knight of the Thistle, and a popular country gentleman. His eldest son, Archibald was born in 1783 and succeeded in 1814.

The 4th Lord Rosebery's first marriage to Harriet Bouverie, a girl of seventeen, ended in a miserable scandal after five years of marriage and the birth of four children. Her elder sister had died a year after her marriage to Sir Henry St. John Mildmay; pity and self-pity beguiled Lady Rosebery and the young widower into romance, and divorce followed in 1814. The passionate couple, more fortunate than those of Rimini,[6] were able to marry in a foreign

---

[5] Readers of Thomas Hardy's *A Pair of Blue Eyes* will be reminded of the funeral of Elfride Luxellian, though her love-tragedy ran on very different lines from that of Catherine Gough.

[6] *Inferno*, canto v, l. 100.

> Amor ch'al cor gentil ratto s'apprende.
> Prese costui della bella persona,
> Che mi fu tolta, e'l modo ancor m'offende.

NEIL, 3RD EARL OF ROSEBERY, AND HIS FAMILY, BY NASMYTH

country, and their eldest son lived into the present century, a well-known social figure.

Lord Rosebery, who had sat for a short time in the House of Commons, was a Scottish Representative Peer until 1828, when he was given a Barony of the United Kingdom. He was a keen supporter of Lord Grey, he was made a Privy Councillor in 1831, and worked actively for the Reform Bill, presiding in 1843 at the great Banquet in Edinburgh, when his leader received the Freedom of the City. His second marriage, in 1819, to Anne, daughter of the 1st Viscount Anson, was singularly happy. She outlived him by fourteen years, and became the much-loved "Grandmama" of the subject of this memoir and his brother and sisters. He himself lived till 1868, a patriarch honoured by his family and by his neighbours.

Archibald, Lord Dalmeny, the elder son of his first marriage, was born in 1809. Like his father, he was an active Liberal, sitting for the Stirling burghs, and being a Lord of the Admiralty in Lord Melbourne's administration until 1841. In one respect he was in advance of his generation by realising the value to the many of the physical education, which, except for those who liked to use their fists, had been considered the privilege of the few. He published in 1848 *An Address to the Middle Classes on the Subject of Gymnastic Exercises.* He may have overstated his thesis that exercise, rather than fresh air, is the one thing needful for physical vigour, and have strained his heart in becoming a swordsman of great accomplishment; for when apparently recovering from an attack of pleurisy, he died suddenly from a heart attack, when only forty years old. He had married, in 1843, Catherine Lucy Wilhelmina Stanhope, the only daughter of Philip, 4th Earl Stanhope. This junior branch of the house of which the Earl of Chesterfield was the head, had for some generations given evidence of originality and of considerable intellectual powers. The first Earl, who married Lucy Pitt, the aunt of Lord Chatham, was conspicuous as a soldier and in Parliament in the reign of George I. The second was highly distinguished as a mathematician. Charles, the third Earl, who lived till 1816, was equally well known for his republican sympathies, which earned him the sobriquet "Citizen Stanhope," and for his attainments in applied science. The improved printing press, the earliest introduction of steam vessels, the possibilities of electricity,

Amor ch'a null'amato amar perdona;
Mi pressi del costui piacer si forte,
Che come vedi ancor non m'abbandona.

[7]

all engaged his agile attention; but he must have lacked the concentration and the balance of the scientific master mind. Lord Stanhope was twice married, first to his second cousin Lady Hester Pitt, sister of the younger Pitt, and secondly to Louisa Grenville, niece of Lord Temple and of George Grenville. His son by his second marriage, who succeeded to the title, showed some of his eccentricity in a less conspicuous form, and also pursued some of the scientific researches of his father.

At the same time, however, Lord Stanhope was a greater subject of interest from the promise of his children. I have heard from a contemporary how it was a common saying that Lord Stanhope was a lucky man to be the father of the cleverest son and the most attractive daughter in London. The son, another Philip, who in due course became the 5th Earl Stanhope, did not literally justify this verdict of a limited social jury; for he was the exact age of Disraeli and but four years older than Gladstone. But he became a considerable figure in Parliament, and a genuine man of letters. Those who care to go behind the slapdash histories that crowd the lending libraries could do worse than take up Lord Stanhope's *Reign of Queen Anne*. With a little more attraction of style it would be a very good book indeed. He was a Fellow in the Royal Society, being the fourth in direct descent to receive that distinction. It may be questioned whether the British peerage can present any parallel.[7] At any rate, there could be no dispute about Lady Wilhelmina Stanhope's charm. Of middle height—her features not of a classical model—her brilliancy of colour, her play of expression, her intense vivacity, disarmed all criticism and left her an unchallenged beauty, both before and after her marriage. Four children were born to Lord and Lady Dalmeny during their married life of eight years:

Mary Catherine Constance, *b.* 1844.
Constance Evelyn, *b.* 1846.
Archibald Philip (the subject of this memoir), *b.* 1847.
Everard Henry, *b.* 1848.

For some years their headquarters in London were at Lord Stanhope's house in Charles Street, Berkeley Square, where Archibald Philip was born on May 7th, 1847. When the lease of this house came to an end in the following year, they moved to the rather

[7] Until 1778, when Sir Joseph Banks became President of the Royal Society, it sometimes happened that Fellows were elected rather as patrons of scientific learning than as experts; but the earlier Fellows of the Stanhope line do not seem to have fallen into his category.

monotonous formality of Eaton Place. There the widowed Lady Dalmeny and her children continued to live, spending part of the summer with her father at Chevening in Kent, and the autumn with her father-in-law at Dalmeny. In 1854 came a change which brought much colour into the children's lives by their mother's marriage to Lord Henry Vane, brother and heir of the 2nd Duke of Cleveland. He had a house in Grosvenor Place, where they all settled. By a rather unusual chance, the vast Cleveland possessions, comprising, besides the wide stretch of farmland and moorland in County Durham of which Raby Castle was the centre, estates in ten other English shires, did not include any secondary house of importance which Lord Harry might naturally have inhabited. So that, for several years after his marriage, he rented such well-known places as Brocket, the home of Lady Palmerston, and the Priory at Reigate. The winter of 1854, however, was spent abroad by the newly wedded pair and by Lady Harry's children. This was the period of transition between the old leisurely travel by chaise or diligence and the universal reign of railways. The Paris-Mediterranean line then ceased at Lyons; so the travellers made their way by river to Marseilles, and from Nice by ship to Naples, which was then the resort of many cultivated English and French visitors. Among the favourite Italian playmates of the Primroses was Princess Maria Camporeale, destined later to adorn the diplomatic world as the wife of Prince Bernard von Bülow, the German Chancellor.

In the following year Archibald Dalmeny went to his first school, Bayford, near Hertford. Few intimacies are closer than those of boys at preparatory schools, fresh from home, and not yet making cardinal virtues of reticence and self-reliance; but unless these friendships are continued and reinforced at a public school or college they are apt to die early. Two of the Beresford[8] brothers, Lord Claud Hamilton[9] and George Bridgeman,[10] were among his fellow pupils.

His letters to his mother show a budding interest in public affairs, for in 1857 there is a list of relatives of his schoolfellows who were likely to stand for Parliament. All of them glow with affection for herself and for the whole family. When his brother arrived at

[8] Lord Charles Beresford (1846-1919), Admiral; created Lord Beresford 1916; Lord William Beresford, V.C. (1847-1900).
[9] 1843-1925. Son of the 1st Duke of Abercorn, M.P. from 1865.
[10] George Bridgeman, 4th Earl of Bradford, 1845-1915. In a touching letter of condolence to the Dowager Lady Bradford, January 10th, 1915, Rosebery described it as "the Bayford of many jokes."

school in 1857, the responsible ten-years-old senior writes: "Evy is a hero. There never was a braver boy. He came to me last night and cried on my shoulder, and said he was homesick. That is all over now however. They bully him rather, but a braver boy I never saw. I try to be as kind as I can. I never try to mention your name between us, it might make him sad." Some of his holidays were spent at Dalmeny, in the surroundings which remained dearest to him throughout all the excitements and chances of the richly coloured years to come.

He was eleven when an accident happened of which the exact gravity remains uncertain. In the course of some game he ran blindfold into an iron gate, striking the hasp, which made a deep wound in his forehead, and caused some concussion of the brain. He was invalided home, kept in a darkened room, and, according to the recollection of his sister, "remained ill for a long time, with fits of deep depression, hating all exercise and conversation, only asking to be left alone." The scar on his forehead was patent to the end of his life, and his family sometimes wondered whether this mishap was directly responsible for the nervous irritability which, as we shall see, now and then afflicted him in later years, and for the craving for solitude which was liable to puzzle his dearest relatives and most congenial friends. It may be, on the other hand, that the severe blow simply gave premature life to innate tendencies which would have matured in any event, and could not have been evaded altogether. While his slow recovery was progressing, the school at Bayford was closed, and Dalmeny joined Everard at Mr. Lee's well-known school at Brighton.

Meanwhile Lord Harry Vane had bought Battle Abbey, one of the shrines of English history, and the boys' holidays were spent there or in Scotland until, in 1860, Dalmeny went to Eton. Then, and for many years later, entrance to the public schools was graded on a purely classical standard. He was a promising scholar, and was placed in Remove. But he came from a cultivated home, and was early encouraged to read soundly outside his regular curriculum. The poems of Gray and of Scott, and the *Lays of the Scottish Cavaliers*—early gifts from his grandfather and his grandmother— remained in his bedroom to the last, with the *Arabian Nights*, in which he noted, years later: "This is the copy which we all read out of as children. It afterwards was given to me by my mother when I was at Bayford." Four volumes of Macaulay's *Essays* were a New Year present from his mother in 1858. More than fifty years later, sending to Sir George Trevelyan a letter of warm thanks for his gift of some of Macaulay's own volumes, he wrote as follows:

July 13th, 1911.

". . . This only increases my overwhelming debt to Macaulay, for in truth I owe him everything. He first touched my trembling ears. On such an occasion it may not bore you to know how this came about. At Christmas 1858, when I was eleven, we were all playing snap-dragon at Chevening. The flames burst out of the dish, and I, among others, was cruelly burnt. That night I was introduced to Walter Scott by my mother's reading to me the Legend of Montrose to keep me quiet. A day or two afterwards I was wandering about the delightful Chevening library (which you know well), and quite by chance took down Macaulay's *Essays*. I fell at once under the wand of the enchanter. I began with Milton, and read no other book till I had finished the three volumes. And at the New Year my mother, seeing my absorption, gave me a copy.

"There was much, of course, that I could not really understand. But I delighted in the eloquence, the grasp and the command of knowledge, the irresistible current of the style. And to that book I owe whatever ambitions or aspirations I have ever indulged in. No man can intellectually owe another more."

Before long another current of influence flowed into that young mind. A translation of Thiers' *History of the Consulate and the Empire*, published in 1850, has the inscription "Dalmeny, March 7, 1859," and the following pencil note: "This book I bought when in quarantine at Mr. Lee's school after the measles. I read it right through.—R. 1885."

This book, surely, also nourished, if not ambitions and aspirations, at least admirations and sympathies destined to colour the web of the boy's approaching manhood.

Dalmeny's house at Eton was a "Dame's," that of Mr. Vidal; but, by an uncommon chance, his tutor, being the unmarried brother of Mrs. Vidal, made it headquarters for himself and for his pupil room. That tutor was William Johnson, "Billy" to his intimates, and (behind his back) to his pupils; perhaps better known to the public as William Cory, the name which he assumed in respect of an inheritance, but also, it appears, because it sounded more distinguished than Johnson.[11]

Not a few headmasters of the great public schools have, in various ways, left an enduring mark on the life of this country. Arnold, the Butlers, Thring, Warre, and Sanderson are familiar names out-

[11] His elder brother similarly changed his name to that of Furse, destined to become celebrated by the admirable art of his son Charles.

[11]

side the bounds of their respective schools. It is difficult to cite under-masters equally famous, beyond William Johnson and his friend Edward Bowen of Harrow.[12] And each of these, possibly, is as widely known by the evidence which he left of a "deep poetic heart" as by his conspicuous service as a teacher. Some of William Cory's exquisite verses will continue to adorn every lyrical anthology.

In a long and cheerful letter to his mother, just after his arrival at Eton, Dalmeny remarks that "fagging is very nominal," and he is evidently not made anxious by the length of school hours, of which he gives a detailed time-table. A letter of a year later, 1861, to his mother, when he was a spectator of the school Confirmation, shows a depth of seriousness unusual in a boy of fourteen.

"Oh Mother," he writes, "the Confirmation was so beautiful you can't imagine. . . . When the Bishop had finished the last prayer in burst the organ and it played while one party was returning and the other coming up. I think almost every one felt it very much indeed and they seemed almost crying except one who laughed I believe while the Bishop was actually laying hands on him at any rate immediately after it. I think this was the most horrible thing ever thought of. Just when God was about to admit him to his table—laughing. I prayed Mother that I never should commit such an enormous sin . . . now you darling you must not show this to anyone the offspring of my sentimentality, but I cannot help feeling sure that God has sent this Confirmation for my special good as it impressed me so much."

The severe criticism of boyhood could make no allowance for the nervous crisis which reduced the one unlucky candidate to hysterical laughter.

When Dalmeny reached the age of sixteen, and the time arrived for his own Confirmation, he was disappointed by the postponement "of what I looked forward to so much, (though I confess that the feeling of my own unfitness made me almost dread the ceremony) as a high and holy privilege." These sound like the utterances of a thoughtful boy, looking piously forward to a clerical Fellowship at

[12] It may not be fanciful to ascribe some part of the influence which each of these remarkable men gained over a succession of pupils to their common love for military history and patriotic prowess. In Sir Henry Newbolt's noble elegy on William Cory the refrain rings with the "splendour of England's war." And Bowen's "Modern Side" at Harrow had many of the elements of an "Army Class," while he was fond of conducting parties of boys over the battlefields of Flanders and of Alsace Lorraine.

the University. They are noted here because they illustrate one element in a complex character—an element which the passage of years never served to dissipate.

But it was far from being the sole, or even the most obvious element. In 1862 he tells his mother, "I wish I wrote oftener, but you must excuse me a little on account of Summer half, when one is always out in a boat or playing at cricket or sapping," and continues with a comical account of the downpour which ruined the 4th of June, when at Surley the rain drove everybody back to the boats, leaving a dozen of champagne behind them, and nobody got drunk, partly because there was not time, partly because "the rain very considerably adulterated the champagne"—though some of the younger boys of the party seem to have tried their best. He steered one of the boats "in a kind of midshipman's cap which is if possible worse" than a cocked hat. Later he had a place in the ten-oar *Monarch*, but the pastime that he most enjoyed was fives. This probably led, when he went to Oxford, to a fondness for racquets, which were not then played at Eton.

In the meantime his tutor was eagerly watching a rare mind breaking gradually into flower. When Dalmeny was fifteen Johnson wrote to his friend, Henry Bradshaw:[13]

"But come, anyhow, to see the boys and young men. My friend Dalmeny is looking forward to making your acquaintance, with the natural eagerness of a budding bibliomaniac. I took him last week to Lilly's, and he forthwith enquired for rare tracts printed by his ancestor Primrose. We went on to Evans', and there he picked out another print representing another Primrose of the seventeenth century, preacher to the French Church in London. At Holloway's he bought autographs, and finally went and made acquaintance with my brother and sister, and showed as much interest in a live child as in dead books. He has the finest combination of qualities I have ever seen. He was quite taken, as I was too, with Dufferin's show speech (do you remember Dufferin, how Cookesley called him the "orator"?); and when Wayte set theme out of it the boy put the peroration about "Laboramus" into flowing, simple, dignified Latin, and then went with me through the last book of *The Princess*. The night before I had translated to him most of the beautiful bits of *Agamemnon*, and I assure you he enjoyed the old poetry nearly as much as the modern. I am doing all I can to make him a scholar; anyhow he will be an orator, and, if not a poet, such a man as poets delight in."

[13] *Letters and Journals of William Cory.* (Oxford, 1897, p. 75.)

Later in the same year, when illness had driven him to seek a spell of rest at Cambridge, he wrote to F. Warre Cornish, who was then taking charge of his pupil room:[14]

". . . I have sent these lads some modern history questions: and Dalmeny promises to do them, that he may thereby induce me to come back—rather a circuitous reason. I would give you a piece of plate if you would get that lad to work; he is one of those who like the palm without the dust. He wrote me a word that he got 'fair' for his lyrics. . . ."

The Horatian metaphor,[15] familiar to English readers from its reproduction in the famous passage of Milton's prose,[16] undoubtedly represents the teacher's verdict at the time, and it has since been quoted a dozen times by critics of Rosebery's public career.

But it should not be misapprehended. Milton, of course, was thinking of those who avoid, in conventual seclusion, the coarse contacts of a sinful world; the common interpretation of the phrase would apply it to the superficial and indolent, who try to find short cuts to distinction instead of toiling up steep and stony roads. Neither of these readings, it will become clear, covers the idiosyncrasies of Rosebery's character. He often enjoyed rubbing shoulders with the everyday world; and he was capable of severe and continuous industry. But he displayed fastidious distaste for "dust," or rather, if the metaphor is to be rendered into English, for mud; so that thus far William Johnson's prognosis is as accurate as a schoolmaster's need be.

About the same time he writes to his pupil:[17] "I have been qualifying for an interview with *you* by reading the *Family Life* of Pitt,"[18] and gives a careful estimate of the book, with some acute observations on passages in Pitt's career. Another letter[19] tells of a visit to Boconnoc and its relics of the younger Pitt and the Grenvilles.

[14] *Op. cit.*, p. 78.
[15] ". . . . . cui spes
cui sit condicio dulcis sine pulvere palmae?"
Hor., Epp. I. 1. 50.
[16] "I cannot praise a fugitive and cloistered virtue, unexercised and unbreathed, that never sallies out and sees her adversary, but slinks out of the race, where that immortal garland is to be run for, not without dust and heat."—*Historical, etc., Works, Areopagitica.* (London 1753, p. 156.)
[17] Cambridge, April 20th, 1862.
[18] Lord Stanhope's *Life of Pitt.*
[19] Penzance, August 29th, 1862.

But the boy did not limit his literary interest to correspondence with his tutor. About 1863 he boldly wrote on some point of Scottish knowledge to Mr. Robert Chambers, one of the famous publishing firm, and author of *Traditions of Edinburgh*—"quite an adventure to me at that tender age."[20] He was asked to luncheon in London in consequence, and was shown a copy of *The Lyon in Mourning*.

In several ways he was not an altogether easy boy to deal with. If he forgot to wipe his feet at the pupil-room door and received a book at his head, accompanying his tutor's cry of "Shoes! shoes!" this may have happened to many others, but, in the words of Lord Esher, who was one of Johnson's favourite pupils a year or two later:

"Lord Rosebery as a boy was difficult of access, even to his tutor. So much so that the unusual method had on one occasion to be adopted of tearing over his verses in order to secure his presence in 'pupil room.' It had the desired effect, and to his enquiry of why that indignity had been put upon him, he was told the story of how Absalom burnt Joab's corn when he found that an interview could not be obtained by less drastic means."

This episode earned Lord Rosebery a nickname.[21] For years afterwards Johnson spoke of "Joab's" doings without further explanation.

Likewise in his relations with his schoolfellows there was a shade of constraint, which did not prevent him from being admired and popular. As Walter Bagehot puts it, "We see but one side of our neighbour, as we see but one side of the moon: in either case there is also a dark half, which is unknown to us. We all come down to dinner, but each has a room to himself."[22] Then and always his "room" had almost the properties of a secret chamber. However this may have been at Eton, many of his closest and most enduring friendships dated thence. The accident of placing in "school" produced the following line, treated as an hexameter by outrageous mispronunciation of the last three names:

"Alexander, Lamb,[23] Dalmeny, Palairet, Hamilton,"[24] Of the above, Hamilton remained a most intimate ally throughout his life;

[20] Lord Rosebery to Mr. C. E. S. Chambers, June 26th, 1910.
[21] *Cloud-capp'd Towers.* (London (Murray), 1927, p. 21.)
[22] Shakespeare, "The Man."
[23] Sir Archibald Lamb, Bt.
[24] Rt. Hon. Sir E. Hamilton, G.C.B.

[15]

others, some of whom survived him, were Frederick Wood,[25] Lascelles,[26] Aboyne,[27] and his fag William Portal.[28]

When he was about fifteen his tutor, ever on the alert to practise mental gymnastics, suggested that he should begin the "Memoirs of His Own Time." Accordingly, for two years at any rate, he jotted down at uncertain intervals reports of events important to Eton, such as the election of a new provost and headmaster, comments on political affairs, social anecdotes told by fashionable friends of his family, and some special experiences of his own. Among these last is an account of a day spent at St. Anne's Hill, with a full description of the house and the formal gardens. "Altogether," he writes, "I came away with increased love and veneration for Mr. Fox and his whole race." Time, and his absorption in the career of the younger Pitt, tended to dim this sentiment for the Whig leader himself, but not for the Lady Holland who then reigned at St. Anne's Hill. Her gift to him of Charles Fox's *Virgil* had a permanent place on his personal bookshelf. The notebooks have also a series of pages on a scandalous blackmailing accusation against Lord Palmerston in his advanced old age, which naturally thrilled every *gobe-mouches* of the day. The charge against the famous Harrovian Prime Minister percolated to the amused ears of Eton boys.

"If not a poet . . ." his tutor had written; but he had his full share of the lyrical faculty so frequent in cultured youth, so rarely destined to mature with the passage of years. Of some Latin verses, his tutor had written: "I looked over Dalmeny's verses: to alter them was a long, delicate job, as they were not commonplace, *pro forma* things, but an honest attempt to turn (of his own accord) some rhymes of mine which he had read in manuscript." But he did not stop at classical exercises. In 1862 a slim volume containing *The Marriage of Peleus and Thetis*, together with *Two Efforts in Blank Verse*, were "Privately printed for the Author" at Eton. His version of the Greek legend shows remarkable promise for a boy of fifteen. The metres are skilfully varied, and the atmosphere is well sustained. The author had evidently read his Milton, his Dryden, and his Keats; but his poem is none the worse for that. The two poems in blank verse, one telling the story of Rizpah, from

[25] Fourth son of the 1st Viscount Halifax. Assumed the name of Meynell on succeeding to the Hoar Cross estate (1846-1910).

[26] 5th Earl of Harewood (1846-1929).

[27] 11th Marquess of Huntly. Succeeded his father while at Eton.

[28] Sir William Wyndham Portal, second Baronet.

[16]

the Second Book of Samuel, the other a Cornish tale, are less distinguished, as might be expected. Blank verse defies the craftsmanship of almost every young writer. "Please show the little book to *no one*," he writes to Lord Stanhope, when sending his literary uncle a copy gorgeously bound in green morocco.

As the delightful years passed at Eton, William Johnson's uneasiness at the irregularity of Dalmeny's genius seems to have increased. In September 1864 he wrote in his journal: "Received a very good, thoughtful letter from my employer, the mother of the beloved Archie and Everard, of whom I was glad to be reminded. If they were only as fond of knowledge as Cambridge men!" The "employer" was seriously impressed by the tutor's complaints that her son's work was not up to the mark, and with the impulsiveness natural to her, she determined that he must leave school at Easter 1865, when not yet eighteen, in order to read elsewhere before going to Oxford. This may have been to take Johnson more literally than he intended, for he wrote a long letter from Cambridge in January, condoling with Dalmeny for missing "the last summer, which is often so full of interest as to blot out the memory of all earlier years." The letter goes on with an eloquent appreciation of the boon granted to "a genuine Eton playmate," and of what tutors can and cannot do for their pupils, hard-working or idle.[29] Perhaps some veiled irony peeps through these last sentences. To the boy himself this unexpected summons was a matter of deep chagrin. To miss the "jolly boating weather and a hay-harvest breeze" of his tutor's song was bad enough; but he was now an active member of the Eton Society, famous as "Pop" even outside Eton. In the end, youth and the Eton tradition won the day; Lord Rosebery was appealed to, and gave his verdict in favour of the summer half; whatever domestic friction had occurred quickly disappeared, and soon the home letters exhibited no diminished freedom and interchange of affection.[30]

He was elected a member of the Eton Society in October 1864; receiving but four black balls, while twenty-three voted. The debates, which took place about once a month, were often on an historical subject, generally in the form of an inquiry whether the character

[29] William Johnson to Lord Dalmeny. K.C.C., January 10th, 1865.
[30] It is interesting to recall that in 1863 Lord Lansdowne's tutor had urged his father to take him away at Easter, because he would "treat work lightly and pleasure as the main object, which Christ Church will set for good"; and he was sent to a tutor for the summer before going up to Oxford (*Lord Lansdowne*, by Lord Newton, p. 5).

of a particular personage was to be admired. Many of the speeches were long and serious, showing not a little careful study and research, but members of an ironical turn, like Dalmeny, were able to enjoy themselves when on their legs, and even more in writing the reports, all of which have been carefully preserved.[31] It thus often happened that a speaker was able to immortalise his own effort in a comic vein. Dalmeny's maiden speech was on the character of his brother Scot, Dundee, and we read that after a long debate he said: "I think Dundee was a very brave man. His life and death were equally romantic. I therefore give my vote in favour of Dundee." It proved to be the casting vote, for Claverhouse was approved by 11 to 10. He also argued in favour of Lord Chatham, and we read that "his polysyllabic arguments occupied 5¼ minutes (for a bet)." When Mary, Queen of Scots, was being weighed in the balance, "Lord Dalmeny then addressed the House in his usual eloquent manner: he pointed out that there is a great difference between regarding a person with admiration and hatred, with many other wise remarks." He joined in the unanimous vote condemning Bolingbroke, and when it was asked, "Was the execution of Strafford unjustifiable or not?" Lord Dalmeny, having controlled his risibility, took the opposite side, for the sake of practice, perhaps, in these memorable words. But the presence of strangers of distinction made him forget the arguments he had intended to bring forth. "I hold that Strafford was justly executed. I cannot but consider him a base apostate—baser and less able than Bolingbroke (Oh! Oh!). There are some to whom liberty is dearer than life . . . if it had to be done again, I would have it done again." Boys appreciate "thorough," and Strafford was exonerated by 15 votes against 4.

He was more successful in taking away the character of Sir Robert Walpole, both in public and private. Fifteen this time voted against the Minister and but four in his favour. It is noted that "Dalmeny spoke in his usual vein of sarcastic and cutting wit, making several of the members look very small."

On subjects of more current interest—he took the part of the North in the American Civil War, and when it was asked, "Ought England to part with Canada?" we read that "Dalmeny arguing somewhat against his private convictions, said that we ought to keep Canada." In the course of his speech he said that the Biographical Dictionary had been exhausted in search for characters who

[31] I have to thank Mr. D. McKenna, when he was President of the Eton Society, for permission to examine these.

ought to be admired. If America desired Canada, he doubted whether it would be well to yield to their pride of conquest. The Americans never cease to revile us, and in a glowing peroration he protested that we must not give up a country which had been gained by the sagacity of a Chatham and cost us the blood of a Wolfe.

The sole record of his interest in the social amenities of the Society is dated a fortnight before he left the school. "Dalmeny moved that Baily's Turf Magazine be taken, but on the disapproval of the House, the motion was withdrawn."

As this half ended, a lady wrote to Lady Rosebery:

"I cannot refrain from repeating a passage out of my boy's letter, as it made me feel how good and wise a friend he had found in your grandson, and it will also gratify you. After speaking very pathetically of his sorrow in leaving Eton for ever next Thursday, he says, 'Dalmeny asked me to go to the early Communion with him and Wood on Sunday morning; was it not thoughtful of him?' "

The boy whose mother wrote this was Scott Holland, afterwards the famous Canon of St. Paul's. The third boy was Frederick Wood, the younger son of Lord Halifax.

All his life long he remained subject to the indescribable charm of Eton, as different from that of Harrow as the flavour of first-rate claret is from the flavour of first-rate burgundy. His love never weakened or changed, and it was quickened afresh by his appointment to the Governing Body, and by the entrance to the school of his two sons. To his last days, whatever honours the years might heap on him, he was prouder of being an Etonian—next to being a Scotsman—than of anything else in the world.

CHAPTER II

Raby Castle—and Oxford

H<small>E WENT</small> from Eton straight to Raby, now the home of his stepfather and his mother. Lord Harry had succeded his brother as 3rd Duke of Cleveland in September 1864, and the great castle where the Nevills had formerly reigned became their principal home. Unlike many mediæval strongholds, Berkeley, Warwick, and Windsor itself, Raby does not tower above a town nestling for protection at its feet, but stands at some distance in a great deer park. On a red October evening, with the stags roaring through the rising mist, it was a stately picture of feudal grandeur. The arrangement by which carriages actually drove into the castle, depositing guests at one end of the great hall and passing out through an archway, was startling and effective. On the other hand, in the days of which I am writing, there was little concession to modern ideas of luxury. Critical visitors shook their heads over the *cuisine* and the cellar, and those who wished to smoke in the evening were relegated to an apartment in a distant tower, in the unmistakable neighbourhood of a well-stocked cheese-room. There was the terrifying possibility for a solitary late-sitter that his candle might be blown out by a gust of wind on his way back to his bedroom, and that he might be marooned till dawn in the great hall, unless he were rescued by a friendly watchman. It was a hospitable house; and the wide sympathies of both the Duke and the Duchess opened it to visitors of opposing views in politics, and of many varieties of intellectual eminence, in a degree unusual in those more restricted days. Dalmeny, afire with interest in everything that was not commonplace, was prepared to profit to the utmost by such opportunities; and although, as we shall see later on, he came to distrust the activities of social diarists, he noted at length some of his impressions of this first prolonged introduction to social life as a young man whose school-days were over. It was early in August, and with a new twelve-bore gun he made his first acquaintance with grouse shooting, on the famous High Force moors, part of which the Duke kept in hand. At first he shot walking with his cousin, Edward Stanhope, but driving was beginning to be fashionable, and he wrote: "Aug. 16, Wednesday. We shot 83½ brace of grouse (driving), of which I shot about 15 brace, which was very creditable, considering that it was my first day of driving, that my gun would not go off during one whole drive, and that I got the worst place (of course, as the son of the house each drive). Walked to the beat and back. Everyone else rode on ponies." This was a satisfactory day, as earlier he had written: "I am not yet an average shot, I fear," and now, as one of five guns, always on the outside, he had all but killed his fair proportion of the bag on his first day's grouse driving. It was an augury of his later brilliance as a shot.

When the party returned to Raby, life resumed its even flow, of gentle exercise, family prayers, and regular churchgoing. Both prayers and services were sometimes prolonged, and the fine Nevill tombs in the church were continually inspected: "The monuments were again looked over. If they are shown every Sunday, I shall be brought to an early grave."

Visitors came and went, among them Robert Curzon, the author of the delightful *Monasteries of the Levant*, who told many good stories, and "Mr. Trevelyan,[1] the Competition Wallah."

August 24th.—"I had at dinner an interesting conversation with Trevelyan about his books. He hinted at writing his Uncle's life, but confessed that at present he was absorbed in politics, and felt no great inclination for the task."

August 25th.—"Played at billiards with Trevelyan and took a walk with him afterwards. He told me that he had written two articles in the *Saturday Review*, but that he could do nothing well anonymously, for he did not think it worth while. He promised me the Prince of Wales's autograph and a copy of *Cawnpore*. He told me much about his Uncle, and recited to me a passage of *Lake Regillus*, which he thought more like Homer than anything in the language. I asked him if he had lost his taste for Juvenal, taking it for granted that he had one. He said *No*, that he delighted in it, and that his favourites in the Classics were Juvenal and Aristophanes."

This was the beginning of a long and affectionate friendship.

One evening the Duke had to go to Durham to read his Address as President of the Archæological Society, where "the Duke, the owner of half the County, was introduced to the assembly by Lord

[1] Sir George Otto Trevelyan, Bart. (1838-1928), M.P. 1868-97, Chief Secretary for Ireland 1882-4, Secretary for Scotland 1886 and 1892-5, Nephew of Lord Macaulay.

Houghton, who has nothing whatever to do with Durham. Lord Houghton did it as ex-President." In spite of this outrage on territorial privilege, my father was a welcome guest at Raby after the meeting, being already intimate with the host and hostess. His acquaintance with the younger generation developed into a close friendship, lasting till his death in 1885, in spite of the difference in their ages of nearly forty years.

A large party at the end of the month included Mr. and Mrs. Disraeli and Mr. Montagu Corry.[2] As these notable actors advanced on to the stage, Dalmeny settled down to a more elaborate record of the day's doings:

August 31st.—"Mama came in from riding when they were all in the library; so she said, 'I was so sorry to be so rude as not to be here to receive you, but the fact is that I had such a bad headache that I was obliged to go and take a ride.' To which Dizzy replied with an air, 'The pleasure of seeing Your Grace in your riding habit makes up for the loss of your society'—the kind of compliment in fact that one sees in *Coningsby*.

"I sat next Mrs. Disraeli at dinner. May I have memory and strength to write down some of our conversation. She began by asking me where I was going to. I replied 'Oxford'; so she exclaimed, 'Oh, yes, I love Oxford, they are all so fond of Mr. Dizzy there, they all applaud him so.' So I said, 'Yes, I suppose Mr. Disraeli took an Honorary Degree there?' 'Yes,' said she, 'he was made a D.T.C.L., or something of the sort.' She then asked me if I were fond of reading, and after a little talk, she said that the only novels she liked were those that improved and instructed her. 'I think *Coningsby* is that,' I hinted. 'Of course,' she said, 'written by a clever man like him.' She then gave a long description of her life in the country, how she managed everything, even to ordering Dizzy's clothes—'I have to go out planting, too. I take a little lunch, and some bottles of beer for the workmen, and sit there all day.' 'Is not that very fatiguing?' 'Ah, but the mind overcomes the body,—and then he is so glad to see me when I come back, and he comes out and sees what I have done, when it is all finished, and says sometimes, "This is delightful, better than anything you have done yet." And then I feel quite intoxicated for the moment, and quite rewarded. And though all my friends have grander places than I have, yet they all come to me and see my walks (not rides or drives, but walks) and say, "These are the prettiest walks we have ever seen." And Dizzy sometimes says that

[2] Lord Beaconsfield's well-known private secretary (1838-1903). Created Lord Rowton 1880. This was Disraeli's first meeting with his famous private secretary of the future.

he would be quite happy if he lived there alone for the rest of his life; but I say, "No, dear, I will never give you the chance," for it is quite dull in the country when we are alone together, for Dizzy takes his book —(he does nothing but read books, old Greek and Latin books) and I take my book, but I am so tired with planting that I am afraid it often falls out of my hands and I go asleep. I never allow Dizzy to come and see me while I am planting, because he would lose the *coup d'œil* of seeing it when it is finished.'

" 'Do you care for politics, Mrs. Disraeli?' 'No, I have no time, I have so many books and pamphlets to read and see if there is my name in any of them! and I have everything to manage, and write his stupid letters. I am sorry when he is in office, because then I lose him altogether, and though I have many people who call themselves my friends, yet I have no friend like him. I have not been separated from him since we have been in the country, except when I have been in the woods, and I cannot lose him (here her voice trembled touchingly). He is always at his office, and gives two dinners to his party every week, to which I am not invited. But I know many Whigs, the Duke and Duchess of Wellington, and my dear friend there'—pointing to my mother. '*He* is so fond of her, he says she is the only witty woman he knows. . . .[3] How has your sister got her hair done to-night? She is just like Marie Antoinette with her hair like that. She is so beautiful. . . . I am looking to see if Dizzy is sitting next any pretty woman that he would like to sit next and admire.'

"I think this half-crazy, warm-hearted woman's talk is worth setting down, for she is an uncommon specimen. Parts are very touching. . . ."

September 1st.—"Mrs. Disraeli greeted me at breakfast with 'We have been talking about you.' 'I am indeed honoured, Mrs. Disraeli.' 'Oh, but I did not say it was very good.' 'But to be talked about by you is enough honour.' I cannot help quizzing her by talking in this way, though I really like her. She praised me in her own and her husband's name very warmly this evening."

September 2nd.—"After breakfast Dizzy came up and asked me how much we had shot. I said that partridges were scarce and that we intended, therefore, to kill nothing but time to-day. 'Then you have a certain bag.' "

Several walks and talks with both Mr. and Mrs. Disraeli followed during the week's visit.[4] The recent stay of Lord Houghton probably made him a subject of conversation, in which Disraeli repeated much of the inaccurate and ill-natured gossip which he set down

[3] Lady Constance Primrose, *m.* 1867 Henry, 2nd Lord Leconfield.
[4] "Dalmeny seemed to me very intelligent and formed for his time of life (not yet of age) and not a prig, which might be feared."—*Life of Lord Beaconsfield*, vol. iv, chap. xii.

in a memorandum at about this time.[5] But the great man, to whom eager youth always made appeal, enjoyed amusing his young friend with reminiscence and observation.

"The first news I ever had of the repeal of the Corn Laws was when I was on a visit to Louis Philippe. . . . So the King one day said to me, 'They are going to repeal the Corn Laws in England,' on which I saw there was business for me, and hurried over to England. . . . Lord Monmouth was Lord Hertford. Thackeray also sketched him, but I think it is a pity to do anything anyone has done before you over again. Besides, Lord Monmouth required delicate touches. Lord Steyne is a mere brutal voluptuary,—not the character at all. For Lord Hertford was a very clever man indeed.

"Talking of the speakers in the House of Commons, I said that Horsman seemed to me one of the best orators I had heard. 'Yes, Horsman is a perfect orator. Some people say that he would not stand wear and tear, but I do not see why he shouldn't. . . . Lord Derby is a wonderful debater, but when he has to make a set statement I think he fails. I always thought his leaving the House of Commons a mistake.' . . . We also talked about Lord Brougham, whom Disraeli ran down very much. He professed himself much delighted with his walk and talk. I took in Mrs. Disraeli to dinner this evening—'He is so delighted with his walk, and so pleased with you. He is so sorry there is no chance of your being in the House of Commons. He would so like to have some young men like you to follow him. But then you are a Whig.' 'Who told you so?' 'He did.' I will leave a page or two here to put down anything of interest which he said and I have forgotten for the moment.

"Your stepfather has got the Whigs out of several scrapes when they sorely needed a man of standing and honour to take their side . . . the late Lord Fortescue did the same thing for them."

He also recorded at length the curious tale of Mr. Pitt *in extremis*, asking for one of Bellamy's veal pies, which Rosebery set down later when he wrote the *Life* of the statesman.[6]

Sunday, September 3rd.—"Went to Church. Mr. ——— preached abominably. I never was made so angry by the manner or matter of any sermon, perhaps the manner set me against the matter. In the afternoon

[5] *Life of Lord Beaconsfield*, vol. iii, chap. ii, *Tancred*. They had been intimate for many years, with many tastes in common, and Disraeli always professed a great admiration for my grandfather, Robert Milnes. He had introduced my father, not unpleasantly, in *Tancred* as Mr. Vavasour, and the reason of this increasing bitterness towards him is not clear, either from the memorandum or from this journal. On the other side the response was indifference, rather than any reciprocal dislike.

[6] *Pitt*, Lord Rosebery (Twelve English Statesmen), chap. xiv and appendix D.

I walked with Eliot.[7] He told me that, at the wish of both parties, his father had asked Disraeli and Sir Robert Peel to meet each other. Something went wrong, and they both took a dislike to each other, which lasted for the rest of Sir Robert Peel's life. He told me that although he had had the mortification of being beaten for Cricklade, yet that after all he had been not so very sorry about it. For he could see that a division must take place in the Whig party on Lord Palmerston's death, and that he should like to shape his conduct by the course of events.

"In the evening took in Mrs. Disraeli. She told me as a secret that Lord Derby gave hardly anything to the Conservative Election Fund : Lord Salisbury and Lord Lonsdale gave the most; that they had not had enough money during the last election. . . . Mrs. Disraeli said that she had been present at the reconciliation between Lord Robert Cecil[8] and Lord Salisbury which took place within the last year, and also at the reconciliation between Lord Robert Cecil and Disraeli. She promised to give me a set of Mr. Disraeli's studs, which she said she had taken away from him to give to young men that she liked !"

September 5th.—"Walked with Mr. Disraeli in the morning. He said that the wonder was how the Conservative party had kept together in spite of the want of patronage. He had only had two Garters to give during the last Ministry. He gave them to the Duke of Northumberland and Lord Londonderry. They had both of them since died, and the Whigs had given away their Garters: 'But what I regret more than anything is the Lord Lieutenancies. For they influence the County gentlemen to a great extent. For instance, suppose a gentleman wishes to be on the Commission of the Peace, he makes up to the Lord-Lieutenant by exerting himself for his party. Now we have hardly any Lord Lieutenants. Lowther[9] is Lord-Lieutenant of two, but then he is a very old man. Garters are difficult to give away, for they are so invidious. I hear Lord Palmerston is much embarrassed about who he shall give the next Garter to. He has made very ridiculous appointments already. Then about Peers, when we were in office I proposed to Lord Derby to make four Peers and he agreed. We wished to raise the Order of Baronetage to the rank at present occupied by the Peerage and raise the Peerage. In this the Queen and Prince Consort cordially concurred. We offered the peerage to four persons, all men of about £90,000 a year. . . . We also gave Baronetcies to six men of £20,000 a year or so. There was great difficulty at first in inducing them to accept, but at last they all consented on condition that each other should accept. The Whigs came in and broke the compact. . . . The Duke 'of Argyll is a clever man but a prig.

[7] 1829-1881. Succeeded as 4th Earl of St. Germans 1877.
[8] 1830-1903. Succeeded his brother as Viscount Cranborne 1865, and his father as 3rd Marquess of Salisbury 1868.
[9] The 2nd Earl of Lonsdale.

"'Lord Granville is a man of the world, which gets him on. He might have been Prime Minister once, and he ought to have accepted even with a certainty of failure, as it is a great thing to have one's name on the list of Prime Ministers.

"'Sir Charles Wood[10] is a first-rate man, etc.'"

A third person, overhearing these conversations, might have thought, without incurring the charge of priggishness, that the leader of a greaty party in the House of Commons, on the edge of the Premiership, could find a better subject of political conversation with a lad of eighteen than the enumeration of peerages and baronetcies conferred mainly because of large fortunes. But the incident illustrates one facet of Lord Beaconsfield's many-sided character. Nobody would have approved more cordially than he the saying of Southey, an evangelist of Toryism, that "Your great Whig landowner is a leviathan with the intellect of a dodo." But he was the friend and guest of one of the principal Whig magnates, and, as this passage shows, only regretted that he could not create more leviathans himself.

Such conversations as these, and the enjoyment of sport, had not occupied the whole of Dalmeny's time. In the month of August he read all Congreve's comedies, especially noting *The Double Dealer* as a "very amusing and good play," leaving *The Way of the World* without the particular commendation which most readers would give it. He passed on to Wycherley, mentioning four famous plays—"of these I think *The Country Wife* the best. But the wit of all of them is indecency." He also enjoyed Bubb Dodington's *Diary*, and read old volumes of *Fraser's Magazine* and of the *Quarterly Review*.

Except for one or two brief visits in the north, Dalmeny remained at Raby until the end of September, when he settled down at Revesby in Lincolnshire, as one of the pupils of Mr. Warburton, the Rector of the parish. Revesby Abbey was the home of his cousin James Banks Stanhope,[11] so that he was not in a strange land, and his fellow pupils were mostly Etonians. He wrote of them: "I like them all very fairly. It is wonderful how much they have improved since they left Eton," a remark to which no double edge was intended, we may be sure. There was some shooting, and there were guests at the abbey, but there was not much to record dur-

[10] Sir Charles Wood, *b.* 1800, created Viscount Halifax 1866. Chancellor of the Exchequer 1846-52, President of the Board of Control 1852-5, First Lord of the Admiralty 1855-8, Secretary of State for India 1859-66, and Lord Privy Seal 1870-4. Died 1885.

[11] 1821-1904. M.P. for North Lincoln 1851-68.

ing his stay at Revesby. There was the necessary study, but more miscellaneous reading of good literature.

The regular sequence of visits to the beloved grandparents at Dalmeny had been rudely broken so far back as 1861. By that year their daughter Louisa Primrose had become a hopeless invalid, unable to travel, so that, from 1862 until his death in 1868, Lord Rosebery never saw Dalmeny House. The grandson used to spend part of his holidays, usually at Christmas, with his uncle Bouverie Primrose in Edinburgh, so that he never lost touch with his Scottish home. Bouverie Primrose, four years younger than Dalmeny's father, had made an unusual, but very happy, alliance with his stepmother's sister, Frederica Anson. The marriage took place in 1838, nineteen years after that of Anne, Lady Rosebery. The elder sister outlived the younger by fifteen years. Bouverie Primrose remained a popular and respected figure in the Edinburgh world until his death in 1898.

Dalmeny matriculated at Christ Church in January 1866, at the beginning of the Lent term. Etonians of the country gentleman class gravitated easily to "The House," where pleasant society was assured, and there was no undue pressure for distinction in the Schools, though a fair proportion of Christ Church men took Honours. It is clear from Lord Lansdowne's biography[12] that Balliol was considered a safer college for a young man just succeeding to great possessions. Dalmeny was not yet "his own father," as the phrase runs, but his mother would have been glad to see him settled at Balliol. His grandfather was a Cambridge man, but favoured his going to Oxford, on the rather singular grounds that it was not quite so far from Battle Abbey. He must have recalled the posting days of his own youth.

Among the older undergraduates at Christ Church when he went into residence were Lord Harrington, a man of great popularity and personal charm, who died just as he came of age;[13] the Duke of Hamilton, who had been a playmate of the Primrose children at Nice in 1854;[14] Lord Warkworth;[15] George Monckton;[16] and Arthur Smith-Barry.[17] His more immediate contemporaries and intimates were Philip Wroughton, known to his friends as "Peter,"

[12] *Lord Lansdowne*, by Lord Newton, p. 66.
[13] 6th Earl of Harrington, 1845-1866.
[14] 12th Duke of Hamilton, 1845-1895.
[15] 7th Duke of Northumberland, 1846-1918.
[16] 7th Viscount Galway, 1844-1931.
[17] Created Lord Barrymore 1902; 1843-1925.

later a model country gentleman and county Member; Henry Tolle-mache, an Admirable Crichton at all forms of sport, who became an approved champion of the agricultural interest in Parliament; Lord Bute,[18] whose early conversion to Roman Catholicism created a great sensation, and was supposed to have suggested the story of Lothair, though his respected and uneventful life ran on altogether different lines from that of Disraeli's hero; Lord Ilchester, the chief of the house of Fox; and last, but by no means least, Edward Hamilton, bringing to Oxford all the best atmosphere of Eton.

It was very much of a hunting set, and included more than one future Master of Hounds. Dalmeny never took to hunting, though he went out once or twice with the Heythrop. Later in life he liked a good-looking hack; but he was one of the exceptions in an age when even Londoners rode as a matter of course, and when a string of horses could be seen waiting outside either House of Parliament during the session. Some of his friends had, or would have, large fortunes, and no doubt spent too much money. But others carried on, and enjoyed the usual university amusements, including hunting, on moderate college allowances, and it would be an error to regard them as a specially spendthrift assemblage. Like their predecessors depicted by the poet who was at Cambridge forty years earlier:

"They talked
At wine, in clubs, of art, of politics:
They lost their weeks; they vexed the souls of deans;
They rode; they betted; made a hundred friends,
And caught the blossom of the flying terms."

There were two close friendships outside Christ Church; Lansdowne, two years older—whom he found installed at Balliol, and Randolph Churchill, two years younger, who soon became an undergraduate at Merton.

Dalmeny, naturally prone to pluck the flowers as they grew, felt under no obligation to map out a course of academic study for three or four years ahead, with a First in Mods succeeded by a First in Greats as the final palm of victory. This first Oxford year was unmarked by incident; in the Christmas vacation he buried himself in the country in solitude, refusing six invitations to pleasant country houses of his Oxford friends, finding the park a swamp, and speaking to nobody but the gamekeepers. He wrote to his mother, December 21st, 1866: "I have not seen a newspaper since I left London,

[18] 3rd Marquess of Bute, K.T., 1847-1900.

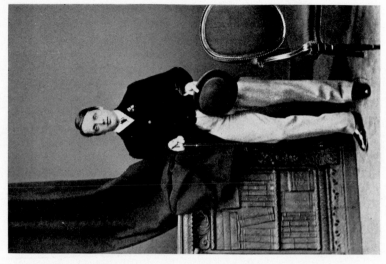

Lord Dalmeny at Eaton

Lord Dalmeny and Lord Ilchester
at Oxford

and for all I know the French may be in London or the Turks in Paris. It is a sort of living death, and I take a grim pleasure in it. It is very good for me to find out how far one can lead a life entirely thrown on one's own resources without vegetating, and I am rather pleased with the result."

In the following spring, March 1867, he set his face southwards. After some sightseeing and play-going in Paris, he made a comfortless journey to Marseilles. "There was a lifelong struggle all night between me and my *vis-à-vis*, a fat French officer, about the arrangement of legs, etc. He had this advantage that he *did* fall asleep, and then his legs were as firm as the rock of Gibraltar." The customary line of steamers had gone bankrupt, so he had to travel on a boat laden with petroleum, which reached Genoa appropriately, as he observed, on All Fools' Day. But he was charmed by a second glimpse of Genoa, which he had once seen in his Eton holidays—"A city of palaces and glowing tints." The steamer struggled on to Leghorn and Civita Vecchia, and on April 4th it was "Naples—at last." But his first grown-up experience of the beloved city was not happy:

"About 11.30 I went off to the Neapolitan Races, which I do not think I shall ever forget. We drove to the Campo di Marte, where, thirteen years ago, I remember seeing Ferdinand II review his troops. It is something to have lived out a dynasty at twenty! When we arrived at the place my driver motioned me to go and get a ticket for the carriage, on which I went off to get one. They cost three francs. To my horror I could only find two half-franc pieces. I had left my gold behind! There I stood, hunting in every pocket, among the jeers of the mob (N.B.—This is metaphorical). My driver now began to use strong language, he thought I did not understand the sum required or the coinage of the country. Alas, I knew both too well. I had to use pantomime. I turned my pockets inside out, I held out my hand as if begging. In fact I showed a neat talent for the legitimate drama. I shouted out 'Ho perduto—tutti—tutti,' which I then thought meant 'I have lost all, all.' I have since reason to think that it means nothing of the sort. My driver now became so violent that I began to think of squaring up to him, as he was not a very strong man. At last I pointed in a commanding way to Naples, so we returned for some way. But the driver met a friend. So he now stopped and conversed with the friend, pointing contemptuously at me. At last the friend produced a heap of coppers, and I produced my two miserable half-francs—so we got in. But it was a poor triumph. Two or three times the horse began rearing and kicking. The first time I jumped out of the carriage—but I did not do so again. My

[29]

jailer motioned me sternly back, and I remembered that I was in pawn for two francs. Whenever my keeper was offered an orange or a cigar he accounted for his having no money by telling the story of my poverty, and little knots of people collected round him frowning at me."

But this was his first and last adventure during a month's stay. He was well looked after by Lady Holland, dining often with her at the Palazzo Roccella, and making expeditions with her and her adopted daughter, Miss Fox, then a girl of sixteen, in the school-room.[19] These included the customary sail to Capri, and the ascent of Vesuvius, which the conditions of the moment made more toilsome than usual. He also dutifully visited the different museums and galleries, and under Lady Holland's auspices became acquainted with the social world of Naples. Though his notes contain some happy pictures of scenery, and some acute personal touches, they are less vivid than those that he wrote at Raby. There was no Mrs. Disraeli to banter, no Disraeli to consult as a benevolent oracle. But there was one lasting result in the conviction that he was unconsciously absorbing that if a man needs an extra home, outside the British Isles, Naples is the one place for it. He returned to Oxford at the beginning of May, "and went to bed for the first time after five nights of railway carriage and diligence." Travellers by Blue and Golden trains should note how their forbears, themselves not despising luxury, made journeys sixty years since.

In the autumn of the same year (October 1867), a messenger from the political world made the first knock at Dalmeny's door. An important neighbour of Raby asked the Duchess of Cleveland whether there was any chance of her son becoming a candidate for the borough of Darlington. Since the death of Lord Palmerston, in October 1865, the outlines of party had become greatly blurred, and the political affinities of some conspicuous politicians were uncertain. Lord John Russell, who had succeeded as Whig Leader, was responsible for the Reform Bill of 1866, which met its Waterloo on June 18th, when by the help of the Anti-Reform Liberals, headed by Lowe, Horsman, and Lord Grosvenor, it was defeated on a crucial clause in Committee by a majority of eleven, some forty Liberals voting with the Opposition. The Tories were in a minority, and the attempts at a Coalition between Lord Derby and the Cave of Adullam Liberals broke down. So a new Reform Bill was introduced by a purely Conservative Government in 1867, and became

[19] This very gifted and charming young lady married Prince Aloysius Lichtenstein five years later, and died in 1878.

law, though only after the sacrifice of three important Ministers, General Peel, Lord Cranborne, and Lord Carnarvon, who were unable to stomach the grant of that unrestricted borough franchise which for a generation had been a bugbear to the Tory party. Party lines, therefore, seemed to be ill-defined for the moment; and a young man, who had lived in a tolerant atmosphere, and had not so far been plied with the strong wine of party controversy, might well be excused for wishing to look about him before sitting down to the feast.

He wrote from Christ Church to his mother as follows:

October 27th, 1867.

"MY DEAREST MOTHER,

"Many thanks for your long letter.

"I was very much interested about Darlington. But there are so many things to be considered, that it seems impossible: though there is nothing I should like half so well as to represent Darlington.

"The first objection is, that though I have no politics, and have never professed any, I am not at all prepared to come forward as a Conservative. Besides the Conservative party has practically ceased to exist, and I think we shall see an entire transmutation of parties before 1869. Anyhow, it is not the time for a young man to commit himself in any way on either side. The next is that my grandfather would probably object, and very naturally, to devote any money which he may fairly destine for his younger children to getting me a seat in Parliament for what might possibly be a very short time. And I should neither feel justified in asking him for money nor my Committee for a subscription. I think the last at any rate an insuperable obstacle; so I shall cease to think of anything of the sort, and if Mr. Surtees ever alludes to it again, please tell him that it is out of the question."

The political curtain was then lowered for a spell, and the course of Oxford life resumed its easy flow. Moderations were passed "triumphantly" at the end of November, and were followed by visits to Blenheim and other country houses. A letter of December 2nd to his mother on the possibility of his going to Dalmeny shows how, at that time, affectionate intimacy with older relations did not prevent formality of access to them, but also throws light on Dalmeny's shy reserve. "I have heard nothing from Lord Rosebery, but if he wishes me to go, I shall, of course, make a point of doing so; but no proposal will come from me."

A few days afterwards he wrote again from London: "Lord and Lady Rosebery are very well indeed. I never saw him looking so well." Three months later (March 4th, 1868) Lord Rosebery died, leaving his grandson two months short of his majority and possession of the estates. Almost immediately afterwards the young man went to Italy for the Easter vacation, this time to Florence, which never engaged his affection as Naples did. He made the rather hasty criticism, "I certainly do not feel to care about the North of Italy so much as the South. The people are so lifeless in comparison, and the scenery round Florence is so comparatively tame. But then I have not seen Fiesole or Vallombrosa."

In the following autumn he paid a flying visit to Russia in company with Lord Bute. St. Petersburg was overpoweringly hot; a forest fire delayed the train journey to Moscow, so that he had only one day there, "infinitely beautiful to see from the top of a tower"; and the expense was formidable, he and his companion paying £14 for one extra day's lodging at a St. Petersburg hotel where they only breakfasted and dined: "I went to a Charity Ball the other night, and saw the Cesarevna, who is very charming.[20] I think the husband played at cards with his aide-de-camp in another room."

The year 1869 opened for him with no clearly defined panorama of life extended before him. He had never entirely devoted himself to the regulation studies of the University, although his tutor, Mr. Owen, afterwards said that he had never seen an undergraduate who gave evidence of having read so widely as he had, and fully expected him to take a brilliant First Class in the Honours School of Modern History. William Johnson, visiting at Dalmeny in the autumn of 1868, had written,[21] "Joab, my host, writes little essays on Luther's times for his Oxford degree, and I look over them critically, touching up the English. He is very clever, and has a peculiar variety of the 'haut ton.'"

Rosebery himself was not too well satisfied. Having returned to Oxford for the Lent term, he wrote that one of his cousins was disappointed at only getting a Third class in Honours—"I cannot see why, as a Third gets him his B.A. without any further examination, and he did not expect a First. If I thought I could get my degree as he has I should be delighted." On the very day that he set down this rather dreary reflection, a second summons to the political arena was being posted, surely a remarkable tribute of confidence in

[20] Princess Dagmar of Denmark, *m.* 1866 the Czarevitch, afterwards Emperor Alexander III. She became the Empress Marie Feodorovna.
[21] To Reginald Brett, Dalmeny, 1868.

an utterly untried man, still some months short of his twenty-second birthday. This was the correspondence:

Private.   *January 29th,* 1868.

"MY DEAR ROSEBERY,

"Your very friendly manner to me encourages me to ask you a favour without any preface.

"If you feel sufficient confidence in Gladstone's Government, will you give a proof of it by seconding the Address.

"The occasion is more important than usual—a new Parliament representing a new constituency about to consider a subject of the greatest interest.

"Yours sincerely,
GRANVILLE."

CHRIST CHURCH, OXFORD, *January* 31*st,* 1868.
"DEAR LORD GRANVILLE,

"Many thanks for your kind note. But it has puzzled me a good deal. I cannot be insensible of the flattering nature of your offer: however incapable I feel of seconding the Address in a way either satisfactory to myself or anybody else. But you probably do not know that I am only a resident undergraduate of Oxford working for a pass degree; and it might damage the Government if, with no counterbalancing quality, the Peer who seconded the Address was a lad *in statu pupillari*.

"I have never yet professed any political principles of any kind; for I think that when special profession is necessary, it is much better for a young man to reserve it, but my private sympathies and my reason have been wholly enlisted in the Liberal cause for some years: and as in June I must take one side or the other, I see no use in postponing that choice for a few months, when I have so thoroughly made up my mind, and so excellent an opportunity occurs of making that mind known to you.

"I can never hope to be of the slightest use to the party, though I should be proud of any opportunity of showing my attachment to its principles.

"Still I sincerely feel that the fact I mentioned at the beginning of my letter might be a disadvantage to the Government; so that I feel I must decline your kind offer.

"I only got your letter to-day. I wish I could have spared you so long a rigmarole as this, plastered with the personal pronoun.

"Believe me,
"Most gratefully and respectfully yours,
ROSEBERY."

[33]

The political curtain was lowered once more, but there was the degree to be taken, and it is impossible to suppose that this presented any serious difficulty. He was reading some Political Economy with Dean Liddell. And there were other interests and occupations. Attendance at the Oxford Union, which has been the ante-chamber of so many oratorical reputations in after life, was not one of these. It may seem strange that, after his frequent appearances in debate at the Eton Society, he should have never made an appearance on this larger stage. But these things are greatly ruled by fashion, and in some periods at both the great Universities it is not the fashion to attend the Union.

In Rosebery's case personal shyness may have been a further reason for this neglect; it was one thing to let himself go at the Eton Society, in a small circle of intimate acquaintance, and quite another to address a large audience of university men with whom he had little in common, and most of whom were strangers to him personally. As has been said, he did not hunt, but he sometimes shot pigeons, played racquets, and was fond of driving, though he never took to coaching, as many of his contemporaries did, becoming afterwards members of the Four-in-hand Club which figured so prominently in the London world. At Oxford dog-carts were in vogue. Rosebery one day was driving Prince Hassan, the Khedive's brother, at that time an undergraduate, when there was one of the mishaps to which two-wheeled carriages were liable, and the pair were tumbled out on the roadside. No great damage was done, but when, not long afterwards, Rosebery offered a lift to the popular Christ Church don, Charles Lutwidge Dodgson (1832–1898), the author of *Alice in Wonderland*, he was met by the Scriptural query, "Intendest thou to kill me, as thou killedst the Egyptian?"[22] Above all, there was the new and absorbing delight in the interest of a racing stable. The charm of the turf, which has gripped so many, was strong upon him. The taste was not hereditary, for the sport had held no attraction in the past for Primroses or Stanhopes, though at Raby he must have seen the sideboards gorgeous with the gold plate won by its owner's father, the Lord Darlington who was dreaded by his baffled contemporaries as the "Jesuit of the Turf." The reigning Duke cared for none of these things. Rosebery had registered his colours for flat racing soon after he came of age, which in itself was something of a provocation to the University

[22] *Exodus*, ch. ii, v. 14.

[34]

authorities, and early in 1869 he blossomed forth as an owner. His principal purchase was a three-year-old colt named *Ladas*, by *Lambton* out of *Zenobia*, of which something more will be said later on; and he made no secret of his hopes that, at the very first attempt, he might grasp the prize on which many owners have vainly set their hearts all their lives, by winning the Derby in the coming June, and creating a precedent by leading in a victorious horse at Epsom while still an undergraduate at Oxford. Some thirty years before, John Bowes, destined to secure four Derbys, had owned the winner of the first when he came of age, and appropriately named him *Mundig*. The home of Mr. Bowes was close to Raby, which possibly may have fired Rosebery to imitate this remarkable feat. But his forerunner was at Cambridge, and Cambridge, with Newmarket at its gates, has generally looked with a more lenient eye than Oxford on those who attended race meetings. *Dis aliter visum* in Rosebery's case. There was no moral offence in owning a racehorse, but it was an arrant breach of discipline for an undergraduate, as it would have been to obtain a publican's licence, or to open a cigar divan in the manner of Prince Florizel of Behomia. If he had agreed to postpone ownership of horses, no doubt he might have stayed on, but pride forbade this sacrifice of independence.

So the axe fell. At Easter Rosebery's name was removed from the books, and he ceased to be a member of the University, with no B.A. to his credit. Schoolboys sometimes feel their sense of fairness outraged by finding a mere escapade not less severely punished than some offence which they know to be really heinous. The claims of school discipline are peremptory. But a University can afford to distinguish the *malum prohibitum* from the *malum in se*: so that, two years later, when Rosebery had given proofs of serious interest in life, his name was replaced on the books of Christ Church. In 1872 he came up for a college "Gaudy," occupied his old rooms in the Canterbury Quad, and returned thanks for the House of Lords. No whitewashing could have been more complete.

But his departure, though not ignominious, was in no trailing cloud of glory. One who knew him well at Christ Church writes that "his influence was always on the side of law and order," while many of his harum-scarum contemporaries were in continual conflict with the authorities. The famous "statue" row, in which some of them were implicated, took place after Rosebery had gone down. The same friend adds, "While he was universally liked, he was not one who at any time had many bosom friends, possibly because he was intellectually immeasurably superior to all his contemporaries." Also, perhaps, because the aloofness which had marked him at Eton, as has been told, still existed at Oxford; and because simpler minds were sometimes puzzled by his ironical turn of banter. He was of middle height, or slightly more, strongly built, with a depth of chest to which the range and flexibility of his voice bore witness. It was not the figure of a horseman, or of a long-distance runner, but he was capable of much endurance, and could outwalk most people. "Just Eton boys, grown heavy," wrote Praed, in the most attractive of all reminiscent poems of school life.[23] Rosebery thickened somewhat, without ever becoming corpulent, and those who knew him through life, looking back on those days noted fewer physical changes in him than in most of their friends. His features were regular, with little play of expression, except when they were lit by a singularly radiant and fascinating smile. The eyes were remarkable. Light blue, and inclined to prominence, they were at times altogether expressionless, like the eyes of a bird. This gave an air of inscrutability, and sometimes of lack of interest in the surroundings of the moment, which many people found formidable. Few realised that they were witnessing the regular discipline of a nervously impulsive nature, at first studied, but becoming almost instinctive. When the charming smile broke out, the air of mystery vanished altogether.

In his Oxford days he was clean-shaven, except for the short side-whiskers which were then common. In a few years these disappeared and he remained beardless. It was easy to picture him in the dress worn before the French Revolution. To his relations, and to one or two of his closest friends, he was "Archie." To his Christ Church allies he was "D," and by that initial they always addressed him to the last. His handwriting, which was neat from the first, was in his boyhood on at least the average scale. It was not till he was leaving Oxford that it began to diminish, and it was some few years before it assumed the exquisite characteristics which it maintained for as long as he was able to govern a pen.

Now the world was all before him, where to choose. He had been a singularly conspicuous figure both at Eton and Oxford, without having tried to win either the academic or the athletic crowns which mean fame at school and college. Anxious mothers would soon be telling their boys at public schools how the sons of some of their

[23] *School and Schoolfellows.*

[36]

friends, such as Lansdowne and Morley,[24] were already started on the steep ascent leading to distinction in public life. Would Rosebery be such a one, or would he use his freedom only for pleasure? To himself, one may be sure, no such Choice of Hercules presented itself. Good literature, Blue Books, and the Racing Calendar all had their uses; there was no hurry, and he fully intended to extract the best from them all. But it certainly seemed to some people that—

> ". . . The busy elves to whose domain
> Belong the nether sphere, the fleeting hour"

were beginning to get the mastery of him. His uncle Bouverie wrote a letter which might be taken as a model for such an intervention. Without a tinge of sermonising, he spoke of the intense attraction of racing, and of the uncertainty which constitutes one of its fascinations. It was the friendly warning of an older man, not a lecture.

It was not until August 1868 that there were some restricted celebrations of his ownership at Dalmeny. Old Lady Rosebery was detained in London by her daughter's illness. His mother and sisters were in the south, and Everard was in Ireland. "All is, I am thankful to say, well over," he wrote, "and it is a comfort to think that the laws of nature prevent anyone coming of age twice." In the same autumn another old family friendship brought about a personal relation destined to influence Rosebery's public life during the next twenty-five years above and beyond any other. Mrs. Gladstone wrote in October that they were going to have a little dance in the house next month, and hoped that he and his brother might possibly be disengaged. She had just missed him at Raby the other day, when Mr. Gladstone and their youngest daughter were there, but having known his mother so long, she felt that they ought to make acquaintance. So that Rosebery's first approach from Mr. and Mrs. Gladstone was not a request that he would help to pass measures through Parliament, but that he would come to tread measures in the drawing-room at Hawarden. In the previous year he had spent three days at Hughenden, and had several hours of walks and talks with Disraeli.

Racing was becoming a serious interest. A colt named *Ladas* first carried the rose and primrose colours in the Derby of 1869, start-

[24] Albert, 3rd Earl of Morley (1843-1905). Under-Secretary for War 1880-85; First Commissioner of Works 1886; Chairman of Committees, House of Lords, 1889-1905.

ing at the odds of 60 to 1 in a field of twenty-two runners, and finishing last. It was a sad failure; all the worse that loud trumpets had been sounded about the colt's merits, and it was to be feared that all Christ Church had backed him for the Derby. There was little success otherwise, and in the result the whole lot went up to Tattersall's for sale on November 1st. Of the seven yearlings sent up none reached their reserves. Their owner may not have been altogether sorry, though he must have wished to repair the losses of a poor year, because Admiral Rous, the Jupiter Tonans of Newmarket, had happened to mention that interest in racing, unless corroborated by ownership of horses, would not be enough to secure a young man's election to the Jockey Club. In the result Rosebery was chosen for that body in the autumn of 1870.

Such a recruit could not but be welcome at Newmarket. What Whyte Melville's heroine described as "the slang aristocracy" in a phrase which now sounds prehistoric, had just lost its leading hero in the Marquess of Hastings,[25] who had died in 1868, leaving little behind him save a reputation for careless good nature and shrewdness in the business of racing, joined to a capacity for lavish expenditure which would have dissipated a far larger fortune than that which he inherited as a minor.

But the famous old town by no means regarded itself as a mere shrine of reckless frivolity. Without harking back to the days of Rockingham and Grafton, there was certainly no incompatibility between devotion to racing and the pursuit of high politics; though at the moment a direct connection had almost ceased for the time being.

Lord George Bentinck was but a memory; Lord Palmerston had died in 1865; Lord Derby had quitted office early in 1868 and was to live but little more than a year longer; General Peel had resigned from the War Office and from Parliament when the Reform Bill of 1867 created a fissure in the Conservative party, surviving only as an honoured Nestor of the turf. But Lord Granville, one of the Liberal leaders, belonged to the Jockey Club, and had occasional interest in a racing stable; while Lord Hartington, who had entered

[25] Lord Rosebery was always interested in the career of Lord Hastings, whom he just failed to meet. He had fancied that the character of Sir Harry Scattercash, in his favourite *Mr. Sponge's Sporting Tour*, must have been drawn from "Harry Hastings"; until he realised that Surtees's book was published in 1853, when Lord Hastings was a boy of eleven. It was asserted that until the final crash of *Hermit's* Derby in 1867 he was well in credit on his racing and betting account; but there is only one end to the finances of a man who treats his winnings as income and leaves his losses to take care of themselves.

[38]

Parliament in 1857, was carrying on, in his easy, unostentatious way, alike the political and the sporting traditions of his famous house. Nor were the frequenters of Newmarket, old and young, by any means a set of Squire Westerns and Tony Lumpkins. Admiral Rous, its undisputed autocrat, had cut a brave figure in the Navy, and sat in Parliament; George Payne, as completely the "gay companion and the favorite guest" as ever Sir Robert Walpole can have been, wasted excellent talents with unfailing geniality, and steadily resisted the prayer of all Northamptonshire that he should sit for the county; Henry Chaplin[26] and James Lowther[27] industriously pursued in Parliament the careers which, later, were to be rewarded by high official promotion; and the presence of such men as Lord Suffolk,[28] Lord Rosslyn,[29] and Gerard Sturt,[30] enriched a brilliant and amusing society. Its feminine element in those days was small in number, but attractive and conspicuous in several aspects. There was "Lady A." Maria, Marchioness of Ailesbury, kind of heart and deep of voice, taking her racing as seriously as she took her evangelical religion. There was the compelling charm and leadership of the Duchess of Manchester.[31] There was the brilliance of the Forester sisters, Lady Chesterfield and Lady Bradford. These were all riding or driving on the Heath, as in those days everybody did, before any stands for visitors existed. Lady Stamford[32] and

[26] 1840-1923. M.P. 1868-1916; Chancellor of the Duchy of Lancaster 1885-6; President of the Board of Agriculture 1889-92; President Local Government Board 1895-1900; cr. Viscount Chaplin 1916. The well-known owner of *Hermit* and other good horses.

[27] Rt. Hon. James Lowther, 1840-1904. M.P. 1864-1904; Parliamentary Secretary to Poor Law Board 1868; Under-Secretary for the Colonies 1874-8; Chief Secretary for Ireland 1878-80.

[28] Henry, 18th Earl of Suffolk (1833-1898), affectionately known to a large circle of friends as "Dover" from his earlier title of Viscount Andover. His contribution to the Badminton Library on *Racing* (London: Longmans, Green & Co., 1886) would do credit to an author of greater pretensions. The figure of Lord Olim Juvabit, in one of his vivid sketches of past days at Newmarket, may well have been modelled on the Rosebery of the 'seventies.

[29] Robert, 4th Earl of Rosslyn (1833-1890). Witty and scholarly, something of a poet, and a personage of unequalled *desinvolture*. My father described him as "One of the few people in the House of Lords who can read and write."

[30] Henry Gerard Sturt (1825-1904). M.P. 1847-76; cr. Lord Alington 1876. A conspicuous figure on the turf, in a partnership with Sir Frederick Johnstone which twice won the Derby. Lord Granville formerly had a share in some of his horses. Lord Beaconsfield christened him "the champagne of society."

[31] Countess Louise von Alten, *m.* first, the 7th Duke of Manchester, second, the 8th Duke of Devonshire.

[32] Wife of Harry, 8th Earl of Stamford (1827-1883). Rosebery knew Lord and Lady Stamford well, and was often their guest at the famous shooting parties at Bradgate and Enville during his unmarried years.

Lady Cardigan,[33] peris kept outside the conventional pale, may have enjoyed themselves as gaily as those who were within it.

In 1870 Rosebery went abroad again, this time with some Eton and Oxford friends, Edward Hope, J. H. Mossop, and J. Shafto. During this sojourn of nearly three months in France and Italy, he kept a journal on a more careful and elaborate scale, which fills a fairly stout quarto notebook. There are humorous accounts of discomforts and mishaps of travel; serious appreciations of works of art; a very few political reflections; and a continual flow of good-natured chaff directed at his travelling companions.

This last feature is a little difficult to understand, unless he intended to circulate the diary in one form or another; but this, apparently, was never done, and the jocular passages must have been sketched in for his own enjoyment. After a week at Nice, with some visits to Monte Carlo, where Rosebery restricted himself to watching the losses of his English friends and acquaintances, the party coasted on to Genoa, where their morning slumbers were disturbed by salutes fired in honour of the birthday of Washington, which evoked the reflection that "the sound of cannon is always pleasant. One is bound to speak with rapture of the possible advent of a universal time of peace, when leopards and lambs shall run about in couples, and a cockatrice's hole be such a desirable residence: but I have a secret feeling that life would lose much, at least, of its outward grace and splendour." They passed on to Florence and its galleries:

"I do not know if after all I like any picture much better than Michael Angelo's *Parcae in the Pitti*. The bridge across the river, which makes the communication between the Uffizzi and the Pitti, is filled with the most beautiful tapestry I ever saw. Much of it is worked with gold thread, to give the metallic gleam to the cuirasses and jewels. There is one piece representing the Morning, which give the gladness and profusion of the light with almost as much force as Guido's picture. I think that nothing teaches you to appreciate a good picture like seeing the copy lying in front of it, the one hard and tawdry, the other mellow and alive. I found one of the copyists explaining to a group of well-dressed Italians (and highly educated, as they understood the French of the Lecture) the astounding fact that Michael Angelo was not merely a painter but a sculptor, and not merely a sculptor but an architect. The Italians listened open-mouthed."

[33] Adeline de Horsey, second wife of the 7th Earl of Cardigan, the cavalry leader (1797-1870), to whom she was married in rather irregular fashion. She was the niece of Admiral Rous.

Rome was reached late in February. It was not Rosebery's first visit, for he had been there at Easter 1864, and he had stood by Keats's grave in the inspiring company of William Johnson. This time he found a polished, and perhaps rather *precieux*, English and American society, with whom he went on the sightseeing round. But he was not entirely dependent on such guidance. He was alone at St. Peter's on Sunday, February 27th.

"As soon as I got up, I went to St. Peter's to hear High Mass. It lasted about two hours, and in the middle of it there was a great procession. These processions are extremely effective, owing to the fact that in the enormous nave you can see the great procession winding about all at once, and to the brilliancy of the colours. The effective part of the service to me is the congregation. Instead of our pews and glossy hats and chignons and neatly got-up lodge-keepers to represent an intelligent and prosperous peasantry, you are elbowed here by real want and poverty and squalor, to whom the Church is the only Home: and it is a home to them at all hours, however splendid it may be. Gibbon called St. Peter's the noblest edifice devoted to the worship of a Deity, and yet the congregation was not at all noble or even respectable in the ordinary sense of the word. There were a great many Zouaves, but there seemed to me to be a still greater number of wild-looking beings in rags and tatters, praying with passionate earnestness, to whom the services of the church were living realities. Nor did it seem to occur to them for a moment that their souls were of less value than those of the very beadles. To them the portion of wine and wafer borne in procession were undoubtedly God's Body and Blood, and the sight of it threw them into a sort of religious ecstasy. One man I can recall in particular. He was a fine picture in himself, and off him I could hardly take my eyes as he knelt next me. I have been much flea-bitten ever since."

A little later on he dined with Bute and met Monsignor Capel, the brilliant Churchman who was reproduced in *Lothair* before his unhappy fall from grace.

"I talked a great deal with Monsignor Capel. He would not hear of secular education, and considered Forster's Bill the best that could be obtained under the circumstances. He told me that Manning was absolutely alone with his nominee Cornthwaite, the Bishop of Beverley, in supporting the infallibilist doctrine. The petition was presented to them this day fortnight, or at least to the English Bishops, for signature, and all, with these two exceptions, refused their concurrence. The Catholics, he said, in England, looked up to two Bishops for guidance—Ullathorne, very senior and an encyclopedia,—Clifford, a great canonist, and the representative of the old Catholic families. These two were entirely opposed to the dogma. Manning is very unpopular. This was all told me that I should spread it. I have therefore kept it to myself, but give it here for what it is worth."

He was by now forming a definite conception of comparative values in art, though neither then nor later did he ever assume the airs of a professed critic.

"This morning we all went (in the great family coach I have hired) to the Farnesina Palace. It did belong to the King of Naples, but, like almost everything else, he has been forced to sell it. There is an entrance hall surrounded with magnificent frescoes by Raphael. The figure of one of the Graces in this series with her back turned is held by some to be the finest female shape in the world. Whether that be so or not, the frescoes are extremely beautiful, and show that Raphael was as great in representing the heathen divine as the Christian divine—two essentially distinct types, of different though hardly unequal majesty. Where you have Jupiter representing merely kingship predominating over a variety of puissant deities each representing some primitive and original power, the idea to me is as sublime as any Christian conception. It is only where the heathens represent him, in their inability to realise perfect justice united with perfect mercy, as the slave of successive and contending fits of weakness and uxoriousness and wrath, that the idea appears wanting in unity and divinity. The face of Zeus is the face of a supreme god, but that will never be realised on canvas. In the Christ of Raphael's *Transfiguration* incomparably the finest figure of a divinity that I have ever seen, and the Christ of Correggio in the same collection, which seems to me to come next to it, you have divinity but not unalloyed with mortality. Christian art, as has been said, is inadequate to its subject; but pagan art was also inferior, and both from the same cause. In Raphael's Christ the face is worn with the cares of ordinary life, and the anguish of a Divine Essence condescending to a sordid humanity, and though it is lit up with an unearthly love and an immortal compassion, mortality is not absent from the conception. In Correggio's Christ, the God, it is true, has freed himself from his humanity; the cere clothes are around him, but not of him, they are below and behind, and the accompaniments of his victory rather than the witnesses of his inferiority. The face wears the gladness of triumph but not the complete resumption of divinity: the cloud of Cherubim glows with a perfect and heavenly joy, but it is rather over the empty grave than the entered Paradise.

"What this remarkable rigmarole has to do with the Farnesina Palace I am at a loss to conceive. In the room next the hall there is a fine fresco of Galatea by Raphael and a head in charcoal by Michael Angelo, which pleased me immensely. I cannot say now that I like Michael Angelo better than Raphael, but he is a great force."

He visited practically every gallery in Rome, and was enraptured by the portrait of a woman in the Sciarra Gallery—

"the most beautiful woman in the world, by Titian. I remember her as a child in my mother's copy, then as soon as I had enough money I bought a print of her, and to-day I had the rarest pleasure I have experienced in Rome of seeing her face to face. I know of no face that touches it in point of dignity, depth and expression. And to relieve the apparent coldness of the face the painter has thrown in a southern warmth of colour, which brings into more forcible contrast the still gravity of her expression. Fortunately these women do not exist in real life, as they would make fools of the world."

On raving about this picture to a lady "who had seen it but too many others on the same day," he was chilled by finding it mixed up in her mind with the picture of Beatrice Cenci. "I met the same lady in the Borghese Gallery, and in the evening asked her if she did not admire Raphael's portrait of Cæsar Borgia, to which she replied with much feeling, 'Yes, she has a sweet face.'"

He had an audience with Pope Pius IX: "He gave me the impression of being the incarnation of what the French call *bonté*, a word for which I know of no English equivalent." So the pleasant days went on: sometimes there were torrents of rain, sometimes the Tramontana blew. The Comte de Montalembert, the most eminent of French Catholics, had just died, and a Requiem Mass to be said at the Ara Coeli was suddenly forbidden, to the great excitement of French sympathisers; but on the following morning the Pope unexpectedly ordered it to be said at another church, and attended in person behind a *grille*. "This has not stopped a single mouth, nor altered to anyone the signification of yesterday's act, except by adding to it a character of petulance and feebleness."

Towards the end of March Rosebery started for his adored Naples. He was welcomed at the Club by many Italian friends, and each page of the journal shows how happy he was to be once more at the place of his choice. There was a "breakfast" of more than a hundred people at Castellamare, given by a Neapolitan princess for the Prince and Princess of Piedmont,[34] where theatricals, dancing, and illuminations lasted far into the next day. Soon afterwards his companions went home, and he paid a short visit to Palermo, which he

[34] Afterwards King Humbert and Queen Margaret of Italy.

duly admired without endangering his loyalty to Naples, whither he returned for a spell of sultry weather, leaving again for Rome in the middle of April. There he came in for the Easter celebrations at St. Peter's, and for the Benediction of the crowd from the lofty balcony of the Cathedral. Like all who ever heard it, he was amazed at the powerful and distinct intonation with which the Pope uttered his blessing—for the last time, as it proved to be—"and so the World and the City were blessed on the seventeenth of April eighteen hundred and seventy." He went out on the Pincio to watch the illumination of St. Peter's dome, half dreading to spoil the splendid impression left from his Eton days, and finding that he was now not less entranced than he had been then. Rome had not ousted Naples from his affections, but he was deeply sensible of the wonder of the city, both in its past and its present. Later in the year (October 3rd, 1870), he wrote: "How curious it is that in this year of horrors and prodigies the, perhaps, most wonderful event of the century—the occupation of Rome by the Italians—has passed as unnoticed as a gipsy encroachment on a parish common."

They journeyed homewards by Pisa and Spezzia, and by *vetturino* along the Cornice, passing each night at some spot on that delicious coast, free at that season from the crowd of winter travellers which would seem so exiguous to-day. They reached Paris on April 25th— "To-day I heard the terrible news of the massacre in Greece.[35] Poor Fred Vyner." This was no light blow. Rosebery was on terms of close friendship with all the Vyner family, the brothers Clare, Frederick, and Robert, the sister Lady de Grey,[36] and the mother Lady Mary Vyner,[37] from whom he had received the utmost kindness. Mrs. Robert Vyner was the sister of his travelling companion John Shafto.

He was in no hurry to embark on the political course for which he was destined by general opinion—partly, no doubt, owing to that very opinion. His days were well filled, and he passed many evenings at the opera and at the play. During the years 1869 and 1870 he did not attempt to speak in the House of Lords, though he

[35] A party of eight tourists, including two Secretaries of Legation, British and Italian, visited Marathon on April 11th. They were captured by brigands, and after a series of negotiations, miserably conducted by the Greek Government, four of the party, including Frederick Vyner, were shot in cold blood.

[36] Married, 1851, Earl de Grey, afterwards 1st Marquess of Ripon.

[37] Daughter and co-heiress of Thomas, 2nd Earl de Grey, *d.* 1892. Her four sons were Clare Vyner, 1836-1882; Reginald Vyner, 1839-1870; Robert Vyner, 1842-1915; and Frederick Vyner, 1847-1870.

attended occasionally, and in the latter year voted for the Bill to permit marriage with a deceased wife's sister.

Later in the same session he found a debate on the affairs of Greece "very feeble and unsatisfactory." But it is not until February 1871 that he really started. Lord Granville, undeterred by the collapse of his premature attempt two years earlier, again in warm terms invited him to second the Address in answer to the Queen's Speech. The mover was Lord Westminster,[38] who had succeeded two years before to the family honours.

There were domestic questions of moment, such as Army Reform and the Abolition of University Tests, but all were overshadowed by the Franco-German war, in which the German victory was already assured, while peace still seemed to be far off. To this subject the greater part of Rosebery's speech was devoted, though he also touched on the Alabama Commission, on the Repeal of University Tests, and on elementary education in Scotland. The following extract shows that he had to some purpose framed his periods on eighteenth-century models :

"I know of nothing in history so grand as the manner in which, when her armies had melted away like snow before the sun, when her fortresses were beleaguered, when her Executive was either captured or fled, when all, in fact, that represented civil organisation or war-like power had vanished, Paris, who for eighteen years had given up herself to luxury and deified pleasure, came forward to endure bombardment and famine and death, in order to become the nucleus of the defence of France. For four months she held on, she fed her population of epicures on husks and rats, yet there was little repining and no crime. . . . And now, at last, there is an armistice,—an armistice, let us hope, that will ripen into a durable peace. Meanwhile we have seen the King of Prussia proclaimed Emperor in the Palace of Louis the Fourteenth. The warmest good wishes of this country must go forth to the new Confederation ; the warm wishes of this country will be to see this historical Empire prove that she cannot merely conquer, but also use her conquests with magnanimity, and that when this disastrous war is concluded she may use her great power in the interests of peace and civilisation."

"What shall we say of France?" he went on. He professed his faith in the destinies of this great country, that she would look back with thankfulness to the crucial trial from which she emerged to a higher and purer state of liberty than she had ever known. He be-

[38] b. 1825, succeded as third Marquess 1869, created Duke of Westminster 1874.

lieved that we should live to see France far greater in the councils of Europe by moral authority than she ever was by her armies.[39]

The speech was well received: he himself noted privately, "Great congratulations, very ill deserved." The Duke of Richmond exceeded the conventional congratulations always offered by the Leader of the Opposition, speaking of "the conspicuous ability of the seconder."

Lord Granville had secured his important recruit, who was encouraged to try his wings more than once during the session. He asked for papers on the Greek massacres of the previous year by which he had been so closely touched, speaking of "that body which was inaccurately called the Greek Government." He had also, for some time past, been exercised by the occasional abuses of lay patronage in Scotland, and he quoted in the House of Lords (May 9th, 1871) the instance of his neighbouring burgh of Queensferry. There the Council of nine members included seven who did not belong to the Established Church, with the result that they appointed Mr. ———, who was drawing large audiences to his lectures in the principal towns of Scotland, and described himself as a person endowed with remarkable wit, eloquence, and pathos. He did not say that there was sufficient cause for objection against Mr. ———, but he believed that if St. Chrysostom had been appointed in this manner he would have had an equally unfavourable reception. A rather heated debate followed, as happens when ecclesiastical matters are discussed in Parliament. A like atmosphere prevailed when he intervened for the last time in this session on the University Tests Bill, which excited the clerically-minded to a degree which now seems barely credible. He was brought into the first of many collisions with Lord Salisbury by his opposition to clerical fellowships, based on the ground that they exposed poor scholars to the temptation of taking Orders. The imputation was exactly of the sort to bring out Lord Salisbury's sting. There were three sorts of gossip at Oxford, he explained—those of the common-room, the undergraduates, and the scouts. Rosebery's facts came from the third source. Lord Granville, winding up the debate, complained of this bitter retort to a speech remarkable for point and for general ability.

[39] In the previous autumn he had written to his mother: "I have, like you, every sympathy for the French army. But at the same time one thinks more highly of the Prussians than we did. They make war *en grand seigneur*. They do not pillage and they treat their prisoners like their own men. It is a great change from Blücher." Alas, there was another great change to follow, years later—William II from William I.

CHAPTER III

Scotland—Three Visits to America

D URING the years which followed his accession to the family estates, Rosebery did not allow the pressure of London, of Newmarket, of English country-house life, or of foreign travel to divert his mind from his Scottish homeland. The inherited property there covered some 21,000 acres in Midlothian and Linlithgow, including the shooting-box of Rosebery, near Gorebridge. There was also a moderate revenue from mines of shale not far from Dalmeny itself. As he admitted when, towards the end of the decade, he brought his bride to Dalmeny, he "had been hitherto somewhat of a roving bachelor," but, nevertheless, he made more public appearances in Scotland than anywhere else. The house of Dalmeny, at which he kept the modest establishment of an uncertain resident, was left in the simple condition which it had worn in his grandfather's time. It was built in the first quarter of the nineteenth century, to take the place of the ancient castle of Barnbougle, of which more will be said later. This was an ivy-mantled ruin when Rosebery succeeded. Dalmeny House is a castellated building of the type familiar in Scotland, where succeeding generations clung to the traditions dating from the French Renaissance, when the two countries were united in common mistrust of England. Standing near the entrance to the Firth of Forth, it looks out on the small islands that break the monotony of the sea-line. The park is charmingly broken into a series of vales and dells, while the size and luxuriance of the timber, both in the open and in the coverts, tell how the harshness of the east coast has been mitigated by the contours of the bay, and by the semi-insular character of the points projecting into the Firth. In spite of its nearness to Edinburgh, Dalmeny remains singularly retired to this day. When Rosebery went there, years before the Forth Bridge was dreamt of, he could fancy himself to be the hermit whose lot he sometimes thought so enviable.

But his native land did not encourage him to adopt a monastic rule of silence. At his coming-of-age banquet thirty-six speeches seem to have been made, of which he had to deliver five, acknowledging enthusiastic tributes to absent members of his family besides the toast of his own health.

In 1871 the Scott Centenary at Edinburgh collected Sir William Stirling Maxwell, Lord Houghton, who was Rosebery's guest at Dalmeny, and a Scottish lettered circle. At the interminable feasts of those days, it was the custom to conclude the entertainment by asking the exhausted company to drink the toast of "The Ladies." This was generally entrusted to a youthful guest, who was expected to treat it with refined jocularity. Rosebery was the victim this time, and finished his speech by hoping that everybody present would silently drink to one, or at most two, of the opposite sex. If not, he trusted that "the short remainder of the night would be spent by him in an agonizing nightmare, in which the ghost of Jenny Geddes would appear to him with her irrepressible footstool." This was better stuff than the audience would have heard as a rule; but it was a poor use to make of Rosebery's faculties at a Scott banquet, and it is not surprising that he privately noted it as "a ghastly ceremony."

His next appearance at Edinburgh was more worthy of his powers. He was invited to address the Edinburgh Philosophical Society at the opening of its session in November 1871. Its rather formidable title did not prevent that important and representative body from inviting men of distinction to enlighten it on subjects of historical and general interest; but the orators were usually far more than twenty-four years old. Rosebery chose the Union between Scotland and England as his theme. His easy grasp of it helps to confirm his Oxford tutor's hopes of his place in the Honours School of History. The debt to Macaulay is traceable, but only in the style, for Macaulay's *History* does not reach the momentous years from 1704 to 1707.

Rosebery realised that he was lecturing, not writing an essay or a history, so he did not dwell on the long negotiations for a treaty in which his ancestor had played a notable part; but he drew some vivid portraits of leading figures in the drama—the Duke of Hamilton, Lord Belhaven, and Fletcher of Saltoun. The sketch of the final negotiations is concise and masterly, as is the series of reflections on the losses and gains which fell to Scotland from the Act of Union, and on the slow processes of reconciliation between the two countries. The peroration shows how the political leaven of the moment was working in his veins, inspiring some thoughts not

DALMENY

actually germane to the subject, but irresistibly rising to the surface of his discourse.

"One word more, and I have done. Our ancestors put their hands to a mighty work, and it prospered. They welded two great nations into one great empire, and moulded local jealousies into a common patriotism. On such an achievement we must gaze with awe and astonishment, the means were so adverse and the result so surprising. But we should look on it also with emulous eyes. Great as that Union was, a greater still remains. We have in our generation, if we would remain a generation, to effect that union of classes without which power is a phantom and freedom a farce. In these days the rich man and the poor gaze at each other across no impassable gulf; for neither is there in this world an Abraham's bosom of calm beatitude. A powerless monarchy, an isolated aristocracy, an intelligent and aspiring people, do not together form the conditions of constitutional stability. We have to restore a common pulse, a healthy beat to the heart of the Commonwealth. It is a great work, the work of individuals as much as of statesmen, alien from none of us, rather pertinent to us all; each in his place can further it. Each one of us—merchant and clerk, master and servant, landlord and tenant, capitalist and artisan, minister and parishioner—we are all privileged to have a hand in this most sublime work of all; to restore or create harmony betwixt man and man; to look, not for the differences which chance or necessity has placed between class and class, but for the common sympathies which underlie and connect all humanity. It is not monarchs, or even statesmen, that give to a country prosperity and power. France in 1789 had a virtuous monarch and able statesmen. But the different classes of the community had then become completely estranged, and the upper crust of society was shivered to dust by the volcano beneath. In this country the artificial barriers which separate class from class are high enough, but, thank God, they are not insuperable. Let us one and all prevent their becoming so. A great page records the bloodless and prosperous history of the Scottish Union. A greater page lies vacant before us on which to inscribe a fairer union still."

His mother, the daughter of one historic house, and married into two others, was quick to notice one phrase in these concluding sentences, and did not hide her disapproval. Rosebery stuck to his guns, which do not nowadays seem to be charged with very high explosive. He wrote to her a few days later (November 24th, 1870):

"I am very much flattered by your having read my address, but I do not conscientiously think it worth the trouble. But the phrase to which you object, I stick to. I never said or hinted that where the heart of the aristocracy is touched, or on a great crisis the aristocracy do not do their duty. But I maintain, and no Liberal can say otherwise, that the House of Lords is isolated in sympathies from the country. And I say that no Liberal can say otherwise because the House of Lords rejects those measures which the country, through its representatives, has ratified. On that ground therefore I hold that I had a perfect right to use the word 'isolated.' At the same time no one can deny the noble qualities and individuals of the aristocracy. But you say that 'Men are not better esteemed in other classes for depreciating their own.' I am not sure that I have depreciated my own, but whether that be so or not, it seems to me that your argument strikes at the very root of political morality. I hope it will be long in England before people act or speak merely to please a class or classes.

"Forgive my long rigmarole suggested by your letter which opened a new light to me, as I did not think that anyone had taken the same view of the expression."

At a time when Local Government, outside municipal areas, was not yet fully organised, it was natural that Rosebery's desire to lend a hand in some national task should drive him to active participation in Scottish educational movements. He had taken no part in the debates on the English Education Bill of 1870; but from 1871 onwards he was in continual request north of the Tweed as chairman and speaker at anniversaries and other educational associations in anticipation of the corresponding Scottish measure in Parliament. As everybody knows, Scotland has long stood in the foremost rank for rational and efficient conduct of the nation's teaching, from the village school to the university. In no field has the *perfervidum ingenium* found finer scope than here. Here Rosebery, eclectic as he was, could find work which he felt to be really worth doing. At one end of the scale were such institutions as the United Industrial School at Edinburgh. Here he presided in 1871, 1872, 1876, and 1877. It was an institution framed on the lines of the ragged schools, for which the conscience of England had been awakened by Lord Shaftesbury and other generous agencies, including the novels of Charles Dickens, leading to the passage of the Industrial Schools and Reformatories Act of 1854. One special element in the situation made particular appeal to Rosebery's mind. Owing to the influx of Irish families into Edinburgh, dating from some fifty years back, a heavy percentage of these indigent children were Roman Catholics. In the first instance, it was arranged that all children should be handed over for one hour each day to ministers of their parents' faith for religious instruction. In such an institu-

tion as this the controversy which has always raged over this solution—whether religious teaching should be given in the school
building and within compulsory school hours—did not arise; but it
was disapproved by some, who held that a Presbyterian country
could not admit the propagation of error in a place of public education. Each year Rosebery set himself to combat this view, and to
plead the cause of the Irish Catholics.

"I do not believe in the charity which meets two ragged children in
the street, which asks them what their religion is, and when one answers,
'I am a Catholic,' and the other answers, 'I am a Protestant,' says,
'Come home, little Protestant, and take your porridge; but as for you,
little Catholic, you may die or starve or emigrate, it is no matter to me.
I do not agree with any of the articles of your dogma, and therefore you
may be left to your own ways and your own doing.' That, as I have
said, is in my view a very narrow spirit of charity."

When the Education Acts were passed, he was able to point out
that industrial schools were intended for those who could not be
reached by the School Board, and that, although in those schools
they considered it not merely a matter of efficiency but of respect
to religion that religious education should be separated from secular
education, yet in that larger sphere of education in public schools
they had to remember that it involved the issues of justice to the
ratepayers, who supported these schools, and the relation generally
of the State to the various forms of religion.

When the Scottish Education Bill was before the House of Lords
(July 16th, 1872), he moved an amendment in Committee, forbidding the teaching in any school of any Catechism or any religious
formulary distinctive of any particular denomination; while admitting that the "religious difficulty" in Scotland was not to be compared with that in England or Ireland, he pointed out that, besides
the one-seventh of the population opposed to Presbyterianism, the
United Presbyterians were in favour of complete separation of secular and religious education. The Shorter Catechism, therefore, was
not welcome to everybody, and yet it was certain as a rule to form
the sole subject of religious instruction. It was a powerfully phrased
argument, but the proposal was naturally unacceptable to the House
of Lords, and it was negatived without a division. Rosebery was at
pains to show that he set himself in no opposition to the Established
Church, or to the Shorter Catechism. In his grandfather's time
Dalmeny had not been a Presbyterian house, and, as a rule, an Epis-

copal clergyman had read the service in the dining-room on Sundays: but the family attended kirk from time to time, and the form of worship that he shared there continued to make particular appeal to one side of his character.

Later in the same year (September 29th, 1872) he was given the Freedom of the Burgh of Queensferry. There he spoke at some length on the claims of agricultural labour and the formation of agricultural unions. But he soon plunged into the education question, defending generally the recent Scottish Act, and specially rebutting the charge of injustice to teachers. "We must remember that the ancient Scotch schoolmaster, if I may so call him, after the passing of this measure, was like Teneriffe or Atlas, unremoved and unremovable practically; in this dignified position and very solitary state that though they were unremovable the parents of the parish did not sometimes consider them fit to teach their children." But he again deprecated the provision made by the Act for religious education. He desired to see religion a separate and careful subject of instruction by the Church and parents of the child, the lay teacher taking no hand in it whatever.

He developed the same thesis in the following year, at a meeting in connection with the Edinburgh School Board election (March 26th, 1873), arguing powerfully against two local schools of thought, one favouring the adoption in Scotland of what was known in England as the Cowper Temple Clause, permitting only "simple Bible teaching," the other desiring this plus the Shorter Catechism.

"Those for whom he spoke threw religion on governmental or accidental agencies, they threw it, in the first place, on the Church, Established or Voluntary; in the second place on that great army of Sabbath-school teachers, which had been such a blessing to Scotland; in the third place —and he was not sure it ought not to have been the first—on the parents; and in the fourth place, on the people of Scotland themselves."

Once again, he addressed, as President, the inaugural gathering of the Glasgow Public School Union, which designed to "unite all parties in a policy undisturbed by theological considerations." Over a thousand people attended, and the religious teaching prescribed by the Act of 1872 was again his main topic. Rosebery's long and witty speech was principally devoted to the personal position and the declared policy of some local advocates of religious instruction by lay teachers.

In the autumn of 1873 Rosebery crossed the Atlantic for the first time, reaching New York on September 30th, after a fine passage, "altogether very good fun," and arriving in the midst of a brief but violent commercial panic. "The surest sign of the times was that at the Manhattan Club fifty dollars more was spent on one of those evenings for drinks than had ever been known before. Now the panic is over." He was appalled by the price of everything, and feared that "the Scotch peerage would soon come to an end in New York."

In a flying visit to Canada he was the guest of Lord and Lady Dufferin at Ottawa, where he noted:

"Canadian oratory is of extraordinary length. What would the House of Lords say to one whole sitting of a great debate being taken up by two inferior speakers? For seven hours did they deliver themselves, and I who heard them am as well as can be expected. . . . One evening a Canadian gentleman asked me what I thought of the debate. 'Well,' I said, with a sort of sigh, 'the speeches were rather shorter perhaps ——' 'Never mind,' he said briskly, mistaking the cause of my sigh, 'you will have some much longer to-morrow!' "

He was greatly struck by the charm of Quebec, thinking it like Edinburgh, with its fortress crown. He was also impressed by the overflowing attendance at the Catholic churches in Quebec, adding: "Oddly enough, though the population is chiefly composed of French Catholics, the Sunday in Quebec is the most rigidly observed in the world. Not an apple stall may be open. There is an old French law against it."

On his return to the United States he enjoyed some varied experiences which are best narrated from the notes which he made at the time. In other countries, but most of all in America, the particular brand of shyness that puzzled many of his compatriots did not affect his bearing either in the company of his intimate acquaintances or among strangers. He sprang into easy popularity there, and established some lasting ties of affectionate friendship. The closest was with Samuel Ward, "Uncle Sam" to a host of Americans, and a man of wide knowledge and great personal charm. He was a scholar and a poet, whose *Lyrical Recreations* were distinguished and thoughtful, though none of them attained the splendid sweep of his sister's[1] "Battle Hymn of the Republic." He was extraordinarily well-read, and was perhaps sometimes guilty of the foible of omniscience; for some of his livelier New York friends insisted that his declared devotion to the charms of the Differential

[1] Mrs. Julia Ward Howe.

[53]

Calculus was based on reminiscences of his youth, rather than on any recent employment of that mathematical method. A brilliant marriage into one of the great New York families had not turned out happily. He had friends in many European countries and followed their political excitements with almost the same interest that he gave to those of Washington. These last, however, were, in a sense, his business, for he was a notable "lobbyist" of the Democratic party, and obtained all the repute, or disrepute, attaching to that profession. Intensely open-handed, he was almost a Leigh Hunt in money matters. Rosebery noted: "I asked Sam Ward what he would do if Providence were to bestow on him a third fortune, say of a million sterling, to-morrow. 'Why,' said Sam, 'appoint three trustees at once, and have myself declared a lunatic: otherwise it would all be got out of me in a week.' "[2]

Sam Ward's closest friend in America was William H. Hurlbert, the editor of the *New York World*, a brilliant journalist, and a man of infinite humour as well as of many solid attainments. He married happily late in life, and afterwards spent much time in Europe. His last years were clouded by a scandal which, if the charges had been proved, would have pointed to a mental degeneration like that which disfigured the old age of Walter Savage Landor. His wife stoutly maintained that he was the victim of a wretched error; and he passed the rest of his days peacefully in Italy, by no means deserted by his old friends.

In a letter full of hints about the United States, dated August 18th, 1873, the Hon. F. Lawley, a cosmopolitan figure on the staff of the *Daily Telegraph*, wrote: "Hurlbert—the most distinguished and visionary journalist in the United States. Now connected with the *New York World*. A man of immense but erratic information: a charming talker: a little mad." The last phrase is illuminating.

Rosebery had always been a clubbable man; not in the way of spending idle hours in the palaces of Pall Mall and St. James's Street, but in the sense of enjoying small, intimate symposia where good talk reigned and good wine was opened. He, "Uncle Sam," and Hurlbert formed one of the smallest possible—the "Mendacious Club" of New York—of which they were the sole members. Sam Ward was the "President," Hurlbert the "Liar," and Rosebery the

[2] His nephew, Marion Crawford, introduced a life-like sketch of him as "Uncle Horace"—Mr. Bellingham, into his pleasant novel *Doctor Claudius*. Longfellow, who was much attached to him, said that at past seventy he was the living example of the Greek adage, "Those whom the Gods love die young," because he would never grow old.

"Sycophant" of this select corporation. A photograph exhibits the three in the correct guise of honest and truth-telling townsmen.

A close ally and frequent *convive*, though not a member of the "Mendacious" party, was Mr. Evarts. In addition to his eminence as a former Attorney-General and as a constitutional lawyer, he was a man of wide knowledge and real wit. And he had the gift, not less socially precious, of saying absolutely irrational things without moving a muscle of his very expressive face. Some of these have survived to this day, as when some serious person asked him whether it could really be true that Washington, in his youth, had paid a debt of a dollar by throwing a coin across the Potomac. He thoughtfully replied, "Well, you must remember that money went a great deal further in those days than it does now." And when asked about a dinner at the White House, where President Hayes had anticipated the national verdict of two generations later by establishing a rule of total abstinence, he answered simply: "It was an admirable entertainment in every way; water flowed like champagne." To the gay companionship of this coterie one contributor was Mr. John Sutherland, proprietor of the famous restaurant at which all the choice spirits of New York foregathered, where he was not only "mine host," but the friend of everybody. There was also the pleasant home life of some of the New York families, particularly of the William Butler Duncans, at whose house on Staten Island Rosebery was a frequent guest. He became a close friend of the whole family, and in 1867 he attended the wedding of Miss Jessie Duncan and Mr. Wilton Phipps. Mr. and Mrs.[3] Phipps afterwards settled in England, and their intimacy with Rosebery and his family became lasting.

Some of the experiences of his first visit are best recorded in the notes which Rosebery made at the time. He was greatly impressed by Salt Lake City, where a wilderness had been turned into a smiling cultivated land by irrigation and sheer hard work. He attended a Mormon ball, at which he was the only Gentile. It opened and closed with prayer, according to the fixed habit of associating every act in life with public devotion.

"Brigham Young told me that it was a physiological fact that polygamy produced finer children than monogamy. I must say I never saw more beautiful children than I did in Salt Lake City.

"The Mormons do not now ask strangers into their houses, or at least

[3] Now Dame Jessie Phipps, D.B.E.

[55]

very rarely. This is owing to the unfair way in which those who were admitted published their experiences. Elder Clawson said to me that Hepworth Dixon was very anxious to see his family, so he admitted him to supper there, but had no idea that Dixon would publish all their domestic details. Dixon's book they evidently consider discourteous: as they furnished him with every document and every opportunity for his book, they laid themselves bare before him and consider that he was at least indiscreet, besides being offensive in tone. However, they speak of him with their customary mildness. Nor do they admire Sir C. Dilke, his travelling companion. George A. Smith, the second man and historian of the Church, told me that Dilke came to his office and asked him innumerable questions and took the answers down in writing, making the gratuitous statement that he did not intend writing a book. Yet afterwards he wrote a book, suppressed this evidence, and inserted all sorts of idle Gentile tales.

"Joseph Q. Cannon also complained. A man—an American—with whom he became pretty intimate told him his desire to be admitted into a Mormon household. Cannon asked him to supper in a few days. Meanwhile he found in an eastern (New York) newspaper personal letters about the Mormons and about the lives and manners of those the writer had met intimately. He traced them to his would-be guest, whom he excused himself from receiving, showing the newspaper as his reason. The guest and correspondent muttered some excuse and disappeared."

On his return eastward he noted several conversations with people of importance in different lines of life.

"I met Dr. Holmes this evening at dinner at Mrs. Winthrop's. He is a small bright man with a mobile face and a kindly expression. There was a good deal of book talk to which he warmed a good deal—and was delighted when I broke in with my fondness for Gray's 'Elegy' which he said Webster desired to have repeated to him when dying. . . .

"He was full of horse talk (which Winthrop introduced) and has seen Plenipo's Derby. He asked about the amount of breeding required in a hunter, and if the neighbourhood of Boston seemed suitable for hunting. He was full of that mysterious American jargon 'a horse low down in the twenties.' He talked about galloping poems, into which he would not admit Longfellow's 'Revere' and Tennyson's 'Six Hundred,' confining himself to Browning's 'News-bringing to Ghent' in which he said one could see each horse do his particular style of going, and Scott's 'Lochinvar.' I told him of Doyle's poem on the St. Leger which he had never heard of but which I must try and find for him."

Senator Charles Sumner (November 9th, 1873).—"I sat for two and a half hours with Senator Sumner to-day in his lodging here at Coolidge House opposite the Revere House. He was in his dressing-gown. With a large head looking larger from a shock of grey hair, a large nose with broad nostrils, a powerful mouth with a pleasant smile and honest false teeth, his only weak facial point may be said to be his eyes which are small and close together. . . .

"He had been much struck by a conversation at Chevening in which Macaulay, Bishop Wilberforce and others took part, in 1858 or 9. They all gave the palm to Gladstone as the first orator of the House of Commons, and Lord Harry, as he was then, alone maintained Bright to be superior.

"He spent 10½ hours at a sitting in November 1872 talking alone with Bright, which was pretty well for two invalids."

December 3rd, 1873.—"I sat next to Sumner at dinner at Sam Ward's and we conversed for three or four hours.

"He did not care for Bolingbroke, though he once had greatly admired him and made a pilgrimage to the Chateau of La Source, his temporary residence when in France.

"No English speaker of this century, not Canning, could have equalled Daniel Webster's speech (which was his best) in reply to Colonel Haynes. We should have to go back to Burke for its equal, whose two magnificent speeches on conciliation with America and on Economic Reform were Sumner's delight.

"He had read every word of Rousseau and made a pilgrimage to Les Charmettes: the care of which was, he said, one of Napoleon's first orders on attaining power: He found the pompous entry of his death at Chambéry. He delighted in parts of the Confessions, but appeared to have had a devotion to Rousseau in early life and to have recovered from it."

Senator Thurman (December 3rd, 1873).—"Later in the same evening Senator Thurman of Ohio the present leader of the Democratic party described Calhoun's speaking as being as close and as hard as a mathematical demonstration, and his delivery being rapid he required a very close attention. Figures he seldom used and then failed in them.

"The finest piece of speaking Thurman had ever heard was Daniel Webster's speaking (off-hand) in an encounter between Webster and Reverdy Johnson.

"He described with great zest the quarrel which he heard between Andrew Johnson and Jeff Davis, both future Presidents, and as such subjects of impeachment."

A. T. Stewart.—"Stewart the immense millionaire who can tell you the value of any article in his prodigious warehouse, told me that Homer and Horace were his favourite recreations. He said that at one time he used to regret the seven years he spent with the classics (I believe he was a schoolmaster) as having been lost to the production of wealth, but he knew better now."

President Grant.—"Grant told me at Mrs. Admiral Porter's 'German' that he had shaken hands with over ten thousand people in a day. Arithmetic stands aghast."

Longfellow (November 23rd, 1873).—"Longfellow was very genial and unaffected at the breakfast he gave Sam Ward and me. He is an older man than I expected to see but he has recently aged, Sam told me. He mentioned having recently looked into Campbell's later poems written in old age, and said sadly and emphatically that they were a great warning.

"He spoke up for sermons and said that he liked sermons to be sermons and not lectures. He said he had heard a very good one by chance when he was staying at the Peacock Inn at Rowsley in Derbyshire, a delightful old Inn which he urged me to go and see. He showed me with great reverence a bit of Dante's coffin. He seemed to enjoy the good things of this life, brought out a bottle of champagne with great gusto and enjoyed his wine and cigars."

Prosperity in America.—"The most conservative country in the world is America—as regards prosperity. Almost everyone has the means of living with some comfort, there is therefore less envy and less desire to disturb the existing order of things than in those old states where the domain of the noble is surrounded by an indigent peasantry, and where there are two classes—those who own principalities and those who own nothing. The policy of the millionaire in England is to isolate himself and weaken his natural supporters by buying out all those who are less wealthy than himself, thereby making himself a more conspicuous object of attack, converting the friends of property into its foes and making apparent to every mind the pitiless rapidity with which humanity is being divorced from the soil. Lord Overstone *may* be secure and *may* buy up Berkshire with impunity : the more splendid fortune of Astor is certainly secure."

American Republicanism.—"I think it might fairly be alleged by an enemy of American republicanism that fortunes are as large, that luxury is as great, that wealth is as insolently displayed in America as in any European monarchy. The marble palace of A. T. Stewart is not the ideal abode of a republican. But such reproaches would miss the point. In America a man is none the better for these splendours, but rather the worse. Liberty indeed is allowed for extravagances which injure nobody, but it is a contemptuous liberty. In Europe a man is made noble by his house and his retinue : in America such a man could only be noble in spite of them."

General Hurlbert and Ben. Butler (December 5th, 1873, Washington). —"These two dined with me to-night.

"I asked what were the mutual feelings of the two armies in the late war.

"General Hurlbert told a story of how he ordered an attack and the picket officer remonstrated because the two sides had agreed that it was damned nonsense going on firing at each other when they did not feel any anger: so they had declared a truce for half-an-hour. The general then proceeding along his line to find out if this were true on the railway track which formed his outpost, found his two sentries playing euchre with the two Confederate sentries. 'Well, men, what are you doing there?' 'Guess we're giving these rebs a damned good hiding, we've got everything out of them except their rebel notes which we won't have at any price.'

"The conscription in the South was exceedingly severe, in the North it was nil. Most of the draughted men from the North ran away. General Butler shot one man who had deserted more than once, re-enlisting and receiving 800 dollars from his township each time.

"General Butler occupied a position near Richmond the lines of which were on a bluff overlooking Dutch Canal, 200 yards from the rebel lines. They never took any notice of each other in a hostile way, but if the order was given to fire along the line would shout out 'Look out Yanks' or 'Look out jolly rebs' so that the targets might retire out of fire.

"General Butler used to go and survey the place regularly with his staff. On one occasion he took a man with a tall (chimney pot as we call it, stove pipe as the Americans call it) hat. On which a Confederate officer shouted out, 'I've seen all you fellows peeping over here for weeks and never minded a bit, but that stove pipe hat is a touch too much: if that doesn't disappear I fire.' The hat disappeared.

"Lincoln came down in his usual rusty black to review the troops once. He rode on Butler's right between the General and the enemy. The troops cheered all along the line, but the Confederates, though they stood out gazing at the important arrival never fired a shot.

"'Do you remember the 20th May?' said a Confederate to General Butler. 'Of course I do.' 'It was,' he added to us, 'the day Beauregard tried to break my lines.' 'Well that I shot at you seven times with a tele-scopic rifle: were none of your staff shot?' An orderly was killed.

"'How was it,' I asked with an apology, 'that your generals acquired their science?'

"'There was no science,' said Butler. 'From '40 to '60 I camped out with the Massachusetts Militia for five days a year—that was all my training.'

"'It was all hard bushwhacking,' said Hurlbert. 'I carried a musket in the Florida war, that was my preparation. I never was at Westpoint.'

"Bushwhacking, I discovered, is tree fighting: by which any European army, they say, would be defeated in America.[4]

[4] On the other hand, Lord Wolseley, who had visited the Southern front, was convinced that at any stage of the war the addition of one army corps from any of the best European armies would have turned the scale in favour of either side.

" 'If a war were to take place to-morrow we could put 700,000 veterans in the field. If we had to fight Spain to-morrow and only took men who had served two years we could raise 300,000 men,' said the General.

" 'At the close of the war,' said Butler, 'we had fourteen hundred thousand men on our rolls. There were, North and South, eighteen hundred thousand men under arms. It was the biggest thing of the world after the French Revolution.' "

Growth of America.—" 'In twenty years,' said Butler, 'we shall own all America from the Northern extremity to Darien: including, I beg your pardon, Canada. We shall then be as compact as the old states. It took Washington three weeks to march from Boston to New York. He could have made the journey in seven hours. It is a great and new experiment. We cannot tell how it will turn out. The Roman Empire fell to pieces because it kept its citizenship restricted. Wherever we go, every inhabitant becomes a citizen; there is the difference.' "

English.—" 'Forty years ago,' said Butler, 'the purest English in the world was spoken in New England, where nothing was read but the Bible and Bunyan's *Pilgrim's Progress*, and Milton and possibly Shakespeare for those who were inclined to read poetry.' "

Washington.—"Washington, according to Butler, desired his style as president to be 'Serene Highness.' At his table he once expressed this desire. One of his friends, a Judge, said, 'That would be all very well for you, General, but how would it do if you were succeeded by our friend here,' a gentleman who was almost a dwarf. Washington never forgave the Judge.

"When he went up to the Capitol he went in a coach with six white horses and outriders.

"There are undoubted descendants of Washington. When he went to Church (according to Cox) he was preceded by a drum and fife.

"Bancroft Davis showed me a portrait of Washington in the State department, which he said is supposed to be the best. Those by Stewart are believed to have been flattering."

Byron and the last Lord Holland.—"Sumner told me that he had heard that Byron had been very fond of the last Lord Holland who was lame like himself. 'But,' said Byron, 'how well he carries it, he seems only to have tripped against a star.' "

Lafayette and Washington.—"Sumner dwelt long on his project of writing on the touching friendship that united Washington and Lafayette. He said that nobody had any idea how tenderly they loved each other who had not gone deeply into the matter."

Disraeli.—"Cushing and Sumner agreed that Disraeli's preface to his father's *Curiosities of Literature* was the best thing he had written, and according to Sumner was one of the most touching pieces of writing and one of the tenderest tributes in all literature."

Speaker Blaine.—"Speaker Blaine told me that his immediate ancestor was in the 'Forty-five' and after Culloden fled to America. He afterwards fought in the Revolutionary War in America, remarking, with great satisfaction, 'What a wonderful bit of luck to have had two shies at those damned Hanoverians.'"

Religion.—"I cannot pretend to say if the Americans are a religious people (as the cant phrase goes) : but I have certainly never seen a nation so given to building and attending churches."

Notes.—"Everything in America appears lean and nervous compared with our robust solidity: look at the men, the horses, even the locomotives.

"There are in America no ruins of antiquity to which they can give sentiment or affection, so they cherish and beautify the industrial objects which form their pride and their means of support: their steam engines and their fire machines are as dainty as crown jewels: their manufactories are often splendid piles—their shops are sometimes marble palaces. There is something very noble in this. In other countries men are too apt to steal down like conspirators to the dingy dens whence they make the fortunes which they display elsewhere. The American, on the other hand, is proud of his work: he links himself to it, while he idealises and decorates it—like the old Venetian merchant princes, and in so doing he dignifies his calling and himself."

Dilemma of American Traveller.—"When one returns to England one finds oneself in a neatly constructed dilemma. If you say you dislike America the answer is 'Ah, I knew you would be shocked when you saw your principles carried into practice: you see what Liberalism would bring us to.' If, as I did, you say that you are greatly pleased with America: 'Ah, I thought you would be delighted at their toadying to you: they always do make so much of a lord.'"

Rosebery could not resist sending to his friend's journal this impression of a torchlight procession for the Democratic Convention, before the Presidential Election of 1873:

Torchlight Procession, for the Democratic Convention before the
Presidential Election, 1873:

"Last night I stood in Madison Square, and, looking down Fifth Avenue there appeared a moving column of lights, clustering and silent. It might have been a squadron of angels marching to encounter the power of darkness. But as it came nearer I saw that it was a great army of human beings proceeding in silence and order to salute their chief.

"The cause, the manner and the surroundings were equally impressive. Along the streets a dense impassive crowd watching with curious respect: the traffic suspended out of deference to the embodiment of so much conviction and so much power: a hush of expectation and critical curiosity: not a policeman to be seen.

"The object of all this interest was a host marching with the precision of veterans, but they were neither the old Guards of Napoleon, nor the Pratetorian legionaries of a Caesar; they shewed neither the disdainful ferocity of an Eastern bodyguard, nor the sullen fury of the Jacobin Clubs: they called for neither blood nor gold. There was cavalry indeed, but it was unarmed, there were banners but they bore the names of peaceful citizens or the shibboleth of political principles, there were cannon, but they were loaded only with ballot balls. All was silence, earnestness and decorum. It was a monster procession of American citizens on its way to salute a political chief.

"To a native there may be nothing remarkable in this. To a foreigner like myself it was a triumph of moral power. Many an American will say as I have heard it said that these men were paid so much a night. It may be so: I can only reply that we would gladly in my country pay twice as much to have such an exhibition.

"It was not the mere numbers though they were impressive enough; it was rather the sign of a civilisation which could not as yet be found in Europe. There was, apparently, perfect sobriety: in my country there would certainly have been no such aggregation of human beings without much drunkenness. There was perfect order without the intervention of the police: in my country there would have been tumult, disorder and a great force of constabulary. Traffic was suspended as if by universal consent, yet there was no word of complaint: it seemed natural to all that private convenience should give way to so great a manifestation: in my country private convenience would have struggled greatly to have its way and would have greatly complained.

"But, more than this, how much must have been sacrificed, time, labour and money to produce this result. The men must have been trained for months, for they marched as soldiers march. Instead of rushing about as is the way elsewhere in times of political excitement to make political centres of themselves, they were satisfied to merge their own individuality in the great mass. There was no anxiety to assert a fitful personality by the delivery of speeches. Though many had to wait long before it became their turn to march, and though the fatigue to many must have been excessive, there was nothing but patience, good humour and alacrity. And all these qualities were displayed in honour of certain principles, and of men who must have been mere abstractions to the vast majority of those who were present: for there was probably not one in a thousand who would have recognised the object of his enthusiasm.

[62]

"I venture to say that this was both a great moral spectacle and a great political lesson. No European potentate, not the Queen of Great Britain saluted by the thunders of her fleet, not the Emperor of Russia reviewing his hundred thousand Guards before breakfast, not the Pope borne amid smoking incense and the blare of the silver trumpets and the awful silence of kneeling multitudes can produce a sight so impressive as this."—FORESTIÈRE.

"The problems presented by this country are:

"1. Size—no republic has ever been carried on on so large a scale.
"2. Difference of races immigrating.
"3. Difference of races as affected by variety of climates.
"4. Differences of the interests of the various regions.
"5. Increase of luxury and expenditure."

In November 1874 he made a second, shorter trip to America, coming in for the Democratic triumph of the election, and finding in consequence that the South offered greater attractions than the West, which had been his original destination. He found Savannah (December 5th, 1874)—

"the most heavenly place except Naples which I have ever seen. Fancy a little city of 30,000 inhabitants, with its streets so lined with forest trees that, looking down the road, one sees a glade and not a row of houses; in which each of the many squares is a shady grove where standard magnolias twenty feet high and more grow by the public way, where the private gardens are thickets of camellias white with flowers and orange trees yellow with fruit, where the sandy roads make the city so quiet that the stillness is broken by the song of birds, where the air is the breath of early morning and the sun is the sun of our summer, and all this on the 5th of December. A little way out of the town there is a place called Bonaventure, formerly the seat of an old English family who planted it out in avenues of oaks. The place is now deserted, and the aisles of overlapping branches with the delicate semi-tropical moss hanging down like snow wreaths look like the naves of ruined cathedrals or the approaches of some sacred sepulchre. I do not know that I ever saw anything so singular in its mournful beauty, and they say that when moonlight shoots the branches and lights up the grey arches the effect is indescribably wild and solemn. Would you not like, as I wish, to live at Savannah, and be buried at Bonaventure? The city has bought it for a cemetery, for which it is all the more suitable that it is too unhealthy to live in.

"From this I go on Monday to the rice swamp inhabited by Chandos Leigh's brother Jim, who married Fanny Kemble's daughter. It is the place at which Mrs. Kemble wrote her book on South America, and I am curious to see it.

[63]

"How thankful our generation ought to be that it was born too late to be intimate with Mr. Charles Greville. I have a holy horror of a diarist which you indeed instilled into me when I was a—(I have just killed a mosquito) child. A man who feels bound to write something and makes a confidante of his journal is subject to every human meanness. But I have not read the book. I only judge from the extracts that I have seen that it must be a sort of posthumous anonymous letter.

"In Annapolis I saw a very painful portrait of Lord Chatham, wigless and in the costume of a Roman Senator, which, by the way, does not suit his legs. He is pointing to a statue of Liberty and looks unhappily like a lean and slippered pantaloon (only with the pantaloons).

"In Baltimore there is a much more curious relic. In a single bedroom without a carpet sits an immensely wealthy old lady who is sister-in-law of the first Napoleon—Jerome's American wife by whom he had several children. She is said to have been so wonderfully beautiful that when she went to her banker's in England they had to let her out by the side door to escape the crowd which was gazing at her. Jerome, when recalled to Europe, brought her with him, feeling sure that the Emperor would sanction the marriage if he only had five minutes' interview with her. Napoleon seems to have held much the same opinion as he refused to allow her even to land. Years afterwards she met Jerome in a picture gallery. He at once exclaimed 'Madame Paterson,' and turned to her, but was hurried away by his companions. She has now turned miser, and intends like Monsieur Thiers to live, considering it more a question of will than anything else. Her son who is now dead was strikingly like Napoleon, they say, but the grandson whom I have seen, though handsome, has nothing of that type about him."

New Orleans followed. He had been told that half the country between California and New York was under snow, so congratulated himself on being in the sunshine.

December 16th, 1874.—"But even had my first plan been practicable, I should not have done so well as in coming here, for the South is the Poland or Ireland of the United States. This place is at this moment in a great ferment, and fighting is expected in the streets next Sunday, as the election returns should then be made, and are expected to be fraudulent. If so our Whites will 'chaw up pretty smart' and 'unpleasantness' accompanied with shooting will take place. The Governor is very much in the condition of an Irish landlord. He has to live in strict seclusion guarded by the police. If any popular excitement is shewn he retires like contraband whiskey into the recesses of the Custom House.

"I have just received and looked through Greville's Memoirs. It would have been better, I think, to have delayed their publication, but

[64]

their suppression would have been a very great loss. I wonder who is doing the same ungrateful duty for the present generation. . . .

"The people are still very French and you hear French spoken in all the streets: but I believe it is not very classical (like the Canadian French) and is popularly called 'Gumbo French.' They have a quarter to themselves. On a hot afternoon the quay gives one something of the same impression as Naples, as it is thronged with noisy, careless, good-humoured, ragged people; the great difference here is that they are negroes. The curious reflection to me in looking at them is that they are citizens, voters and sovereigns."

Christmas was spent in Cuba (December 25th, 1874):

"I do not know how to begin about Cuba, or how to end, everything is so new and so enchanting, except, by the way, the wild beasts. For on arriving here last night just after we had sat down to supper, a scorpion, three inches long, appeared and began to walk deliberately down the table while I gazed at him as if he were the Commendatore in *Don Giovanni*. The cockroaches, too, of great size and activity, are rather depressing. But I am going into the country to-morrow, and am promised greater delights than these—large hairy tarantula spiders, the size of a hen's egg, snakes as thick as my wrist and jiggers. . . .

"The house is very much like a house at Pompeii only ten times as large, and we live practically in the open air. My hostess speaks nothing but Spanish, so we converse by pleasant smiles."

The year 1876 found him once more in America for the greater part of October and November. Life passed much as on his former visits, in the company of Sam Ward and Hurlbert. He also saw much of the Duncans, and something of Evarts. The names of the hospitable James Gordon Bennett and John Hay, and of Laurence Oliphant, recur in his notes, and on one occasion he writes: "Hurlbert and I gave breakfast to Tupper and Barnum. It was inimitable." Mr. Barnum was equally pleased. He wrote: "What a glorious treat Tupper did afford us to-day. I regard him as a benefactor. I am sorry to say that our horse-rehearsals are only from 8 to 10 a.m. If these unearthly hours can be utilised the enclosed order will do the business." The order was one to admit at all times to rehearsals of horse-riding, to show him all objects of interest, and to keep reserved seats for him when desired. But Mr. Barnum's interests extended to a world beyond that of his famous circus. He again wrote recommending Rosebery to hear an eloquent Presbyterian preacher, "Enclosed note to sexton would get you (incognito) a good seat or two. I am not a *proselyter*, but if on your voyage you should have a couple of leisure hours I could supply you a few pages that might open new and lofty ideas, if your Lordship has not looked into new and universal theology." Rosebery announced his intention of hearing the Presbyterian preacher. He also played racquets pretty frequently throughout this visit.

Lord Dufferin was disappointed at there being no visit to Canada this time, but wrote: "However, I daresay we shall be able to have a political crisis for you by this time next year, if you will promise to come."

A review of these American visits during Rosebery's unmarried years leads to the conclusion that to himself they represented the holiday spirit in its fullest form. In America he was absolutely free to go where he wished, and to do what he liked. His extreme quickness of apprehension permitted him to make the most of experiences not in themselves extraordinary. Soon after he returned to England he dined with Ferdinand de Rothschild, to meet Lord Beaconsfield and a cheerful party. The Prime Minister told Lady Bradford: "After dinner there was whist, and Rosebery came up to me, and talked very well—just come from America—his third visit, and full as an egg of fun and quaint observation."[5]

[5] Lord Beaconsfield to Lady Bradford, December 8th, 1876. *Life of Lord Beaconsfield*, vol. vi, ch. iii.

CHAPTER IV

Political Activities, 1871-1879

I T HAPPENED, perhaps unfortunately for Rosebery himself, that the current of events did not automatically carry him along the ordinary routine of party politics. He was too young to take an active part in the Liberal triumph of 1868, and he was not urged by tradition to an early plunge into public life, like a Hartington or a Lansdowne. He had thus missed the brilliant dawn of Mr. Gladstone's greatest administration. His convictions, cautiously formed, were now definitely of a Liberal colour; but even had he been a political conscript from the day when he came of age, nothing could ever have turned him into an unquestioning partisan. In 1871 he had followed up his successful opening as Seconder of the Address by as many interventions in debate as could be expected or desired from a novice; during the session that followed, he was a recognised member of Lord Granville's flock, though never a blindfold follower in its track.

In February 1872 Gladstone asked him to call, said that Granville wanted assistance in the House of Lords, that an attempt was being made to combine political office with the Household appointments; would he consider taking the vacant Lordship-in-waiting on the same footing as Morley and Camperdown, representing in the House the department formerly the Poor Law Board, now the Board of Rating? In his note of the interview he writes: "I said I would, consider the proposal, but I confess in my own mind it never occurred to me to require consideration: what I said was only out of respect to Mr. Gladstone. At the same time, if I wanted political office just now it is quite clear that it is the only thing that I could be offered, and much higher than my deserts. On Friday morning I sent a respectful note to Mr. Gladstone declining the offer."

2 BERKELEY SQUARE, *February 16th, 1872.*
"DEAR MR. GLADSTONE,
"I am sure you will believe me when I say how fully sensible I am

[67]

of your personal kindness to me yesterday, both in manner and in making me the proposal that you did; and also of the honour I should receive in entering public life under your government.

"I need not therefore fear misconception when I say that in addition to my incompetency to perform satisfactorily either class of the duties which would devolve upon me, there are private reasons which compel me with all gratitude and respect to decline your offer.

"Yours faithfully,

A. ROSEBERY.

"The Right Hon. W. E. Gladstone."

In the light of later knowledge the offer looks inadequate if not grudging. But Gladstone held that the rungs of the official ladder must be climbed one by one; he did not like passing over older men who had given good service even of a modest sort, and a good many such had survived from his administration of 1868. So that a man of four-and-twenty perhaps could not have expected more, and Rosebery's private note proves that he himself did not.

A year later Mr. Gladstone offered him the Lord Lieutenancy of Linlithgow, which he declined in the following terms:

Private.   2 BERKELEY SQUARE, *May 2nd*, 1873.

"DEAR MR. GLADSTONE,

"I need hardly say how honoured I am by your kind proposal.

"The office of Lord Lieutenant has, I believe, in Scotland at least, hardly any public duties. This ought to make the undertaking of it very easy: but I confess it weighs with me on the other side. And yet, though a nominal responsibility, it acts as a tie in various ways.

"Besides it involves other obligations of society and residence by which at present I should be very unwilling to bind myself.

"And moreover it seems to me that a Lord Lieutenant should be a person constantly resident in the County and conversant with its affairs. I cannot pretend to this. The office is a high honour, greatly appreciated in the district, and one which there are many joyfully and efficiently to undertake.

"These reasons alone are sufficient to entitle me to ask you to excuse me from accepting the lieutenancy of Linlithgowshire. I do hope I have expressed clearly what I mean, though I am not sure of this. I thank you warmly for the proposal, for I hope I may take it as another proof of your kindly feeling; and I trust you will not consider that, in declining it, I have done anything in the slightest degree inconsistent with that sincere gratitude and respect which makes me always

"Very sincerely yours,

ROSEBERY."

Mr. Gladstone would not accept this refusal, and sent the letter to Lord Granville, writing on a slip:

> "This is wrong.
>   Can you or Bessborough persuade him?
>   His mother could not?
>
>   "W. E. G. May 2."

Lord Granville noted: "We will try. G."

Mr. Gladstone's *entourage* hammered away at Rosebery's disinclination, as did some of his political friends. The sternest remonstrance came from Bouverie Primrose, who covered eight sides of note-paper, and pointed out that to reject such an opportunity was to some extent an offence to his country neighbours, all the more as his grandfather had regarded it as an honour to hold the post. It was also a slight to the Government whom he had publicly supported, because they would be at their wits' end to find an eligible candidate in the county. His uncle concluded by saying:

"Lastly there is incomprehensibility.

"I think everyone does himself injustice when he makes himself incomprehensible. There are no duties or obligations upon a Lord Lieutenant which you could not fulfil and which could have been heavy or restrictive to you, and no one can understand or assign the least reason why you should seclude yourself, in a country of Honours and Titles, from an Honour which fell so naturally and harmoniously upon you, and imposed no toil or restraint to speak of.

"Such incomprehensibility is not to the advantage of a man's public or private character, and is liable to give rise to a number of false surmises which may not only influence the public and private estimation in which he is held, but be made to recoil upon himself in ways he least expects, at moments not the least looked for and in modes most disagreeable and permanently annoying."

This severe and almost prophetic remonstrance from a most affectionate relation, added to further pressure from Mr. Gladstone, had the desired effect, and he wrote again to Mr. Gladstone as follows:

Private.   2 BERKELEY SQUARE, *May 25th*, 1873.
"DEAR MR. GLADSTONE,

"I am truly sensible of your kindness in sending for me and speaking to me the other day. At the same time I cannot feel convinced by what was said as regards the Queen. Such an argument seems to me, to go too far; and I should be very sorry to follow it out to its legitimate consequences.

[69]

"I can hardly tell you how sorry I am that I cannot bring my mind into agreement with the arguments which have been used against my refusal of this unhappy office: nor how sorry I am that my views should not be in exact accordance with yours even on a point like this. For it shews clearly to me want of judgment or discernment on my part: and yet I can but follow my little light. I honestly confess I see no call of duty in the question: but I do see a probability of a very false position for me in future years.

"At the same time though I cannot bring my mind into accordance with the views you expressed, I can bring my will into subjection. This I am quite ready to do. I am sure, where we differ, it is a thousand chances to one that you are right. So, if you still wish or think it proper to appoint me, I will defer to you.

"I hope this note is not presumptuous or pompous. It is perhaps harder to write and to do than you would think; for I have thought a good deal about this, and consequently feel rather strongly.

"But, however you may think proper to end the transaction, it will always leave with me the pleasant memory of your kindness and condescension.

"Believe me,
Yours faithfully,
ROSEBERY."

The session of 1872 was chiefly notable in the House of Lords for an animated debate on the Geneva Arbitration on the American Claims against Britain for damage inflicted during the Civil War, especially by the raiding *Alabama*, improperly allowed to escape from an English port. The arbitration had been agreed in the previous year by the Treaty of Washington, the British side being represented by a Commission, of which Lord Ripon was the chief. The present point at issue was the inclusion or exclusion of what were known as the Indirect Claims, many of them of the most preposterous character, such as the claims for an indemnity for causing increased premiums for marine insurance, for loss by transfer of the mercantile marine to the British flag, and, strangest of all, for causing the prolongation of the war, though it was notorious that the fighting on land had continued for months irrespective of the exertions of two or three privateers. Lord Russell, with all the prestige of an ex-Prime Minister and ex-Foreign Secretary, demanded that the Arbitration should not take place until the Indirect Claims had been formally withdrawn, and he was backed by another *magni nominis umbra*, Lord Grey.[1] Other great guns came into

[1] 3rd Earl Grey (1802-1894); Secretary of State for the Colonies 1846-52.

[70]

supporting position,—Lord Stratford de Redcliffe,[2] Lord Malmesbury,[3] Lord Derby[4] in moderate terms, Lord Salisbury in terms of extreme bitterness against both the Government and the United States. Lord Granville and his colleagues, Kimberley and Ripon, made the best of their case. They were followed by Lord Westbury, who, speaking from their benches, but not concealing his polished contempt for them and their ways, held that it would be highly mischievous to carry Lord Russell's motion.

Rosebery followed, a Daniel come to judgment among orators thirty or forty years older than himself. He began by a reference to "those precious balms with which Lord Westbury was accustomed to break the head of Her Majesty's Government." And I remember his confessing in after years with what terror he uttered this description of the most quietly formidable figure in the House of Lords. His main point, and a strong one, was that the appearance of dictation from England would drive all Americans, even those who most disapproved the Indirect Claims, to a refusal to withdraw them. It was the kind of feeling which, in this country, had caused the rejection of the Conspiracy to Murder Bill in 1858, not so much because it was objected to as because a foreign Power was supposed to have suggested it. He hit out boldly—he "did not admire the position of the noble Earl who had brought forward this resolution with regard to this question. Considering that the acts of the *Alabama* and other vessels out of which these claims arose took place while the noble Earl was Foreign Secretary, this motion would have come with a better grace from anyone rather than him. No one knew better than himself the difference in their relative positions. He well knew the humble position he occupied in their Lordships' House. He well knew that the noble Earl addressed them with all the weight of his great experience, all the lustre of his historic name, with all the prestige of a former Prime Minister. But, knowing all this, he could honestly say, on this occasion and as regards this debate, that he preferred his own insignificance to the eminence, the mischievous eminence, of the noble Earl. It was easy enough to pass votes of censure. During the few years he had sat in that House the annual Vote of Censure had come round as regularly as

[2] Stratford Canning, 1st Viscount Stratford de Redcliffe (1786-1880).
[3] 3rd Earl of Malmesbury (1807-1889). Secretary of State for Foreign Affairs 1852 and 1858-9.
[4] 15th Earl of Derby (1826-1893). Secretary of State for Colonies 1858; for India 1858-9; for Foreign Affairs 1866-8; and again 1874-8; and for Colonies again 1882-5.

the hands of a clock. But it was not every day they had an opportunity of destroying a treaty. . . . They, by their votes, would have done that of which it was easy, though painful, to see a beginning, but almost impossible to see the end. They would have stamped out the last vestige of a treaty; they would have blistered instead of healing an open sore; they would have disturbed, perhaps permanently, the good relations between the two countries. He implored, then, each noble Lord, as he recorded his vote, to pause in face of the responsibility—the tremendous responsibility—which he was about to assume (June 4th, 1872).''

Lord Cairns said that no apology was necessary for a junior Peer's intrusion into this debate, but quite the contrary, and was generally complimentary. A division was happily staved off, and the event altogether justified the Government's caution, for the United States, without formally withdrawing the Indirect Claims, soon announced that they would not be submitted at Geneva. If they did not appear there, they clearly could not crop up elsewhere; but the faces of the President and the Senate were saved with no harm done to anybody.

In the course of the same session, Rosebery had insistently advocated the extension of extradition treaties, and on the Scottish Education Bill, as has already been described, he unsuccessfully brought up a clause similar in form to the "Cowper-Temple" section of the English Act, though he designed it for a different application in the Scottish schools. But he could not yet be counted as a regular attendant in Parliament. Lord Granville rejoiced when he "took any opportunity of adding to the too few proofs he had already given of his power to take a most important part in the House"; and the *Scotsman* echoed the sentiment, urging him, if he spoke from below the gangway, not to turn his back on the reporters' gallery. The Duke of Argyll's enunciation was the model for him to follow, Lord Granville's conversational tone the example to avoid. But it was not only the official mind that was exercised about his future. Prominent Members of Parliament who were also sportsmen and men of the world dropped words of admonition. Horsman, of Cave of Adullam fame, whose oratory Rosebery had praised to Disraeli years before,[5] asked him down to the country for a talk (January 30th, 1873).

"It is a very interesting and critical period for you, and I should like very much to try to show you how much there is both to inspire

[5] See p. 24.

and repay you in the future, if you really brace yourself to a life worthy of your opportunities and gifts. But time is very precious, and great prizes are not won without consciousness of the necessity for great efforts. Excuse this *lecture*, but I am much interested."

And a little later Sir Robert Peel,[6] himself the most careless of brilliant politicians, wrote with an undertone of warning (March 12th, 1873) : "I hear you are doing capitally as Chairman of your Committee, and hope you give yourself all the trouble necessary to carry it through to a successful issue . . . everything will depend upon a well-digested Report, which you are fully capable of drafting."

Even "Uncle Sam's" indulgent sympathies became uneasy as time went on. Rosebery replied to a letter of his (May 23rd, 1874) :

"Many thanks for your pleasant notes and stories. The one which amused me most I confess was the one in which you expressed your fear of my falling into the hands of Padwick and ruining myself on the Turf. Even a Scottish peer cannot be ruined by four racehorses, especially when they win!"

Mr. Padwick was the notorious gentleman who was believed to have played the part of Mephistopheles in the Hastings drama, and a name of terror to parents and guardians.

Rosebery could make a fair case for some political inactivity during these earlier years of this decade, but there were personal causes besides, the outcome of his introspective reserve. A man may be fully conscious of his own powers but be continually dissatisfied with their exercise on succeeding occasions. Perhaps it is only thus that in oratory, as in other arts, the highest peaks are to be climbed. I may be pardoned for quoting in this connection a reminiscent letter, written some forty years later.

Lord Rosebery to Lord Crewe.
                    38 BERKELEY SQUARE, *December 29th*, 1916.
"MY DEAR R.,

"Lying awake last night I was thinking about our conversation about your father, and I remembered an episode which, as one of many, seems to explain the remarkable good-will with which he is treated in current memoirs.

"As a very young fellow I made some speech in the House of Lords (I forget anything else about it), which seemed to me a dead failure, and I was greatly depressed. But next morning I received a note from

[6] The Rt. Hon. Sir Robert Peel (1822-1895). M.P. 1850-80 and 1884-6; Chief Secretary for Ireland 1861-5.

[73]

your father congratulating me upon it in cordial terms. This warmed me once more, and raised me from the ground. It might have been the frigid dignity of the House of Lords which had made me unduly dejected. My conviction, however, still remains that the speech was a failure, and that your father, realising this, and the mortification of a young friend, took the trouble on returning home to write a letter to cheer him from the pure tact of kindness.

"That was the sort of thing that he did I fancy pretty often, and that is why his memory is so sweet to scores of others as well as

"Your aff.,

R."

Outside the House there was no particular spur to oratorical effort: the Government's mandate was not exhausted, though enthusiasm might be waning; the platform, especially for Peers, had, in ordinary times, not yet become the recognised medium for declarations of political faith. So it was not surprising to find Rosebery silent, except for occasional interventions in Scotland on matters of immediate interest in that country. Nor did he show any fresh activity in this direction up to the Conservative victory in 1874, or for some time after it. In the House of Lords in 1873, after once helping to defeat the Government on an amendment moved on a Scottish legal question, after speaking powerfully in favour of an inquiry into the system of patronage in the Church of Scotland, and on the question of judicial peerages, regretting that no special regard was being paid to the Scottish Bench, he asked one or two questions on foreign affairs.

He then settled down to one great effort, in moving for the appointment of a Royal Commission on the supply of horses (February 20th, 1873). At the beginning of a sparkling speech which fills thirteen columns of Hansard, he dealt with a published letter addressed to himself by Admiral Rous, "whose opinion would carry just weight with them, not only on account of his great ability, and because he had added lustre to the Navy and the Turf, but also because he gave up to the horse 'what was meant for mankind.'" The Admiral had written that horses were better and more numerous than ever before, and that the general prosperity had not only sent up their price but that of all other stock. So that a grassland farmer might hesitate to breed horses if he could get a quicker return from cattle and sheep. On the other hand, in Rosebery's opinion, backed by a series of figures, there was a serious shortage both of harness horses and cart horses, and the export of animals of all

[74]

breeds was becoming a formidable menace, especially from the military standpoint. It may be remarked that during the last fifty years similar complaints have even survived the gradual replacement of horses by mechanical power, but Rosebery was entitled to regard himself as something of an authority on light horses, since he was asked more than once to judge the classes of hunters and harness at agricultural shows. In this debate he made, incidentally, a brave defence of racing, which, as he said, Mr. Gladstone had lately described as "a noble, manly, distinguished, and historical amusement," and which hundreds of thousands of the poorer classes of the community enjoyed.

Lord Granville, for the Government, while considering Rosebery's fears exaggerated, offered a Select Committee in place of a Royal Commission, also speaking up for the thoroughbred horse, and mentioning that he had stayed in France with "the only foreigner who has ever won the Derby,[7] whose farm of 2,000 acres, with all its road and market service, was worked entirely by thoroughbred horses from two and a half to five years old, on the system prevailing to some extent in Ireland." The Duke of Richmond, the Leader of the Opposition, agreed with Lord Granville, and the Select Committee was nominated. But *post equitem sedit atra cura*, and the Government soon had greater anxieties to face. Mr. Disraeli's ministry had touched on the thorny question of Irish University Education, but could not grapple with it; Mr. Gladstone, having dealt with the Irish Church, would not leave this more intricate problem unsolved. He won the adhesion of Cardinal Manning; but this was of less moment than the hostility of Cardinal Cullen and the Irish Bishops, who were alienated by a measure which the Presbyterian community in the North found equally unpalatable. Thus the second reading of the Bill was defeated by a majority of three. Disraeli would not form an administration unless a dissolution were to follow; so Gladstone's Government held on through the year, inevitably shaken and weakened.

At the end of January 1874 came the Dissolution of Parliament, and Disraeli sailed in with a triumphant majority. This might be the customary swing of parties; but the portent was the return of fifty-eight Irish Home Rulers, pledged, as a distinct party, to a revolutionary change in their country's government. At this first stage its significance was not properly understood by anybody in England. At any rate, it can never have crossed Rosebery's mind,

[7] Count F. de Lagrange won the Derby with *Gladiateur* in 1865.

as he scanned the election returns, that his own career was destined to be more painfully hampered by the Irish question than by any other. During the election he was, of course, altogether muzzled, like other Peers, and could only vent his feelings in private. In a letter to Sam Ward he protested (February 16th, 1874):

"What nonsense you write about the Tories—as to their being able to be more liberal from not having to make such professions. They are all professions. They profess anything but Liberalism, they would call themselves Communists to get seats, but when they have got them they are as illiberal as ever. . . . The Tories are mad with joy. They condole with one, they sympathise with one, they pat one on the back. I nearly died of it, till I found a certain remedy, which is this: I always say, 'Well, now it is a consolation to think *one* of my friends will benefit by it; what *do* you mean to take? What *will* you accept?' His face drops, his manner becomes mysterious, the words 'Commissioner'— 'Secretary'—are vaguely audible. I reply, 'Too low, you don't know your own position: no fellow occupies such a space in the eyes of the country—of your age.' He beams upon me, but says, 'There is something in that, but you exaggerate.' 'Not a bit,' I rejoin firmly. 'You have a great future. If I were a Tory, I should look to you as my leader.' We part delighted with each other, he not having the most remote chance of ever rising to the position of—say—a parish beadle. But this is a great recipe, and I only tell it to people the other side of the Atlantic."

The untoward issue of the conflict had certainly not dashed Rosebery's spirits. He concludes his letter:

"Dilectissime mi Samuel
vale et jubila

"Sic non plus ab
So no more from

"umbrâ tuâ
"Rosa-bacca."

When Rosebery found himself for the first time on the Opposition benches to the left of the Throne he had no immediate temptation to settle down to parliamentary hackwork. The measure most keenly debated was the Public Worship Regulation Bill, which, from its nature, inspired in celestial minds the fury usual when religious matters are mooted in a deliberative assembly. In these battles Rosebery took no part; but he was keenly concerned with the Scottish Church Patronage Bill, on its first reading congratulating the new Government on tackling a grievance which his friends of the late administration had not attempted to handle. Doubtless the Queensferry case was vividly in his mind.[8] He reserved further observations for the Second Reading, and did not, in fact, speak at this stage, though he once intervened briefly when the Bill was in Committee. The measure which transferred patronage from private individuals to parishioners was approved by the great majority of Scottish Peers, including Lord Rosslyn, who had lately been nominated by Disraeli to the post of Lord High Commissioner to the General Assembly of the Church of Scotland. People remarked with pleasure that he had received this appointment instead of the Mastership of the Buckhounds, because it was feared that his command of explosive language might shock the followers of the Queen's hunt. The Bill passed easily through all its stages, but it had a rougher passage through the House of Commons.

Rosebery's only other appearance in the summer of 1874 was characteristic. He always had a keen eye for personal grievances, and would take any pains to put right a personal injustice. A former official of the House had got into trouble over his accounts as Clerk of the Patent Office. The department of the Comptroller and Auditor-General did not yet exist, and the case was dealt with by arbitrators, with the result that the official lost his pension and passed eight months in prison. He had now presented a petition for rehearing, and Rosebery, speaking forcibly, moved that this be referred to the appropriate committee. He was supported by the great authority of Lord Redesdale, the Chairman of Committees, and by Lord Bath. But the Lord Chancellor and his two predecessors demurred from the purely official standpoint, so that the attempt failed.

Nothing gave Rosebery greater pleasure than humorous exposure of meaningless anomalies based on tradition, if they proved to be really inconvenient, so that when his great friend the Duke of St. Albans pointed out the absurdity whereby theatres in the Lord Chancellor's jurisdiction (March 5th, 1875) were closed on Ash Wednesday, while other places of amusement were open, he chimed in with a merciless sketch of the regulations under which the Court Theatre remained open because it was in Chelsea, not in the Metropolis, and "an exotic body of minstrels known as Negro Melodists could, by a change in the locality of their performance, make that which was illegal in Piccadilly have the odour of sanctity when it was brought within the precincts of Drury Lane." Later in the ses-

[8] See p. 46.

sion he prays for a general measure to deal with the whole subject of licensing of theatres and places of public amusement. His other appearances in the House in this year were concerned with minor points of Scottish Bills, his particular parliamentary business being a Committee of Enquiry into Scottish Representative Peerages, of which he was Chairman.

It is difficult to-day to comprehend the excitement and hostility that were aroused by the Royal Titles Bill, authorising the Sovereign to assume the style of Empress of India. On the one hand it was felt that this title, whatever its past associations, fairly represented the relation of the British Crown to the Princes and people of India; it had not been thought wise to make any change immediately after the suppression of the Mutiny; but the Prince of Wales had just made a successful progress through the Peninsula, and the moment, therefore, seemed appropriate. In opposition, it was argued that the Imperial title brought with it traditions of tyranny and of arrogant domination—*"Tu regere imperio populos Romane memento"*;[9] Queen Victoria was nowise the successor of the Mogul Emperors of Delhi; no position in the world was superior to that of the King or Queen of England, and it should not be implied that there could be; sycophantic people would try to use the title regularly in this country.

The proposal might have had a better reception had it been made by some other statesman; Disraeli was believed to be subservient to Queen Victoria's likes and dislikes, and any woman's fancy, it was thought in those benighted days, would be captivated by the tinsel crown offered to her by his Oriental imagination. So that the attack did not come from the Radical benches. Nor did it follow party lines. In the House of Commons it was led by Lord Hartington; and in the Lords Lord Shaftesbury, who had no party ties, moved an Address begging the Queen not to assume the title of Empress. At an earlier stage, the veteran Duke of Somerset, also no party man, for he disliked Gladstone and despised Disraeli, said that the Prime Minister had become intoxicated by the atmosphere of the Court; Lord Lawrence, one of the saviours of India, thought that a new title in the vernacular should be selected by the Governor-General in Council; Lord Sandhurst, a soldier of long Indian experience, supported Lord Shaftesbury, so that Rosebery found himself in good independent company. He pointed out that, all over the country, meetings were being held and petitions signed against

[9] *Æneid*, vi. 851.

the Government proposal. The title of King might be applied to a ruler of rulers quite as well as that of Emperor. He regretted the absence of Lord Derby, because his forbears had been Kings of Man, and yet had owed allegiance to the Kings of England. Scottish sovereigns had done homage to Kings of England, and King Edward the First would rise from his grave if he could hear some of the arguments that had been used about the title of King as compared with that of Emperor. On the other hand, the Emperor of Brazil had no rulers among his subjects, nor had the Emperor of Hayti. The opposition, he maintained, was in no sense factious, but reflected public opinion, which had obliged the Government to taboo the use of the title in this country. "So that the Bill might properly be labelled 'Poisonous, for outward application only.' "

In the division, Lord Shaftesbury was beaten by only forty-six in a house of 228 peers, a figure which shows how strongly the innate conservatism of all parties reacted, as it continues to do, even in these advanced days, against any suggestion appearing to be merely new-fangled. The event has, on the whole, justified Lord Beaconsfield and his majority. The title of King-Emperor is acceptable in India, not least to the Indian Princes; and the title of King of England has suffered no displacement or diminution whatever, but stands first in security and in estimation among the monarchies of the world.

During this autumn a ferment of greater oratorical activity arose outside Parliament. Mr. Gladstone, no longer leading his party in the House of Commons, had begun to excite the country by his denunciations of the Turkish atrocities in Bulgaria, and both sides had to follow suit (October 4th, 1876). Rosebery made a rattling party speech at a banquet given at Dumfries to Mr. Robert Jardine of Castlemilk,[10] hitting right and left at Conservative policy at home and abroad. In some loudly cheered sentences he said: "To come to the difference between Liberals and Conservatives, it has struck me that it can be defined by a simple mechanical illustration, as the difference between a locomotive and a donkey engine. The locomotive, as we all know, is a swift machine, and a certain sign of progress and of civilisation. The donkey engine is constructed to fulfil its usefulness in a much narrower sphere and to remain stationary the while."

[10] Sir Robert Jardine (1825-1905), first Baronet. M.P. for Dumfries Burghs 1868-74; for Co. Dumfries 1880-92; head of the great firm of Jardine Matheson & Company.

Metaphors sometimes come home to roost, as he realised a few days later on board the *Russia*, where he occupied a large deck cabin in the bows of the ship. "At Dumfries on Wednesday I compared the Tory party to a donkey engine. They are now avenged, as the engine is outside my door and makes an infernal noise."

Rosebery had travelled more and knew more foreigners than most men of his age, so that his interest in foreign affairs was soon reflected in Parliament. He pressed for information about Heligoland (March 13th, 1876), of which, he observed, most people only knew that it had been in moral peril from gambling tables and physical danger from rabbits. He wanted to know how this little dependency was governed, because its minute size did not justify high-handed interference with its constitution. Lord Carnarvon gave a soothing reply, pointing out that some of the islanders had adopted the profession of wreckers; but that all the liberties of the people would be maintained. Egypt, where Mr. Cave's financial mission had lately been sent, also occupied his attention, and he made a request for papers.

It was not until the beginning of the new session in February 1877 that the Eastern Question in its fresh aspect became a subject of serious parliamentary discussion. The tale of atrocious cruelties inflicted on the Christian inhabitants of Bulgaria by the agents of the Turkish Government, with its approval and connivance, from May of the previous year onwards, had filtered slowly to England; and the Government were accused of having carried their indulgence to Turkey, based on their obligations under the Treaty of 1856, to such a pitch as to fall short of the other great Powers in the effort to check these crimes and to insist on the punishment of the criminals. In the autumn, Mr. Gladstone, emerging from his partial retirement, had headed the agitation of protest. The incomparable fire of his speeches, and their effect on the country, began to make shrewd observers wonder what this retirement really meant.

There were animated debates in both Houses early in 1877, first on the Address in reply to the Queen's Speech, and then on special motions. On February 20th the Duke of Argyll, the classical orator of his Liberal generation, asked for information concerning the special mission of Lord Salisbury to Constantinople in the previous November. This mission was understood to be the sign of a bolder policy imposed on the Government by the popular indignation which the Opposition campaign had aroused. The official reply came from the Prime Minister, just installed in the House as Earl of Beacons-

[80]

field. In the course of his speech he produced facts and dates to prove the complete ignorance which pervaded not only England but all Europe at the time when the atrocities were committed. Two days later Rosebery pointed out that the Blue Book did not seem to confirm the Prime Minister's argument, and he was not entirely convinced by the explanation offered in Lord Beaconsfield's reply. Later (April 19th) he called attention to the unhappy position in which this country was left by the Tripartite Treaty of 1856, by which the independence and integrity of the Ottoman Empire was guaranteed: "We might be some day placed in this position, that we should either have to fight for Turkey, a war which the conscience of this country would refuse, or to draw back from our pledged word." Lord Derby, in reply, advanced the rather risky doctrine when thus baldly stated: "No Treaties can be, or are intended to be eternal . . . nothing has been more common in European diplomacy than the recognition of the fact that Treaties do, by the lapse of time and the force of events, become obsolete."

A month later Rosebery developed his thesis still further (May 14th). Russia was now at war with Turkey; Austria might become embroiled in the contest. What was to present her from summoning us to fulfil our engagement of 1856, and to insist on our maintaining the integrity of Turkey? The Russian army was marching into the provinces of the Ottoman Empire. How could it be maintained that the integrity and independence of that Empire had not been interfered with? Lord Derby had said, the other day, that treaties were not eternal. Supposing that to be true, let them be decently buried, and consigned to the sepulchre of archives; but let them not sneak out of existence under the impression that nobody was going to act upon them. Lord Derby could only rejoin that there was in fact little risk of our being called on to fight under the terms of the Tripartite Treaty, and that it was an awkward moment at which to denounce that instrument. Perhaps the main interest of this debate to-day rests on the comparison with what happened thirty years later, when Rosebery was to urge on his fellow countrymen the danger of our being drawn into a European war from engagements contracted with France. No statesman of his generation liked as little as he did to contemplate the necessity of a future war.

Much had happened before Rosebery again intervened in a debate on Foreign Policy in the House of Lords. Russia, after some unexpected checks to her advance, had arrived within reach of Constantinople; she had forced on Turkey the Treaty of San Stefano, which the other Great Powers, under the guidance of Lord Beacons-field, had refused to sanction. The Berlin Congress had been held, and had carried out a qualified partition of the European dominions of the Sultan. Rosebery took no part in the great debate which followed Lord Beaconsfield's long and masterly speech when laying on the table the protocols of the Congress. That was the occasion on which Lord Derby, stung by what he considered the misleading account given by Lord Beaconsfield of his reasons for resigning the Foreign Secretaryship,[11] opened out the detailed story of those reasons, and of the different views taken in the Cabinet at the time. His successor at the Foreign Office, Lord Salisbury, lost his temper at what he considered a shocking breach of confidence, and went so far as to compare his noble relative to the basest figure in all English history, Titus Oates.

Rosebery's opportunity came three months later. At the end of May and the beginning of June the Government had entered into secret negotiations with the two protagonists, with Russia through the Salisbury-Schouvaloff Memorandum, of which a leading feature was the yielding to her of Kars and Batoum (May 30th to June 4th, 1878); and with Turkey by a Convention whereby, in return for our occupation of Cyprus, we agreed to come to the assistance of Turkey in the event of her Asiatic dominions being attacked by Russia from the more advantageous position now secured to the latter. It was the Russian arrangement that caused Rosebery's intervention. Early in June the terms of the Memorandum had startled the world by their appearance in the pink columns of the *Globe*. By an amazing piece of departmental stupidity, this crucial document had been entrusted to a temporary clerk, engaged, so it was said, at 10*d.* per hour, and the paper being worth a great deal more than its weight in gold, the unhappy man was tempted to reveal it to an enterprising newspaper. Lord Salisbury, when questioned in the House, replied that "the statement in the *Globe*, and other statements he had seen, were wholly unauthentic, and not deserving the confidence of Their Lordships' House." The summary first given in the *Globe* omitted to state that Turkey would be able to leave troops in the new province south of the Balkans. This was a point of substance, but it was thought to be a strain of language to describe as "wholly unauthentic" a version which chanced to pass it over, the remaining points being correctly enumerated.

Ten days later the *Globe* had printed the entire Memorandum:

[11] *Hansard*, March 28th, 1878.

Rosebery now asked for it as a Parliamentary Paper in the most considerable speech he had yet delivered. The Government had advanced the excuse that the Memorandum could not be published without other papers which foreign Governments would not allow them to produce. He thought this alarming, because the country might be pledged to something in the future of which the British Parliament was to be left in total, entire, and contemptuous ignorance. He next dealt faithfully with the comedy which, as he put it, had been played in sending a dispatch to Lord Odo Russell, our Ambassador at Berlin, instructing him to press upon Russia, and on the other Powers, the injustice of depriving Turkey of Kars and Batoum. If the English Plenipotentiary failed to persuade the Powers in this respect, he would be made acquainted with the course which Her Majesty's Government had decided to pursue. Rosebery asked whether Lord Odo, when he received that communication, was cognisant of the Agreement which had been signed on May 30th. "Was Lord Odo one of the company or was he a simple actor put up to recite the arguments of Batoum, with the prompter by to keep him to his part?" The whole thing, he proceeded, reminded him of the scene in the *Midsummer Night's Dream* between Starveling, one of the actors in the play within the play, and Bottom the weaver.

After dwelling bitterly on the abandonment of Greece by England, he passed on to a more general review of the situation: "He did not pretend that secret understandings were unknown to us; but he believed this was the first time we had called a European Congress with the view to discussing great Treaties, and standing forth on behalf of public law, we having, at the same time, bound ourselves in private to consent to those stipulations which we had denounced, and which we continued to denounce. . . . This country had always had one or two attributes that distinguished her from many other nations. One of these was unto her a sacred prerogative, —that of standing out on behalf of weak nations; another was that in dealing with the affairs of other nations we were fair and straightforward. Another circumstance marking our history was the openness—the almost faulty openness—of our diplomacy. Another of which we had always been proud heretofore, was the completeness of our parliamentary control. He confessed to the fear that great doubt would now be thrown upon our possession of these attributes, and indeed he regretted that some of them seemed entirely to have disappeared.

[83]

In Lord Salisbury's reply, which followed immediately, he defended his use of the epithet "unauthentic," and in the same circumstances would use it again. Rosebery's complaint that the traditions of English diplomacy were not being maintained "only shows that entire unacquaintance with the inside of a Government Office, which I have no doubt in the noble Earl's case, will not last long." It was dangerous to come into a Congress where opinions were hopelessly divergent, and this made preliminary understandings necessary. It was unfair to say that Lord Odo Russell was playing in a comedy, because, as a matter of fact, Russia did notify at Berlin the terms of her occupation of Batoum by making it a commercial port, not a naval station. In the matter of Greece, Lord Salisbury could only offer her the consolation of bidding her trust to the development of her own resources in comparison with those of her stronger neighbour, Turkey. Other critics of the Government followed, Lord Carnarvon answering his former colleague; Lord Morley, one of the rising Liberals; Lord Bath, another of the Tories who had broken with Lord Beaconsfield over the Eastern Question; Lord Hammond, lately the skilled permanent head of the Foreign Office; and Lord Granville, who wound up the debate. All these gave unstinted praise to Rosebery's speech. No other member of the Government took part in the discussion.

During the remaining life of Lord Beaconsfield's administration, Rosebery abstained from further criticism of its Foreign policy in Parliament, but he carried on the platform war by several speeches in Scotland. Of these, the principal was delivered at a Liberal demonstration at Aberdeen (October 10th, 1878). After indignantly repudiating the accusation that the Liberals were a caucus-run party, he proceeded to dissect a pledge made by Mr. Cross, the Home Secretary, the night before. "No meeting could ever have been more mutually agreeable than the meeting of Mr. Cross and his constituents. The constituents saw that in Mr. Cross they had an able, an upright, and an honourable gentleman as their representative; and Mr. Cross must have been convinced that if they accepted the statement he made to them, the confidence of his constituents must be illimitable and inexhaustible."

After banter of Mr. Cross for a series of unproved assertions, he observed that the Home Secretary

"proceeded in the spirit of a prophet to tell them that the Liberal party, or as he called them, the Radical party, would stop at nothing but a clean sweep of all existing institutions. As regards the word Radical,

[84]

I do not quarrel with being called a Radical, if it means one who looks at the root of things, and is not satisfied with assertion without proof, and with the mere claptrap of invective. When Cabinet Ministers go about and utter statements of that sort about their opponents, it is time for the country to tell that Cabinet what it thinks of it."

Having disposed of Mr. Cross, he turned to the Foreign Policy of the Government.

"Now, I should like to discuss for a few moments what 'peace with honour' really is. I believe there have been few chances of a great European settlement comparable to that afforded by the Congress at Berlin. I believe that the Congress at Vienna and the Congress at Paris afforded no such opportunities. I think there never was a more favourable opportunity for really carrying out a very noble Foreign Policy. Well, the result of it has been that the Congress of Berlin appears to have offered no settlement at all. What have the Government done? They have partitioned Turkey, they have secured a doubtful fragment of the spoil for themselves. They have abandoned Greece, they have incurred responsibilities of a vast and unknown kind, which no British Government has a right to incur without consulting the British Parliament and the British people."

With a touch of platform exaggeration, he went on to describe as "one of the unhealthiest spots on the face of the globe," Cyprus, which, before the other Powers had secured the portions of the Turkish Empire which they desired, another Power engaged, behind the back of the plenipotentiaries, in securing for itself.

"That Power, Gentlemen, I blush to say, was Great Britain. We rendered ourselves by that act *participes criminis*—sharers of the spoil and of the plunder of our ancient ally. Sir, I venture to say that no defeat in battle could have been so prejudicial to our prestige on the Continent as the acquisition of the island of Cyprus in the way we got it. I ask you to think how, after the transactions of the last few months, we can keep up moral reputation on the Continent. We have flaunted the Treaty of 1856 in the face of other Powers as our banner and our motto, and when it came to affect ourselves we treated it as so much waste paper."

From the standpoint of this country's interests, he proceeded to urge, nothing could be graver than our engagement to defend Turkey in Asia in consideration of reforms which would never be executed. "You will have observed, all through these negotiations, that we actually treat Turkey as a great Power. There never was so deliberate a mistake as that. Turkey is not a great Power, she is an

[85]

impotence." He concluded a loudly applauded speech by scouting the plea that this responsibility must be incurred for the preservation of India. "I believe it is no more necessary for the preservation of India than it is necessary that we should damage Spain in order to keep Gibraltar. But I do say this, that we may pay too great a price even for the preservation of India."

A little later, Lord Carnarvon addressed the Edinburgh Philosophical Institution on "Imperial Administration." It was a nonpolitical occasion, but, in moving a vote of thanks, Rosebery made the first recorded utterance of his Imperial faith. He could not be sorry to do so in the presence of an ex-Colonial Secretary who had just severed his connection with the Government.

CHAPTER V

Scotland, 1878-1882: Lord Rectorships: Marriage

IN THE autumn of 1878 the Liberal students of Aberdeen University, politically the most progressive of Scottish universities, had invited Rosebery to stand for the Lord Rectorship. It was an unusual compliment to a man of his age, but a complication arose from the possible candidature of Lord Aberdeen,[1] another young Scottish Peer of promise, with obvious local claims. His political affinities were at the time uncertain, and he wished to stand on a non-party platform. Mr. Gladstone knew that he was a Liberal at heart, and rejoiced at seeing the grandson of his old chief entering on public life. A rather animated correspondence followed. Rosebery was not prepared to disappoint his student supporters by withdrawing for no very urgent reason. In the event Aberdeen had no desire to appear as a rival Liberal; the students stuck to their party nomination, and Rosebery found himself only in competition with Mr. Richard Cross, then a rising, or half-risen, Tory politician. A desperate struggle ended in Rosebery's victory by a majority of three. In due course Lord Aberdeen became an earnest Liberal, and a valued public servant. His and Lady Aberdeen's friendship with Gladstone and with Rosebery lasted through the lives of both.

The Lord Rector of a Scottish university, after his official birth, does not develop immediate activity like the young of some mammals and fishes, and it was not till November 5th, 1880, that Rosebery delivered his Inaugural Address to the Aberdeen students, at the Music Hall. His reception at the railway station the night before had been wildly enthusiastic, his carriage being dragged by the students to his hotel, where he had to address the crowd from a window. When the time came for the address, the respected Principal of the University, by a genial custom not necessarily implying hostile animus, was prevented from uttering a word by an orchestra of "miniature fog-horns, toy musical instruments, bells, and other

[1] 7th Earl of Aberdeen, *b.* 1847. Lord-Lieutenant of Ireland 1886, and 1905-15; Governor-General of Canada 1893-8; *cr.* Marquess of Aberdeen and Temair, 1916.

contrivances." The Lord Rector was heard almost in silence, a thing which does not always happen to Lord Rectors. He began with the modesty of a young man addressing young men: "Chosen I believe as being, like you, a young Scotsman, though much older than yourselves, from sympathy rather than respect, from a sense of kinship rather than a hope of guidance." He went on to tell them of their coming share in the destinies of the Empire and in shaping the character of the nation, touched on the meaning and purpose of university training, and then reached his central subject, the crucial importance of the study of mediæval and modern history, and, for his audience, of Scottish history. He lamented the absence of any provision for its teaching, at Aberdeen as at the other universities,[2] and devoted the rest of his address to a brilliant sketch of the Scottish character as it developed through centuries of poverty and agonizing struggle up to its last two hundred years of prosperity and calm. It is a most penetrating analysis, of which a cavilling critic could only observe that the example of Macaulay had perhaps led the speaker to indulge in an excess of topical allusion and a plethora of proper names. But considering the audience and the occasion, such a reservation would scarcely be just. The concluding passages of the Address are marked by the deep gravity that Scotsmen understand and value.

"But I do not wish to weary, but to attract you, if possible, to the close study of Scottish history. I have thought that by so doing I could, without presumption or didactic affectation, best fulfil the duty imposed upon me. You are the best judges how far such a pursuit would suit your manifold dispositions. Around you learning spreads her various wares; you have but to pick and choose. You are the generation that holds for the present the succession to the long roll of famous men who have adorned this University. They have handed to you the light; it is for you to transmit it. The vestal lamp of knowledge may flicker, but it never dies; even in the darkest hour of dormant civilisation, it found loving hands to cherish and to tend it. To you that lamp has been given by those who have watched over it in these ancient colleges. I hope and believe it will not wax duller in your hands, but rather that you will show forth its radiance in whatever part of the world you may be called upon to wield that influence which every educated man must exercise.

"And how solemn a moment is that passing forth from the cloisters of learning into the great Vanity Fair of the world, there to make, for

[2] Sir William Fraser, the Scottish genealogist (1816-1898), founded by will a Chair of History and Palæography in the University of Edinburgh.

[88]

good or for evil, the choice of Hercules and abide by the result. Even I may, without presumption, indicate to you the crucial importance of that crisis of your lives, when it lies with you to decide whether your career shall be a heritage of woe or a fruitful blessing and an honoured memory. Day by day, the horizon of human possibility, which now lies so unbounded before you, must contract; the time must come when, under the stroke of illness or the decay of nature, hope, and health, the pride and power of life and intellect, which now seem so inseparable from your triumphant youth, will have passed away. There will then be no surer consolation, humanly speaking, than the consciousness of honest hope fulfilled, of health not abused, of life and intellect exerted in all its strength and fulness, not like water poured upon the sand, but for the raising and bettering in some degree of some portion of your fellow-men. I would fain hope that this living mass of generous youth before me was animated by no less a hope, by no lower an inspiration, and that in coming years it will be my pride and privilege to hear of some of you at any rate receiving the merited praises of grateful mankind.

"And if I might address your venerable University which has conferred so gracious and so undeserved an honour upon me, I would say, in the words with which the Psalmist hailed the sacred city, 'They shall prosper that love thee'; that love thee aright, that love thee not merely as an end, but also as a means, as the blessed link with splendid traditions and with noble men, as the faithful guide and the unfailing friend."

By coincidence, a contest for the Lord Rectorship of Edinburgh University reached its crisis at the same moment. These honourable offices enjoy the almost unique distinction that battles are fiercely waged, often on purely political issues, with no preliminary canvassing or speaking by the candidates themselves. Rosebery, therefore, had been selected by the students, and had agreed to stand, while still holding his office at Aberdeen. It was, in fact, on the morrow of the Aberdeen Address that he became Lord Rector of Edinburgh by a majority of thirty-nine over his Conservative opponent, Sir Robert Christison. It was an extraordinary tribute to his popularity, for Sir Robert, just fifty years his senior, was not only the *doyen* of the great medical school at Edinburgh, and a toxicologist of European reputation, but an engaging and impressive personality, preserving full mental and bodily activity in his old age. Mr. Gladstone had recommended him for a baronetcy in 1871, in spite of his pronounced Tory views.

Again just two years passed before the delivery of the Rectorial

[89]

Address (November 4th, 1882). Sir Robert Christison had died earlier in the year. The Synod Hall of the United Presbyterian Church was the scene of undergraduate rowdyism surpassing ordinary manifestations of the sort. Professors were violently hustled and bombarded by pea-shooters, furniture was damaged, and the offering of prayer was accompanied by castanets and yells. Party feeling was at a higher temperature than at Aberdeen, parties being more equally balanced. It was all the clearer evidence of Rosebery's power of speech that the Address itself was undisturbed by anything worse than a few chaffing protests and interruptions. He started with grave words of homage to Sir Robert Christison's memory, and then plunged into the main theme of his discourse—the patriotism of a Scot. After some lively sentences on the freaks to which the unhappy word "patriotism" is subject, the company and costume in which it finds itself, the crime, volubility, and virtue which it inspires, he defined it as "the self-respect of race." Irish patriotism was too dangerous a ground to venture on; "the English feeling shows itself chiefly in an impatience, if I may so call it, of Scotsmen and Irishmen: perhaps not an unnatural emotion, but not one on which I propose to comment." After some shrewd observations on reunited Italy, he declared that a country like Scotland, "self-sufficing," in a real sense, should keep its nationality intact, both for its own sake and that of the Empire of which it is part, "preserving it internally by development, and externally by emulation." Scotland, he went on, retains the ancient symbols and facts of independence in its systems of religion, and law, and of education, and these are to be watched with special care, because of the excellencies dividing them from other such systems, not mere peculiarities and catchwords of form. Ease of communication and "the centralisation of Anglicising empire" had destroyed and was destroying many of the old land-marks of national character, "effigies and splendours of tradition." These leave and teach their lessons; but

"the dream of him who loved Scotland best would lie not so much in the direction of antiquarian revival, as in the hope that his country might be pointed out as one that, in spite of rocks, and rigour, and poverty, could yet teach the world by precept and example, could lead the van and point the moral where greater and fairer states had failed."

The Address closed with an appeal to his young students to make the best of their wide opportunities of influencing their fellow-men in different walks of life, trusting that "the great wave of learned life that will roll from these walls . . . will neither wreck nor strand the vessel of State, but help to bear it safely on."

Rosebery became Lord Rector of Glasgow in 1899; but St. Andrews, the most cautiously conservative of Scottish universities, did not honour him thus till 1910. These later Addresses will be noticed in their time.

Through those years of political movement and sociable diversion Rosebery's friends kept asking themselves whether he intended to marry, and how soon. William Cory wrote to Reginald Brett[3] (1878): "I am sorry Rosebery is still addicted to *badinage*; let him fall in love." When he went repeatedly to America, it was thought not unlikely that he might return thence with a bride. In 1874 his close friend Randolph Churchill became engaged to the brilliant and beautiful Miss Jennie Jerome of New York; and, two years later, Lord Mandeville, the Duke of Manchester's heir, married Miss Consuelo Yznaga, whose wit and high spirits were to charm her own and the next generation in London for many years. Then, as now, there was plenty of beauty and attraction in the West. In a letter to Sam Ward he wrote (February 16th, 1874): "Make it a point to tell me in your next how Miss ——— (not yet formally 'out') whom I took in to dinner at her uncle's house, and who lives at Washington, is looking. She is a thing of Beauty, and I meditate over her as over a sonnet." And with another charming and most admirable young lady, not of Washington, things went further, so that an engagement between them was freely reported on both sides of the Atlantic. But unless his affections were irreparably involved, there was nothing to make an early marriage urgently desirable.

He was warmly attached to his brother Everard, who would carry on the succession in case of accidents; he had troops of excellent and amusing friends, men and women, old and young. He was pleasantly quartered in his bachelor's house, No. 2 Berkeley Square, where he could return, on a small scale, the profuse hospitality which sought him from all sides. Money was also, in some degree, a question. He had started with a good income, but always gave generously, and liked buying many things, some of which were costly. There was his racing-stable, and, in spite of his reply to "Uncle Sam's" friendly hint, he became in a degree "dipped" by this, or, rather, by occasional betting on a high scale. He lived in a wealthy and lavish world, and did as others did. Survivors of that generation will recall that to avoid a long wait at a cold country

[3] *Ionicus*, p. 88.

station, or even a crawling train journey, it was comfortable to take a special train; it might cost five-and-twenty pounds; but "What's a pony?" was a natural question in those untaxed days. A dowerless marriage might mean, then, a reduced scale of living of a kind galling to a proud nature. His public career, of which the lines could, by now, be pretty nearly traced, would be hampered by the necessity of taking thought for the morrow. It was therefore wiser to wait. But, liking women's society as he did, he was intensely attractive to them; once, certainly, there was the possibility of an English alliance for which the high-bred beauty and womanly charm of the other partner would have justified a happy forecast.

Meanwhile, he had long inspired the most utter devotion in a heart capable of the finest feelings. He had been introduced to Hannah de Rothschild—in a strange enough combination of place and person—by Mrs. Disraeli at Newmarket. The anomaly came from the matron, not the maiden, for her father, Baron Meyer de Rothschild, was a leading figure at "Headquarters," and had a house there.[4] He was the youngest of the four sons of Baron Nathan Meyer de Rothschild, who came to England in 1798 and founded the London branch of the cosmopolitan banking house. He with his two elder brothers, who were partners—the third having settled in Paris—when not immersed in European finance at New Court, led the lives of country gentlemen in the Vale of Aylesbury, where they occupied a remarkable enclave of more or less contiguous properties. The Rothschild stag-hounds brought crowds of hard-riding visitors to hustle over a fine grass country; and all the brothers took an interest in the Turf. Baron Meyer was the most conspicuous and successful, his great year being 1871, when he owned the champion colt and the champion filly of that season, the latter being named after his daughter. He married in 1850 Juliana Cohen, a most accomplished wearer of that well-known name, and Hannah was their only child. The health of both parents broke down early; in 1873 the Baron's nephew, Baron Ferdinand, wrote to Rosebery that Mentmore was completely shut up (November 5th, 1873), adding: "I feel a bitter pang for the owner, who has been so cruelly smitten in the prime of life."

In the following year Baron Meyer died, and his wife's nervous illness became more and more acute until her death in 1877. He left an enduring monument in Mentmore and its village; an amazing

---

[4] In some books of reference the name is given as Mayer, which may have been the original form in Germany, but he was always known here as Baron Meyer.

creation of a great house, a wide park, and noble gardens, transmuted, as by the hand of a genie, from its first state of rolling pastures sloping up to the crest of a foothill of the Chilterns, and dotted with fattening bullocks. Joseph Paxton, more famous as landscape gardener than as architect, built the house, borrowing the general plan from Wollaton, the famous home of the Willoughby family near Nottingham, but using the lovely buttercup Oxford stone, and not conforming slavishly to the Tudor model. Such an exterior positively cried out for splendid fitting within. The great central hall was exactly framed to show tapestry at its best, and to display, as few rooms in England can, the massively gorgeous furniture of the Italian Renaissance. The very finest French work of the eighteenth century, some of it with Marie Antoinette's own cypher, found a place in the drawing-rooms, and there was a wealth of Limoges enamels and of Sèvres china, together with some Italian and Dutch masterpieces. Seventy years ago good taste, backed by a large fortune, could acquire such treasures at prices which nowadays sound moderate, and Baron Meyer, with his wife and her devoted sisters, made many journeys to Italy and Germany in search of them. Everything passed to his daughter. It is often an irreparable misfortune either for a young woman or for a young man to succeed early to a great inheritance; but nobody was ever less spoilt by it than Hannah de Rothschild. Divine wisdom warns, "How hardly shall they that have riches enter into the Kingdom of Heaven"; but if that Kingdom is a place into which unkindness, and petty self-love, and lack of charity cannot penetrate, and where only things of good report abound, those who knew Hannah de Rothschild, either in her girlhood or through her married years, could never doubt that she was one of the happy souls for whom its gates are always standing open. It was indeed a very noble character, and she added to much native wit and no small intellectual capacity all the accomplishments encouraged by elaborate training in the best schools.

Rosebery was on terms of friendly intimacy with Baron and Baroness Meyer, and was several times their guest both at Newmarket and at Mentmore. With much community of tastes and serious interests, it might seem natural that he and Hannah de Rothschild should contemplate a life partnership. Her feelings, as I have said, were early awakened. But obstacles existed on both sides, particularly hers. One of her aunts, and two of her cousins, had indeed married Christians; but she was devoutly attached to her faith, and for her such an alliance necessarily meant a severe moral wrench. In the Rothschild family intermarriage between the different branches had become almost a custom: Baron Lionel's eldest son and both his daughters had married cousins of the French or the German house, and it may have been anticipated that the only child of another English partner would do likewise. She was completely independent, and had nobody's permission to ask; but the disapproval of a singularly united family would not be an easy thing to face.

Nor was such an alliance altogether easy for the bridegroom, in spite of all its material advantages. His family was ancient, though not so illustrious as to suggest an Austrian attitude towards a marriage lacking sixteen quarterings; but he felt, and continued to feel in a degree which few of his friends realised then, or since, the invisible but impassable barrier which difference of faith erects between those who believe at all, without the slightest impairing of trust or of affection. It will be told how, when the end came twelve years later, he had to suffer on his side of the dividing gulf. On the other hand, he was entirely devoid of the anti-Semitic prejudice which socially was less acute throughout Europe fifty years ago than it afterwards became; he was on very friendly terms with the three sons of Baron Lionel de Rothschild. One of these, Leopold, wrote in 1877: "You are always such a true friend to all our family." And at that time he was more intimate still with their Austrian cousin and brother-in-law, Baron Ferdinand, who had settled in England and entered Parliament after the tragically early death of his wife Evelina, Baron Lionel's daughter. Baron Ferdinand was a man of the finest taste in art, and created on a hill near Aylesbury the palace and park of Waddesdon. He was one of Rosebery's most regular correspondents both before and after his friend's marriage to Hannah de Rothschild, and a repertory of social and political gossip, presented with much detail and some humour. As early as 1876 there were rumours of an engagement, and even unauthorised announcements in newspapers. Eighteen months passed, and the reports were confirmed. Three-and-twenty years later Rosebery wrote to Mrs. Leopold de Rothschild (January 3rd, 1901): "This is not New Year's Day, but far more sacred to me, for it is the anniversary of my engagement." La Rochefoucauld lays it down: "Il y a de bons mariages, mais il n'y en a point de délicieux." This will be denied with righteous indignation, but there are many prosperous alliances based on warm liking and mutual esteem. This was

MENTMORE

of another sort. It was founded on admiration and warm affection on the one side, admiration and adoring devotion on the other. For all its glittering outside it possessed the quality of wearing well, which has made proverbial the wedding-gown of a very different Primrose bride. The marriage was celebrated on March 20th, 1878, first civilly at the Board-room of the Guardians in Mount Street, and afterwards at Christ Church in Down Street, Piccadilly.[5] The latter ceremony was attended by troops of friends of both families, headed by the Prince of Wales and the Duke of Cambridge, and Lord Beaconsfield gave away the bride. William Rogers, the Rector of Bishopsgate, officiated. This admirable and liberally minded man, like some Abbés of the best sort, made it his business to interest his friends of the more fortunate class in the educational and social good work of which he was an apostle. He had the gift of doing this effectively and manfully, without a tinge of sycophancy or any sacrifice of principle.

Rosebery had long enjoyed his friendship, and since 1874 had been interested in the schools at Bishopsgate. Prebendary Rogers, in return, looked out keenly for the racing successes of his friends, just as Charles Kingsley might have done. Lord Dalhousie, a dear friend of Rosebery's, well noted by John Morley[6] as "one of the truest hearts ever attracted to public life," was one of the Rogers circle, and Lord Londonderry was another. Sadly crippled by arthritic rheumatism, he was always gay, and always helpful.

Socially there was no abrupt change in the life of either partner in the marriage. They started with a large common acquaintance, and each became more and more friendly with the special allies of the other. Rosebery's intimacy with the Rothschild cousins grew closer, and in January he assisted at the wedding of Leopold de Rothschild with Miss Marie Perugia (January 19th, 1881). Her elder sister Louise, Mrs. Arthur Sassoon, was already an admired and popular figure in London. A lifelong bond of affectionate friendship united Rosebery and his wife to both the sisters and their husbands. There was a large circle of political affinities whose names recur throughout this story, and there was a smaller coterie of which Marlborough House was the central luminary, some mem-

[5] The diary volume for 1878 is almost blank except for the entries:
January 3rd: "Engaged to be married at 4.20 p.m." and
March 20th: "Married. 1. At the Workhouse in Mount Street and
2. At Church in Down Street.
To Petworth for honeymoon."
[6] *Life of Gladstone*, bk. ix, ch. v, p. 2.

[95]

bers of which also frequented Newmarket. Rosebery's list of special intimates included Francis Knollys, not less distinguished for his office of trusted Private Secretary to the Prince of Wales than for uncompromising utterance of Radical sentiments; and Harry Tyrrwhitt-Wilson, later Knollys's brother-in-law—gay, reckless, the ideal companion of an idle hour, gifted with no small share of native wit. Another intimate was Christopher Sykes, often Rosebery's companion in visits to Paris. It was still the custom fifty years ago, in some stately country houses, to find huge amusement in the generally harmless but often rough pleasantries popular with subalterns of a sporting regiment. Christopher Sykes was often the subject of such jokes, for no very obvious reason. He joined in them with sufficient good humour; but he was in reality a man of no little shrewdness and observation, who, when it came to repartee, could give his not too brilliant banterers more than they bargained for. Lord Carrington, a cousin of the Primrose family, and another close associate of the Prince of Wales from early childhood, was an intimate of the circle. He was one of Rosebery's most regular correspondents, unlading a copious farrago of social and political doings and chances. Always an enthusiastic party man, he can hardly have foreseen, in those gay days, the tribute of admiring affection which Lord Lincolnshire, five-and-forty years older in years, but not a day older in heart, would receive from all Liberals, and from many who were not Liberals.

Lord Fife, lately succeeded to the family honours, was another star in the Marlborough House firmament; and of the racing contingent Rosebery's closest intimates were Sir Frederick Johnstone, cynical and rather caustic, but a most loyal comrade; William Gerard, rather similar in type, but in addition a dispenser of the most reckless good humour; and, of a slightly later generation, Lord Durham. Some of the attributes of his famous grandfather had descended to this last. Destined to suffer the cruellest blows of fortune, he was endowed with such courage and persistence and loyalty, with capacity for single-minded affection, as, his friends will agree, have hardly a parallel in their memory. From his Oxford days Rosebery had also been closely bound to the Vyner family. Lady Mary Vyner, the last representative, with her sister Lady Cowper, of the great family of Grey, Earls and Dukes of Kent, had always shown him kindness. Her son Frederick was one of the victims of Greek brigands in the Marathon tragedy, and Rosebery organised the memorial to him in Christ Church Cathedral. The eldest brother

Clare, and Robert, the youngest, were both active on the Turf. Clare never married, and died comparatively young; but Mr. and Mrs. Robert Vyner remained close friends of Rosebery's as long as they lived. Such, in outline, was the lighter side of Rosebery's existence. But in this country, as in no other, there is sometimes an intermingling of orbits, as when, on the Friday of one Epsom Summer Meeting, Rosebery's guests at dinner at the Durdans were Mr. Gladstone, Clare Vyner, Frederick Johnstone, Billy Gerard, and another votary of the Turf. There is no record of that evening, but it may well have been a pleasant though an unusual one.

Somewhat to anticipate events—Lady Rosebery entered keenly into the marching and countermarching of the political field. Before her marriage she had been acquainted with most of the principal figures that thronged it, and friendly with some of them, for the Rothschild filaments were widely spread. She meant to be in the thick of the fray, after winning her spurs in the Midlothian campaign. Through the months of 1880, when Rosebery had to decline office, first from scruple, afterwards from illness, the party leaders were perpetually consulting her, and urging her to influence him. In reply she kept dwelling on the depression of his spirits and on the certainty of his speedy recovery. She had to realise that the political veil has its seamy side. "I was perfectly astounded to hear of the numbers of people who ask for office." And some of the Ministers could not, or would not, understand Rosebery's attitude. Even Mr. Gladstone, she thought, did not take it in.

"Mr. and Mrs. G. dined with us [August 1880]. After dinner I seized a moment to talk about Archie, and said I wished he had some work to do, as I believed it was what his brain required and should do good to his physical health. He answered, alluding to official work, 'But then there is nothing now to give him.' I was horrified at seeming to hint at office, when I meant nothing of the sort, and endeavoured to explain I meant to work at a subject. Mr. Gladstone may be a marvel of erudition, but he will never understand a man, still less a woman."

A harassed Prime Minister may be excused for supposing that this particular woman, an adoring wife, was thinking of her husband's political future. At the same time she observed how kind Sir William Harcourt was in often coming to see them, and how Sir Charles Dilke was equally thoughtful. He and Joseph Chamberlain evidently hoped to secure Rosebery as an adherent to the Radical wing of the Ministry; but in the early summer of 1881 the wife's

[97]

eagle eye remarked a change, because nothing more had been heard of the project that Rosebery and the two Ministers of the Left should jointly address various meetings in the country. Lord North-brook was another who found favour in her eyes. But she thought that Lords Granville and Hartington kept somewhat aloof; and in spite of Lord Spencer's pleasantness, "I never can look on him as a great motive power. Besides he does not mention Archie to me."

CHAPTER VI

Midlothian: Gladstone's Second Government

THE Administration of 1874 had expended its debonnair youth; in its maturity it had revelled in the spectacular return from Berlin; though beset by some fears, it was beginning to count on a renewal of its mandate at a not distant General Election. The Opposition, if not exactly distracted, was certainly not united; and the formal retirement from the stage of Mr. Gladstone was seen to be compatible with the occasional emergence of his figure from the wings, when it attracted greater attention than those of the other actors. He had denounced in trumpet tones the barbarities inflicted on the Christian subjects of the Porte, regarded by Lord Beaconsfield's Government as unlucky incidents in a complicated political story. A great moral issue had been raised, to which Britain, mindful of past crusades, might not remain indifferent. It was thus beginning to be clear that the leader's retirement was not in truth final. His physical powers were as amazing as those of Lord Palmerston and his electric mental energy had in no way abated. Oxford had long since rejected him; he was member for Greenwich; but if he were to resume great place, he ought to represent some town of historical fame, or some centre of industrial activity. The West Riding of Yorkshire (*quantum mutatus* in these advanced days) was then a rallying-post of Liberalism. Leeds was the Mecca of the faith, where the commercial magnates were for the most part pillars of sturdy Nonconformity, and where the *Leeds Mercury,* owned by the powerful Baines clan, and skilfully conducted by T. Wemyss Reid, was the official Liberal organ in the provinces. It would be all the more natural for Mr. Gladstone to contest a Leeds constituency, as one of his principal lieutenants, Lord Ripon, the most prominent of the Radical Whigs who were political heirs of Fox and Grey, was a near neighbour and actively interested in the industrial and educational progress of the city. However, a contest for a selected Yorkshire seat would be little more than a walk-over for Mr. Gladstone. If he could be got to assault some Tory stronghold he would not be electorally wasted.

Just such a Giant's Castle was the county of Midlothian, for which Lord Dalkeith, the son of the fifth Duke of Buccleuch, was the sitting member. He had been first returned in 1853, when only twenty-two years old; he had shared the defeat of many Tories in 1868, but had regained the seat in 1874 by a considerable majority. Not a man of commanding ability, he was of distinguished manners, sound intelligence, and the highest character. The family influence was overwhelming, based on the possession of some 430,000 well-administered acres in eight different Lowland counties, including a moderate-sized, but very valuable, estate close to Edinburgh. But the fifth Duke was no mere Marquis de Carabas. He and Mr. Gladstone had been colleagues, for he had been first Lord Privy Seal and afterwards President of the Council in Sir Robert Peel's second Government, resigning with it in 1845, and not rejoining to drink his share of "the poisoned chalice." Mr. Gladstone once told me that Sir James Graham agreed with him that the Duke was fully competent to take charge of any great Department of State. This was "approbation from Sir Hubert Stanley," for Sir James, by common consent, was the ablest of Victorian administrators. So that, when the Midlothian Liberals, at Rosebery's instance, urged the veteran champion to enter these lists, they were hazarding much. The failure of such a raid would verge on the ridiculous; and Rosebery would incur the reproach of compromising the cause in Scotland by an ill-timed adventure. But the prize was proportionately rich if it could be won.

Thus began Rosebery's close personal intimacy with Gladstone and his family. They had been well acquainted for years. Rosebery had been pressed to join the Government, and he had often been a guest at the Downing Street breakfasts and other entertainments. On April 5th, 1875, he wrote that he had brought from Scotland the American madeira of which he had spoken, two or three bottles of which he asked Mr. Gladstone to do him the honour to accept. "I now forward them," he wrote, "and hope you will be interested in these specimens of perhaps the only aristocracy which the United States deigns to recognise, for Murdoch Madeira there may almost be called a governing caste." But to a superficial onlooker it might have seemed that there was little in common between the old and the young man, separated by the gulf of nearly forty years. The one was a life-long scholar, the fine flower of academic culture, a

Churchman first and foremost, and a grave figure in the social world. The other was brilliant as a meteor, a favourite in gay coteries, and a votary of the Turf. It might appear to represent the contrast between the library of the Athenæum and the bow window of White's Club. But the onlooker would have been wrong.

One thing intolerable to Gladstone was a flippant approach to grave matters. He found in Rosebery a character that might take some trivial things too seriously, but would never treat serious things lightly. Nor could Gladstone ever comprehend how any superior intellect could be disfigured, as some are, by a shallow streak of coarseness. Rosebery certainly never posed as a Puritan to him or to anybody else, or affected to be insensible to some of the allurements of "the nether sphere, the fleeting hour." Genuine humour always appealed to him, even in unpresentable forms. But his mind was essentially refined, and he was capable of the utmost disgust where his taste was offended. Again, there was much common ground, not obvious to the bystander, in Rosebery's genuine bookishness, and in his perpetual interest in ecclesiastical personages and their doings. Lastly, his leader could not fail to recognise in him a touch of the quality ever-present in himself—the moral indignation that blazed up at the view of anything cowardly or treacherous or tyrannical. We sometimes smile at those who, not sharing their friends' pleasures, are less tolerant of these than of their vices. Gladstone never fostered such small prejudices and disapprovals. He was not interested in racing, though there was a legend that he had once surprised a convivial party by reciting a long list of Derby winners. But he liked the old ways; and if Hartington or Rosebery enjoyed breeding or running horses, as landowners and statesmen had done for generations in the past, he saw no reason to object to them, any more than to Spencer's hereditary pack of hounds.

Rosebery was now becoming the most conspicuous figure in the Liberal group of the Scottish Lowlands. The Duke of Argyll's impressive character, and his gorgeous eloquence, had hitherto won him undisputed supremacy not only in the Western Highlands but in the academic world of all Scotland; but here, close to the capital, stood out a younger man, giving promise of similar oratorical power, with the added grace of wit, captivating to the university mind, and likely to appeal equally to a wider circle outside. This first Midlothian campaign was to establish Rosebery once for all, before he was three-and-thirty, as the standard-bearer of Scottish hopes and Scottish ideals.

Since October 1878, and his slashing attack on the Government at Aberdeen, Rosebery had not been active on the platform. The Midlothian campaign of 1879-80 belongs to Gladstone's biography, not to his, and must be briefly treated here. It was suggested in 1878 that Mr. Gladstone might contest an Edinburgh seat, but it was not till January 1879 that the Liberal Committee of the County of Midlothian made their offer, which was strongly backed by Mr. W. P. Adam, the Scottish Whip. It would be a "tooth and nail affair," Mr. Gladstone noted.[1] In August Rosebery wrote offering the hospitality of Dalmeny to the candidate and his family, and on November 24th the triumphal procession from Liverpool to Edinburgh, punctuated by speeches at Carlisle, Hawick, and Galashiels, opened the campaign. The drive from Waverley Station, *à la Daumont*, through thronged streets with lights gleaming in every window, is still remembered by Edinburgh veterans. On the last day of the month Rosebery presided at a great meeting in the Corn Exchange, and at a huge open-air "demonstration" at Waverley Market. At the former he recalled the banquet to Lord Grey in 1834, at which his grandfather had been Chairman, "the deliverance of our country from the house of bondage—bondage of mock constituencies, controlled by great landowners and crafty wire-pullers" (laughter and cheers).[2]

"Full of years and honours, followed in his career by his country with a strange mixture of tenderness and pride, at an age when body and mind alike invite repose, the illustrious statesman has come down to fight one supreme battle in the cause of freedom. He has passed through one long series of well-ordered triumphs. From his home in Wales to the Metropolis of Scotland, there has been no village too small to afford a crowd to greet him—there has been no cottager so humble that could not find a light to put in his window as he passed. Mothers have brought their babes to lisp a 'hurrah,' old men have crept forth from their homes to see him before they died. These have been no prepared ebullitions of sympathy; these have been no calculated demonstrations. The heart of the nation has been touched. And, Gentlemen, we to-day have nothing to do with the special business which has brought Mr. Gladstone down to Scotland. This is no electoral meeting. We are here to-day, electors and non-electors, Liberals from every part of the United Kingdom, one with another, come to pay respect to

[1] Mr. Gladstone to Lord Granville, January 11th, 1879. *Life of Gladstone*, bk. vii, ch. vi.
[2] At this election the creation of "faggot votes" was understood to have been undertaken on a vast scale by the Tory organisers in Midlothian.

[102]

BARNBOUGLE—GENERAL VIEW

the intellect which has inspired our Liberalism and to the leader who has led our party to victory. On the colours which were borne to triumph in 1868 his name is inscribed. And, though these colours are tattered now, they are none the less glorious for that. Others may enjoy the place—others do enjoy the place and the power which he held so worthily then. But there is one place and one power which, as none can give him none can take from him, the power is the power of a great intellect, moved by the highest virtue and the purest patriotism—the place is the place in the hearts of his fellow-countrymen."

On the tremendous day of December 5th at Glasgow, when Gladstone, after his Rectorial Address of an hour and a half, and a speech after luncheon in the University Hall, enthralled an audience of 6,000 for another hour and a half in the afternoon, and finished his day by an address after dinner to a great audience in the City Hall, Rosebery was not allowed to be silent, though he naturally confined himself to a short, telling improvisation. But the shouts that dragged him to his feet showed that it was not Edinburgh alone that hailed him as the rising star of Scotland.

Christmas came, and a short stay abroad for Rosebery and his wife. Hannah Rosebery had come to Dalmeny at the end of October to prepare for the political visit. They returned from Nice in February 1880, and Rosebery was almost at once laid low by a sharp attack of scarlet fever, at that period the most prevalent and the most dreaded of zymotic diseases. So that when Mr. Gladstone turned north again in the middle of March, Rosebery had by no means recovered his full strength. But he was again host at Dalmeny, this time for three weeks; and his disability as a Peer served to spare him most of the daily and nightly exertions which would have tried even his powerful constitution. But he attended the dinner of the Glasgow University Gladstone Club (March 29th, 1880), and fastened sharply on the Foreign Policy of the Government, dwelling caustically on the tributes of admiration paid to it by statesmen of the Continent whose interests were directly opposed to our own. "We are told that the Opposition to which we belong is detested by the Powers varying in importance, and all quoted *in extenso*." He asked who was so much disliked by every foreign Power as Lord Palmerston, who was regarded by the Tories as the *beau idéal* of a Foreign Minister.

"I believe that our watchword in Foreign Policy will be the cause of England, peace, and freedom throughout the world. When I say peace I do not mean peace at any price, when I say freedom I do not mean licence; when I say England, I mean not merely these two islands; I mean the great Empire throughout the world, which we are as proud of as any Tory possibly can be, which we will maintain even with our blood if necessary, but which we will not recklessly increase at the cost of the people of England."

A still more important occasion, just before the poll, was the Inaugural Banquet of the Scottish Liberal Club at Edinburgh (March 31st), when Mr. and Mrs. Gladstone were among the guests. A number of Scottish Peers were present, and other representative Scotsmen, among whom the name of Campbell-Bannerman is conspicuous. Rosebery, speaking from the Chair, again dealt mainly with foreign politics, but he also referred to an observation of the Chancellor of the Exchequer in the House of Commons a month before. Sir Stafford Northcote had said that whenever the subject of Peers' interference with elections occurred to his mind, it was always associated with the name of Rosebery. The object of this attack had already consulted Mr. Gladstone. Writing from his sick-room at 107 Piccadilly by his wife's hand, he asked:

"Ought I to take any notice of the Chancellor of the Exchequer's little innuendo last night? I call it 'little' for the Leader of the House of Commons: in a lesser personage I should call it an impertinence. I have, as you know, never interfered in Midlothian: I have never canvassed for you: I have never spoken on your behalf: I have not even attended your meetings. The most I am guilty of is the having had the honour of receiving you at my house, which even in the present ostracism of yourself and the Liberal Party can hardly be deemed an offence against the privilege of the House of Commons. However, on the whole, I am inclined to do nothing. If you agree with this view, take no notice of this letter. If I do write a note I would enclose to you a copy of the one I should send."

In the result Rosebery confined himself to an expansion in this speech of what he had written to Gladstone:

"During last November I had the public misfortune, as regards the good opinion of Sir Stafford Northcote, but the great happiness of my life as concerns myself, to entertain in my house your distinguished guest. Prescribed and hunted as our party is, I never knew, till it fell from the lips of the Chancellor of the Exchequer, that the very right of asylum is denied to the arch-criminal of his country."

Party feeling was running high, but it is singular to note Rosebery's use of expressions which sounded excessive at the time, but became literally applicable a few years later, when the Irish Question was not only to rend the Liberal party but to shatter not a few private friendships.

The poll was declared on April 5th, Gladstone's majority being 211. The voters numbered 2,947, a ludicrously small figure for an earth-shaking contest, it would be said to-day. Meanwhile, at Leeds, where he had been nominated without his consent, over 24,000 voters had returned him, with a majority of upwards of eleven thousand over his Conservative opponent. Rosebery had taken a house in George Street, Edinburgh, for the Midlothian contest, and the victor noted: "Fifteen thousand people being gathered in George Street, I spoke very shortly from the windows and Rosebery followed, excellently well." Rosebery's was also a very brief speech, celebrating the victory won for constitutional government, and for oppressed nationalities throughout the world, concluding thus:

"To use the words of Mr. Pitt, I will only say that I trust that Midlothian, having saved herself by her exertions, will now save Great Britain by her example."

Gladstone's letter of thanks to his host and hostess is given at length in the *Life*[3]; I quote a few material sentences:

"As to Midlothian, the moral effect, before and after, has I think surpassed all our hopes. The feeling until it was over was so fastened on it, that it was almost like one of the occasions of old when the issue of battle was referred to single combat. The great merit of it, I apprehend, lay in the original conception, which I take to have been yours, and to over-shadow even your operations towards the direct production of the result. But one thing it cannot over-shadow in my mind: the sense of the inexpressible aid and comfort derived day by day from your considerate, ever-watchful care and tact. . . . It is a very pleasant subject of reflection to me that the riveting effect of companionship in a struggle like this does not pass away with the struggle itself, but abides."

This letter crossed one from Rosebery to Gladstone dated the previous day:

"MY DEAR MR. GLADSTONE,
"I cannot tell you the immense and overpowering sense of relief that I feel after the events which have occurred. I always thought that the stimulus and inspiration which Liberalism required must come from

[3] Bk. vii, ch. viii. Hawarden, April 10th, 1880.

you and that the proper tripod for you was Scotland; and if Scotland then Midlothian. The intensity (to put the qualities aside) required was only to be found in Scotland and yourself. But I have never disguised from myself that we had to fight agencies extremely powerful and absolutely unscrupulous, and that in engaging you to lend us your name and your energies we were accepting responsibilities which in my view were quite appalling. These pressed upon me when physically weak perhaps even more than when I was stronger, but I have often thought during the last two months that I could not have survived your defeat.

"And now all is over I am lost in an immense thankfulness, and I have had an overpowering reward. Our little country has answered its purpose, and has been the pivot on which you have turned the country. That has been my first happiness. My second has been this: that owing to this contest I have had the privilege which I could never otherwise have had of seeing you and knowing you (if I may use the word without impertinence) more closely than I could ever otherwise have done. The reverence I had before has become enveloped in a warmer feeling to you and yours, and I cannot help on this one occasion, what I could not do again without disrespect, signing myself as I feel

"Yours affectionately,
ROSEBERY."

It is, a pleasant reflection, and one that could hardly arise in any country but Britain, that this vehement political struggle did not break up Rosebery's personal relations with the Buccleuch family. The old Duke died in 1884: Rosebery maintained a cordial friendship with his successor, the defeated candidate, and with the new Duchess, one of the Duke of Abercorn's daughters, of a family with which he had been intimate from his boyhood—and the following generation at Dalkeith and Drumlanrig did not fail to continue the tradition.

The inevitable return to power of Gladstone, and the formation of his second Ministry, form part of the history of the country. It was generally surmised that Rosebery would receive some office, and the usual crop of newspaper conjectures placed him in a Viceroyalty, in an embassy, and in the Cabinet itself. Mr. Gladstone always desired to follow "Peel's rule against admitting anybody straight into the Cabinet without having held previous office." He had to break it sometimes, as with Bright in 1868 and Joseph Chamberlain in 1880; but these were older men, picked from outside the traditional band of young Peers and Members of Parliament, for whom an Under-Secretaryship in their thirties might mean admission to the Cabinet in ten or fifteen years' time.

Rosebery himself found it difficult to think of office at all. Sensitive to a degree which few comprehended then or afterwards, he had been cut to the quick by such criticisms as that of Sir Stafford Northcote, repeated in a coarser form by less refined opponents. Queen Victoria, noting for Sir Henry Ponsonby her conversation with Lord Granville, wrote (April 28th, 1880): "Lord Rosebery would accept nothing, as he said it would look as if Mr. Gladstone had paid him for what he had done."

His letter to the Prime Minister, in answer to the offer of the Under-Secretaryship of the India Office, states his attitude less crudely (April 25th, 1880):

Most Confidential.

"MY DEAR MR. GLADSTONE,

"In the first place let me thank you for the great honour you have offered me. There could not be a more attractive post for a young man; for there is real distinction to be won in holding one's own against such odds in the House of Lords, while defeat would not necessarily imply disgrace; there is much to gain and little to lose.

"As regards the labour of it, anybody beginning departmental work for the first time must expect hard work, and one can only do one's best. People cannot rise in politics by sinecures, and I being new to the business should have to work hard in any department.

"As regards the chief of it, I do not think I need say anything.

"I have lain awake nearly all night thinking it over, for of course to me it is the most critical moment of my life. I cannot deny that for some time past it has seemed to me possible that this period of trial might come: otherwise it would have been useless for me to take the resolution that I did. But now that the crisis has come I must face it. If I take this appointment, I lose the certainty that what I have done in the matter of the elections, however slight, has been disinterested. In losing that I lose more than political distinction could repay me: I should feel that where I only meant personal devotion and public spirit, others would see, and perhaps with reason, personal ambition and public office seeking. If either Hartington or Granville had been Prime Minister, kind friends as they have always been of mine, they could not have given me so high a post, for I have done nothing to deserve it.

"No, with all gratitude to you, I must remain as I am. Yesterday is a day I can never forget, when I sat with you treated like a son and in possession of this high proof of your confidence and esteem. The memory of that no one can take away from me, whatever motives may be assigned for my answer (which however no one need ever know) while I shall always continue in however obscure a position

"Your sincere and devoted follower, A R[4]

"This is for your eye alone—I am writing to Hartington by this same messenger."

He also wrote to Miss Mary Gladstone, her father's confidante, with whom he and his wife had established a firm friendship (April 27th, 1880) :

"Many thanks for your kind little note which has cheered me very much. I find heroism is difficult to people who are not heroes.

"There is nothing 'grand' in what I have done, for I had literally no option in the matter. Nothing but the resolution I took could have enabled me to get through the election, or to have lived with your father on terms of frankness and freedom. When you analyse my motive it is little more than a half selfish sacrifice to peace of mind. Moreover, my real motives are so well known that it would be waste of time in me to dilate on them. They are :

"1. Annoyance at not being asked to join the Cabinet.

"2. Dislike of hard work. 3. Passion for the Turf.

"However that may be, my heart is so full in response to your note that I do not trust myself to write. God bless and preserve your father in the great work before him, and all of you to help and sustain him."

For a man in his thirty-third year, generally credited with a political future, to decline a secondary office to which nobody could have thought him unequal, simply because he had been the host of the Prime Minister during his election, might seem almost morbidly scrupulous. But few will blame such an excess of carefulness on a field where fine scruples are apt to grow stunted and to wither. As a matter of fact, there were physical reasons besides. In June Hannah Rosebery wrote to Mrs. Gladstone in answer to inquiries about her husband :

"Your letter is more than kind, and if anything could encourage Archie to three months' exile, it will be your affectionate recommendation of fresh air and rest. He has promised to endeavour to carry out the doctors' injunctions, and though they assure me there is no cause for any nervousness, still I am much relieved at his decision to follow their advice."

[4] For convenience in printing, the "A" and the "R" are separated, though Lord Rosebery always used them in monogram, as may be shewn in the reproduction of the letter on page 340.

He himself noted that the stars in their courses fought against him, and the warning of the famous Edinburgh physician, Matthews Duncan, that if he neglected his cure he might become useless for life—"he has a friend, a doctor, who was in the same position and neglected it, and is now done with. They say scarlet fever changes or affects, every pore in one's skin." There can be no doubt that Rosebery paid for his too early activity in the Scottish campaign by perilous approach to a complete breakdown. It was thought that the gradually ascending levels from Homburg to Gastein, and Gastein to St. Moritz, would restore the tone that he had lost. And so it proved, though there were one or two disappointing relapses of great fatigue. The offer of the Indian Under-Secretaryship was renewed, rather prematurely, as it happened, and was again declined, in the following rather depressed terms:

Confidential.   [5]HOTEL DE L'EUROPE, SALZBURG, *July 14th,* 1880.

"MY DEAR MR. GLADSTONE,
    "Your kind note was put into my hand as I was leaving Homburg on Monday.
    "It is quite unnecessary for me to thank you for this new proof of your confidence. You will know what I feel without my telling you.
    "As regards the reason I gave before for my inability to accept the same invitation you now renew I confess it seems to me no longer applicable. There have been intervals, stormy intervals, since then, which make the place appear at the present moment less an unde-served reward than a call to duty.
    "On the other hand I may say in strict secrecy that I no longer feel the confidence I did then that my position with regard to my immediate chief would be as mutually agreeable as I then fancied. That opinion however regards him and not me, and is not one perhaps that I have any right to mingle with the general question.
    "But the absolute, miserable, and decisive reason that now compels me to hold aloof is my health. It is a disagreeable subject to dwell upon. Yet I must say that I am not as well as when I went to Homburg, in spite of two days when I thought otherwise. I do not know what is the matter with me, medically speaking, but speaking as the patient, it is prostration physical and mental. I felt tired when I left London, but not the annihilation of the present moment. As it happened, two hours after I got your letter, I saw a famous doctor in Frankfurt, who had never seen me before. He knew all about the Midlothian business and about me, and, strangely enough, said, 'I saw that Mr. Gladstone had offered you office and that you had refused.' I replied that you had

[5] This letter was posted from Gastein on July 16th.

[109]

offered me office again that morning, in order to find out what he thought. He screamed out at the idea, said it was out of the question, and that three months' office now would do me more harm than ten years' hard work hereafter. I believe he is right, but at present I know I am good for nothing. Whether I shall ever be good for anything is a question I ask myself all day long. You offer to let me remain abroad for a time, but I do not feel as if I could do that. I doubt if I could remain in the state of absolute inactivity that the doctors say is necessary for restoration to health, if I felt that I had duties elsewhere to the public: more especially if I knew, as I know, that my post should be eagerly coveted by some who would be of real use in these troubled times.

"It is a strange fate that compels me to refuse the same position twice in three months and for different reasons. It is needless for me to say how painful it is. I hope I am neither a fool nor a hypochondriac. Whether I ever become one or the other I know that I am like a sucked orange now, and that it would be criminal in me to undertake any public function.

"Excuse the length of this letter and believe me always

"Yours very sincerely,

A. R."

The passage referring to Hartington reads strangely, for there was no Minister with whom Rosebery was on closer terms of friendship based on community of tastes and on mutual respect for each other's personal qualities. Hartington himself wrote at length (August 9th), pressing him to reconsider the offer:

"I think you would like the office. At this moment I hate it as I should hate any office; but if it were not for the waste of time in everlasting attendance at the House, which makes all official work a burden, I cannot imagine anything more interesting than the work of the India Office. I can assure you that it would be a great relief to my mind if you could accept."

He went on to say that he missed Lansdowne much more than he expected. Rosebery was touched by the kind terms of this letter, but replied begging him to fill up the post at once, having no hope of ever being able to fill that or any other post. To another correspondent he wrote (August 18th) that he considered himself henceforward as a country squire of a mild type. He would be humbugged by no more cures, and was returning to England next week. As late as November he still described himself as "rather in the dumps at being so easily tired."

Scottish affairs, public and private, absorbed his full attention during the autumn of this year. There was talk of a tunnel under the Forth, to be approached through the policies of Dalmeny, condemned by Mr. Auldrjo Jamieson, Rosebery's legal adviser, as a wild project to be firmly opposed. Mr. Joseph Chamberlain, now at the Board of Trade, when privately appealed to, thought there was no fear that the project would mature. Lord Reay, the Dutch diplomatist who had succeeded to an ancient Scottish title and had married a wealthy Scottish wife, was a regular correspondent of Rosebery's and kept him posted on party politics and on doings in Scotland. He had written at length in the summer (July 3rd and 8th) about Heriot's Hospital in Edinburgh, now the subject of parliamentary inquiry and bandied about between the Home Secretary, the President of the Council, and the Lord Advocate. This was a typical example of the eddies in which Scottish parliamentary business was made to swirl; and more and more its reform became Rosebery's main preoccupation. At Mentmore in October he had this out with Sir William Harcourt, and found a sympathetic hearer in the Home Secretary, who enjoyed Scottish visits and Scottish sport, but did not wish to be plagued with the settlement of Scottish problems in the company of a Lord Advocate of whom he had a poor opinion. He agreed that there ought to be a distinct Scottish Department, with a full-blown Minister. At the close of the year he explained that he had written to Gladstone (December 23rd) on the basis of Rosebery's representation:

"But the only reply was that his whole mind was full of Ireland, and that 'the land of brown heath and shaggy wood' must wait for the inhabitants of the shores of the melancholy ocean. He also told me that I had a Solicitor-General and should have a Lord Advocate soon to help me, which looked as if he thought the whole thing was a fit of laziness on my part, which is not the fact. So it is clear that we must wait for the *mollia tempora fandi*, and if we survive Ireland, we will yet do justice to Scotland. You may rely on my not letting the thing drop, as you have convinced me more than ever of its expediency.
"Yours ever,
W. V. H."

The fruit of this agreement was not long in ripening, as will be seen directly.

Rosebery was now the accredited champion of national claims. His Edinburgh friend, Professor Donaldson, wrote (October 6th):

"You can scarcely have an idea how strong the affection of the Scottish people for you is. In all political and very many social gatherings you are the first they think of, and when you refuse, as in many cases you must, there is genuine vexation and grief."

This autumn witnessed his Rectorial Address at Aberdeen and his election as Lord Rector of Edinburgh University, which are noticed separately. The latter was followed by the foundation of a Rosebery Club, on the model of the Glasgow Gladstone Club, at the suggestion of an intimate Edinburgh friend, Sheriff Holmes Ivory. But his sympathy was not limited to the high academic field. He liberally supported the fund for boys attending the Watt School of Art through the medium of the Edinburgh Trades Council. On the political side he presided at the Edinburgh banquet to Mr. W. P. Adam, who, as Chief Whip, had been the Carnot of the Liberal victory, and was just appointed Governor of Madras (November 2nd).

In the *Life of Gladstone* (bk. vii. ch. i.) Lord Morley sets forth convincingly the elements of disruption inherent in the powerful and representative Government which met Parliament in 1880. In the spring of 1881 the prospect of Irish land legislation drove the Duke of Argyll from the office of Lord Privy Seal. Rosebery, as we have seen, had not been available for the Indian Under-Secretary- ship when Lansdowne resigned it, but a fresh shuffle of the cards might now find him a fitting post. Harcourt, genuinely anxious to secure this valuable recruit, again approached Gladstone at Easter. He had been staying at the Durdans, and wrote:

"Rosebery says he did not expect to be appointed, though that I consider is not quite an accurate view of the matter."

He went on to explain that at any rate Rosebery was irritated and disappointed because he seemed to have expected confidences which he did not receive. Something, therefore, should be done to soothe him. This was not a happy line to advance towards Gladstone of all people. He replied curtly:

"The notion of a title to be consulted on succession to a Cabinet office is absurd. I believe Rosebery to have a very modest estimate of himself, and trust he has not fallen into so gross an error."

Gladstone's choice of Chichester Fortescue, just created Lord Carlingford, for the Privy Seal was natural enough. Ireland had been placed in the first line, he was an Irishman, and had been Chief Secretary so long ago as 1865. Later in the session he took charge of the Irish Land Bill in the House of Lords and assisted its passage loyally and capably.

Such considerations, joined to Gladstone's conservatism in the matter of official promotion, prevented Rosebery's admission to the Cabinet at thirty-four, the age at which Canning, Peel, and Gladstone himself entered the inner circle of government. But if he had been given the Privy Seal, with the charge of Scottish business, pending the creation of a Scottish Secretaryship, a just and sensible reform would have been accelerated, while Harcourt and he having started in friendly accord, some later occasions of personal friction and misunderstanding might have been escaped. In the House of Lords early in the session he only intervened in a discussion on the administration of the Burnett bequest, a religious endowment at Aberdeen University to be regulated under the Endowed Institutions (Scotland) Act. In his capacity of Rector of the University he came into collision with the Duke of Richmond, its Chancellor, a frequent antagonist on other occasions. He spoke wittily for Lord Dunraven's resolution in favour of opening museums and galleries on Sunday, which was lost by but seven votes in a tolerably full House.

Scotland claimed him again on the Court of Session Bill (March 22nd), when he was asked to protest against the proposal to reduce the Lords Ordinary from five to three. He asked questions on the persecution of Jews in Russia, and on the Convention between Turkey and Greece. Lord Fife, a Liberal who had lately succeeded to a seat in the House, pressed the Government to consider the appointment of a Minister for Scotland other than a law officer, on the lines of a report issued twelve years before. It was suggested that a Parliamentary Under-Secretary with a seat in the House of Commons would satisfy the Scottish demand. The Duke of Argyll thought that the Lord Advocate could only be displaced by a Cabinet Minister, and, since this was not proposed, he hoped the Government would not be in a hurry to make a change. Rosebery drew a rapid but exhaustive historical sketch of Scottish administration since the Union, pointed out that much Scottish business was not legal; that no Lord Advocate had been in the Cabinet, though he had to act as Minister for Scotland; that Scottish members of the House of Commons had signed a memorial in the sense of Fife's question but had received no reply; and, most of all,

"the words Home Rule have begun to be distinctly and loudly mentioned in Scotland. . . . I believe that the late Lord Beaconsfield, on one occasion in Scotland, implored the people of Scotland to give up 'mumbling the dry bones of political economy, and munching the remainder biscuit of effete Liberalism.' I believe the people of Scotland, at the present moment, are mumbling the dry bones of political neglect, and munching the remainder biscuit of Irish legislation."

To his horror, *The Times* reported him as saying, "The Government are munching, etc.," and he wrote at once to Gladstone, explaining that the *Scotsman* had given the correct version.

Later there was a discussion on the recently delimited Greek frontier and the European Concert (June 30th). That cumbrous piece of machinery then inspired lofty hopes which later events tended to depress. Lord Salisbury, indeed, pointed out that it was the authority of Prince Bismarck, rather than that of the Concert, which had settled this particular difficulty; Rosebery, on the other hand, congratulated Lord Granville "for having kept together a most splendid yet efficient instrument." His last unofficial appearance was in a debate on the subject of Scottish Peerage claims to vote for Scottish Representative Peers, which ended in the appointment of a Select Committee with the most exiguous functions (July 8th).

University College was in the habit of holding an annual public debate, and this year Rosebery presided over a discussion on the motion that the Advance of Democracy tends to strengthen the Foundations of Society. Winding up a debate on this pompously worded thesis—a debate which had produced predictions of the abolition of the monarchy and of the House of Lords—and the institution of manhood suffrage and equal electoral districts, the Chairman summed up by assuming a position well to the Left, though not to the Extreme Left. If the House of Lords should impede the march of democracy, it would meet the fate of Stephenson's cow. But were the forces of beneficent democracy to be employed at the moment in sweeping away a practical Second Chamber? A Tory speaker had regarded America with disfavour. He, on the contrary, had the greatest warmth of feeling for America and the American people. "I am one of those who think that a person who elects a very moderate intellect to carry out his transactions, and chooses him of his free will, is better off than the man who has a leviathan set over him against his will." On paper, the main elements of the British constitution were not congenial to democracy. No doubt the advance of democracy would largely affect the power and influence of the privileged classes. He did not regret that, because they would have no reason to exchange part of their privilege and power for the secure enjoyment of the remainder. He confided in the good sense and practical ability of his countrymen, and therefore desired to give a large share of responsibility and power to them. Above all, responsibility.

As the months flew on, the absence from the Government of such a conspicuous figure, in no way disabled from lending a hand, became more and more noticeable. Scottish friends were puzzled, and said so. John Morley, with whom a friendship was budding,[6] and who had told him, "It would be of great use to me, as well as a great pleasure, to have a chance of knowing your ideas from time to time" (May 20th, 1880), wrote later in the same year: "I hope it is not an impertinence in me to say that I am getting rather impatient to see you among the Government magnates."

The Under-Secretaryship at the Home Office fell vacant by the elevation of Mr. Leonard Courtney. Harcourt wrote to Gladstone: "I think you know how sincerely I am anxious that Rosebery should join the Government for all reasons, and particularly on the ground of my great personal regard for him" (July 27th, 1881).

It was understood that Rosebery would have special charge of Scottish business, of course in concert with the Lord Advocate. He wrote to Gladstone (August 1st): "You are always devising some friendly plan for me, and I fear you must often have thought me crotchety with regard to them." He was afraid that the shifting of offices might cause inconvenience, but was indifferent to the possible attribution of personal motives in having urged a change in the management of Scottish business. He concluded: "I am pleased and proud to think that at last I shall serve under you." Congratulations poured in. Arthur Godley, Mr. Gladstone's trusted private secretary, was "glad you are to be Minister for Scotland"; Edward Hamilton, also from 10 Downing Street, set him in the foremost place among his contemporaries, and hoped he would mollify the somewhat rough manner of his Secretary of State; Reay wrote he would be supreme in his sphere till promoted to the Cabinet; Sir Charles Dilke said they must congratulate *themselves*, and when he got office worthy of him, would congratulate *him*. Rosebery had written to Dalhousie an affectionate note full of compunction, having heard that his friend, who had been working at the Home

[6] The intimacy had not progressed very far, for the writer added, "Pray do not call me Professor, I am not, nor ever was, nor shall be professor of anything, not even of hairdressing or corn-cutting."

Office, had bidden a melancholy farewell to Harcourt. Dalhousie replied that Rosebery was tormenting himself about nothing, for he was bound to conform to the new arrangement. He himself had only made civil regrets to Harcourt, who had been very kind to him. He felt sure that Rosebery must be out of sorts. Nevertheless, the seeds of future difficulties lurked in the arrangement.

Harcourt was anxious to secure Rosebery, but he also wanted an Under-Secretary in the Commons. This he could not have. On Rosebery's side, he found himself not only Under-Secretary at the Home Office, but in a sense subordinate to the Lord Advocate—a very different affair. Still, things worked well enough at first. The Harcourts stayed at Dalmeny on their way north, and Rosebery wrote to Mary Gladstone: "The Home Secretary, the Lord Advocate (regnant), and I have been like lambs and lions and cockatrices." And he noted later visits to Dundee Prison in the morning, and Perth Prison in the afternoon, "and so home to bed in the evening." His parliamentary duties for the session were limited to answering in a sentence a question about pawnbrokers. During the prolonged discussions in committee of the Land Law (Ireland) Bill, Rosebery regularly supported the Government in the Lobby till it passed on August 22nd. His sole intervention in debate was on a minor amendment of Lord Salisbury's, modifying in the land-lords' interest the functions of the Land Court, the central pivot of the measure. "The Government, as I understand it, considered that the Court was a necessary evil. They wished to encourage recourse to it as little as possible." This was not exactly the tone of an impassioned disciple. His abstention, however, was fortunate, for early in the month he was again in the hands of Dr. Mathews Duncan with a slight relapse of his last year's illness.

The autumn of this year kept Rosebery active in Scotland. Sir William Harcourt was made a Freeman of Glasgow, where he and Rosebery interchanged jocular compliments in scenes of unbounded enthusiasm.

Two days later (October 27th) Rosebery spoke at a great Liberal meeting in Dundee, after receiving an address from nine important Liberal associations of the surrounding counties. He declared his attachment to Liberal principles, and hoped that as age creeps on, and pulses grow colder, it would be his fate not to be a backslider in the cause. At the evening meeting, after sketching sarcastically the efforts of Sir Stafford Northcote and Lord Salisbury, he touched on the management of Scottish affairs in Parliament.

It was impossible to lay down a rule that there must always be a Scottish Cabinet Minister. He himself had neither the necessary ability nor experience, and nobody else was available. The Lord Advocate was fully competent to represent Scotland in the House of Commons, and he would do his best, in spite of criticism from some of their own party, to serve Scotland with a special sense of responsibility to the whole country, though not to a single constituency.

A month later he was at Greenock, addressing a great party meeting (November 4th). After a picturesque and reasoned comparison of Tory with Liberal Foreign Policy, he devoted the rest of his speech to Ireland. At that date fully ninety per cent. of Liberals would have adopted the tone that he did. He did not believe that Home Rule would ever be granted by a British Parliament, but oppression and confiscation had affected the very basis of society in Ireland, and Gladstone, broadly speaking, was the only man who had done anything for Ireland. How could he be the object of the bitterest malignity of Ireland? The Government had given the Land League every chance of showing itself to be a peaceful tenants' association, and only quelled it after it had run up the black flag. Britain must continue to have patience. "We are dealing with an exceptional race, and an exceptional state of things; but even in dealing with these we need not tremble nor falter, if we are guided by the light of justice and truth." He concluded by the belief that, though we were paying for the sins of our forefathers, unborn generations would rise up in Ireland to bless, as in reason they must, the name of their latest and greatest benefactor, the Prime Minister.

He lived to see the Government of Ireland reconstituted in a fashion which neither he nor the Prime Minister expected or desired.

At Hull he also devoted to Ireland the bulk of a long speech (December 7th). Sir Stafford Northcote and Lord George Hamilton had lately spoken, and Rosebery reiterated the argument that however partial the victory over disorder might be, and however slow the operation of Gladstone's remedies, at any rate Conservative orators had nothing to boast of, either in the past or the present. The condition of Ireland was the fruit of English misrule.

"Have we advanced an inch, have we advanced a foot, have we advanced a yard, in the last century, towards making Ireland more reconciled and more prosperous under our rule? . . . We can but sow the seed hoping that if we ourselves are not spared, others may reap the harvest. I do maintain that it is not for the Conservatives, who have never lifted their hands to help Ireland, to hinder the Government in the task in which we are engaged."

Only two other political occurrences of the year 1881 need be recorded, each in its way a tribute to his rising reputation as a party man. In January he was blackballed for the Travellers' Club, a non-political institution of the highest standing, and was almost tearfully assured by his sponsor, the accomplished Edward Cheyney, that the axe fell solely for political reasons. In August, when the Queen visited Edinburgh for a Volunteer review, he was sworn of the Privy Council at Holyrood. This gave him full standing in the conduct of Scottish business.

Home life passed tranquilly throughout the year, with no foreign travel to speak of. In the previous year much correspondence had taken place about the purchase of a piece of land at Knightsbridge, west of Albert Gate, on which a great house was to be built overlooking the park. The project fell through, and pending the choice of a home for themselves, the Roseberys took a lease of Lansdowne House at the end of the year. Its owner was absent from Europe as Governor-General of Canada from 1883 to 1888, and as Viceroy of India from 1888 to 1894. It was a heavy blow, he wrote, to let his house at all, but he would sooner have the Roseberys as tenants than anybody else that he knew.

The year 1882 opened propitiously with the birth of the first son. He was christened Albert Edward Harry Meyer Archibald—"names enough in all conscience," as his father noted. The godfathers were the Prince of Wales and the Duke of Cleveland. During Lady Rosebery's convalescence and throughout the spring the weeks were passed in London and at the Durdans, broken only by a brief visit to Trinity, Cambridge, as Harcourt's guest, and by a couple of short flights of a day or two to Edinburgh, where Rosebery attended Sir Robert Christison's funeral, and for the first time slept at the restored Castle of Barnbougle. "It was a strange feeling re-inhabiting the disused home of one's predecessors. It was beautiful sleeping in the room over the walnut room with the outlook entirely sea." He got through some Scottish business, and opened the Fisheries Exhibition at Edinburgh with a "wretched little speech" (April 12th, 1882).

He kept himself in condition when in London by early walks in Hyde Park, a practice which he maintained for many years. It was his delight to secure a picked companion for these trudges, and to

[118]

take him back to breakfast at Berkeley Square. At the Durdans he enjoyed continual rides, and in the previous winter he had started playing football with the servants. On the first day, in a frost, he "had had enough of it in half an hour," but he persevered for many more games during the cold weather.

During the session of 1882 Rosebery's parliamentary attendances were purely departmental. The important Scottish matters that emerged included the Entail (Scotland) Bill, a complicated subject with which Rosebery dealt skilfully and tactfully, in face of powerful opposition from old-fashioned Scottish landowners. Queen Victoria, sharing their standpoint, directed Sir Henry Ponsonby to write (June 19th): "The Queen laments the change of Scottish Entails." Rosebery replied that the measure was "not revolutionary"; but she wrote again (June 24th), fearing that many old properties would be alienated: "Would many people wish to convert their estates into money?" Of the Educational Endowments (Scotland) Bill, a valuable measure complementary to the English Endowed Schools Acts, something will be said later.

In English affairs it fell to Rosebery to answer a question asked by an eccentric politician, Lord Stanley of Alderley, about the recent Macclesfield election (February 10th). There had been extensive bribery, two solicitors had gone to prison for corrupt practices, and the election was declared void. In pleading for mitigation of the sentences, Lord Stanley took the most offensive tone he could, asking how much Rosebery had spent on the Midlothian election, and other Liberals on other candidatures? Rosebery's brief reply was a pattern of scornful good-humour; but his own comment was, "My first official answer,—very bad."

Soon afterwards Lord Stanhope introduced a measure regulating the hours of women and young persons in a limited class of shops. The machinery of the Bill was criticised by many who were not merciless upholders of universal freedom of contract. Even Lord Shaftesbury pointed out the risk of diminishing women's employment (February 28th), so that Rosebery, abounding in sympathy with the purpose of his noble relative, had an easy task in refusing Home Office countenance to the Bill. Lord Stanhope was more successful in winning its sympathy for a measure prohibiting the payment of wages in public-houses—a necessary reform too long delayed (May 2nd). Other topics discussed were precautions against fire in theatres, and the gates and bars obstructing, in private interests, some of the busiest thoroughfares in London. It was not until several years later that these were removed by Act of Parliament. At the very close of the session Rosebery came into collision with the masterful Chairman of Committees, Lord Redesdale, over the Scottish Fisheries Bill, and got the best of the encounter.

The social revolution in Ireland, as Mr. Gladstone called it, from the very first menaced the unity of the Government. In 1880 the House of Lords rejected the Compensation for Disturbance Bill by a vast majority, and the Government lost in Lord Lansdowne one of its most valuable juniors. The Land Act of 1881 changed the Duke of Argyll from a comrade prompt for occasions of ardent oratory into an undiscriminating critic of Government policy, while it shook the faith of many other supporters. From the opposite standpoint, the Government measure of coercion, the Protection of Life and Property (Ireland) Bill, introduced by W. E. Forster in the same session, from its suspension of the Habeas Corpus Act only secured the consent of Gladstone himself after deep searchings of heart.[7] 1882 was not old before it was clear that neither the Coercion Act nor the Land Act had pacified the country. Parnell had appeared to be irreconcilable, and to be trying to wreck the Land Act. After Gladstone's stern warning that the resources of civilisation against its enemies were not exhausted,[8] the Irish leader had been lodged in Kilmainham Gaol.[8] But the state of the country grew worse, and in April, there being some evidence that Parnell would not be inaccessible to reason, the policy was modified, chiefly through the agency of Joseph Chamberlain. Lord Cowper had resigned the Viceroyalty, and at the beginning of May the Cabinet decided to release Parnell and the two other imprisoned Members of Parliament, bringing in a new Protection of Life and Property Bill to replace that passed the year before. Forster resigned, and his place was taken by Lord Frederick Cavendish, Lord Spencer having agreed to return to the Viceregal Lodge.

Rosebery played no direct or responsible part in these events, but he was in the innermost circle, as is shown by his notes made at the time:

May 3rd.—"Talked with Frederick Cavendish about his appointment to the Chief Secretaryship, which was not yet announced. He low at leaving his place by Mr. Gladstone's side. Harcourt had been the only man he could not get on with. H. had said to him the night before: 'You give Rosebery any money he asks because he is such a friend of

[7] *Life of Gladstone*, bk. viii, ch. iv, p. 2.
[8] Leeds, October 8th, 1881.

Mr. Gladstone's, and you won't give me anything.' His father and Hartington had been against his taking it; H. because he thought F. did not speak well enough. He told me he was not to be in the Cabinet, but was doubtful how that would work. I said he would probably be put in within a few months, and that he would have been in long ago if Hartington were not there already."

May 4th.—"Situation of affairs gloomy and desperate. I was given to understand that three suspects had given pledges but these deny them."

Rosebery and his wife went quietly down to the Durdans, greatly disquieted.

May 6th.—"Much perplexed as to my position, as to which I wrote a paper.[9] I am clear that I disagree with the policy of Govt. but am almost clear that I ought not to resign. Finally wrote to Mr. Gladstone to ask him to give me five minutes on Monday morning; this with a view to asking him what is the exact position of a subordinate like myself with reference to Cabinet policy."

May 7th.—"Rode from 10.30 a.m. to 1.15. A melancholy and perplexed ride.

"On my return at 2.15 learned the news of the assassination of poor F. Cavendish and Burke. They might have taken a more brilliant life, they could not have taken a nobler life than F. Cavendish's.

"Of course this event cleared my course completely. All hands are wanted at the pumps."

He returned to London and wrote to 10 Downing Street: "I can only say 'God sustain you all. It is past all words.' "

At the moment it was difficult to gauge precisely the political outcome of the crime. A trusted Scottish correspondent[10] wrote that it was difficult before Sunday to find any Liberals who heartily approved the release of the suspects. There was now a general agreement that a firm vindication of the law ought to be followed by remedial legislation on Arrears, etc. Such violent manifestations as that of a Trades-Unionist who advocated martial law for Ireland could only be transient. But Rosebery's depression of spirits continued. Another frequent Edinburgh correspondent, Charles Cooper of the *Scotsman* (May 14th), combated his pessimistic outlook, and maintained that the tragedy of May 6th had in effect cleared the political air. But it was an anxious time. When Mr. Gladstone stayed at the Durdans late in May, Scotland Yard, through Lewis Har-

[9] This does not exist.
[10] James Patten, May 10th.

court, begged Rosebery not to let his guest walk in the grounds after dusk, though it was difficult to conceive danger in that quiet corner.

Scotland was still dissatisfied with the arrangement whereby her popular hero remained an Under-Secretary, in charge of her business, but meanly ranked in the official hierarchy. Cooper wrote from the *Scotsman* that he meant again to push "the Privy Seal view," of which several Scottish members had written their approval, a sentiment also held generally throughout Scotland. Other Scottish friends sent letters at the same time in a similar sense, begging that he would not refuse a seat in the Cabinet were it offered.

Throughout the year Rosebery had tried to keep the Prime Minister abreast of Scottish business, and to make him realise its relative importance. In the spring he wrote at length about Scottish judges and their salaries, and, a little later begged that the vacant Junior Lordship of the Treasury should be conferred on a Scottish member (May 18th, 1882).

"Though I do not pretend in any sense to represent Scotland or to assert that Scotland will be seriously outraged if you do not appoint a Scottish Lord of the Treasury, yet I would venture to remind you that 'many a little makes a mickle,' that Scotland is the backbone of the Liberal party, and that, if I am rightly informed, there is some discontent as to her treatment. If this discontent, instead of being floating and partial, should become consistent and general, one article in the indictment would certainly be the missing of this obvious and easy opportunity of supplying that omission of a Scottish Lord of the Treasury which was the subject of complaint on the formation of this government."

The reply was to the effect that there was only one vacancy, and that it was reasonably asked that it should be filled from below the gangway. This was the sole impediment. Rosebery replied at once (May 18th) :

"Dear Mr. Gladstone,
"I am obliged by your note, and beg to express my regret for having interfered in the matter."

On this the Prime Minister minuted: "Assure him that his interference was quite right, and such as I desire and am thankful for."

The Scottish Entail Bill was in danger of delay. It was unpopular with some landlords. Rosebery, however, warned the Private Secretary at 10 Downing Street of the Scottish discontent at the slow progress of the measure, with good effect. But a more serious situation arose over the Scottish Endowment Bill. It is nakedly set out in the following letter:

HOME DEPARTMENT, *June 27th,* 1882.

"MY DEAR MR. GLADSTONE,

"I am sorry to trouble you in the midst of your labours with a letter. I would not do so did I not think the matter one of the greatest importance both to Scotland and the administration of Scottish affairs by the present Government. Moreover your statement on Tuesday and Mr. Duncan McLaren's letter appear to make it opportune.

"I do not think from what you said on Tuesday that you are aware of the almost vital necessity of passing the Scottish Endowments Bill this session. I say 'almost vital,' which is a strong expression, with reference to Scotland and the position of the Government there. The Endowment Bill has been introduced three times by this Government. It has received the general support of the Scottish members, and, if I might employ a much abused term, of the intelligent people of Scotland. As a measure, no impartial person will, I think, deny its merits. But were it the worst measure ever brought in, its position as regards the Government would be very much the same. Three times in three successive sessions has the Government introduced the Bill to Parliament. By a combination of what I fear our enemies would term indifference on the part of the Government, and very unscrupulous lobbying on the part of a small and corrupt clique which opposes it, it has twice been allowed to lapse. It is now for the third time in danger. The clique I allude to already boasts that it has again beaten the Government and that the Bill will again be allowed to drop. That means that the recess will again be passed in intrigue and wirepulling in Edinburgh, in renewed vapourings over the defeat of the Government, in unscrupulous charges against all connected with the Government or the Bill, in reiterated complaints as to the neglect of Scottish business and the impotence of Scottish administration. What are indeed the facts as they appear to the most impartial eye? The Prime Minister was returned by a Scottish constituency, backed by an overwhelming majority of Scottish members. From the day of the first meeting of the new Parliament until the present day of its third session, if I am correctly informed, not one minute of Government time has been allotted to Scotland or Scottish affairs. Can you be surprised that the people of Scotland complain? Of course the first persons to bear the brunt of this are the Lord Advocate and myself. We are not conscious of deserving blame; in and out of the session we have done all we could. But I do not see what more we can do, and our reward, more especially mine, will be to return to Scotland to be taunted with our incapacity to get any attention paid to Scotland. More especially mine, because my appointment was supposed to indicate that greater attention would be paid to Scottish business, whereas it indicates nothing of the sort.

"Were it not for this, you might well ask what business it is of mine: the Bill is not in the Home Office, and it is for Mundella to speak. But unfortunately the view is taken in Scotland that I have a considerable share in the responsibility; and certainly wherever the Scottish half-pence may go, I shall get the Scottish kicks.

"That is an eventuality which I am not prepared to face, when I am of opinion that the aggressive boot contains a toe of justice. I literally do not know how Scotland is to be faced during the recess if this Bill be not passed: and as we all hope that you are coming to Scotland we trust that it may not be under any imputation of neglect of Scottish affairs. And apart from all, I repeat as regards the special evil which this Bill removes that it corrupts the very foundation and source of public life in Edinburgh.

"Believe me, dear Mr. Gladstone,

Yrs. always,

(Signed) A. ROSEBERY.

"P.S.—I think it right to add that so far as we know there are not eight out of all the Scots members who even profess to oppose any part of the Bill."

Mr. Gladstone replied with the suggestion that the Bill should go upstairs to a Grand Committee, then a novel method of accelerating the march of important measures of special interest to a section of the House. Rosebery pointed out the objections to this course:

HOME DEPARTMENT, *June 28th*, 1882.

"MY DEAR MR. GLADSTONE,

"With reference to your note of to-day I have to express a hope that you may soon see your way to giving a day for the second reading of the Scottish Endowments Bill even though you cannot do so at present.

"As regards the project of a Grand Committee I have to observe:

"Firstly, if the Grand Committee be a formal and parliamentary one, the reference will not be allowed without a debate on procedure which would take longer than to pass the Endowments Bill in the regular way.

"Secondly, if it were not a formal one, it would not really advance the Bill and would in any case have to be preceded by a discussion on the second reading: while the treating of a Scottish Bill in an exceptional manner would certainly be unpopular in Scotland.

"Thirdly, this Bill is the least fitted of our Scottish Bills for such a method, as there is little difference in detail to be thrashed out, but a fixed determination by the Heriot ring to obstruct, so that the Grand Committee would only be an additional stage for the Bill.

"Fourthly, such a reference would be used by the opponents of the Bill to prove that the Bill was treated in a 'hole and corner manner'— a favourite phrase of theirs. On the other hand a public discussion would betray the utter weakness of the opposition in fair and open field.

"In fine I venture to think that this Bill would not be a good *corpus vile* for the experiment of a Grand Committee whether it be regular or informal.

"Believe me,
Yr. affy.,
AR"

The climax came in December, after a conversation in which the Prime Minister, always personally affectionate and appreciative, but immersed in Irish and foreign troubles, did not recognise the urgency of meeting the claims of Scotland, or those of Rosebery himself. It may be easy to comprehend the reasons which caused delay, but not the absence of explanation by one who could explain anything. Rosebery felt it necessary to make himself clear on paper. He wrote on December 6th and, more categorically, on December 10th and 16th:

Confidential.   HOME DEPARTMENT, *December 6th*, 1882.

"MY DEAR MR. GLADSTONE,

"While I am sincerely obliged to you for your frank intimation of yesterday, it places me in a position of extreme gravity, personally and officially.

"I need hardly say that I should never have connected myself with what I must regard as a very imperfect system of managing Scottish affairs, or indeed have surrendered my liberty at all, had it not been for the paragraph in your letter offering me the appointment:

"'I do not think that the arrangement would last very long in its present form. There *must* be within the next six months further manipulation of political affairs: and with this there is the likelihood of development uncertain as to time, but certain, and so more than a likelihood except as to that element.'

"Your explanation of yesterday so completely removes the meaning I had attached to this sentence that I am compelled to view the situation altogether in a new light.

"Family reasons oblige me to hurry to Scotland to-night. If I am able to leave my wife I will ask you to grant me an interview on your return: if not, I must write what I have to say. But I hope I may consider myself at liberty to consult (in strict confidence and without mentioning any names but yours and mine) one or two of my principal supporters in Scotland, and to ask that permission is the main object of this note.

"Believe me,
Yr. affy.,
AR"

Confidential. DALMENY PARK, EDINBURGH, *December 10th,* 1882.

"MY DEAR MR. GLADSTONE,

"Many thanks for your kind letter.

"I have no difficulty in explaining what I meant. I understood your communication on Tuesday to consist of two parts: one was that only Lord Derby and Sir C. Dilke would at present be admitted to the Cabinet; and secondly, that, though an arrangement might be made about Easter to fill up the Presidency of the Council, which has now been in commission for many months, that claims of seniority, with regard to which you mentioned a name, would have to be considered.

"Under these circumstances, I felt that my appointment, which I had understood from your letter of July 31, 1882, would only be a temporary one, would assume a very different aspect. I have never considered that the responsibility for Scottish administration should rest with the Under-Secretary for the Home Department. On two occasions last summer I ventured to point out to you that the arrangement could not last, and I understood that you assented. The experiment was always believed by me to be purely tentative, but in my humble opinion it was open to the reproach of being both undefined and undignified. But I believed that it was intended to mark a new departure, to be a step in the right direction, and to contain the germ of a new office which would satisfy the country. I gathered, however, on Tuesday that it was your intention to enter upon the next session of Parliament with this system of administration unaltered.

"That intention, I confess, I found it difficult to reconcile with the passage of your letter which I quoted, and raised a question to me of much gravity with reference to public affairs in Scotland.

"The personal question is a minor one. If a somewhat Chinese principle of seniority is to prevail in promotion, it will be many years before I cease, except by my own act or a party defect, to be an Under-Secretary. I am almost, if not quite, the junior member of the Government. In merit I have no doubt that my inferiority would be equally undoubted. If I could ever hope to rise higher, it could only be by the favour and support of my fellow countrymen. But if seniority is to be reckoned against me, that, and the probable succession of one, as well as the probable elevation of other ministers to the House of Lords, would keep me for ever in a subordinate position.

"I do not value office at all. It is a sacrifice of much that renders life pleasant to me, leisure, and independence, and the life of the country. But, unattractive as it is, your remarks appeared to me to open a gloomier vista still: and if the result of all this should be my retirement into private life, I should have nothing personal to regret, while I should feel that I could be of more use both to Scotland and yourself as an independent member than in my present position.

"I am sincerely sorry to trouble you with all these trivial and tiresome details. But if you knew how I hate writing them you would pity rather than blame.

"Believe me,

Yr. affy.,

AR"

Confidential.   Dalmeny Park, Edinburgh, *December 16th,* 1882.

"My dear Mr. Gladstone,

"My domestic anxieties have prevented my answering your letter before this, and I fear they will equally prevent my going to you at present. I should be glad to rest on the constant kindness of your expressions, were it not that this very kindness makes it necessary for me to clear up the position so far as I am concerned. You are so strong that you can afford to disregard any claim or interest you please. I, on the other hand, am obliged to keep in view the one interest of the nation which I serve and which made me what little I am. I cannot, therefore, honestly remain, if I wished it, a party to an arrangement which I think derogatory to the national position and injurious to the national interests. That you have been too busy to attend to Scottish business arrangements I can readily believe. But that is exactly where the mischief lies. No minister of importance has the time to look after Scottish matters, and so they have to be dealt with by subordinates who are not of importance, an arrangement which I know to be—as I have already said —derogatory and injurious. Large changes are now being made which it is found possible to consider, but as usual the question regarding Scotland is the one which must be shelved or adjourned.

"I never thought to find myself engaged in an argument with you on what may appear to be a question of my personal advancement. I can only hope that you know me well enough to understand and believe that this is not the case. I serve a country which is the backbone of our party, but which is never recognised.

"I, and those whom I have consulted, feel that it is necessary now to make a stand on its behalf, and that is why I am obliged to take up the present position. But let me add that if you can see your way to developing an arrangement for Scottish business and putting some one

[127]

else at the head of it (and there are several persons eminently fitted for it) I will gladly serve in any subordinate post you may choose.

"As to 'patience and faith,' I have perhaps exercised more of both than you imagine: while the best proof I can give of the little regard that I have to my own interests and happiness in taking my present course is the risk I run of forfeiting your affection and esteem: the more so as I know that in any case all this can but end disagreeably and painfully so far as I am concerned: and indeed political life can never be the same again to me.

"Y. affy.,
AR"

Scotland and he himself had been lightly treated, he felt, and he did not scruple to say so, even to his revered chief. The Prime Minister's notes in reply continued affectionate but vague. Mrs. Gladstone also wrote, and elicited this answer:

DALMENY PARK, *December* 15*th*, 1882.

"MY DEAR MRS. GLADSTONE,

"I was greatly touched by your kind and affectionate letter, which was just like yourself, and I cannot praise it more.

"However, I know you will forgive me if I cannot write more about this business, which is absolutely nauseous to me from every point of view. As regards politics and office, I do not think I shall ever get the taste of it out of my mouth.

"Yours ever,
AR"

Meanwhile, throughout the autumn, Scottish business had been absorbing, and Rosebery, except for a brief sojourn abroad, had been immersed in it at Dalmeny. The case of the Skye crofters produced an article in the *Scotsman* sharply criticising the Government, on which Harcourt wrote furiously to Rosebery that the newspaper was malicious and malignant, and trying to do all the harm it could to the Government, as, for instance, by suppressing a generous speech made by Lochiel as spokesman of the landowners. Rosebery drove into Edinburgh to remonstrate with his friend Cooper, the editor. He was very busy, and Lord Dalhousie wrote (November 24th): "How you find time for all the work you get through is marvellous to me."

There had been an idea that Gladstone would visit his constituents in the autumn, but the engagement to Dalmeny was deferred until some date in January. Early in the New Year it was abandoned for a time under doctor's orders. Meanwhile, Edward Hamilton had consulted Rosebery on the merits of postponement until Easter at any rate, as there could be no immediate Cabinet reconstruction, and no provision for a revised Scottish administration was therefore possible. It would be awkward for Mr. Gladstone to appear in Edinburgh with nothing done, or even announced.

Egyptian affairs, with which Rosebery had no direct concern, had been the second main preoccupation of the Government. The collapse of the dual control by England and France at Cairo, the military rebellion under Arabi, the massacre of Europeans in Alexandria, and the consequent bombardment of the forts by the British fleet (July 11th), followed in rapid succession. The last development cost Gladstone the co-operation of John Bright. For some days his resignation seemed doubtful, and between the 12th and the 15th of the month Rosebery received notes from 10 Downing Street that "things are looking very bad" or that "there is a gleam of hope." On July 13th he notes:

"Marlborough House breakfast.[11] Had a talk with Bright. He said Dizzy had never done anything worse than, or so bad as, this bombardment. I excused it. He said, 'Say no more about it, it's damnable!'"

Two days later, when the resignation was announced, he met Bright again at Lady Aberdeen's.

"Had a talk with Bright. He said all the Government had lost our heads: Gladstone had not, but he had a flexible conscience: meaning that he was not unscrupulous but that his conscience followed the bent of his mind. I regretted his resignation (1) because the peace party would have less confidence in the Government, (2) because it might precipitate Mr. Gladstone's own retirement. He thought the latter very likely."

On the 17th, at the Opera, the Prince of Wales sent for Rosebery to talk about Egypt.

"He wishes his views transmitted to Mr. Gladstone. His views are comprised in the wish to see the Khedive declared an independent sovereign. He told me that the Khedive was the only one of Ismail's sons who was brought up entirely in Egypt, and he is the only one who is worth anything."

Very early in June the health of old Lady Rosebery began to cause anxiety. She was now bedridden. Her grandson paid many visits when she was able to see anybody.

[11] This old term for an afternoon garden-party was still in use.

"When I went she thanked me in the dear old formula again for coming, 'So good of you to come, dear Archie.'"

The end came on August 19th:

"She who had loved me longest and whom I loved tenderly would no more be the centre and point of contact of so many different persons whose only link was their affection for her."

The letters that he received, including many from Hannah Rosebery's relations, showed the impression made on a younger generation by the gentle, dignified old lady. She had not been laid in the grave before her grandson had to face another shock. He was riding to Leatherhead Downs when the groom with him, a great favourite, was bolted with, his horse charging an iron gate and giving him a ghastly fall. He was dead before he could be got to the nearest house.

"I had left home at 10. It was 11.20 when I returned, and what an abyss of horror between the two dates."

He had to start for Edinburgh the same night for his grandmother's burial. After the ceremony he caught the train to London, and the next day attended the inquest on Dick, the groom, and his funeral, returning to Edinburgh the same night. A fortnight later he and his wife started for Naples, pausing at Lucerne, where he thought Thorwaldsen's Lion memorial to the Swiss Guard "surely one of the noblest monuments in the world," and at Milan. They reached Naples on September 17th, and Rosebery, as cicerone of his best-loved spot in the land of olive, aloe, and maize and vine, must have felt, as the poet of "The Daisy" did, all the pleasure of happy understanding with a beloved companion. There was a great deal of rain, and at least one sirocco, but these did not prevent a great deal of joint sightseeing. At the Palace at Capodimonte:

"I had forgotten the portrait of the Duc de Reichstadt as an Austrian Grenadier,[12] which I suppose was painted for the Bourbons to gloat over. They should have had a pendant painted of Louis XVII as a cobbler."

Here, surely, spoke the ardent Bonapartist.

The miracle of St. Januarius "was duly performed in an hour and forty minutes." But the call of Naples was irresistible. On the morning of departure:

[12] A copy of this picture was made for him.

"We drove to the dear Villa Delahante which looked sublime. I long for it and dread it. Without resolution it would be a Capua. With a heavy heart left Naples by the 3.47" (September 27th).

The greater part of the autumn was spent at Dalmeny. Regular attendance at the office in Edinburgh, some desultory shooting, the entertainment of many Scottish neighbours and of a few friends from the South, including a long visit from Sam Ward, brought the year to its close. Little or no progress had been made with plans for the rearrangement of Scottish business and with the recognition of its importance. Rosebery continued to make it clear that he could not long remain in his anomalous position of Under-Secretary in Downing Street. Scotland would no longer be content with such a wraith of a Scottish Secretary. During a flying visit to London (December 4th), amid the strains of *Iolanthe* at the Savoy Theatre, Gladstone told him that the larger Government changes had been postponed, and that only Derby and Dilke would be admitted to the Cabinet. The next day the Prime Minister supplemented this information by saying that there might be rearrangement of the Presidency of the Council about Easter. There was also some vague talk about Gladstone's "probable retirement" (which was in the meantime deferred till Easter).

At Christmas the atmosphere was unexpectedly cleared by letters from the Prime Minister himself, and from Harcourt and Dilke, holding out more hopeful prospects.

The year 1882 had been an eventful one for Rosebery. It had witnessed the birth of his two boys, in January and December, and with them the advent of hopes which after years were to fulfil abundantly. But it brought private sorrows as well, and the prospects of public life were without comfort. These must have been in his mind when he finished his diary with the words: "Goodbye, thou damnable year."

Rosebery hoped that the mists surrounding Scottish business might evaporate with the new year, and in this spirit he journeyed to Hawarden on January 4th. He was welcomed there as always; but the mists did not roll away of themselves, and his reserve kept him silent.

January 5th, 1883.—"Lady F. Cavendish here, beautifully calm and simple. After breakfast Mr. Gladstone put on a little Inverness cape and a straw hat, and invited me to walk round and round the square garden. Talked much of his health, excellent except in one point, that the night's sleep, eight hours or so, which is what keeps his brain and nervous energy going, he cannot depend on. Much discourse on this. He generally has neuralgia at the end of a session, and pays for his work in that way. He spoke of his troubles. 'The Queen alone,' he said fiercely, 'is enough to kill any man.' I could not help laughing at his manner, but he said, 'This is no laughing matter, though it may sound so,' and proceeded with all their mutual troubles—Derby, Dilke, the Archbishop, the Duchess of Roxburghe and the Robes. In the midst of this he saw that the dog had been making a hole in the flower-bed, and became fierce at once, pursuing him, and throwing the stick he had been shaking at him, in doing which he dropped his hat. He then picked up his hat and stick and resumed discourse. He soon got tired however. We had another walk in the afternoon together,—talk of indifferent subjects. He is reading *The Antiquary* to rest his mind."

January 6th.—"Mr. Gladstone had not realised that I was going early so he took me off at once after breakfast. He had only slept two hours, and Mrs. Gladstone was expecting Andrew Clark.

"At 10.50 took my departure, not a syllable having been said about the subject of our previous correspondence and the object of my visit! Arrived about 3.15 in London. To Harcourt, with whom a long talk."

Hannah Rosebery, however, gleaned a store of knowledge during January. On the 12th of that month Mrs. Gladstone passed through Edinburgh, and the two wives engaged in a fencing-match, of which the younger left a record in eight closely written pages of her journal. Mrs. Gladstone first touched on the political gossip of the moment—the Prime Minister's difficulties with the Queen, how he often had to write two letters a day to appease her, and how even Lord Beaconsfield had said she was very difficult to manage; the troubles caused by Sir Charles Dilke's republican opinions; by the vacant post of Mistress of the Robes; and by the Archbishopric of Canterbury. Lady Rosebery defended Sir William Harcourt against the criticisms of Mrs. Gladstone, who "seems strongly to dislike him." It was only at the last moment that they got on to the subject near to Lady Rosebery's heart. A cynic might smile at her tale, but there is something touching in the cross-purposes that it describes. The elder woman, entirely absorbed in her famous husband, investing him with a more than papal infallibility, regarding all other Liberal public men as his satellites, and Rosebery in particular as a brilliant and charming youth who must bide the time fixed by superior wisdom—the younger adoring wife, conscious of her husband's supreme ability, of his intense sensitiveness, and of his keen desire for a career of public usefulness—how were these two to understand each other? Mrs. Gladstone kept on repeating, "It is all right now," adding, "He must not be in a hurry to mount the ladder, he is very young." "It is Scottish business, not himself, that he is anxious about," replied the other. "Oh, that will be all right and will be seen to," said Mrs. Gladstone, "in a careless manner." But her young friend persistently harped upon Scottish business and on the anxiety felt in Scotland concerning it. If that were only properly dealt with, Rosebery would be only too pleased to resign.

"'No,' said Mrs. Gladstone, 'four months ago he told Lord Granville that politics was the only thing in the world he cared for.' I said, 'Yes, then politics seemed different.' She said, 'Oh no, he could not give them up, it would be such a pity, a wasted life,' I said, 'I am right though.' She said, 'To do nothing but the Turf?' I kept my temper and replied, 'There is nothing of the Turf.' She said, 'It will be all right.' I said, 'He knows best.' She said, 'He is so young.' I said, 'Not of head or heart, he knows what is right.' She went downstairs, and I had no need, thank God, to kiss and shake hands. . . . The remark of Lord Granville's is not correct, Archie says."

The circumstances of the moment made inevitable the clash of these two warm hearts and loyal natures. It happened that a week or so later Hannah Rosebery came in for a more satisfactory interchange. On her journey from Scotland to Mentmore she descried Hartington at Preston and invited him to her carriage. Three hours of talk followed. He had heard of Rosebery's wish to resign, "but then we all wish to." She replied that this was really serious. Hartington had told Harcourt, he said, that Rosebery ought to have the Privy Seal with Scottish affairs, but Gladstone wanted that office for Agriculture and Commerce. "Gladstone," he went on, "is very strange and old-fashioned in some ways, and in other ways radical: he takes Sir Robert Peel as his model, and talks of seniority and previous claims."

When the Government was formed Rosebery had been spoken of for the Cabinet, and Hartington could not understand how the present situation had arisen. Lady Rosebery proceeded to tell him of her husband's abortive visit to Hawarden and her own "irritating conversation" with Mrs. Gladstone. The sound sense that kept her from being entirely blinded by wifely devotion must have made her glad to lay her woes before a listener of absolute fairness, a staunch friend, and one who hated exaggeration and could not comprehend sentiment.

At headquarters nothing occurred to change Rosebery's determination. When Parliament was meeting and Harcourt telegraphed to ask what Scots measures were ready, Rosebery in reply, after giving the required information, stated that, after a recent correspondence with Mr. Gladstone, he did not conceive that he had any special connection with Scottish business. But Lord Granville, the next day, spent three-quarters of an hour of comment on this note. Meanwhile, the Prime Minister, whose nights had got worse instead of better, had started off for the South of France, all letters being kept from him, so that no new development could be anticipated from that quarter. Scottish correspondents kept on inquiring when a Minister for Scotland would be nominated. The ordinary business of the Home Office was steadily carried on, including inspections of prisons. In the House of Lords the Bill forbidding the Payment of Wages in Public-houses received its second reading by a large majority (March 6th), but the House agreed with the Home Office in refusing to sanction the Performance of Stage Plays for Charitable Objects, without a licence (April 19th). Rosebery was also responsible for the early stages of the Criminal Law Amendment Act for the better protection of young girls "and almost old women," as he noted. This measure became law after he had resigned his office.

Friendly and hospitable converse with the Gladstones continued, and they were fellow-guests at Sandringham in March. At the end of this month he fulfilled an engagement to speak at Birmingham as the guest of Joseph Chamberlain. Lord Salisbury had spoken just before, and Rosebery's host had written, "I hope you will make mincemeat of him." But a terrible contretemps occurred, of the sort that most public speakers have experienced once, but not more than once.

"To Birmingham by 1.30 train. Meant to put speech together in train, and found *en voyage* that I had left all my notes and materials behind. I never was in such a cold sweat. Arrived at Chamberlain's at 5. Large dinner to be at 5.30. Dismay of C. In despair I knocked some notes together, and recalled some of my meditations. Sat between Miss Chamberlain and Wiggin, M.P. at dinner. Afterwards with butler to station to meet notes, which arrived ten minutes before meeting,— too late.

"Great meeting. Spoke very indifferently, but not an utter breakdown."

The speech as reported does not warrant such a note of depreciation. A little earlier Rosebery, at Glasgow, had paid an eloquent tribute to Mr. Bright, on whom the Freedom of the City was conferred. He had recalled the sympathy and affection of his fellow-countrymen for the great member for Birmingham, resting not so much on his unattainable eloquence as on the brilliant transparency of his character. He had recalled the battle for cheap bread for the people, and Bright's immortal protest against the Crimean War. He had touched with tactful reticence on Bright's resignation from the Government on the Egyptian Question. "It was a disappointment to many who had hoped like myself that Mr. Bright and Mr. Gladstone hand in hand would finish their course of fire and of usefulness together." It was a fine little speech, greatly applauded, but here in Birmingham it was an easier task still to defend Mr. Bright from the sarcasms which Lord Salisbury had scattered on his head as upon those of all other leading Liberals. A considerable part of the speech was devoted to Ireland, for which the Prime Minister had striven "with more than human earnestness in a case where success was doubtful and triumph impossible." It was true that Ireland might be more agitated under a Liberal than under a Conservative administration, but for the reason that from the Liberals they also had learned to expect something, and from the Tories they knew they had nothing to expect except a Coercion Bill. Rosebery proceeded with a cutting attack on the Conservative party on their lack of any coherent policy at home, their dangerous activity abroad, and their unwearied policy of vituperation. To judge from the laughter and applause with which the report of the speech was punctuated, the speech was one of Rosebery's complete platform successes, and well deserved the expression of thanks from Chamberlain for the "able, pointed, and interesting speech to which we have just listened."

In May a change seemed to be impending.

May 5th.—"A note from Harcourt to say Cabinet had decided to bring in Bill to provide Minister for Scotland. He said to me after the Academy Dinner: 'Well, you ought to be greatly flattered : the Cabinet agreed to-day to do a thing they do not care about doing, simply to please you. I agreed that reference to a Committee was impossible, indeed only Gladstone and Granville were at all for that.'"

At the Banquet he sat by Lord Shaftesbury, who told him that all the great speakers had prepared immensely, Canning especially.

" 'How about Pitt?' I asked. He said Pitt reserved himself entirely for the House of Commons struggle, and did no business."

[135]

The political atmosphere remained cloudy.

"Dilke told me that matters are coming to a crisis in the Cabinet between the party that wants to do something and G.'s inactivity. Things will probably come to a head in the first two Cabinets after Whitsuntide."

Rosebery discussed his position with Hartington, and on the same day (May 29th) talked with Dilke and with Harcourt at the Queen's Ball. Two days later a debate in the House of Commons put a match to the bonfire. In a debate on the Civil Services Estimates strong exception was taken to the arrangement whereby the Under-Secretary to the Local Government Board took charge of Home Office business in the absence of the Home Secretary. It was contrary to Liberal tradition that the Under-Secretary for the Home Department should be a Peer. Harcourt, in defence, said the work of the Home Office had increased five times in twenty years : it was "inadequately represented, not only in the House of Lords, but also in the House of Commons." The present arrangement was not meant to be permanent : it was made to meet the exigencies of the Scottish members. Sir Richard Cross asserted the absolute necessity of an Under-Secretary to the Home Office in the House of Commons. Rosebery had to go to Edinburgh for a couple of nights, but on his return told Hartington of his letter of resignation to Mr. Gladstone.

June 4th.—"To H.O. as usual. Had a note from Hartington to say that he had been summoned by Mr. Gladstone to confer on my resignation. At 4 had another note from him to say Mr. G. wished him to see me before I finally settled. I saw H. at the House. He said he supposed it was of no use asking me to stay. Mr. G. wished for two stipulations : (1) that the separation should be amicable and so represented by me, especially in Scotland. I replied that that quite fell in with my ideas. (2) That I should declare that this was no obstacle to my returning to the Government next week if possible. I agreed, but said that of course I should judge of any particular proposal on its own merits. He said that Mr. G.'s view was that the future Minister for Scotland might or might not be in the Cabinet, as it suited."

June 5th.—"Mr. G. wished to see me, so I saw him for two minutes (Mrs. G. in the room). Nothing of importance passed, but his manner was very cordial and he said : 'God bless you' with great warmth when we parted."

Rosebery retreated to Ascot for the week, but the Home Office had not done with him. On the Tuesday afternoon a messenger arrived from Harcourt, followed by three others on Wednesday. The Home Secretary had been pardonably excited by an article in the *Standard* imputing Rosebery's resignation to his language and temper. The result was an arranged question in the House of Commons, to which Harcourt replied that there was not a word of foundation for the statement that Rosebery had taken amiss something he had said or done.

"As to the relations between Lord Rosebery and myself, they have been for many years, and, I am happy to say, are still those of closest political friendship and personal affection which has never been disturbed for a single moment. . . . Lord Rosebery wrote to me this morning: 'I know what you must be feeling under so undeserved an innuendo, but I am quite as indignant as you are.'"

On the same day Gladstone promised the Bill for the conduct of Scottish business for an early date.

Rosebery was now a free man, and meant to remain so as long as he could. The London season was a gay one, and there was much entertaining at Lansdowne House. Sam Ward and W. H. Hurlbert were both frequent guests. Friendship with the Gladstones was unimpaired, and the Prime Minister passed a Sunday at the Durdans, where there was "much talk of Chamberlain's late indiscretion." At the end of July Rosebery received the offer of the Scottish Office if the Bill should pass. He declined:

[*Copy.*]
Private.   HOUSE OF LORDS, *July 30th,* 1883.

"MY DEAR MR. GLADSTONE,

"I have just returned from Chevening and found your very kind letter, for which many thanks. But it is just because this is an 'unencumbered interval' in my life that I wish to go to Australia. I am still young, my children are still younger, and each year will diminish my opportunities.

"I will not profess to have put aside the possibility of the Scottish Ministership being offered me. But I have weighed the matter carefully, and have come to a distinct conclusion. Before I mention that conclusion, however, let me thank you cordially for your offer, and the terms in which it is conveyed.

"In the first place I have been so much the advocate for the office being formed, that, if I should accept it I am open to the accusation, which has been freely urged in the candid press, of having pressed for it in order that I might fill it myself. I do not indeed attach much weight to the character of such imputations. But if I had felt myself free to take it, I should not have spoken at Edinburgh as I did. I there put on record my view of the necessity for a minister in terms which I could not have used had I not thought myself precluded from taking it: and it has for some little time been my intention if I made that speech to also make my tour. I am not conscious of any unworthy motive in advocating a Scottish office.

"But suppose I urged in Parliament that there should be another railway commissioner or another land commissioner, and, having convinced Parliament and the Government, became myself that commissioner, I should give people the right to say things which they have no right or power to say now.

"There are other minor considerations which I need not intrude upon you now. They are swallowed up in two greater ones. One of these is that in my opinion the first Scottish Minister, in justice to Scotland, the Lord Advocate and himself, should be a Cabinet minister. At any rate I have always been clear that I could not be an efficient minister for Scotland without a direct voice in the Cabinet. The other is personal, and it is this; that I have made up my mind never to re-enter the Government except as a member of the Cabinet. I can quite understand that you will think this very presumptuous on my part. But the fact is that for office, quâ office, I do not greatly care. I am convinced that for me there is no middle term of usefulness between that of absolute independence and Cabinet office. As absolutely independent I hold a position in Scotland, of which I do not think so highly as some others may, but one which I greatly cherish. As a Cabinet minister I should hold a position in Great Britain which it is an honour to covet. But by accepting office outside the Cabinet I lose both positions. On that point I have some experience to guide me.

"I hope I have made myself clear. I value my independence and its advantages much, and perhaps too much, but at any rate so much that I will never surrender it again except for the position which ought to be preferable even to independence such as mine: nor should I surrender it then with indecent alacrity.

"Now I know your views on this point, and it is for that reason that I consider the next six or eight months as an 'unencumbered interval': and indeed as regards office I regard the rest of my life in much the same light.

"I am, therefore, about to fulfil a long cherished purpose, and I feel that I can do it without any sacrifice of private duty or public advantage.

"With renewed thanks, believe me,

"Y. affy.,
AR"

THE DURDANS

He was troubled by scruples similar to those which had made him refuse any office three years earlier, but equally he did not hesitate in estimating his own capacity for public service in the light of his recent experience as an Under-Secretary. On the same day "Harcourt came to luncheon—very cross." On August 15th the Gladstones dined, and he was again pressed to take the Scottish office. Three days later he had a long talk with Harcourt on the subject. Gladstone made a last effort on the 20th, and Rosebery definitely declined. On the following day the Local Government Board (Scotland) Bill came up for second reading in the House of Lords after a rather lively passage through the House of Commons, when Rosebery's name was freely canvassed. It was a very pusillanimous measure, but was strong enough to frighten Lord Salisbury and the Conservative Peers. Rosebery wound up the debate, saying that he would not reply to aspersions made on him in the House of Commons, because those flowers of rhetoric betrayed by their flavour and their fragrance the soil from which they sprang. He pointed out that though the measure came late to the House it contained only six clauses, the outcome of discussion on every platform in Scotland and in every newspaper in Scotland, which showed that it was the desire of Scotland that it should pass. All was of no avail. The Bill was rejected by a majority of fifteen in a House of seventy-seven members. This was Rosebery's sole appearance in this session of Parliament after his resignation.

In the early summer he became a Trustee of the British Museum, to Gladstone's great delight, but he hesitated for some time before accepting the post, in spite of Edward Hamilton's insistence. He may have thought acceptance hardly consistent with his discontent at Gladstone's attitude towards Scottish political affairs. Lord Reay wrote with great candour that he would commit a great folly if he refused this real distinction, and that the notion would be strengthened that he was too sensitive for the wear and tear of public life, while suspicion of Mr. Gladstone's motives in making the offer, as a sop in place of office, would be equivalent to a break-up of his and Rosebery's confidential relations. Nobody in Scotland would be grateful for the refusal. These and similar appeals carried the day.

CHAPTER VII

World Tour and Politics, 1883-1884

AFTER Rosebery's two short visits to Dalmeny in August and explanations with his Scottish supporters, and after a parting interview with the Prime Minister, he and his wife sailed from Liverpool on September 1st, for the travel which he had advanced as one of his reasons for quitting office. They arrived in New York on the 12th, and though they had left behind their two friends of the Mendacious Club, they found a warm welcome from others, such as the Duncans, Mr. Choate, Whitelaw Reid, John Sutherland, and the Oliver Belmonts, with whom they stayed at Newport and met most of the gay world of New York. Towards the end of the month they were the guests of Mr. Carnegie and his partners at Pittsburg, spending the day at the steel works—"on the scene of Braddock's defeat," as Rosebery did not forget to note. They passed on to Chicago, having hired a Pullman car for the journey west, and under the guidance of its enterprising inventor they visited the model settlement of Pullman, with its 64,000 inhabitants, churches, theatres, athletic ground, and all the amenities of a considerable town. Chicago had then almost recovered from the fire of eight years before, but was conspicuous for solid, rather than exciting, elements of interest. After a day there, they passed on to Colonial Bluffs, where 107 dollars had to be paid for extra luggage. But in those more spacious days—"much of it is wine, which has a gradual tendency to diminish." Then to Omaha, past a station which a few years before had been sacked by Indians, and so to Cheyenne and Denver—amazing in the wide prairie, with its 50,000 inhabitants, its sudden splendour, its electric light, and more telephones than any other town in America.

They pursued their way by Utah, and over the Sierra Nevada to San Francisco. Here they were received hospitably by the local magnates—Sharons, Mills, Floods, and many others. During a fortnight's stay, interrupted by a brief visit to Monterey, they savoured all the wonders of the Western capital—Chinatown; some neighbouring ranches; and even an earthquake—the most severe for fifteen years, but not severe enough to awaken Rosebery. There was also a little shooting of duck and other game. One remarkable day produced "about two dozen quail and rabbits, and a yellow-hammer."

On October 20th the party embarked on the s.s. *Zealandia* and rolled heavily all the week's way to Honolulu. The few hours' stay there was given to sight-seeing, and to a visit of ceremony to the affable chocolate-coloured Sovereign of the islands (October 28th).

The Line was crossed with no greater hardship than a subscription for the benefit of Neptune and his court. The heavy weather did not prevent the mock trial of a teller of travellers' tales, to which a charge of breach of promise was added. Rosebery assisted as Council for the Defence, in a gown devised from a waterproof, an imitation wig of muslin, carrying a green baize bag stuffed with papers adorned with enormous seals.

Auckland was reached on November 11th, and they were hospitably entertained by Mr. Clark, the Mayor. But they saw none of the wonders of New Zealand, going on the same night to Sydney, where they arrived after six days' more heavy rolling. It was the worst weather known for twenty years, as travellers are apt to be told. They had their first sight of the famous harbour by moonlight (November 17th).

Lord and Lady Augustus Loftus entertained them hospitably at Government House, and Lady Rosebery, much tired by the rough voyage, remained there quietly for the first three weeks. Of these Rosebery spent ten days in a journey to Queensland, going by sea and returning overland, enjoying a sheep-shearing, putting up at bush hotels, and seeing some of his Primrose cousins settled in the Colony.

Melbourne was the next stopping-place (December 12th), and the travellers were the guests of Lord and Lady Normanby. Rosebery wrote to his mother:

"One misses Sydney Bay very much, which is next to Naples the finest thing I have seen. This is what is called a noble city,—great wide streets like Edinburgh New Town or St. Petersburg, but I am not sure it has the charm of the winding irregularities of Sydney and its hills. However it has no mosquitoes, and not even any mosquito-nets, which shows an appalling sense of security. The people here are much more energetic and pushing than the Sydney people, which is partly the effect of climate, partly the result of a strong American infusion at the time of the discovery of gold."

From Melbourne a flying visit was paid to Ballarat, where they went down a mine and wielded unremunerative pickaxes. Rosebery returned to Sydney alone (December 22nd); attended a Press dinner; received some political news from England; was impressed by the excellent racing, and the order kept on the race-course; was gorgeously entertained by the sporting magnates; attended a rollicking expedition of drag-net fishing which concluded with a game of rounders, unknown since Bayford days; and felt very unhappy at leaving Sydney. From Hay he made a long drive over the Old Man Plain in a dust-storm:

"An endless, dust-coloured plain, occasionally a cinder coloured tree, the dust skimming swiftly after us like Furies, or any hostile pertinacious spirits. At the change, a lonely inn with a thirsty and exhausted host and hungry and animated flies, I sitting silent in the buggy for fear I should swallow dust, my companions exchanging an occasional murmur: this is a picture of that day, a fair shadow of Purgatory if not worse; and yet—we were not unhappy."

Warbreccan, a pleasant station of Sir Patrick Jennings's on the Edwards River, was the destination, whence he passed on to the mining centre of Sandhurst, which reminded him of the pictures of Jerusalem, "and if really like it, is certainly Jerusalem the Golden"; and so back to Melbourne. The officer who had captured the Kelly gang of bushrangers showed a suit of their armour made of ploughshares heavily padded within, and described the exciting scene of their destruction. Rosebery was again impressed by the excellence of the racing arrangements at Flemington, except for the undue punishment inflicted by the jockeys.

Both the travellers were fascinated by Tasmania, where they spent four well-filled days (January 3rd): "A pretty enclosed country, ridiculously like England, and stations with names from Scotland." The stage coaches were of the old English type: "I saw these venerable relics of antiquity and thought, not without emotion, of the House of Lords."

At Hobart the Governor, Sir George Strahan, was "a perfect host, so genial, and kindly and energetic." A ghastly experience was the visit to an old prison where the convict lunatics, the dregs of the extinct convict system, were dragging out the rest of their degraded lives. The Superintendent had been at Port Arthur, and had given the author of *His Natural Life* much of the information on which that appalling story is founded. The details were in no way exaggerated: "He astonished me by saying that Maquarrie Harbour was the worst of the convict settlements, then Norfolk Island, then Port Arthur. But I suspect that Dante would have got a hint or two from any of them."

All their impressions of Tasmania, its officials and its inhabitants, were of the most agreeable sort, and no happier days were spent anywhere throughout the tour. They returned to Melbourne before starting homewards. At the wedding of a member of the Governor's staff (January 8th)—

"the bridegroom cooler than a cucumber, the church prettily decorated with flowers: the ceremony vague and impulsive, with the impression every now and then 'a sudden thought seizes me, let us sing a hymn'; and so hymns were sung. Miss ——— at luncheon said that the bridegroom had wished the whole church to be decorated, but as he found it would cost £500 insisted on the adornment of certain parts, the altar, the font ——— 'And why, in Heaven's Name,' I broke in, 'the font?' We all laughed consumedly, and Miss ——— blushed in the same ratio."

There was a banquet given by the Mayor:

"The principal feature was a captain in the Messageries who was brought by a friend and treated by the friend as a Marshal of France. I returned thanks for him, and as soon as I sat down he returned thanks for himself in a language which, as it was something between English and French, I informed an inquisitive neighbour, was the tongue of the Channel Islands,—'Is it really now?' Then one of the Ministers set him up figuratively and pommelled him, and gave him so many messages to take back to his Government and people that his own steamer would not have held them."

Another visit to Flemington on "The Bookmakers' Day" when the Ring borrowed the course, gave the prizes, and took the receipts, was followed by a short stay at St. Hubert's, the pretty centre of an extensive wine-growing estate, whence an expedition was made in blazing heat through glorious scenery and vegetation to Fernshaw and the Black Spur. The last excitement at Melbourne was an exhibition of buck-jumping by the rough-riders of the police:

"It quite came up to my expectation, which is rare. The horse was blindfold when saddled and mounted. The moment the bandage was removed, off he went in the attitude of the Order of the Golden Fleece. But generally after his first mad bucks he turned sulky, a frame of mind from which no amount of flogging would rouse him. The horsemanship was magnificent."

They started in the s.s. *Adelaide* for the port and capital of that name (January 17th). Sir William Robinson, the Governor, brother of the better-known Sir Hercules, received them. There was an official reception at the Town Hall, and a banquet, adorned by pipers, in the evening. It was so stifling that on emerging the Governor said that it had changed to a cool breeze, though in fact the hot wind was still blowing. One meeting was destined to bear fruit later on:

"I had the great pleasure of meeting my old school-fellow Kennion, now Bishop of Adelaide. Fancy one's contemporary being so shabby as to take a Bishopric and make one feel a hundred. But I forgive him: I believe he is both a saint and a man of business. I have rarely been so fascinated."[1]

It was not to be supposed that, during a sojourn of nearly ten weeks in Australia, Rosebery would be able to abstain from public speaking. He was a notable Scot, and Scottish societies abounded in all the Colonies, which owed so much to the Northern country. He was a Liberal already conspicuous as a brilliant orator; Liberal ideas were generally in favour overseas, though the attitude of some Liberal doctrinaires towards the Colonies was freely resented. Speechifying was popular, for the fluent facility which those of British race seem only to acquire when they quit these islands for good had already begun to blossom in Australia. On two occasions the entertainment was Scottish. At Sydney the banquet was given by the Highland Society (December 8th, 1883). In a forty-minute speech, after a tribute to Scotsmen in the Colony, that though imported thistles had become a pest, yet his fellow-countrymen had at any rate managed to gather figs from them, and a half apology for not being a Highlander himself, he explained the prompt result of his visit to Australia, that the abstract sympathy and interest felt all through his life was now quickened into an actual entity, a living and tangible thing. He would carry away two main impressions. The first was that the great masses of the people had an opportunity of living a happier existence than in anywhere else within the British dominions. The second was the boundless future of the country. Its growing population was equal to that of the United States when she declared and wrested her independence from the mother-country. He passed on to touch on the Convention which had just been sitting in Sydney, the first at which the different States, as they now are, met for the interchange of ideas on subjects not merely local. It had reached two conclusions: the first the exclusion of convict

[1] Dr. Kennion was appointed Bishop of Bath and Wells during Rosebery's Premiership.

settlements from the Pacific; the second the cautious encouragement of federal relations between the Australian Colonies. He approved of both resolutions, and trusted that Scotsmen, their sons and their sons' sons, might be privileged to bear a part in building up in this land of milk and honey, secluded from the curse of rivalries and traditions and strifes in our older world, a state which shall have the prerogative of peace, which shall satisfy the imperious instincts of a dominant race, and not merely these instincts, but also some of the noblest and some of the happiest aspirations of suffering mankind.

The second national occasion was the Speech Day of the Scotch College at Melbourne (December 19th, 1883). After the usual request for a whole holiday, he claimed that the Scottish race have the greatest thirst for knowledge of any nation that is known in this world. In a country of universal suffrage such as Australia, everybody's duty is to fit himself by education for the task of government, so he called on the students to fit themselves for the high duty of citizenship for the sake of Victoria and for the greater Australia looming in the future.

On December 10th, Mr. E. Barton, the Speaker of the Legislative Assembly, gave a dinner to both Houses of the New South Wales Parliament, which both the Governor and Rosebery attended. He said that his early hopes of beginning a speech with "Mr. Speaker" had been frustrated, so his pleasure in doing so now could be imagined. It amazed any Englishman to see how far local government could be carried with efficiency and self-respect, as a contrast to the single government exercised at home over thirty millions of people, many of whom were supposed to be incapable of self-government. He again dwelt on the Convention and an Englishman's interest in the Federation of Australia, which would enable her to speak with a broad voice entitled to respect in the civilised world. Australia could thus speak to the mother-country with the voice of an eldest son who has attained his majority, and on whom the property is strictly entailed.

"I will ask you only to remember one thing in your dealings with the old country, as I wish statesmen in the old country to remember it in their dealings with you. It is that neither you nor they should reason too much from precedent or from history. It has made its own history; it is creating its own precedent, it is steering its path into the future, where no chart and no compass can guide it. Least of all can she forecast her own relations with her own Empire, and God forbid that you or I, or any of us, or any of them in the old country, should attempt to do it at this time. Let us do the best we can, and work for the best. She can only blindly work, trying to do her best for these her children—for her greatest children as for her least children—and in that attempt I pray she may be successful. He relations with her colonies cannot any longer be defined. People talk of the Roman colonies, of the Greek colonies, of the military colonies, and of the American colonies. We have nothing to do with those colonies. They have interesting records, but they furnish no guidance now for the British Empire. We have outlived that time of minority and instruction. Her relations with her colonies are, it seems to me, of a complicated and of an intricate nature. They are connected by a golden thread of affection and of descent. They are cemented, Gentlemen, more closely than anything by the fact that there are few of us in England who have not got relations or kinsfolk working among you here. When they talk of cutting us adrift from you, or cutting you adrift from us, people do not seem to remember that that is the case, and that we do not care deliberately to cut ourselves off from our own blood and our own flesh. But as regards your relations with the mother-country, I would sum them up in a single sentence, by saying that, in the strict sense of the word, she does not attempt to guide, she does not pretend to control, but she does regard her giant offspring with a pride which it would be the merest affectation to conceal."

This address was enthusiastically applauded, and there was surely no little foresight in this early recognition of the practical independence of what were then styled the Self-governing Colonies in managing their own affairs.

At Melbourne also the Mayor entertained the Governor and his guest (January 9th, 1884). Rosebery again laid stress on the Convention. Like Sancho Panza, who had been forced by the stern doctor beside him at the banquet to forgo all the daintiest dishes, he had been compelled by Dr. Time to sacrifice such dainty fare as a visit to New Zealand, one of the most energetic of colonies. Everything had been sacrificed to arrival in Australia while the Convention was still sitting. One speaker at a previous banquet had seemed to think that the great object of the Convention was to have one Parliament alone for the whole of Australia.

"However that may be, let me impress one thing upon you. Our bitter experience in the old country should lead you to prize local government as the greatest of all gifts. We are endeavouring in Great Britain to recover our lost local government. I hope that you in the colonies will never make such a mistake as to forfeit that local government.

[146]

If I remember aright, I have heard a dread murmured that if federation took place, and if Australasia became a dominion as Canada is, there would be some danger of Australasia desiring to separate from the mother-country. (No! No!) I only mention that as an argument that has been used, and I am quite sure that everybody here has heard it used as an argument against confederation.

"Now, I don't profess to define for one moment what is the basis on which the British Empire rests. I do not believe that such a conglomeration has ever been seen since the world began, and I don't believe that anyone here or outside this room can give any satisfactory account to the logical mind of the basis on which that Empire rests, because it is not a matter of compact or of civil contract. The connection between Great Britain and her colonies is a marriage of the affections, or it is nothing at all. It has been said very lately by a writer who has visited Australia, Mr. Forbes, and who is entitled to great weight on his own account, that the connection of Australia with the mother-country would not survive a war (dissent). Well, that is a question on which I am wholly incompetent to judge. I have naturally no experience, nor have you, to judge whether that is so or not. But my belief is that the connection of loyalty between Australia and the mother-country would survive a war. And would survive, as long as other things were equal, as long as the home country and the daughter-country were allowed to preserve their positions of mutual independence and mutual self-respect. I believe that if those are observed, the connection of the colonies,—and I am speaking of Australia more particularly—with the mother-country will become closer and not looser than before.

.   .   .   .   .   .

"There is no subject so interesting to Englishmen as the future of the British Empire. To many it is merely a fortuitous agglomeration of nations and of countries. To some it is simply a series of accidents. To others it is only a grammatical expression. I believe it is none of these, but at the same time when we come to think how many climates, how many races, how many religions, how many forms of government are comprised within the British Empire, we cannot be surprised that it is beyond the minds of those who have endeavoured to define it. What can be more puzzling than the fact that this city, which can only send a letter and receive an answer to it from London four times in the year, should remain attached by sympathy and by affection to the centre of our Empire? It would seem that there could be no common interests and no common affection. But there is an old tradition, I don't know if it remains good—that in the British Royal dockyards every rope that is manufactured, from the largest cable to the smallest twine, has a single red thread through it, which pervades the whole strand,

and which if unpacked, destroys the whole rope. That was the sign of the Royal production of those ropes. Though I distrust metaphors, I believe that that metaphor holds good to some extent of the British Empire. It is held together by the single red line and that red line is the communion of races. I have always hoped that that communion of races might exist as long as my life lasted, but since my visit to Australia it will become a passion with me to endeavour to preserve that union and to serve this country of which I can never have any but the happiest and most delightful memories; while if there is anything that I can do to serve either this or any of the other colonies of Australia you, Gentlemen, may reckon upon my doing it."

Rosebery's farewell message to Australia was delivered at Adelaide (January 18th), in the surroundings of grilling heat to which allusion has been made:

"What with the hot wind my audience was languid. What with the hot wind and the difficulty of coping with the Town Hall, I was languid. I had not had enough preparation, and there was an old drunkard who interrupted. The result was that though I spoke for an hour, it was uphill work. It was not an after-dinner speech, but I had to deliver it, and had no other opportunity."

It was indeed his most finished utterance in Australia, grave with the consciousness of departure from the glorious country which probably he might never see again, and animated by the confession of his faith in the future of the British Empire. After touching on the special characteristics of South Australia, and the achievements of the Sydney Convention, he went on:

"Now, sir, what conclusion do I draw from this recital? Why have I told you things which must be more or less familiar to yourselves? I do it for this reason. I say that these are no longer colonies in the ordinary sense of the term, but I claim that this is a nation—a nation not in aspiration or in the future, but in performance and fact. I claim that this country has established to be a nation, and that its nationality is now and will be henceforward recognised by the world. Sir, that is a great position to take, and I think the facts I have stated substantiate it. But there is a further question, and it is this: Does this fact of your being a nation, and I think you feel yourselves to be a nation, imply separation from the Empire? God forbid! There is no need for any nation, however great, leaving the Empire, because the Empire is a commonwealth of nations."

Fifty years later the phrase has become a commonplace of political terminology. Then it was the announcement of a new gospel. He proceeded to dwell on the anomaly of asking the Parliament at

Westminster, oppressed by the appalling problem of Ireland, puzzled by the adaptation of ancient institutions to the needs of the nineteenth century, and by the riddle of the government of London, to devote its energies to Australian affairs. He asked Australians to be tolerant, because they were much better left alone, and because the time must come for some adjustment of the burden which would bind the Empire closer together. Australia could claim to be a nation, making its own history, since it had won self-government, and isolated in a manner which no other nation has been or could be for the purpose of remaining an Empire of peace. She would not desert the old country if war should come, but the British fleet must be strong enough to protect their shores.

"I may say that with every day the chances of England being at war with any other European power grow less, because every day she looks less to other people's empires and more to her own."

He concluded with the recital of his Imperial creed:

"It seems to me that hand in hand they may yet follow up a career of usefulness to mankind—led by those common and eternal principles of justice which alone can exalt and sustain a nation, and which we proudly boast and humbly hope have long guided and directed the British Empire; which have been the pillar of cloud by day and the pillar of fire by night that have guided us to so many achievements and through so many troubles. I believe that every day we remain united we shall be less anxious to part. I believe that every day we remain united it will be considered more desirable that we should continue so, not merely for our own selfish interests, but for the interest of humanity at large: because it is on the British race, whether in Great Britain, or the United States, or the Colonies, or wherever it may be, that rest the highest hopes of those who try to penetrate the dark future, or who seek to raise and better the patient masses of mankind. Each year the power and the prerogative of that race appear to me to increase; each year it seems to fill more and more of the world. I believe that the connection of the British Empire will remain, for the reason that it is desirable for civilisation that it should continue to exist. I confess I think that each day that we live we shall be more and more unwilling to see this ancient Empire of ours—raised with so much toil, colonised with so much energy, cemented with the blood and sweat of so many generations—pass away like a camp struck noiselessly in the night, or split into isolated and sterile communities, jealous among themselves, disturbed by suburban disputes and parochial rivalries, dwindling possibly, like the Italian States of the middle ages, into political insignificance, or degenerating into idle and polite nonentity. And, sir, let me remind this assemblage of the fact—that empires, and especially great empires, when they crumble at all, are apt to crumble exceedingly small.

"I have only a word to say now, and that is the saddest of all words, because it is good-bye. My visit to Australia, short as it has been, has had this result—that it has quickened my feelings of interest in Australia into affection, and has divided my feeling towards your country between my head and my heart. We do not indeed have the same aspirations as to weather. The divinity that we worship in Great Britain is the sun; but here the object of adoration and desire are the clouds. And now I feel I have to leave your sunshine for our clouds; but I can safely promise that among our clouds I shall cherish the recollection of your sunshine. Whatever I can do in the smallest way to justify the kindness with which I have been received here I will do. I shall form aspirations for your future even higher, perhaps, than you now form for yourselves. And I shall not be accused of any unnatural or excessive unselfishness in forming these aspirations, because I think that the majority of Englishmen have come to know this—that in forming good wishes for the future of Australia they are forming good wishes for the future of our Empire."

Rosebery spoke informally on several other occasions, but such were the prominent utterances of his Australian sojourn. They were recorded by him in detail, because the tour came to be something of a turning-point in his career. The doubts that had long floated in his mind concerning the destiny of the British Empire in the fast-changing conditions of the time were now crystallising into the conviction that a new outlook was imperatively demanded at home. At this moment Australia presented the finest field for the birth of such a conviction. The gold fever of the fifties had given place to a vast though wavering production of the precious metals; the convict settlements had become a painful historical memory, almost as unreal as the fires of Smithfield. The great squatting estates and urban properties begat vast fortunes with no present menace to the claims of humbler folk, and thus did not excite general envy; the facilities of transport and communication multiplied day by day. There was little poverty and no mendicancy. No wonder that a perfervid Scot like Rosebery, seeing what a part Scotsmen had played in this marvellous pageant of prosperity, was altogether captivated. His deep absorption of the Imperial idea, destined to colour his after life so powerfully, dates from this year of travel.

The s.s. *Paramatta* started on her voyage to Ceylon. There was a brief pause at Albany, where there was a show of native dancing and spear-throwing, but Perth could not be visited. The fifteen days to Colombo were for the most part passed in ideal weather. "It is impossible to conceive anything more perfect than gliding along this blue sea under the sunshine of this blue sky." On another day he noted:

"In the afternoon there were athletic sports. There is on board an 'Amusements Committee,' which fully justifies Sir George Lewis's sensible remark."

But there was variety in conversation with personages such as Sir Frederick Haines, the Indian Commander-in-Chief, and Joe Thompson, the leviathan book-maker from Melbourne, who sang comic songs one evening. Reading was a great resource. *The Wealth of Nations; The Life of Hook* ("What a noble fellow!"); Carlyle's prose translation of Dante; Mrs. Howe's "well-written life of that vast impostor *Margaret Fuller*"; Burke's *French Revolution* —"I am rather disappointed with it, though of course no one else could have written it. But he is so completely, though naturally and accountably in the wrong"—novels by Trollope and one or two others; these make up a good bill of fare.

The arrival at Colombo inspired Rosebery to an almost dithyrambic flight of fancy which must be recorded:

"I left land, when I saw it last, which was instinct with the rude life of the future of England making her way in the wilderness. And now, when I land again, I set foot in the mysterious East, glowing with its sunlight and its myriad colours, with its petty eagerness, its hand to mouth existence, and its ant-heap swarms of population. This not an hour or a morning or a year: it is nothing less than an existence teeming with new impressions and boundless vistas of idea. I can describe nothing, I could not criticise or even notice, I remained in a passive receptive state, plunged with every mental pore open in this vast ocean of ancient novelty. The outriggers, with naked bronze figures guiding them, the lonely, skinny fisher in his frail boat, the solemn Mohammedan merchant with his singularly inconvenient basket cap on the back of his head, the diver plunging for his sixpence, the washermen with their greasy certificates of worth by former passengers tendered to their successors, the hungry jewellers with their choicest gems tendered for a few shillings, every head turbaned, every form lean, every mouth blood red with betel, all this one saw before one landed."

Sir Arthur Gordon,[2] the younger son of the statesman Lord

[2] (1829-1912) G.C.M.G. M.P. 1854-7. After holding several Colonial Governorships, Governor of Ceylon 1883-90. *Cr.* Lord Stanmore 1893.

Aberdeen, reigned at the Queen's House as Governor. Rosebery enjoyed hearing the political verdicts of an older man brought up in the very centre of affairs, but professionally aloof from them.

"We talked over Gladstone's (ecclesiastical) patronage. I told him that I had repeated Sir R. Peel's phrase 'the odious power conferred by patronage' to Gladstone, applying it to his probable feelings, and that Gladstone had at once replied that he enjoyed his patronage very much. 'Yes,' said Sir Arthur, 'many persons dislike patronage, because they know that every appointment they make creates one ungrateful person and a host of enemies according to the old saying, but it never occurs to Gladstone for a moment that anybody may be disappointed or aggrieved.' I added that Gladstone has the valuable faculty of always making up his mind, when he has made an appointment, that it is the best possible, and that no other would be one quarter as good. This is an immense saving of mental worry. But I also said that once I had a long talk with him when the air was dark with difficulties, but he spoke of the filling up of a Welsh bishopric as the most important of them all. 'Yes,' said Sir Arthur, 'what my father always said of him is very true, he has no sense of mental perspective.' Sir Arthur did not speak, I thought, very warmly of Gladstone, but with a lurking bitterness. He said that the man Gladstone really detested was Palmerston, that he (Sir A.) had lately had a conversation with Mr. G. on Mr. G.'s own position, which Mr. G. had begun by asking him if he remembered a conversation of theirs twenty-one years ago, in which Mr. G. had spoken of the horrible spectacle presented by an 'old man clinging to power long after efficiency had left him, i.e. Palmerston. Gladstone hoped he would never appear to the world in that light. Sir A. believes him to have an ardent anxiety for retirement. I said I did not think it was so strong as it had been in 1881 and 1882. . . . He told me he had once seen Metternich completely put down. After the great smash at Vienna in 1848 he was fond of reading his memoirs aloud. One day at Richmond in 1849 he was doing this when, on a pause, Madame de Lieven threw herself back with a desperate gesture of weariness, and said aloud: 'O! Mon Dieu! que cela m'ennuie!' Metternich collapsed."

Rosebery went with Sir Arthur's other guest, Sir William Gregory, to visit Arabi Pasha, the interned Egyptian exile.

"A fine-looking man, with broad powerful face, and a forehead which, though not high, is instinct with capacity."

The interpreting was weak, but Rosebery gathered that Arabi had intended to make the Mahdi Governor of some part of the Sudan, and that he could not see why parliamentary institutions should not work in Egypt. When Rosebery mentioned the sixty million Mohammedans in India, Arabi observed that people who were well governed would stand by their rulers, rather boldly applying the same consideration to the Government of Turkey.

"On leaving him he informed me that this was the happiest hour he had spent in Ceylon, the Oriental method, I suppose, of saying good-bye.

"Thompson, the Australian book-maker, and his family, five in number, had come to see the famous exile, lying in wait under the verandah. When I looked round Joe had got Arabi tight by the right hand, which he was shaking with agonizing vehemence."

The other event of their stay was an excursion to Kandy (February 5th). It is a fascinating place, and the travellers were enchanted by the gardens of Perediniya, with their colossal bamboos and flowering trees, and by the town with its temples and silent lake. The same evening they started homewards. Rosebery left Ceylon in a mood not less exalted than when he first got sight of it, and again tried to embalm his sensations in words:

"In these two days it seems to me that I have lived nine lives of a cat. I have never in years, I think, received so many absolutely new impressions. I feel like the blind man whose eyelids were anointed with the clay laid on by the Messiah's hand: I did not believe there was a sensation so novel left in the world, or rather a world so novel left for sensation. It is a golden dream to carry through life, a life which must always be brighter for this one little ray of the rare Eastern sunshine let in through a chink of time into the foggy chamber of a British existence."

To Hannah Rosebery, too, Ceylon was an indescribably beautiful fairyland.

The voyage to Suez was like all other voyages, diversified by such incidents as the abstraction of a silk kammerband by a female rat as a nest for her family, and a wordy dispute between passengers on the proceedings of the Amusements Committee. Of this last Rosebery set down an Homeric account. But he got through plenty of reading: the translation of the *Inferno*, Plutarch's *Life of Alexander* ("What a marvellous vision!"), and the *Life of Alcibiades*:

"One never realised sufficiently his great ability. The Duke of Wharton, I think, must have taken him as his model. It is the only way to explain him. Read also Gehring's little *Life of Mozart*, what a prodigy! Yet perhaps he did not die prematurely. For he began so early and worked so hard that he had lived for at least thirty years of intense composition and suggestion. 'Few people live more. Nothing is more futile than to measure life by years."

But the plum was the correspondence of Lord Aberdeen, which Sir Arthur had had privately printed for his own use, and of which he lent four volumes to Rosebery for the voyage.

"But I conscientiously fear that he should never let them go 'out of his own hands. The imagination cannot picture what the Queen must think about it if she knows it. Heaven forfend!"[3]

The customary pause at Aden awakened fresh thoughts of the Empire and its meaning:

"After all, one's final reflection on Aden is *Quæ regio in terris nostri non plena laboris?* That we should have established ourselves, our coal, and fortifications to protect our coal, on a parched rock in Arabia, is full of suggestion. That we 'should have done so as an incident of our Indian Empire is a fact of tenacity. That we should there have received and revived the tanks of Solomon is a singular succession 'and a pregnant thought."

Before reaching Suez, Rosebery filled several pages of his diary with a descriptive report of his fellow-passengers, their looks, and their ways. He concluded mysteriously:

"Why do I scribble all this insignificant balderdash? I have my reasons. More I will not and cannot say."

They dawdled through the Canal, past Ismailia, which reminded him "of a small pot of French polish upset on the desert," to Port Said, which "gave the impression of a town composed of the packing cases left by passing ships." There they changed into another steamer, obliged to occupy seven whole days on the journey to Marseilles, so as to avoid three days of quarantine there, "which makes one feel as if one was riding a horse in a race which one knew to be drugged." Thus it was again a dawdle, though sometimes a less flat dawdle, through the Mediterranean, past "the jagged rock of Scylla with its little town flung over it like jetsam," and Charybdis, unidentifiable among several whirlpools; past "the charred cone of Stromboli with vineyards soothing its scarred sides, and on the side of the summit, like a wound, the crater rolling out dense clouds of

[3] The whole correspondence was placed at the disposal of Lady Frances Balfour for the *Life of Lord Aberdeen* published in 1923. It is now, with other papers of Lord Aberdeen's, in the British Museum.

smoke; on the left the islands, once, if I am not mistaken, the Insulæ Æolides, all silent volcanoes, watching Stromboli as old men watch the sports they once loved,"[4] the travellers reached Marseilles, lunched at the Réserve, where all the world goes for *bouilla-baisse*, and found themselves at Paris at the opening of spring (March 2nd). It was early days for the *dimanche anglais*, but Rosebery was surprised to find almost all the shops shut. He and his wife shopped inveterately in Paris, so this made a greater kindness of his hurry to reach London.

"We had meant to stop over to-morrow, but letters came from Reay saying that he had been offered the governorship of Victoria and could not make up his mind without consulting me. So we proceeded this evening to London."[5]

The Government still seemed prosperous enough, if it could survive the approaching conflict with the House of Lords on the terms whereby household suffrage should be extended to the counties. The Roseberys had gone straight to the Durdans, where the children were settled, but in a few days he saw Gladstone in London.

"He seemed changed. Talked to him about Lord Aberdeen's correspondence. He replied 'Nobody cares a d . . . for Lord Aberdeen.' He also said that the Government wished Ripon to stick to his guns in the Ilbert Bill. The House of Lords could not force a dissolution on the Franchise Bill, but the Government might go to wreck on Egypt. Hartington and Granville both came in."

A little later the Gladstones spent part of the Easter vacation at the Durdans (April 8th), when the Prime Minister

"talked about Reform. I argued with him about the Irish.[6] He suddenly broke off: 'I am sick of contention: I cannot at my age spend the rest of my life in contention.' As to minorities, the best plan would perhaps be to establish wards as in Municipal elections. He passed on to the difficulty of either leaving or governing Egypt, a country in which slavery and corporal punishment existed, but he saw no difficulty in its finance. No parallel was to be drawn with India, which was not a Moslem country, and had behind it the history of the East India Company. If we were to govern Egypt we give up French alliance forever.

[4] Rosebery's classical memory was almost correct: the Lipari, a group of ten islands, had several names in ancient times, Æolidæ Insulæ for one.

[5] This appointment was not made. Lord Reay became Governor of Bombay in 1885 till 1890.

[6] The extension to Ireland of the new Franchise would make the case for Home Rule infinitely stronger, as Hartington and others foresaw.

Not but what we need no alliance and are strong enough to stand alone. The Government might break up on Egypt. He asked what I thought. I told him. He remained silent, and after a minute said 'You could probably not put that view of the case more forcibly' and retired into the house."

Rosebery's view, needless to say, was not that of divesting this country of responsibility for Egypt or of dependence on agreement with France. During their walks, the Prime Minister astonished Rosebery by not knowing that Chamberlain wished to be Irish Secretary when Frederick Cavendish was appointed, and said that, though he did not wish it done in his time, the Privy Seal should be held by the Prime Minister. Rosebery gathered that he might take it, but that, being a Commoner, he would require a regulation of the Queen to give him the proper precedence. "Dizzy" had taken it at the beginning of a financial year, and took the salary which had been voted.

There was also a long talk with Goschen (March 23rd), when walking the Derby course, Rosebery's favourite promenade with his guests, whether interested or not in that Isthmian track. Rosebery somewhat evaded questions about his political programme, but summed up his position as being able to support the Government on Reform, after Hartington's speech, the only black spot being the retention of the number of Irish members.[7]

The Durdans was their headquarters till Easter, when Rosebery repaired to Scotland for a week, when he received the Freedom of Dundee.

The Provost welcomed him (April 15th) as the man Scotland needed in the difficult future. Rosebery devoted most of his speech of thanks to the Colonies. He was surprised at the indifference with which Britain regarded her great possessions all over the world. France, far less densely populated than we, was making efforts to create a Colonial Empire. There was a school of economists who would limit our dominions to the three countries of these islands, of which one by no stretch of the imagination could be considered attached to the other two. He, on the contrary, thought it mattered enormously that the stream of emigration should flow to other parts of the Empire. Were it not for the flag the trade of Australasia would naturally flow to America. Separation of the Colonies would be like building over the open spaces of a large town, for they are

[7] See *Life of Gladstone*, bk. viii, ch. viii, p. 5, for the great debate on this question in the House of Commons in May.

the breathing spaces for the Empire to depend on. But Parliament would never find time for Imperial questions without extension of local self-government and administration. He begged, too, for expression of that sympathy which might be felt but never reached the outlying parts of the Empire—they were left to believe that they were ignored and forgotten in the councils of the nation. Sympathy would reap its own abundant harvest of reward.

The ceremony at Edinburgh was followed by a banquet starting at 6.30. After the twenty-six speeches had been made, at 10.45, Rosebery "sneaked away" to Barnbougle, where he spent the next day arranging books. He returned to Epsom and a bachelor party for the Spring Meeting, but the old Duke of Buccleuch had died, and he found a letter from Lord Dalkeith asking him to attend the funeral. A night journey made this just possible. At the "tender and impressive" ceremony he kept out of the way, but was observed by the grandson. The new Duke, the defeated candidate of 1880, "sent me frequent messages to say how sorry he was to miss me, and that he should never forget my coming till the end of his life." He was right in feeling that Rosebery's presence meant more than a courteous formality to a neighbour. Personal liking and Scottish sentiment alike directed him to Dalkeith. On his return he found a letter from Gladstone, offering him the Lieutenancy of Midlothian, in succession to the late Duke. This he at once declined. But there was no Liberal landowner of sufficient standing as an alternative, and after being begged to reconsider his refusal, he wrote agreeing to become a *pis aller* as Lord Lieutenant, though he was giving up more than his Chief could guess in surrendering at all. The Prime Minister did not often find such coyness in the ranks of possible office holders.

It was sixteen years since Rosebery took his seat in the House of Lords. He had played a fair part in its current business, without becoming one of the worker bees who can collect no honey except in its Committee-rooms or on the Committee stage of some involved Bill in the House itself. His ready wit, not less than the capacity for hard work and close investigation proved by some of his speeches, had made him the most conspicuous figure of his generation on the red benches. But he could not feel entirely satisfied with what he saw there. Whatever the ideal Second Chamber might be, nobody could imagine that the House of Lords approached that ideal either in theory or in practice. At any rate it was worth while to examine the possibilities of improvement by constituting an organ which, if not altogether impartial, should be strictly well-balanced, to make a report to the House itself. A Select Committee, carefully chosen, would be such a body. Rosebery accordingly moved (June 20th) :

"That a Select Committee be appointed to consider the best means of promoting the efficiency of this House,"

not starting an academic discussion as he said, but making a practical proposition. After admitting that there was no precedent for such a committee, he sketched the different changes in the composition of the House during the six centuries of its existence. The greatest was the swamping of the House under George III. At his accession there were 174 Peers, of whom 149 had seats in the House. During his reign 388 were created, 140 on the advice of Mr. Pitt. A curious proof of the change was that on the first reading of the first Reform Bill, of the Peers created before 1790, 104 voted for the Bill, and only four against it. The Bill was thrown out mainly by Mr. Pitt's Peers. Then came other innovations, such as the abolition of proxies, and lately, the admission of judicial Life Peers. But infinitely more marked were the movements outside —the enormous powers now vested in the House of Commons, the creation of the Newspaper Press, and of the Colonial Empire.

Is the House of Lords efficient? A delicate question, but at any rate not so efficient as it might be made. Take 120 Peers, official, diplomatic, naval and military, and men of letters. The Senate at Washington surely could not produce so many distinguished individuals, yet it carries greater weight, not because it is an elected body, because many elected Second Chambers are not valuable institutions. It was absurd that the House of Lords should be content with a quorum of three, and that after an idle session all the legislation of the year should be crowded into "one hour of glorious life." The system of joint committees ought to be examined, both for public and private legislation. The popularity of the House was neither so great as its friends assert nor so small as its enemies made out. But it might represent some vital principle more powerful than popularity by including more of a great variety of complex interests—the various operations of our vast Empire, commerce, the professions, the Church. The dissenting bodies ought to be represented; while, though the Army and the Law were there in numbers, and the Navy to some extent, medicine was entirely absent, and science would be, except for the happy accident of Lord Rayleigh's presence. Four or five Peers spoke for the banking and railway interests, but commercial interests generally could not here compare with the enormous weight they carried in the other House. Again, there was too much receiving and too little paying of rent. A noble lord from Ireland shook his head,[8] and Rosebery had to admit that he understood his meaning, but said that everybody was in the same boat. Again, the Arts were not directly represented.

He passed on to quote a long extract from a speech by Lord Salisbury in 1869 when the creation of Life Peers was being considered. The Conservative leader then said that the Peers were too much of one class, and therefore often too much of one mind; they wanted more representation of diverse views, and more antagonism. Rosebery held that the question of Life Peers was too large to discuss at the moment, but his Committee could consider the possible extension of the principle already admitted by the nomination of Law Lords. He suggested a select committee "which might either be a hatching machine or a sepulchre," because he did not think that any individual Peer, whatever his authority as leader of a party, could hope to carry any substantial proposition of reform. Therefore the chance for any suggestion of his own would be small indeed. He would gladly have waited if anybody of more importance had taken up the question, but he believed that every day of postponement did harm. This was in the best sense a conservative motion. Its only meaning and scope was investigation. Some of the ardent spirits of his party did not wish to see the House reformed.

"They wish to point it out as a mediæval barque, stranded by strange chance, or irony of time, across the teeming harbour of the 19th century, and acting only as an obstacle to more active and useful shipping."

He hoped that their Lordships would not play their enemies' game on this occasion, and concluded with the belief that the Peers could best guard the honour of generations, both living and dead, and yet unborn, by embracing vigilantly every opportunity of testing the soundness of the structure of the House by examining its foundations. The motion was shortly seconded by Lord Onslow, a few

[8] It was a joke at Trinity College, Dublin, that factory of happy jokes, that an Irish M.P. had quoted the line:
"O fortunatos nimium sua si bona norint!"
and that the goddess Echo had answered from the Irish mountains:
"No rint!"

years younger than Rosebery, and just becoming prominent as an active Conservative of the forward school.[9]

Lord Granville spoke of the mover's "incisiveness and sympathy and more than usual ability," but politely sprinkled cold water on the plan of a select committee with a wide reference. At the same time he indicated his liking for Life Peerages. Lord Salisbury was not less complimentary to the great eloquence and ability of Rosebery's speech. He also favoured Life Peerages in principle, but, while willing to consider any special proposals, did not think that "a mere fishing committee" would be an advantage. It was a time of rapid transition, and therefore not one for gratuitous changes. Lord Kimberley thought the select committee an indignified and vague conclusion for the House to adopt, and begged Rosebery not to force them to vote against his proposal. In the event a division was first taken on the suggestion that Life Peerages should be specially named as a subject for the committee's consideration. This was defeated, the Government voting with Rosebery but the Conservative phalanx opposing. When the original motion was put, Lord Granville and his colleagues walked out; but Rosebery was joined by some independent Conservative Peers, so that his defeat was a shade less severe than on the first division. He was genuinely annoyed by the half-heartedness of his former colleagues, noting in his journal that "our front bench got into hopeless and ridiculous confusion," and in his bound volume of *"Hansard,"* "the Government walked out amidst jeers." And he was not alone in being indignant. Reginald Brett, with whom he was intimate both as a later pupil of William Cory, and as Hartington's secretary, was a frequent correspondent. He wrote (June 24th) : "The impression is strong that Lord Granville ought to be rid of (1) Egyptian negotiations,[10] (2) reply to Rosebery's speech. Fowler of Wolverhampton was saying so."

The speech itself received many compliments. Lord George Hamilton wrote enthusiastically as a Conservative onlooker (June 23rd) ; and Lord Houghton :

"You could not have done it better. It was the most amusing speech I have ever heard in the House, and reminded me of the old days before

[9] 4th Earl of Onslow. Several times Under-Secretary of State; Governor of New Zealand 1889-92; President of the Board of Agriculture 1903-5; Chairman of Committees in the House of Lords 1905-10.

[10] Lord Granville had made a statement in the House of Lords on June 23rd on the exchange of views with France on Egyptian finance and the British occupation.

all the champagne was dry and all the ale bitter, and clever men were not ashamed of being pleasant."

Nearly fifty years have passed, and the fact that the composition of the House of Lords remains as it was in 1884, though circumstances brought about some restriction of its powers, may or may not be taken as an excuse for the Liberal apathy shown on this occasion and the subsequent neglect of Conservative Governments to tackle the question of reform. It will be seen how, in later years, Rosebery clung to the hope that something definite should be done.

So much for the House of Lords. It aroused a passing breeze, but the Representation of the People Bill, which was to affect the composition of the next House of Commons—and Governments and Oppositions alike find it difficult to look beyond the next House of Commons—threatened a tempest that might develop into a tornado. Extension of the franchise to householders in the counties must involve some redistribution of seats; but how, and when, was that redistribution to be accomplished? Tories feared that if the Franchise Bill were passed, then redistribution might be gerrymandered wholly to their disadvantage. The Government saw that if the passing of the Franchise measure were contingent on the Redistribution Bill, the latter would in fact be framed by Lord Salisbury and his majority in the House of Lords. This extension of the franchise had been mooted by resolution in 1876 by Mr. Trevelyan, when Disraeli was in power; it raised no new principle, and was known to be inevitable at some not distant time. The Bill passed the House of Commons by a large majority; but when the second reading came on in the House of Lords, Lord Cairns did not move its rejection but an amendment, demanding that the Bill should not come into operation except as part of an entire scheme of redistribution. A great debate ensued, displaying the Second Chamber at the height of its oratorical powers. Rosebery spoke on the second day. He followed Lord Brabourne, a country gentleman of lettered tastes, who, having accepted a peerage from Gladstone in 1880, had seldom supported the Government and now sorrowfully announced his intention of voting for the amendment. His speech was frankly hostile to the Liberal party, and the opportunity was too good for Rosebery to miss. "The anguish," he said, "with which the noble Lord found himself obliged to vote against the Government showed that his coronet must be a crown of thorns, because ever since he had a seat in the House it had been his consistent and inevitable fate thus to vote."

[161]

Having planted this fatal dart, Rosebery asked the House what it would gain by retarding this measure of justice? It was impossible now to combine redistribution with franchise, not only because every member who might be affected would join in the discussion, but because questions must be raised touching the root of the administration of the Empire. There was the complex question of Ireland. Scotland was under-represented and could not be overlooked. There were questions of proportional representation and the claims of minorities. The Opposition had stultified themselves in the House of Commons by proposing to add 500,000 women voters to the 2,000,000 named in the Bill. And the country would not stand the postponement of redistribution, if that was what the Opposition feared. The measure could not have been produced before because it obviously was a prelude to a general election; the House of Lords had no more moral claim to reject such a measure than the House of Commons would have to reject on second reading a Bill passed by the House of Lords to reform itself; and therefore the technical prerogative of rejection should not be exercised. The House, that ancient institution, was being placed in the risky and unsuitable position of trying to dam a torrent of popular feeling:

"I see a situation as grave as the unwisdom of a leader and the misguided strength of a party in this House are able to produce. I do not pretend to say that we have at stake to-night the existence of this House, because I do not think so; but we have at stake that without which existence is not valuable or tolerable,—the weight and authority which are given by wise decisions and by sympathy with the nation,—that nation for which we legislate, but which governs us."

He appealed to the independent Press and to the Episcopal bench "who preach a Gospel which is not merely a message of peace and goodwill to the world, but which is also the highest and purest conception of democracy yet vouchsafed to mankind."

Among the later speakers, the Archbishop of Canterbury,[11] as though in response to this appeal, urged that a second reading be given to the Bill, the necessary redistribution to follow immediately. Lord Salisbury, in his most bitterly sarcastic mood, mocked at Rosebery's description of the Bill as a matter of justice and principle, whereas it was a mere exhibition of parliamentary tactics by a Government which, having a majority, did not wish to lose that

[11] Edward White Benson (1829-1896). Bishop of Truro 1877, Archbishop of Canterbury 1882.

majority. He utterly scorned the threats that public opinion would resent the action of the House.

Lord Granville wound up the debate in a more systematic speech than he usually found necessary, covering all the ground with singular skill. Of Rosebery's speech he asserted:

"One of the most remarkable speeches I have heard delivered in this House was from the noble Earl, who I think may be complimented on the share he had in the Midlothian campaign. His was a blast which not only filled this House, but will reach the furthest confines of the United Kingdom."

The division was remarkable, the Government securing no less than 146 votes against 205 strict Conservatives, whipped up from the highways and hedges. The minority counted some hundred more votes than in an ordinary party division. Dukes had begun to mistrust Mr. Gladstone, but no less than eleven of these personages voted for the second reading, against twelve who sought the opposite lobby. More significant still, whereas only one Bishop supported the amendment, both Archbishops and ten Bishops voted for the second reading, giving a gallant response to Rosebery's appeal. Still more amazing was a note which reached him before the division:

Private.   MARLBOROUGH HOUSE, *July 8th*, 1884.
"MY DEAR ROSEBERY,

"I must write you two lines to tell you *how* I admired your speech. It was simply splendid, and so much to the point in every sense of the word. You spoke for upwards of an hour—and it seemed to me like ten minutes.

"Tell me candidly your opinion whether you think there would be any Constitutional objection if in my position I voted with the Government.

"I am,
Yours very sincerely,
ALBERT EDWARD."

It was not exactly a party division, but it is safe to conclude that Windsor Castle would not have approved of the inclusion of that illustrious name in the division list, in which, needless to say, it did not appear. Rosebery noted of his own effort: "I spoke from 7 to 8 with some success." A stream of congratulations flowed in from England and Scotland. A letter worth mentioning came from one of the finest minds among journalists of that day:

[163]

July 12th, 1884.

"My dear Rosebery,

"I cannot abstain from troubling you with this line expressing all my deep appreciation of, and conveying my best congratulations on your really splendid speech. I heard it all, and it was incomparably the best speech in the whole debate. I have heard many great speeches in the House of Lords during the last eighteen years, and I cannot recall that I ever heard anything finer.

"Yours sincerely,
T. H. S. Escott."

The long and wearisome negotiations, conducted with much patience, tried by occasional breakdowns of temper on both sides, which concluded by the device of an autumn session and the ultimate passage of both Bills, are part of the history of the country. The successful issue was largely due to the personal intervention of the Queen, and the difficulties which she encountered with tact and firmness are fully set out in the collection of her letters.[12]

The position which Rosebery had attained in the councils of the party, added to the special weight recognised after his speech in the House, gave him definite *locus standi* in these colloquies. And we find him at 10 Downing Street (July 1st), "determined to try and compromise this silly franchise business. Gladstone very strong for it." Lord Wemyss, the most open-minded and undisciplined of Tories, had put down a motion which proved to be identical with Rosebery's solution, that of an autumn session to deal with redistribution, the Franchise Bill being permitted to pass now. Gladstone wrote to the Queen favouring Rosebery's idea in principle.[13] Lord Salisbury remained obdurate, and secured Lord Wemyss' defeat by a reduced majority, to the great chagrin of Rosebery, who had told Gladstone that the compromise was sure to win on a vote. But the parleys proceeded, at last good humour reigned, and neither side could boast absolute victory, or had to confess absolute defeat. Later in the year Lord Houghton wrote:

"The Queen told Carlingford that from the way that Gladstone and Salisbury buttered each other, she does not see how she is to have an Opposition again—exactly the reverse of the Duke's difficulty[14] in 1832."

[12] Second Series, vol. iii, ch. vi.
[13] *Loc. cit.*, p. 514.
[14] At the crisis in the fortunes of the Reform Bill in May 1832 the King amazed everybody by inviting the Duke of Wellington to form a Government in order to pass it—in the manner that Catholic Emancipation had been carried three years before.

Her Majesty's fears soon proved to be ill-founded.

Rosebery's other interventions during the summer session were less important. The Secretary for Scotland Bill was dropped in company with other Government measures, after the adverse vote on the Representation of the People Bill, and Lord Salisbury (July 10th) accused the Government of acting like the mediæval Popes, who, when they could not get the thing they liked out of the King, interdicted all the religious services of the inhabitants of his kingdom. Rosebery made the disappointment of Scotland clear by a question on the future of the measure. It did not get an encouraging reply. When Rosebery was in Australia he found opinion highly excited by the reported intention of the French Government to ship an increasing number of habitual criminals, *récidivistes*, to New Caledonia. There was no little risk that escaped convicts might be able to land at points on the thinly populated coast, but, apart from this, Australia objected to the arrival on her shores of time-expired French criminals, some of whom had been guilty of most atrocious crimes. France was still sensitive on Egypt, and this was a delicate matter for our Foreign and Colonial Offices. Rosebery, who had already raised the matter in Parliament, recognised that the Bill then before the French Senate could not be altogether challenged, so he set himself to suggest safeguards which would remove the strongest Australian objections. He enumerated these in a letter to Lord Derby (June 11th); and the outcome was satisfactory enough for him to withdraw a notice of motion which had been on the paper of the House of Lords for some weeks. In doing this he sketched out the general outlines of the story, and professed his willingness to leave the question in the hands of the Foreign Office. Lord Granville explained that urgent representations had been made to the French Government. The scheme was modified, and the substantial service rendered to Australia by their recent visitor was warmly recognised by some of his correspondents, especially in Queensland which had seemed to be particularly threatened. At the end of the month W. E. Forster presided at a Conference on Imperial Federation. Rosebery seconded the first resolution as a declared supporter of the movement. A little later he paid a flying visit to Amsterdam on the Duke of Hamilton's yacht, and went sight-seeing in her launch to Haarlem and other points accessible by canal. The family moved to Dalmeny in August, entertained the Prince and Princess of Wales for the opening of the Forth Bridge, and immediately afterwards received the Gladstone family. Gladstone was oppressed by the dread that the obstruction of reform by the House of Lords might drive the Liberal party to attack the hereditary principle as such, and had sent a note on the subject to the Queen.[15] "Very good and powerful" was Rosebery's observation. The Queen also was greatly impressed by this memorandum. Mr. Gladstone made three successful speeches, the last on September 2nd, when Rosebery also went south. He visited Postwick Hill, near Norwich, a small house which he had lately bought as a residence for a little property which had come into the family by the marriage of the 3rd Earl of Rosebery with the heiress of the Ward family. There he shot partridges, and visited neighbours near Cromer. Felbrigg, the home of the Windhams, always had a particular interest for him. He then returned to Scotland, where he fulfilled a double engagement at Aberdeen.

The meeting of the Trades Union Congress gave an opportunity which he seized with adroitness in a speech of nearly an hour. Henry Broadhurst was largely responsible for his appearance. Starting from what he called the federation of unions in the Congress, he treated it as applicable to the concerns of the Empire. Historically, the notion of making the Empire a single centralised union had failed; now there was the danger of its having no cohesion at all. The impulse for Imperial federation must come not from Parliaments, but from the people; that was why he wished to interest this Congress in it. For a united Empire the connection should be a little stronger than the mere practice of sending out Governors and vetoing Bills. Meanwhile France and Germany were both extending their Colonial Empires. In this country the working classes were more interested than others, because both in Canada and Australia these classes had made far greater advances than here in hours of work, in representation in Parliament, and even in payment of members, though this last provision, on which he expressed no opinion, was not altogether approved even in Victoria, which had adopted it. From such experiments we could learn much in this country. Emigration to the Colonies, only about a half of emigration to the United States, had not been carried out by Government with sufficient regard either to employers or employed. But the maintenance of the bond of nationality touched the Trades Union Congress. This was a practical question which could not be put off from day to day until it might be too late to do anything; whereas a league of English-speaking peoples, which a later generation might hope to see,

[15] *Letters*, Second Series, vol. iii, ch. vi, p. 531.

was a sublime conception, but not to be achieved in this time. The bond of Empire must either become stronger or weaker; and to strengthen it must become an article of creed with the working classes both at home and in the Colonies before becoming a question of practical politics.

At this date it showed some courage to devote to hopes and problems overseas almost the whole of a speech made to a working-class audience; but the frequent applause with which it was punctuated proved the success of the experiment.

On the afternoon of the same day Rosebery received the freedom of Aberdeen, his hat, by a time-honoured custom, being decorated with the diploma and long streamers of red ribbon. Here he dwelt on the rapid growth of cities, and the training they offer for great affairs, as in the case of Chamberlain. There was a shifting of the balance of power away from the country district, and a corresponding weight of responsibility in the towns. He looked forward, also, to local government in the counties and the smaller communities which the counties include, thus freeing Parliament for Imperial work. In Scotland the demand for more local administration was urgent, and they must begin by securing the nomination of a Secretary for Scotland.

The pleasant, varied life at Dalmeny was resumed, but was broken by a mishap. Rosebery rode most days, and one afternoon his hack "came down a burster" a hundred yards from the house, giving him one of the worst of falls, an unforeseen fall on the flat. He broke a collar-bone and also sustained an internal bruise which caused acute pain and prolonged discomfort, compelling the use of powerful sedatives. Mr. and Mrs. Gladstone had been invited, but he was only just able to see them. Other visitors came, but Rosebery remained an invalid, passing most of his time in bed until the whole family moved to London. Another visitor, his brother Everard, he saw for the last time. He and Everard, the "Tiny" of early days, had always been close friends, but never close companions. Everard Primrose, a year younger, inherited many of the qualities which made the union of the Primrose and Stanhope stocks so remarkable in that generation. From Trinity, Cambridge, he joined the Grenadier Guards, and was devoted to his profession. Generally popular, cultivated, ironical, an excellent linguist, and no ascetic, he was the ideal military attaché at such a capital as Vienna, where he was now serving. But he wanted to see active service, and in August Rosebery had asked Hartington to give him a chance in Egypt. He was now soon due to start for the Nile, from which he was not to return.

Lord Spencer came, having been closeted all the morning with Campbell-Bannerman, urging him to accept the Irish Secretaryship vacated by Trevelyan's move to the Duchy of Lancaster.

"While we were talking C-B's answer arrived, refusing: he knew his own capacity, and its limits, etc."

Three days later Rosebery heard that Campbell-Bannerman had revoked his refusal, and, after the move to London, Spencer told him that in spite of this the Government were going to make an effort to get Sir Henry James to take the post. Fortunately nothing came of this. In reply to Rosebery's warm congratulations, Campbell-Bannerman wrote that he was honestly opposed to taking the place, because he did not feel qualified for the work:

"I carried, in truth, the line 'nolo secretari' to the extremist point permitted by honour."

In one respect the change to the South was not a success. The ordinary routine of London, and a visit to Newmarket, proved to be too exhausting. At the beginning of November the first renewal of his favourite walk of the Derby course, in the congenial company of Henry Calcraft, tired him out. He began to sleep very badly, and to feel languid. Accordingly, when the Prime Minister (November 9th), in the course of a walk at the Durdans, asked him to take the Board of Works, with a seat in the Cabinet, he was not in a mood to accept work immediately. He said that his difficulty was Egypt, and a long talk on other subjects followed. It will be recalled that by the cutting to pieces of Hicks Pasha's force in November 1883, not merely did Egypt lose all hold of the further Sudan, but it was evident that the Mahdi could advance to Khartoum if he wished, and possibly to Wadi Halfa, or even Assouan. It was decided to withdraw the Egyptian garrisons, and in an ill-starred moment it was decided to send General Charles Gordon, of Chinese fame, to carry through the evacuation.[16]

The succession of events,—the discussion over Gordon's request for Zobeir Pasha to succeed him as Governor; the fall of Berber

[16] The despatch of Gordon was decided by Lords Hartington, Granville, and Northbrook, and Sir Charles Dilke, the Prime Minister being at Hawarden. It is safe to assume that Lord Wolseley's unstinted admiration and personal affection for "Charley Gordon" did more than anything else to impel Ministers to this hapless decision.

in May, and the consequent isolation of Khartoum; the disputes about a relief expedition and its route—all these created an impression of infirmity of purpose in Downing Street. Rosebery could not pretend to be satisfied with his forecast of future Egyptian policy. Mrs. Gladstone warned Hannah Rosebery that refusal to take office might compromise her husband's future, that it would arouse a new rumour of his fickleness which would be encouraged by Harcourt, whereas Lord Granville was really friendly. Two days later Lady Rosebery saw the Foreign Secretary, who dwelt on the extraordinary effort made by the Prime Minister to get Lord Carlingford to resign in Rosebery's favour. Lady Rosebery mentioned Egypt. "Does he want to seize Egypt?" asked Lord Granville, going on to point out that Rosebery would have no responsibility for past policy, and would influence future policy far more from within the Cabinet. The Government could not last long; good speeches were all very well, but they were not the same thing as official education: Rosebery was none too young for the Cabinet. Soon the offer became known in political circles, and Rosebery received congratulations from John Morley, Dilke, Broadhurst the Labour representative, and others. But he showed Hartington his letter practically refusing, and the grounds of his refusal are best set out in his letter to Lord Granville:

LANSDOWNE HOUSE, *November 12th*, 1884.
"MY DEAR LORD GRANVILLE,

"Your kind and frank conversation with Hannah yesterday encourages me to write to you on a matter personal to myself, even if I did not feel it my duty to you as leader of our house.

"From the moment that Mr. Gladstone offered me this Commissionership of Works on Sunday afternoon I have felt that I must refuse it. It is not indeed an attractive post, having neither dignity nor importance, and is I think the least of all the offices, being only a sort of football for contending connoisseurs. But if the Pope be *servus servorum* I suppose I may be too. However, this is merely an innocent digression, for I hope you will believe that no personal consideration or silly fastidiousness has anything to do with my feeling in the matter. But Egypt is a great obstacle—I have written to Mr. Gladstone as to this to point out why I think it impossible for me to come in now. Not merely is Egyptian policy to be decided now, and I have never disguised my difference from the Government on that point, but Egyptian finance.

"You can guess the extreme delicacy of my relation to that question, for though I am not a member of the House of Rothschild, I am allied to it as closely as possible by kinship and friendship, and I feel therefore strongly the difficulty of entering the Cabinet at the moment of the discussion of Northbrook's Report.

"As to both policy and finance I could probably accept a *fait accompli*; but I do not see how with self-respect I could swallow all the considerations and enter now.

"If I disagreed with the conclusion arrived at I could indeed resign. But resignation is almost impossible to me after resigning last year and the resignation of even the humblest member of the Cabinet on such a question could only do harm.

"The consideration alluded to in connection with Egyptian finance would equally prevent my speaking much about Egypt in my present position (I have only alluded to it once in a speech), and on almost all other questions I am so wholly in accord with the Government that I could be of as much use (or as little) to them out as in just now.

"Believe me, dear Lord Granville,

Sincerely yours,

ROSEBERY."

Two days later he again saw Hartington, and agreed to the Prime Minister's request that the offer should be kept open for a week. In the event it was kept open into the next year, Lord Selborne and other members of the Government encouraging Rosebery with expectations of a favourable development in Egypt. A week was spent at Sandringham (November 24th), when the Prince of Wales, in a frank talk with Lady Rosebery, observed that the post was not equal to Rosebery's claims, and that the Government now needed him but ought to have invited him before. At the same time, patriotism might oblige him to accept it if the country were to be left in the hands of such men as Chamberlain and Dilke. All through the autumn Cooper of the *Scotsman* had been hammering away at the thesis that high office, if offered, must not be refused. But Rosebery must assert himself. When the Prime Minister was going to Scotland for his summer campaign, Cooper wrote to Rosebery (August 11th, 1884):

"The position is not what it was five years ago. You need not be overshadowed by Mr. Gladstone. You have a position which entitled you to a place of your own. The public will want you, and you can come to their call if it suit you, but you will, I take it, be Mr. Gladstone's host, and in no sense his appendage."

A flying visit to Liverpool followed (December 3rd), with a speech at the Reform Club. Here he first touched on the naval expenditure, in which public opinion, following the lead of the *Pall*

Mall Gazette, had put pressure on the Government, and proceeded to speak of Egypt and of British responsibility there. First to the Egyptians, because at Alexandria and Tel-el-Kebir we had destroyed a government, "a very loose and rough government, it is true, and grounded on insurrection, but a government popular and national," and were bound to set up something in its place; secondly, to ourselves, to see that no other foreign nation should take our place. When we depart we must leave a monument of the liberty and civilisation of which we boast. He touched on the settlement of franchise and redistribution, as a prelude to a longer disquisition on reform of the House of Lords, which that House should itself undertake. A seat in the House, he boldly asserted, should not be a matter of hereditary claim. And the new Chamber should be one of the greatest possible simplicity, without fancy franchises, but strong enough to be a real Second Chamber, or they would end by not having a Second Chamber at all.

He made a rush to Scotland for H. M. Stanley's lecture at Glasgow, and a short stay at Dalmeny was interrupted by a summons to Windsor. It was supposed that one or two of the estates near Balmoral might be sold, and the Queen expressed a hope that he would buy one: "We should like so to have you as a neighbour."

In conversation with Princess Beatrice he said that the Queen ought to go to India. The Princess thought that she would, but for the long sea voyage.

The rest of the year was spent between Dalmeny and Mentmore. As it was ending, Hartington wrote, enclosing a letter from Gladstone, who had seen the circular which Rosebery had issued to his supporters on House of Lords Reform.

Mr. Gladstone thought that its circulation looked so like a deliberate plan of separate and continuing action that he asked Hartington to ascertain whether Rosebery's hesitation was really caused by doubts about contingencies in Egypt. If he had definitely abandoned the idea of office, the place had better be filled up at once. In transmitting this letter Hartington said that he did not himself regard the letter to the Peers as indicating any settled plan of separate action. Rosebery, in his reply, confirmed this, and explained that he felt he must pursue the question of reform whether he took office or not. In the former case, the question would at any rate be in proper train for someone else; but if not, he could not find himself at the beginning of the session without having done anything, and without any ostensible excuse for having done nothing.

The new year opened peacefully at Mentmore. Spending a day in London (January 3rd, 1885), he heard that:

"Mr. Gladstone, who is low and sleepless, dined with Lord Reay the night before, and had said half to himself: 'rest will not come to me, but I shall go to it.' I went to Downing Street and met him in the passage. We talked for two or three minutes: he seemed weary and unhinged. He went to Hawarden after the Cabinet, and if he got any better there is to go to Cannes."

Jowett and the ever delightful Henry Cowper[17] spent a few days at Mentmore, as did Reginald Brett and "Jowett's friend Milner," who in reply to the master's question had written that he would be delighted to make the acquaintance of one with whose views on foreign and colonial policy he greatly sympathised. This was Rosebery's first acquaintance with the young civilian, then only conspicuous as a typical product of Balliol. The "Colonial Confederation League," soon to take shape as a regular organisation, was beginning to hold meetings. The position at home grew no clearer. Rosebery showed Hartington the heads of the letter he proposed to send the Prime Minister in refusing the new offer of the Cabinet (January 28th):

"He seemed to concur. But wished to talk to me about his own position. He, H. had a talk with W.E.G. last week as to the break-up of the Liberal party, which seemed to him inevitable. W.E.G. concurred, or rather thought there was too much reason to fear it, but advised Hartington not to resign, if he must resign, on the Egyptian question, a question no one cared a button about."

He found at Edinburgh that Cooper of the *Scotsman*, to his surprise, concurred in the refusal of office. The letter to Mr. Gladstone was posted on February 1st. He was south again on the 3rd and heard of the conclusion of the temporary agreement with France about Egypt. A day later the news of the fall of Khartoum reached him at Mentmore. Here was a startling aspect of "the question that nobody cared a button about." Where Gordon was concerned, "the nation was in one of its high idealising humours,"[18] and went wild over a truer hero than it has sometimes thought fit to worship. Rosebery saw that for himself the situation had changed: it was no moment to foster personal scruples and reserves. As he had said two years earlier, "it was all hands to the pumps."

[17] (1836-1887). Second son of 6th Earl Cowper. M.P. 1865-85.
[18] *Life of Gladstone*, bk. viii, ch. ix.

So he wrote:

Secret. Mentmore, Leighton Buzzard, *February 8th*, 1885.
"My dear Mr. Gladstone,

"Ever since the disastrous news from the Soudan reached me I have felt impelled to write to you: but I waited to be sure of the soundness of my impulse; while I confess the statement in your letter, which I received the next morning, that your constructive work in Egypt was nearly accomplished ran counter to my strongest convictions in the matter and made me pause again.

"But the question now is one less of policy than of patriotism. We have to face a crisis such as rarely occurs in a nation's history, which the nation therefore should face with a united front. The Government at such a juncture has a right to appeal to the public spirit and place under requisition the energies of everybody.

"If therefore you think that my services can be of any use to the Government you have the right to claim them, and they are fully and freely at your disposal.

"I cannot disguise from you however that my opinions on the situation in Egypt are unchanged, and that it is for you to judge if under these circumstances I can enter the Government. I cannot profess to alter my convictions in consequence of the fall of Khartoum, but I can offer to put them on one side for the moment in view of a public calamity and its consequences. I do not myself see how I can be of use to you, but that is for you to decide. Moreover you may no longer have any post at your disposal. These however are not questions for me: my only call of duty is plain and simple—to place myself at your disposal in the hour of difficulty and disaster.

"Believe me,
Yours affectionately,
AR"

10 Downing Street, Whitehall, *February 8th*, 1885.
"My dear Rosebery,

"I have just received your letter and I highly appreciate the patriotic spirit in which it is written.

"I believe that the resolutions at which the Cabinet has arrived under the painful circumstances recently made known are such as you would thoroughly approve.

"When I said that our constructive work in Egypt was so advanced, I did not mean that I thought the time was close at hand when the question of evacuation would come up.

"The present juncture overshadows all the future: and you would certainly form your own ultimate conclusions on our position in Egypt

[173]

proper with much greater advantage from within the Cabinet than from beyond its precinct.

"I therefore from my point of view do not see reason for throwing any difficulty in your way, and as the office is still, happily, open (which to-morrow in all likelihood it would have ceased to be) I will with your permission submit your name to the Queen.

"I presume that the secondary arrangement for the discharge of business in the House of Commons will hold good, as you expressed I think a favourable opinion of it on its merits.

"Unless you telegraph to me to hold my hand I will proceed not later than to-morrow morning.

"I remain,

Affectionately yours,

W. E. GLADSTONE."

February 10th, 1885.

"MY DEAR ROSEBERY,

"The Queen has approved, and is pleased at your accession. Lefevre also joins the Cabinet.

"I am glad to say that Granville made to me a happy suggestion which I ought myself to have thought of.

"We propose that you shall hold the Privy Seal[19] with the Board of Works: (salary is attached to the latter only). I think you will like this.

"Yours affectionately,

W. E. GLADSTONE."

He was able to make a public profession of his duty and the duty of all patriotic citizens when going with Lord Carrington to a meeting at Epsom (February 9th). There he rapidly indicated how moments of disaster in the past had brought out the best in other great nations, and spoke of the heroism of the troops in their magnificent march across the desert. He was shocked at the feeling that the fall of Khartoum should involve the fall of the Government. He did not pretend to have concurred altogether with the Government's Egyptian policy: more than once he had thought that a bolder and clearer course might have been adopted. But in his view every Englishman ought to strengthen the Government in every way he could. He hoped the disaster, if only for a moment, might unite the nation. All Europe was watching to see if we were enervated by our long years of prosperity. The rest of the speech was devoted to colonial policy. He regretted being at issue with Bright, the greatest man but one in the party, who at Birmingham

[19] Making him the fifth personage in the realm, outside the Royal Family.

had stigmatised the policy of Imperial Federation as "childish and absurd."

"I suppose the position of the Imperial Federation League is this. The armaments of this country may have to be increased, in order to afford protection to our coaling stations and our Colonies. In that case the Colonies might wish to contribute, in some form or other, to the support of these armaments; and the contributions would be raised in any way the Colonies thought fit, whether by a protectionist tariff, or on Free Trade principles.

    .   .   .   .   .

"It is with regret that I have appeared to differ in the remotest degree from one whom I admire and love so much as Mr. Bright. We cannot be snuffed out by epithets. Much was said about the divergent doctrines held by leaders of the party. The Liberal party was always going to break up but never did. Liberal Cabinets had never been of perfect unanimity. In Lord Grey's Cabinet was Lord Durham. Sir William Molesworth was able to work in harmony with Lord Palmerston, and I do not suppose that Mr. Stansfield and Mr. Bright were in harmony with all their colleagues."

Perhaps the recitation of these past divergencies, and of their failure to break up the party, would not have been out of place in later years.

The Times reserved its congratulations for the country and for Rosebery's colleagues, rather than for himself, and as letters flowed in, almost all the writers—Ministers, Conservative opponents, Liberals who were next door to opponents—dwelt on his courage and self-sacrifice in lending a hand at such a moment. W. T. Stead, who was so nearly a great man, and yet so definitely failed to be one, wrote:

Private.   PALL MALL GAZETTE, NORTHUMBERLAND STREET,
                  STRAND, *February 12th,* 1885.
"MY LORD,
"I hope that the occ. note in the P.M.G. to-night does not jar on the feelings of the Privy Seal.
"I think you have done a right noble act, but I fear that you will have to follow it up by one as noble and even more difficult before six weeks are over.
"Unless I much misread the signs of provincial opinion, Chamberlain will rat and the Cabinet will be exposed to a frightful strain. But, when the poltroons peel off the patriots will have their chance.
"I hope you will pardon me, for saying that you have an immense

chance if you have but stuff in you to play a man's part in politics instead of merely a politician's.

"I am almost in despair when I look at our 'Statesmen.' What a puny breed they are, compared with Gladstone! What preoccupies our Radicals? England? The Empire? Nothing of the kind. It is the distribution of places when Gladstone goes, this man's petty ambition, the other man's personal ends, etc., etc.

"Unless we can rise above all that, block out the Empire as a whole, and think out a policy, colonial, foreign and domestic that will be at once consistent, moral and practical we are undone.

"I shall always at any time be glad to hear from you or to see you.

"And when in my wrath I blaspheme the Ministry, pray consider that my objurgations are framed with a saving clause exempting from their scope the present holder of the Privy Seal.

"Again begging you to pardon the liberty which I have taken in addressing you thus frankly.

"I am,

Yours truly,

W. T. STEAD."

The Master of Balliol, from a more sublime height, said (February 15th):

"Two persons have asked me whether I thought you ought to join the Ministry in their low estate. I said No to the first, I was inclined to say Yes to the second, but the truth is that both answers might be given with equal reason: for whether it was or was not a mistake to cast in your lot with them at this moment, must depend on the use which you can make of the position. . . .

"Milner tells me of the great pleasure which he had from his visit to you: I certainly think that one of the surest elements of political success is the friendship of young men. No statesman has made a full use of it."

There spoke the wisdom of age. And among the many letters of that date was one vivid with the keenness of youth. Laura Tennant, the exquisite girl just affianced to Alfred Lyttelton, wrote:

"The step you have just taken is, to my mind, one of the noblest things I have lived to see."

She was not to see many more, for, after a short year of wedded happiness her eyes were closed for ever. Rosebery had for long been on terms of close friendship with Sir Charles Tennant and with his family.

He attended his first Cabinet of two and a half hours on the 16th.

It is a pleasant custom of Cabinets, sometimes humanizing dull discussions, for Ministers to exchange brief confidences on half-sheets of note-paper. On this occasion Lord Granville tossed Rosebery this query:

"I wonder what you thought of us all?"

The reply was just barbed with recollection:

"More numerous than the House of Lords and not quite so united."

A similar note from Lord Northbrook was candid:

"I think you have joined a very short-lived Cabinet,"

and Rosebery thought that they certainly did not seem very harmonious.

Such was Rosebery's first entrance to the inner councils of Government. A Minister of the Crown is always *homme enchaîné*, his time is no longer his own; and in a sense his opinions are no longer his own, for, where no deep principle is involved, he must often subordinate his preferences to those of his colleagues, and he must keep silence out of doors. But one man knows that he is bound by the golden chain of willing service; another feels that he is bearing an iron yoke imposed by imperious duty. It was the irony of Rosebery's political life that, gifted as he was with all the powers and graces apt to lighten the official burden, from first to last circumstances made it uneasy to bear. He just missed the triumphant election of 1868; when victory blazed again in 1880, he thought himself debarred from office; when he felt able to join, the tide was already on the turn. He joined because Scotland needed him, and the work was otherwise uncongenial. To change the metaphor, he was taking a commission in a force distracted by internal differences, and only held together by an aged leader whose health seemed to be breaking down. As the tale progresses it will be seen that never once, during the forty years of his active life, did political office present itself to him dressed in the glowing colours which, for a season at any rate, it ought to wear for a man who entered a Cabinet before he was forty, and was twice Foreign Secretary and once Prime Minister.

Another Cabinet on the following day (September 17th) led to this rather significant observation:

"I was more accustomed to the abruptness of manner which surprised me yesterday."

The most interesting subject of discussion was the answer to be sent to the Canadian offer of troops, a memorable step in Imperial relations. This and other offers came up again a day or two later, when "we succeeded in impressing on Mr. G. the necessity of putting strongly what he had to say about these offers, and he afterwards did it very well." This was the debate on Sir Stafford Northcote's vote of censure, when the Government scraped through with a majority of fourteen (February 28th).

CHAPTER VIII

Ireland: Germany: Foreign Office

AS MIGHT be expected, the Left Wing members of the Cabinet, Joseph Chamberlain from 1880 and Sir Charles Dilke from its reconstruction in 1882, were bitterly opposed to special criminal legislation for Ireland; and Chamberlain had been the principal intermediary when the so-called "Kilmainham Treaty" was contemplated. Rosebery, he knew, was more accessible to fresh ideas than many of his colleagues, and the fact of his being a Scotsman made approaches hopeful, for Scotland also hankered after more local government. But from first to last Rosebery never looked on the claims of Ireland with an eye distracted by emotion or sentiment. To indulge in metaphor—Dark Rosaleen, the wayward and reckless gipsy of those days, never struck him as a particularly romantic figure. He thought her untidy, almost squalid, and rather foolish, compared to his adored Caledonia, inheritress of all the gifts of Pallas Athene. He had never visited Ireland, he did not care for the prime Irish sports, fox-hunting and fishing, and he did not enter into what those acute Irish observers, the chroniclers of the *Irish R.M.*, so well call "the lethargic and pessimistic humour" of a certain type of Irishman, who is "always a critic in the stalls, and is also in spirit behind the scenes." But he saw that there was a complex problem of government to be solved, and he always believed that people have a right to look after their own local affairs, even though in certain respects outsiders might manage them better.

Meanwhile the question of "coercion or no coercion" was becoming imminent. The Crimes Act would expire in August; was it to be re-enacted, or maintained in part, or repealed altogether? The Cabinet was at sixes and sevens. Spencer, the most responsible actor in the piece, demanded retention of some special provisions; and at last those who would have liked to see the Act disappear altogether agreed to a two-year term for these. But it was found that their agreement was conditional. A Cabinet committee had been considering Chamberlain's proposal for a Central Council or Board on an

[179]

elective basis, but strictly subordinate to Parliament. This would be above and in addition to county councils, and would take over education, poor law, and other local services, except the police. It was understood that Parnell would accept this, and even assent to some stiffening of the criminal law. There was ample cause to think that the Irish leader might be open to reason. In the early spring (February 25th), after a conversation with the Prime Minister, Rosebery had noted:

"Mrs. O'Shea, wife of the member, whose relations with Parnell were said to be guilty, whom Mr. G. had seen something of but had now handed over to R. Grosvenor, and who had great influence with Parnell, told Mr. G. that Parnell was a changed man since he had been in Kilmainham, and was now, so far as he dared, on the side of moderation."

Chamberlain's proposal was submitted to the Cabinet in due course. Gladstone's biographer states: "All the peers except Lord Granville were against it. All the commoners except Lord Harting-ton were for it. As the Cabinet broke up, the Prime Minister said to one colleague, 'Ah, they will rue this day.'" Perhaps he was right, but Rosebery's conclusion was less dramatic. After telling how Chamberlain said he could turn his scheme into a Bill in a week, with the requisite expert help, he noted:

"No one seemed to like it much, and eventually Spencer and Chamberlain pinned themselves down,—Spencer not to swallow Chamberlain's Bill, Chamberlain not to swallow Spencer's Crimes Bill."

This being so, it is not surprising to read, two days later:

"There was a severe crisis yesterday. After the Cabinet on Saturday, Mr. G. wrote to Spencer to say he must resign, as no agreement could be come to about Ireland (for he is with Chamberlain, but he will not desert Spencer). All yesterday he was packing up, and pacification was going on, at 7 an arrangement was made, Chamberlain rather giving in in order to preserve the P.M."

But Chamberlain was not the man to accept a rebuff, and it would be a mistake to regard Rosebery as definitely hostile to his plan. At a later Cabinet Rosebery wrote on a half-sheet:

"Would you take a stroll to-morrow morning, or dine quietly to-morrow evening. I am a Scottish home-ruler as well as Irish."

The reply came back:

"Your last remark is most to the point. I had a talk with Cooper the other night and found him in favour of a scheme for Scotland which is exactly my own for Ireland. I suspected that you might have been prompting him. I cannot walk to-morrow, first because I never take exercise, second because I have a Royal Commission. But I will dine with you quietly if I can leave the House."

About the same time he wrote:

Secret.   40 PRINCE'S GARDENS, S.W., *May 17th,* 1885.
"MY DEAR ROSEBERY,

"I send you the papers re Local Government in Ireland.

"I need not point out that such a scheme as I propose would be applicable to Scotland and if desired to Wales.

"The letter enclosed from Lord Spencer shows that his opposition has been intensified if not created in the last few weeks.

"I had every reason to hope that he would have assented to the principle.

"The present object of 'the Castle' appears to be to retain, as much as possible, its existing powers of interference and control.

"My object is to get rid of everything which is not absolutely essential to the security and integrity of the Empire.

"It is only in this way that we can relieve an over-burthened Parliament of work which prevents it from giving due attention to Imperial affairs.

"A small scheme will be a mere sop to Cerberus—stimulating but not satisfying the appetite of the creature.

"A large scheme would content all reasonable Irishmen, and the agitation for Separation would soon be confined to a mere Rump of politicians without influence or character.

"My proposal would protect the English taxpayer, now certainly menaced by the demand for bribes of money for all Irish purposes.

"Nothing will induce me to join another Government, or to meet a new Parliament except as the advocate of some such plan,—failing which I am convinced that a repeal of the Union is only a matter of time.

"Please return all the papers when read.
                              "Yours very truly,
                                        J. CHAMBERLAIN."

It must be observed that while Chamberlain did not contemplate the creation of an Irish Parliament, he meant his scheme to be large, and one to content all reasonable Irishmen.

At a meeting of some Cabinet colleagues Rosebery said that

Spencer must write down the irreducible minimum with which he could govern Ireland. By June there was still no complete agreement.

In a general discussion on Ireland (June 5th), Shaw Lefevre, Dilke, and Chamberlain were all against "Coercion," and Chamberlain wrote on a piece of paper, "Can you not give us a lift in this matter? I fancy you agree with us, though I have not liked to ask you your opinion." Rosebery replied that he was in favour of a strong local government measure, but could not throw over anything which Spencer declared to be the least possible special legislation with which Ireland could be governed. Three days later Spencer made his statement, warning his colleagues that a considerable part of Ireland would have to be proclaimed when the Act should come into force. There were loud protests, and after "a confused and simultaneous discussion" the question was adjourned. But this particular issue never fell to be decided by the Liberal Government. On the same evening it was defeated by twelve votes on a Conservative amendment to the Budget supported by the Irish members. An interval of some confusion succeeded, since Lord Salisbury was unwilling to take office without either a majority or assurances from the Opposition, while a dissolution was impossible until redistribution had taken effect. Ultimately Lord Salisbury formed his Government on June 24th, 1885.

It will probably be convenient to pursue here the story of Ireland, so far as Rosebery was concerned with it, until the General Election.

In a long talk with Gladstone on his way to Windsor (June 18th), Rosebery, on his way to Ascot, urged the Prime Minister to form a fresh government, either parting with Spencer and those who agreed with him, or with the Ministers opposed to what was falsely called coercion. By forming a fresh Cabinet on whichever principle he might adopt, he would have all the offices at his disposal, and get rid of the existing difficulty. "True," said the Prime Minister, and plunged in thought. But probably he considered that the simplicity of such a procedure was more apparent than real. Had he attempted to carry it out the arrangement of pieces for his game would doubtless have proved to be different from that which appeared on his chess-board the next year.

In a later conversation he said that Rosebery's speech at Edinburgh seemed to indicate greater contiguity to Chamberlain than to Hartington. This was at the meeting of the Midlothian Liberal Association on June 29th, where Rosebery invented a popular formula by stating his willingness to walk under an umbrella with both

Gladstone and Bright. He spoke of local government for the three countries as the main problems for the coming election. To give Ireland real control over her affairs was an experiment which might fail, but at any rate they would be treading in the path on which Liberal Governments had lately proceeded with so much consistency and some success.

"If we fail, we fail in a good cause, and at any rate we cannot be much worse off than we have been; but if we succeed, it will be the greatest feat that the Liberal party has ever accomplished."

By this time the Prime Minister had become convinced that the notion of a Central Board was done with. Rosebery, on his side, had a long talk with Hartington, proposing a meeting of the late Cabinet to try and arrange an agreement. And he attended the banquet given to Lord Spencer as a response to the discreditable attack made upon him by the Irish, and a section of the Conservatives, in the so-called Maamtrasna debate. In the course of that tragic farce John Morley had heard Parnell say, in great excitement, to one of his party: "This is the greatest thing we have accomplished." The Radical ex-Ministers did not attend the banquet, and Hartington told Rosebery that he did not believe Liberal unity to be possible, and that the only consideration that prevented him from throwing up the game was that the moderate Liberals would be left without a leader.

In the autumn, at the Paisley Liberal Club, Rosebery delivered a scathing attack on the Tory alliance with the Parnellite party, with scornful disbelief of the Government denials. The Conservative chiefs, he pointed out, held a meeting many weeks before they came into power, and decided that if they had a chance, they would do without exceptional legislation in Ireland. They had no evidence to go on, except what they saw in the newspapers. It was surprising, knowing their utterances, that they were able to meet in a room at all.

"I never heard of any violent assault, though we know that they were in a state of violent and very critical difference, which was only appeased by the sacrifice of Sir Stafford Northcote, who was offered up like the Greek virgin of antiquity, to assist the success of the enterprise. There were frequent outrages in Ireland. But this is the moment at which the Tories decided, with a light heart, not to renew any part of the Crimes Act. While this is the state of matters in Ireland, Lord Carnarvon is engaged in the peaceful duties of a sort of serenade,

If he cannot soothe Ireland by dulcet strains no one can. Day by day, year by year, in season and out of season, in bed and out of bed, Lord Carnarvon is engaged in pouring little drops of oil—infinitesimal drops of oil on the stormy waves of Irish wrath and Irish discontent. When the cruet-stand fails he falls back on the Consolidated Fund, and if the British taxpayer does not weary in well-doing neither will he. What is the result? The Irish vote is to be cast against the Liberal party."

With great insight he lamented the effect on many honest members of that party of creating the feeling that it was hopeless to do anything for Ireland. He was right: the majority of the Liberal-Unionist party thus came into being. He went on to deal with Parnell's extended demands:

"What is proposed is this, as I understand, that Ireland should be treated as a colony,[1] and that the Crown should be the only link between Ireland and the mother-country. . . . Is Ireland loyal to the British connection, or is she not? If I had the power, and if I were convinced that Ireland were loyal to the connection with this country, there would be no limits to the concessions that I would offer to Ireland. No demands formulated by Mr. Parnell should appal or deter me if I were sure of that one feature in the problem; no price should be too great to pay for a loyal and contented Ireland. But now, if we had to pay the price, what should we get? We can only surmise; but I am afraid the surmise of everyone in this hall would point in the same direction."

These sentiments are significant, falling from one who could be almost intoxicated by the romance of Australasia, but was chilled to the bone by Parnell's frigid aloofness. They typify the inner sentiments of not a few supporters of Gladstone's policy. A resuscitated O'Connell might have secured Home Rule in 1886.

Rosebery was at Acton Park for a great meeting at Wrexham (October 27th), and "walked with R. Grosvenor.[2] He discoursed on the future Prime Minister. Hartington, Chamberlain, Spencer, Granville, etc., etc., and at length said, but for my age, he should consider me the best! I burst out laughing in his face."

He was twice at Hawarden, and on the second occasion there was much talk of Ireland. "I told him plainly he could not decline to form a government. 'Am I,' he exclaimed, 'to remain at this work till I drop into my grave?' Meanwhile his family has settled the question for him."

[1] As we should now put it, a "dominion."
[2] Lord Richard Grosvenor, the Chief Liberal Whip.

The great leader came to Dalmeny in November, and made a series of election speeches which Rosebery was precluded from attending (November 14th). He sent his host "a letter which he had composed yesterday about Ireland, and why (rightly) he will not put a plan before the public." This letter is printed in full in the *Life of Gladstone*.[3] It sets out the reasons for not accepting Parnell's invitation to frame a plan for Irish self-government, the paramount reason being that its production would concentrate opposition to it and destroy all hope of its adoption.

The Conservative Government from its inception in June 1885 had been pursuing a policy of general conciliation in Ireland. It was the rule that the Lord-Lieutenant should not intervene in debate, but this was broken by Lord Carnarvon who, with Lord Salisbury's countenance, declared that he was prepared to rely on the ordinary law (July 6th). A considerable measure of Land Purchase (the Ashbourne Act) was passed (October 7th). Lord Salisbury's speech at Newport undoubtedly gave the impression of an open mind, with a bias in favour of some sort of central body subordinate to Parliament. On November 21st Parnell's manifesto ordained that the Irish vote in Great Britain should be assured to the Conservative party, and its effect was far-reaching. When the Election came, it was estimated that Parnell's action meant for the Liberal party a loss of forty to fifty votes on a division.[4] Perhaps the impression of Conservative pliability left on the minds of moderate Home Rulers like Rosebery has not been sufficiently recognised.

The headship of the Board of Works had not greatly appealed to Rosebery beforehand. It was not a Ministry of Fine Arts, and its relation to other public bodies, especially the Metropolitan Board of Works, was ill-defined. But during the four months of his tenure, he gave full attention to the work of his office. Herbert Gladstone, now a Junior Lord of the Treasury, represented the department in the House of Commons. It was a period of some movement in the reconstruction of public offices: Dover House, one of the isolated survivals of the days when Whitehall was a centre of fashion, was designated for the Scottish Office, whenever that could be created; and another, Gwydyr House, brought Rosebery into sharp collision with the Treasury on the question of some minor interior altera-

[3] Bk. ix, ch. i, p. 4.
[4] But of course it cannot be asserted that all the Liberals who would otherwise have been returned would have supported Home Rule in the form in which it was finally presented to the House of Commons.

tions. That department had sent him a blank refusal with the brutality of tone which it sometimes employed. He wrote fiercely to the Secretary:

"I do not of course question the right of the Treasury to make any order they think fit, but they must find another First Commissioner of Works to execute their behests."

Herbert Gladstone soothingly intervened with success, and he remained on friendly terms with the Treasury officials. There was a solemn expedition to Aldershot with the Prince and Princess of Wales and the Duke of Cambridge to choose a site for the huge statue of the Duke of Wellington, removed after much argument from its perch on the arch at Hyde Park Corner. Altogether his recollection of this brief interlude, and of his association with Bertram Mitford,[5] the brilliant Secretary of the Board, was one of enjoyment.

Amid the political distractions of this spring the hand of death made the first gap in the happily united family. Everard Primrose had obtained his desire, and had joined the river column whose march to rescue Khartoum, unavailing as it proved to be, wrote a chapter in the history of the British Empire, of which no tale of endurance or bravery in the Great War has obliterated the memory. At Abu Fatmeh on the Nile he was laid low by enteric fever, the scourge of nineteenth-century campaigns. On Easter Sunday (April 5th) Lord Wolseley telegraphed an almost desperate account, and on Wednesday Everard died. The *Ave atque vale* in Rosebery's journal is in a handwriting broken by emotion:

"And so I strike the word brother from my dictionary. How hard it is to have been so hopelessly separated from him in this long illness, to have so realised him sinking slowly, homelessly, in the hard, hot glare of the desert sun, caring so much for all the people, and all the things from which he was cut off. We know no details, nor shall we for three weeks at least; shall we indeed ever know what we want to know? There is so much that perhaps none can tell. What love, what faith, what sorrow moved him, or was he too feeble for thought? Farewell, Brother,—word and fact—on this side time. Would that I could fill up the irreparable blank by calling my suffering fellow-men by that name, in action as well as speech, or rather by action instead of by

[5] (1837-1916.) In the diplomatic service. Secretary H.M. Office of Works 1874-86, Cr. Lord Redesdale 1902.

speech. The brotherhood of man is so noble and difficult in action, so silly and easy in mere speech."

The next days were crammed with political business, but early in the following week he was able to spend a night at Battle Abbey, where both his sisters also were:

"A soft, melancholy, and yet pleasing evening,—so much to talk about, so much love and sympathy in the air."

Everard Primrose was indeed much missed. He was very popular in his battalion, and in the world of Pall Mall, but also in cultivated coteries like that of Holland House, where he was a favourite guest. There were messages from those whose opinions counted. Lord Hartington wrote from the War Office that since he had been there he realised how much was expected of Everard in his profession; and Lord Lansdowne from Canada:

"He had everything to make life worth living, and he could have taken a prominent place wherever he might have wished to take it."

One immediate consequence of the bereavement was the abandonment, for the moment, of a visit to Berlin, for which Rosebery had been starting on Easter Monday.

Foreign policy, and especially the relations of Britain with the Great Powers, continued to engage Rosebery's attention, notwithstanding his preoccupation with Scottish government and the uncertainties that harassed his own career. Most of his speeches showed this; and now that he was a responsible Minister men began to think of him as an active force in this region of affairs. One friendship certainly contributed towards this impression. At the beginning of 1882 he had asked one of the German Embassy to bring Count Herbert Bismarck to Lansdowne House. The acquaintance, based at first on Rosebery's intense admiration for the great Chancellor, in time developed into a close friendship. At the end of that season Count Bismarck was enthusiastic for further visits to England. When Rosebery joined the Cabinet his friend wrote warm congratulations, and may have equally congratulated himself on finding a safe channel for semi-official communications. His father had no liking for Mr. Gladstone or Lord Granville, and the relations between the two Foreign Offices were none too genial. German colonial expansion, especially in Africa, was destined to create friction with us for the next few years. In the spring of this year trouble flared up over the Cameroons.

"MY DEAR ROSEBERY,

"I was delighted to receive your kind letter and to hear from you again and I must write you these few lines to express you my very best thanks for it.

"I quite agree with what you say about the political situation and the English-German relations: the latter ought never to have come to the uneasiness in which to my great sorrow they are now, and I think it would not have been difficult to avoid every sort of ill-feeling on both sides, had your Colonial Office from the beginning shown a little good-will and treated us in the same friendly way, as we always treated England in all political questions up to the last summer.

"I, do not know who is the moving spirit of all the notes that are evidently elaborated in the Colonial Office and pour in here by dozens. If you will take the trouble to read Lord Granville's note of the 21st inst. about Kameroons you will see that it is not written in a very civil form, I might say next door to rudeness.

"Lord Granville used to be always so civil and polite, that I hardly can believe he has read that note before he signed it.

"My father is particularly vexed, that some of his most confidential conversations with Malet[6] have been published without asking him—a proceeding which never yet took place.

"I am more sorry than I can tell you that you have given up the idea to come to Berlin: we would receive you 'à bras ouverts.'

"Perhaps I can manage to come to England in March or April. I trust I should see you in that case: I deeply regretted that I could not avail myself in autumn of your kind invitation to Dalmeny because of your accident, but I hope it will not be long ere we meet again.

"Please remember me kindly to Lady Rosebery and believe me

"Ever yours,

H. BISMARCK."

At Count Herbert's anxious request for an interview Rosebery carried him off to Kensington Gardens, where, after running up against the French Ambassador, M. Waddington, to his amazement, they walked and talked for a couple of hours. Later in the day Rosebery saw Lord Granville, and Bismarck's conversation at the Foreign Office was "stormy and recriminatory." But on the following day peace reigned, and before Bismarck left for Berlin he and Rosebery had another talk of three hours.

March 9th.—"I took him to the station. He told me that he had shown my letter to his father, who had been greatly pleased by it,

---

[6] Sir Edward Malet, British Ambassador at Berlin.

particularly by a phrase about the Teutonic race. He pressed me very earnestly to come to Berlin at Easter."

As has been said, the visit had to be postponed. But meanwhile a complication developed of even more formidable possibilities than any that could arise on the Nile. Russia had annexed an area of Turcoman territory in Central Asia, and a Commission had been appointed to delimit its frontier and that of Afghanistan (March 31st). Suddenly the Russians attacked the Afghan troop at Penjdeh. But before this the situation was menacing, and at a Cabinet on the 23rd the Russian Minister was to be informed that an advance towards Herat would be *casus belli*. It was resolved to take power to call out the reserves. After this firm stand negotiations with Russia went on, but Rosebery's private trouble kept him in the background. It was difficult for the Government to agree on anything.

April 24th.—"Our draft despatch proposing arbitration to Russia came round. I assented, but said I wished to know what our next move was to be. Hartington and Harcourt objected. So we three, with W.E.G., Granville, Northbrook, and Kimberley met in Mr. G's room at 6.30. Long wrangle. Harcourt, because Kimberley interrupted him, said he had better leave the Government at once. He had never been so insulted, etc. On some other point he said he must resign. Granville protested against the perpetual threatening of resignation taking the place of argument."

The despatch went in a modified shape. Rosebery wrote a strong memorandum on our situation with Russia (April 26th), pointing out that the *Pall Mall Gazette*, the organ of W. T. Stead, which preached conciliation, was not told what the Russians really think, but what they wished to appear in print. While we had been honourably negotiating Russia had been grabbing, and we might find ourselves accepting a frontier condescendingly offered by those who had no right to be there at all. The effect of weakness on India and Afghanistan would be deplorable, and no better in the West.

"All Europe is laughing at us, our nose has been pulled all over the world. Throughout next week we shall be undergoing the process with France. Our Government smiles over it, and thinks it is not humiliating. But it *is* humiliating. And they further say that we are so strong we can afford it. But are we so strong? Nations with armies of two millions do not consider us strong."

But he was preaching to the partially converted. A few days later the Prime Minister asked for a credit of eleven millions. On May 2nd news came that Russia had accepted the principle of arbitration, and the chief danger was at an end.

Not the least important element in the Russian business was its repercussion on Egyptian policy. After the failure to rescue Gordon the Government left further advance to Khartoum to Lord Wolseley's discretion, but in no case could a push be made before autumn. There was some feeling that at any rate Khartoum should be retaken to satisfy national honour, the reconquest of the Soudan being left an open question; but meanwhile a force was to be dispatched to Suakin, to crush the elusive Osman Digna. This was done, but the situation on the Indian frontier, and our apparent friendlessness in Europe, seemed to render impossible the locking up of any large force in Africa.

A long speech at the meeting of the National Reform Union at Manchester (April 1st) was mainly devoted to the Soudan. At this distance of time it would be wearisome to reiterate details of a policy which at the time aroused deep passion on both sides. Rosebery offered a closely argued defence of Government action both on the Nile and on the Red Sea. To this audience he had to exculpate his colleagues from the charge of needless slaughter of unoffending Arabs quite as earnestly as to vindicate their care for the national honour. The Liberal party, then as afterwards, attracted men of opinions not less definitely opposed than those of Palmerston and Cobden when it came to fighting or a threat of fighting. Touching on the Central Asian difficulty, he doubted the applicability of arbitration to the particular case. As a matter of fact, he was never a fanatical devotee of arbitration in itself, believing, as many sensible people have, that it is a poor second-best to agreement reached through argument and conciliation. At the close of his speech he was able to slip in some phrases on Imperial federation, using as his text the offers of military aid received from Australia and Canada. He defended the advocates of federation from the charge of not having produced an actual plan. The idea must first soak into the minds of people here and in the Colonies:

"The maintenance of Empire,—though I believe that Empire means the girding of the world with a broad belt of British populations which shall ensure the maintenance of peace—demands self-sacrifice and exertion."

Lord Hartington had been in hot water with Windsor Castle over various actions or derelictions of the War Office. This seemed unfair, for he had never been in favour of retirement from the Soudan, and as they took Rosebery's favourite exercise of "walking the course," he announced his determination to resign. Rosebery pointed out that he could not choose a worse opportunity. Two Cabinets followed, and Rosebery sent Hartington a careful memorandum on the subject. In this he fully and ingeniously stated the arguments on both sides, reaching the conclusion, not that we should hurry away or abandon our plans, but that we should concentrate our forces and modify our plans.

"This would meet all your strongest arguments, satisfy our consciences, and maintain the honour of the country."

Next day the opposing views were compromised, partly because both Lord Wolseley and Sir Evelyn Baring had modified theirs so that the resignations of Hartington and Childers, Chancellor of the Exchequer since 1882, were averted. It is not uninteresting to speculate what would have been the effect on the party fortunes of a break-up on this question in 1885, in place of that which marked the following year. Possibly there would have been but little difference in the long run. The Queen was greatly disturbed by the decision of the Cabinet, as appears from her correspondence. Sir Henry Ponsonby wrote to Rosebery asking for his opinion, and the reply is given in full in the Queen's *Letters*.[7] He was morally in a strong position, for he had no responsibility over the earlier steps taken, and he made out a good case for the present policy as the choice of the least of great evils. Ministers went on threatening resignation on one subject or another. Defeat was in the air, and some thought it would be better to be beaten on a minor Government proposal rather than on the Budget, thus avoiding a public break-up over Ireland. Once, when the Chief Whip did not seem to be enjoined to exercise his duty with the utmost zeal, Rosebery felt bound to remind his colleagues that they appeared to be contemplating a course of conduct which on the Turf would bring them under the notice of the Jockey Club. But before the curtain fell, Rosebery was able to pay his visit to Berlin. It was no Government mission, but he had to be primed for the coming conversations, and his packet of information was not entirely made up of sugar-plums. A farewell talk with Gladstone, in a harassed mood over personal ques-

[7] Second Series, vol. iii, ch. vii.

tions and more resignations, only elicited the remark that in the Denmark affair he had discovered Bismarck to be a liar. The Foreign Office was more formal. Rosebery was given a Memorandum, largely in Lord Granville's own hand, covering the particular points at issue. It opened with the complaint that while Prince Bismarck professed that his relations with the British Government are now of a perfectly satisfactory character, the action of German representatives are almost uniformly unfavourable to us. In the matter of the Egyptian loan they had perpetually hampered agreement on the Convention. On the Suez Canal Convention the German delegate almost always supported the French view; on the Afghan Frontier Question, it was believed that Prince Bismarck had urged Russia to stand firm. The German attitude in Turkey had throughout been disadvantageous to us. He was also furnished with papers on the African colonies, touching some of the questions which Lord Salisbury was to handle six years later.

Travelling by Flushing, Breda, and Hanover, twenty-five hours brought him to Berlin (May 22nd) in time for supper with Herbert Bismarck at the Radziwill Palace, a splendid house, nearly all reception-rooms, so that Rosebery put up at a neighbouring hotel. After some sight-seeing, he was presented to the great Chancellor at luncheon, and had an hour and a half tête-à-tête in the garden afterwards. Dinner at six, and then "hot political talk" with Herbert Bismarck Unter Den Linden for a like period. It was more natural to pour out Foreign Office grievances to the son than to the illustrious father in a first conversation. The next morning Baron Bleichröder called at the hotel.

"As he was talking, the door opened, and George with an alarmed countenance ushered in Prince Bismarck, for all the world like Leporello and the Commendatore: he was very gracious and sat till 12.30."

In after years, Rosebery was fond of saying that the only two people who had thoroughly frightened him were Queen Victoria and Prince Bismarck. No doubt that was true, for his shyness, and he was very shy, was not of the sort that makes a bogey of an individual. It was Queen Victoria's birthday, and though he had been excused from dining with the Crown Prince and Princess at Potsdam, he was asked for late tea (which proved to be a substantial meal) and to stay the night. He revelled in the beauty of Frederick the Great's Neues Palais, was taken to Sans Souci for a drive in the country, and over the Palace—

"Great complaints of the Princess not being allowed to arrange and preserve, and the Palace offices turned into barracks,"

—and so back to Berlin.

Bismarck's talk about Sedan, etc., was incomparably interesting, on public affairs there was an atmosphere of good-will, and the marked personal liking which Rosebery awakened in Berlin was soon to stand him in good stead. He and Herbert Bismarck set off for The Hague (May 26th). He spent a day at that delightful spot, and reached home via Brussels, to unfold his budget of information at the Foreign Office. He felt some difficulty in doing this, writing:

"There is indeed something intensely repugnant to me in being a man's guest and writing down his careless utterances like an interviewer, and I only did it under the impression that no eye but my own would ever see the non-political part. I almost feel as if I were doing something ungentlemanlike even now, but I would rather risk this than the impression which seemed upon you in the House of Lords that I was trying to conceal or hold back anything. I cannot, however, forget that the Chancellor spoke to me in his own phrase 'as one gentleman to another,' and I feel certain that you will not allow any other human being to see my notes."

In less than a fortnight the Government fell, and after all on the Budget.

June 9th.—"Government were beaten last night by 12. 252 to 264. Amid cries of 'Foxy Jack' from Parnellites. Cabinet at noon. All in high spirits except Mr. G. who was depressed. He began by saying anxiously that he would like to have announced that the Cabinet had come to agreement about Ireland, but unless he is now told there is such agreement he must take the reverse for granted. No one speaking, he proceeded to the result of the division. There was no question as to reasoning with anybody. . . . I asked if we could not resign by telegraph,[8] which horrified Mr. G."

A moment of peace followed. At Mentmore he drove about, and sat out and meditated, thinking that he had never seen the place looking so beautiful. Then came Ascot, with a strong reminder of Berlin:

"The Prince of Wales at once took me aside and gave me a long confidential letter from the Crown Princess to read. She said that there had been a dead set made at her in Berlin at the time of her marriage,

[8] The Queen was at Balmoral.

[193]

and that it had never entered Fritz's head to think of doing without Prince Bismarck should he survive his father. It was so interesting and confidential that she ended by adjuring the Prince to burn it. The Prince in reply announces his intention of specially preserving it, and the fact of his having shown it to me."

The following week came the farewell to office at Windsor, and the return of seals:

"When I went for my audience the Queen was alone with the Prince of Wales, and only said 'I am very sorry to take them from you, Lord Rosebery.' "

Possibly all the holders were not so pleasantly dismissed.

Though out of office, Rosebery moved the second reading of the Secretary for Scotland Bill in the House of Lords (July 9th). It was almost the sole survivor from the late Government's programme, and could now be treated as sailing into harbour. The most striking new feature of the measure was the assignment to the new Minister of control over education, and this produced much discussion in its later stages. The outcome was not exactly as Rosebery desired, but he was able to note, as it were with a sigh of relief, "Secretary for Scotland Bill through at last." A month later he met the Duke of Richmond abroad and heard of his having accepted the office. Lord Salisbury had shown no enthusiasm for the measure, but desired to give the office a good start by appointing a Minister of the first class, recently Lord President of the Council, so Rosebery was well content.

The Duke of Argyll and Rosebery, two loyal Scotsmen, two sensitive spirits, and two eloquent voices, could seldom see eye to eye. Rosebery's Edinburgh speech of June 29th had somehow excited the elder man's wrath, with the result that—

"the Duke of Argyll made a long *omnium gatherum* speech [June 10th] in which he dealt so much with my Edinburgh speech that I had to get up after him, and having nothing to say spoke quite inconceivably ill. However I am sure it is profitable to make a bad speech, it teaches one so much."

For an unprepared rejoinder, the speech does not deserve so harsh a verdict, and at the time it was reckoned as a success. He was candid on the portentous indictment which the Duke had drawn against his former colleagues, and on the lack of fairness manifest in his attacks on individual Ministers. The phrasing was less distinguished than in some of Rosebery's considered efforts, but was by no means inadequate.

The Roseberys went to Homburg for a mild cure which, for him, included fairly regular lawn-tennis, until in the fierce heat it was impossible to hit a ball, and some elementary German lessons. Princess Bismarck was staying there, and Herbert Bismarck was often over, to retail the current political gossip. There were frequent visits to Frankfort and raids on the choice curiosity shops there.

The early autumn was spent at Mentmore with a come-and-go of friends (September 3rd).

"John Morley and I took a walk: he confesses to a certain weariness of politics. I triumph over him as always hating them."

Another guest was Prince George of Wales, who arrived from duty at Portsmouth. Rosebery went for a day or two to Hawarden.

"Discussion at breakfast on correspondence: Mr. G. said peers did not know what it was. He averaged 100 letters a day (received) during the Bulgarian agitation. I retorted that he encouraged it, that he never received a volume of bad poetry without writing a long letter in reply, and that he was an easy prey to crafty autograph hunters."

After his return to Mentmore Goschen was a guest, and Rosebery told him that he would make a fatal mistake if he did not join the next Gladstone Government, for it was unfair to leave Hartington to fight alone the battle of the moderate Liberals. Whatever split might take place later, Goschen would be stronger for having served under Mr. G. for that time. It was eleven years since he had been in office, and it was doubtful whether Hartington would join without him. Goschen seemed to be impressed by these arguments, but later influences prevailed against them.

The sorrow that had stricken the family in the spring found a certain counter-weight in the marriage of Lady Mary Primrose to Henry Hope of Luffness, which took place at Raby in October. She had been the popular daughter and deputy hostess of that house and of Battle Abbey since she grew up. It was an alliance with a Scottish neighbour which gave pleasure to the whole circle of her relations.

During this autumn of opposition in 1885 no hostile critic could accuse Rosebery of shirking his share of the party burden. Besides the great Paisley meeting,[9] during October, November, and December he addressed Liberal meetings at Reigate, Sheffield, Slaith-

[9] Pp. 183-184.

waite, Wrexham, Bo'ness, the Scottish Liberal Club, and Glasgow. Some of these speeches dealt with Ireland or with foreign affairs, as has been described, and in most of them the chord of Imperial responsibility and Liberal Imperialism was firmly touched. At Reigate (September 20th), something of a Tory stronghold, he had the unusual experience of speaking through a fire of interruptions. There was much banter of the Government; but in the more serious passages of the speech, he preached against the excessive hours of labour in some occupations which trades unions could not protect. Girl dressmakers were a notable instance of this; but the hours of railwaymen, stretching sometimes to as many as twenty, were a personal injustice and a public danger. He was not much enamoured of socialism, but if it, or any other "ism," would help, he would not disdain to borrow from that science. The system sapped the life of the men and, putting corporal punishment aside, no greater sufferings existed under negro slavery.

Just a month later (October 20th), at Sheffield, he developed this theme at greater length in that centre of trades-unionism. After his former speech, he said, he had been styled a coroneted socialist, but he had never seen a coronet in his life, and doubted whether the socialists would welcome him as a fellow-labourer, but he firmly believed that the hours of railway servants were a public scandal, and that there might be a case for legislation assuming that trades-union power was not effective. He compared the eight-hour day he had seen in force in Australia. In view of existing controversies, it is curious to note that, after expressing a favourable opinion on state-aided emigration as a relief to unemployment, he added that he did not propose to consider that night the solution offered by some artisan clubs in working-class centres, where the question was treated from the Malthusian point of view.

Soon afterwards he was at Slaithwaite, the West Riding town whose name remains the despair of those born south of the Trent. There he discussed, for the first time in public, the land, which Chamberlain's condemnation of landowners, migration to the towns, and the fall in the price of wheat had placed in the forefront of current questions. It is a fact worth noting, since it seems to exhibit one of the contradictions of his character, that Rosebery took little direct part in the ordinary interests of a landowner. He had early inherited a large estate in the Lothians—that Mecca of high farming; at his marriage he stepped into ownership of a wide pasture domain in the Vale of Aylesbury, to which he and his wife added materially. He rode around the countryside, and was always happy with a gun. But he never made any study of agricultural details, and had no enthusiasm for the various crops and live-stock of a farm, though he owned a first-class herd of Scotch-bred short-horns, and when fresh varieties of disease-resisting potatoes were being evolved, the Dalmeny home farm produced one of the most famous. He liked talking with most specialists and picking up their knowledge; but those "whose discourse is of the stock of bulls," as the Revised Version has it, did not appeal to him. Even with the thoroughbred stock to which he was so much attached, his verdicts always seemed to be rather those of the skilful outside critic than those of the born stableman.

Here in Yorkshire he spoke up for greater distribution of inter-ests in the land, for the abolition of the law of primogeniture and of all entails save marriage settlements; for the simplification of transfer, so that land should pass as easily as consols; and for a national register of titles. He favoured a great multiplication of allotments, but doubted whether the local authorities of those days would be active in supplying them. He thought embarrassed owners should sell, painful though it would be; but he frankly doubted the possibility of establishing a peasant proprietary, believing land to be a good supplement to wages, but a bad substitute for them. Their opponents spoke of the rights of property, but he wanted the rights of property to preserve and, if possible, to restore the commons and the common-rights of the people. Lord Spencer, a practical judge, thought this the best speech on the subject that he had seen. But advanced agricultural politics were not popular everywhere. Joseph Arch, the champion of agricultural labourers, had made trouble in the eastern counties, and an inquiry came from Sandringham whether Rosebery had subscribed to the agitator's election fund. He replied to Francis Knollys:

November 15*th*, 1885.

"It is quite true that I subscribed to Arch's expenses, under the following circumstances and for a single reason.

"In April or May last I was asked to give to a fund for enabling Mr. Arch to enter Parliament, and I sent £50.

"It was not then settled for what constituency he was to stand. I did not and do not know any one opinion of Mr. Arch's on any subject whatever. I strongly suspect that I should differ from him on many things, though I suppose he is called a Liberal. But I subscribed to assist him to enter Parliament on the sole and simple ground that it seemed to me a farce to give the agricultural labourer the franchise, and then not to admit their chief representative to Parliament. Without extraneous assistance he could not enter Parliament. Without him the new House of Commons as a representative assembly would be glaringly incomplete, and I subscribed. I hope he is not raging or doing anything appalling!

"Yours affectly.,
AR"

Both these Yorkshire utterances went well, though before he started he wrote: "I have been worrying myself all day with my speeches without the slightest effect."

The three Scottish speeches were made in the atmosphere of the General Election; two of them in its approaching shadow, the third after the results were declared. At Bo'ness, the port on the Firth of Forth, he opened a Liberal Club (October 31st), and after congratulations on the Scottish Secretaryship and Scottish education, he devoted most of his speech to a plea for Liberal unity. Mr. Gladstone's manifesto (addressed to the country through the electors of Midlothian) did not pretend to exhaust the future; but any Government, whatever its complexion, would be face to face with Parnell's ultimatum. It could not be ignored; if they meant to comply with it, it would be because its demands were just, not because it made them tremble. But they found Liberal members at each other's throats, because this or that man did not pledge himself to this or that particular reform.

"There are many causes with which I sympathise from the bottom of my heart, though I do not think this is the moment for saying so—many causes from which I may be supposed to hang back just now—causes to which I may be considered a laggard at this moment. I quite admit that I am a laggard on the present occasion as regards some of these, because I see a greater danger before me.

.   .   .   .   .

"What does it avail me to keep an outlying position if I find on my return that my camp is in the hands of the enemy? What is it to me to carry out any of those great reforms which Mr. Gladstone does not consider pressing—and his judgment is surely as good as yours or mine—if I find that in promoting these reforms I have left everything—Church and State, Parliament and Government—at the mercy of a dictator, who openly avows his hatred of each and all?"

This was not the language of a timorous Whig. And dread of an Irish dictatorship in Parliament was never more strongly expressed

[198]

than by his leader in the hundred times quoted speech of November
9th. The same evening at Grangemouth, the neighbouring rival
harbour to Bo'ness, Rosebery developed the same theme, begging
for a united Liberal party in Scotland.

On November 13th the Scottish Liberal Club presented Rosebery
with an address. The Gladstones were at Dalmeny, and electioneer-
ing had begun, but such an occasion was not an infringement of the
rule banishing Peers from the scene. Rosebery kept away from the
regular meetings. It was a dull November day:

"Low about my speech. But took a long walk after luncheon and
it came all right. The banquet to me came off this evening. It was very
splendid. The electric light was used in the Music Hall for the first
time."

He received many congratulations on this speech of forty-five
minutes, but as a matter of fact it does not read as vividly or
freshly as many others. No doubt he was hampered not so much by
Mr. Gladstone's presence as by the knowledge that in a sense he was
a spectator, not a combatant in the ranks.

The Midlothian poll, with its vast majority for Mr. Gladstone,
compared with the modest 211 of 1880, was disclosed on November 27th.

"We drove into Edinburgh to the Rosebery Club meeting, which
Mr. Gladstone addressed, and I afterwards for a moment. Then to
the Corn Exchange, where I in the Chair. Speech for thirty minutes.
Mr. G. for forty minutes. Somehow I felt the whole thing melancholy. We took him to the station. I was a good deal mobbed coming
out and going home.
"To-day struck me as very sad, I know not why. Mr. G. was older,
feebler, less victorious by much than in 1880 if victorious at all, and
somehow one felt as if one were witnessing the close of that long and
brilliant career. Several of our party wept at the Rosebery Club
Meeting."

Many borough elections in England had gone against the Liberals, so that Rosebery could utter no note of triumph except for
the Scottish Secretaryship and for the "great national thanksgiving
for the health and strength and the personal triumph of our great
Chief."

Glasgow had returned her full complement of seven, all Liberals,
and Rosebery went to a great meeting there (December 4th), with
Campbell-Bannerman and other Scottish members. In the last

Parliament there had been fourteen Liberals from Ireland, to-day there was not one. It is not surprising that Rosebery denounced the ingratitude thereby shown to Gladstone. "No man who ever lived had done one-twentieth of what he had done to right the wrongs of Ireland. The new Parliament was a rickety infant that could not live long, and Scottish Liberals must make ready for an early dissolution."

In the midst of this series of speeches, Rosebery, always critical of himself, was anxious to know whether practice was bringing about its due result. George W. Smalley, an American publicist of high standing, spent a great deal of time in Europe, and was thoroughly conversant with politics and politicians both in England and abroad. Rosebery and he corresponded frequently, and on this occasion he was asked for his judgment on the recent efforts.

November 9th, 1885.

"A very great improvement. The change was marked after your return from Australia. You must be aware what a different impression you have since made on the public. Before that, people thought your speeches clever, but the tone of them hardly that of a man who had flung himself into public life body and soul with serious purposes and a settled resolve. You did not always seem quite sure of yourself. A speech in those circumstances may be brilliant but scarcely impressive. I do not think you then had with the public the weight to which your abilities and sincerity entitled you. The place you have since taken is very different—I am speaking of the English public, not Scotch—and I should say the English are now coming round to the Scotch view, and coming rapidly. The recent series of speeches in England I think far stronger than any you have before made, and the effect on the public mind is in proportion to the thoughtfulness, the definiteness of aim, and the power of statement which characterise them. But I still say you have never done, on a given occasion, quite so well as you might, simply because of a want of an absolute completeness of preparation. You trust, as you have a right to, to your gift of thinking on the legs, but except in debate I consider that improvisation ought to be mainly confined to diction. That the substance and order of a speech ought to be fully thought out in advance and the different parts *fused* into a whole. A man in your position, with your career before him cannot take too much pains. You have the natural gifts; whether you are to be a speaker of the highest order depends wholly on the amount of trouble you are willing to take. There are parts of the Bo'ness speech which, from another point of view, are better than anything before. There is passion in it, in the oratorical sense, and such an expression of strong feeling as you seldom allow yourself. Don't be afraid of letting yourself go. There was a passage in the Dumfries (Burns) speech admirable in a different way, because equally suffused with genuine sentiment picturesque and imaginative also. Now the public judges a man by his ordinary performance, by his average, and rightly, but when it is a question of what a speaker *can* do, the test is to be found in the best he has hitherto done. Those are the passages which tell you what is to be hoped for from him, and what flights he may be expected to take hereafter. You keep Bright in mind, and you know his method, and there is none better. You must have observed how his orations flow from end to end with an unbroken current. No man ever prepared more carefully, and no man ever seemed to speak so easily and simply."

This judgment by a skilled observer from the land of orators, a man of wide general experience, may be taken as a sound appreciation of Rosebery's speeches throughout the ten years during which he considered himself tied to political life.

Soon after the Glasgow expedition a summons to Hawarden arrived. Lord Spencer came at the same time. Rosebery urged his host to call a party meeting: "This he always hates." The leader's view was simple. He would support the Tories if they could come to agreement with Parnell. Otherwise they should be opposed at once; this by a vote of want of confidence without reference to Ireland; if Ireland must be brought in, it must be not by Parnell, but by the Liberal leaders. At present he leaned to proceeding by resolution. The other subject was destined to affect Rosebery personally:

"I had a talk with Mr. G. about Granville, as to whom he opened out to me. He fears G. wishes to return to the Foreign Office. Mr. G. appears to know that this is inexpedient."

Two days later (December 9th) he was warned by telegram that an important letter was coming. It proved to contain the wish that Rosebery should see Labouchere, enclosing a letter from him, with extracts from a letter from a leading Irish Member of Parliament. Rosebery felt he could not but comply, but said he did not know how far Labouchere was to be trusted and that Parnell at any rate was not to be trusted.

Henry Labouchere was a cadet of a distinguished family of Huguenot origin. His uncle, Lord Taunton, had left him (unwillingly, it was said) a considerable fortune, to which he had been able to add largely by judicious dealings on the stock exchange. Diplomacy, in which he had started, had proved to be too cramping for his careless independence, and he had taken to politics, sitting for Northampton as an extreme Radical. With Dilke, and other members of a small group, he was one of the evangelists of republicanism on the French model. This rather crude conception of a bourgeois republic is as extinct here to-day as Jacobitism; but fifty years ago it represented a distinct type of public opinion, before Socialism had obtained a footing in England. Labouchere was also the proprietor of the weekly journal *Truth*, which, while freely purveying social gossip, also did good service by exposing fraudulent money-lenders and other malefactors. Mr. Gladstone neglected no genuine current of opinion, however divergent from his own, and thought that Labouchere, who was in close touch with the Irish members, might be serviceable. From Queen Victoria's letters it can be seen that, in the view of Windsor Castle, he was nothing but a desperate revolutionary. Labouchere was genuinely cynical; but in public life he credited everybody, including himself, with the basest motives to a degree that became almost wearisome. He was always the centre of a circle in the House of Commons smoking-room. One day, after a speech of Mr. W. H. Smith's, he said thoughtfully: "It is sad to see how that good old man has learnt to lie; he will soon be running our Old Man hard." Everybody laughed, but neither the character of Mr. Gladstone nor that of the Conservative leader suffered materially. As a matter of fact, Labouchere was a kind and generous man, free with his money in cases that appealed to him. Where he did good by stealth he did not blush to find it fame, because he never blushed; but he was assiduous in showing that it was not really good at all, but something quite different. Mr. Joseph Chamberlain told me that once when Labouchere had been caught out befriending some unlucky person, at no little trouble and cost, he set himself to explain that he had thus purchased a useful tool who could be used without shame or scruple. If it could not be said that he touched nothing that he did not adorn, he certainly made everything seem amusing. Rosebery had long known Labouchere as the agreeable playmate of an idle hour; so long ago as 1871, he, Francis Knollys, and another had joined Labouchere in giving dinner at the Star and Garter to the Royalty actresses, Miss Hodson and three others. Miss Hodson, in the course of her brilliant stage career, had already become Mrs. Labouchere.

Now there was sterner business on hand. Labouchere had told Herbert Gladstone that if anything was to be done, a definite programme must be put before Parnell, "Otherwise, he will maunder about Grattan's Parliament, of which he knows nothing." There was some hurry, because the Tories would make every effort to capture Parnell, whose tendency would be to shilly-shally, and for the time to agree to nothing. Labouchere's Irish correspondent, who had not seen Parnell for over a fortnight, was extremely candid about his chief's limitations and peculiarities. He concluded:

"In my deliberate opinion Mr. Gladstone is the only man who can settle the Irish question. He is the only man with hand and heart for the task; the only man who can reduce to decency the contemptible wretches who so largely compose the Liberal party. I thank God that so many of the howlers and gloaters over our sufferings have met their fate."

But the Liberal leader was wary. He drew up a note pointing out that the Tories and Nationalists had been in alliance for years, that the Government of the day should bring in a measure at once, which would receive fair play from the Liberals. Liberals might put out an outline of essentials, but a plan could only be carried by a Government. It will be seen that the prospect of a Liberal Government, though not explicitly indicated, was not ruled out, and Rosebery was told that he might go a little farther with Labouchere. When they met on December 12th, Rosebery repeated his extreme aversion from negotiation with Parnell at this stage. But the talk was not purely political. Labouchere was intimate with Randolph Churchill, and was full of gossip about him, and also about Dilke, who had become involved in unhappy scandal earlier in the year. Rosebery was in Scotland till almost the end of the year. While there, he received half a dozen letters from Labouchere, some of several pages, with inimitable stories of the negotiations. How Parnell had disappeared "with an Egeria of some kind," and his colleagues were hunting for him; how some days later they believed that he had "retired to warm salt water baths with a new Egeria, they did not exactly know where"; how Lord Carnarvon had told Justin MacCarthy that he was in favour of a large measure of Home Rule but the party would not hear of it, so would the Irish accept an inquiry? how this was considered simply a trick to remain in for six months, and how Randolph Churchill called Carnarvon a damned traitor; how the Hawarden proposals remained full of ambiguities; how "Joe" was furious over the newspaper revelations which afterwards became known as the Hawarden Kite, and at the Irish preferring "Short" Gladstone to "Codlin" Chamberlain; how the Irish party wanted a Royal Viceroy, to be advised, Labouchere

[203]

hoped, by a Privy Council containing a number of Liberals and some Irish; how a leading Irish member, quite seriously and with tears in his eyes, had told of the beautiful loyalty of his supporters, instancing one who, on his deathbed, had adjured his son to impersonate him at the coming election, and how the son had shown equal loyalty by doing it; and finally how utterly unlike English Liberals these Irish were.

Rosebery was in London at the end of the year, seeing Hartington, who said he would not join Mr. Gladstone's Government, and asked Rosebery to come to a meeting, which he declined to do.

"Then Harcourt, furious with Mr. Gladstone, talking of 'lying' etc., full of pique: he says Mr. Gladstone's experiment must now be tried, though it is insane folly. I said to him that it would be awkward for him to sit by Mr. Gladstone and defend it. 'Oh, but I should not go back to the Home Office,' which remark, if it means anything, must mean that he would also leave the House of Commons, but he would not get the Woolsack for all that.

"Washed all this sort of thing out of my mouth by going to the Lyceum and seeing *Faust*. Irving at his best. Went and saw him."

At the same time he received from Lord Spencer the following avowal:

ALTHORP, NORTHAMPTON, *December 30th,* 1885.

"MY DEAR R.,

"You hate compliments of the season, but as I cannot omit them for Lady R.'s sake, I at once get over this stumbling-block, and wish her and you a very happy new year, well out of all disagreeable Home Rule in public and private.

"I have been meditating a letter for some days, as I feel that you and I will be looked upon by ex-colleagues as co-conspirators in aiding and abetting the G.O.M. in his wickedness.

"Since we parted, as you may suppose, I have been in the thick of the controversy.

"I never felt so disgusted in my life as I was by the *Standard* and *Pall Mall*, not to say Leeds revelations.

"The letter to the travelling Artist was bad enough, but my hair well-nigh bleached when I read the disclosures. I have the shrewdest suspicion that it came from Herbert.

"I doubt whether Mr. G. even winked at what was done, but he was too loyal as a parent to raise his hand against the indiscretion of the infant H——s.

"Of course some will say it did good by showing what the feeling in England really was. But to my mind it did much more harm. It upset the whole of the sensitive Irish, such as Police and R.M.s. It threw distrust among colleagues, raised a storm in the London Press urged on by the monied men who I fear have 100 millions lent on land in Ireland. All this turned back the commencement of concession among Irish Tories who had begun to say 'This tension is intolerable, terms must be made, the sooner the better.'

"But to what is more serious. As far as I can judge, you and I, and I know not whether you still hold the views you did at Hawarden,— you might well have gone back from them—will stand alone among Mr. G.'s colleagues. Possibly Lord G. will follow Mr. G. but I know of no one else inclined to do so. We three peers and John Morley could not form a Gladstone Government, and at present I see no prospect of Mr. G. getting a following enough to justify his going on.

"The question then is, ought he to join the Home Rulers with his voice and support them, or ought he and those who may agree with him to keep silence, lest Ireland should become ungovernable. I cannot yet answer this to my satisfaction.

"I fancy that Mr. G. would like to move an amendment on the Address clear of the Irish question, if it is shown that government stand unsupported by the Irish.

"I look on that as impossible without facing the next question, can he with his views form a government?

"There is a great deal against having a meeting of the ex-Cabinet, but it is essential that Mr. G. should see and talk to leading members of that body. I hope he will move towards London next week. This is essential before he settles anything. After all the Tories may take the thing up, what a blessing if they could!! I still hold to the necessity of guarantees, but I think, they could be got. Underlying all this how odious (and maybe wicked) it is to think that Parnell and his crew are to govern Ireland. I have personal difficulties about contact with them, but I need not say anything about these at this stage. I expect that unless the Tories act, all will end in smoke.

"Yours sincerely,

SPENCER."

At the dawn of the new year, Rosebery, through no conscious effort beyond increased activity in speech-making, and by the aid of no dramatic incident, had become in a real sense a central figure in the Liberal party. Mr. Gladstone's authority was supreme and unquestioned except so far as his reiterated intention of resigning had impaired it: it was now assumed that he would remain until the Irish Question was out of the way. But he was almost twenty years senior to most of his colleagues, and far ahead of all in official experience and prestige. So he could not be the confidant of their hopes and fears. Rosebery's letter bag, since his return from his tour, had been filled to bursting with such confidences. With the Gladstone family he held a special place. Not only Gladstone himself, but Mrs. Gladstone and Mary Gladstone, whose happy marriage was celebrated about this time, were continually writing to him. And he was in regular communication with Granville, Hartington, Harcourt, Goschen, John Morley, Dilke, Chamberlain—men at the opposite poles of opinion, but all prepared to put trust in his judgment and his sympathy. And it was not only that he was charming and receptive. He did in reality occupy a central position, as Gladstone himself did in a different way, between Whigs and Radicals, and at this time he attracted both equally. Perhaps he was touching now the true zenith of his political influence. There was as yet nothing to awaken jealousy or hostility in the minds of any section of the party.

The understanding between Conservatives and Irish had not survived the election at the close of 1885, with its figures of 251 of the former and 85 of the latter against 333 Liberals of all shades. There were no common convictions or common realities to prolong this unnatural connection. The day before Parliament met, Rosebery

"called on Mr. Gladstone. He subdued but manly and firm in tone. . . .

"At 11 p.m. the late Cabinet peers met Harrington and Harcourt in Mr. G.'s room. They had been talking over the Queen's Speech with Mr. G. and were in a fine taking as to what Mr. G. would do. It reminded me of the Duke of Grafton's Cabinet talking over the possible intentions of Lord Chatham."

The next morning the late Cabinet met, when, after much fencing over Ireland, it became evident that Hartington had definitely broken away from any policy of Irish self-government, and so from Gladstone's leadership. Rosebery went down to Mentmore, where Sir Henry Ponsonby was one of a small party.

"Sir Henry Ponsonby after dinner said 'I have a message for you from the Queen which I had better give you at once. She thinks you too much under the influence of Herbert Bismarck, who is not of the same ideas as his father. I do not know what she means.' 'Nor do I. Herbert and I hardly correspond about politics, and I write nothing to him which might not be read at Charing Cross. He on his side writes much the same to me.' On reflection I suggested that he must have been making contemptuous remarks about the Battenberg dynasty in Bulgaria and elsewhere, which must have reached H.M.'s ears. . . . The Queen anxious to send for Hartington, on the ground that W.E.G.

in his letters on resignation had intimated his intention to retire. I said I thought that it would be a great calamity and blunder, and would defeat H.M.'s object, as I explained. He asked me if he might tell her so, and I agreed. The Queen very anxious about Granville. I said so was I, but could not remonstrate as I should be countered with the demand—'Whom would you suggest instead?' which I could not answer. 'But the Queen would like Salisbury to be Foreign Minister under Hartington, but failing that has fixed upon you.' I told H. P. that was impossible. Much talk with him. He acknowledged that *Truth* had wonderful information."

On January 26th, Rosebery attended the fateful debate when the Government were beaten by 329 to 350 on Jesse Collings's "Three acres and a cow" amendment. "There was a smart schism on our Bench." Two days later he went with Lord Spencer

"to see Mr. G. Found him with Wolverton discussing Granville's return to the F.O. Wolverton gave message from Harcourt to say he would not remain in the House of Commons. 'But I am determined he shall,' said Mr. G. Much talk about Lord Granville. I put difficulty of replacing him as he had been Foreign Minister for thirty-three years, more or less, and had absorbed all the experience of the party. Mr. G. said Kimberley would do."

The next morning he saw Mr. Gladstone for a moment, reading *The Court of Louis XIV*, which he said rested him. He was tired out with writing an answer to the Queen's possible objections. She had not sent for him, though Salisbury had returned from Osborne three hours before.

After a few quiet days at Mentmore, winding up the shooting season, Rosebery returned to London. He was summoned to Carlton House Terrace by Mr. Gladstone (February 2nd).

"When he came into his little room he at once offered me the Foreign Office. He said he was bound further to state that he saw no alternative for me but the Scottish Office. This he repeated. He further said that the office had the advantage or disadvantage of bringing the holder into the most constant relations with him. I said it was too big a thing for me, that at any rate I must have an hour or two to consider. He admitted that that was fair, but asked me to be as quick as possible. He promised Granville's hearty co-operation.

"At 3 I sent an acceptance. It is an awful scrape.

"At 11 p.m. I was sent for by the Prince of Wales, who knew of my appointment. At 11.55 to Epsom."

The supersession of Lord Granville was a painful matter for all concerned, not least for Rosebery himself, from his real affection and respect for the late Foreign Secretary. In the practical conduct of public life statesmen have to be treated as being what common opinion judges them to be. By this often unfair test Lord Granville had not of late been a successful Foreign Secretary. If blame had to be apportioned, the Government as a whole, not he as Minister, should have been held responsible for the failures in Egypt, and for difficulties due to the German zest for colonial expansion. But it was felt that in a degree he had lost his grip of critical affairs. Though six years junior to Gladstone, he was in some respects an older man, and he was troubled by frequent attacks of gout. He was besides somewhat harassed in his private affairs, as, in the general depression of business, the great ironworks in Shropshire, which were his family inheritance, had of late suffered severely. Thus not only Queen Victoria, but all his senior colleagues believed that foreign affairs ought to pass into younger and stronger hands. Mr. Gladstone's rule, as we have seen, favoured promotion by seniority; but though circumstances had prevented Rosebery from pausing for the proper interval on each landing of the ministerial staircase, yet a man in his fortieth year, by no means unbroken to official work, could not be regarded as a raw novice. He wrote at once to Lord Granville:

LANSDOWNE HOUSE, *February 3rd*, 1886.
"MY DEAR LORD GRANVILLE,[10]

"I must intrude on you with one line. You will know otherwise that I have been nominated to the Foreign Office, but you can only know from myself with what real misgiving and reluctance I go there.

"No one is so convinced as I am of my unfitness for that post, and no one is better aware that all the knowledge and experience of foreign administration is concentrated in yourself. Your advice and assistance are therefore as indispensable to the Government in foreign affairs as your leadership of the House of Lords is to the smoothing of its path in Parliament. Indeed, had not Mr. Gladstone promised me your generous co-operation, it would have been hardly possible for me even to make the attempt. I hope I am not presumptuous, therefore, in venturing to reckon on your kindness, and your guidance in the overwhelming task which I have undertaken.

"Believe me,
Yours sincerely,
R."

[10] Also in *Life of Lord Granville*, vol. ii, p. 483.

In his conversations in later years Rosebery never would admit that Lord Granville in his prime had been anything but a highly competent Foreign Secretary.

His new post brought Rosebery into more intimate connection with the Court, since, as appears from almost every page of Queen Victoria's correspondence, and from the memoirs of the statesmen who served her, she regarded the Foreign Office, like the War Office, as being the special domain of the Crown. So far back as 1870 Rosebery had been invited to Balmoral, and had there several times dined with the Queen, but he probably was bidden rather as a Scottish magnate, the son of one of her bridesmaids, than as a rising politician. But as the years passed, the shrewd eye of the Sovereign did not fail to watch his progress in public life. And it has been noted[11] that he was asked for his opinion about the Soudan soon after his admission to the Cabinet in 1885, though he had no departmental knowledge of the circumstances. The Queen, as has been seen, now favoured his promotion to the Foreign Office as a second choice. For some obscure reason, she seems throughout to have entertained a strong official prejudice against Lord Kimberley, than whom there was no more capable administrator and no more loyal and generous-minded man. Sir Henry Ponsonby was instructed to tell Mr. Gladstone that the Queen would never agree to Lord Kimberley's appointment to the Foreign Office. The Prince of Wales had written to the Queen: "If Lord Kimberley is an impossibility, how would Lord Rosebery do? I cannot help thinking he would be a good appointment." Rosebery, therefore, entered on his new duties with no other disadvantage than the Queen's general disapproval of a Government led by Mr. Gladstone.

Rosebery's audience at the opening Privy Council at Osborne is fully recorded in the Queen's Journal, including his remark that the Foreign Office was "too much."[12] His own brief account runs:

"H.M. very gracious—very anxious about Greece. Radowitz not to be trusted. Herbert Bismarck very hostile to Battenberg of Bulgaria, who is very anti-Russian. General tendency of Europe peaceful, I said, except in the wretched Balkan kingdoms. H.M.'s face fell. I explained I meant Servia and Greece. Ireland quite secondary to foreign politics."

The Queen's face might well fall if she thought that Prince Alexander and his Bulgaria were reckoned among the "wretched king-

[11] See page 191.
[12] *Letters of Queen Victoria*, 3rd Series, vol. i, p. 47.

doms," and she noted in her Journal that Rosebery "made one very strange and naïve observation, viz. that he hoped Sandro was not Russian!!"

Lord Salisbury's report of Rosebery's official visit to him is also given at length in the Queen's Letters.[13]

"Lord Rosebery," he said, "expressed several times his intention of maintaining the continuity of English politics in foreign affairs."

This was the case, but it is necessary to note the conditions under which the doctrine of "continuity" appealed to him. Earlier in the year (January 17th), Count Hatzfeldt had stayed at Mentmore, and had complained that the foreign policy of one British Ministry was overturned by the other. Rosebery replied that this was true, but a successful foreign policy would not be. The condition of continuity was success. Rosebery was able to reassure Lord Salisbury in this instance, because he and Gladstone both felt that their predecessor's policy had been prudent, both in south-east Europe and in Egypt.

Arising out of the position of Bulgaria, squeezed between Russia and Turkey, not a buffer state but a territory which each desired to dominate, Greece had threatened war on Turkey, her secular enemy. This could not be permitted, for none could tell how far such a blaze might spread, and having secured the assent of Prince Bismarck, Lord Salisbury had informed the Greek Government that a naval attack on Turkey was prohibited. This was the sound policy, but Greece could not entirely apprehend the situation. For fifty years some of her Western friends had been asking, in the Byronic vein, where had the Pyrrhic phalanx gone? and now not only was that formation not permitted, but there must be no attempt at another Salamis, and even Navarino seemed to be forgotten. Besides all this, the King of Greece was brother of the beloved Princess of Wales, and this must excite English sympathy, while Rosebery himself had been Chairman of the Greek Committee in London. But it was thought wise in Downing Street to encourage Prince Alexander to come to terms with Turkey, and it must prepossess Turkey in his favour if Greece were restrained by the action of the Powers. So, at Rosebery's first official interview with M. Gennadius[14] (February 8th), he explained that there would be no change in policy or in the instructions to our representatives. He had seen the French Ambassador on the same day, and reported that it struck him, more

[13] *Loc. cit.*, p. 49.
[14] The Greek Minister.

from manner than anything else, that M. Waddington was more disposed than before to join the Government in action against Greece. He could not help thinking that the French Government had reckoned completely on a change of attitude towards Greece by Mr. Gladstone's Ministry, and now finding its mistake was anxious not to be left out in the cold.

He was not unduly elated by the pomp of his first reception of the diplomatic body. After sending off the consequent telegrams, he noted "What a fly on a cartwheel."

Greece continued to give anxiety. Rosebery wrote privately to our Ambassador at Berlin:

Private.　　　　　　　Foreign Office, *February 24th*, 1886.
"My dear Malet,

"Many thanks for your letters. It almost looks as if Servia and Bulgaria would now make peace in a few days, which I hope will have its effect on Greece.

"It would be an excellent thing if we could get Greece to give way without the portentous machinery of a blockade. But I regard the maintenance of the present fleet and every part of it at Suda Bay as a matter of vital necessity until the question be settled.

"John Hay[15] has replied to our enquiry as to the facility of a blockade by a raw head and bloody bones telegram saying that it would involve the destruction of batteries, the occupation of islands, and the sinking of ships: sketching operations compared to which Navarino would be amicable and Alexandria a flea-bite. None of us who are represented in the allied fleet would contemplate such measures; and we have now telegraphed out further questions.

"Bismarck must not think me slack in this matter. I have indeed obtained the consent of the Cabinet to the blockade, but I am anxious only to try it as a final resort. And I should like to await the effect of the probable Servo-Bulgarian arrangement, and the conclusion of the Turco-Bulgarian business, before taking this ponderous step, which is always liable to petty and indeed ridiculous obstacles while it will not be particularly popular anywhere. I believe the Greeks are only too anxious for an excuse to give in and that the population is quieting down; while our demonstration might resuscitate the excitement. This is Rumbold's[16] opinion.

"But do not mistake me. I am as determined as ever to proceed with the blockade should the Greeks not give way. Meanwhile, I repeat, it is

[15] Admiral Lord John Hay, commanding the Mediterranean Fleet.
[16] Sir Horace Rumbold, 8th Baronet, Envoy-Extraordinary and Minister Plenipotentiary to the King of Greece 1884-8.

vital that all the ships should remain where they are, or the Greeks will see disagreement and consequently hope.

"Yours sincerely,

AR"

Rosebery was at Windsor with the Greek Minister (March 1st):

"And the Queen said: 'Did you remark when I asked how the King and Queen were, he replied that they were well in health, with great emphasis. I did not know what he might not be going to say, so I thought I had better put an end to the interview.' She was quite right. Gennadius, who was evidently full of speeches, was a little disappointed, but confided to me on the way back that his people were caving in."

The Queen was to open the Indian and Colonial Exhibition, and Rosebery, always impressed by the value of symbols, wrote to Sir Henry Ponsonby:

FOREIGN OFFICE, *April* 13th, 1886.

"MY DEAR PONSONBY,

"Many thanks for your note, which is, I suppose, conclusive. But it is a thousand pities. The symbol that unites this vast empire is a crown and not a bonnet. These colonists and Hindoos who have come from every part of the world to see their Sovereign open this exhibition regard her as their Sovereign. They will never have another opportunity as long as they live of saying 'We saw our Queen come as Queen and Empress to perform her part as head of this Empire, wearing the Sign which unites us all; by which she is Queen of New South Wales and the Cape of Good Hope, Queen of Newfoundland, Queen of New Zealand, Empress of India, etc., etc.' To have seen their crowned Queen will impress their imagination; and they will go to their various homes feeling that they realise the monarchy under which they live as an institution and not a person. To see the Queen in morning dress will gratify their personal loyalty, and interest them profoundly, but it will not impress them with the fact that they have seen the ancient and permanent symbol as distinguished from the personality of the monarch.

"You must remember that to nine-tenths of these colonists a Queen without a crown is hardly a Queen at all, and that, if the Queen on this historical occasion appears before them as the lady president of a republic might, you lose the opportunity of a political inspiration and a cohesive memory. Alas—however—we cannot struggle with the inevitable.

"Yours,

AR"

[212]

It was not until late in April that France joined the other Powers in presenting an ultimatum to Greece, and in May a notice of blockade by the combined squadrons was presented, it being necessary to restrain the Greek fleet from any adventure against Turkey. In the House of Lords Rosebery laid papers covering the action of the Government since it took office, with copies of the collective notes addressed to Greece and the replies made to these and to the notice of blockade. Greece, he stated, had not placed its army on a peace footing, and refused to disarm. The result was that the land forces of the two countries remained drawn up face to face. Turkey had ceded Thessaly to Greece five years before, and was not now prepared for another cession. The Turks had to keep an army of 300,000 men in Europe, which meant employment of the Reserve, with such loss of agricultural labour as to cause famine in some districts. It was important to uphold the European Concert, and this had been achieved, even though France had taken some separate action. Lord Salisbury, while reserving a final judgment, said that the policy which the country was pursuing was that of all parties in the State.

It was not only the French who had anticipated that the new Government in Downing Street would initiate a new policy in southeastern Europe, and the supposition added not a little to Rosebery's difficulties. The German Ambassador believed that both Greeks and Servians were counting on such a change, in spite of Gladstone's and Rosebery's public declarations. The Queen's special interest in Prince Alexander made her the central figure in this particular tableau. The Prince was brother of Prince Louis, who had started the career of brilliant service in the British Navy which he concluded as an admirably efficient First Sea Lord. He was brother, too, of Prince Henry, who filled with tact and discretion the difficult position of being resident at Windsor as the Queen's son-in-law. The Sovereign was thus in specially frequent communication with the Foreign Office at this moment of many complications between Turkey and Greece, Russia and Bulgaria, Austria and Servia. Rosebery wrote gratefully:

February 14*th*—"Your Majesty's great experience and Lord Rosebery's absolute inexperience in foreign affairs do indeed represent the opposite extremes, and he can only congratulate himself and the country that the one is used to correct the other. With such guidance and the absolute devotion to the service of Your Majesty and the country which is the only quality he claims, he hopes that these difficult and complicated negotiations may be brought to a successful issue."

This was a charming valentine for Her Majesty, and it was indeed a complicated situation. Servia would not demobilise, waiting on Greece. Rosebery's only hope at the moment was that the three empires might arrive at a united opinion on the agreement which Prince Alexander had made with Turkey.

The Queen may have conceived that his alleged inexperience might extend to carelessness about her private communications; for he had to tell Sir Henry Ponsonby:

"Please assure Her Majesty that no one opens any boxes she is pleased to address to me except myself. Indeed, I open all my boxes, except some purely departmental ones."

The Queen's opinion of Rosebery as "the only really good appointment" in the entire Government was frankly stated to the Prince of Wales.[17]

Rosebery had on the belated adhesion of France to the European Concert said in a letter to the Queen:

April 28th.—"The French diplomatic triumph does not amount to much. The French, while negotiating with us as to joining the Concert of the Powers, and quibbling over a word to cause delay, telegraphed to the Greeks that they had better give way, for the Powers were really going to act. It is a proceeding of a little boy who runs to tell a pilfering comrade that the policeman is round the corner. Lord Rosebery, however, is sure that Your Majesty does not care who takes the credit so long as the object is attained."

France was not in the good books of the Foreign Office. A little later, news came from Paris that a reception held by the Comte de Paris had caused very strong feeling against the Royal Family, and that M. de Freycinet would probably not be able to resist the demand for their expulsion from France. Rosebery wrote to the Queen in reply to a question from her that a representation by her Government would do more harm than good:

"To expel the Orleans princes, and to disoblige the English, would, in the eyes of many Frenchmen, be killing two tempting birds with one stone."

Later there was trouble with France in the New Hebrides. Some French traders had been murdered, a French ship was sent with

[17] Letters of Queen Victoria, 3rd Series, vol. i, p. 58.

troops, and it was asserted that the French flag had been hoisted. Opinion in Australia became excited, and Rosebery, after interviews with the French Ambassador, drafted a strongly worded dispatch to Lord Lyons. On this Mr. Gladstone wrote:

"Though the case for the New Hebrides is unsatisfactory and warrants suspicion, I would suggest for your consideration whether it is not rather more acid in expression than the present stage requires. What appears to me is that Freycinet's declarations (I have no very good opinion of him) in themselves are not unreasonable."

He went on to ask whether in a similar case we should not have taken much the same action. Rosebery replied that he had struck out one paragraph suggesting that the French attached insufficient importance to their obligations. He added:

"The despatch is not to be read to M. de Freycinet. It is for Lord Lyons' guidance who is always suave and cautious. But in the present state of colonial feeling, and in view of the suspicious action of the French, it is necessary for us to leave on record a despatch of considerable firmness. The French sent this expedition without telling us a word, to avenge murders of which they knew nothing, and as to which even now they give shuffling answers. Their soldiers are building wooden barracks. They have notified the missionaries that they are establishing military posts, and they are sending 360 *récidivistes* to New Caledonia. The latter circumstance will set Australia in a blaze which the other proceedings are not calculated to assuage. If our despatch is not recorded in a serious form we alienate the Colonies (whose views as to language are primitive and spicy) while we neither strengthen our position with the French nor express the full force of an overwhelming case."

In very early days at the Foreign Office Rosebery was challenged to show whether he could do more than drive his team with a light hand and whether he could use the whip on occasion. Sir Robert Morier, our Ambassador at St. Petersburg, was one of the ablest figures in the Diplomatic Service, but a man very conscious of his own powers, and impatient of official control. The Foreign Office regarded him much as the Cabinet regarded Sir William Harcourt. He had received direct instructions (February 16th) to inform the Russian Government that Germany had been invited to join in representing to the Sultan that he would do well to sacrifice one of his conditions in his arrangement with Prince Alexander. This, it was thought, should remove the objections felt at St. Petersburg. The

Porte agreed to give up this stipulation, which was for mutual military assistance, and Morier was told (February 19th) to urge the Russian Government to drop their other objections to the agreement. Instead of doing this, he wrote a dispatch of some length, giving his reasons, good or bad, for not following the instructions, the main reason being the impermeable attitude of his German colleague. This was a little too much, for it meant that Sir Robert, from his local knowledge, was better able to conduct these European negotiations than the Foreign Office, with its command of information from every point of the compass. He was coldly informed:

"I must request, if on a future occasion Your Excellency should see serious objections to the execution of such instructions as you may receive, that you will communicate such objections to me by telegram, and will report the course which you are taking or which you desire to take."

The whole story is told in the *Letters of Queen Victoria*[18] as she evidently took keen interest in this first court martial held by her new Foreign Secretary. She must have been amused by Rosebery's comment:

"It is no consolation to Lord Rosebery to read in the *Times* of this morning that Sir R. Morier has given one of the most successful balls of the season: or to hear from Sir R. Morier that the Tsar is greatly pleased with Lord Rosebery's method of conducting business, of which, indeed, owing to Sir R. Morier's proceedings, the Tsar can know nothing."

But no rancour persisted, and a letter from the Private Secretary (March 17th) assured the erring Ambassador that the matter would drop, so far as Rosebery was concerned, with a good-natured message from him advising Morier to be careful not to say anything at St. Petersburg which might do prejudice to him in high quarters in England and Germany if it came round "as everything does." Morier was intimate with the Royal Family at Berlin, which made the warning necessary.

Sir E. Thornton at Constantinople, Sir F. Lascelles at Sofia, and Sir William White at Bucarest were all in perpetual communication with the Foreign Secretary, officially and privately. Prince Alexander, overborne by Russia, misused by Servia, and the subject of endless Turkish intrigue, was not always amenable to advice from Downing Street, or even from Windsor. Instead of ruling over a

[18] Third Series, vol. i, pp. 67-72.

united Bulgaria, as was his right, he was to be merely Governor-General of Eastern Roumelia under the suzerainty of Turkey, and there was much discussion of the term for which he should be nominated. Rosebery explained to Sir E. Thornton (March 24th) that our position was simple, that we had fought as long as we could for an appointment for no fixed term (to which Russia had strongly objected), and only joined in signing for a term of five years because all the other Powers did the same. Prince Alexander had not complained or protested during all the time, but lodged a protest at the end, so they had to agree to sign without him, and Rosebery told Sir F. Lascelles that this might not be a bad thing, because if the settlement were unpopular in the Principality he would be divested of responsibility. The Prince was taking a dangerous attitude to which he could give no support (March 28th).

"If the Prince can keep on the throne five years he will be safe for an unlimited period. If he cannot, what is the use of a longer term?"

The fatal answer to this query was not given while Rosebery was Foreign Secretary. The kidnapping of Prince Alexander and his deportation to Russia (August 22nd), his return to Sofia amid the apparent applause of the population, and his final abdication (September 6th) after finding disaffection general and the support of Europe lacking—these occurred after the fall of the Government.

But on the eve of its defeat Rosebery had to encounter another Russian manœuvre, and to encounter it alone. By Article LIX of the Treaty of Berlin Batoum was declared to be a free port. The Emperor of Russia had decided to put an end to this régime, on the ground that the Treaty only registered a spontaneous declaration, not a stipulation. All the Continental signatory Powers discussed the matter, and agreed that it was not of much practical importance. Neither Prince Bismarck nor the Austrian Chancellor, Count Kalnoky, took it very seriously, the former believing it to be a step towards conciliating national opinion brooding over recent disappointments, and the latter simply saying that he did not admire the mode of proceeding, but that there was nothing to be done. Rosebery told one Foreign Ambassador that in his opinion we ought to decline to recognise the Russian declaration, and to leave Russia, as it were, in a state of illegality and outlawry against the public law of Europe. He accordingly addressed a dispatch to St. Petersburg (July 13th), in which, after closely arguing the case from the Treaty of Berlin protocols, he said:

[217]

"One direct, supreme, and perpetual interest is no doubt at stake in this transaction—that of the binding force and sanctity of international engagements. Great Britain is ready at all times and in all seasons to uphold that principle, and she cannot palter with it in the present instance. . . . Her Majesty's Government are compelled to place on record their view that this proceeding of the Russian Government constitutes a violation of the Treaty of Berlin, unsanctioned by the signatory Powers, that it tends to make future Conventions of the kind difficult, if not impossible; and to cast doubt at least on those already concluded.

"It must be for the other Powers to judge how far they can acquiesce in this breach of an international engagement.

"But in no case can Her Majesty's Government have any share in it. It must rest on the responsibility of its authors."

This was pretty sharp wording, and the Russian Chancellor, M. de Giers, who, according to Morier's information, had strongly opposed this action unless it were taken by previous agreement, took the reproof hardly, and as Sir Morier reported:

"Losing his self-control he exclaimed, trembling as he spoke, 'This is the most wounding communication that has ever been addressed to one Power by another. It has gone straight to my heart, and will remain there till I die; and when it is published in the blue book, it will go straight to the heart of every Russian and will rankle there.'"

When the Emperor was informed, "he was painfully affected by the accusation of having violated the Treaty of Berlin . . . but he sincerely desired the maintenance of the good relations at present subsisting"; and Rosebery could not resist writing privately to Morier that M. de Giers' appearance of having received a slap on the face and his intention of carrying the dispatch in his heart till he dies seemed rather theatrical, as Morier had made it clear in his dispatch that he had been using the same arguments, couched in language quite as forcible.

Egypt was technically at peace, but her frontier was insecure, her finances were embarrassed, and there was "the hindrance which is offered to all effective administration by the peculiar international obligations which Egypt has incurred." Chief among these were the Capitulations, on a system said to date back seven hundred years to privileges granted by Saladin to one of the small Italian republics, and a cause of general inconvenience down to our own day. There were also the mixed tribunals—a regular source of international friction. Sir Henry Drummond Wolff, one of the lights of the Fourth party, quick and amusing, playing to a Conservative Government the part which Labouchere took when the Liberals were in power, had been sent on a Special Mission to Cairo by Lord Salisbury. Rosebery desired its continuance, but wrote:

"As I am the least of the apostles, and some nine or ten years younger than the youngest member of the Cabinet, I may not carry so much weight as I could wish."

He asked Sir Henry (February 19th) to continue writing dispatches as interesting and valuable as those addressed to his predecessor:

"But your stumbling-block will be expense. Remember what a fierce and drastic economist is our present Dictator. And that if you were to make Egypt happy, contented and prosperous next week, your present expenditure would cause him a pang and make him desire your instant removal. . . . I daresay you will think me very Scotch in emphasising expense, but it is only from the friendly wish to remove one of the greatest obstacles in the reception of your mission in Parliament and at home generally."

The presence of Moukhtar Pasha, the Sultan's envoy, did not make the Egyptian situation less complex. He had taken too much on himself, and Rosebery wrote to Sir Henry:

March 19th.—"While I am anxious that you should keep up your friendly relations with Moukhtar, I hope you will equally display great firmness if necessary, and if for instance he should attempt to interfere with the moving of British troops to Assouan, you will give him blandly to understand that his own business should keep him fully occupied without making it necessary for him to interfere with other people's.
"We are quite willing and anxious to work with him if possible, but he must not become a mere perpetual purposeless obstacle. Are these diplomatic oilwells that Nubar has gone to visit? Or is it a genuine desire to sniff petroleum?"

Nubar Pasha, the famous Armenian Minister of the Khedive, was sanguine about a great oil development in Egypt; but as Rosebery wrote later:

"It will take a good deal of petroleum to pay off the debt of Egypt in twenty years."

[219]

Before the Government fell there was much discussion about the blockade of the Soudan, which from time to time was exercised to prevent the passage of arms to the Khalifa. Drummond Wolff took the side of the Cairo merchants, who professed to be ruined by the prohibition of harmless exports. Rosebery objected, "What we have too often displayed in Egypt, a shifting policy without aim or principle," and he asked:

June 25th.—"Are we to be the only sufferers in Egypt? Is the shoe not to pinch the Egyptians at all? Is she not to have a share in the disadvantages of defending the country? We are to find trade for the Cairo merchants, at the expense of our own troops and our own tax payers, who will be called on to defend the frontier against the troops that this trade is to furnish forth for attack."

A week later he wrote:

"I shall not enter now into questions of *haute politique*, for I am in an interesting condition, electorally speaking, and shall not know for a few days whether I am a man or a mouse."

It turned up mouse, and in his final letter of good-bye he wrote:

July 30th.—"My idea has been to give Egypt some little opportunity of working out her own salvation without constant interference from without. Circumstances have favoured that policy, not the least of which have been your industry and spirit of conciliation. It will always be a pleasant recollection to have worked with you."

Almost every letter contained references to Randolph Churchill, the close friend of both, and the author of Rosebery's friendship with Drummond Wolff. Rosebery was also in frequent communication with Sir Evelyn Baring, quietly carrying on, amid innumerable difficulties, the work which was to prove so fruitful and to make him so famous.

The only speech of any length that Rosebery had to make in the House of Lords as Foreign Secretary was on an Egyptian subject. Lord Salisbury was a merciful master of legions when foreign matters were at issue, and was content with the attitude taken by his successors in the Balkan complications. But some independent Peers asked why Zobeir Pasha could not be released from detention at Gibraltar and permitted to go up the Nile. For upwards of a year that remarkable personage had been interned at the request of the military authorities in Egypt, it having been found that he was in communication with the Soudan tribes. Rosebery had no difficulty in showing that after the refusal, by the country rather than by the government of the day, of Gordon's request for Zobeir, it would be impossible, now that the Soudan was by general agreement being abandoned for the time, to send him back there as a sort of British agent. The motion was therefore negatived without a division. Rosebery's only other interventions in the House were brief replies to ordinary questions.

During Rosebery's tenure of office there were no troublesome questions with America; and though there was frequent correspondence about the Russo-Afghan frontier, its details were more directly the concern of the India Office. During his brief term in Downing Street he had not only confirmed the opinion that he was a man of outstanding ability, but he had gained a reputation for moderation and reason. He had seen the advantage in the conduct of foreign affairs of gaining the confidence of Queen Victoria; for her unrivalled experience, and her prestige throughout the continent of Europe, formed a backing which no Foreign Secretary could afford to neglect. Where her family affections were involved, as with the fate of Prince Alexander of Battenberg, her opinion might be strongly biased, but as a rule, in external affairs, she was singularly free from deep-seated prejudice of the sort which precluded her from contemplating a scheme of self-government for Ireland in any shape whatever. She not only thought Rosebery "a very clever pleasant man, and very kind," but she opened out to him her confidential opinion of the Prime Minister and his intentions in a letter printed in the collection of her correspondence,[19] to which Rosebery replied as follows:

FOREIGN OFFICE, *July 12th*, 1886.

"Lord Rosebery with his humble duty respectfully submits his thanks to Your Majesty for Your Majesty's gracious letter; which he cannot but consider as a mark of confidence most gratifying to him.

"He need hardly repeat his strong opinion in favour of resignation. Ever since April he has been of opinion that if the Government were beaten on the second reading of the Irish Bill they should resign. Some of his colleagues at first appeared to agree with him; but before the division took place they had changed their minds. He therefore did not urge the question in the Cabinet. But on this occasion he feels sure of a much larger support, if not of that of Mr. Gladstone himself.

"Mr. Gladstone has, however, written him a letter which he thinks shows that the Prime Minister leans at present to immediate resignation.

[19] *Queen Victoria's Letters*, 3rd Series, vol. i, p. 159.

"The only alternatives would appear to be to resign at once or receive the *coup de grâce* at the meeting of Parliament in the beginning of August.

"Lord Rosebery cannot conceive it possible that any of the present administration should seek the support of the dissident Liberals; or seeking it, obtain it.

"Lord Rosebery ventures to think that Mr. Gladstone's is not a nature which could endure power on sufferance. Considering that there will be four distinct parties in the new House of Commons, none of which will work together for all purposes and all occasions, it will be difficult enough to form a sufficiently strong administration to carry on the affairs of this country at home and abroad with due efficiency. No one, he thinks, is likely to see this more clearly than Mr. Gladstone, or to perceive that his own party has by no means the best chance, or perhaps even the second best chance, of securing this desirable result.

"Lord Rosebery is not sure if he has answered fully and satisfactorily the points raised in Your Majesty's letter, but he need not say that he will be only too glad to supplement this letter in any way or on any questions that may be desirable.

"He humbly thanks Your Majesty for Your Majesty's gracious reference to himself."

According to plan and to precedent, Rosebery, throughout his term at the Foreign Office, was in almost daily communication with the Prime Minister, often by brief notes, oftener still by stepping across Downing Street to secure five minutes of advice. Mr. Gladstone was ailing in the winter, and Rosebery's first note from the Foreign Office ran:

"I am very sorry to hear of the rheumatism which, according to song, lives in damp attics, which is an abiding reproach to Mentmore."

Even through his Irish pre-occupations the leader kept in close touch with the tangle of south-east Europe, and with Greece in particular. He was for determined use of the fleet as the surest method of keeping the peace. Rosebery was able to write on April 17th that Greece had yielded, though ungraciously. In the same letter he touched on our relations with Germany in East Africa, which were not finally adjusted until fourteen years later.

"Bismarck is rather difficult to deal with. Things are not going as he wishes at Zanzibar, and he is very much put out, accusing all our agents of hostility. I am inclined to think that the best solution of the question would be that the Sultan should cede part of his territory to Germany in exchange for a guarantee of the rest from France, Germany and ourselves. However, I cannot propose this. . . . I had to give Hatzfeldt a strong hint that they must take care at Berlin of the style of their communications, which is apt to savour distantly of menace.

"There is nothing to take hold of, but the tone is not altogether what it should be."

No admiration for Prince Bismarck could make the Foreign Secretary submissive to the faintest rattle of the sabre.

Every man on leaving a public office feels emotion at his farewell to his loyal companions of the Civil Service with whom he has worked. He is fortunate if he can write as Rosebery did (July 29th): "Engaged in distributing Honours and making people happy. The greatest joy in the world."

In the course of Mr. Gladstone's amazing campaign he spoke at Manchester (June 25th), and, after running through the names of the colleagues who had stood by him, he came to "the youngest member of the Cabinet, of whom I will say to the Liberal party of this country, and I say it not without reflection, for if I said it lightly I should be doing injustice no less to him than to them—in whom I say to the Liberal party that they see the man of the future."

Rosebery wrote:

June 29th, 1886.—". . . Since the Ambassadors have left me more alone I have begun to read a few speeches. I did not quite like your first, but that was only the lowest step of the ladder which you have been mounting ever since. Now, however, the eminence is gained, and in my humble judgment in all the history of your marvellous efforts you have never made a campaign so splendid as this last. I put age aside as a preposterous and bewildering consideration. I regard you as having surpassed yourself in a way I should have deemed impossible. If you win this election, it will be your victory alone, no army, not even an imperial guard, hardly a staff, with perhaps Morley as an esquire or aide de camp. It will be a rare and incredible achievement, and I shall only regret having not heard one single syllable, or witnessed one single reception.

"I was arrested in your speech at Manchester by your unexpected outbursts about myself. It is a delicate subject to speak about, but I wish you to understand that I feel from my heart you are mistaken, through partiality and kindness. I have attained much more than the highest summit of my ambition, and the furthest reach of my capacity. I can hardly hope to keep my place. Napoleon said of his marshals that he knew the *tirant d'eau* of each of them. Look over your marshals again and you will know that I am right. My draught of water is that of a punt, and I remain gladly in the shallows.

"I doubt if a peer can ever lead the Liberal party again: he has the gain of comparative ease, against which he must set the disadvantage that he must not wrestle for the prize. I indeed count that no disadvantage, for I am more than satisfied and have won a greater prize than I could ever have dreamed of. I shall gladly serve as long as I remain in public life.

"This is a strange letter, for I do not often venture to offer you praise or consideration about myself. But I am stimulated to write thus, without intending it when I began, by your achievements and your praise. Though the latter is wholly unmerited and must in my opinion be flagrantly falsified, it will remain a heritage for me and an heirloom for my children.

"Yrs. affly.,
AR"

Nothing that might have shaken Rosebery's judgment during the progress of the swaying battle on Home Rule had so far affected him. Chamberlain and Trevelyan went, but there was nothing to make him abandon hope. At Christmas of the previous year he had written to Reginald Brett:

December 23rd, 1885—"I cannot understand people preferring separation to Home Rule. I detest separation, and feel that nothing could make me agree to it. Home Rule, however, is a necessity both for us and for the Irish. They will have it within two years at the latest, Scotland will follow, and then England. When that is accomplished Imperial Federation will cease to be a dream. To many of us it is not a dream now, but to no one will it be a dream then."

Holding this faith, and up to the neck in the European whirlpool, he did not attempt to follow the details of the Irish measure, crucial though they proved to be.

Journal

February 24th.—"Gladstone beginning to expound his Irish plan, with which he said he did not trouble me as he knew how busy I was, and then he was acting within the scope of what he knew to be my ideas. I implored him to spare me. But when he sketched a vast skeleton, I could not resist saying slyly, 'Is it six or seven years since you told me you had lost all power of constructive legislation?' Mr. G. could not help chuckling."

In June (17th) Rosebery devoted the whole of a long speech at Glasgow to the Irish question. The man who would deny that the

Irish were in favour of local government would deny anything. The Conservatives had put an end to exceptional legislation in Ireland, and after the election the Liberal Government tried conciliation of parties to the utmost, and asked for a vote on the simple proposition of a legislative body for Ireland. The supremacy of the Imperial Parliament was to be maintained. The Conservative policy was simply twenty years of coercion. As to Ulster, speaking as a Scotsman, he could not understand why 1,200,000 Protestants should fear to throw in their lot with Ireland. He did not believe in the bloodthirsty theologians who came forward with the Shorter Catechism in one hand and the revolver in the other. He believed that in a few years the complaint would be that Ulster, with its Scottish ancestry, would have more than its fair share of predominance. He concluded: "Are you as weary as we are of that fatal and dreary policy of giving Ireland everything except that which she wants, and that which, according to every principle of Liberalism, we have ever held she has a right to obtain?"

His own comment on the speech was: "Spoke for 1 hour 20 m. Eheu. Enthusiasm enormous, not for me but the thing."

After the Conservative victory at the election (October 19th), he spoke once more on Ireland at the meeting of the Newcastle Liberal Club. On the text of the unity of the party he examined the remarkable figures of the late election, drawing from the extraordinary number of abstentions the conclusion that the country was asking for time to make up its mind, but had not rejected the policy. Now that they were in opposition, their function was to watch and to criticise. Between Liberals and Liberal Unionists there was a difference of degree, not of principle, because most of the latter held that the Irish ought to manage their own internal affairs in their own way. Some give and take ought to bring about an arrangement with them.

Such were the hopes that, at the beginning of the following year, brought Liberals and Liberal Unionists to a brief and fruitless colloquy at Harcourt and Chamberlain's Round Table.

A flying visit to Hawarden followed.

Journal

"Mr. G. said he had heard Chamberlain was exasperated at the allusion to me as man of the future. He had not meant it offensively to J. C., who was in the House of Commons, while I was in the House of Lords, and therefore did not compete with him. In speaking of me he had thought of age and the proved capacity for development. He said he agreed with me in going for conciliation, but what middle course was there? I said 'Suppose the Irish M.P.s were to be constituted a local government for Ireland?' He said he had thought much of that, but the Irish Peers were the difficulty. I said, 'Let them alone, or let them elect representatives as at present.' He mused, 'That would be a Conservative element, but there would be no harm in that.' He seemed rather taken with the idea. Full of gloom about Churchill and Chamberlain in the future, and of wrath over England's treatment of Ireland. Gave me a little book with a Latin inscription and blessed me tenderly on going."

CHAPTER IX

Visit to India, 1886-7—Egypt—The Irish Question—The Queen's Jubilee—Imperial Federation

O N OCTOBER 28TH the Roseberys started for India. Their companion was Ronald Munro Ferguson of Novar and Raith, who had been a private secretary at the Foreign Office and, as Rosebery told his mother, "insisted on continuing so." Raith was just across the Firth of Forth from Dalmeny, and there was a family association of long standing; but this was the real beginning of a close intimacy, personal as well as political, marked by genuine affection and respect on both sides, and by unstinted loyalty on that of the younger man. Sir Arthur Hardinge,[1] just appointed Governor of Gibraltar, was going to be landed at the Rock, and as far as Egypt they had the congenial society of Henry Calcraft. Short of Gibraltar there was the excitement of collision with a large sailing ship, only not sunk because they were going at half speed— "What was strange was that within five minutes of the catastrophe the saloon sounded as if dinner were going on—full of chattering females. I remained lazily in bed." But when they reached Gibraltar, having their victim in tow, it was found that necessary repairs to their own bows, where some plates were sprung, meant a short delay in their journey. Asked by the Governor to find their way to the official house, the Convent, they walked up there, and to their horror found themselves in the midst of a levee held by the outgoing and incoming Governors.

"There was a pause, the Governors looked at us, Henry Calcraft groaned 'Go on.' I saw what was expected, and with the sensation of taking a header walked forward in a grey tweed suit, a pot hat in my hand, a large white cotton umbrella under my arm, my race glasses slung round me—in a word the British Tourist in his most excruciating form. Shook hands with the Governors, bowed deeply and passed to the left followed by the somewhat less seedy Calcraft and Ferguson.

[1] General Sir Arthur Hardinge, K.C.B., second son of 1st Viscount Hardinge. Governor of Gibraltar 1886-00.

Afterwards all Gibraltar, the Chief Justice in his wig, the Vicar Apostolic in purple, the military in their uniforms did similar homage. It was a very funny scene so far as we were concerned."

They saw the sights of the Rock, though not the monkeys, and were even able to pay a flying visit to San Roque across the Spanish frontier. They sailed on the evening of November 3rd.

"I watched for some time the splendid trophy. From the Mediterranean side the rock seems to face Africa with the head of an elephant, and Europe with the head of a lion. We have held it for two centuries, and the power of man has vainly tried to wrench it from us. It should be the symbol of England. Till I saw Gibraltar I never fully realised why we are so hated in Europe."

At the short pause at Malta Rosebery was fascinated by the "Barocco, or cloistered walk where the monk-knights used to walk, chafing in their limits and eyeing the sea as comported the frontier sentries of the Christian world." The armoury appeared to him the most interesting he had seen, because it gave the impression of being the most genuine. He had been entrusted with some parcels for Prince George of Wales, then serving on board the *Dreadnought*, a name then without the formidable significance that it held twenty years later. "He had grown a beard, and seems to have shot up," was Rosebery's description of his future Sovereign.

Malta, take it for all in all, did not strike him as so imperial a monument as Gibraltar, but much more likely to be coveted and much more difficult to defend. There was a Radical party, he was told, favouring annexation to Italy, while many of the peasantry believed the island still to be governed by the Knights.

There was no special incident at Port Said, whence they had the company of intimate friends in the Duke and Duchess of Manchester and Lord Fife; or at Aden, except that at the latter Rosebery had a long walk with a leading official who had been there for sixteen years, and explained that it was because he had not been allowed to accept promotion elsewhere:

"The last time he had been so prevented was by me. He had been offered an appointment in the Bombay Presidency[2] which he had been debarred by me from accepting. I exclaimed indignantly, 'It must have been under my successor!' 'No,' he replied firmly in a voice which vibrated with sorrow and essential veracity, 'I well know it was your

[2] Aden was under the Bombay Presidency.

LADY ROSEBERY, BY G. F. WATTS, R.A.

lordship.' What remained for me but to point out that there were persons in the world who could not be replaced: this was the penalty they had to pay for extraordinary merit: and that in the critical state of the Somali question it would have been madness to separate oneself from him. It was not a very promising commencement for our interview, but he is an excellent fellow, and we were soon wallowing in the alluvial mud of Zeyla, Berber, Harrar and the Somali. I was delighted to hear that my anxiety about Socotra was well founded. Two or three days after I had got the treaty concluded and the flag delivered, a German ship of war appeared and asked to whom Socotra belonged. On the Union Jack being hoisted she at once disappeared."

There was fair time for reading throughout the voyage. Rosebery began with Eliot Norton's two new volumes of Carlyle's letters, in which he found little or nothing, and "finished, too, the much more interesting biography of that wild poetic antediluvian parson, Hawker of Morwenstow." He read a great deal of Balzac, Burton's *Mecca*, and the volume of Lord Aberdeen's private letters.

Bombay was almost a welcome home (November 22nd), for Lord and Lady Reay were at Malabar Point. There was frequent entertaining there, and everything that Bombay had to show, including a rather ghastly visit to the Towers of Silence, at which some other Englishmen of the party displayed a ghoulish interest in the obsequies. Rosebery's leading impression was of pity for the distinguished Parsi gentleman who was their guide. "Fancy if, whenever an eminent person came to London, I had to take him to Kensal Green and there listen with him to a lecture on decomposition and the funeral service." But all experiences were not so grim. He visited the temples and the markets, had pleasant meals at the club, long walks and talks with Reay and his officials, and made an expedition in a launch to the caves of Elephanta.

On December 2nd they set out for Ahmedabad and the relics of its vanished glories of mosque and tank, this last—

"an exquisite lake constructed in 1451 and restored by Mr. Borrodaile, a public spirited Collector, with all the private funds he could extract and all the public he could economise; for which last proceedings he was incredibly snubbed and wigged. Honour to him forever, say I. A road connects the mainland with an island of trees and flowers, on which we stood and mused watching the gay groups of holiday makers reflected brilliantly in the smooth waters as they wended their way home, and the rich deep afterglow of the sunset. I have enjoyed nothing in India so much."

[229]

Jaipur was the next stage (December 5th):

"Just before we arrived I tossed Ronald his Panama hat, which however skimmed gracefully through the window into the jungle. If events are to rank according to their real importance, this deserves the first place."

The travellers missed the unrivalled glories of Udaipur, for the Resident was absent, but found plenty to occupy them at Jaipur in the lovely gardens, in the animal fights where no animal or bird was injured, though "the rams rushed at each other and banged their foreheads till they recoiled and our heads ached to see it; and the pigs of pigsticking, sulky, truculent, and extremely like the British householder of the middle class"; and most of all in the climb to the deserted city of Amber, with its great empty palace-halls and noble views through the range of hills.

On to Agra to the hospitable house of Colonel Euan Smith (December 8th).[3] From all the scenes that nature or art have made famous, fewer travellers, perhaps, have returned disappointed from Agra than from any other. Assuredly Rosebery did not.

"THE TAJ

"What a day in one's life. We spent three hours beside the marble lily, virgin in silent and exquisite triumph over her eternal chastity. I was so moved that I broke into what I am pleased to call verse, so will desist from prose. We climbed minarets, we walked round it, we sat in contemplation before it, we were intoxicated with it."

Rosebery jotted down some isolated lines, such as "A gate of heaven, could we find the key," and "A flash of moonshine petrified; the door of gracious dreams."

But his final sonnet took the form:

"THE TAJ

"Image of Heaven! unto him that sees
Thy portal, earth and death and time are past:
He moves in spirit o'er the pathless seas,
To that dread Vision which shall be the last.
His gaze discerns the palaces that crown
Thy mount, O Sion! Immortality
Breathes o'er the 'peerless Tomb.' Hence grief hath flown
Death has no sting, and grave no victory.

[3] (1842-1910) Cons. Gen. Zanzibar 1887-91. Min. Res. Tangier, K.C.D., etc., 1891-93.

'My father's house hath many mansions': fair
Fell here their shadow in some straying beam:
And we who watch can see the glory there,
The nightless day and the eternal dream.
So let us gaze a moment free from care.
The Christian prays, the Moslem built a prayer."

There is a note of Keats and a note of Wordsworth in these verses. Nothing of the still surviving Tennyson or Matthew Arnold. His farewell to the dream-temple four days later may be noted here:

"In the afternoon at sunset we paid our last visit to the Taj. It was bathed in the lemon light of the sunset, a Moslem was shouting his appeal to Allah, not unmusically, the divine building seemed more serene and matchless than ever. I left it with emotion: shall I ever see it again? It is not likely, but it is hard to part for ever with so beloved a dream. It is not too much to say that I am in love with it. I cannot tear myself from it, or keep my eyes off it. It is a sublime madness of which I am not ashamed."

But there was also the noble tomb of Akhbar at Sikandra, with a marble pillar at its foot in which once stood the Koh-i-noor.

"Honest times. Lord Northbrook when Viceroy gave a covering worth £500 to the tomb of Akhbar which was at once stolen. But then Christianity and superior civilisation had intervened."

And there was the abandoned city of Fatehpur Sikri, with its gorgeous red sandstone mosque, and the intricate palace of the great Emperor:

"But Akhbar neither *lassatus* nor *satiatus* left this splendid creation and built Agra! What lives those men had,—and yet no longer than ours."

There was the jail, where prisoners make carpets, "cheap, durable, and extremely lovely," and last the fort, "a splendid assemblage of stern and exquisite beauties."

After he had "imitated my lineal but remote ancestor (as the Prince of Wales said of King Alfred), Moses Primrose, and bought green spectacles," the party passed on to Delhi, where the architecture of mosque and fort seemed to Rosebery less impressive than at Agra, but where he "visited bareheaded" the place where Nicholson fell and others consecrated in the siege.

Lahore came next. It was beginning to be cold—bracing and delicious—but the temperature of 46 degrees in the Lieutenant-Governor's sleeping tents made an abrupt change from Bombay. Here Rosebery met a long list of the officials active in the north-west, where the heart of India beats strong, and he was introduced to the savage squalor of the Afghan horse market. They started by train for Peshawar, fascinated by the novelty of the landscape, and by the Indus "flowing composed and conscious in a strong deep stream between two rocky banks, the most striking piece of scenery I have seen in India." The bazaar at Peshawar was a novelty, being Asiatic, not Indian, and another novelty was the escort of two mounted sowars in front and two behind when he and Ferguson walked in the bazaar.

"While in front again and around were policemen on foot attacking everything living with their truncheons, hustling the people from their doors as they sat, and sending them flying like bundles of old clothes going to the wash. It was an amazing spectacle, but one must not judge the East at first sight, it is clear. No one seemed to mind the least. In the afternoon I had a conversation with Abdul Kader Khan, the prime minister of Shere Ali, the very man who proclaimed the *jehad* against us; very interesting it was."

An expedition to the Khyber was signalised by the unforeseen meeting of one of their party, a young Afridi chief, with his half-brother, who appeared with some forty or fifty armed followers. There was a deadly blood feud between the two, and anything might happen:

"I saw our chief dismount and hurriedly shake hands with his brother, and remount with a sensible look of relief. I afterwards found out that he had said to the native officer, 'Subadhar, if I shake hands with my brother, will you promise to come and stand close beside me?' And it was on the promise of the Subadhar faithfully performed that he saluted his excellent relative. He had indeed good reason for uneasiness. Had we not been there he would have been killed like a dog as a matter of course."

Rosebery and Ferguson made another expedition to Kohat, the genuine frontier post, with its Sikh garrison, where they were interested in observing the methods whereby young Indian "politicals" learn their job. A tonga drive of thirty miles, which disreputable horses, with some stray old rusty straps as harness, performed at a gallop in two hours and a quarter, brought them to the nearest station for a seven-hour journey to Rawal Pindi, and so back to Lahore. Leaving Lady Rosebery in friendly care, Rosebery and

Ferguson started for a wild dash upon Quetta. At Sukkur, on the majestic Indus, the great railway bridge was still three years from completion, and they turned north to Jacobabad, all along the line coming in for festive Christmas celebrations. After various contretemps due to the season or the newness of the railway, and a long spell on an open truck in bitter cold, they were safely deposited at Quetta, and well looked after by the guardians of the frontier. Rosebery had the luck to have a discourse on the North-West Frontier from General Browne,[4] "commonly known as Buster Browne," the engineer officer who superintended all the strategic lines of railway, and made careful note of it.

On December 28th they started for the railhead, some eighty miles from Kandahar, and turned back to Kach, being the first passengers who travelled on the line, and finding "the creaking of the sleepers and the slight-looking bridges sufficiently exciting." A five-mile walk across country in the dark brought them to Kach, whence they started on foot the next morning, as from rotten ice riding was difficult, with the thermometer at 19 degrees. The walk, in its turn nineteen miles, finished up with the Chappa Rift tunnel of some two miles, with sublime views from the windows piercing one side overlooking the gap below. As the tunnel was lined with pointed stones and feet were sore, it was agreeable to reach a train at the end, and to be landed at Sibi at 10 p.m. They found the town illuminated by "the Municipality," assumed to consist mainly of Colonel Bruce, the political agent, a "keen silent Irishman." The two inscriptions he noted were "Welcome Lord Rosebery" and "Income Tax hard." These in some cases had become combined, and after they had proceeded a short way some crackers went off, and the ponies in the carriage bolted, so that when they arrived at the principal decorations in the square it was at a gallop, with "the Municipality" and the honoured guest each sawing and tugging at the reins for dear life. However, all ended well, and Rosebery, from the roof of the political agent's house, thought "the little town a fairy scene, it was all howling desert seven years ago. One of the chuprassies with us had helped to build the first house."

The trip was over: they journeyed to Sukkar, thence paused at Lahore, were joined by Hannah Rosebery on New Year's Day, and reached Lucknow the next morning. Every Englishman sees Lucknow with a blend of pride and amazement, and Rosebery was duly

[4] Maj. Gen. Sir James Browne, K.C.S.I. Bengal Engineers. Engineer-in-Chief Sind-Pishin State Railway 1884: Quarter-Master General in India 1889.

impressed, though one mosque struck him as "a curious mixture of a place of worship and Cremorne." Cawnpore followed, "altogether a worthy object of pilgrimage," and they proceeded to Allahabad as guests of the Lieutenant-Governor, Sir Alfred Lyall. "A lovely quiet day of pure enjoyment" (January 4th), Rosebery noted; and no wonder, with the delightful companionship of his host; and there were other congenial figures in Sir Douglas Straight, who had left British law to become an Indian judge; Mr. Allen, the agreeable proprietor of the *Pioneer*; and the Chief Justice, Sir John Edge. A few days later the party stayed at Benares, fascinated by the alternate splendour and squalor of the town, and by the river view—with something of Venice in it, with the palaces overhanging the ghauts along the Ganges.

They arrived at Calcutta, on January 9th. The weather was delightful, bright and not too hot. It was a quiet, uneventful week, punctuated by walks and talks with their host Lord Dufferin, by some races, by the usual viceregal dinners and dances, and by a visit to the Legislative Council, which reminded Rosebery much of a sitting of the House of Lords. A flying visit to Chandernagore was distinctive, with the tricolour sashes of the officials in evening suits and opera hats; but the one failure of the tour was the ascent to Darjiling, where three days were spent in dense fog, with no glimpse of the famous mountain prospect. The only consolation was a visit to a tea plantation, followed by a visit from a "swarm of dirty good-humoured pedlars, from whom we made many purchases, Ferguson standing by like Judas with a great bag of silver."

The following week was spent peacefully at Calcutta, occupied with successive interviews with notable Indians and a service of the Brahmo-Somaj. The return to Bombay was on January 26th, and three days later the travellers left for Hyderabad—"full of character and beggars, a real native city, not too much veneered by Western civilisation." This accent was pronounced when Rosebery and Ferguson walked in the Indian quarter of the city, where English people seldom went, and were formidably stared at. In Hyderabad an Englishman was a stranger, not always a welcome one. The Nizam showed much attention, and Rosebery, not impressed by him at first, on further acquaintance recognised dignity and capacity in his small personality—an opinion which later experience by the Government of India confirmed. Salar Jung, Minister like his more famous father, was absent for the moment. The return to Bombay was followed by a visit of the men of the party, headed by Lord

Reay, to the Portuguese settlement of Goa. Of this expedition Rosebery wrote a long, serio-comic account, in portentous English, narrating how Governor Reay carried to a successful issue the expedition partially undertaken by Vasco da Gama and Albuquerque. The "topical" humour of this has necessarily somewhat evaporated; but there is no mistaking the serious impression left by old Goa:

"A hamlet of cathedrals in a forest. There is no trace of life: nothing but an arch which conducts to a city which no longer exists, and beyond the arch vast silent churches and a jungle of palm trees. Yet once it contained 120,000 souls. But fever was too potent for the city and it faded away. The fever—and the snakes—still remain."

After two more days at Bombay, the party, with Lord Fife, started homewards in the s.s. *Verona* (February 11th). "The ship is clean and empty, Hallelujah." Plenty of incident had been crammed into these eleven weeks in India. Many influential and communicative people had been met, and many places visited in different ways characteristic of Indian life. No time had been given to sport, which is seldom at its best until a good deal later in the year. Altogether the tour was a thorough success. But Rosebery's record of it does not leave quite the same impression of an awakened soul as does that of his Australian journey. Many Englishmen, when they visit India, feel that for the first time they are learning what the British Empire is. That consciousness was roused in Rosebery by the spectacle of the British race creating a new world out of emptiness. Perhaps he was less stirred by the thought of our succession in the continuity of Indian rulers:

"How Sultan after Sultan with his pomp
Abode his destined hour and went his way."

And this in spite of the keen historical sense which was always on the alert, in India as elsewhere.

The voyage was propitious, except for one day in the Red Sea when "we had the sort of weather which the deceased Pharaoh once encountered, and which I thought was reserved for the security of an ancient race. A violent wind from the S.W."

He got through a fine mixed lot of reading, generally at it all day. Gladstone's *Irish Speeches, The Tale of a Tub,* and the *Journal to Stella,* Hübner's *A travers l'Empire Britannique,* Lecky's *Leaders of Irish Opinion,* the *De Corona* in Kennedy's translation, some Burke, *La Guerre et la Paix,* and in a light vein *Pêcheurs d'Islande* and Mrs. Walford's *Mr. Smith.*

After this uneventful voyage, the travellers reached Suez on February 21st, and journeyed straight to Cairo. Rosebery's brief experience as Foreign Secretary opened as many doors as he desired into official life during his sojourn of ten days, and he did not fail to take advantage of these opportunities. Egypt was settling down; but her finances had not yet recovered from the fabulous extravagance of Ismail Pasha's rule and the cost of military adventures in the Soudan. It was felt that unless the search for oil on the Red Sea coast proved richly successful, Egypt had no chance of meeting the enormous interest on her debt without aid, presumably a British guarantee. Ismail Pasha was an unfailing topic.

Journal

"If you find conversation flag in Egypt, if a dinner wane, or your company be dull, you have only to mention the name of Ismail to effect an instantaneous and refreshing change. 'I have searched Greek and Roman history, and all history indeed in vain,' said Nubar Pasha, 'to find a parallel. What became of all the money he spent? I have no idea.' I suggested that much went at Paris and Constantinople. 'I doubt if three millions were spent at Constantinople altogether.'

". . . On the other hand, the Khedive told me that whenever his father went to Constantinople he spent millions, and Tewfik Pasha, the Governor of Suez, told me that out of the last loan of thirty million sterling Ismail only received five, the whole of which he spent at Constantinople in two months. The same authority stated that one of Napoleon III's Ministers received four or five million francs for giving the consent of France to the International Tribunals, and two others received pensions from Ismail Pasha. Blum Pasha[5] told me that Ismail's Civil List was £1,300,000 per annum. When, however, Blum went to him at a critical moment to say that he must make some financial sacrifice, Ismail received him in the great room at the top of the stairs where he always sat. There were as usual only ten or twelve candles lit, though there were many chandeliers. When Blum had finished his appeal, Ismail said it was impossible for him to make any sacrifice,— 'You see, even now, I can only afford these few candles to be lit out of so many.'

". . . This was at the period of his wildest extravagance. Once, Blum Pasha told me, he was at Vichy and sent to Cairo for two millions worth of Treasury Bonds (sterling). They were despatched to him, and a month afterwards he sent for two millions more, which were equally despatched. What became of all this? When Ismail wished to add Darfur to his dominions, Nubar Pasha went to him and asked him if

[5] At the Ministry of Finance. "An exceedingly agreeable Austrian with a strong sense of humour, who has been in Egypt 22 years. He would shine in any society."

[236]

he knew about the country, representing to him what a harassing and undesirable acquisition it would be. 'Are there not five millions of inhabitants?' inquired Ismail. 'It is believed so,' said Nubar. 'Then at 10s. a head capitation tax, that represents £2,500,000 per annum,' was Ismail's only remark. 'That is the sort of man he was,' says Nubar, in a sort of despair.''

The most sinister event of that sinister régime was the sudden disappearance of the all-powerful Finance Minister, Sadyk Pasha, known as the Muffetish, Ismail's factotum and confidant, and the possessor of a colossal fortune. As Rosebery put it, "Wolsey and Séjanus were nothing to it."

As the story reached Rosebery, when Goschen came to Egypt with M. Joubert, he refused to have any dealings with Sadyk Pasha, who wrote an angry letter to the Khedive, and was rebuked for its tone. Such a rebuff was a danger signal, and it was noted later that about this time Sadyk asked one of the principal European bankers if it would be possible for him to become a French subject. His friend guessed the reason, but asked why he desired it. "I do not know," said Sadyk, "why it is, but I have a sort of feeling as if something were going to happen which might make it desirable." A day or two later the Khedive asked the Minister to come and see him at nine o'clock at the Abdin Palace. When he arrived, a brougham was at the door, which he entered at Ismail's invitation, who got in with him. They drove to the Abbassiyeh Palace. There they had some conversation in the hall, but Ismail presently said he must go for a moment into the harem. When he had gone, Prince Hassan appeared and told Sadyk that he was under arrest. "Why?" "I do not know: that is not my business, I am a soldier obeying orders." Next morning a Dahabyieh took the Muffetish up the Nile. From the moment he entered Ismail's brougham with his smiling master he was never seen again. Then came the part said to have been played by one of the best and most respected Egyptian Ministers, "thin, intelligent, and agreeable," according to Rosebery's description of him. The day after Sadyk's disappearance he set off up the Nile with Ismail's signet ring—a sign of full powers conferred upon him. He returned some time later with his arm in a sling. It was supposed that the jailors attempted to drug the Muffetish under his superintendence, and that a violent struggle ensued, in which the Minister was wounded in the hand.[6]

[6] Rosebery did not note the story which was long prevalent in Cairo that, in his desperate struggles, the unhappy victim had bitten to the bone the hand of his former colleague.

Sir Evelyn Baring asked Rosebery whether this need prevent him from recommending the Minister for the K.C.M.G., as he had been on the point of doing when the story came across his mind. Rosebery declined to give advice, as he could form no opinion of the credibility of the story.

Rosebery had much intimate conversation on the future of Egypt with Nubar Pasha, the powerful Armenian Minister, with Riaz Pasha, a Turk of Jewish extraction, and with Moukhtar Pasha, the representative of the Sultan. Riaz held that Egypt should be left to herself, subject to the supervision of some Power, which he considered necessary.

"I defined his view that there should be an European directing spirit but an Egyptian hand. He assented, declaring that some European Power should have a right of surveillance. But he would not have English Ministers 'as there could not be two captains in one boat.'"

The connection of Moukhtar Pasha, an agreeable soldier, with Constantinople was not immediately important.

"He is supposed to have received but two telegrams from the Sultan during his stay in Egypt, both referring to a supply of delicacies for the Imperial table."

But in a long talk he detailed the causes of alienation between England and Turkey:

"He says 'chose' once in every three words.
"There were half a dozen specific grievances, one the question of reforms in Armenia. The Porte acknowledges no such name as Armenia."

Rosebery did not mince words in reply.

"I told him frankly that if I were in office now I should be angry and hurt at the total want of gratitude of the Turks for our services in the Greek blockade, when we had prevented the outbreak of a war which could not have been limited, when the present friends of the Porte, the Russians, were actively intriguing the other way."

The party left Port Said for Naples on March 4th, and after only five days of that paradise and its "happy walks and shades" in the always congenial company of Sir James Lacaita, sped on to Rome, where interviews with the Pope, the King, and the leading Ministers broke into the ordinary sightseer's routine. Hannah Rosebery went on to France, and Rosebery paid brief visits to Vienna and Berlin, where he again spent most of his time at the Radziwill Palace, joining his wife at Paris, to reach England just before Easter and settling down at the Durdans for the month of April.

During Rosebery's absence abroad the two outstanding political events were the resignation of the Chancellor of the Exchequer, Randolph Churchill, and the attempt to reunite the Liberal party by the meeting of Harcourt, Chamberlain, Morley, Herschell,[7] and Trevelyan at the Round Table Conference on Ireland. Rosebery wrote to his leader from the Suez Canal on his way to India:

November 12th, 1886.—"I got a paper yesterday with the report of the Leeds meeting[8] which filled me with pleasure. The note of political thoroughness and of loyalty to yourself, the temperate earnestness of all, or almost all, the speeches made me think it one of the best of these political conventions. At the same time, I adhere strongly to the belief that your strength and the strength of the party lies in silence: that is, as much silence on the part of the leaders as is consistent with keeping the party in heart—good heart (Glynnese).[9] What talking has to be done should be done by members to their constituents, in the sense of educating them. Meanwhile, let our governors have their fling. Randolph has I imagine exhausted himself for the present, and I suspect we shall soon perceive considerable fissures in the Tory surface. But let them have rope: I am sure little more is needed."

Two months later he wrote from Government House, Calcutta:

Confidential.   *January 11th*, 1887.

"My dear Mr. Gladstone,

"It may amuse you to have the innocent impressions of an unguided and uninstructed . . . mind as regards the position created by R. Churchill's resignation. We have only here some barren and possibly inaccurate telegrams to go upon, so that I may be in a fool's paradise.

"It seems to me that the Government has received a shot between wind and water, and that even if there is not a mutiny on board, there are at any rate not many efficient hands left to work the pumps. They have got Goschen it is true, but they have bought him much too dear. They had him already, and he was quite as useful to them in a private capacity as he can be officially. But Goschen's adherence, when Hartington refuses to join, gives the Unionists much the same blow that New-

---

[7] Lord Herschell, G.C.B. Born 1837; died 1899. Solicitor-General 1880-5; Lord Chancellor 1886 and 1892-5.

[8] National Liberal Federation.

[9] The Gladstone and Lyttelton families maintained a dialect of such expressions, thus styled.

man's admission to Romanism gave the Tractarians: it justifies all the hard things said as to their secret tendencies. To my mind this discrediting and impairing the Unionist position is a fatally high price to pay for the pleasure of seeing Goschen on the front bench. (I am glad he is there as it seems a great step in the direction of an honest and high-minded Tory party which I long to see.) Then if it be true that Northbrook has been compelled to throw up the India Office by an angry clamour of the Tories who cannot bear to see a crumb or a fishbone distributed outside the Carlton, a lurid light is cast on the Unionist position to which the most zealous of that party can hardly blind themselves. They are in the position of beasts of burden, or strictly of Roman allies contrasted with Roman citizens: they may bear any amount of burden and heat, but are not qualified to receive the rewards. Surely this must leave a rankling sore in the Unionist relations to the Tories.

"Then Salisbury exchanges Randolph as a leader for the respectable but inadequate Smith. Randolph becomes a bitter, dangerous, and unscrupulous enemy, who will not rest till he has overthrown the Government.

"Lastly Chamberlain has found in these transactions an excuse for holding out an olive branch, and escaping from his difficult and almost impossible position.

"The strongest government could hardly survive these disasters; but this weakly infant can hardly be kept alive by all the wet-nursing of Hartington, or the bottle of Cross, or the Daffy's elixir of the soothing Smith.

"We have a telegram which announces a conference between Chamberlain, Morley, Harcourt, &c., which you will bless but not attend. All this gives me sincere pleasure. I am confident that a common ground of action can be discovered, for I know your moderate and conciliatory frame of mind. And I think that the Irish having found themselves weaker in the constituencies than they expected will be satisfied with less than they were last year.

"Forgive this long and crude dissertation, but I have no one here on whom to pour my impressions.

"We are living in a splendid palace in a delicious climate with perfect hosts. I feel myself a Stoic to be able in such a Capua to turn what I am pleased to call my mind to the affairs of that foggy and immoral island which you inhabit.

"Y. aff.,
"R.

"All this is for your own eye alone."

About the same time (January 26th, 1887) he wrote to Reginald Brett:

[240]

"Here one watches your political crisis with a philosophy tempered by ignorance, with this minor advantage that one has to think out the situation for oneself, without having that trouble removed by the inspired surmise of the daily press.

"I could wish to see the Government either a stronger or weaker. In some respects indeed it could hardly be weaker. But I have always been a believer that the Jubilee year would not be a year of peace, and war on the Continent makes it desirable to have a strong government in England. Moreover the duration of Athenian Cabinets compares favourably now with that of British administrations and I am a little ashamed of my country. However, we can have no government of average strength until this silent Irish revolution be accomplished; and we should be grateful for the exiguous mercy of a government supported by 319 votes,—for I suppose we may deduct Randolph's. Of course we shall rub through all this distressful series of complications as British good sense will rub through anything. But all the same it is not a bad moment to be perched on India's coral strand. Indeed, if all we hear be true, Greenland's icy mountains should be preferable to my native city and its snowbound fog."

Rosebery went to Glasgow at the end of April, and spoke at the meeting of the Liberal Association (April 29th) "for 1¾ hours, appalling," as he said. Ireland was his principal topic.

"He doubted reunion of the Liberal leaders, but had unlimited faith in the common sense of the rank and file. They were told, for instance, by the Duke of Argyll, to forget party. The Duke could not forget party, because his party was himself. But he would warn the Liberal Unionists that if they forgot their party too long, the party would forget them. After a general election a clear line would be drawn; but though after being buffeted on one cheek the Liberals had meekly offered the other, the time might come when thy would come to the end both of their patience and their cheeks. Then would come the final and total and permanent disunion of the Liberal party."

Throughout the year Rosebery was active on many platforms. He was becoming a familiar figure everywhere, and was easily the most attractive speaker that could be secured, next to Gladstone himself. At Plymouth (May 20th) where there was an audience of 3,000, at Ipswich (October 5th) at a gathering at least as large, and at Castle Douglas (October 20th) when he spoke for an hour amid much enthusiasm, and at Edinburgh (October 5th) where Lord Spencer was the other leading attraction, Ireland was always the central subject of the discourse. The Ipswich speech called forth a long and bitter leading article in *The Times*, in which Rosebery was accused of condoning violence, and generally of presenting a mere travesty of Irish affairs. Before the Edinburgh speech he wrote to Spencer:

"Do not disparage yourself by placing your utterances below mine. Nothing can be tamer or feebler than my orations. I speak worse and worse, while you speak better and better. I see no prospect of improving. I am in the very depths now about my speeches, whereas yours are the weightiest in many ways that can be delivered on this absorbing Irish question. You will have a splendid reception in Edinburgh, and I shall swing the censer by your side."

But it would be tedious, at this distance of time, to make any detailed examination of the series of speeches on Ireland which Rosebery delivered in this and the following year. The vexed problems of that day—the position of Ulster, the retention of Irish members at Westminster, and so forth—have found their solutions, good or bad, long since, but in view of the part played by the Irish Question in Rosebery's later years, his absorption in it at this time cannot be passed over. But it by no means represented his only contact with public life.

From May onwards Rosebery's intervention in the Lords' debates touched oftenest on Imperial affairs. On May 2nd he indicated the disappointment which the Australian colonies would feel at the rather colourless reply which was all that Lord Salisbury could give to a question about French action in the New Hebrides asked from his own benches; and the same matter came up a day or two later, when the *Standard* had published what Rosebery called "the somewhat spicy details" of proceedings at the Colonial Conference. "New Hebrides papers are still not presented," he complained on August 1st, and finally on August 12th agreed to Lord Salisbury's plea for further delay.

He asked questions on the Anglo-Turkish Convention (May 23rd, June 28th, July 5th), and on Afghan affairs (June 13th). He favoured State-aided emigration of service pensioners to New Zealand, shook his head over the reappointment of Sir John Pope Hennessy after squabbles with his Council in Mauritius, and inquired whether an American bank had been established in China with a capital of two hundred millions sterling. Rosebery's most vigorous contribution to a debate was made to a discussion on the Criminal Law Amendment (Ireland) Bill conducted with singular ill-humour by the Government party, particularly by the Liberal

Unionist Peers. He followed Lord Northbrook, who had made a speech generally denouncing Gladstone and his adherents, with small reference to the Bill before the House. In the House of Commons such a speech would have been out of order, like a good many others in the earlier course of this debate. Rosebery indignantly denied the right of the majority to ask for an alternative policy to that of the Bill, which differed from all previous Coercion Acts in being a permanent alteration of the law. He asked whether a great national franchise had been deliberately extended to Ireland with a full and steady determination to refuse the main proposition which would be brought back by the members elected under that franchise. Why did the Liberal Unionists reserve all their anger for those who sat on the same benches? Lord Carnarvon had refused powers of coercion, quoting Cavour's statement that it was easy to govern in a state of siege, and saying that to do so permanently was impossible. Yet here was to be a permanent Act. The Liberal policy continued to be one of conciliation as opposed to coercion, by the remedy of Irish grievances.

On August 1st the Secretary for Scotland moved the second reading of a Bill strengthening his office by transferring to it many of the powers of the Home Secretary. It did not, however, promote its holder to a Secretaryship of State. Rosebery cordially approved, but thought that the office had suffered even more from the fact that there had been five Secretaries for Scotland in sixteen months.

Looking on at one of the Irish incidents in the House of Commons, he observed, "The conduct and manners of the House have become painful." John Morley told him that in the last Government Labouchere had strongly pressed to be made an Irish Privy Councillor, which would give him a footing in Ireland. Early in July a by-election at Spalding gave the Liberal candidate an unexpected majority of over seven hundred. One Conservative was not displeased:

July 3rd.—"Had an anxious conversation with Randolph. He did not disguise his joy over the election. If it were followed up by another victory the Government could not last three weeks. He then boldly asked me if I should feel inclined to join the 'National party.' I said I did not believe in it. 'But,' he said, 'if it were a success? I acknowledge the difficulty, but could you not serve as Foreign Secretary under Hartington?' I told him that I was not specially anxious to be Foreign Minister, and that there were too many jarring personalities and principles in the 'National party' for me. I was delighted with our present position. We were not as we had been a flabby disconnected majority, but a compact minority united by a principle. 'But a principle you cannot put into a Bill?' 'That remains to be proved.'"

September 20th.—"Went to town to see John Morley. He told me that Chamberlain had wished to submit his new plan of Home Rule to Mr. G., who had declined, though expressing every wish to reunite with him. J. M. very low. He had seen Parnell, who had come over to J. M.'s views about settling the Land question and not leaving it to the Irish Parliament."

"Broached to J. M., W. H. (William Harcourt) as probable and not undesirable P.M. He horrified, but promised to think it over."

Mentmore, September 24th.—"Hartington came by 6 train. Hammer and tongs with him all night till 1.30 a.m. on Home Rule and politics. . . . H. not strong in argument, or sanguine, but evidently in sympathy with Tories. Says they do unprincipled things but are not animated with Liberal hatred to property. Pointed out Liberals not likely to love property if property deserted *en masse*. Has not much hope of Tory success in Ireland, but prefers the bare hope to an experiment of Home Rule which he does not think will work, and which he is sure will require remodelling of the British Constitution. As regards H. R. he cannot bring himself to more than a local government of a humble kind similar to anything done for England and Scotland. He acknowledged it was likely he would have to join the Government. He is in a very weary state of mind, but the rock on which he pillows himself is distrust and dislike of the G.O.M. He openly regrets his election address of last year as going too far."

London, September 27th.—"Met John Morley. He had had a letter from Chamberlain saying he would give up public life if a satisfactory solution of the Irish question were arrived at, otherwise it was his duty to persevere! I pointed out to J. M. that the announcement of the settlement would run, 'The Liberal party is at length reunited. Mr. G. accepts all the Liberal Unionist points : in return for which Mr. C. retires into private life. J. C. has sometimes a grim turn of humour.'"

A little later Rosebery found Harcourt most anxious to get Chamberlain back.

September 28th.—"Stead came and spent seven hours with me tête à tête, rather too much of a good thing, but he was very agreeable. When he regretted in the P.M.G. that our younger statesmen were not religious, Dilke wrote to complain that he, Dilke, was. Stead says that land purchase in Ireland must be settled by commune or parish buying and becoming landlord."

Hawarden, October 11th.—"Went away at 10.30. W. E. G. came to the door. Said, 'I hope you are well with Morley?' I said, 'We are twins, except in intellect.' 'I say nothing about intellect, but I am delighted to hear it in the days of Chamberlain and Randolph.' He had previously said that Hartington had 'done more to push forward Liberalism than anyone else: in fact the pace would probably be too fast for Granville and such like, but not for me."

But there were non-political engagements as well. Rosebery had always been interested in shorthand writing, and when an International Congress was held in London (September 26th), he delivered the Presidential address of fine quality, animated by illustrations gathered from his wide reading of political history and memoirs. There were delegates from all over the world, and they were greatly impressed.

He also spoke of technical education, once at the Society of Arts, with Hartington, one of its keenest advocates, in the chair and a galaxy of M.P.s and men of science round; and again in the industrial atmosphere of Keighley. Of this speech he wrote to Lord Spencer:

"I should have answered before had I not been bothered with leaving home and technical education, which latter topic produced a discourse from me so long and tedious that I fancied myself by Stratheden out of Hobhouse's dam."[10]

The Times, however. was kinder this time, speaking of the effective appeal made by him on a topic that interests all parties and irritates none.

The brilliance of the London season found its focus, of course, in the celebration of the Queen's Jubilee, favoured by the gorgeous sunshine of June 21st. Rosebery's devotion to his Royal Mistress was deeply chivalrous, and the following letters show that he wrote from his heart. Queen Victoria was really touched, as her reply makes clear.[11]

HOUSE OF LORDS, *July 7th*, 1887.

"MADAM,

"I have not hitherto ventured to address to Your Majesty any congratulations on the auspicious occasion of Your Majesty's Jubilee; for I feared to intrude on Your Majesty, at such a time, and was doubtful

[10] William, 2nd Lord Stratheden and Campbell (1824-1893), and Arthur, 1st Lord Hobhouse (1819-1914)—two serious and weighty speakers who did not cultivate brevity.
[11] These letters are printed in full in the *Letters of Queen Victoria*, 3rd Series, vol. i, pp. 338-42, but it is impossible to omit them from this biography.

moreover whether it was proper for one in an unofficial position to do so. But now the ceremonial pressure of festivity has to some extent subsided; and I am informed that Your Majesty has been graciously pleased to receive communications from some of Your Majesty's former servants. And so I cannot resist the impulse to send Your Majesty a few humble lines. If in so doing I have offended I feel sure Your Majesty's constant and abundant kindness will excuse me.

"Last year on the occasion of Your Majesty's birthday I ventured to express my feelings on the memorable year that was then opening, being well assured that I should not be in Your Majesty's service when the Jubilee actually occurred. Now it may be perhaps permitted to rejoice at the unclouded consummation of this national and historical festival.

"Few even of those who are not Your Majesty's subjects could view unmoved the procession from the palace to the abbey with its proud cavalcade of princes, its majestic representation of the sovereignties of the world, and the enthusiastic multitudes that hailed its passage: but fewer still that touching and magnetic moment in the Abbey when Your Majesty appeared alone and aloft—symbolising so truly Your Majesty's real position—to bear silent testimony to the blessings and the sorrows which it had pleased God to bestow on Your Majesty and Your people during two generations. And when later Your Majesty passed from the Sovereign to the Mother, the touch of nature which has brought Your Majesty into sympathy with the humblest of Your subjects added the supreme emotion to a matchless scene. None who beheld that spectacle can ever forget it: for it was history and human nature blended and compacted in a single glowing picture.

"There appears to have been not the slightest failure or the most trivial drawback. All was worthy of Your Majesty and of the Empire: all has tended to strengthen and to deepen the foundation of a monarchy which overshadows the Globe, and represents the union and aspirations of three hundred millions of human beings.

"I could not help feeling, as I gazed at the Thanksgiving, that Your Majesty's mind must not improbably have returned to the past, and to those who are gone who would have rejoiced to witness and to share the triumph of that day. But when Your Majesty turned to the present it could hardly be in a spirit of dis-satisfaction with the august and genial Ceremony, or the universal and unaffected joy. Neither class nor party had any monopoly of that festival: it was as national and spontaneous as the loyalty which dictated it.

"I humbly hope that Your Majesty has recovered the fatigue that could hardly fail to attend so much exertion, however pleasurable and gratifying; and that Your Majesty may be spared to witness many years, which, though they will not be Jubilee years, will nevertheless be

[246]

years of loyalty and thankfulness for the benefits and splendour of Your Majesty's unrivalled reign.

"I again hope that Your Majesty will excuse this intrusion and allow me to subscribe myself

"Your Majesty's devoted Servant and subject,

ROSEBERY."

The Queen to Lord Rosbery.　　　OSBORNE, *July 21st*, 1887.

"I cannot answer your beautiful and most kind letter in the third person, which is so formal,—I would at once have answered it, had I not been just starting for Aldershot, and had I not also wished to send you the accompanying Jubilee Medal which I hope you will wear in recollection of those never to be forgotten days, but of which I had none by me just then. You have indeed so truly and kindly described those scenes and the very mixed feelings which filled my heart, that I would wish to thank you warmly for it. It is impossible for me to say *how deeply, immensely* touched and gratified I have been and am, by the wonderful and so universal enthusiasm displayed by my people, and by high and low, rich and poor, on this remarkable occasion, as well as by the respect shown by Foreign Rulers and their people. It is very gratifying and encouraging for the future, and it shows that 50 years' *hard* work, anxiety and care, have been appreciated, and that my sympathy with the sorrowing, suffering and humble is acknowledged.

"*Alone*, I *did* feel, in the midst of so many, for I could not but miss sadly those who were so near and dear, and who would have so rejoiced in those rejoicings, above all *Him*, to whom the Nation and I owe so much!

"Yesterday afternoon, I was most agreeably surprised by your kind and most valuable present, accompanied by such flattering words.

"It is the beautiful little Miniature in its quaint setting, which you once sent for me to see, and which I shall greatly value, though I fear I have no sympathy with my great Predecessor, descended as I am, from her rival Queen, whom she so cruelly sacrificed. Still I am delighted to possess this exquisite gem, which I *intend* to *wear*.

"In renewing my thanks,

Believe me,

Always yours very truly,

VICTORIA R. & I."

Lord Rosebery to the Queen.　　DURDANS, EPSOM, *July 23rd*, 1887.
"MADAM,

"It has been the singular fortune of Your Majesty to make millions of people happy during this Jubilee, but none I think happier than I was on receiving Your Majesty's gracious communication yesterday.

"It was not only the winning acceptance by Your Majesty of the little

[247]

locket, and the even more gratifying intimation of an intention to sometimes wear it, nor yet the undeserved honour of the medal, but it was the eloquent condescension and simplicity of Your Majesty's beautiful letter that I can never forget.

"I can well understand that Your Majesty should feel no very cordial affection for Queen Elizabeth, who, with all her force of character, seems to have been wanting in that very quality of sympathy which has been the subtle and pervading distinction of Your Majesty's reign. By it Your Majesty has cemented the strength of this ancient Monarchy, for it has the magic prerogative of uniting the highest and the lowest, without impairing but even increasing mutual respect and regard. Never did I feel this so deeply as in reading last night Your Majesty's affecting words, which can leave me only with my life.

"I will not further intrude on Your Majesty except to hope what I cannot doubt that the pageant of to-day is worthy of the occasion, and of Your Majesty, and of the Empire.

"I have the honour to be,
Your Majesty's devoted Servant and subject,
ROSEBERY."

Lansdowne House was the scene of many festivities, some of which were attended by the foreign Sovereigns and Princes who had thronged to honour the most venerated of their caste. And it was the Roseberys' farewell season at the beautiful Adam pa'ace of which they were the tenants. In July they became owners of 38, Berkeley Square, a fine and commodious *hôtel*, but naturally not graced with the unattainable distinction of Lansdowne House.

Much of the autumn was passed at Dalmeny, whence rapid excursions were made for some of the speeches that have been mentioned, and for a few visits to the country houses of friends. At one of these, Ashbridge, Rosebery in a walk with the Prince of Wales pointed out to him the great danger of the present horizontal division of politics. The Prince, who some time before had given Rosebery particulars of his stormy conversation with Prince Bismarck, this time observed that Germany could put a million of men on her frontiers, but wanted another million.

Two of the children, Harry and Peggy, had been seriously unwell in the late autumn, but were out of danger before the year ended.

Since its inception in 1885 the Imperial Federation League had pressed on its activities in the face of some opposition and mistrust. The Colonial Conference of 1887 was a signal for the League to stand up and speak for the nation. On July 6th of that year a banquet was given to Rosebery's cousin Edward Stanhope, who was the author of the Conference, and to Sir Henry Holland,[12] who had presided over it as his successor at the Colonial Office. Rosebery was Chairman, and was able to speak of the League as the established mouthpiece of Imperial sentiment in the country. He enumerated the four heads under which its activities ought to develop—political connection, defence, communication, and commerce. He asked for a guarantee fund, to be made up to a thousand a year, to carry them on for three or five years longer. It was, he added, a pleasant feature that Ministers and ex-Ministers met on the Executive of the League.

In 1888 Rosebery read a paper at the League's Council on its present position, and at the annual meeting he explained that it was not its present object to convert Parliament into a senate in which the Colonies should be directly represented. That might come, but it would be a revolution of the first magnitude. Federation did not imply a written constitution, but an Empire of which even the most distant parts are closely leagued together for common objects under a supreme head. It existed already, and it was their task to carry this idea to its fullest possible degree of development. It would not do to take a doctrinaire attitude: let the recent Colonial Conference be the first of a series, and let us take every opportunity of drawing our different commonwealths closer and closer. He added that so far the League had been largely concerned with Australian interests, and he was glad to see that Canada was beginning to take an active part in their proceedings.

At the banquet the same evening he compared the growth of the Empire to a game of chess, which had begun with castles, such as the acquisition of Malta, Gibraltar, and Quebec. Then came the scheme of colonising from Downing Street by knights and bishops. Highly competent gentlemen sometimes went out whose views were rather a relief to the Home Government than an absolute bounty to the Colony. But whatever the system, the Queen still remained; and lastly, where the pawns go the Empire goes. The emigrant who leaves these shores as a rule takes the Empire on his back, and the purpose of the Imperial Federation League was to make this a vivid notion. He repudiated the charge that the members of the League were "visionary dreamers." Their work was eminently practical, though animated by a great, lofty, historical, and Imperial sentiment. In conclusion, he paid a pleasant compliment to the Governor-

[12] (1825-1914.) G.C.M.G. M.P. 1874-88. *Cr.* Lord Knutsford 1888, and Viscount 1895. Secretary of State for the Colonies 1887-92.

General designate of Canada, Lord Stanley of Preston (16th Earl of Derby), a political opponent, but honoured for "the honest steady work he has done for the interests of the State."

In July, at a meeting of the League to welcome a Canadian statesman, Rosebery notes: "A Mr. Parkin of New Brunswick spoke with great force and volubility." This was his first meeting with the man whose name is most nearly connected with the Imperial Federation movement.

The Leeds Chamber of Commerce offered Rosebery an address of welcome in the autumn (October 11th), and speaking of foreign policy, he pointed out how closely it had become entwined with colonial policy, now that the Powers had begun a career of colonial aggrandisement. We now had neighbours everywhere all over the world. He favoured the extension of commerce by purely peaceful methods, and pointed out that the Colonies in proportion to their population took a larger share of British goods than foreign countries. Chambers of commerce could mature public opinion on the retention of colonies in the Empire, and if they did not want to be left alone in the world with Ireland, they must give a larger share to the Colonies in our affairs, and give them a right to prompt the voice of England when it speaks abroad to a much greater extent than at present.

They must be prepared for demands, sometimes unreasonable. They must be prepared in some respects to diminish their own insular freedom of action on behalf of their giant offspring abroad. The cause called Imperial Federation, for want of a better name, was worthy of the devotion of the individual lives of the people of this country. If they would forgive him this little bit of egotism, he could say from the bottom of his heart that it was the dominant passion of his public life. Ever since he had traversed those great regions that own the sway of the British Crown he had felt that it was a cause for which anyone might be content to live: a cause for which, if need be, anyone might be content to die.

This speech, an advance, considering its date, in its conception of the true future of the Empire, evoked loud applause from the Leeds commercial magnates. Apart from its fine rhetoric, a reader of to-day will not deny it the merit of sound foresight. It may not be easy for such a one to realise how little in those years the average Briton thought about the Empire, and how general was the mistrust of those "visionary dreams" with which Rosebery and his allies were credited. As he observed in a speech at Glasgow, Lord Brassey, whom he was introducing to a Scottish audience, was not a visionary philosopher or a random rhetorician, but the most travelled of men of business, who had looked into every chink and crevice of the British Empire, and was a convinced believer in Imperial Federation.

During 1889 Rosebery was bound hand and foot by the London County Council, but he presided at the fourth annual meeting of the League, and made a considerable speech. He began with a triumphant notice of the progress of the League in Canada, which had not been thought a good field for their exertions. There were now eighteen branches in the Dominion, and Ministers, Senators, and Members of Parliament thronged the Council. He went on to expose the fallacy of supposing the old country to be played out and to be seeking Federation in her own interest. On the contrary, she might be self-sufficing, with no relations with the Colonies, and he, for one, wanted more. His aspirations leant to the absolute predominance of the Anglo-Saxon race throughout the world. The United States had federated under the utmost difficulties, and there was no reason to despair of our future. Responsibility for foreign policy, and for defence, were the two practical considerations in view. He was sure that any plan for federation must arise from a colonial, not from a British demand, and the watchword must be equal social, moral, and political rights for every subject of the Queen, whether white or coloured, whether he lands on these shores or whether he lands in some other part of the Empire.

In replying to the toast of his health he reminded his audience that whereas we had started a colonial system with governments closely modelled on our own, we now had exactly changed. The colonial Governments had become much more democratic, and the movements that we take are a closer approximation to their forms of government. The Federation Question, therefore, had an incalculable influence on the future of this country.

Later in the year, Rosebery, on behalf of the League, asked whether the Government would convene a conference to report on the possibility of closer union. Lord Salisbury warily answered that they would receive with all respect any suggestions that the League might make for modifying Imperial relations, but they did not think it within their province to summon a meeting of delegates. If the Colonies desired to consult they could do so without help from us. The intervention of Her Majesty's Government might be taken to imply that they were prepared to make representations for establishing closer and more substantial union.

Undeterred by this shower of cold water, Rosebery rejoined smartly repudiating the notion of a conference summoned by the Colonies among themselves, both from the point of view of Imperial unity and the supremacy of the Crown. And he reminded the Prime Minister that five years ago Mr. W. H. Smith had moved a resolution demanding some form of federation to avert the disintegration of the Empire.

And when the City branch of the League met at the Mansion House (November 15th), a powerful platform, including Cardinal Manning, supported Sir Henry Isaacs, the Lord Mayor. Rosebery seconded the main resolution. The word "Imperial," he said, was not popular in the Colonies, because it represented red tape and bureaucracy, with the Imperial foot put forward and hastily drawn back.

He repeated his objections to producing a cut-and-dried plan. It was impossible now to introduce colonial representation, as such, into the House of Lords, the House of Commons, or the Privy Council, or to found a Customs Union. The method of conference was the right method of advance, and for the time being the League was prepared to limit its energies to seeing that conferences are constantly and permanently renewed. He went on to indicate the other necessary conditions for their success. The very best men should attend them, and they should be invested with all the authority and splendour which the British Government could give. They would not produce statutes, but recommendations.

"You may say that a congress that only meets to report and recommend has but a neutral task before it. I think that those who take that view hold a very inadequate view of what the utterances would be of a conference that represents a quarter of the human race, and represents the immeasurable opulence and power that have been garnered in the past century of her history."

The question whether Imperial federation is an impossible dream would be brought to the touch by the adoption of this scheme. Every possible topic could be discussed with authority and weight. He looked forward to a time when the Empire would be almost self-sufficing, not perhaps commercially speaking, but in its foreign and external policy—a pledge of peace and prosperity not merely for our own race, but for all mankind.

It is clear, I venture to think, that Rosebery did no little service to the Empire by inducing his keen colleagues of the League to advance step by step, not quenching their enthusiasm, but keeping it under control.

At the fifth annual meeting of the League in the following year (May 22nd, 1892) Rosebery again touched on the Conference Question. It had proved to be as well that a Colonial Conference had not been summoned last year, because the minds of Australians were preoccupied by the movement for their own federation. On the other hand, the Fisheries Questions between the United States, Canada, and Newfoundland had accentuated the need for an Imperial foreign policy.

At the Canada Club (July 2nd) Rosebery took occasion to preach from the text of Heligoland, whose unimportant cession had caused heartburnings, a discourse on the impossibility of parting from Canada or Australia. There would be a feeling of regret, almost of degradation, which would shake the Empire to its very foundations.

All this time Rosebery had been diligent in attending the Committee Meetings of the League whenever possible, in addition to the larger gatherings mentioned above. The successive appearance of such books as Dilke's *Greater Britain*, Froude's *Oceana*, and Seeley's *Expansion of England*, the product of very different minds, turned to the anxious study of Imperial questions many who had accepted the existence of the Empire as an everyday phenomenon, like the tides. There still survived thinkers, of whom Goldwin Smith was the most prominent, who held that the dissolution of the Empire, and the independence of the greater Colonies, would be the saving both of them and of the mother-country. Goldwin Smith, an exile from the Oxford professorship which Disraeli had derided, had settled in Canada, and there published *Canada and the Canadian Question*, in which he urged the Dominion, if she did not wish to stand alone, to ask for admission to the American Union. Rosebery directly combated the Professor's arguments. His Australian experiences had not led him to dread an active spirit of disintegration there, but it was not absent, especially in New South Wales and Queensland, where an active minority, with a section of the Press, strongly advocated Australian federation as a step towards separation from Great Britain. Both in the Colonies and at home there was much general discussion on Defence questions, and in particular on the dilemma which seemed so real to some of the overseas statesmen, and has proved to be so purely academic—whether the

Colonies might not be dragged into wars with which they had no concern. There was the corresponding dread here that the rash action of an individual colony might involve us in trouble with another nation. When Lord Salisbury received the League's deputation in 1891 he "was aware of the large portion of our foreign negotiations, our foreign difficulties, and the danger of foreign complications which arise entirely from our colonial connections," and in the following spring (March 23rd, 1892) Rosebery himself, speaking at the City Liberal Club, observed:

"Our great Empire has pulled us, so to speak, by the coat tails out of the European system, and though, with our great predominance, our great moral influence, and our great fleet, with our traditions in Europe and our aspirations to preserve the peace of Europe, we can never remove ourselves altogether from the European system, we must recognise that our foreign policy has become a Colonial policy, and it is in reality dictated much more from the extremities of the Empire than from London itself."

It will have been noted that the actual conditions for Imperial approximation remained undefined. The League was inclined to welcome the scheme of an Imperial Budget of Defence, to which Great Britain should contribute the principal share, the self-governing and Crown Colonies according to their capacity and their need for protection. Some favoured the imposition of special duties for this purpose. As we know, this project did not formally mature, any more than did the grandiose plan of which it originally formed part, that of a federal constitution for the Empire, with some form of government or council which would not detract from the local independence of each unit.

All this is ancient history, and many of the vexed questions found their answer in the course of the South African War, others in the Great War. But it should be remembered to the credit of the League, and of Rosebery's foresight as an Imperial statesman, that their hopes were based on periodical conferences; on the admission to the Privy Council of Colonial Ministers, and of Colonial judges on its judicial side; and on the appointment of representatives of the self-governing Colonies in an official capacity. The achievement of "Dominion status" (to use an unfortunate because undefined expression) has closely followed these lines. Finally, when we puzzle over the apparent eagerness of some Dominion statesmen to secure "the right of secession," we note that the authorised spokesman of the League wrote:

"Every responsible British statesman of the last half century has said that when the Great Colonies wish to go, Great Britain will raise no objection, that this view has been re-echoed unanimously by the press and by public opinion, and that no advocate of Imperial Federation, National Unity, or whatever other name we apply to British consolidation, has ever hinted at the union of self-governing portions of the Empire as anything else than a pact entered into voluntarily by communities free to choose or refuse as they please."[13]

[13] *Imperial Federation.* (George R. Parkin, London, 1892.)

CHAPTER X

Reform of the House of Lords—London County Council—
Home and Foreign Politics

THE early days of the new year were spent at Sandringham, with the enjoyment of four days of the lavish and varied Norfolk shooting. One of the party was a favourite guest of the Prince's, the Marquis de Galliffet, the Prince Rupert or Hodson of 1870, the hero of the last desperate charges of Sedan, when the day was lost past hope, and of the fine response, *"tant que vous voudrez, mon général! tant qu'il en restera un!"* It was known that on the hill opposite the old King, whose first battle had been Ligny, put down his glasses with the simple tribute of *"tapfere Leute!"* But General de Galliffet was also remembered as the pitiless executioner of files of defeated *communards* in 1871.

January 3rd.—"He told me after dinner that he was 57 and extremely ambitious; that Boulanger could have walked into the Elysée at one time, but is now forgotten; B. went into Bourse speculations at the time of the war panic with Mackay the American and won largely. Galliffet told Napoleon III in 1869 that the army was not ready. He acknowledged that the French hated England more than any other country, for which he blamed our policy in 1870."

But General de Galliffet was no Boulanger, and a few years later he played a fine part as Minister of War in upholding Colonel Picquart at the crisis of the Dreyfus trouble.

The political atmosphere remained chilly, both as between the parties and within the Liberal party. Arthur Balfour as Chief Secretary for Ireland had displayed unforeseen qualities of energy, and in the House of Commons maddened his Irish opponents by his supple skill in debate.

Early in February Gladstone came to the Durdans and—

"Talked of the future. Of Harcourt's qualifications for leadership— his ability universally acknowledged, an equally universal determination to have nothing to do with him. From this I strongly dissented. The

[256]

future black because of Chamberlain and Randolph: 'I am reproached with being too sanguine, but on this point no one can be less so. I pity you, I pity chiefly John Morley as being in the House of Commons!' We talked of the past. I said that if we had proposed a Royal Commission we should have carried our measure through the House of Commons after the pause of a year that it would have given us. He generally concurred."[1]

Early in the new year Rosebery believed that it was a propitious moment for grappling once more with the reform of the House of Lords. At the beginning of March he expounded his plan to John Morley, and a few days later (March 8th) collected his leading peer colleagues, Spencer, Kimberley, Granville and Ripon for the same purpose. All of these except Granville were disposed to agree: then came George Curzon and St. John Broderick, who set forth their scheme for making qualifications of efficiency. Rosebery pointed out to them that this would not touch the real weakness—the want of some basis of election. On March 11th he brought forward his motion for a Committee to inquire into the constitution of the House. Lord Dunraven had withdrawn a similar motion to make room for him. He spoke for an hour and three-quarters—"a *succès d'estime*" as he put it himself. He recapitulated firstly the circumstances of his motion of 1884, and the agitation against the House of Lords which followed the rejection of the Franchise Bill in that year. Recently Sir Michael Hicks Beach and Mr. W. H. Smith had expressed themselves in favour of Reform of the House of Lords by its own act. He dwelt on the omnipotence of the Government in the House; there were only some thirty in favour of Home Rule. The weakness of the House was the untempered application of the

[1] It is interesting to compare Lord E. Fitzmaurice's verdict on the Bill of 1886: "It is not difficult to see, especially at this interval of time, that, quite apart from the merits of the question, the attempt to deal with Home Rule in 1886 was premature. A nation will make a great alteration of its constitution in one or other of two sets of circumstances. It will do so either after long and careful enquiry, such as preceded the Act of Union with Scotland, when time has been given for the opinion of the country to become convinced of the wisdom of the proposed change; or it may be forced by adverse circumstances such as those which compelled the British Parliament in 1782 to grant complete legislative and judicial independence to Ireland, in the same year as that in which it had to submit to the final loss of the American Colonies and to unfavourable treaties with France, Spain, and Holland. Neither of these two sets of circumstances existed in 1886. The nation had not been prepared by previous discussion; and in the external relations of the country there was nothing to compel an unwilling consent to change. . . . On June 7th, 1886, the Home Rule Bill was rejected on the second reading by a majority of thirty votes. The numbers were 343 to 313." (Lord E. Fitzmaurice, *Life of Lord Granville*, vol. ii, p. 486.)

hereditary principle. It was a false analogy to say that the Crown would suffer by departure from it. Since the great Reform Bill the House had been converted into a party instrument, since which its control over Governments had ceased to exist. But the arguments for a Second Chamber were conclusive. He proposed a Committee to investigate, because the Government would not take up the business, and no unofficial individual could undertake it. Various plans would be before the Committee. He did not think the simple addition of Life Peers would be sufficient—"the mere zoological collection of abstract celebrities." The Privy Council would be an ideal Second Chamber, even if the 109 Peers in it were alone nominated. But there might arise the same practical difficulties as with the creation of Life Peers. He would suggest that a delegation from the whole peerage, Scottish and Irish included, should represent the hereditary element, with safeguards for minorities. Then there should be an elected element, chosen by the County Councils that were just coming into being, by the larger Municipalities, or by the House of Commons, or by all three. Again, there was the principle of life peerages and official peerages, a valuable element when limited in number. He would like to add representation of the Self-governing Colonies, and in every case would fix a proportion of the various elements.

He passed on to meet the formidable argument which Lord Salisbury had advanced in a speech in the country, that, after all, political power is a constant quantity, and any addition made to the powers of the Lords can only be at the expense of the Commons. Rosebery tried to show that a distinction could be drawn between increased power and increased efficiency, while admitting the possible disturbance of balance if a new Second Chamber were devised, not subject to the creation of Peers. To meet this objection there might be joint sittings of the two Houses, or recourse might be had to a suggestion of Mr. Bright's, that when a measure had been once or twice rejected by the House of Lords, the House of Commons might, in the language of diplomacy, *passer outre*. He disliked this last remedy, because he thought it would be used to excess.[2] Peers who were not selected for the new House should be freely able to stand for the House of Commons. In conclusion, he pointed out that it was the Conservative party in the country who

[2] This, as we know, has not actually happened with the Parliament Act; but we shall see later on that Rosebery's objections of five-and-twenty years back had not been overcome.

were pressing for this reform at a time of political calm. Lord Wemyss, who followed, did not think it safe to trust the constitution of the House to the chances of a Committee, and reform should be on the responsibility of Ministers of the Crown. Lord Dunraven, ardent for reform, thought that a Bill should be introduced, and was prepared to do it. Lord Kimberley would have preferred a Government Bill, but would vote with Rosebery, feeling that the last Reform Act made some reconstruction of the House of Lords necessary. Lord Salisbury replied at length, with a compliment, to the mover's remarkably able and eloquent speech: with its fertility of illustration, it should have been justified by laying on the table the measure to which it referred. It was a speech with a foregone conclusion, and in itself seemed to be the only Order of Reference to a Committee. He went on to challenge the assertion that the House was inveterately and permanently Tory. Mr. Gladstone's recent measures had drawn a new dividing line which unfortunately coincided with classes. But would Rosebery's proposals give a sound democratic basis to the House? A House of Lords with a Radical majority would be a very odd assembly. He agreed that black sheep ought to be excluded. But if certain peers were elected for life by the rest, what was to prevent an elected peer from becoming a black sheep? He favoured the nomination of a limited number of Life Peers, but doubted whether they would be very effective. Only former members of the House of Commons, or of the Bar, had the *robur et aes triplex* not to be extinguished by the most terrible audience a man can address. Lord Salisbury boldly concluded by asserting that no Second Chamber would answer in the long run, in this country, but one based on the hereditary principle. Its composition gave it the easy-going tolerance for accommodating itself to the difficult part of playing second to the House of Commons. A reconstructed chamber of active politicians would insist on sharing the powers of the other House. The Peers would be touching weapons of a terribly keen edge if they undertook to reconstruct that ancient assemblage.

Lord Granville wound up the debate. Nobody could really deny that the House was permanently Conservative, and he felt that Lord Salisbury's unyielding attitude was doing much to shake the position of the House of Lords in the country.

Rosebery's motion was defeated by 97 votes to 50, the minority being composed of Liberals of all shades, with half a dozen Conservatives.

[259]

This debate has been dwelt on at some length, partly because its subject captured Rosebery's special attention throughout the whole of his parliamentary life; partly because no final conclusion upon it has been reached by the country. It has been usual to blame Lord Salisbury for having neglected to grapple with it during the two periods of office when he was dictator of Parliament. The latter passages of his striking speech in the debate show why he never seriously attempted any reconstitution of the House of Lords. Lord Salisbury did not live to witness the passing of the Parliament Act, and it is possible to imagine how the lightning of his sarcastic wit would have played about that measure. It is too soon as yet to gauge the precise outcome of what was undoubtedly intended to be the prelude to another Act remodelling the constitution of the House. Hitherto its effects have not been notable in any direction. But at any rate, if Lord Salisbury were here, he could point to the complete failure, so far, to devise departure from the purely hereditary basis of the Second Chamber.

To conclude this year's dealing with the question, Rosebery took no part in the long debate on Lord Dunraven's House of Lords (Constitution) Bill (April 26th). It was a far-reaching measure, but was withdrawn on Lord Salisbury's undertaking to bring in a Bill for the creation of some Life Peers, and to make possible the expulsion of "black sheep."

The engagement regarding Life Peers was fulfilled on June 18th by the first reading of a Bill empowering the creation of not more than three of these exalted beings in a year, belonging to certain categories in the Navy, Army, Diplomatic or Civil Services. Two others of some special qualifications might, but need not, be created, making five in all as a maximum. Power would also be taken to expel a "black sheep" by the cancellation of his Writ of Summons.

Rosebery followed, and thought that in view of the wide discussion of reform in the Press and on platforms, and of the danger of complete want of sympathy between the two Houses, these small proposals made one feel that the subject is almost hopeless. He thought that a system of delegation would answer far better than one of expurgation of the undeserving. He would support the Bill as a precedent for larger proposals. The Duke of Argyll—always on the alert to suspect any action of Rosebery's—asked what his noble friend was driving at by his speeches in and out of the House? It was pretty plain that he only wanted a Second Chamber that would always say "ditto" to the House of Commons. Rosebery had said that the House of Lords had obstructed Liberal measures. This the Duke denied, and proceeded to a long diatribe against Gladstone and Rosebery for their recent conduct.

The Bill came up for second reading in due course (July 10th), but it had been announced in the House of Commons that legislation in general would be postponed till the Autumn Session. Rosebery, as "a somewhat platonic admirer of the Bill," derided the carefully guarded categories of Life Peers, which would turn the House "into a sort of legislative Bath or Cheltenham, or, perhaps, if it is not disrespectful to say so, into a sort of legislative hydropathic establishment, where these noble persons will take more care of their constitutions than of the constitution of this House." He then rounded on the Duke of Argyll, who on the first reading had made his customary attack when Rosebery could not reply, having already spoken. And he went on to show how the Duke had attributed to him a series of statements that he had never made.

The Discontinuance of Writs Bill, whereby "black sheep" were to be cast out, shared the fate of the larger measure. Neither, as a matter of fact, reappeared in the short Autumn Session.

Otherwise, politically it was not a year involving any particular heart-searchings on Rosebery's part. Ireland boiled up anew with the fresh agitation over the charges connected with the alleged letter of Parnell's published by *The Times* in April 1887, and the remotely connected legal proceedings instituted in the following spring.

In a letter to Lord Spencer, written during his Italian tour, he showed his liking for what was afterwards known as the "step by step policy." The Government were going to extend some local government to Ireland:

April 3rd, 1888.—"With regard to the Local Government Bill, I hope our people will support it in the main with ardour. We cannot, it seems to me, show too much enthusiasm for the democratic parts of the measure, as I understand it. I do not say this in the cynical belief that no course will cause more annoyance to the Tories. But I say it because in principle it seems a measure such as we should have wished to carry, though of course the House of Lords would have thrown it out. If my view be correct we are bound as honest men to promote the Bill. Secondly, as regards expediency, it seems to me clear that this Bill lays a basis for the Liberal party in England such as it has never had before; while it makes Home Rule in Ireland a logical necessity in addition to being a political necessity which it was before."

Then came the appointment of the Parnell Commission in July. Rosebery kept Ireland to the front in his speeches. At Inverness, on June 14th, he dwelt on the falsity of the Liberal Unionist position. If it was true that they were good Liberals in the green-room, and influenced the Government, why did they not show their Liberalism before the curtain and on the stage? The Liberal party, having put its hand to the plough, would never draw back—where would the Liberal Unionists be then? He had to recognise that the exclusion of the Irish members was not popular, so it might have to be dropped. He developed a most caustic account of the Tory-Parnellite alliance of 1885, and the attack on Lord Spencer. "History may record more discreditable acts; it can hardly record any more contemptible." He spoke bitterly of new instances of coercion, and of Mr. Dillon's recent committal to prison by a magistrate not by a jury. The whole of this speech vibrates with feeling, as much as any that he delivered on Ireland.

He reverted to the subject when addressing the Home Counties Liberals at Willis's Rooms (June 21st), describing Mr. Dillon as a martyr to his great cause, and at Stansted in Essex (July 25th), dealing with the Statutory Commission, he accused the Government of purposely mixing up the inquiry into the letters with their general indictment of the National League.[3]

At Bolton (July 28th) he again depicted the harsh incidents of coercion, and said that all the tentative schemes for Ireland, all the roads, local government, provincial councils, even separate Private Bill legislation—all would lead to Home Rule.

He thus did his duty as a loyal party man; but he never permitted anything to stand in the way of attention to Scottish affairs, and when the Secretary for Scotland, Lord Lothian, brought in the Scottish Universities Bill, modifying in important respects the constitution of the Universities as designed thirty years before, Rosebery, while supporting the measure generally, delivered a series of studied criticisms relating particularly to the proposed powers of affiliation of other colleges to the universities, under undefined conditions. Subsequent speakers followed his example in this, and secured promise of reconsideration from the Government.

Meanwhile an entirely new vista of occupation and usefulness was opening out. From early days Rosebery had been moved by the spectacle of the vast unregulated city in a corner of which he and

[3] The whole story of this sinister business is told at length in Morley's *Life of Gladstone*, vol. iii, bk. x, chap. iii.

his like were congregated. Before his marriage he was well acquainted with Mr. Henry Solly, then the head of the Artisan's Institute in East London. But he carried on his more intimate friendship with William Rogers,[4] Prebendary of St. Paul's, and Rector of Bishopsgate since 1862. He and Rosebery corresponded regularly and candidly. Rogers, the contemporary of Queen Victoria, was a son of Eton and Oxford, where he had rowed for the University. As "perpetual curate" of a poor East London parish, for many years he had been an evangelist of education, cleanliness and the provision of rational amusements for neglected people. His alleged dismissal of doctrine by the phrase "hang theology" offended many worthy folk; but there was no doubt of his absolute devotion to good causes. Like other broad-minded ecclesiastics of the century, Sydney Smith, his close friend Jowett, and Charles Kingsley, he was enthusiastic in bringing the fortunate folk of the world to comprehension and into association with the less fortunate. Like Charles Kingsley, he was much of a sportsman, and could be excited by the racing triumphs of such friends as Lord Falmouth and Rosebery. But no man was less of a social sycophant, or more utterly independent in expressing his opinion to anybody, rich or poor. Rogers was greatly crippled by a painful rheumatic affection, by which he refused to be disabled; and once or twice Rosebery had been able to force him to a short spell of rest at the Durdans.

County Councils came into being by the legislation of this year, and the new County of London was carved out of Middlesex, Kent and Surrey. It was clear that the new body, taking the place of the somewhat discredited Metropolitan Board of Works, might assume functions of the weightiest character.

On December 1st Rosebery saw Canon Rogers, and intimated his intention of standing for the London County Council. "He to consider." The next day he met another active Londoner, and spoke of standing, preferably for Whitechapel. His candidature for the new body belongs to the story of the next year; but London had been much in his thoughts before its new scheme of government had come to maturity. The opening of the Swimming Bath at the People's Palace in the Mile End Road—the concrete expression of Walter Besant's vision—was on May 14th. Rosebery and his wife had made a gift of it, and the little ceremony was followed by supper at Toynbee Hall to meet "some working men, very pleasant and

[4] P. 95.

[263]

interesting." And all excursions eastward were not official, for instance, on a Sunday morning:

July 1st.—"With John Morley to the City. We walked to Houndsditch and all about any nooks we could find. Stood on London Bridge, and went in reverence to see the house in Bolt Court, where Johnson lived and died. A happy reverent morning."[5]

Before this the usual current of the year had been broken by a visit to Italy (March 25th), a day or two at Milan followed by a fortnight at Naples. A happy spell of irresponsible occupation, with many visits to the Rendel Villa, and an excursion to Taranto as the guests of Sir James Lacaita at his country home, which seemed to be just like what an old Roman farm was, with its culture of pollarded olive trees unaltered since the time of Varro, and the labourers dancing the tarantella in the afternoon. The cultured Sir James as a busy landlord was a new character. Three days at Rome, of no special interests, started them for Paris, which they found still restless, with Boulanger's intentions uncertain, and crowds in the streets "mainly good-humoured but irritable."

Rosebery went to Cambridge as the guest of Oscar Browning at King's College, to receive the honorary LL.D. degree (June 9th). In the morning he and Lord Salisbury had met at the Mansion House, urging the claims of the South London Technical Institute. The evening found them fellow guests at the banquet at Trinity College—

"sat between Salisbury and St. Germans. Answered as one of the doctors designate. S. asked me how much I was going to subscribe to the South London Institute. I told him I had resolved to give what he did."

The next day at the Senate House, when he received his degree, he was able to note "not hooted, cheered even. Balfour most cheered." The following day he visited William Pitt's rooms at Pembroke; saw the old Provost Okes, ninety, but keeping Eton as his chief interest; and attended Service at King's, "very fine—noble effect of great west door open at the end."

There was a short summer visit to Sandringham. The Prince's visit to Berlin had been painful:

[5] Later Rosebery wondered whether this was the occasion on which Morley asked him to write the little book about Pitt, and on reflection concluded that the suggestion was made, but that he did not take up the subject till after 1890.

"He gave me a long narrative of what passed. Very indignant; and a little put out, I think, by my silence and reticence. The clock struck nine (the dinner hour), and guests arrived while we were still in conclave."

The Bismarcks were the main cause of the trouble; and Rosebery's special relations with them must have placed him in an awkward position at the moment.

Scotland, however, had a good share of attention this year. Flying visits to Edinburgh at the end of January and late in April were followed by a stay with Mr. John Hamilton,[6] at Dalzell, when excursions were made to Hamilton Palace and the Glasgow Exhibition. He was still farther north in June for the Liberal meeting at Wick. After receiving the freedom of the town—

"At 1.30 to John o' Groats. Never have I enjoyed an afternoon more. At the inn there was a deputation of one, or at most two, with an address the most northerly ever presented in Great Britain. Then we walked over springy turf to Duncanshay Head, passed over the Goes (great fissures made by the sea), sate on the edge of the cliff and watched Swona and Ronaldshay and the currents all smiling and sunny, usually so terrible. The gulls were a delightful addition. Then to look at the Stacks, and home by the beach composed of pounded or broken shells—picking buckies. Everywhere the simple people hoisted flags and cheered and showed cordiality."

The spectacle of this ironical figure, half student, half sportsman, happily picking shells on the extreme northern shore, would surely have puzzled some of his acquaintance of southern lobbies and race-courses. A meeting at Inverness followed, and then by pony and launch to Assynt and Ronald Ferguson's northern home at Novar.

Much of August was given to grouse shooting, first with Lord Hindlip at Invermark, where his old school friend Newport at a drive, not on the moor but the forest, performed the remarkable feat of killing forty-six birds in one drive with a single gun, and running out of cartridges. Then to Mr. Arthur Sassoon's delightful lodge on the Seafield estate, Tulchan. The rest of the late summer and the early autumn were spent at Dalmeny, receiving no large parties, but a succession of friends from England, America and France, and with many outings with the children in gorgeous

[6] John Glencairn Carter Hamilton, 1829-1900; M.P. for Falkirk Burghs, 1857-9; for South Lanark, 1868-74 and again 1880-86; created 1st Baron Hamilton of Dalzell 1886.

[265]

weather. On October 31st there was an Imperial Federation meeting in Edinburgh, with a forty-five minutes' speech from Rosebery.

There was a brief stay at Hawarden (October 11th), where he sat up till 1.30 talking to Harcourt and his son in the smoking-room, a haunt not frequented by their illustrious host. The next day (October 12th)—

"Spoke to Mr. G. earnestly about his Leeds speech, urging a great statesmanlike broad speech, avoiding detail. He agreed, murmuring, 'It makes a very dull speech, but never mind.'"

"Met Mr. G. coming from church at 8.50 a.m. and told him that as regards dullness of speech, that could be prevented by a very small spice of political and personal reminiscence."

Two visits to the splendours of Longleat and Wilton, where the company was choice and the pheasants flew high, were followed by a short stay with Harcourt at Malwood, his cherished home in the New Forest. Rosebery had been going the year before, but the illness of one of the children had interfered.

The year opened by a dinner with Canon Rogers at Bishopsgate Rectory, to meet City celebrities, legal and financial, with the City Police Ball to finish the evening. A few days later he addressed his first meeting as an independent candidate, not for Whitechapel, but for one of the four City seats allotted to the London County Council. In his short electoral address, dated January 1st, he declared his absolute freedom from party politics in this campaign, and indicated his belief that the Council would prove itself worthy of larger powers than were already conferred on it. But speaking at the Bishopsgate schoolroom (January 7th), with his staunch old friend in the Chair, he thought the enlargement of the Council's powers was a matter for Parliament, and that for the present it should devote itself to perfecting its organisation, on the three foundations of absolute incorruptibility, of personal efficiency, and of rational economy. The Metropolitan Board of Works, it should be recalled, had come under some suspicion of jobbery and "graft."

Three days later, at the Memorial Hall in Farringdon Street, Rosebery further pressed the need of abstention from party politics as such. The City, he thought, could maintain the leading position in London, and renew its youth, as the city guilds had done, by being awakened to their responsibilities. The City, where 50,000 slept but a quarter of a million spent their lives, should set the example, and let London save London. He answered with adroitness and humour questions from doubting hearers, and promised regular attendance at the Council, a point on which he was not unnaturally heckled.

At Houndsditch (January 16th), with a City Conservative in the chair, he reiterated his independence of party for the purposes of local government, and declined to state opinions on questions within the purview of Parliament. Nevertheless, these speeches were as fully reported in the Press as if they had been concerned with party issues. This was in some degree a personal tribute : many Londoners could not make up their minds whether the new Council was going to be really a dominating municipal authority, or only the Metropolitan Board in a fancy dress. Polling was on January 18th. Sir John Lubbock, a famous City figure, combining fine cultivation with a great position in business, was returned at the head of the poll with 8,976 votes. Rosebery followed with 8,032, and was warmly received at the declaration at the Guildhall. The City Council, with the affability of the aged to the young, had lent the infant County Council the Chamber at the Guildhall one day a week for three months. The first meeting, of two hours, was inconclusive, and ended in an adjournment; but the second, also of two hours, and a "jarring debate" as he put it, ended in his election as Chairman by 104 votes against 17. Some of the minority, men who to-day would be Left-Wing Socialists, were discontented at the election. They did not want an ex-Minister, and a wealthy man, holding that all officials of their body should be its paid servants. But it was a small minority and, the election once over, Rosebery soon secured the personal goodwill of most of its members. This was the first occasion on which it was publicly important that he should make friends with people of different upbringing from himself and with tastes and habits foreign to his own. He had been doing it all his life, for no man had less of *morgue*—to use a foreign expression difficult to render exactly into English—nor did his special brand of shyness and reserve give that appearance of *morgue* by which shy but genuinely modest men are sometimes misjudged. He got on just as well with a Scottish labourer whose native wit supplied the place of book-learning, as with a poor student whose life was centred in his books, or with a bookmaker whose only book was his own. In a way it was a singular gift. Most often those who are so happy as to possess it win their way by an openly natural bearing, and by seeming the same to everybody. A man of close repression, like Rosebery, rarely so shines. His was an individual power of suiting not only his conversation, but his whole identity to the company with which he was in sympathy. His sympathies were numerous, and his toleration was large. There is amazing attraction in a man of first-class intellect who, *in loco,* is quite indifferent to the intellectual equipment of the hour's companions. As Gibbon said of his society at Lausanne: "I am too modest, or too proud, to rate my own value by that of my associates; and whatsoever may be the fame of learning and genius, experience has shown me that the cheaper commodities of politeness and good sense are of more useful currency in the commerce of life." Most of us have known two or three such social philosophers, but I have never quite seen Rosebery's equal in this respect. Not that he ever suffered fools gladly, or endured boredom for long, for he showed remarkable skill in slipping away from uncongenial surroundings when unrestrained by shame or duty.

Thus did Rosebery start on his voyage of municipal discovery, for discovery it certainly was. The London County Council came into being, overshadowed on the one hand by the majestic traditions of the Guildhall and the Mansion House, and somewhat tarnished on the other by the recent ineptitudes of London local government. When the full Council met, there were no established rules of order for a body of 137, too large for committee procedure, and barely large enough to accept the discipline of a legislative assembly. Then some twenty committees had to be formed. Rosebery's absorption in the work of these was no little surprise to the Council and to some of his friends. Charles Fox, asked at St. Anne's Hill why he was doing some laborious and monotonous work in the garden, replied, "Because I am a very painstaking man." Rosebery shared some of Charles Fox's tastes and foibles; but he too was a very painstaking man.

From February 13th, committees met every day, sometimes sitting for five hours on end; and now and then two or three met consecutively. The notes of these consecutive days are instructive, just as he jotted them down. Before his election he had pledged himself to a Liberal meeting in the Edinburgh Corn Exchange. There were 4,000 people present, and a row of Scottish M.P.'s on the platform. The story begins on the previous day:

February 18th.—"Committee of Council Meeting at 12 till 4.30. Then to Harcourt."

February 19th.—"Left by 10 train for Scotland. Arrived at Edinburgh at 6.30. Crowd. To Royal Hotel, where H. Then with her and

[268]

Lord Hamilton to meeting. Spoke for one hour 20 minutes. T. P. O'Connor spoke for 30 or 40. At 10.20 left meeting for London."

February 20th.—"Arrived in London. Bought a horse at 9. To John Morley at 11 and walked with him. Attended Metropolitan Board of Works Parks Committee."

"Gave dinner to about 20 of the Opposition leaders. Mr. G. fresh from Italy very well but voice husky."

"To Durdans by last train."

The next day he was back in London, attending committees in morning and afternoon. This was an unusual rush; but he was always tempted to try a splendid constitution too highly. Possibly, but for the calamity that soon broke up his home, he might have done so with impunity for many years.

Four-fifths of the Edinburgh speech were devoted to Ireland. He made excellent play with the effort of the English minority to excite Protestant opinion in Scotland against Irish Catholics:

"You are familiar with our visitors from the South, the sort of gentleman who in the railway carriage between Berwick and Perth thinks it his duty to assume a kilt. I have observed that in the same way it is customary for the random Unionist who visits Scotland to assume as he passes the border the aspect and guise of a beleaguered Protestant."

The whole speech was full of banter, and concluded with a grave appeal for Imperial Unity.

In London relations with the expiring Metropolitan Board were at first difficult, and it fell to Rosebery (March 20th) to give three instances in which the County Council, still a provisional body, had been treated with neglect and contempt by their moribund predecessors. Consequently the emergence of the Council from its chrysalis stage could not be delayed; and on March 21st, meeting at the Board room of the extinct body in Spring Gardens, it fell to the Chairman to review for his colleagues the work done in their provisional stage. The Metropolitan Board had failed in collective courtesy, but their Chairman, Lord Magheramorne, had been most helpful. They themselves had found how little they disagreed, and that they could trust each other. It was altogether a very cordial gathering, and of good omen. The Council continued to hold its weekly meetings at the Guildhall until April in the following year, when the Chamber at Spring Gardens was reconstructed, but the latter building housed most of the Committee meetings. In May, a salary of £2,000 a year was voted to the Deputy-Chairman, it being thought convenient to appoint a salaried officer under this name in the first instance, instead of a Clerk instituted with a permanent title.

Mr. J. F. B. Firth, M.P., a man of large municipal experience, was first appointed, but he died in the early autumn. Rosebery paid his memory the high tribute that, having given up his position as leader of a party to become the servant of the Council, he had disarmed every antagonist, and shown absolutely unrivalled capacity for the place he filled.

The Improvements Committee was keenly active, and wished to begin the widening of the Strand by clearing the south side of Holywell Street; Rosebery, with excellent foresight, pleaded for a large and comprehensive scheme, though trusting that preliminary plans should be lodged by the end of November. This would show that they were at work, and meant to take power to improve London. There were one or two personal disputes, some of them acrid, over loans and contracts, but the chief excitements of the autumn were connected with licences for music and dancing. At the first meeting at which the Council sat as Licensing Authority Rosebery, for once making a regular speech, reminded his colleagues that they were not meeting as a popular representative body for debate, but in a quasi-judicial capacity, and should endeavour, without the spirit of harmless repartee, to arrive in a spirit of dignity at a resolution on the very arduous problems to be submitted to them. Several bodies had wished to send deputations, but the Council would have had to spend days in the blameless and insipid occupation of receiving them. The appeals from the Licensing Committee were mostly granted. They had secured the incomparable services of Sir Charles Russell,[7] and Rosebery observed with pleasure how he recited music-hall songs, with the same modulation he might have used for Tennyson. In announcing the Council's decision Rosebery paid compliments to the Licensing Committee, who had undertaken serious exertions (in attending music-halls) when others were endeavouring to obtain rest and recreation elsewhere. He could see nothing to laugh at in this tribute. He also praised Sir Charles Russell's conduct of the principal case, and went on to speak of the standards of wit and taste that obtained at music-halls. If they were going to insist on a higher standard, they ought to give warning of this intention to the

[7] (1832-1900.) G.C.M.G. M.P. 1880-94. Lord of Appeal and Lord Chief Justice 1894.

proprietors. It would not be fair first to condemn persons for maintaining the existing standard because they wished to establish a new one, thus causing injury and injustice to innocent parties. In the second place, he dreaded going beyond the temperature of public opinion in these matters. Public fastidiousness had greatly increased since Thackeray wrote about the "Coal Hole"; and if they tried to outstrip popular progress there was risk of reaction, which would cause the very evils they were trying to eschew.

On November 7th, at the Guildhall Statutory Meeting, Rosebery was unanimously re-elected Chairman amid a chorus of grateful praise. He replied congratulating the Council on its neglect of political considerations. His only complaints were, first, that the Government had declined to meet, by a simple Act, their distinct needs as the London Council; secondly, that they had been badly treated financially, losing the old Coal and Wine dues of London without receiving the promised compensation to the rates; and thirdly, that a dead set had been made against them by the public, and by the majority of the Press. Superior people preferred the classic quietude of their predecessors, that slow but deep stream. Nevertheless, in their short stormy life they had gained a great deal of esprit de corps. He spoke of the future County Hall that would have to be built some day; meanwhile, they would be regarded by their more splendid successors as men, who in difficult circumstances endeavoured to do their best. For himself, he asked that his re-election might hold good only till the summer recess, not until that time next year. To carry on the tale of Rosebery's first connection with the County Council, Council and Committee Meetings continued congestedly till December 17th, when the Council met at noon and cleared off arrears till 7, enabling him to catch the 8 p.m. train from King's Cross to Edinburgh for the winter holiday.

When the Council reassembled (January 14th, 1890), there was a curious dispute over the proposed municipal welcome to Mr. H. M. Stanley, just returned from his famous expedition in search of Emin Pasha. Mr. John Burns did not question the traveller's ability or pluck, but he had been responsible for the death of hundreds of human beings when trying to get the 160,000 tons of ivory which Emin Pasha had gathered. The reverend gentleman who had suggested the welcome complained that his own Christian character was being aspersed by these comments. A long discussion ensued, with Rosebery refusing to admit any points of order in what one of the speakers called the most disagreeable discussion into which the

Council had ever entered. The motion was finally withdrawn; but one can picture the fires which would have blazed under a weak or excitable chairman. Humanity is the most intoxicating of senti-ments—*bhang* or *ganja* in a controversy.

There was much discussion (March 14th) over the proposed Blackwall Tunnel, a legacy from the Metropolitan Board, and it fell to Rosebery to close the debate in a closely divided session of the Council. He thought there was something of a pledge to East Lon-don for its construction, but had long hesitated because hundreds of acres of marshland would appreciate in value, possibly fifty-fold, and there could be no provision for betterment in the rate-payers' interests. If they could secure this, it would be right to wait, but he saw no prospect of a Parliamentary measure, and had come down on the side of proceeding at once. In the event, this course was favoured, but only by a majority of nine.

At a later meeting (March 25th) the scheme again only scraped through by small majorities.

Rosebery's unfailing attendance at Council and Committee meet-ings went on till July 16th, when his resignation was handed in, and the Vice-Chairman, Sir John Lubbock, said all that an accom-plished speaker could say at such a moment. Three leading members followed, including the Deputy-Chairman. All of them laid special stress on his work in the Committees, besides, of course, referring to his brilliant chairmanship. Said one: "The whole work of creat-ing committees and forming and marshalling the staff was done with the instincts of a man of business and the judgment and au-thority of a statesman. His watchfulness of the smallest detail in committee absorbed his time to an extent hardly appreciated." An-other declared that a few months ago the Chairman had found them a mere collection, so to say, of atoms, and it had been his labour of love to weld those atoms together, apart from opinions, into one harmonious whole, and to convert them into a machine of no mean working order. The Deputy-Chairman dwelt on Rosebery's willingness to give help and guidance to individual members, and on his ubiquity in and out of the Committee rooms, and his power of instantly taking up the questions there under consideration.

It was estimated that, from the opening meeting to his last ap-pearance as Chairman on July 8th, he had presided over the Council forty-four times, and had attended 280 committee meetings. It has been noted above how mischance dogged Rosebery's footsteps in his successive admissions to political office: to vary the metaphor, his boat was never borne on the rising tide. This time fortune was kinder, for though the difficulties were many, in overcoming them he attracted universal admiration and applause. It is not too much to call it the truest success of his whole career; a success won in a minor field, if you will, but a success unalloyed by any jealousy among colleagues, or any misapprehension of his motives or of the purposes for which he was striving. Not least, he was given the chance of making friendships which would not have blossomed otherwise, but which bore fruit for many years. His coadjutors in office have been named, as has John Burns; but there were others, like John Benn, an embodiment of London energy and observation, with whom intimacy increased as time went on.

The main current of life through 1889 flowed on, though more slowly, past the great central shoal of County Council work. To anxious gazers westward the murky atmosphere of Ireland seemed to grow somewhat clearer. The merciless exposure of the Piggott forgeries in February—which the Government endeavoured to counter by insisting that, after all, the Irish leader and his band had applauded intimidation and had not denounced crime—was followed by a mutual effort to forgive and forget on the part of Liberals and Home Rulers. There was an Eighty Club dinner (March 8th) with Frank Lockwood, the most popular of Liberal lawyers and wits, in the Chair.

"Spencer, as guest, spoke for an hour with an interesting statement as to his change in 1885 and 1886. Then Parnell asked for, and made an admirable speech. I proposed vote of thanks. Insufferable heat. Eighty ladies lined the room. Charles Russell next to me: introduced me at once to Parnell, his guest on the other side. Then Spencer introduced and shook hands. A striking occasion."

On May 17th the Prince and Princess of Wales dined at 38 Berkeley Square:

"The Princess told me she should like to go to Dublin, as she liked the Irish. The Prince told me it was all premature, but that he thought the right Prince to go in, say, a year was the Duke of Connaught. I told him it would be fatal to mix up Royalty with the present régime —until it had at least been confirmed by another general election."

The general result of the Parnell Commission's findings was beyond doubt the progress of public opinion in favour of Home Rule. The political history of the year, with the steady gains of the Opposition in by-elections, is fully narrated in the *Life of Gladstone*

[273]

and elsewhere. With the rising tide, Rosebery was anxious that the course through the difficult channel into harbour should be charted beforehand, as is shown by the following letter to his leader on the subject of nominating a small committee of Liberal hydrographers. Gladstone had written dubiously on this expedient.

1, FERDINAND STRASSE, HOMBURG, *August 11th*, 1889.
"MY DEAR MR. GLADSTONE,

"I was greatly pleased to receive your letter this morning. . . . As regards the Irish Question, I would urge against your passive position that the committee is needed not merely on the ground of preparedness for the crisis when it comes, but as regards the party. The party is in a somewhat critical condition. There is a tendency to follow any Appollos who announces that he is in possession of the true doctrine; a disposition to cavil at the front bench, and also a movement for rather postponing Home Rule to vague Socialist schemes. I am all for the combination of domestic reform with Irish policy, but I am not for the obliteration of a definite cause to which we are pledged by vaporous views which have at present no ripeness or consistency. I am all for the free play of individuals in the party, but not for chaos. And I believe that nothing would restore faith and discipline more than the knowledge that the late Cabinet or a part of it were maturing details of Irish policy and measures.

"And whereas you yourself have limited the field of your future operations, the party would feel that this subject to which you devoted yourself to the exclusion of other topics was receiving your strict attention. This is no mean gain: but we should further demonstrate that the cause, if in the background, was in the immediate background, and ready to take the field at the first opportunity. Again, it is clear that the Government must deal with Irish local government. They may even dissolve upon it. They may bring in a Liberal scheme, including perhaps provincial councils or a central board (like Chamberlain's) but stopping short of Home Rule. On this they may go to the country and say: 'Here is our scheme, uniform, and applicable to England, Scotland and Wales: giving Ireland all that can be given short of creating a separate State. What is the alternative? The bill of 1886 is dead, disavowed by some, amended by others. What else is there?' If Ireland then be quiet, if trade be good, if administration be generally adequate, such a course might damage us more than I like to contemplate.

"What you incidentally say about jealousies is a strong but not insurmountable objection. We could either (1) remit it to the Committee which aided you in 1886: or (2) we could form two committees, one for land and the other for constitution, which together might include all the ex-Cabinet; or (3) we could subdivide the bills and have committees on the different parts; or (4) we could strain the bills through two or three committees, each so to speak affixing their marginal notes; or (5) a small committee might first go through the Home Rule Bill and send round the result in a box for individual annotation. In all cases the result to come before you for your final pronouncement, and, if you thought fit, the convocation of a Council.

"What you say as to your habit in the preparation of your great measures is undoubtedly true and very remarkable. But this is not a Bill. It is rather in the nature of what would be called in the United States a constitutional amendment. It involves the greatest principles of constitutional law, and is worthy of a conference such as that which met to lay down the relations of the different American States to each other in 1787 (I think). As we are not likely in this country (though it is not impossible) to adopt so large and dignified a procedure the next best thing is that those who are responsible for the proposal should turn it over and mature it: not individually, for then it will never be done, the stress of present politics being too great, but collectively and under an impulse from yourself.

"I do not think it would be fair to ask you to preside at any preliminary committee: you have earned exemption from such drudgery. But after conference with Parnell you might well address a paper to your colleagues inviting such a committee or committees, and giving indications both of your views and of Parnell's.

"Has the time not now arrived, by the bye, when you might invite Parnell to Hawarden?

"I am not losing sight of the value of Irish co-operation: but for their sake and ours it should be no more, it should not be amalgamation. And I believe it would cause pleasure to them if they knew that the Irish question was still employing the best energies of the late Government, while I am sure that in the country it would impart confidence to our scattered congregations, and strengthen followers who are bewildered as to the scheme of 1886.

"I do not moreover underrate the force of what you said to me as to the future bill necessarily being adapted to the temper and exigencies of the moment at which it has to be produced; I less than any, for I believe the longer it is deferred the more it will approximate to the federal principle. But that does not seem to me to countervail the advantage of having on record the edition of 1889-1890.

"I must close this interminable letter without exhausting my arguments. I will only add that if there were one small committee it should consist of Herschell, Spencer, Harcourt and Morley. All I think are generally favourable to the idea, and would serve: nor could that selection excite jealousy. Spencer is here, and I shall see him to-day, and take the liberty of showing him your letter. But I will not wait to see him

[275]

before despatching this dismal volume; though you know it is sent with complete deference to your unrivalled judgment and experience.

"Yr. Affly.,

AR"

At Norwich on April 12th, and at the Colston Banquet at Bristol on November 13th, Rosebery spoke on Ireland. The first of these occasions—"I spoke for fifty minutes, I fear dully. 7,000 people"—was almost unpunctuated by a laugh, an unusual event. It was a grave indictment of English government in the past, and a condemnation of the Union, almost solemnly worded. At Bristol he also spoke bitterly of the "part of the Constitution that was sown in corruption and raised in dishonour," but the speech was full of deft hits at the Liberal Unionist dissentients. Perhaps they were represented at the banquet, for he noted: "A fine fellow in the chair,—the Rev. U. R. Thomas,—but they were all Thomases."

In six weeks the crash came.

Journal

December 28th.—"O'Shea's suit against Parnell announced."

Foreign policy had to be watched, whatever other preoccupation might be present or impending. Rosebery wrote to Mr. Gladstone on January 15th:

Confidential.   38 BERKELEY SQUARE, *January 15th,* 1889.
"MY DEAR MR. GLADSTONE,

"I ought long ago to have answered a kind letter from Mrs. Gladstone; but I am in a fair road to become a vestryman, which takes up a good deal of time. But John Morley has brought me a letter from you which turns out my epistolary hose on to you.

"I am in truth rather dismayed at your idea of speaking your mind about the Italian alliance with Germany. Now is this necessary? I remember when I took the Foreign Office you said to me that the important matter was to keep foreign affairs from disturbing us in England, where we had a great enterprise on hand which would fully occupy our energies. Does this not apply now with equal force? Have we any need to raise further animosities against us? Your allusion to Austria produced a strong feeling of hostility to us in 1880. But if you make this declaration of hostility to the Italo-German alliance, you will range against us Germany and Italy besides (for the alliance is popular in Italy,—at least in the main). All this we might disregard if it were your duty to make it. But is it your duty? I admit that your past services to Italy give you a *locus standi* in regard to any advice you may

[276]

think it right to offer her. But from even your elevation is it judicious to offer suggestions to her about her foreign policy? How should we relish it in England if a foreign statesman were to offer us advice or remonstrances about our alliances?

"Again, could your utterance have any effect? I think not. Supposing you carried half the nation with you you could not extricate them from their alliance. It is as I believe for a fixed time—at least the last one was.

"Again and finally, is it worth while to add to the divisions or causes of division in the Liberal party here a difference on foreign policy— more especially when that difference does not effect ourselves?

"There are many Liberals I think who would be of opinion that Italy has acted wisely in entering upon this alliance, and could not well otherwise have secured her own safety. But whether there be many or not, there are some; and what counterbalancing advantage would be obtained by your declaration to weigh against the alienation of even a few members of the party? Forgive me if I have written bluntly and strongly in favour of non-intervention on this occasion. It is because I feel strongly in the matter, and am anxious to avoid what I cannot help thinking would be a grave mistake.

"Yrs. affly.,
AR"

38 BERKELEY SQUARE, *January 24th*, 1889.
"MY DEAR MR. GLADSTONE,

"Many thanks for your letter and for the generous spirit in which you accept my remonstrances.

"I admit that I raised questions which cannot be discussed in a letter. But my excuse must be the deep feeling I entertain that even from yourself an expression of opinion on this subject would be less likely to bring peace than a sword.

"I do not in the least wish you or England to stand under the shadow of Bismarck, and at this moment there is little likelihood of this nation assuming that position. But Europe is a powder magazine, in which a spark, even of genius, may have effects impossible to calculate.

"That is all I have to say. *Liberavi animam meam*, and I am quite satisfied to leave the matter to your better judgment, now that my side of the case is fully before you.

"Y. affly.,
AR"

When the article was in print, he wrote:

Private.   SPRING GARDENS, S.W., *May 8th*, 1889.
"MY DEAR MR. GLADSTONE,

"It is very good of you to refer your article to me. It seems to me that you have avoided the danger which I feared. At the same time I still retain my own opinion that Italy could not in the present state of Europe stand alone, and that her relations with France are more uneasy than you judge them to be.

"Two other points strike me. It is possible that the Italians may dislike what you say about torture, as being insufficiently corroborated: though I am aware that you have already touched on the subject. The other statement you make which fills me with surprise is that the priesthood are Italian and not Papal in their sympathies. I know nothing for or against, and so I do not doubt its accuracy, but it is startling.

"Forgive these free remarks on your very interesting article.

"Y. affly.,
AR"

In the House of Lords there were no debates on foreign affairs demanding his intervention.

The friction between the British and German Courts was marked in the early months of the year. Rosebery was received by the Empress Frederick at Buckingham Palace (February 25th). She told him how King Frederick William IV used to say of her husband, "This is my successor, for my brother can never reign." "She was pleasant and soft,—wept once." But it was not only sorrowful reminiscence. " 'Your friend Herbert has it all his own way now: he has got rid of us.' I took the opportunity of saying just afterwards, 'The young Emperor seems to show much energy.'—'Does he? I know nothing about him.' This the only jar, otherwise all cordial and pleasant."

Herbert Bismarck came to London on a soothing mission in March, but did not venture to apply for an audience of the Prince of Wales. It was six months before peace was restored between H.R.H. and the Emperor. At Homburg, where the Prince and the Duke of Cambridge were doing the cure, and Herbert Bismarck paid a visit, Rosebery noted:

"All was reconciliation at Osborne. The best of uncles and the best of nephews."

The Emperor had been at Cowes at the beginning of the month, when he became an Admiral of the Fleet, and the Queen a Colonel of German Dragoons.

Earlier Rosebery had been interested by an item of Herbert Bismarck's news:

"He told me that Chamberlain had suggested exchange of Heligoland for Angra Pequena and Walfisch Bay, and said he would support it. J. C. strongly Germanophil."

It will be noted later how this notion matured.

In domestic politics the House of Lords Question still simmered, with small prospect that a substantial meal would be served (February 28th). "Black sheep" were to be cooked first, and Lord Carnarvon asked a question about them, urging that the "few, but still notorious" sinners should be treated like men in the Services guilty of conduct unbefitting a gentleman and an officer. By the convenient practice of the House, a debate followed, though there was no motion. One Peer asked how many times might a man rat and not be an unworthy member of the House? Lord Salisbury thought Lord Carnarvon's case overstated, but would not mind creating some power of expulsion. Rosebery defended Mr. Gladstone from the charge of having obstructed the two Bills of last year, but had to shed a tear over the abandonment of the Life Peerages Bill. He was followed by a noble friend who thought that any Peer convicted of having been twice in any one year at a race meeting, or of owning racehorses, should be incapacitated from sitting; and Rosebery retorted by asking if that proposal was retrospective?

Lord Carnarvon duly introduced his "Discontinuance of Writs Bill" (March 21st) in a speech of much grace and accomplishment. Its rejection was moved on the grounds that it only touched the fringe of the Reform Question, and on others, and an interesting but rather confused debate followed. Rosebery declared himself in favour of Lord Herschell's suggestion that a Select Committee should examine the situation. But convinced reformers would in no case get much from this measure. The real difficulty consisted in the purely hereditary character of the House.

The Bill ultimately perished by the application of "the previous question."

During this session one or two matters affecting the County Council and his old post of the Office of Works invited comment from Rosebery, but there was nothing of great import. He had no direct concern with the disputes over Royal Grants on which Gladstone supported the Government against the Left of his own party. But Rosebery was informed and consulted and attended the principal debate on July 25th.

"Sat out dreary speeches by Smith, Labouchere (1½ hours) and Storey (1 hour). Then came Mr. G. with a fine 50 minutes, ending with a most pathetic touch."

Some other notes on public matters, old and new, may be included in the review of this year:

"Charles Villiers told me Canning the best speaker he ever heard,—appearance, face, eye, went for much. Some good judges, though, preferred Plunket.[8] He remembers old Wilberforce introducing young Macaulay to some benevolent meeting, and Macaulay's speech.

"Granville says that Lord Aberdeen preferred Canning's speaking to Pitt's; but his mother told him that if Canning came in at one door to pass through a room he would not go straight to the other door, but circumnavigate every piece of furniture:—not a bad metaphor.

"Mr. G. furious after dinner about Pitt's later Irish Policy—the worst thing in history, worse than St. Bartholomew's. Acknowledged afterwards 'I am in a passion.'

"John Morley said he was thinking of retiring from politics—the strain was too great. He had just had letters from Carnegie enclosing a sort of blank cheque to pay Chamberlain if that was what J. C. had meant by 'obligation.'[9]

"Mr. G. said, 'I speak as a dying man, but I confess I look back with pleasure to the times of liberation in which my political life was cast, and with doubt to the coming times of construction.'

"Dined with Asquith and Haldane at the Blue Posts. Sate next A. Balfour. Took John Morley on to the National Liberal Club Reception."

This is the first conjunction of these names, of which several were to be so closely connected.

Outside the small group of literary politicians such as John Morley and George Trevelyan, Rosebery did not mingle greatly in the world of letters. He met George Meredith at a small dinner and was not captivated, thinking him "affected like his books"; but at a similar feast, where George Russell[10] was host, he found "Browning very agreeable. Spoke of himself. He had always been independent, and so indifferent to reputation. Wrote for himself and could not trace any sudden rise of fame. His wife's works still sold better than his own. The Browning Society by no means complimentary in B. discussions." Matthew Arnold was a favourite guest at Aston Clinton, Lady de Rothschild's home near Mentmore, and thus the Roseberys knew him well, and enjoyed seeing him also at

[8] William Conyngham Plunket, 1st Baron Plunket (1764-1854). Appointed Lord Chancellor of Ireland 1830.
[9] This was evidently a ludicrous misapprehension by Morley's kind American friend.
[10] Rt. Hon. G. W. E. Russell (1853-1919). M.P. 1880-85, and 1892-5. Three times Under-Secretary.

the Durdans. Tennyson, as we know, lived in a small circle which never intersected Rosebery's.

After the County Council rose for the summer vacation six weeks were spent abroad. Lady Rosebery had not been in the best of health, and they began by spending most of August at Homburg. This was the most fashionable moment of that fashionable centre of mild air, mild distractions, and a mild cure. The Duke of Cambridge took them over to his ancestral home at Rumpenheim—

"A homely whitewashed barrack of little cells opening into one another, stiff and simple beyond words, a few yards from the Main. He showed us the summer-house whither his family took refuge while Napoleon's army was marching home to France along the opposite bank from Hanau and Leipsic. It was there that the old Duchess[11] who died this year saw Napoleon. The Duke would not give up his position in England for the Regency of Brunswick."

They passed on to Coburg and Nuremburg and Munich. Thence to the Bavarian Alps and the series of tastelessly extravagant splendours for which King Ludwig, on the border-line between genius and insanity, and most nearly allied to the latter, was responsible. Flying visits to Salzburg and Vienna brought them home via Paris, and the rest of the holidays were spent in Scotland. County Council work filled up the rest of the autumn and early winter.

[11] Augusta, daughter of the Landgrave Frederick of Hesse-Cassel; *m.* 1818, Adolphus, 1st Duke of Cambridge, and *d.* April 1889.

CHAPTER XI

The Turf—Earlier Years

THE Rosebery colours of primrose and rose hoops, rose cap, were registered in 1868, soon after their owner attained his majority. The safe path of a breeding stud, formed by the purchase of a mare or two and some well-bred yearling fillies, seems a slow business to keen youth; and Rosebery looked out for quicker returns. Mr. W. Cowen's *Ladas*,[1] by *Lambton* out of *Zenobia*, started thrice as a two-year-old in 1868, winning each time. One of the races was the considerable Convivial Produce Stakes at York.

It seemed, therefore, to be a hopeful purchase for a tyro at the game. A substantial sum was paid (1869), and the colt was entrusted to an experienced trainer, James Dover of Ilsley. He ran first in Rosebery's colours in the Derby of 1869, starting at 66 to 1 in a field of twenty-two runners, and finishing last. He ran again badly in the Cesarewitch, carrying 6 st. 7 lb., and at the same forlorn odds. At the Houghton meeting he carried 7 st. 13 lb. in the Cambridgeshire. There were twenty-nine runners, he was not quoted in the betting, and ran nowhere. But on the Friday in The Houghton week he gained his only victory by giving 9 lb. to Prince Soltykoff's *Badsworth* in a match over a mile, and beating him. *Badsworth* cannot have been a good horse.

In the following year *Ladas* did no better. Credited with some speed, he was started four times over short distances, running nowhere in the Stewards' Cup at Goodwood and in the Great Eastern Railway Handicap at Newmarket. In 1871 he ran twice unsuccessfully, and was sold for a trifle to Mr. Henry Chaplin. This was "the Baron's year," when *Hannah*, named after Baron Meyer's only child, won the Oaks and the St. Leger.

In 1869 Rosebery's stable consisted of one five-year-old, two four-year-olds, two three-year-olds (including *Ladas*), and four two-

---

[1] *Ladas* is said to be an obscure Greek word for a young stag; but the colt was no doubt named after a famous runner, said by one authority to have been the messenger of Alexander the Great. His name became proverbial for speed in later times, as appears from *Juvenal*, Sat. xiii, ll. 96 *et seq.*, and from *Martial*, bk. ii, 1. 86.

Lord Rosebery in his Cab

year-olds. One of the four-year-olds, *Athena,* won a couple of races, but there were few victories, and though he was successful at Doncaster, it must have been a poor year for a heavy bettor.

In 1870 the well-bred two-year-old *Ellesmere,* by *Elland—Lady Audley,* won the valuable Gladiateur Stakes at the July meeting, but failed later. Another *Elland* two-year-old, *Andorra,* won two matches. Matches have almost died out nowadays, but in the seventies and eighties they still flourished. Rosebery delighted in making them. There was little racing for him in 1870, and in 1871 he won nothing. But in reality it was one of the most fateful years of his turf career, destined to retrieve his first disappointment, for in October he bought *Paraffin,* by *Blair Athol* from the famous *Paradigm,* as a brood mare. After his purchase of the Durdans he started a breeding stud there. Eighteen seventy-three produced some better luck. He won the Gimcrack Stakes with *Padaroshna,* bought after winning a small race at Stockton. Other two-year-olds did not do much, but Dover won a Maiden Stakes with a two-year-old by *Lecturer* named *The Teacher.* Rosebery bought the colt late in the season, and re-christened him *Aldrich,* after the seventeenth-century Dean of Christ Church, the founder of Peckwater Quad. In the spring of 1874 *Aldrich* won the City and Suburban for Rosebery— his first important race. The colt was no marvel: in a field of nineteen he carried 6 st. 4 lb., and started at 40 to 1. But he was the hero of the most singular racing dream on record.

Lord Vivian[2] ran a horse now and then, but he was not of the circle of racing pundits. One night before the race he dreamed that the City and Suburban had been won by a horse called *The Teacher.* He told the rest of the party, and the entry was examined. No such name was found. Later on, when Lord Vivian was told of the changed name, he was quite positive that he had never heard of it, and no explanation was ever forthcoming. It can only be surmised that he had in fact been told of it at some time, and that it passed out of his conscious mind. But even so, it would be a curious freak of the subconscious mind to make the substitution in sleep, about a horse whose chance of winning cannot have been seriously discussed beforehand.

In the same spring Rosebery bought the three-year-old *Couronne de Fer,* by *Macaroni—Miss Agnes.* This was a possible Derby hope. He improved on the hapless *Ladas* by running second, and Rosebery kept him for a time as a sire.

[2] 2nd Lord Vivian 1806-86.

Two useful animals ran as two-year-olds in 1875, *Levant,* by *Adventurer—Repulse,* winning the Acorn Stakes and July Stakes, and *Father Claret,* by *d'Estournel—Defamation,* winning three times.

Eighteen seventy-six was still better, for *Controversy,* bought in the previous December, won the Lincolnshire Handicap and six other races, beating the brilliant *Lowlander* in a match at Ascot. *Levant* carried off two valuable stakes; but *Father Claret* did nothing. An old horse, *The Snail,* bought early in the year, carried off the Northumberland Plate, and the two-year-old *Touchet,* by *Lord Lyon,* won four matches and two small races.

In the following year Rosebery, on the look-out for promising blood, bought out of a selling-race Count Festetic's two-year-old filly *Bonnie Agnes.* This proved to be another lucky stroke. He won the New Stakes with another filly of his own breeding, *Bellicent,* by *Cremorne—Lynette.*

Eighteen seventy-eight witnessed the union of the Durdans and Mentmore studs. Since the death of "the Baron," the latter had been carried on at Crafton on behalf of his daughter. *King Tom, Favonius* and *Lecturer* had stood there; and after Baron Meyer's death the great *Macaroni* was bought, and reigned at the stud till 1887.

It was a moderate year's racing for Rosebery. *Touchet* won a race at Ascot, some old horses, such as *Kaleidoscope* and *Oxonian,* bought to carry the colours, picked up some moderate races. One two-year-old winner, *Casuistry,* by *The Miner—Lady Caroline,* gained a name later for another stable as the dam of *Paradox.*

The opening of 1879 was propitious. *Touchet,* now five years old, won the Lincolnshire with 8 st. 4 lb. The year closed equally well, for the four-year-old *La Merveille,* by *Blair Athol—Cauldron,* who the previous year had run third for the Cambridgeshire for Robert Peck with 6 st. 3 lb., now won it for Rosebery with 8 st. at the pleasant price of 30 to 1. Nor were the two-year-olds idle. Of the five that won races, *Cipollata,* by *Macaroni—Duckling,* and *Illuminata,* by *Rosicrucian—Paraffin,* who won the Molyneux Stakes, were the most hopeful.

Much was hoped from *Cipollata* the next year, but she was nowhere in the One Thousand Guineas, though she won races at Ascot and the July meeting. None of the other dozen winners of races in 1880 was of great account. The two-year-olds *Town Moor* and *Voluptuary* were considered the best.

[284]

Eighteen eighty-one was more striking. *Town Moor* ran third for the Derby; *Voluptuary* won three races, was sold, and later finished up his career on a London stage. Several two-year-olds won races, and two of the fillies became historical. *Vista,* by *Macaroni—Verdure* (sister to *Corisande*) was pure Mentmore in descent. She stayed well, winning the Prince of Wales' Nursery at Doncaster and another mile Nursery. The other mare *Kermesse* was probably the best animal Rosebery ever owned. A brown, by *Hermit—Hazeldean*, she was bought as a foal from Mr. Henry Chaplin. At two years old she was once beaten a head by *Dutch Oven*, but won her other five races, including the Champagne Stakes and the Middle Park Plate, in which she beat all the best of the year.

Everything promised grandly for the next season, but in the early spring *Kermesse* got loose at exercise and split both pasterns. She was wonderfully patched up, and won two races at Newmarket in the autumn, after missing her classic engagements. This was the most remarkable mare's year in turf history. Besides *Kermesse—Geheimniss, Shotover, Dutch Oven* and *St. Marguerite* between them would have won every classic race five years out of six. In other respects it was not a bad season for Rosebery. The five-year-old *Pruhomme* won the Chester Cup; one promising two-year-old *Bonny Jean*, daughter of *Bonnie Agnes*, secured three races; and another two-year-old, *Narcissa,* beat the great *Geheimniss* in the Fernhill Stakes. Altogether Rosebery won twenty races this year.

Eighteen eighty-three was still better, with about the same number of wins, since they included the Oaks, won by *Bonnie Jean*, the second string *Etarre* running third. *Vista* won two races, and there was a hopeful two-year-old *Kinsky, Illuminata's* first foal, by *Kisber*, a sire much favoured by Rosebery.

The next two seasons were inconspicuous, but not deplorable. In 1884, sixteen races were won, four of them by the three-year-old *Kinsky*, sold at the end of the season to Colonel Crewe-Read. Later he won the Chester Cup. The four-year-old *Polemic*, with 6 st. 1 lb., ran second to *St. Gatien* in his famous Cesarewitch.

The next year was also uneventful. *Cipollina, Cipollata's* sister, won the Newmarket Oaks, and three two-year-olds took half a dozen races; but there was nothing in the stable of which to dream dreams; public affairs were absorbing, and Rosebery decided to sell the Mentmore yearlings. Genial Mr. Edmund Tattersall wrote (September 30th, 1885):

[285]

"We do not want you to go off the turf. . . . Politics and giving up the turf killed Lord George Bentinck, and we do not want you to injure your health for the good of the country."

Sixteen yearlings sold for £4,715. In the year following five older horses remained in the stable. Three small victories can have brought little grist to the mill. In 1887, 1888, and 1889 Rosebery ran nothing, and the yearlings were sold. Thus closed the first chapter of Rosebery's racing career. It had opened in blank disappointment, but was not altogether a fiasco. Many owners have raced a longer time without winning a classic event.

CHAPTER XII

Home and Foreign Politics: Visit to Vazin—Lord Hartington—Lady Rosebery's Illness and Death— European Travel

THE year 1890, destined to close in black gloom, opened with the customary prospect of congenial labours and sufficient diversion. The County Council reassembled early in January, and Rosebery's work in it has been described above. The early spring was chiefly spent at the Durdans.

February 10th.—"The Gladstones and Mrs. Drew, Granville, Spencer and E. Hamilton dined. Mr. G. like a boy, and a very pleasant dinner. The discussion on the Queen's Speech not oppressive. Granville told me that old Lady Jersey (in this house)[1] always expected presents on her birthday. Alvanley was one of the first to arrive and always took some little object out of the drawing-room which he presented to her with an exquisite speech, in her boudoir."

In the previous year there had been some coolness between the Prince of Wales and Rosebery, and the Prince had contemplated a visit elsewhere than at Dalmeny for the opening of the Forth Bridge. This would have been a marked rebuff. But in January H.R.H. relented, and he stayed a night at Dalmeny for the ceremony.

March 4th.—"Opening of the Forth Bridge: a gale from the west. I crossed the bridge on the outside of the railway carriage, and was nearly blown away. . . . The Prince very civil and confidential—hoped he might consider me a friend. . . . Showed me a very disparaging letter from the Empress Frederick about her son."

Late in July the Roseberys left for Geneva, for a short fortnight's stay. There he enjoyed following up the memories of Voltaire and of Rousseau, and the treasures of the Musée d'Antiquités. Mr. Barton, the British Consul, of the Bordeaux branch of his Irish family, Mrs. Barton, and her mother, Lady Emily Peel, were at

[1] 38 Berkeley Square.

[287]

their hospitable villa, and were the kindest of guides in many expeditions. One was to Baron Adolphe Rothschild's villa at Pregny, lunching at Bellevue, the "little house by the water, with a charming dining-room with four Tiepolos in it. I have not liked a room so much for some time." But, not for the first time, he was more completely intoxicated by glimpses of the pageant of nature than by any display of luxurious art. Witness his Journal:

July 29th.—"The evening sultry as hell. A cloud overhanging, full of wrath and portent, the lightnings forked and sheeted playing on the opposite mountains, as if Beelzebub were giving a ball on the summit. One top was kindled with a dull lurid flame like a volcano, where I suppose the lightning had set the woods on fire. Below, the Lake, black and terrible as impending revolution."

And in a less terrific vein:

July 31st.—"A glorious night. Mont Blanc frozen clear, with one cold glittering star in chilly sympathy: then of a sudden a golden gleam, and in a moment the whole saffron moon, genial as a sun, filled and absorbed and warmed the heaven. For an instant it rested on the summit of Mont Blanc as though saluting it, and then rose on its own solitary imperial course. I could hardly go to bed."

Impressive, too, was the junction of the blue Rhône and "muddy democratic Arve."

After the return to England came the news of Cardinal Newman's end. A year before, Rosebery had been at Birmingham but had not been able to pay his respects at the Oratory, for the Cardinal was not visible.

August 13th.—"While at luncheon received telegram from Father Neville to say that if I wished to see Cardinal Newman's remains I must come at once. So caught the 2.10 train. Arrived at the Oratory at 5. Met Father Neville who took me to the Church, then to the little sitting-room and tiny oratory, where he produced a good portrait of the Cardinal which the Cardinal had proposed to give me when he heard I had been disappointed of Millais's, and had been over-ruled, I suppose, very naturally: then to his admirably planned library. The sitting-room a mere cell filled with books.

"The Cardinal just like a saint's remains over a high altar, waxy, distant, emaciated, in a mitre, rich gloves whereon the ring (which I kissed), rich slippers. With the hat at the foot.

"And this was the end of the young Calvinist, the Oxford don, the austere Vicar of St. Mary's. It seemed as if a whole cycle of human thought and life were concentrated in that august repose. That was my overwhelming thought. Kindly light had led a guided Newman to this strange, brilliant, incomparable end.

"Seeing him on his right side in outline one saw only an enormous nose and chin almost meeting—a St. Dominic face. The left side was inconceivably sweet and soft, with that gentle corner of the mouth so greatly missed in the other view. The body, so frail and slight that it had ceased to be a body terrestrial."

Soon after this solemn pilgrimage Rosebery moved to Scotland. There was again grouse shooting at Invermark and at Tulchan, but it was a poor year, and by the end of the month he was established *en famille* at Dalmeny. September was amazing, as in the north it can be:

September 7th.—"I never remember such weather as the last two days in Scotland."

In home politics the Report of the Special Commission marked the dividing line between parties with brutal clearness. It has been noted how ingeniously the Government had striven to confuse the issues: the Piggott letters, which had been relied on to blow the Home Rule fabric into atoms, now that they were known to be forged, were treated as of minor importance.

In the House of Lords (March 21st) Lord Salisbury proposed that the Commissioners' Report be adopted and that they be thanked for their just and impartial conduct. On the Liberal side all the heavy artillery was brought up. Lord Herschell, in a long and masterly speech, directly opposed the motion. It was his contention, and that of Lords Kimberley and Spencer who followed, that the whole business was in no sense judicial but a political manœuvre directed against political enemies and carried out by political methods. When Rosebery's turn came, following Lord Derby, he developed this theme, and pointed out that all the speakers who supported Lord Salisbury had been ex-Liberals, not Conservatives. The objection to the Report was that it made no attempt to discriminate between moral crime and political offence. As to violent language, equally violent had been used by Ulster partisans, and Lord Wolseley had never contradicted the story that he had offered to organise the forces of disorder if a Home Rule Bill were passed. Lord Salisbury himself had sat approving speakers inciting to revolution in certain contingencies. But for the forged letters there would have been no Commission at all, and the language used by *The Times* was parallel to that used by the *Irish World*. No apology was offered to

Parnell, who had been tried by a tribunal chosen by the Government, had been found innocent, with the net result that he was fined £40,000 of expenses. When Lord Salisbury embarked the country on a war with Afghanistan he had been arraigned for a gross political offence by many, including some eloquent voices now dumb and supporting his present policy. Suppose some forged document had also been produced? If it were found to be forged, the amplest reparation would have been offered, though the grave political offence would have been the same, as the speaker still considered. He concluded by an appeal to the Irish Peerage. They were standing on one side, the Irish people on the other:

"If there be one truth more strictly and universally written than another by history, it is this: that an aristocracy divorced from a nation is a doomed aristocracy. I regret it with all my heart, but it is a truth written on the ruined Palaces of Venice and Versailles. . . . It is not a hundred years ago since we had your Charlemonts and Cloncurrys and FitzGeralds, Charlemonts who were not ashamed to lead the Irish Volunteers, Cloncurrys and FitzGeralds who were not ashamed to share the aspirations of Ireland, even to prison and the grave."

He read the list of Irish Peers who had signed the protest against the Union in 1800, including many of the greatest names in Ireland. And not only the Irish Peers, but Government and Parliament had lost the opportunity of presenting to a generous and high-spirited people a resolution of regret for the charges founded on fraud and forgery. The debate lasted till past midnight, and concluded without the farce of a division.

The Anglo-German Agreement, wide in scope and far-reaching in consequence, was the other Parliamentary subject that diverted Rosebery's energies from London administration. The cession of Heligoland, a small and loyal colony, close to our shores, as a consideration for the settlement of vexed questions thousands of miles away in Africa, excited some feeling.

Rosebery asked (June 30th) whether the wishes of the people had been consulted, and if those who objected to the transfer would be given the option of settling elsewhere. Lord Salisbury replied that they must wait till the Convention could be laid on the table, and when asked what were the means taken to ascertain the feelings of the people of Heligoland, announced that they were of a confidential character, and could not be discussed. "Confidential with the population?" asked Lord Granville.

The Bill came up for second reading (July 10th). It referred solely to Heligoland, but Lord Salisbury naturally made reference to the African negotiations for which Parliamentary sanction was not formally needed. He dealt fully and fairly with the whole business, but could not say how the wishes of the inhabitants of the little island had been ascertained. He did not dispute that it might be of strategic value to Germany, though it was of none to us. Coming to Africa, we could not claim the right to lock up the whole of it. He elaborated a defence of Germany's claim to territory north of Lake Tanganyika, and to access to the River Zambesi in the south.

Rosebery could not refrain from reflecting what the reception of such an agreement would have been if Mr. Gladstone's Government had submitted it to the House, but he was determined not to cavil at it. The whole business was rather like the apportionment of the New World by Pope Alexander VI. He wished that some formal Conference on Congress could sanction such agreements on behalf of the communities of Europe at large. He did not press the value of Heligoland to us, but present Ministers in 1885 had scouted the notion of ceding it. The precise extent of the Sultanate of Zanzibar had been doubtful, and now the consent of France, one of the guaranteeing Powers, did not seem to have been secured. One thing was clear. Since the Liberal Government left office in 1886 the prestige and influence of the Sultan of Zanzibar had diminished. Now we were buying back a small part of what we had in 1886, and the protectorate of Zanzibar, by a cession of British territory, one of our few assets from the war with Napoleon. But of course there was no question of opposing the plan as a whole.

Outside Parliament Rosebery's oratorical engagements were limited by County Council work, but he attended the Co-operative Congress in Glasgow as its President. In a long inaugural address he disclaimed any special knowledge of the subject, wishing to speak as a learner. As a politician he was first interested in the moral effect of the movement on the State. Then, more technical, there were the soundness of its economic basis and the possibilities of its extension in different directions. After dealing with the first two divisions of the subject, he observed, speaking as an ignorant outsider, that there were three directions in which advance might be made. The first was building societies, the inception of which could be claimed by the county of Clackmannan before they gained an impulse in America. The second was insurance. He did not believe that a system of national insurance, which was being tried in Germany, would apply here at all. It would be resented here as complicated and compulsory, but should succeed admirably by co-operative agency. These remarks were loudly applauded. In the third place, he believed that in spite of some well-known failures there was a great future for co-operative farming, not starting on an ambitious scale, but in imitation of some of the dairy-farms successfully run by companies.

At the conclusion he was presented with a writing-table of Co-operative manufacture, and, thanking for it, remarked that he was also wearing a pair of Co-operative trousers.

It happened that Rosebery and Herbert Bismarck were in frequent communication this year, and it is worth noting that in their correspondence there is not a word of Heligoland. It was sometimes suspected that Rosebery's admiration for the Chancellor and liking for his son might deflect his judgment in matters of foreign policy. But with him the Foreign Office came first, whichever party might be controlling it. The great event, of course, with the Bismarcks was the resignation (as the Emperor called it) or abrupt dismissal (as they called it) of the Chancellor. Rosebery wrote to Herbert Bismarck:

March 20th.—"I can hardly trust myself to write of this stupendous news. One paper (a French one, I think) describes best what I should say, 'When one has the luck to have a Bismarck, which does not happen to everyone, one does not throw him away.' Of course I do not presume to judge the Emperor, but when I think of the weary and painful and unending toil and combination by which the fabric of your policy and the peace of Europe have been maintained, I envy his courage. . . . And now as to yourself. You speak of your political career as closed, but that is not so. I know it was always your wish that it should end with your father's, and that you should obtain an interval of rest and enjoyment. But your experience and ability must always be at the service of your country. The holiday will have one great advantage for you, you will know your real friends. You have been so near the seat of power that it has not been easy for you to find this out. And now I doubt not that many envious asses who fear to kick the old lion may vent their spleen on the young one. I see the beginning of this in the Times telegram of to-day. I only hope that I may have the opportunity of showing how truly, whether you are in or out of office, I am,

"Your affectionate friend,

AR

"Pray salute your father and mother from me. I hope they will not dismiss hastily the idea of a little tour here. . . ."

The "little tour" Rosebery hoped would include a stay at the Durdans, which was to be lent to the distinguished travellers, or a visit to Dalmeny in the late summer. The Prince, however, could not give up his custom of visiting one of the German or Austrian watering-places. Rosebery bought the original of Tenniel's famous cartoon "Dropping the Pilot," with the solemn form of the old statesman, in jacket and sea-boots, coming down the ship's side, watched by the smaller figure of his Sovereign, with the Imperial crown, leaning over the bulwarks. Rosebery sent an impression of this to Prince Bismarck, who expressed himself as deeply touched. Herbert Bismarck wrote that the Emperor had wished him to remain in office, but he had excused himself on the ground that his health had given way, and he could not adapt himself to a new Chancellor. He added: "The gentleman who is going to be my successor comes from the Grand Duchy of Baden, where he has formerly been a Public Prosecutor. His name is Herr v. Marschall, and he has never been conversant with the a, b, c, of foreign affairs. I wish him good luck."[2] Prince Bismarck's comment on the whole affair was simple:

"It is very strange, the Emperor names his best general a Chancellor, and his best Chancellor a field marshal."

It ended by Mohammed going to the mountain, as the mountain could not be moved. Rosebery proceeded to Ostend (September 24th), where Herbert Bismarck met him. They glanced at the glories of Bruges, and passed on to Hamburg, where the principal glory was a restaurant, reputed to be the best in Germany. They passed through Berlin and Stettin on a day's journey to Varzin.

Prince Bismarck met them on horseback, and drove with Rosebery in the victoria to the house. There was a family party, and a few neighbours dropped in. Each day Rosebery had a drive of two or three hours with his host. Prince Bismarck knew French and English well, so converse was easy. Herbert Bismarck was entirely fluent in English, and his letters to Rosebery are singularly free from errors. Rosebery himself was a competent French scholar both for speaking and writing, though he could not claim the mastery given by Lord Lansdowne's French descent, or by Lord Granville's youthful years passed in the Faubourg Saint-Honoré. But he never

---

[2] These rather acidulated good wishes were in a manner fulfilled many years later. Baron Marschall von Bieberstein was the most active agent in the subjection of Turkey to German Imperial ambitions.

learned any German, except for his few elementary lessons at Homburg, and he could not read the language. It is, perhaps, stranger that his adoration for Naples never impelled him to the study of Italian. It certainly was not from indolence, for he was always studying something. But though he retained rather more Greek and Latin than most public school boys who have not been classical specialists, it is probable that he never had the facility in acquiring languages that sometimes adorns powerful intellects, like Gladstone's, but may equally accompany others the opposite of powerful.

From Varzin Rosebery and Herbert Bismarck made an expedition to Danzig, Marienburg, the huge palace of the Teutonic Knights, and Königsberg. At this last the great hall in the Schloss was declared to be 137 yards long, which taxed Rosebery's credulity, though it was the longest room he had ever seen.

"At the end of it is a little horseshoe salon with its prim furniture and cracked harpsichord untouched. Here, separated from the palace and espionage by the vast hall, Queen Louise held her evening parties and planned German regeneration."

This must have been a pilgrimage of the heart, for the Prussian Queen was one of Rosebery's special heroines.

Rosebery reached London on October 5th, and went straight on to Scotland. He found his wife in bed with an attack of low fever, but not seriously unwell. So on the next day he kept his engagement to address the Glasgow Trades House annual dinner. He replied for the House of Lords, in the vein of pleasant banter which that toast used to encourage in great industrial centres. But he was serious in pointing to the dangers—the possible claim of the House to equality with the House of Commons, and the fact that men might become members of it against their will. He dreaded, too, lest the reform of the House might be undertaken not at a moment of political apathy, but of political paroxysm.

The next day he returned home, and the consulting doctors declared Hannah Rosebery's illness to be typhoid fever—as it was then always called. But there was no immediate alarm, and her husband returned the next day to Glasgow to receive the freedom of the city. The doctors, as he told his friends after the ceremony, had been anxious that the patient should not be alarmed by the abandonment of an engagement by which both of them had set such store.

When receiving the freedom he was able, from his double experience, happily to express his belief that in the practical work done in municipal life a man gets a quicker return than from work done in Parliament.

It had been arranged that Mr. Gladstone would come to Dalmeny on October 20th, for the toil of four large meetings, and a series of drives through his constituency, varied with short speeches, on the days of relaxation. Rosebery had to write his bitter disappointment at the loss of the visit; he had looked forward to this campaign with pride and pleasure.

At first Lady Rosebery's malady pursued its ordinary course, with high fever but strength well maintained. The children went, two at first to Dr. Donaldson's hospitable roof at St. Andrews, two to the castle close by. Lady Leconfield was her brother's support through the phases of alternating confidence and terror, which reached a climax on October 25th, when the doctors thought the end was near. The patient faced it calmly, and the two were together all day, talking of many things. She sent a message to a London friend whose illness was declared to be the same as hers. The next day she rallied, the symptoms that had alarmed the physicians proving to be salutary, and she seemed to be marvellously better. Her illness had moved many to sympathy, even outside her large circle of acquaintance—within it there was affectionate anxiety. Cecil Spring Rice had been one of Rosebery's official private secretaries at the Foreign Office. He was the reverse of sentimental, but a staunch friend. He wrote to Ronald Ferguson on October 27th, "I do hope Lady Rosebery's illness is taking a good turn. I don't know any one who deserves so well of fate as she does."[3]

The first fortnight of November found the doctors well satisfied, though recovery was not in sight. Rosebery was able to wear a brave face, as this letter shows:

DALMENY PARK, EDINBURGH, *November 6th*, 1890.
"MY DEAR MR. GLADSTONE,

"Your unexpected letter this morning gave me the greatest pleasure. I fully appreciate what you say about Hannah's illness being so near the heart of things during the late campaign; and if I could have avoided sending that telegram on that initial Saturday how gladly would I have done so. After Hannah, I thought most of you and the strain of speaking with so cruel a drain of sympathy.

"As to the campaign itself, of the speeches and the effect produced I hear nothing but good. I reserve the perusal of Hartington for a rainy

[3] *Letters and Friendships*, vol. i, p. 109.

day—a rainier even than to-day: in fact indefinitely. I should like to have seen you at the Glen, where you must have had a time only less agitating than the baronet's. I hear Margot put you through a most searching cross-examination, and I am sure that your faculty of admiration was not suffered to rest. But I regard the Glen as the most perfect of all modern country houses, architecturally speaking.

"I have been printing an old list of the Jacobites involved in the 1745 affair, and giving it to the Scottish Historical Society (of which you should be a member). A particularly choice copy was being prepared for you, when it was discovered that the index was imperfect—the pivot of the whole thing. So now I wail among my broken potsherds! And now for the bouquet—Hannah's progress is absolutely uninterrupted.

"Yr. affly.,

AR"

And the ill wind blew away one painful misunderstanding. The intimacy of Rosebery and Hartington had been based on community of many friendships and many tastes. In political warfare Hartington's broadsword cut deep and true; his admiration for the wrist play of Rosebery's rapier was unbounded. His mind moved surely but not fast; and, as was shown in the fiscal controversy thirteen years later, he did not always anticipate the effect that his own action would produce on others. He now wrote to his friend a letter of sympathy with his trouble and of inquiry about the cooling off of their personal relations. When they had last met on the neutral territory of Sandringham Hartington said to a fellow-guest, "I think Rosebery really hates me," which was the opposite of true; but this letter shows how deeply the younger friend had been hurt. An easy-going man might have let the occasion pass with a shrug. Rosebery never shrugged his shoulders, and he took it seriously, as he did everything of which he thought at all.

Private.   DALMENY PARK, *November 7th,* 1890.
"MY DEAR HARTINGTON,

"Thanks for your letter. I have no difficulty in giving you the explanation you ask for in terms so kind.

"It never occurred to me that a difference of opinion as to the proper course to pursue with regard to Ireland in 1886 could affect our friendship in the slightest degree. Nor did it, so far as I know.

"But in 1887 I was asked to stand for the rectorship of Glasgow. I do not like rectorships as they entail rectorial addresses. But when I saw that you and the other Unionist leaders warmly approved the idea of such a candidature, but more especially you, I thought it my duty not to avoid the opportunity of re-uniting the Liberal party even in so small a matter. And so I stood. But within a day or two of the election you published another letter urging your followers to vote against me. I offered to bet 100 to 1 that that letter was not genuine. But it was. It was not for me to judge whether it was fair or not. I could only be clear of one thing—that it was not the act of a friend. And as a friend —much against my will—I ceased to regard you.

"In spite of the letter I was elected, but by the form of election the ultimate decision rested with the chancellor—one of your principal adherents. He gave his vote to my opponent; although he was in a minority, and although he was that Lord Lytton who had been most reprobated by every branch of the Liberal party. But on that I lay no stress, nor do I wish to hold you in any degree responsible. I cared nothing for the election, and after your second letter I hated it: for the iron of that transaction entered into my soul.

"There! you have brought this outpouring caused by the re-opening of an old wound, on yourself, or I would apologise for the length of this letter.

"Believe me,
"Very sincerely,
AR"

Evidently Hartington, knowing that the contest for the rectorship was political, treated his own intervention as that of a political leader. Personal considerations did not arise, any more than they would in a debate in Parliament. The Chancellor, Lord Stair, doubtless thought the same. He was an old family friend of Rosebery's, but he was a very strong Unionist and felt entitled to give his casting vote to an ally. But there was this difference, which Hartington at the time did not apprehend, it seemed. The Chancellor had a duty to fulfil, and carried out the obligation conscientiously, possibly with reluctance. But Hartington had no more official or local connection with Glasgow than with the North Pole, so that his intervention seemed purely gratuitous. However, these candid explanations cleared the air and the close friendship was renewed in full vigour.

The first half of November seemed a little brighter. One or two intimate friends came, and Herbert Bismarck made a short stay. The bulletins became more satisfactory, but Rosebery could not feel greatly relieved. He wrote to Mr. Gladstone on the 17th:

"My invalid progresses slowly if indeed at all. To my mind she has not done well for some days, but the pundits continue to issue reassuring bulletins, more or less, so that I suppose I ought to be reassured. It cannot be far from the fiftieth day of fever, and how the human frame resists such a strain is more than I can understand."

On the very next day the brave resistance failed. I cannot help interposing a vivid personal recollection. I had been going to Dalmeny on October 18th for a quiet Sunday, to remain on through Mr. Gladstone's campaign, which was to begin after his arrival on Monday. Now, exactly a month later, I was to spend a few days, quiet in a different way, but helping, as I hoped, to divert my kind friend's thoughts into other channels while the beloved patient's slow recovery went on. On arriving at the station I was given an agonized note telling me that she was in a most critical state, and I went on south in deep sorrow. There was indeed a bare twenty-four hours of real anxiety before the end came.

The broken emotions of the next few days, spent with the grieving children, cannot be detailed here. It was settled that the funeral should be in the Jewish cemetery at Willesden, for Hannah Rosebery remained a loyal daughter of her ancient faith. The ceremony was on November 25th, when all the Rothschilds and most of Rosebery's colleagues of the Cabinet and of the County Council attended. At a Jewish funeral only men are present. Sir Henry Ponsonby, who was there on behalf of the Queen, wrote her a full account of the grave simple service and of Rosebery's self-control: "He wishes to show in public that he is able to put aside his sorrow, but in private he breaks down." The Queen's motherly solicitude was offered to any troubled heart, but specially to one who, like Rosebery, looked up to her with knightly devotion. She had thoroughly liked Lady Rosebery, so could write with comprehending sympathy. His acknowledgment of her letter tells the story of the thoughts that crowded on his mind at this supreme moment.

MENTMORE, *November 28th*, 1890.

"MADAM,

"I have I confess found the greatest difficulty in addressing myself to the duty of acknowledging Your Majesty's most gracious letter. Five or six times have I begun and laid down the pen. But Your Majesty's indulgence, the fruit I fear of sad experience, has deigned to allow me a pause. I find however that delay is fatal in this case, and that the lapse of time only makes it more difficult to write. I dearly loved my wife, and our home was happiness itself: but I only now know what I have lost, and each new day represents a new desolation.

"I need not speak of her illness, for Your Majesty was better informed of its various stages than I was. The only circumstance of interest that I can supply is this: that on October 25, when she was given over she knew of her danger and was then able with calm courage to have a long conversation with me, as it were in the hand and presence of death, and which was, so to speak, her dying message. Afterwards her recovery was so rapid that we dismissed the thought of danger, and for the last ten days she was delirious, so that that last solemn talk is a great comfort. On me, and I think on my sister, the end came as a surprise, for the recuperative power had been unfailing: and we were perhaps dazed with the length and alternations of the illness, as the day of her death was the fiftieth of her fever.

"I very humbly assure Your Majesty that Your Majesty's constant signs of sympathy were of priceless value to my patient, who ever cherished an ardent affection for Your Majesty; and who, on her bed of intolerable discomfort (rather than pain) was inexpressibly solaced by Your Majesty's tender solicitude. It is impossible to over-estimate the pleasure, in sickness or in health, that Your Majesty's mark of kindness gave to my wife.

"To turn to another source of strength and comfort I would venture to say that what my sister has been to both of us in this long agony, God only knows.

"There is, however, one incident of this tragedy only less painful than the actual loss; which is that at the moment of death the difference of creed makes itself felt, and another religion steps in to claim the corpse. It was inevitable, and I do not complain: and my wife's family have been more than kind. But none the less is it exquisitely painful.

"Your Majesty has passed but too often through the Valley of the Shadow of Death, and will understand me when I say that there seem to me only two consolations. The one that the Almighty and All Good has certainly ordained all for the best. And the other that love, such as my wife's, cannot perish; that it is with me as much as my skin or the air I breathe; and that so it must be to the end. Great love I firmly believe never dies or runs dry, but is part of the poor heritage of mankind.

"It is also a melancholy pleasure to witness the universal feeling for her and the great measure of affection which she had almost unconsciously accumulated all around her.

"But perhaps the nearest thought to a bereaved soul is contained in the lines Your Majesty wrote in my wife's album, and the lighting upon which has given me the desire to write to-night—

> " 'I hold it true whate'er befall,
> I feel it when I sorrow most,
> 'Tis better to have loved and lost
> Than never to have loved at all.'

"I humbly beg Your Majesty's pardon for allowing my pen to run on. For this once, however, I cannot but see in Your Majesty less my Sovereign than the wife who has known the same sorrow and deigns from the sad summit of her experience to associate herself with those that grieve below. And I am,

"Your Majesty's

"devoted Servant and subject,

"ROSEBERY.

"I would venture to beg that Her Royal Highness Princess Beatrice would be pleased to accept my thanks for her gracious sympathy."

What the memory of that long intimate talk in the midst of the illness meant to the bereaved husband is shown from a letter of the same time to Mrs. Drew:

"On October 25th we believed that she was dying and she knew of our belief. She bore herself with so beautiful and pathetic a calm that it remains with me as the most exquisite memory of my life. And so, when it came to the point, her noble nature had quenched the fear of death."

Just before Christmas the Queen again wrote, knowing from her own repeated experience how poignant to the stricken heart is the coming of that season of traditional joy. Rosebery replied in deepest gratitude, and continued:

"And there is so much sorrow now. Three of the friends who grieved with me have themselves passed away. The procession passes swiftly on from the seen to the unseen; and while we are still straining to catch the last glimpse of one we loved, another has gone: and we begin to feel that our hearts and our interests are not here, but in the great silence."

Thus closed a chapter of Rosebery's life—perhaps the best chapter, because, though the succeeding years brought him high honours, "great place," successes in oratory and in letters, and some friendships that grew in value, he remained a lonely man. To have complete, unquestioning confidence in anybody was his chiefest difficulty. He came near it with one or two of his friends; but he only achieved it in perfection with her. She had seemed to be of sound constitution, with promise of a long life. Once or twice she suffered from fainting attacks, but they were not thought serious. But at the end of the year 1890 the London doctor who had treated her told Rosebery news that in a way brought some comfort, if comfort it could be called—that she had suffered from a fatal malady which must have carried her off within two years.

How real and deep his affection for her was the world outside did not realise. A great heiress always has to surmount the critics' doubts whether she herself, or her possessions, constitute the central fact of her marriage. But apart from this, Rosebery's manner to her in public was sometimes abrupt, and he now and then seemed impatient of her obvious devotion to himself. Obvious it was, as when, for instance, her wish to hear the epigram with which he was delighting one side of the table, made her ignore the existence of her neighbour at the other. But any such irritation sprang from the shy element in Rosebery; and nobody who saw the two together at home, or in a small congenial party, could doubt the affection as well as the comprehension that united them. Nor could such a one fail to find what good company she was. She was also a writer of excellent letters, full of just the news and gossip that her correspondent would like to hear told.

The close of the year was spent at Mentmore, mostly in greyness and snow. It was a wrench to see even intimate friends. As he wrote to Reginald Brett (December 15th): "I should greatly like to see you, if anybody. But the fact is I am antigregarious just now, and perhaps morose." He read much, because he always read, and he was deep in the eighteenth century, because the *Life of Pitt* was in view. But he wrote to me that he could not find much solace in reading any poetry, even "In Memoriam."

Just at the same time died one of Rosebery's favourite companions, Harry Tyrwhitt. He was gaiety personified, and even when rapid consumption claimed him as its victim he remained imperturbable, humorous, and refusing to be an invalid, only talking of a troublesome cough. He was the most conspicuous of a light-hearted group that, in those eighties which the present generation believes were so solemn and decorous, turned night into day and yet by day were everywhere. Each of them might have said with the dying versifier:

> "Life's opening chapter pleased me well,
>   Too hurriedly I turned the page:
> I spoiled the volume: who can tell
>   What might have been my Lost Old Age?"

Between Rosebery and public life the curtain remained drawn throughout the year 1891. He made no speeches either in the House or on the platform. But his political friends did not want to lose him, and Gladstone in particular kept him in strict view. In April he wrote to Rosebery for his opinion about the vacant Liberal leadership in the House of Lords, suggesting that it might remain vacant. Rosebery replied at once (April 12th), strongly objecting, on the grounds that without a chief the little party of thirty or forty would drop to pieces. They must have a rallying-point—a leader chosen by themselves, who would not necessarily be the principal figure in a new Government. Lord Granville's guidance had been consummate, but an occasional division on a question of principle might have been a good thing.

"He did not like to reveal the nakedness of the land. But that nakedness is notorious, and there is a sense of notoriety and responsibility attaching to a vote in a small minority which is not so disagreeable, I suspect, as is generally supposed."

In reply to his chief's acquiescence he wrote again from Madrid (April 16th) :

"What has been done seems to me a very fair arrangement. There will be a head to the party or rump; and Kimberley who is an admirable debater and accustomed to the House of Lords, will, I have no doubt, keep the remnant together."

In the early summer he saw Mr. Gladstone twice in London, and Campbell-Bannerman once, but that was all. During his stay abroad he wrote to his chief from Gastein :

July 16th, 1891.

"1. I am entirely in agreement with you as to the paramount necessity of holding aloof from the Triple Alliance, or any other such engagement; for the same reason for which I am hostile to the Channel tunnel :—that I am anxious to obtain the full advantage of the insular position with which Providence has endowed us.

"2. In saying this I lean neither to the right nor to the left—neither to Germany nor to France. My wishes and sympathy are entirely with whichever side most promotes peace.

"3. I do not think that Salisbury has given or can have given any tangible support or adhesion to the Triple Alliance : for he is a very different Salisbury to the Foreign Minister of 1878 or the Prime Minister of 1885. Should he have done so, he will have ruined his reputation as a British Foreign Minister.

"4. For my part I am content with Fergusson's[4] last answer; and so, I thought, was the House of Commons.

"5. If, however, that is not so, and it is felt that the Liberal party should say anything further, I feel strongly that that should be said, in the first place at any rate, in the House of Lords. There is the Foreign Secretary, and there is the Prime Minister. Why then not drink at the fountain head instead of once more seeking the muddy tap, so often tasted, of Fergusson? No one could raise the question with more knowledge, judgment or experience than Kimberley: unless

"6. You could say something yourself. A measured, guarded, weighty deliverance from yourself, as brief as you like, (and indeed the shorter the better) would be invaluable. Personally I should prefer a speech to an article which must be relatively long and expanded.

"7. I earnestly hope that if Harcourt speaks he will also be measured, guarded and brief. To raise false expectations in France would be as fatal a policy as to join the Triple Alliance.

"I hope these views will not be unacceptable to you, (except the playful poke about the Channel tunnel), although possibly very ignorant; as, for the present at any rate, I am only a spectator, 3,500 feet above the sea and 3,500 miles from public life.

"Y. affly.,

AR"

In October he spent a couple of days at Hawarden. The only guests were Scott Holland and Mr. Gladstone's trusted secretary, Algernon West.

October 29th.—"A. West's idea is that Mr. G. should be in Cabinet without office. I pointed out two radical difficulties. 1. Mr. G.'s consent to such an arrangement. 2. The finding of a person sufficiently self-sacrificing to be a dummy premier. I sent for the boys and they arrived this evening. They went to a performance at the Hawarden gymnasium, sitting on each side of Mr. G. The latter came back chilled and tired, and lost control of himself (for the third time in my experience) in speaking of the Irish rebellion of 1798. In vain did I try to keep him off and turn the subject."

Rosebery went quietly to Althorp early in December, and took part in "a long palaver" with Spencer, Harcourt, and Morley, with Mr. G. presiding.

"We discussed every imaginable subject from a list brought down by Mr. G. Egypt, as to which I said that the Government which

[4] Sir James Fergusson 6th Bart. (1832-1907) M.P. 1854-68, and 1885-1906. Governor of New Zealand 1873 and Bombay 1880. U.S. for India 1886-7 and for Foreign Affairs 1886-91. Postmaster General 1891-92.

simultaneously gave Home Rule to Ireland and evacuated Egypt would be a bold one, finance, etc. etc."

On the next day Mr. Gladstone came to Mentmore.

"After dinner, Mr. G. in the amber room hoped that I should soon find it possible to return to public life. On this we talked with some fulness. He was emphatic on the point that when one had attained to a certain point in politics it was not possible to retire."

The old year ended by the transport of the whole party to Petworth to greet the new one in an atmosphere of loving companionship.

It was rough snowy weather after the New Year and until Rosebery started alone for Milan on January 17th. It was equally cold there, though dry during the week of his stay, when for the first time he was able to devote himself to the picture galleries and the library. He wrote:

"Spent some of the day with Leonardo's Last Supper. What a divine legacy for a man to leave. Its very damaged condition makes it more venerable and striking. The Christ is the fated, weary man of sorrows. On each side Leonardo has introduced alternative figures of Christ,— as if to show that it was not for want of realising the possible types that he has chosen the one that he has. The one is the soft almost feminine angelic face,—on the right. On the left is the keen, suffering, brilliant face. But Leonardo has chosen best."

He passed on to Brindisi, where he saw an Austrian-Lloyd steamer which one of the Vienna Rothschilds had hired for his own use "waiting by the wharf for him, blazing with electric light. It has been there these eight days. I entered my oil-lit vessel at 1 a.m." He preferred the full journey by Cape Matapan to the short cut from Patras, and thence had the whole deck to himself, basking in warm sunshine.

"I am reading Gibbon and Casanova through. The latter is unexpressibly long, but is an extraordinary picture of manners and morals in the eighteenth century, which should not be banished because of the occasional obscenity, which is no worse than Smollett, and is not in all the eight volumes equal to a page of Zola. After reading Casanova no explanation is necessary of the fall of Venice. She had evidently fallen long before Napoleon arrived: he only picked her out of a dunghill."

[304]

He found Athens a French provincial town with a German Schloss tacked on to the Acropolis, and seeing the troops drilling, felt confirmed in the wisdom of his discouraging action in 1886. But he visited all the great historic temples and theatres in close detail, not less than Schliemann's extraordinary spoil from Mycenæ. Marathon had a personal message for him from his happy Christ Church days, as well as its famous old story.

"I started at 9 for Marathon with the same coachman who took poor Fred Vyner. He had little if anything new to tell. I thought the peasantry looked hungrily at me as I went, and regretfully as I returned. This may have been fancy. We stopped on the bridge where Fred and his party were captured.

"Alas! Alas! We thought it an excellent joke at the time, and were only undeceived by his murder. Marathon is a little mound with excavations like a gravel pit in the midst of a parochial plain like a village common. I lunched on the mound and meditated sagely on fame."

He made more pilgrimages to the Acropolis, worked on the character of Pitt, and "had cuttlefish for luncheon, a great delicacy here. But I could not eat *pieuvre* with enjoyment." He started for Sicily (February 8th), and found snow falling and Lent beginning. So he hastened on to Naples. There were Italian friends to greet him, but he had said the last good-bye to the godmother of his early Naples days, Lady Holland. She died in London in September 1889. It was still wintry, but he was busy, because, besides his customary visits to book-shops and curiosity shops, the idea of a Naples villa was maturing in his mind, and he visited various houses, all unsuitable, under the care of a young Italian friend who knew every palace and every inhabitant of every palace. Herbert Bismarck arrived, but after some five days the weather broke again, so Rosebery went on to Rome and Venice. All this time he had been reading Gibbon: "What a solid dignified piece of work, with his buffoon face smiling a fat smile of smug raillery now and then." He never felt well at Venice, and after two days there the sight of a party of English acquaintances goaded him on to a direct journey to London, where he found his children dumb with astonishment at his arrival. He made the Durdans his headquarters, riding most days, spending time with the children and noting the different ways in which they were changed by the break-up of home. He was restless and slept badly. Mr. Gladstone came one day, and they talked of a thousand things; and Rosebery often saw Canon Rogers, now at Mickleham. The last day of March brought the death of Lord Granville.

"Alas! Alas! No man can fill, or ever I think take an interest in, the place he filled so conspicuously well in the House of Lords."

A day or two later:

"After dinner drove to John Morley's to take him at his word as to coming with me to Granville's funeral to-morrow. It is extraordinarily kind of him. Sat with him till 11.15."

His friend knew the pang that it must be for him to stand so soon at another graveside. The next day Reginald Brett came for a great part of it, full of kindness; and then Rosebery started off again for a foreign tour. Kindness greeted him again at Paris, where Baron Alphonse de Rothschild offered him the use of Ferrières or of his Cannes villa; but he carried out his plan of passing on to Biarritz. It was stormy there, and on the second day he wrote, "Spain is tempting," and on the fifth, "Spain is not only tempting, but has tempted successfully." He reached Madrid on April 15th, and was taken care of by Sir Clare Ford, whose inherited knowledge of Spanish art made him a perfect guide to the galleries and sumptuous palaces. But he went to the Escorial alone.

"It did not disappoint even my expectations, yet I had come to Spain on purpose to see it. Grey and grim with a bleak mountain range behind, and a wilderness like the sage brush country of the Rocky Mountains around, it is the most sublime sepulchre for the quick and the dead ever devised by man. For the dead alone the Taj is of course supreme. The Church, more especially if the frescoes were removed and Cellini's Christ placed over the high altar, is internally the most expressive church I have ever entered; with its cruel grey granite and its crushing silence it is the very valley of the shadow of death. The Escorial is the gloomy and costly embodiment of Philip II's character and reign—one of the most interesting and wonderful things in the world."

Since his calamity Rosebery had lived at his beautiful homes, and had visited some of the most beautiful places in Europe. But nothing had suited his mood so well as the Escorial. To borrow Thomas Hardy's plangent phrases:

"Fair prospects wed happily with fair times; but alas, if times be not fair! Men have oftener suffered from the mockery of a place too smiling than from the oppression of surroundings too sadly tinged."

[306]

Sir Clare took him to Toledo, where they were received by all the magnates of the province, civil and military. "The (too) civil ones remain with us all day, and I can understand the anguish of Royalty." With the Ambassador he also attended a bull-fight, and found—

"By judicious shutting of my eyes during the horse scene one can enjoy a bullfight very well. There was one incomparable matador Rafael Guerra (Guerrita) whose grace, coolness and dexterity made one in love with bullfighting."

The next day he came on a large crowd following an arrest, as he thought:

"But it turned out to be, between two obsequious gentlemen, smiling with condescension, Guerrita."

Then to Cordova and the delights of Seville, where the cathedral was in the course of reparation, but he was able to see its gorgeous treasures, the Alcazar, and the gallery of Murillos. Also the cigarette factory:

"Myriads of young virgins with babies. Statue over entrance with trumpet—to be blown whenever real virgin enters."

Also more than one variety of *olla*. After a few more days at Madrid Rosebery returned to France, laden with some attractive purchases from Madrid and Seville curiosity shops. On the way home he spent a day at Fontainebleau, which he had never seen, and found the forest quite equal to his expectations. His driver, a furious Bonapartist, who had served with Bourbaki, admitted that "President Carnot greatly strengthened the Republic by spending his money and giving without regard to party in charity." He emphasised the last. "But," he said, "all we demand is peace. We will never go to war again, unless attacked." "Not even for the provinces?" "No, No," he cried. "This is what I have always believed to be the real feeling of the peasantry in France."

And the event proved that Rosebery was right.

He returned to the Durdans, to unsettled weather, and to many sleepless nights. These sometimes drove him to ride at six in the morning, or even earlier. Thus passed May and early June, and on the doctor's recommendation he started for Marienbad, not as yet made fashionable for loyal Britons by the presence of their Sovereign. Pausing at Brussels, he visited the picture gallery:

"There was a portrait of Alva by A. Moro exactly like Reay. Dutch pictures do not appeal to me: faithful reproductions of the aspects of humanity which we most wish to forget."

At Marienbad he began by overwalking, and was depressed by wet weather. His good friends the Butler Duncans arrived, and became his companions in more measured excursions. At the beginning of July:

"This morning I woke for the first time unfatigued. The moment I appeared on the parade Mr. and Mrs. Duncan separately and without agreement exclaimed, 'Why, how well you look this morning!' So much for one good night."

General de Galliffet also appeared at the baths. "He comes to thin himself: though he is not very fat 'a soldier is never thin enough.' "

Rosebery's cure was to be completed at Gastein in fresher air, and during his fortnight there he was able to indulge his passion for walking without overdoing it, except on one occasion when, in a severe tramp of over four hours, he climbed a hill perpendicularly for two hours, and had to leave off before reaching the top for fear of being benighted.

He was back in England by the beginning of August, to find two more causes for sorrow. His stepfather was dying, longing to be released, but lingering on till the twenty-first of the month. He and Rosebery had always been on affectionate terms, and Rosebery never wrote to his mother without a message, "Love to the Duke." He was a man of dry manner, sometimes speaking of politics with old-fashioned pomposity, but he never deserved anything but respect. William Cory described how in a quiet visit at Battle he enjoyed the plain dignified talk of his host. He had always been a rich man, and of late years one of the richest in England, but avoided any sort of ostentation. He was buried at Raby, amid a crowd of younger relatives between whom his millions were divided. Rosebery of course escorted his mother, and had to act as momentary host, for nobody knew to whom the inheritance would fall. When leaving, Rosebery left this note for his mother:

RABY CASTLE, *August 31st*, 1891.
"MY DEAREST MOTHER,

"I must write a line to thank you for these two happy days, for such they have been to me. I cannot recollect that we have ever been two days alone together in our lives, and I have enjoyed them greatly: the more, as, widowed mother and widowed son, the hand of God has brought us so near to each other. If my staying has been any solace to you it will be an additional pleasure.

"I need not say how great a happiness it will be to me to be of assistance to you, and how entirely I and my children and my houses will be at your service.

"Your loving son,

AR"

CHAPTER XIII

County Council: General Election: Foreign Office: Labouchere

EARLY in the new year Rosebery took advantage of his freedom for a jaunt to Italy, Naples of course being the main point. There was snow at Milan followed by a drizzle, so he hurried south, and found his adored city bathed in sunshine—which was far from being a certainty. Sir Thomas Farrer, one of the bright lights of the Civil Service, and an old friend, was there, and Rosebery spent much time with him. On most days they sat and talked for an hour or more. Rosebery made a number of not distant excursions, and visited several villas, including the Villa Delahante, to the charms of which he was destined soon to succumb. Two days at Rome were mainly spent in the company of Lord Dufferin and his family at the Embassy.

February 2nd.—"To St. Peter's. I really think that the Church of the Escorial on the whole is more terribly impressive, more overwhelming. Walked to the Ara Cœli in honour of Gibbon (they *were* saying vespers), to the Capitol, the Forum, and Palace of the Cæsars."

It will be recalled that Rosebery resigned the Chairmanship of the County Council in July 1890; and now that new elections were pending in March he was urged to become a candidate. He had already (January 11th) explained to the electors for the City that, since contests this time would evidently be on political lines, whereas he had stood on non-political grounds, he could not now appear there as a candidate. Then St. George's in the East, comprising the district long notorious as Ratcliff Highway, appealed to his sympathy for the workers and invited him to stand. He declined, but in doing so issued what amounted to a manifesto defining his policy for London. He demanded the removal of petty restrictions on expenditure, the control of the water supply, the readjustment of rates, the control of the police, and, as infinitely the most important, the union of the City and County with as little friction as possible, so as to create a London Council in fact as well as in name.

The development of London, as we all know, has not followed these lines; more especially, perhaps, owing to the almost fantastically rapid growth of outer London than for any other reason.

All through the spring Rosebery was in frequent communication with Mr. John Benn, his close ally in Council politics. He attended a dinner given by Sir John Lubbock, his successor as Chairman, and several meetings held on behalf of Progressive candidates. At one of these for the City of London, with Prebendary Rogers in the Chair (April 30th), he developed the theses of his manifesto, carefully guarding himself against the supposition that he was attacking the City of London, but definitely forecasting the abolition of the Corporation as a separate existence within a short time. For once his gift of prognosis was quite at fault.

On the following evening John Morley presided over a great meeting in St. James's Hall, Sir Charles Russell and many other Members of Parliament being on the platform. Rosebery spoke at length in defence of the Council against the hostile criticisms of Lord Cross and Sir Henry James. It was these attacks, he said, which had made him leave the shadow where he was. To his hearers he seemed somewhat aged and tired, and showed signs of unaccustomed nervousness.

Meanwhile Mr. Benn had not been idle. As candidate for East Finsbury, a workers' constituency, he persuaded it without difficulty, and Rosebery with a great deal, that the late Chairman would make him an admirable colleague. The passive candidate merely stipulated freedom from meetings and canvassing. He was duly elected by a majority of over a thousand, and the Progressives won a goodly victory throughout London. When thanking the electors at a meeting in the Clerkenwell Road (March 14th) he dwelt on the present impossibility of non-political candidatures, bantered the Liberty and Property Defence League, and then spoke seriously of the coming reorganisation of the Council, pleading for an unpaid executive, and with deep conviction of the need for a unified London.

At the first meeting of the Council Rosebery was invited to resume the Chairmanship, and agreed to do so for a time, describing himself as a stopgap for the weeks needed for reorganising the conduct of business. He soon (March 22nd) indicated in detail the directions in which the Council would have to decide between different methods of prescribing the functions of its Chairman, the size of its committees, its financial policy, etc.

On June 27th he wrote resigning the post of Chairman, explaining that the work for which he had given his help to the Council was in a fair way towards completion.

The life of the Duke of Clarence, with all its great prospects and fond hopes, had been cut short on January 14th, and in February Rosebery paid a visit to the bereaved parents at Eastbourne, where the Duke of Devonshire had lent them his beautiful house of Compton Place. There was much intimate talk of the past and of the future. And there was one allusion to *Pitt*:

"The Prince as he lit his candle to go to bed said, 'By the by, you have been very hard on my great grandfather George III, but the Queen rather takes your view, and thinks you are right."

Two private troubles followed, serious though not crippling. Since his wife's death Rosebery had largely reduced his establishment of house and stables, and had cut down his general expenditure. But now appeared the reverse of the medal. A brilliant young American friend, charming himself, and married to a charming English wife, was over-sanguine in finance, and Rosebery had invested considerably in a Western mine, of which the American had charge. The enterprise collapsed entirely, and its unlucky promoter was due to return home from a fruitless voyage to Europe.

March 1st.—"He leaves for America to-morrow: I was told that a kind message from me would be welcome: I at once wrote that if he would not come to me I wished him Godspeed, etc."

March 2nd.—"At breakfast at 8.30 a note arrived to say that he had shot himself in the night. Alas! Alas! It turns out that he called on me at 10 last night. What an end to what a splendid glowing life. . . . Thank God I never said or wrote an unkind word to him; or even thought one of him that I can remember."

Three days later a telegram came—

"To say all my Australian money gone plus certainly £3,300, probably £10,000E., and that to avert further calls I must commence legal proceedings. Verily misfortunes never come single."

On the fatal March 1st Rosebery had been spending the evening with Rogers at Bishopsgate. He had ventured on one more field of enterprise, having written a sermon which his old friend delivered in St. Paul's the following afternoon, Ash Wednesday. The author attended the service, and concluded:

"It was not very successful, I think! I had no time to give it."

Only a rough draft of this discourse exists, the manuscript having been destroyed after Canon Rogers's death. The text was Ezekiel xxvii. 3, the marvellous vision of the valley of the dry bones, and of the winds of Heaven that breathed life into them. The sign, the preacher said, was given not merely to Israel, but to all humanity. And therefore to each nation, and to this city, under the fatherhood and guidance of God. The draft proceeds to enlarge on conditions at home and in the British Empire. It is unfinished, and it is doubtful whether Canon Rogers delivered it precisely in this form. Such a wealth of rhetoric was foreign to his own manner of preaching, at any rate.

The discourse was to pay a double debt, for a day or two later Rosebery drove from the Durdans to Mickleham—

"Where I gave Rogers a tag to adapt his Ash Wednesday sermon to one for the re-opening of Mickleham Church."

On April 7th Rosebery started alone for Portugal, thus completing his itinerary of South and Southwestern Europe. He saw all the sights of Lisbon, visited Fielding's grave, and was enthralled, as every traveller must be, by the unrivalled charm of Cintra, an unparalleled sight of verdure and wide prospect for the palaces of kings, and by the tasteful Moorish splendours of Montserrat. He passed on by Bádajos to Seville, again coming in for the gorgeous ceremonies of Easter. It was fitfully wet, but there were processions day and night. One was to start at midnight (April 13th), with a party dressed as Roman soldiers—

"So I determined to wait up and see the original sight. Alas, I little knew what I bargained for. One, two, three, passed. It rained heavily for an hour. Yet in the Calle de la Sierpe there were always many people. After 4 it became so crowded that one could hardly move, as many who had been to bed returned. At 5 came broad daylight, and at 6.30 the procession. The crowd was flippant and rather drunk. . . . I tottered to bed (for I had been on my feet for eight hours) at 7. At 8.30 I was woke by the procession returning."

But the great religious ceremonies were more successfully seen; and he also witnessed the curious arrival of six bulls for the next day's fight. They came from the meadow which they inhabited at

[313]

full gallop, escorted by three horsemen, and thirteen trained oxen. The Comtesse de Paris and her son rode at the head of the charge. When the bulls arrived at the enclosure, by an ingenious arrangement the oxen, like the trained elephants at a *keddah*, helped to hustle their doomed brethren towards the line of boxes facing the ring.

"As each enters his cell the door is deftly shut and the lamp withdrawn. The bull is left in solitary darkness till he shall come out next day into the full glare of the bullring and die. It struck me as tragic and pitiful."

But the next day:

"Guerrita is one of the most graceful of human beings."

Three days at Granada in perfect weather followed. The Alhambra—

". . . surpasses expectation in delicacy, refinement, and idealism. Two or three Moorish embassies have been here and have been observed to weep, and there are families in Tetuan who have preserved the keys of their Granada houses for generations, against the time they shall return which will be when the stone hand on the Gate of Justice grasps the stone key."

There is a note of rapture in Rosebery's musings on Granada, only surpassed by his musings on Naples. Had his affections not been pre-engaged, he can easily be imagined as investing in a *château en Espagne*. He spent (May 1st) a pleasant day or two at Madrid, and a couple in Paris, which he found as *triste* and deserted as Edinburgh. In the carelessly scandalous London world there had long been a story ascribing irregular parentage to Lord Dufferin. That distinguished man's features were not of the accepted British type; but there was nothing in them to warrant the rumour here disposed of.

"Dufferin said, 'I want to speak to you on a subject which would make some people very angry, but not me, I mean the story of Dizzy being my father.' He then told me that his parents were married in 1826 (I think), and went abroad immediately, and that he was born ten months after marriage. They did not return to England until 1834, when they made Dizzy's acquaintance. As to the alleged fondness of Dizzy for him, he had hardly spoken to him above three or four times in his life, on one of which occasions Dizzy had been almost rude. I said I was not sure if I ought to give up my authority. He said, 'I know who it is, and I have had a long talk with her.' 'What did she say?' 'That if it had been true it would have been equally creditable to all parties.' He is going to set matters right in a short preface to his mother's works."[1]

After his return home he was installed an Elder Brother of the Trinity House (October 25th), and in the autumn spoke at the banquet given by the Lord Mayor to that famous Corporation.

The months of May and June passed much as usual, with some quiet entertaining, and the resumed gathering of old friends for the Epsom summer meeting.

There was also a return to the arena of politics. Rosebery had been busy with the County Council reorganisation; but this was being concluded, and he had to decide for or against a definite resumption of the heavier burden. It is evident that he did not appreciate how deeply he was committing himself. Now, just as happened several years later, he could not recognise the fact that once a man in middle life has won the confidence of his countrymen in high office, he must be prepared either to take up work again or to disappear altogether. So that when he took part in political conclaves and attended political meetings he did not realise that the net of the veteran *retiarius* of Hawarden was already over his shoulder, and that he would never extricate himself.

A great meeting at Edinburgh (May 13th) welcomed "the occasion of his return to political life." In a long speech he deprecated the use of that phrase, for he was not sure of his intention. He was only there lest it should seem that he was not loyal to Liberal principles, or to the leader whom he had introduced to Midlothian—the proudest reflection of his life. After touching on Scottish questions, he devoted the rest of his speech to Ireland, and particularly to Lord Salisbury's recent address to the Primrose League. The Prime Minister had spoken of "a hostile Ireland on our flank." Rosebery fastened on the phrase like a terrier, and said that to win the country to Home Rule nothing else was needed than to rub that speech into every voter in the United Kingdom.

At the end of the month (May 26th) he was in Birmingham, the hostile stronghold. His speech, in his most effective strain of humorous argument, was mainly devoted to the Liberal Unionists, Jesse Collings, the subordinate, and Joseph Chamberlain, the master of eulogy and invective—"I think he prefers the power of invec-

---

[1] This was done in the "Account of the Sheridan Family," prefaced to the edition of her *Songs, Poems and Verses*, published 1894.

tive." Home Rule, compared with the watery proposals of the Ministry for Irish Local Government was again the principal theme, and was uncompromisingly urged on the meeting.

Next he went to support T. A. Brassey (June 9th), his old friend's son, in his assault on a purely Tory fortress at Sutton in Surrey, presenting a general indictment of the Government's policy.

There was a great Roxburghshire meeting at Kelso (June 16th), with more staunch advocacy of Home Rule and the query whether Ireland only exists for the benefit of Ulster; and another in support of the Liberal candidate for Edinburgh City. Here the opposition was in the hands of Lord Wolmer,[2] a rising light among Liberal Unionists, and Rosebery held him up as a striking instance of the absorption by Conservatism of men who had before been really Liberal and still used the name. Rosebery's last appearance before the election was at Whitechapel, in support of the ever-faithful John Benn. There would be no disturbance of foreign policy, he said, if the Liberals were returned to power. He again dealt with Ulster, and devoted the rest of his remarks to the vexed questions of London government.

Parliament was prorogued on June 28th, and the election followed. Liberal hopes had flown high. Gladstone, we are told,[3] reckoned on winning by eighty or a hundred. Such by-elections as that at Rossendale had stimulated such forecasts. A month earlier Mr. Gladstone had told Rosebery that the Queen had intimated through Ponsonby to Harcourt that her exclusions were Dilke and Labouchere.

May 28th.—"He discussed Labouchere as a Minister, spoke of his own deafness as a Cabinet disability, and was in the highest spirits. He was averse to giving Asquith Cabinet office, as to Bryce he spoke doubtfully."

Now, when the leader and John Morley arrived at Dalmeny, the framework of a possible administration was discussed and re-discussed. Harcourt also sent a list of names.

July 3rd.—"Morley came to my room at 11 p.m. In confabulation till midnight. 'If you do not join the Government it is hamstrung; it cannot last three weeks after Parliament begins, etc., etc.'"

July 4th.—"Mr. G. came to my room with his lists, which we talked over till luncheon without touching the capital point."

[2] Second Earl of Selborne, *b.* 1859.
[3] *Life*, bk. x, ch. vii.

It was windy, rainy weather, and the electoral barometer also sank to "stormy." By July 6th the hope of a good majority had faded, and Mr. Gladstone began to show signs of depression.

"Were he twenty years younger he would care little, but he now stood on the razor's edge with regard to his power of work. His great comfort was that all was in the hands of Almighty God. He evidently wanted to talk to some sympathetic person, so I sate with him in the library."

July 8th.—"Mr. G. and I drove about the park in my phaeton this afternoon. He was depressed and feeble, saying that he supposed I had no comforting consideration to offer him—which indeed I had not. He said, 'A great trial of this kind throws one back on oneself, and makes one examine oneself, and I now see how for the last six years I have been buoyed up with the belief that we should have a great majority and that the Irish business would be a very short business.' He bears up with wonderful courage."

Then a few guests arrived, including Bouverie Primrose.

July 10th.—"An amusing scene. My uncle says to Mr. G., 'I will move round to the left, as the left is my bad ear,' and acts accordingly. Mr. G. then, not hearing a word, composedly moves round in turn to my uncle's left, saying, 'I will come round here, as the right is my best ear.' Mr. G. said with some animation, but perfect good humour, 'After being shown all over the country for four hours yesterday, like a dwarf at twopence a head, I have some right to privacy.'"

The next day Gladstone opened up the subject of the leadership of the Lords. It would be the general opinion, he observed, that Rosebery would be the fittest person to cope with Salisbury in debate. This he put very strongly. Rosebery demurred, saying that Kimberley was the best. His chief believed that Kimberley would not continue, and that Spencer would be the fittest, failing Rosebery himself, in view of his mastery of the Irish Question. Rosebery thought that Spencer would do very well, but that all round Kimberley was best.

The last blow fell on July 13th, when Gladstone's own majority fell to 690. He had hoped for some 3,000, but Rosebery had some reason to fear that he might be beaten outright.

Rosebery had faced the fortnight's campaign manfully, but the strain had been terribly severe, apart from any heart-searchings about his own future. With a wearied captain, a discouraged crew, and an ebbing political tide, it seemed a ghastly parody of the voyage of thirteen years before with youth on the prow and happiness at the helm. Lady Fanny, the wife of Edward Marjoribanks and sister of Randolph Churchill, a woman of the finest sympathy and understanding, was one of the small party. She saw how her host was being tortured by memories, and in the middle of the contest sent him a note begging him to leave his guests and seek quiet for a few days elsewhere. But he saw it out, and only on July 16th joined a yacht on the west coast, in company with two Scottish political friends, one of them his faithful friend and regular correspondent, William Patten. Starting from Wemyss Bay, round the Mull of Cantire, for a night at Jura, and so to Oban. This little tour relaxed the strain somewhat, as the notebook shows. After fetching his two boys from Dalmeny, he started again from Oban for a longer trip. It is only possible here to record his visit to Dunvegan in Skye (July 29th), though other of his impressions were memorable. He was equally impressed by the chief and by his home.

"Macleod is a noble looking old man of 80 with an even nobler sister of 82, who has been the guardian angel of the people. She remembers Walter Scott at Abbotsford, as she told me, commending warmly Miss Ferrier's novels, with his heavy face lit up. (She rather prefers Ferrier's novels to Sir W's.) She sate sunning herself. I did not see enough of her. . . . There is nothing like Dunvegan that I know of in hoary antiquity and tradition and genuineness."

August 1st found him back at Dalmeny. On his peaceful cruise he must have been reminded that romantic Scottish mountains and cherished feudal towers did not tell the whole story of our islands, for from the start he read *Castle Rackrent* again, and much of *The Absentee*. But he was also directly bombarded from many quarters. His long intimacy with his chief did not prevent the existence of cross-purposes between them. The reserve of the one, and the qualifications with which the other guarded most of his utterances prevented the interchange of simple statements. Lord Acton, who enjoyed Gladstone's fullest confidence, wrote (July 18th) that the leader had thought the question of office really settled, because he and Rosebery had gone into matters of detail which implied that he would join. If there were really a hitch, the whole scheme of negotiation and distribution of offices would have to be begun over again. Acton could not believe that Rosebery would keep Gladstone's offer in suspense, or that he would refuse the great position and the greater inheritance which were his. Rosebery replied:

[318]

LORD ROSEBERY, ABOUT 1892

"MY DEAR ACTON,

"I duly received your kind letter at Portree, but am in some perplexity how to answer it. For Mr. Gladstone did not make me an offer
of any kind at Dalmeny: indeed, he hardly had the opportunity of
doing so. I was anxious that he should not: as my personal views—
I mean those as to my own future—are unchanged, and, had an offer
been made I must once more have stated them. That is all I have to
say. I wish it were more acceptable.

"Yours sincerely,

AR"

Acton replied:

August 2nd, 1892.

"If so, it will be a festive day for a variety of people, at home and
abroad, and a very sad one for

"Yours truly,

A."

On August 3rd Rosebery wrote to Harcourt, Spencer, etc., and
sent a letter to Arnold Morley, the trusted Liberal Whip, for delivery to Mr. Gladstone. Spencer had begged him to come within
consulting distance: "Pray think of us, and come and help us." The
answer was:

"The reason I do not come South is not that I am happy here, or
that I am indifferent to my friends, but because I have never wavered
in the resolve that so far as my own will can avail, my political career
should end with the General Election."

Harcourt's appeal was more subtly persuasive.

"You will have seen in the papers," he said, "the account of Gladstone's illness. . . . I need not picture to you what are the heavy
responsibilities and cares that fall upon us all in such a situation. . . .
I greatly mistake your character if you should be unwilling to give us
your aid and counsel and support in this critical conjuncture, and I
sent a telegram to Oban entreating you to return to London. . . . I
feel sure you will not be wanting in the offices of friendship to your
friends who so much desire and need them."

Mr. Gladstone was laid up with a severe cough, and Harcourt
wrote again the next day, saying that the attack was causing some
anxiety. He repeated his appeal in moving terms.

In his reply (August 3rd) Rosebery explained:

"The eighteen months that I have spent in seclusion have convinced me that I was not intended or fitted for political life: all my interest is now divorced from it: should I be forced back into it again future extrication would be difficult if not impossible. . . . I have dwelt on the whole case in my letter to Mr. G., but cannot repeat all that egotistical detail even to so true a friend as yourself."

Spencer tried again (August 4th), and after dwelling on the blow to Gladstone, concluded:

"Personally I do not know what I shall do: I looked forward to serving under you in the House of Lords, and later on, as I hoped, in the Cabinet. Pray think what an opportunity you will lose, one which your ability, your aptitude for political life, your experience and hard work have created. The country will lose a Leader marked out for the times of change and difficulty which are coming."

In writing to Mr. Gladstone, Rosebery reiterated his distaste for political life in similar terms to those cited above, but explaining that he had twice left his seclusion, once to help Liberals on the London County Council, the other to make some political speeches lest it be said that he held aloof from differences of opinion. But he could not conclude with a blank negation:

"One word more. The sole consideration that weighs with me against every other consideration is the fact that at an advanced age you are once again about to commission the ship of state with a courage which I can only call sublime and which lays almost an obligation on your friends and followers to stand by you. But that is not an overpowering consideration except to those who are conscious of being able to render efficient service. I am not. And I could now retire without inconvenience."

He went on to represent that Kimberley, he had long thought, would make an admirable Foreign Secretary, and that without himself there were four Liberal Peers of Cabinet rank.

The bombardment continued from all quarters, and from artillery of every calibre. Several relations wrote: Edward Hamilton set before him his duty in terms so frank as to risk the loss of friendship: Reginald Brett appealed in a tone of unusual seriousness and depression. Ronald Ferguson, no unquestioning Gladstonian, and living much in a Unionist circle, was sure that the Liberal party as a whole would go to the devil before long if Rosebery left it.

The fact would be established that "Joe" had chosen the better part in trying to make the Tories good instead of trying to make them out bad.

John Morley, however, took the literal part of the *deus ex machina*. He jumped into the Scotch express, having fired off this note:

SPENCER HOUSE, *August 4th*, 1892.
"MY DEAR ROSEBERY,

"To your disgust and indignation you will see me about an hour or so after you get this. I only come as bearer of a letter from Mr. G. You'll give me some breakfast anyhow?

"Ever your affectionate,
J. MORLEY."

The host noted (August 5th):

"J. Morley arrived early. Walked with him most of the day and rode. The children dined with us at 7—a fascinating little banquet. At 8.30 I drove him into Edinburgh, and we went to London by the 9.30. He told me that Mr. G. before talking to me about the leadership of the Lords (on July 11th), and as he fancies offering it to me and my accepting it, told him he considered it carried with it the *jus successionis*, as he did not believe that Harcourt could ever lead the Liberal party. Harcourt has written Mr. G. a secret letter about his eyesight. He has been leading Mr. G. a terrible life, had a tremendous interview with him on Wednesday, and spoke of standing aloof."

Mr. Gladstone's letter must be given in full.

Secret.   1, CARLTON GARDENS, *August 4th*, 1892.
"MY DEAR ROSEBERY,

"My first duty is to thank you most cordially for the personal kindness, indeed I must say tenderness of your letter. But the letter is an event, with which you will I am sure desire me to deal frankly according to my sense of the facts.

"There are three points to which I must refer.

"The first is your conviction of your own unfitness for public life. I distinguish between this conviction and your desire to escape from public life, for I am quite sure that, under the circumstances of the case, you would regard that desire as no more than dust in the balance.

"With respect to the conviction I have only to say that I have never known a case where such a conviction on the part of the person concerned was allowed by him to prevail against the clear, unhesitating,

[321]

unanimous judgment of friends, and the no less unequivocal judgment of the world.

"Your most touching reference to me leads me to say a word upon this isolated aspect of the case; to repeat, in fact, to you what I have more than once during the last six years urged upon others, sometimes with success. It is the undeniable truth, that in contemplating what may happen next week, and what has to follow the probable event, I am simply waging a daily and hourly battle against Nature, with no sort of personal assurance as to my capacity to sustain it. On the contrary, full of apprehension and misgiving; but yet inevitably forced on by the knowledge or belief that the demand is one made upon me by the crisis, and that that demand is morally inevitable. I have not the same command over the actions of others as over my own. But my convictions about them may be as clear, or even clearer. And in this case I feel that the very same appeal, which the facts make to me, they also make to you; and that the appeal entails the very same obligations.

"I will not now dwell on what happened at Dalmeny, further than to say that, when I left in your hands provisional statements connecting your name with the Foreign Office; when I discussed with you, and leant to its association with, the leadership in the Lords, and when I also spoke of the representation of the Department in the Commons, without receiving from you an adverse sign (nay more than one positively favourable), my impressions were such, that I am now taken by surprise.

"But I go back, as you do, from that period to our conversation at Mentmore in the winter; when you made the same plea, and when I found myself compelled to offer the same reply. It is my fixed assurance, founded on all I know of public life, of Great Britain, and of its people, that what I then said was right; that you had no open choice before you; that your acceptance was predetermined by previous acts, and that the nation would not tolerate your refusal.

"What I then stated was, I think, absolute; and did not need, and scarcely admitted, strengthening. Nevertheless, much corroboration has been supplied to it by the varied and admirable services which you have since rendered to the public cause.

"I am aware that we, your friends and colleagues, are deprived of all semblance of a title to urge this plea with respect to your public speeches in the interval. But the main element of the whole case, in my mind, is the solid, permanent judgment of the nation. And, as regards that judgment, and the grounds which the nation will think it has for forming it, the force of the facts is I think stubborn, and not to be denied.

"I am sure I may rely upon your kindness not to send an unfavourable decision in this important matter without seeing me; and you will believe me to remain,

"Always affectionately yours,
W. E. GLADSTONE."

Meanwhile, Windsor Castle was also wondering. At the end of May, after Rosebery's Glasgow and Birmingham speeches, he had fallen from his eminence of favour. The Queen wrote to Sir Henry Ponsonby (May 30th), announcing that the Dissolution would come at the end of June, and proceeded:

"First of all she must say how dreadfully disappointed and shocked she is at Lord Rosebery's speech which is radical to a degree to be almost communistic. Hitherto he has always said he had nothing to do with Home Rule and only with Foreign Office affairs, and *now* he is as violent as any one. Poor Lady Rosebery is not there to keep him back. Sir Henry must try and get at him through someone so that he may know how grieved and shocked the Queen is at what he has said. In case of the Govt.'s defeat the Queen meant to send for him first, but after his violent attack on Lord Salisbury, this attempt to stir up Ireland, it will be impossible, and the G.O.M. at 82 is a very *alarming lookout*. . . . She thinks sometimes it will come to Sir William Harcourt! But he would command neither respect nor confidence."

Now that the crisis was come, and the dreadful names of Labouchere and Dilke were bruited abroad, minor delinquencies must be overlooked, and Sir Henry Ponsonby wrote (July 20th):

"Lord Rosebery's position is a mystery, and as he has gone on board a yacht he is not at this moment accessible."

On the next day (July 21st) he described a conversation with Edward Hamilton, who did not know what Rosebery intended to do, but felt that if he stood aloof now he would probably be rejected by the Liberal party, and might retire from political life. Hamilton asked whether the Queen could write to Rosebery, insisting on his taking the Foreign Office. Sir Henry, the sagest of counsellors, proceeded:

"Sir Henry thinks that a little time should be taken for consideration before any letter of this sort should be written. At present, although there is every probability, there is no certainty of a defeat of the Government, and it would not do to assume that Lord Rosebery would be called upon to take office yet.

"And then Sir Henry Ponsonby cannot quite make out what Lord Rosebery meditates.

"It may be health that keeps him afloat just now, it may be dislike of the Gladstonian programme, or it may be that he wishes to retire from public life.

"But it is also possible that he is waiting till the party ask him to take the Foreign Office, when he will make his own conditions which are believed to be that he shall not be interfered with especially on the question of Egypt, or briefly that he will not abandon Egypt as many insist upon. If this is correct, it may be as well not to interfere at present or at any rate till the views of the chiefs become a little clearer."

Hamilton, equally loyal to his chief and to Rosebery, persevered, and having seen Francis Knollys, again wrote asking that whenever the Queen had to send for Mr. Gladstone she should simultaneously communicate with Rosebery; and lay special stress on the necessity of securing him when giving her orders to Mr. Gladstone. This would be more effective than sending a message through the Prince of Wales.

But Sir Henry, ever prudent, objected even to this. He told the Queen that the matter must be fought out between Gladstone and Rosebery before she could interfere. After his interview with the new Prime Minister, he told the Queen that Rosebery had been informed of her wish that he should take the Foreign Office, but Mr. Gladstone feared that he would refuse on the ground of *insomnia*.

It ended in a letter from the Prince of Wales (August 14th), who had been told by the Queen that she herself could not put pressure on anybody to join this iniquitous Government.

Confidential.   R.Y.S. "ALINE," COWES, *August 14th*, 1892.
"MY DEAR ROSEBERY,

"Nobody dislikes more than I do to interfere in matters which not only do not concern me—but which might be looked upon as indiscreet—but as we are such old friends and have so freely talked on so many subjects especially regarding politics and the probability of a Liberal Govt. coming into power which has now become a fact—you will I am sure forgive my writing to say—with what deep concern I have learnt from public rumour that you are disinclined to accept office in Mr. Gladstone's Govt.

"That you may differ with him on many salient points I can easily understand and appreciate—but I for one—who have my country's interest so deeply at heart—would deeply deplore if you were unwilling to accept the post of Secretary of State for Foreign Affairs! a post which you have filled before with such great ability and which has not only been appreciated at home—but by all foreign countries.

"Though I know that the Queen has no desire to press you to

[324]

accept this post—which for reasons best known to yourself you are disinclined to take—still I know how much she wishes for it, and I for one do most earnestly hope that you will reconsider what I understand is your present decision—or at least undertake to preside over Foreign Affairs for six months.

"There are many grave questions at this moment affecting our interests in India, Egypt and Morocco, and it requires a very watchful eye—to prevent Russia and France from harming us—and a thorough knowledge of the subject which nobody possesses more than you do. Let me therefore implore you to accept office—(if Mr. Gladstone will give you a free hand in Foreign Affairs—and not bind you to agree with him in *all* his Home measures) for the Queen's sake and for that of our great Empire! Forgive me bothering you, my dear Rosebery—but I should not write so strongly if I did not feel the grave importance of your accepting office in the present serious political crisis.

"I am,
"Yours very sincerely,
ALBERT EDWARD."

The quarry was now captured. Accordingly he replied to the Prince of Wales as follows:

38 BERKELEY SQUARE, W., *August 15th*, 1892.
"SIR,
"I have just received the more than gracious letter which Your Royal Highness has been so kind as to write to me.
"The difficulty that I have found in going to the Foreign Office is not public but private; for I have the gravest doubts as to whether my long loneliness and sleeplessness have not unfitted me for public life.
"However, the matter has now been practically taken out of my hands and settled in the way that Your Royal Highness wishes.
"More I cannot say now, except to beg that this communication may be considered as strictly private and personal to yourself.
"But I must be allowed to offer my sincere thanks for this fresh proof of Your Royal Highness's constant friendship for

"Your obedient servant,
ROSEBERY."

The victim narrated the whole story in a rough note:

August 11th, 1892.—"I went to Mr. G. at 2, at 1, Carlton Gardens. We sat on the sofa side by side. I said I feared I could not announce any change. He, much taken back, urged me to take advice. I said that in these cases a man must judge for himself. He broke out against this, said that there were men such as the late Lords Granville and Clan-william who were the sort of men to seek counsel of in such affairs. I admitted that I knew what the advice would be, but that no one not in my skin could conceive the loathing of politics that I had conceived. Perhaps it was that my nervous system had sustained a greater shock in 1890 than I was then conscious of, but there it was and he could not understand it. He said with great vehemence that he did, that for years past he had abhorred and loathed the contentious side of politics. I cited Lord Althorp and said that my case was stronger because of my orphan children. He denied the analogy and implored me for the sake of my children themselves and my posterity not to take such a course. He added that in these cases frankness was the truest kindness and that it would be said of me 'relicta non bene parmula.' I said that I had discounted all that. After about ¾ of an hour I rose to go. I stood in front of him as he sate on the sofa. He clasped my hand in his and said with the most pathetic violence, 'God Almighty in His infinite mercy and goodness guide you to a right decision,' repeating this two or three times with the greatest solemnity.

"This was on Thursday, August 11. No further communication passed between us till Monday, August 15. Arnold Morley called and left a note from Mr. G. saying that he was just off to Osborne to submit my name to the Queen for the F.O. Late in the afternoon I telegraphed to him 'So be it.'

"On the next day I went to him by appointment at 3.30 p.m. I said to him, 'Well, you have got your way and I have not got mine, but it is on your responsibility—not mine.' He said that the Queen had insisted on it and offered to press it personally on me, but had not, 'Can you guess why?' I said 'No.' 'Because she thought this affair seemed loosely hung together and hoped it might fall through.' I said I was glad she had taken no part: she could only have secured my refusal, for I could not have yielded to her instance what I had refused to that of my friends and colleagues. He said with intense passion, 'You do not know what I have gone through in the past week. Do not repeat what I am going to say to a living soul—I have been treated BRUTALLY by one man. Never have I been so treated.' At last I had to remind him that it was I who had received the commission. 'But,' he replied, 'it is for us to consider whether we will join you.'

"He said that the French were well affected and I said that I hoped so, that I should tell Waddington that it was a mistake to suppose that I was hostile to France but that I should hint that goodwill to be fruitful must be mutual and practical.

"I also told him that the way in which my appointment had been brought about was probably the only method by which it could have been accomplished."

[326]

A day or two later he was at Osborne for his first audience:

"She held out her hand warmly. I kissed it. 'It is so long since I have seen you and you have gone through so much.' I said I wished she could have left me where I was. 'Oh no, I hope the work will be good for you, and then think of the reception of your name.' 'It is nothing but a name.' 'Oh no, much more than that. You know I have always given you good advice'—or words to that effect, quite maternally."

Nobody had followed this shifting scene more attentively than George Buckle, the Editor of *The Times*; because no publicist more entirely realised what was at stake. He had been over to Mentmore on the 14th, when he and his host had a long and earnest talk: "In the afternoon he sent a further powerful and affecting letter." He therefore hailed the news of Rosebery's acceptance with joy, feeling sure that the strenuous collar-work of the post would be the patient's best cure.

Another welcome letter came from Charles Cooper of the *Scotsman*. The newspaper had gone over to the enemy, so that personal association had greatly ceased, but Cooper now wrote that nothing could lessen his conviction that Rosebery, if he were willing, might be the staff and guide of the Empire. Countless letters came, signed by distinguished names—one from Cardinal Rampolla with a message from Pope Leo XIII, who had retained, he said, a most agreeable recollection of Rosebery's audience at the Vatican.

Much space has been given to the events of these few weeks, since they seem to mark a principal turning-point in his career, and to show up his state of mind in bright relief. "Incomprehensibility," his clear-headed uncle had said years before. This time he was equally puzzling to Harcourt's *esprit positif*, to Spencer's grand simplicity, and to Campbell-Bannerman's shrewd tolerance. John Morley, himself with a surface equally sensitive but of a different texture, sometimes lost patience, as in a letter to Harcourt of January 26th.[4] Even some of these intimates may have been tempted to believe, as many of the crowd did, that all this hesitation was not quite genuine. The story will have been poorly told if any reader concludes that there was any tinge of affectation in these comings and goings, or if he does not credit the reality of the conflicting emotions which seethed in that unresting mind.

At the Cabinet on the following day, compromise was in the air. A subsidy of £1,000 a year to King Mwanga of Uganda was the

---

[4] *Life of Sir W. Harcourt*, vol. ii, ch. x.

first step; then a telegram from Portal justified a three months' postponement of evacuation.

"In Mr. G's sitting-room, much walking about of Mr. G. between Harcourt and me. We did not sit down till 12.30. Bewildered colleagues in knot all round."

Harcourt, Herschell and Rosebery met to draw up a *procès verbal*. This was done in terms stated by Harcourt, and as he wrote grimly to his son—"so far so good, for the present"; Rosebery took Kimberley and Campbell-Bannerman off to luncheon. "This morning I did not think I should eat lunch as Foreign Minister." It indeed was for the present only. On October 20th another deputation from the British and Foreign Anti-Slavery Society, comprising many leading Members of Parliament, attended at the Foreign Office. Its special object was to press the construction of a railway from Mombasa to the Victoria Nyanza. This was the only way, it was suggested, in which the behests of the Brussels Anti-Slavery Conference could be obeyed. Rosebery was again cautious. He was not a dictator, but a single member of a Government which had responsibility not only in respect of the slave trade, but to the taxpayers. After briefly reviewing the circumstances, he said that his visitors represented that continuity of moral policy which Great Britain could never afford to disregard. That policy, he declared, is the salt that savours our history, and by it when we have passed away, we shall come to be judged. Greece remains by the spiritual force of her literature; Rome not by her campaigns, but by her laws and works of civilisation.

"And in the same way I believe that this country, when it stands before history, will stand, when all else has passed away, not by her fleets and her armies and her commerce, but by the heroic self-denying exertions which she has made to put down this iniquitous traffic."

He repeated that he could not pledge the Government to pursue any course of policy in Uganda; but the cause they advocated must occupy a commanding place in the balance of considerations.

Those who thought with Harcourt that the anti-slavery movement was a mere cloak for annexationist ambitions remained on the alert, seeing that the real struggle on Uganda was yet to come. Rosebery asked the Prime Minister and Harcourt whether it would be better not to compromise, but that he himself should go. Walking with Asquith, he met Mr. Gladstone and Morley, who stopped them:

"Mr. G. took my arm (for the first time that I remember) and we walked round and round the Downing Street garden. He hinted vaguely at the Mombasa railroad, and said with much feeling that my behaviour had been beyond reproach. I said with more that he would not believe perhaps the pain it had given me to give him so much trouble—that it wrung my heart. He said he needed no such assurance. The interview was signally warm and tender."

So Rosebery stayed on.

The other breeze that ruffled the autumn calm was started by Rosebery's old friend Henry Labouchere.

"Oct. 1. Spencer and J. Morley dined with me. Labouchere has written to Wemyss Reid to say he will accept the Legation at Washington, leave Parliament, bury the hatchet, and come to a concordat about the succession to Mr. G.! Otherwise he promises triple venom after that event."

As has been said, Labouchere's professed republicanism, his fierce opposition to the Royal Grants, and his editorship of a journal which recalled the *Age* and the *Satirist* of a former generation, had kept him from receiving even a subordinate place in a Government to which he had undoubtedly helped to attach the suffrages of the extreme Left. He had written to Wemyss Reid,[5] the trusted confidant of all Liberals:

"Rosebery's gain would be clear. I have no personal dislike to him —quite the reverse. But he is much too clever a Peer to have as P.M. to my thinking. But were I in America neither this nor Egypt would be my affair."

Wemyss Reid wrote to Morley, setting out the whole story; Labouchere had, as always, been candid. He was indeed bitterly incensed, and had written, "I am quite prepared to use the arms put into my hands for my own advantage, not being of a modest or retiring habit of mind." "The dangerous nuisance," as he described himself, explained to John Morley that he wanted the matter settled before Parliament met, because he would get into a mess with his Radical friends were he to shirk Uganda, while if he were put into antagonism with Rosebery and an appointment were made later, it would be deemed a matter of buying and selling. The next move came from Mrs. Labouchere who, without telling her husband,

[5] Sir T. Wemyss Reid (1842-1905). Editor of *Leeds Mercury* 1870-87, of *The Speaker* till 1899. General manager of Cassell & Co. Author of several biographies of public men.

sought an interview with Rosebery at the Foreign Office, "of not more than ten minutes." He was somewhat touched by her persistence in her husband's cause; and I remember his contrasting the brilliant actress of the "seventies" with the very plainly attired lady who sat in his official room. From his record of the conversation, which lasted not ten but forty-five minutes, he evidently was kindness itself; but he could not help asking "what would be the position if this proposal were made not on behalf of a Radical leader, but of a destitute duke? Would not the columns of *Truth* teem with violent diatribes against so colossal a job?" There followed explanation of some misapprehensions, and allusion to possible scandals, and the meeting closed amicably. Then came a note from Labouchere himself, stating how the idea had originated, and describing his conversations with Ministers. Morley had spoken of insuperable difficulties, which in reality were "blessings in disguise," but, Labouchere observed—

"I don't quite believe in disguised blessings; in fact, I never heard of them except in a tract, and in Balfour's speeches, when he put the Nationalist M.P.s in prison. As regards my attacks on Rosebery in *Truth*, the Liberal party are divided as to what our principles of foreign policy ought to be in Europe and Africa. He takes one side and I take the other. Of course I fight for my side. There is nothing personal in this. I did not adopt my opinions in order to attack Rosebery; but I have always held them and always fought for them. In America, however, there are no heathen to convert, there is no Egypt to retain, and there is no Triple Alliance."

Rosebery thereon wrote to Labouchere, establishing direct communication, and sent the papers to the Prime Minister. The Laboucheres suggested further ways of meeting the difficulty of a diplomatic re-shuffle, and the business trailed on into the following year. Labouchere (January 4th) announced his intention of bringing in a Bill to allow Peers to surrender their peerdom, and stand for the House of Commons. Rosebery expressed his concurrence, and this may have encouraged Mrs. Labouchere to call on him again in Downing Street to describe a scheme for her husband's immediate resignation of his seat, the appointment to be made later. Labouchere himself wrote three or four times, letters so excellent that they ought to be recorded in full, did space permit. Mrs. Labouchere, he said, had got it into her head that Washington was an Elysium, though Chamberlain had said it was a dreary hole, stiff and dull. He himself in this damp atmosphere suffered from a rheumatic affection in the neck and throat, which made sitting in the House like the torments of the damned. If he got to Washington he would stay there, like St. John in Patmos, and give up Parliamentary life. As to buying and selling, he would lose in the money sense, because from investments he had three times what he could spend, while *Truth* brought in more than twice a Cabinet Minister's salary. (Rosebery had offered to talk it over again with Mr. Gladstone, and if it were desired, with Harcourt and Morley.) This was very kind, but all the Ministers had already spoken of insuperable difficulties, although each individually favoured the appointment, while wondering how Labouchere could give up the paradise of Parliament. "A Cabinet, in fact, is the firm of Jawkins and Spendlow on a large scale."[6] He thought that Rosebery overestimated his opposition. There would always be a section for non-intervention, but the safety of any Foreign Secretary is that not ten men in the House know anything about foreign politics, and, provided there is no war, want to know nothing.

"As for Washington, a man must be an utter fool who does not get on with the Americans. This is done by never expressing an opinion on party issues; by occasionally making a speech at a dinner about the language of Shakespeare; by feeding Senators and others; by carrying out instructions like a machine; and by generally professing that, if there are two countries made to love each other, they are England and America."

In his last letter of reply Rosebery wrote:

"Many thanks for your letters. One of my main regrets is not being able to do as you wish is that I shall not be in regular receipt of such fascinating despatches. . . . I can only repeat that I am very sorry that circumstances do not enable me to give you the promise you ask for."

Labouchere replied:

"*Fiat voluntas tua.* I daresay that if rheumatism will keep off, I shall get as much enjoyment out of the H. of C. as in writing you dispatches about seals from Washington."

Labouchere's enjoyment had not long to wait; but for the moment the final scenes of the comedy were played by Mr. Gladstone and Mrs. Labouchere. The Prime Minister had entered into the

[6] The misspelling of the famous partnership in *David Copperfield* is of course intentional.

sport with great relish, and had suggested some phrases in Rosebery's first formal reply. Now he wrote (February 18th, 1893):

"*Ecce iterum Crispina.* My poor dear wife was horribly shaken this morning by a card inscribed Mrs. L., and a request for a moment's interview. This proved to be intermediary. I was to be the victim for 'five minutes': you know how these minutes stretch from the small photographs to the life size."

Needless to say that the veteran fencer, equipped with all the courtesies of the duelling ground, was not touched. "All things end at last, and we parted, seemingly in good blood."

The episode had a prompt sequel; and in its effects on Rosebery's position proved to be really important. For Labouchere, by capacity and ruthlessness, was the leading Radical figure: and a breach with him meant a breach with much of the fighting strength of the party. He might very possibly have made a success of the American mission, though it clearly was impossible to send him there at the time. As the correspondence shows, Rosebery was far from dismissing the notion off-hand.

During the year Rosebery still took no part in the doings of the House of Lords. Apart from his County Council work and the few political occasions that forced him to the platform, he spoke eloquently at Glasgow on housing and the need for playing-fields, and at the opening (May 13th) of Brockwell Park, Herne Hill, he described London as the prey of builders, and urged (June 6th) his friends on the County Council not to be remiss in securing open spaces, so fast disappearing under red and yellow villas. This was forty years ago, and we still keep on saying the same thing. The opening of the Polytechnic in the Borough Road was his last civic duty of the year, and he presided on St. Andrew's Day at the dinner of the Scottish Corporation in London. He was at Sandringham for the Prince's birthday party, and was three times summoned to Windsor, where he was invested with the Order of the Garter on November 21st. When he had received Mr. Gladstone's proposal he had written as follows:

Private.   FOREIGN OFFICE, *October 6th,* 1892.

"MY DEAR MR. GLADSTONE,

"I am much honoured by your proposal to submit my name for the vacant Garter.

"My first impulse is, I confess, to ask you to excuse me. It seems to me that the time for Garters and the like has long gone by for me, and there is no one now to be pleased.

"Moreover I cannot help feeling that this decoration might well be utilised to lure some big fish who might be useful to the party; and this solution would be much the most agreeable to me.

"But it has been my unwilling fate during the last two months to be engaged in so much irksome and painful correspondence with you that if you prefer to press your present proposal I shall not be so ungracious as to resist. Only I would ask that whatever you decide I may for this reason not hear any more on the subject.

"I have written exactly my whole mind on this subject and it reads very ungratefully. But I hope and believe that you will understand me. If I have omitted anything it is this—that it seems to me, particularly in these days, so much more distinguished to be undecorated (like yourself) than the reverse.

"Believe me,
Your affectly,
AR"

The Queen asked if he already had the Thistle, for if he had, she would not allow him to give it up. On one of the other occasions conversation turned on names and titles, when Rosebery complained of his name having been taken for the Primrose League—"She did not quite like this, I think."

"HONI SOIT QUI MAL Y PENSE!"

"This Garter, brighter from the knee
Of him who uttered nothing—important."

"Mister" Rosebery loquitur:

A Star and Garter! Here's a go!
Well, well, no doubt 'twas to be worn meant;
And, as mere personal adornment,
It does look smartish, dontcher know!

All personal adornment's vain,
Held Dr. Watts, holds dear McDougall;
For dowdy dress and habits frugal
Befit the Democratic strain.

And I'm a Democrat—of course!
The Benjamin Franklin of the Peerage!

[333]

And yet—ah! truly 'tis a queer age—
A Decoration has *some* force!

I wonder what the L.C.C.
   Will say to this! That I should spurn it?
   John Burns may swear I ought to burn it.
Still—it looks natty round my knee.

I need not wear it when I sit
   Among the broadcloth'd heirs of Bumble!
   But Foreign Minister too humble
Were butt of diplomatic wit.

Battersea's pride my pride may scourge,
   Well—he may find he's caught a Tartar.
   A robe—a coronet—a garter!—
Materials for a new "Pride's Purge"!

The keen-eyed Democratic lynx
   May watch me with alert suspicion,
   As but a half-disguised patrician,
But—shame to him who evil thinks!

                  (Left posturing complacently.)

He paid a flying visit to the unknown shores of Ireland, as the
guest of John Morley, spending his time between two Lodges, and
seeing the sights of Dublin. Dining with me at the Viceregal Lodge
he made the acquaintance of our delightful friend Father James
Healy. He was deeply impressed by the Library of Trinity College,
and noted at Glasnevin Parnell's grave like a flower-bed, and the
cross erected to the slayer of James Carey, "who died for his country
at London, England."

Two years had passed since Lady Rosebery's death, and some of
her husband's friends were surprised at his persistently continued
display of household mourning, in various ways that seemed to
them extravagant and unreal. His children were too long dressed in
black; and for four or five years he went on using notepaper with
the broadest black edge obtainable. For many years longer his letters still bore signs of mourning. In these days, since the Angel of
Death has hovered over almost every home in the land, the custom
here has changed—for the better, as most would admit. But at that
date the era of professional mourners, and nodding plumes, and
streaming hat-bands, had scarcely closed. In some foreign countries,

By kind permission of the Proprietors of "Punch"

KNIGHT OF THE GARTER, 1892

even yet, much of the old pomp remains; and the different religious faiths expect their own injunctions to be observed. It is idle to judge harshly the ways whereby our poor humanity, at its wisest or at its weakest, seeks for itself some shred of passing comfort, or tries to pay its empty tribute to the dead. One may compare the confession of another powerful mind: Disraeli, the most loyal and grateful of husbands, was teased by Lady Bradford for his indulgence in this fancy. This, we are told, was his rejoinder:

"It is strange, but I always used to think that the Queen persisting in that emblem of woe, indulged in a morbid sentiment. And yet it has become my lot and seemingly an irresistible one. I lost one who was literally devoted to me . . . and when I have been on the point sometimes of terminating this emblem of my bereavement, the thought that there was no longer any being in the world to whom I was an object of concentrated feeling overcame me and the sign remained."[7]

The recollections and prospects of the two men were far from being identical. One of them was seventy years old when he wrote, the other at this time was five-and-forty. But the words of the older man give some clue to the sentiments of the younger. And there we can leave it.

It is only fair to add that the children were not restricted to a régime of sable garb and excerpts from the Burial Service. The two girls paid their visit to a theatre to see *Walker, London,* and were kindly received by John Toole. Later the whole party went to see *The Private Secretary.* "It was a great success, for we all laughed amazingly."

[7] Letters of Lord Beaconsfield to Lady Chesterfield and Lady Bradford, edited by the Marquess of Zetland. Introduction.

CHAPTER XIV

Foreign Office, Egypt; Siam; The Irish Government Bill; Navy Estimates; Gladstone's Retirement

A LITTLE ceremony early in the new year only claims record in the light of later events. A presentation was made to Lewis Harcourt on his resignation of the Secretaryship of the Home Counties Liberal Federation. Rosebery presided, and dwelt on the brilliant distinction which the recipient would have won, even if in office, had he not chosen perhaps the nobler and certainly the more laborious part of working in obscurity for the regeneration of the Cause. Lewis Harcourt, in his reply, said that they recognised in Lord Rosebery all that was best in the English character. In him they saw the model citizen, the brilliant writer, the eloquent orator, the admirable municipal reformer and, above all, the practised and practical statesman. Both speakers strewed roses with ungrudging hands.

Later in January the Foreign Office was agitated by the ministerial crisis in Egypt, where the new Khedive Abbas Hilmy Pasha, a schoolboy in age and capacity, dismissed three ministers whom he considered too submissive to Downing Street. Rosebery's position was not easy, for several of his colleagues were so anxious to get out of Egypt that they would not consider a mild humiliation too great a price to pay. On the other hand, Lord Cromer's suggested measures reminded Rosebery of the *coup d'état* of December 2nd, 1851, and after a long Cabinet he drafted (January 17th) two compromise telegrams which were substantially accepted. "The Khedive gave in," he noted, "but snake scotched, not killed." Two days later the fight in the Cabinet was renewed for two hours, at the end of which Rosebery carried his further compromise telegram. Harcourt took Rosebery's view in the main, and was conciliatory, but his one real supporter was Bryce. Mr. Gladstone was very hostile, and fertile in historical precedents; Kimberley, Herschell, and Spencer did not support Rosebery, and all the rest looked on mutely.

[338]

April 16. 1893

Mentmore,
Leighton Buzzard.

My dear Mr Gladstone

many thanks for
letting me see Dilke's letter
which I return.

It is interesting and able,
bar perhaps that Dilkerian
assumption of an omniscience
and precision which he
does not possess.

But much that would have
been possible and practicable
has been prevented by the
action of the young Khedive

/pp

Aj.

At the same time Rosebery told the Prime Minister that the army of occupation ought to be strengthened:

"Prevention is better than cure at all times: we have had a significant warning, and I fear if we do not take it we are at the beginning of a new and alarming phase of the Egyptian question . . . though it may be desirable to evacuate Egypt we cannot be jockeyed or intrigued out of it."

Later on he repeated to the Prime Minister his general reading of the situation. Sir Charles Dilke had written to Mr. Gladstone an expression of the Radical view.

MENTMORE, April 16th, 1893.

"MY DEAR MR. GLADSTONE,

"Many thanks for letting me see Dilke's letter, which I return.

"It is interesting and able, bar perhaps that Crokerian assumption of an omniscience and precision which he does not possess.

"No one is more sensible than I am of the delicacy and perplexity of our position in Egypt. Were we out of it I should on the whole rejoice. Nor am I insensible to the advantages offered by a convention on the basis of that of 1887 with a modified clause as to evacuation.

"But much that would have been possible and practicable has been prevented by the action of the young Khedive."

The Queen, always dreading the Liberal Government's attitude towards Egypt, complained that instructions had been sent to Lord Cromer without her sanction. Rosebery trusted that he would be acquitted of precipitation or neglect. Cromer had proposed to occupy all the Government offices and to seize the telegraph office. Had this somewhat violent scheme been adopted the Queen's assent would have been necessary, but its rejection merely meant more time being given to the Khedive for reflection. A tumultuous storm of sinister telegrams had rained on the Foreign Office, so that it had been difficult for the Prime Minister to send details to Windsor.

A day or two after the Cabinet (January 18th) Rosebery described to the Queen the difficulties he found in commending Lord Cromer's views, with which he was in general agreement, to some of his colleagues, loyally concluding:

"Sir William Harcourt holds very heartfelt feelings in favour of general evacuation, but it is doing him no more than justice to say that he has been extremely conciliatory and good tempered in this business."

And there was even an element of discord on the side of the great public servant on the spot. The Foreign Secretary wrote to the Queen:

"Lord Rosebery makes every allowance for the crisis and the strain to which Lord Cromer has been subjected. But he cannot think that the tone of his telegrams was judicious, and this constituted indeed the greatest obstacle in Lord Rosebery's path.

"Lord Cromer is gouty; but gout, though a disease by no means incompatible with statesmanship, is an element in the situation which requires vigilance on the part of the sufferer. That is to say, he must watch himself to see that it does not affect his manner or style. The French proverb might be converted into 'Il n'y a que la vérité et la goutte qui piquent': there were traces of both in Lord Cromer's telegrams. Hence the Cabinet was irritated.

"Lord Rosebery does not say this in detriment of a public servant whom he trusts, admires, and respects. But he is certain that had Lord Cromer simply telegraphed 'Pray give me authority to announce reinforcements, as the General and I cannot respond without them,' he would have had them without demur on Saturday morning; and saved Your Majesty and one at least of your Ministers much anxiety."

Rosebery's correspondence with the Prime Minister on the Egyptian crisis shows no sign of the "hostility" which the former noted on January 19th. It was evidently only directed against drastic military measures, and there was no copious interchange of letters such as had marked the Uganda crisis of the previous autumn.

The Queen, however, kept a vigilant eye on the Diplomatic Service. Rumours had reached her concerning two of its prominent members; and Rosebery had to admit that Her Majesty's gracious letter had somewhat disconcerted him. Of one of the officials in question Rosebery had hoped that in the torpid and somnolent atmosphere of his present post his proverbial irritability would have lost something of its keen edge. To learn, therefore, that he had managed to tax the endurance of his phlegmatic and impassible surroundings was almost more than Rosebery could bear.

"For it is impossible to move him. It would be wrong on the one hand to foster by his promotion the race of impracticable diplomatists of which he is the ideal, while on the other hand it is clear that the Court does not exist which would not, after the briefest experience, pant for his removal. A post as Queen's Messenger of an exalted and special description, which would keep him in constant flight through the principal Capitals of Europe, would alone meet the case of this bird of sinister passage, but this unfortunately does not exist."

With respect to the other diplomatist, Rosebery, though he had long been assailed by the rumours in question, was not inclined to credit them:

"He thinks that the Ambassador having closed his garden to the public has given rise to these malicious reports. He may add that in spite of pertinacious enquiry on the subject he has never been able even to hear of anyone who has even seen the lady, the supposition of whose existence has caused so much searching of heart. He is inclined there-fore, judicially as well as benevolently, to doubt her being more than a phantom of local gossip."

In the very middle of the Egyptian excitements befell a domestic event of the sort that seems so trivial to those who have not ex-perienced it, so unforgettable to those who have—the boys' de-parture to their first school. Rosebery's private record of it reads thus:

January 20th.—"The little boys rather low. Neil got me to read *The Sick Stockrider* to him,—a poor consolation, as he had wept the last time I had read it. We dined all five together,—not cheerfully. After-wards I walked to Bishopsgate and back, and saw old Rogers in bed."

January 21st.—"We all spent a miserable makeshift morning, but boys very brave. I made all the children write their name in my bible, (Harry for the first time as Dalmeny) and read John XIV. Then I went and bought the boys bibles, and frames to hold their parents' portraits. At last at 3.25 they went off. Shall I ever forget the cab with the precise initialled new luggage on the top?

"To-day is the centenary of the execution of Louis XVI. I console myself by the incomparable anguish of the parting of Jan. 20, 1793.

"Before the Cabinet yesterday I sent the boys to Mr. Gladstone to ask for his blessing before going to school. It was a touching and beautiful sight. They, and I think he, deeply moved. Alas—five minutes afterwards he and I were hammer and tongs over Egypt."

He wrote to Lady Leconfield the same day:

"Within five minutes of the boys' going I received distracting tele-grams. The strain on public grounds would have been very severe all this week, and I think the private strain has, so to speak, tugged me straight. When I am anxious abroad I think of my trouble at home and vice versâ, and like a whipping top am kept going by constant stripes."

[343]

Two days later, when he was seeing Mr. Gladstone on business:

"He spoke about the boys. Said he saw I was moved when he blessed them: 'I thought of the time when I first took Willie to school and cried like a child.' "[1]

Have these simple emotions died out with the passing of Queen Victoria's reign?

Mr. Gladstone, as has been noted, attached importance to Rosebery's leadership of the Lords; but Rosebery thought differently, and had written before Parliament met:

December 14*th*, 1892.—"As to the leadership of the Lords, I was clear in August that it should remain where it is; but I did not wish to trouble you more then, and so only communicated my views to my colleagues in the House of Lords, shewing that there were six months before us.

"Lord Salisbury indeed combined the Foreign Office with the leadership of the House of Lords. But, putting aside the intellectual disparity, there is a vast difference between leading a party of 500 peers and a party of 25. Were I well versed in the questions at issue I should rather enjoy this, but I am not, and should have laboriously to master them. Now I fear that night-work may bring me back to insomnia, and I can just get along without night-work or discreditable arrears under present circumstances. But if I were leader I could not. . . . I seem to have left you under the impression that I had agreed to lead; whereas *I* really went away under the impression that you would weigh my written objections at your leisure. Forgive this long story."

The result was that Lord Kimberley stayed on, and Rosebery attended his official dinner before the opening of Parliament. Thus during the session which opened on January 31st he confined himself mainly to departmental speeches, with a few exceptions, one of the first importance.

The Uganda squabble, which had so nearly closed Rosebery's career as Foreign Secretary, had been compromised by the dispatch as Commissioner of Sir Gerald Portal, whom Rosebery had observed in Egypt years before, to "endeavour to make British influence felt by the natives, to maintain peace and order, to develop legitimate trade . . . and generally to pave the way for conferring on the natives the benefits of civilisation which, on the suppression of the evils of the Slave Trade, should accompany the revival of prosperity." Portal was to have a considerable force of Zanzibari troops, and to be given as free a hand as possible.

[1] William Gladstone the younger had died in July 1891.

This was on a fair way towards the establishment of the Protectorate which was announced in Parliament on April 12th. One cost of the exhibition was the promising life of Sir Gerald Portal. Sir William Harcourt, his biographer tells us, had yielded to the arguments for settled control in that distracted region, and was immersed in his continual controversies with the spending departments. But he cannot have promulgated the Government policy in Parliament with much enthusiasm. On the other hand, Lord Salisbury gave it marked approval.

While the debate on the Address was in progress, Rosebery wrote to the Prime Minister:

"Pray forgive my writing a hint which I forgot to give this morning. Do not ignore Edward Grey, who is able and ready to speak if the discussion on foreign affairs goes on tonight."

It did continue, Labouchere having already violently assailed Rosebery at home and Captain Lugard[2] in Africa, and having encountered a crushing answer from the Prime Minister. Sir Edward Grey intervened in due course, and was complimented on his first appearance as spokesman for the Foreign Office.

Questions relating to Central Africa and the Congo (April 4th) did not flare up this year, but a letter to Sir Henry Ponsonby shows that the train was laid. The Queen thought that Sir E. Monson, her Minister at Brussels,[3] had not shown due consideration to the King of the Belgians. Rosebery replied:

"The fact is we have strong reasons for separating the King of the Belgians from the Sovereign of the Congo. The one is monarch of a guaranteed and friendly nation, the other is ——

"A pinch of fact is worth a bundle of epithet. The Sovereign of the Congo has sent a large filibustering force into the British sphere of influence, and it has occupied Lado, an important post on the Nile. The Sovereign of the Congo says he has no idea where the expeditionary force may be. It is the King of the Belgians then that has been in constant and notorious communication with them (for we know it as a fact). We can only regret that the separation of the function of the two sovereigns is so complete. . . . Possibly something of all this has percolated into Monson's manner, if so I am not surprised and cannot blame him.

[2] *B.* 1858. *Cr.* Lord Lugard 1928. G.C.M.G., etc.
[3] Sir Edmund Monson, Bart., G.C.B. (1834-1909). Minister at Athens 1888-92, and at Brussels 1892-3; Ambassador at Vienna 1893-6, and at Paris 1896-1904.

"I will leave you to judge how much of all this you will communicate to the Queen."

In other communications to the Sovereign in the spring (March 29th) Rosebery tried to soothe the concern which she had expressed at the possible payment of Members of Parliament by saying that Mr. Gladstone was not in love with the proposal, and financial considerations would prevent its being "forthwith" carried into effect. But a grievance was felt, and—

"In himself, Lord Rosebery is well aware that it has not always worked well, and that it may probably lead to demands for payment by local bodies; but he is inclined in this as in much elsewhere to trust to the good sound common sense of the people of Great Britain.

"Mr. Labouchere has hitherto dealt tenderly with Lord Rosebery, leaf by leaf, like an artichoke. But he has now wearied of such untimely delicacy, and is moving to strike Lord Rosebery's official salary entirely off the estimates!"

The frontier between Siam and Cambodia, part of the Annamite Empire under French protection, was beginning to create some uneasiness. We were not concerned with the particular matter at issue; but it was the happy lot of the great European Powers to have no contiguous frontier in Asia, and any subjection of Siam by France might bring Indo-China into undesired proximity to Burmah and India. When the question was raised in the House of Lords (June 15th), Rosebery gave a guarded reply, pleading lack of information. A month later the same Peer, Lord Lamington, asked a further question, and this time Rosebery read a written answer. The frontier question at the Mekong Valley was still unsettled, but the more serious matter of the ascent of the river Menam by two French gunboats was believed to have occurred against orders. British property at Bankok was safeguarded by our ships, and the French declared themselves equally anxious to secure the integrity and independence of Siam. Later in the month Rosebery found the whole business weighing heavily on him, and for a moment it appeared extremely critical. It was important to know what the attitude of Italy and of Germany would be in the event of war with France. The German Government thought that Italy would respond to "the somewhat dramatic confidences" made to her, and would have to intervene. From Germany's own standpoint :[4] "From the point of view of domestic politics, a war would not be undesir-

[4] *German Diplomatic Documents* 1871-1914, vol. ii, pp. 238-40.

able if supported by public opinion. From the military point of view
it is just as good now as later." Rosebery asked for a Cabinet on
July 1st, telling Gladstone that the French persisted in their blockade in spite of the unconditional surrender of the Siamese to the
French ultimatum, and that they had ordered our gunboats to leave
Bankok. The situation, therefore, was grave. Happily the rumour
proved to be untrue. Rosebery had at once telegraphed that the vessels were to remain, which would have meant a collision, but the
British officer commanding found that he had misunderstood the
French Admiral. So the Cabinet was not called, and the incident
closed. Harcourt, who had been abroad, wrote hearty congratulations to Rosebery on his settlement of the question. But Rosebery's
opinion of the French proceedings was candidly given to the Queen
at the height of the crisis:

FOREIGN OFFICE, *July 26th*, 1893.
"Lord Rosebery with his humble duty returns his respectful thanks
for Your Majesty's gracious letter and telegram.

"He does not disguise from Your Majesty his belief that, if a note
were presented at Paris saying that Your Majesty's Government could
not accept the position created by the Siamese cessions of territory, the
French Government would yield; more especially if that note were
supported by a similar one from China. But there would be the chance
of refusal, and a refusal would mean war. The two questions that
Lord Rosebery has to ask himself are: would the Government run this
risk, and would the House of Commons support them if they did. To
both these questions the answer would in his opinion be, undoubtedly, No.

"These questions and problems have been actively employing Lord
Rosebery by night and by day ever since affairs have taken this acute
turn. He would not shrink for a moment in staking his official existence
on the risk he has mentioned, and he may yet have to do so. But the
moment for that has not yet come, and, if it did, his retirement might
not greatly further the solution of the difficulty.

"In all these questions it is of the first importance to distinguish the
material from the immaterial. The behaviour of France to Siam has
it appears been base, cruel and treacherous. Perhaps nothing so cynically
vile is on record. But that is not our affair. We cannot afford to be the
Knight Errant of the World, careering about to redress grievances and
help the weak. If the French cut the throats of half Siam in cold
blood we should not be justified in going to war with her. In all this
matter we have only one prime interest, and, strangely enough, that
interest is equally French. It is to keep a buffer between the French
frontier and that of India, in order that a vast expenditure and danger

may not be incurred by the immediate proximity of a great military power on our South Eastern flank. If we can secure such an intermediate zone, state, or territory we shall have obtained all that Great Britain really requires. A short telegram just this moment received from Lord Dufferin gives some hope that this may be secured.

"Lord Rosebery fears that Your Majesty will think all this very cold blooded. He at any rate is not so. It makes his blood boil to read of the French proceedings. They invade and butcher the Siamese, and demand two-fifths of Siam for doing so. The Siamese indeed are not a very truthful or respectable race, but that is no excuse for treating them like vermin, and for behaving to them not with common honesty, but with uncommon dishonesty. We cannot however keep the police of the world: the Empire is a sufficient responsibility without that. The French must bear the burden of their own misdeeds, and Lord Rosebery does not doubt that as there is a God in heaven, these will find them out.

"Nor, with great deference, would Lord Rosebery wish to appeal to the Triple Alliance. It becomes Your Majesty's dignity to settle this matter without such assistance. Resort to the Triple Alliance may some day be necessary, and no doubt the French are trying their best to drive us to it: but this should be in some direr strait than the present.

"Lord Rosebery begs that Your Majesty will excuse this tedious but very secret rigmarole."

Rosebery's verdict that nothing so cynically vile as the conduct of the French was on record is Gladstonian in its vehemence. Perhaps it goes somewhat far, if one were to examine the history of European expansion in Asia and Africa by the Great Powers. But Rosebery's experience at the Foreign Office had bred in him deep distrust of the French policy of those days outside Europe. Nor was he by any means alone in so thinking.

Apart from these grave affairs, the Foreign Office was not greatly harassed this year. Armenian Christians were being tried at Angora (then an unfamiliar name), and the Archbishop of Canterbury pleaded for them. Rosebery was able to show that his intervention had secured banishment instead of death as the fate of the chief ecclesiastics, and if the trial of the other prisoners proved to be the mere mockery that theirs had been, he would make the same representations.

He was also able to show that he was keeping a vigilant eye on Persia and the Persian Gulf.

Mr. Gladstone had said that the result of the General Election smote him under the fifth rib; but Home Rulers were in a majority and to drop the subject was impossible. Rosebery, as we have seen, was a bearer of the thyrsus, but did not boast the Bacchic inspiration. Neither he nor Harcourt formed part of the Cabinet Committee of six whose task it was to frame a measure better balanced and more acceptable than the Bill of 1886. The Queen had somehow persuaded herself that Rosebery, chained to his chair at the Foreign Office, was little more than nominally adherent to Gladstone's Irish policy, and did not scruple to confide to him the dislike and dread with which she contemplated it. His acknowledgment must be given in full, for it exactly presents his candid opinion:

FOREIGN OFFICE, *June 9th,* 1893.

"Lord Rosebery with his humble duty begs to express the feelings of pleasure and gratitude with which he has received Your Majesty's gracious letter, and the expression of confidence contained in it.

"It is however for reasons which are sufficiently obvious, not very easy for him to discuss the topic on which Your Majesty dwells.

"He is not an enthusiastic Home Ruler, in the sense of believing that it is a certain panacea for the secular ills of Ireland; nor would he pursue that remedy to the length of civil war, for of course it would then be worse than the disease it is designed to cure. But he regards it as on the whole the most practicable or least impracticable method of governing that country, and, indeed, until it shall have been tried, he knows of no alternative: for he believes that were the hope of Home Rule to be removed the latent forces of anarchy and revolution would break out with renewed horror.

"He considers therefore that the Government have no choice but to go on with their measure, to which they are pledged in honour, and which a majority of the House of Commons supports. It will no doubt be rejected by the House of Lords, and the result of that rejection remains to be seen. Lord Rosebery will utter no forecast with regard to it. But, in the meantime, by the unwritten laws of politics and of the existence of Governments, the bill must inevitably proceed through the House of Commons. There is indeed no choice in the matter.

"Lord Rosebery deplores Your Majesty's misgivings and distress, the more so as he can fully enter into Your Majesty's point of view. But even should the Home Rule Bill be as full of danger as Your Majesty believes, Your Majesty can surely place sufficient confidence in the robust common sense and overwhelming power of Great Britain to be certain that the ultimate result cannot be disaster. Lord Rosebery's own prognostications are of course much more sanguine, though falling short of course of the hopes entertained by some of his colleagues. Indeed he is not sure that he does not consider the London County Council a more portentous circumstance than an Irish Local legislature.

"Should Your Majesty care to see Lord Rosebery, or could it be the least relief for Your Majesty to discuss this subject with a devoted servant, he would leave for Balmoral on Wednesday, June 14, as was originally proposed."

After its laboured transit through the House of Commons, the unheard-of vigour with which the champion of eighty-four fought its battle, and its final passage by a majority of 34—impossibly puny for a great constitutional change—the measure reached the House of Lords. It was not debated there until September 5th, when Lord Spencer moved the second reading of the doomed Bill and the Duke of Devonshire its rejection. Four days of debate concluded by a vote of 419 against a poor 41 in favour of Home Rule. All the principal orators in the House, and some others not exactly orators, took part.

Nearly forty years have passed, and Ireland, then governed in practice as a Crown Colony,[5] has become a self-governing Dominion. So the interest of the discussion is now purely historical. Rosebery spoke at length on the third day, following a powerful speech from a former pillar of the Gladstone Government, Lord Selborne. The unreality of the present discussion was Rosebery's first comment. Then he turned to the Duke of Argyll, who had quoted from his *Pitt* some observations on the Union, and called him the victim of the fatal and malignant disease, *lues Gladstoniana*. Lord Londonderry, on the other hand, with his mass of quotations, was a sufferer from *morbus Spenceranus*.

He himself would not discuss details, because the point at issue was far larger than any Bill. The debate would be elevated by making it a discussion on policy; the two parties disagreed on the method of governing and conciliating Ireland. He did not pretend to be certain, but he had reached the convictions he held in the teeth of almost all that would tend to make him take the other side. In the House of Commons the Tory party had voted recklessly for incompatible amendments, as it seemed in order to bring Parliamentary institutions into contempt. But in the Lords their responsibility was tenfold greater. It would be a standing reproach to Lord Salisbury that in six years of office he had made no attempt to reform the House. An Irish Peer had said that he knew all about Ireland; but that was not the question—Did Ireland know about him? Did he represent Ireland in any shape or form? Passing from that, he had

[5] The presence of Irish members in the House of Commons did not really contradict this, highly inconvenient as they could make themselves there.

sometimes felt that the Irish Question would be settled by an agreement between the two political parties. The Liberal Unionists at any rate had admitted that Home Rule was merely a question of degree. If, instead of rejecting the Bill, they had defined their policy by moving amendments, the final issue would have been a conference of the two Houses, which might have led to a fruitful result. He proceeded in the tone of his letter to the Queen to describe himself as a witness, but not an enthusiastic witness, in favour of Home Rule. With him it was not a fanaticism, but a question of policy alone. He touched upon the Tory abandonment of coercion in 1885, and asked how Austria could have held Venice if every four or five years a party had announced that it would drop coercion. Again, there could be no equal devolution in the countries of the United Kingdom, though at first he had hoped there might be. But what policy, what scheme had the Opposition in view? When they were in power Irish business still consumed as much parliamentary time as before: "Whether you plaster Ireland with your garrisons or with your gold, the end of it by some devious path or other will be only some form of Home Rule." It, the Bill, was an experiment, but so had been the establishment of the London County Council and the Reform Act of 1867. This Bill was not, like that, a "leap in the dark," but a leap towards the light.

Lord Balfour of Burleigh, who followed, said that the speech was full of chaff, but not of argument: Lord Halsbury, the next day, regarded it as an exhibition of tactics and diplomacy. Lord Salisbury, in winding up the debate for his side, said that Rosebery—

"did what I often observed in speakers with a singular facility for the lighter and more humorous kinds of speech. He took refuge in that in order to save himself from the necessity of expressing a grave opinion on any grave subject whatever . . . it seemed to me that the problem which he set himself to solve was 'How shall I get through an hour-and-a-quarter's speech without undertaking any pledge which may be inconvenient to me in the future?'"

This was hardly fair, as Lord Kimberley in conclusion pointed out:

"My noble friend the Foreign Secretary is like one of those actors who possess in the highest degree both a tragic and comic vein, and if he commenced with a number of witty observations which I am sure delighted the House, he did not forget to turn in the latter part of

[351]

his speech to the graver aspect of the subject. I do not think it possible that any more impressive appeal could have been addressed to this House than that of my noble friend on the general policy of the question."

Rosebery's private comment was:

"Ill prepared, and by an unlucky muddle thought I had been speaking two hours instead of one. This made me omit some important arguments, and disturbed the balance of the speech. Went home profoundly disgusted with myself. But some people were pleased."

Francis Horner wrote in 1809 that no legislative measure had ever been carried against prejudices that was not prosecuted with as much ardour as if it were expected to prove a very panacea—though none could with truth be so proposed. He was not far wrong, as the later history of the nineteenth century showed; but Rosebery did not think Home Rule a Panacea, as he had told the Queen, and was not prepared to say that it was. But he was not a bad prophet of the methods whereby the Home Rule ship would at last be brought to harbour.

Hard driven, but not over-driven, by his Foreign Office duties, Rosebery found it possible to appear this summer on several uncontentious fields. He presided at the twenty-fifth banquet of the Royal Colonial Institute (March 2nd). His office, he pointed out, was concerned almost daily with colonial questions, such as frontier delimitations. He repeated his conviction that in frequent Imperial conferences would be found the solution of "what was called Imperial Federation." Some thought the Empire large enough, but it was part of our responsibility that some of the undeveloped regions of the world should receive the Anglo-Saxon character.

More congenial still was the stone-laying ceremony at the Bishopsgate Institute (May 15th). Canon Rogers, said Rosebery, had been a civilising agency for thirty or forty years. He had lately (and here, surely, was a touch of *malice*) preached a sermon on "Can these dry bones live?" and life was being breathed into the dry bones of the City charities. He hoped the Institute would provide innocent enjoyment, because the thesis that life could be reduced to a Blue Book for mental and a biscuit for physical nourishment did not stand the test of time or experience.

He next opened the new Town Hall at Battersea (November 15th), with a cordial speech on municipal institutions and the new-

THE HANDY BOY!

The Missis: "I knew you had plenty to do, Primrose, but I was quite sure you wouldn't mind taking up those coals!"

born pride of Londoners in London. He spoke at the Royal Academy banquet (June 25th), and at the Trinity House, where he had a bantering match with Sir William Harcourt, but, like the other speakers, turned gravely to the naval calamity which had just stricken the nation in the loss of the *Victoria* and Admiral Tryon.

Two other Imperial occasions were a paper read by Lord Onslow at the Colonial Institute (November 14th) on State Socialism in Australasia, and a dinner at the Imperial Institute (November 16th) to an old friend, Lord Elgin, on his appointment as Viceroy of India. But these were *parerga*. He was entrusted by the Cabinet with the chairmanship of the Conference between Federated Coal-owners and the Miners' Federation on the dispute which had brought about a general strike in the industry. It met at the Foreign Office on November 17th. The Chairman's account tells the story:

"One of the most anxious and happiest days of my life. The Coal Conference assembled at 11 and rose at 5.20 having come to a treaty of peace.

"I gave a plain luncheon. Afterwards the masters retired to discuss a proposition of mine, and remained away fully two hours. The men were away, later, and for about twenty minutes.

"Dined alone, very tired. But it would have been a good day to die on."

The terms included the creation of a Board of Conciliation composed of fourteen representatives of each side, with a neutral chairman, to meet in a month's time. The Board to have power to determine the rate of wages as from February 1st, 1894. The men to resume work at the old rates till that date.

It had been an overwhelming week, with great pressure at the Foreign Office, the outside engagements that have been mentioned, and new private cares from the default in money matters of a financial agent of the highest personal connections in London.

Rosebery had been tied to London for most of the year. He had snatched an odd day or two at Newmarket, but had seen little racing, except for going for the day to Ascot with the Prince of Wales, where he saw his *Illuminata* two-year-old, destined to make history the following year, win the Coventry Stakes in a canter. His visits to Osborne and Windsor were chiefly official; but at one audience the talk was on languages, when the Queen said that she had never had any difficulty with French, in spite of Rosebery's urging the niceties and difficulties of the language,[6] but that she always had her German letters overhauled before they went.[7]

During a week at Balmoral in September Rosebery met the Empress Eugénie, the Grand Duke and Duchess Serge, and other magnates. Once he went out deerstalking, an unusual enterprise for him, but he "never saw a horn."

Before Lord Elgin was selected for the Indian Viceroyalty the post had seemed difficult to fill:

"Kimberley came in something like despair about a Viceroy. I said, 'You know, if I am fit, and if there is no one else, I would go, rather than see the place jobbed away.' K. 'Nonsense, if you go, the Government will go too.' I. 'Then let us all take cabins.'"

Rosebery's only other absence was a spell of three weeks at Homburg, by the doctor's orders. Royal personages were as thick as peas, but Rosebery made solitary expeditions to the curiosity shop at Frankfort, where he was guilty, as he said, of "sad extravagance." External repairs and alterations were going on at his house in Berkeley Square, which needed remodelling from top to bottom.

At the very opening of the new year an alarm sounded over the Navy estimates. During the autumn of 1893 an animated correspondence, adorned with much warm language, had passed between Sir William Harcourt and the First Lord of the Admiralty, Lord Spencer, and the naval situation had been angrily debated in Parliament. The opposition of the Treasury was to be anticipated, but when the Prime Minister took up the cudgels the matter became serious. At the end of the previous year Rosebery had done his best to persuade the Prime Minister that some increase of the fleet was reasonable:

Confidential.   FOREIGN OFFICE, *December 18th*, 1893, 11.30 *p.m.*

"MY DEAR MR. GLADSTONE,

"I will not trouble your eyes with many words. But if, as I think possible from your letter to-day, you are prepared to fall in with the general anxiety for the increase of our fleet, I would most earnestly urge you to let this be plainly evident in your speech to-morrow, and I do this on the sole ground of the interests of peace.

[6] An illustrious French lady told me that she had never heard her language spoken with such exquisite precision as in a conversation between the Queen and the Duc d'Aumale at which she had been present.

[7] This demonstrates the untruth of the prevalent story, which gave much annoyance to the Royal Family, that the Queen made frequent use of the German language at home.

"Prevention is better than cure, and I firmly believe that the spontaneous expenditure of a few millions now may prevent the compulsory expenditure of many hundred millions later. And, as the effect of this immediate expenditure is ever more moral than physical, I lay the greatest stress on an early intimation—not necessarily to commit or forestall the Cabinet—but to prevent vain delusions being nourished on the Continent. If we are to spend the money let us get our money's worth: and half the worth will lie in the promptitude of the announcement that we are ready to spend it.

"Forgive this brief intrusion, but I feel on this subject more deeply and strongly than I express, or can express.

"Y. affly.,
AR"

Ten days later he wrote:

"I would beg you to remember that what I wrote to you on the eve of the Navy debate applies to all questions of European policy. Europe is in a parlous state, and any words that may intimate a weakening of our position may have a far reaching effect. A single sentence in your Navy Speech of the kind I begged for would have had an incalculable value for peace. But that word was not spoken, and the opportunity is gone. Only do not let us now give any idea that we do not stand where we did last February, or we may revive forces and passions that we should find it difficult to control.

"Forgive the heartfelt earnestness of these words; dictated as they are by a pervading sense of the gravity of the situation.

"Y. affly.,
AR"

Mr. Gladstone indeed went farther than Harcourt, who thought that they must make the best of a bad job and accept the estimates, little as he approved them. It was reported that he followed the Prime Minister into his room at the House of Commons, in spite of the warning. "I really cannot discuss this matter with you."

January 3rd.—"Harcourt however persisted, and had a terrible interview, denouncing Spencer (as Mr. G. says,) speaking with extreme bitterness to Mr. G. himself, according to Harcourt. Mr. G. seems to have practically ordered him out of the room. Spencer this afternoon low and tired. He wanted me to go and see Mr. G. Harcourt, who followed, said that would be fatal, but urged me to go and see Mrs. G."

The Queen had naturally from the first taken the part of the Admiralty, and had hoped that Rosebery would support Lord Spencer. In the autumn Rosebery had written (November 15th, 1893):

"With respect to the Navy Lord Rosebery shares Your Majesty's feelings in the fullest degree, though of course in *The Times* articles—as is right for the purpose aimed at—the shadows of the picture are laid on too lavishly.

"Lord Rosebery is in reality more interested in this matter than any of Your Majesty's Ministers, for the authority and weight of the Foreign Office suffer obvious diminution when the Navy is suspected of weakness and are perhaps impaired by that suspicion at this moment.

"Lord Rosebery therefore viewed with pleasure the utterances at Manchester of so strong a Cobdenite as Mr. John Morley.

"Lord Rosebery hopes he need not assure Your Majesty that he has already given Lord Spencer promises of the most earnest support, and has frequently urged the paramount importance of the question. But the initiative in the Cabinet and elsewhere must come from Lord Spencer."

A day or two later, at Windsor, the Queen recurred to the question, saying that the Navy must be increased:

"I agreed. She added 'And the Army,' or something to that effect. When I was doubtful, she said 'Ah, I cannot agree. I was brought up so to speak with the feeling for the Army,—being a soldier's daughter,—and not caring about being on the sea I have always had a special feeling for the Army.' "

Colloquies proceeded daily between colleagues. Rosebery was in continual conference with Morley, Spencer, Asquith, and Edward Majoribanks. On the 10th he saw the Prime Minister, who said, "The dead are with me." The differences were so far patched up that Mr. Gladstone went to Biarritz for a month, but from there came news that he had said to Sir Algernon West:[8] "You might as well try and blow up the Rock of Gibraltar with your own hands as try to move me."

For a short time Rosebery was crippled by a strained ligament. Soon after his recovery came the announcement that Gladstone, sending a message like Tiberius from his island, proposed an instant dissolution of Parliament. Half a dozen of the principal Ministers met, and not one would entertain the proposition. The Prime Minister returned and gave a Cabinet dinner on February 17th. Rosebery, seated on the host's left, noted:

"When dinner was over I said to him, 'If any secret matters are going to be discussed we ought to look to the doors.' 'Certainly,' replied

[8] (1832-1921). Private Secretary to Mr. Gladstone 1868-73. Chairman Board of Inland Revenue 1881-92.

Mr. G. airily, 'if anybody has any topic to raise it might be done now.' This was all that passed."

A week later at a Cabinet the Prime Minister uttered a few vague words as to the time when his co-operation with the Cabinet would cease, but no one said anything. The final scene came on March 1st. It is depicted in the *Life of Gladstone* with the emotion of a faithful follower parting from a glorious chief. Rosebery, not less moved at heart, described it for himself in a different tone:

"Kimberley said three words of adieu and broke down. Harcourt burst into sobs before beginning, and then read his own pompous letter to Mr. G. A horrid scene."

Rosebery had written his own adieu a few days earlier:

Secret.   FOREIGN OFFICE, *February 24th*, 1894.

"MY DEAR MR. GLADSTONE,

"I cannot forbear writing you a few words, and the bitter thought is that they may be the last that I shall address to you as a colleague. For, though you have never told the Cabinet expressly or in terms, I can scarcely doubt after what you said yesterday that it is your intention to retire from office in the forthcoming week.

"Since I entered Parliament I have always been your follower. Since 1879 I have been more closely and personally attached to you. And though there have been differences, and are, there are many fewer than might have been anticipated in view of the difference in age and conditions. We have seen, if I may say so, glorious days together—the recollection of which still stirs my blood—you as chief and I as esquire. And now all is passing or past, and it is a moment of anguish,—to all your colleagues I believe,—most certainly to me.

"I fear that the present, but I hope temporary, condition of your eyesight gives you only too good a reason for resignation. But it would be affectation to deny that there is also a difference of opinion;—opinion perhaps is too weak a word, for with me it is a matter of faith. In this one point at any rate we are agreed—that it involves the peace of the world. Unfortunately we are at the two poles asunder as regards the means.

"On this point I could say much. I have held aloof of late—partly because I could not bring myself to believe in your intention, much more because it is painful to be in a relation of acute difference on so vital a point. Nor do I believe for a moment that anything I could say would change your views, for I am no more your equal in argument than in anything else. But I could at least convince you that from my point of view my policy is not less than yours founded on peace and not on oppression.

"It is hard to be thus parted; and once more I deeply regret that you did not leave me, as I so ardently wished, in my retirement. But whatever happens you cannot change my present feeling to yourself. Goodbye is a hard saying:—hard at all times, but scarcely tolerable when I think of what you are and have always been to me, of the old Midlothian days, of the times of storm and sunshine in which I have stood by your side, and, above all, of the time to come, when that may not be.

"Y. affectionately,

AR"

Gladstone's last audience was at Windsor on March 3rd, and it afterwards was known that, had his opinion been invited, he would have suggested Spencer as his successor. He had no prejudice against a Peer as Prime Minister; and when I was at Hawarden in the winter he indicated that the best man for the place would probably be found in the House of Lords.

It can only be assumed that his experience had convinced him, as it had the rest of the Cabinet without exception, that Sir William Harcourt's unquestionable claims to the succession were overborne by paramount objections. A later generation was puzzled by all this. That a man so genial, so humorous, so thoroughly kind-hearted, should be an impossible colleague was a mystery to those who had never served with him. But so it was.[9] The 15th Lord Derby, the least excitable of men, had found him so when he joined the Government in 1882. Campbell-Bannerman could get on with anybody, but he had been bullied over his Army estimates and, as I knew at the time, did not want to see Harcourt ruling at No. 10 Downing Street. John Morley's attitude, as Harcourt's biographer observes,[10] needs more explaining, and the reasons suggested by him seem to me entirely correct. Harcourt's lukewarmness on Home Rule went for something; but his roughness and sharp tongue for a great deal more. It is all very well to say that after his frequent rows he forgot all about them, and bore no malice; but since his colleagues were peaceable people and the provocation invariably came from him, they were apt to remember what form the rows took: *"si rixa est,*

[9] I had the benefit of an old family friendship, and always received every kindness from Sir William Harcourt. We were amazed at the legends of his early unpopularity, such as the famous, and obviously untrue, one that three men agreed to make up a dinner of six at a club by each asking the most unpopular person of his acquaintance, and that only four covers were laid, for all three had invited William Harcourt.

[10] Vol. ii, p. 264.

ubi tu pulsas ego vapulo tantum." But perhaps they were all wrong. Difficult characters are sometimes mellowed by success to an extraordinary degree. As president of the Cabinet he might have sought for harmony, and not have engaged in perpetual protest. Lewis Harcourt, too, might have employed his skill in making things go well instead of going awry. Still, so far as the Foreign Office was concerned, a Harcourt premiership could not have been peaceful. The causes for friction which in fact ensued would have been the same, and the resignations which bade fair to break up the party might have happened before the Government fell, instead of afterwards.

There was no other possible Prime Minister in the House of Commons. Either Kimberley or Spencer ranked as *papabile*, but either was willing to serve under Rosebery, for whom it was assumed that the Queen would send. Conversations had started even before the last Gladstone Cabinet.

February 25th.—"Asquith came. He and C. Bannerman had been listening to Marjoribanks. He had been summoned to Harcourt yesterday to listen to a long memorandum. It set forth that the P.M. should be in the H. of C. But that he if it were the general wish would lead the H. of C. under conditions: 1. that he should take independent decisions in the House; 2. that he should see all F.O. despatches; 3. that he should have some control of patronage; and another which I forget.[11]

"I remarked that it might be difficult to serve under Harcourt, but that it would be still more difficult to serve over him. Marjoribanks also said that there was a growing feeling in the H. of C. against a peer. I said I was delighted to hear it.—Might it grow! Asquith and Campbell Bannerman came to see me. Both, I could see, much disquieted by E. Marjoribanks' tidings."

[11] This was the understanding that a Cabinet should be called at his request.

CHAPTER XV

Prime Minister, 1894

O N THE day after the farewell Cabinet the Prince of Wales sent for Rosebery and gave him a message from the Queen, that she hoped he would stand by her in the difficulty in which she was placed. On the next afternoon (March 3rd) Sir Henry Ponsonby brought a letter from her appealing to him on behalf of herself and the Government to form an administration. Later in the day he saw Harcourt, who left a long account of this interview and of one which took place on the following morning.[1]

Rosebery, in writing to accept office, had told the Queen of the difficulties ahead of him. He would renounce the undertaking rather than not submit the name of the best successor to himself at the Foreign Office. He felt deeply, too, the prospect of finding himself in acute conflict with some of the Queen's views. He also wrote to Sir Henry Ponsonby (March 4th) :

"Things are not going very well. One or two of my colleagues in the Commons are endeavouring to impose conditions upon me—one of which is that the new Foreign Minister shall be in the House of Commons. I have refused to submit to any conditions not ordinarily imposed on a Prime Minister. I don't want to be Prime Minister at all, but if I am to be, I must be a real one. I have told them that if this condition is pressed I will throw up my commission at once. That is how matters stand. Of course, all this is for the Queen, but I prefer to tell her informally through you."

In answer to his personal letter the Queen wrote:

WINDSOR CASTLE, *March 4th*, 1894.

"The Queen thanks Lord Rosebery for his kind confidential letter.

"She is sorry to hear that he apprehends any trouble which might alienate him from her. The Queen can hardly think this possible, or at any rate probable.

"She does not object to Liberal measures which are not revolution-

[1] This is printed at length in the *Life of Sir William Harcourt*, vol. ii, pp. 271-2.

ary & she does not think it possible that Lord Rosebery will destroy well tried, valued & necessary institutions for the sole purpose of flattering useless Radicals or pandering to the pride of those whose only desire is their own self gratification."

Meanwhile John Morley had suggested becoming President of the Council, but was induced to remain Irish Secretary. He may have hoped for the Foreign Office; and if the very tart entry in Lewis Harcourt's journal is to be considered accurate,[2] he was in a state of acute discontent. He dined alone with Rosebery on the 4th, but it is recorded the next day:

"A small conference of 5 at 11.30. Harcourt sulky. Morley went off in a huff. No more conferences."

That afternoon he kissed hands as Prime Minister and First Lord of the Treasury, saying farewell to the Foreign Office. He did not enter light-heartedly on his task. The morning before he had been at 8.30 to Communion in Down Street—"the church at which I was married." Thoughts of his life of the past, and of the life of the future, were a help in the present hour of triumph chequered by doubts and regrets. On the following Sunday at Epsom his friend and Vicar, Canon Hunter, asked the congregation to remember in their prayers "our neighbour the Prime Minister."

Not long after, he wrote to Arthur Godley:[3]

"I am very grateful for your kind note. Your letters always have a stamp about them which no others quite possess. I am very homesick for the Foreign Office, and I do not think I shall like any of the duties of my new position. Patronage is odious: ecclesiastical patronage distressing. It is in consequence, indeed, of a Dean having died that I dictate this from my bed."

The first Cabinet was held at the Foreign Office on March 8th. The difficulty arising from the choice of Kimberley as Foreign Secretary was not composed until two days later. On the 12th he went from the Durdans—"a terrible day." It opened with a party meeting at the Foreign Office, and this passed off well. Rosebery declared, "We stand where we did. There is no change in measures,—there is only a most disastrous change in men." The question of the Welsh Church was to be dealt with promptly, and to the Irish Question they were bound by every tie of honour and of policy. The

[2] *Life*, vol. ii, p. 269.
[3] *b*. 1847. Private Secretary to Mr. Gladstone 1872-4 and 1880-2. Permanent Under-Secretary for India 1883-1909. G.C.B. *Cr*. Lord Kilracken 1909.

presence of Morley as Chief Secretary was a guarantee of that. He spoke firmly against the pretensions of the House of Lords, and in conclusion asked to be judged not by his words but by his acts. Harcourt followed with a speech in his best vein.

It was by Rosebery's words that he was destined to be judged later the same day, when, after having taken his seat at the Treasury Bench, he attended the debate on the Queen's Speech in the House of Lords. There Lord Salisbury assured him of the heartiest welcome from the majority of the House, and went on to point out that Home Rule was now in suspense, that the issue depended on its acceptance by England, and that its decision should be asked at once. When Rosebery, after touching on Gladstone's retirement and on foreign and domestic affairs, came to Ireland, he followed the Tory leader's argument with needless fidelity:

"The noble Marquess made one remark on Irish Home Rule with which I confess myself in entire accord. He said that before Irish Home Rule is concluded by the Imperial Parliament, England as the predominant member of the partnership of the Three Kingdoms will have to be convinced of its justice and equity."

He went on to express the assurance that this conversion would be neither slow nor difficult, and that Ireland would prove herself entitled to the boon. At this distance of time, after all the unforeseen events of forty years, the excitement aroused by these phrases seems surprising. *The Times* declared that Rosebery had at one blow shattered the fabric of Liberal policy. As Rosebery observed later at Edinburgh (March 19th), the statement was a platitude in the sense in which he uttered it. Clearly a Home Rule Bill would never be carried without more English votes. But as a Scotsman he repudiated the doctrine that every measure must be approved by England before it could be passed.

Still, the expression was unhappily used at the particular moment. As the French thinker puts it, *"Toute verité nue et crue n'a pas assez passé par l'âme."* Except as an element in Imperial Federation, Irish Home Rule was not for Rosebery a thing to move the soul, but to convince the head.

Punishment was not tardy. On the following evening (March 13th):

"At 10 Campbell-Bannerman came to announce that the Government had been beaten at 8,—by Labouchere and by two!"

The debate on the Address in the Commons had been carried on by Randolph Churchill, who maintained that the famous phrase was only used to lull the fears of Unionists; John Morley made a gallant defence of it; John Redmond denounced Rosebery in unmeasured terms; Joseph Chamberlain was sarcastic; and Labouchere proposed his amendment practically abolishing the powers of the Upper House. Its success in a House of under three hundred of course proved nothing; but it had the effect of making the Government look ridiculous, and reflected cruelly on its head.

An address from the Progressive majority of the County Council at St. James's Hall brought together a great band of Peers, Members of Parliament, and citizens. Whoever might be faithless, London was faithful; and the welcome was to the Councillor for East Finsbury no less than to the Prime Minister. In reply, he praised the salvation from building of a thousand acres of land, and the wise labour policy of the Council, and passed on to a general survey of the social progress made under the Liberal Government. The new Home Secretary, Asquith, loudly called on, said that the creed of the Liberal party had been proclaimed by the one man who had authority to do so.

The Prime Minister's work, though continuous and often harassing, does not involve the fixed hours and the daily drudgery of a great department, and Rosebery was occasionally able to enjoy the marvellous spring weather at the Durdans, and once or twice to spend a night at Newmarket. High hopes were beginning to centre on the *Illuminata* colt, now named *Ladas*—after the unlucky purchase of Oxford days—with a defiance of luck which made gamblers shake their heads.

It will be remembered that the Uganda difference had been composed for the moment by the dispatch of Sir Gerald Portal as Commissioner. But there was no real agreement between Harcourt and Morley on the one side and Rosebery and Kimberley on the other, not merely on this question but on all those affecting African colonisation. The two former and their supporters thought that the Empire was as large as it ought to be, and apparently would have been content if the whole continent of Africa, except Cape Colony and Natal, had fallen under foreign influence and control. Sir William Harcourt had imbibed much wisdom at the feet of Sir George Cornewall Lewis, but he may not have seen that what was true in the 'fifties might not be equally true in the 'nineties. As his biographer tells us, he was proud of being a Little Englander in one sense; but he seems to have supposed that this country, while avoiding much contact with the Great Powers of Europe, could exercise, by possessing the strongest navy, a controlling influence over European politics in case of need.

In a Cabinet system it is an advantage to a Minister to have served as subordinate or chief in an office outside the run of his ordinary interests. Harcourt had plenty of knowledge of the outer world. This he showed not only as *Historicus*, but in many speeches and addresses. But he would have gained by serving at the Admiralty or in the Colonial Office. To him his opponents were all Jingoes of the worst sort. This, needless to say, was a complete injustice to Rosebery and Kimberley, who were no more Jingoes than Lord Salisbury was. But Rosebery doubtless held that certain elements in the problem were changing rapidly. The awakened consciousness of our own Colonies, joined to the eager creation of great colonial Empires by France and Germany; the possibility of mitigating the grouping of Powers into alliances by inducing all to combine in the Concert of Europe—these, it seemed to him, made impossible that aloofness from the affairs of the Continent which even the United States, not themselves of it, have found impossible to maintain.

The question of the Upper Nile was nearly connected with the retention of our influence in Uganda and with the possibility of our complete withdrawal from Egypt. A complication arose over the proposal to transfer to the King of the Belgians (and Congo) our sphere of influence on the Upper Nile on a long lease. Kimberley wrote to Rosebery on March 27th: "Ought we not to let Harcourt know of these negotiations? He ought not to kick at it as it really tends to narrow our responsibilities." This was done at once, but Harcourt made no comment until April 22nd, when he wrote one of his dictatorial letters of protest, accusing the Foreign Secretary and the Prime Minister of transacting foreign affairs in the House of Lords and of taking particular care that he should know nothing of them. Through the spring and summer constant communications passed between Kimberley and Rosebery, the former sometimes narrating Harcourt's arrival at the Foreign Office in a worse temper than usual. Germany demurred to one of the most important articles in the Agreement. The French objected on the curious ground that part of the territories affected belonged to the Ottoman Empire—which had no more control of them than had the Empire of China. Rosebery jumped at the contention, and drafted a memorandum

[366]

(June 17th) declaring that the Nile is Egypt and Egypt is the Nile, and that as the occupying power our first interest was to obtain a recognition of this principle by the Great Powers. A conference should be proposed in which with the support of Germany we should get our sphere of influence defined. A protocol to be added that whenever Egypt is in a position to reoccupy it we should with pleasure hand over to her that part which is at present under our control. France, he believed, desired a conference, and the real object of the Anglo-Congolese Agreement would thus be attained.

He wrote to the Queen (June 13th) :

"The Anglo-Congolese agreement is causing disproportionate excitement; in France, because France had endeavoured to do the same thing, and had failed; in Germany, from jealousy and an anxiety to obtain compensation for acquiescence."

And the following day (June 14th) :

"He sent for Count Deym and held language to that Ambassador[4] which will ricochet through Vienna to Berlin.

"He told Count Deym that the style of the German note, though not unusual in communications from Berlin, was insufferable, and that if Germany were going to side with France or appear to side with France in this or other African questions, we must reconsider our position as regards our general attitude in Europe, more particularly in the Mediterranean and the East.

"Lord Rosebery would humbly suggest that, should the time come for Your Majesty to write to the Emperor, it should be pointed out that Germany is playing an extremely dangerous game. She is alienating this country, and instead of making friendly remonstrances and proposals for reconsideration she takes a tone which she might properly use in addressing Monaco. Moreover she is encouraging France to bully Belgium. It is never wise to fan a French flame, and Belgium might easily become the cause as well as the scene of a European conflagration. Should the French come in contact with British or Belgian posts in Africa, whether the conflict were slight or not, British or Belgian blood would be shed, and a war might easily ensue. From such a war Germany would not hold aloof, and it is thus difficult to see the motive of her policy."

In the event, the objection of Germany and France prevailed, and the King of the Belgians asked that the agreement should be abandoned, to the supreme joy of its opponents in the Cabinet.

[4] Austro-Hungarian Ambassador in London.

Uganda remained as a bone of contention. On June 1st Lord Stanmore, Rosebery's old friend of Ceylon days, moved for papers, and a debate followed. After Lord Kimberley had replied on the religious disturbances and other local matters, Lord Salisbury uttered a powerful plea for immediate consideration, if not immediate construction of the railway from the coast. One reason, he argued, was the opening up of new sources of consumption, which, unlike other countries, we leave all others as free to use for commerce as we do ourselves. Rosebery replied with general agreement, but ardour for the railway must be combined with general discretion. We had to make great sacrifices to maintain our naval position, which was more important to the interests of the Empire than a hundred Ugandas. It might have been wiser to construct a line of telegraph at once, and the question of the railway was one for mature judgment.

In fact, however, things had gone farther. On the previous day Rosebery had noted at the Cabinet, "Delicate and critical topics handled with creditable moderation," though it was nearly a year before the railway was actually sanctioned.

In April trouble arose over the treatment of British subjects in Nicaragua, and the exequaturs of both British and United States Consuls were withdrawn, though afterwards restored. Kimberley thought the main point was to avoid ruffling the susceptibilities of the United States. Later the question of coercing the recalcitrant little state, in the absence of explanations from her, had to be considered. "A pacific blockade" was suggested—rather a *brutum fulmen*, it was thought. Rosebery preferred making preparations to making an immediate decision, and inclined to the seizure of customs if necessary. In October, no step having been taken, Rosebery protested to the Foreign Office against ignoring the United States. He did not know that they had shown much jealousy of us in recent Mosquito affairs[5] and would like to say to them, "Your citizens have been seized and arbitrarily imprisoned like ours. Would you be disposed to take joint action to demand reparations? We must take such action and we should prefer to act with you to show that we have no wish for a separate position or advantage in Mosquitia." The matter dragged on into the spring of the following year. Harcourt thought that damages should be settled by arbitration,[6] but

[5] The implications of the Monroe Doctrine had not then been extended to such cases. At this time the Indians in the Mosquito Reserve claimed British protection.
[6] *Life,* vol. ii, pp. 330-31.

to this Kimberley strongly demurred. Harcourt also complained that "Lord Rosebery" had not consulted him or summoned a Cabinet.[7] The American Minister, Mr. Bayard, thought that we were entitled to demand redress, and French opinion took the same view. In May 1895 some ships were sent, and Nicaragua complied with the British demand.

The attitude of the House of Lords, in its unreformed state, towards the Liberal party was a perpetual anxiety to Rosebery, and his manner of encountering it brought him for the first and only time into direct collision with his Royal Mistress. The whole episode is delineated in *The Letters of Queen Victoria* more completely than is possible here; but Rosebery was so greatly affected by his necessary part in it that it cannot be passed over, even with the repetition of some facts and documents.

The Queen went to Florence in the middle of March, and there heard of the defeat of the Government in the debate on the Address (March 17th). She wrote sharply that the Whips must have been very neglectful, and that Rosebery must insist on more care in future. She added that if Ministers themselves held language like Mr. Gladstone, Sir William Harcourt, and (though in a much less strong degree) even Rosebery, one could not be surprised when a regular revolutionist like Mr. Labouchere became very bold. She went on to say:

"The House of Lords might possibly be improved, but it is *part and parcel* of the *much venerated* and *admired* British Constitution, and *cannot* be *abolished*."

Rosebery, in a respectful reply, announced the dispatch of the following memorandum. It reached Florence on April 8th.

10 Downing Street, Whitehall, *April 7th*, 1894.

"The present position of the House of Lords must be a subject of anxiety to every one who considers the conditions and possibilities of politics.

"It is not too much to say that that position is, as I have said in public more than once, a source, not of security but of danger. I do not say that this is the fault of the House of Lords—it might easily be argued that it is—but I wish to put that on one side and to confine

---

[7] Sir William Harcourt was mistaken (letter to Kimberley, April 18th) in thinking that the Foreign Secretary had asked for a Cabinet and been refused. The Cabinet had been offered and not required.

[369]

myself to stating that in my opinion the peril of the situation arises from circumstances beyond the control of the Peers.

"In 1831 the position of the House of Lords was more attacked than it is now. Had the Peers not yielded then with regard to the Reform Bill they would in all probability have produced a revolution. They did yield, however, and the country turned eagerly to the other questions then opened out, so that, partly from this circumstance, and partly from the difficulty of dealing with it, the question of the House of Lords sank into the background. From 1832 to 1885 the question of the House of Lords had been mainly academical—parties in it were pretty equally divided; the Conservative majority was on the whole wisely led, more especially by the Duke of Wellington; and occasions of friction were comparatively few. But in 1884 the question was anew forced upon the country by the rejection of the Franchise Bill by the House of Lords. There is no doubt that a very strong feeling was then produced. The Franchise Bill was however passed in the Autumn of that year, and in 1885 the House of Commons was elected on the new democratic suffrage. This was in itself a new complication in the position of the House of Lords. For here was a Chamber elected by six millions of voters, all exulting in the exercise of their powers, which was liable to be controlled by another Chamber, not elected in any sense, not representing anybody, and one hereditary in its character.

"In 1886 a further change took place, also disastrous to the House of Lords. On the subject of Home Rule for Ireland a schism took place in the Liberal party, which threw the great mass of the Liberal Peers into the arms of the Conservative majority—so much was this the case that, in addition to the other disadvantages already referred to—the hereditary, irresponsible and unrepresentative character of the House —there was the further embarrassment of its being practically limited to a single party. It was obvious then that, although from 1886 to 1892 there was no difficulty, because the same party was dominant in both Houses, when a House of Commons should be elected in which the majority should be Liberal, there would be immediately an acute conflict. This has soon come to pass. It did not take place on the rejection of the Irish Home Rule Bill, because on that point there was a majority of 70 purely English members on the side of the House of Lords. But on the occasion of the Employers Liability Bill the opportunity was seized. Some Liberals like Lord Farrer, for whom I have a profound respect, are of opinion that the Peers were justified in the course they then took. If that be so it is a conclusive proof of the strength of the feeling against the House of Lords. Because, if on a point on which people are divided, and on which the House of Lords certainly appears to be defending freedom of contract, there can be the bitterness of feeling which at present exists, it is obvious that in a dispute with the

House of Commons on any great popular issue, the feeling would be overwhelming. Of the strength of the present hostility I have little doubt. Everyone who speaks in the country is astonished at it: I myself have been struck by it in the same way. The apparent slightness of the cause that elicits it is a conclusive proof of its dominant vigour.

"I personally have always been in favour of a Second Chamber, and was an advocate of the Reform of the House of Lords. On two separate occasions I brought the question of its reform before that House, and spoke as plainly on the subject as I do now. It is possible that on those occasions, in 1884 and 1888, reform might have been effected. During the late Government it might also have been managed, but it is not now, I fear, practicable. The House of Commons are violently hostile to the idea, and so is the Liberal party throughout the country; while the Conservatives are not friendly to it.

"It is easy to understand how galling this House is to the party to which it happens to be opposed. When the Conservative Party is in power, there is practically no House of Lords: it takes whatever the Conservative Government brings it from the House of Commons without question or dispute; but the moment a Liberal Government is formed, this harmless body assumes an active life, and its activity is entirely exercised in opposition to the Government.

"Therefore while the Conservative party is in, we have not the control of a Second Chamber, but when the Liberal party is in it has to encounter not merely the control, but also the determined hostility of this body. It is in fact a permanent barrier raised against the Liberal party.

"I point this out to show the practical difficulty. For it is of no use to say of the House of Lords that the Peers are conscientious in their action, that they are honestly Tory and honestly Unionist, for the point of the objection is that they are so honestly of one party that they feel it is their duty on all occasions to oppose the other, a course which, however conscientious the Government which they thus oppose naturally resents.

"I have drawn up this memorandum to show exactly how the matter stands in my opinion, not to blame the Peers, or indeed to blame anybody, but to show the dangerous incompatibility of their relations with the House of Commons, and the hopelessness of the present position as regards the Liberal party.

"I cannot suggest any remedy, for any remedy which would be agreeable to the House of Commons, would be revolting to the House of Lords, and any remedy which would please the House of Lords would be spurned by the House of Commons.

"But it is well to look this serious situation plainly in the face: it is a permanent and not a fleeting danger to the Constitution. It may be said that if the Tories came in to-morrow the question would cease to exist, for the want of harmony would then disappear. But this would only be a postponement, for the Tory party could not hold power for ever and the feeling would simply accumulate against the coming of the next Liberal Government."

The Queen replied at length the next day. She took exception, as so many have, to the description of the House of Lords as unrepresentative, and to his application of the epithet "disastrous" to the Liberal Unionist action in 1886. She did not believe in a strong feeling in the country against the House of Lords, and thought Rosebery unfair in assuming that on any great popular issue it would conflict with the House of Commons. She thought that some day even Rosebery might be thankful for the power and independence of the Peers, and solemnly conjured him not to excite the passions of the people on this subject.

Rosebery replied a week later, first explaining the sense in which he had said that the Peers represented nothing, and why he had called the secession of 1886 "disastrous." It was disastrous to the House of Lords by completely upsetting the balance of parties there and converting it into an entirely anti-Liberal body. No one would blame Lord Hartington for an entirely conscientious act. However, he himself had used the same language about the Lords for the last ten years, but had never denounced it with the invective employed by Lord John Russell, Mr. Chamberlain, and the present Duke of Devonshire.

"But these statesmen Lord Rosebery is not concerned to defend. His line is simply this that it is idle to blind oneself to the danger of the present state of things, and that true patriotism consists not in concealing it but in stating it and inviting a remedy."

While the Sovereign was still on her travels he wrote in depression (May 7th):

"At the Foreign Office he had the happiness of being able constantly to report to Your Majesty on matters of European interest, and his endeavours to maintain the proper position of Your Majesty's Government abroad. Now he has nothing to write about which does not appear in the newspapers: sterile and endless discussion in the House of Commons which he himself can only read in newspapers."

A day or two later the Queen replied:

"She too regrets having no longer his able reports on Foreign Affairs. *There* indeed he was a great support to the Queen. . . . The Queen forbears entering on other subjects which might be painful, but cannot help grieving at speeches which she thinks are uncalled for."

There was no mistaking the Royal displeasure. The letter of acknowledgment shows that it was keenly felt:

10 DOWNING STREET, WHITEHALL, *May 14th*, 1894.

"Lord Rosebery with his humble duty submits his reply to Your Majesty's gracious letter.

"He cannot but first offer his respectful thanks for the kindness with which that letter is expressed, as he can readily perceive that Your Majesty feels some disapproval if not disappointment.

"He feared that this would be the case when he most reluctantly obeyed Your Majesty's summons, and he then urged on Your Majesty that he should be allowed to remain at the Foreign Office. Your Majesty says that '*then* he was a great support to the Queen.' That he hoped was indeed the case, and it was thus that he desired to remain. It was however otherwise decided, to his deep and heartfelt regret.

"He is still serving Your Majesty with earnest and loyal zeal, according to his imperfect lights, and he would ask Your Majesty to realise his position before withdrawing confidence from him.

"He is as Prime Minister more unfortunately situated than any man who ever held that high office.

"He has inherited from his predecessor a policy, a cabinet and a parliament; besides a party of groups—one of which is aimed against himself. All this is kept in existence by a narrow majority which may at any moment break away. He himself is only able to guide this tumultuous party through a leader, bitterly hostile to himself, and ostentatiously indifferent to the fate of the Government.

"Lord Rosebery in the meantime is shut up in a House almost unanimously opposed to his ministry, and, for all political purposes, might as well be in the Tower of London.

"Under these circumstances, though he hates making speeches anywhere, he has no course open to him but to speak in the country. Otherwise, little known as he is, he would be completely eclipsed by the Leader of the House of Commons, and obliterated as Prime Minister.

"As to policy, he is pledged to the policy of Mr. Gladstone's Government, having formed part of that Government. He has no power (even had he the desire) to dissociate himself from it. He did not indeed take an active part in the framing of the measures of that government, but he is none the less responsible for them.

"What then does Your Majesty expect of him? He cannot now honourably withdraw from the post of hazard, however irksome it may be, and, without presumption, he does not believe that Your Majesty would

[373]

find in the Liberal (or any) party a minister more truly devoted to Your Majesty. He cannot, even if he wished to do so, withdraw measures which are part of the programme of the Liberal party; for the only result would be that he and not the measures would disappear.

"All that he can do, which some other Liberal ministers conceivably might not, is, while pursuing a Liberal domestic policy at home to take care that the interests of Your Majesty's Empire are maintained abroad.

"He believes that he has now laid the whole truth of the position before Your Majesty, he humbly hopes not too unreservedly. But he has written, less as a minister to a Sovereign, than as a gentleman grateful to One who has shewn him so much kindness, and whose good opinion he hopes never to forfeit. He therefore begs that his letter may be seen by Your Majesty's eye alone.

"He does not know that he has anything to add except that, when his Ministry falls, he hopes to extricate himself from politics for ever, as he believed that he had done in 1890."

This letter throws strong light on the writer's inner character. Queen Victoria's reply, in its brevity, its good nature, and its gentle reproof, surely somewhat illuminates hers:

BALMORAL CASTLE, *June 8th,* 1894.

"The Queen has never yet answered Ld. Rosebery's long and confidential letter of the 14th of May & therefore wishes *now* to say a *few* words on the subject. She fully realises the extreme difficulty of his position, having inherited some such (as she must call them) dangerous & almost destructive measures from his Predecessor, which she deeply regrets. But she still hopes that he will act as a check & drag upon his Cabinet.

"What she would however wish to say, speaking *very* openly to him, is that in his Speeches *out* of Parliament he should take a more serious tone, & be, if she may say so, less *jocular* which is hardly befitting a Prime Minister.

"Ld. Rosebery is so clever that he may be carried away by a sense of humour, which is a little dangerous. It is as a sincere well wisher of Lord Rosebery that the Queen says this.

"She does not see how he can disentangle himself from politics, he will be too much wanted."

Queen Victoria disapproved of platform speeches. Parliament was the only stage on which the political drama should be played. In her girlhood campaigning in the country was unknown. Speeches were made on the hustings at elections, and sometimes at farmers' ordinaries, but rarely elsewhere. Once or twice Mr. Canning's gorgeous eloquence sounded outside Liverpool; but that was something of a novelty. So that she blamed Gladstone for instituting a practice which her more sober-minded statesmen were compelled to follow. It is not easy to judge from this letter whether the Queen mistakenly thought Rosebery to be, in fact, lacking in seriousness or merely to be doing himself an injustice by ill-timed exhibitions of oratorical humour. If the first, she was only in accord with very many others.

Nothing further happened until the autumn, when Rosebery had to wound the Queen's susceptibilities once more. He wrote on October the 24th:

"Lord Rosebery with his duty humbly begs to refer to the correspondence that passed between Your Majesty and himself with regard to the House of Lords in March and April of this year. He does so with sincere regret, as always when he is so unfortunate as to differ in opinion with Your Majesty.

"But he has no choice in the matter, for it will shortly be his duty to lay before the country his policy with regard to that question.

"That policy will consist, in the first place at any rate, in moving a declaratory resolution in the House of Commons of the impossibility of the elected representatives of the people allowing their measures to be summarily mutilated and rejected by the House of Lords.

"This is the least that can be done. The cry in the Liberal party is for the abolition of the House of Lords or of its veto. Lord Rosebery does not believe these measures to be constitutionally practicable, and moreover he is in favour of a Second Chamber of some sort; though he has long believed that the House of Lords, as at present constituted, cannot continue to exist, and has always frankly and publicly avowed that opinion. What will be the result of such a resolution? In the first place, the country will have at some time or another to decide upon it at a General Election. Lord Rosebery thinks it possible and even probable in view of the opposition of the English constituencies to Home Rule that the House of Lords may obtain a majority in its support. In that case he hopes that the Government which would then come in, and which would have the power, would also have the will to bring about a thorough reform of the House of Lords.

"On the other hand, should the constituencies support the Government by a majority which would shew the House of Lords that the country was in earnest, he apprehends that the result would be a complete reform of the House of Lords and a revision of its relations with the House of Commons.

"He does not believe that in any case the country will be content

[375]

with a single Chamber or content to give uncontrolled authority to the House of Commons.

"But these forecasts may well fail to interest Your Majesty as being empirical. The practical matter is the resolution, and Lord Rosebery can assure Your Majesty that no less will content his party, and he doubts much if that will. He himself though firmly convinced of the necessity of this policy could not go further at this stage.

"Lord Rosebery must again humbly express his regret at reiterating opinions and proposals, with which he has too much reason to fear Your Majesty does not agree. He may however express his hope and belief that it will not be necessary to include any allusion to this topic in the gracious speech from the Throne at the opening of Parliament."
DALMENY,
October 24th, 1894.

The Queen at once sent a telegram of strong protest, to which he replied thus:

October 26th, 1894.

"Humble duty;

"He has to-day received at Sheffield Your Majesty's gracious telegram which has distressed him much.

"He earnestly believes that the best and the highest interests of the country are involved in settling the Constitutional question in a time of calm like the present.

"Did he think otherwise he would humbly ask leave to retire from Your Majesty's Council.

"Later on in time of passion, nothing less than revolutionary proposals will satisfy and even now he is doubtful if he can hold his own ground against the extreme party.

"The Resolution itself would be of a kind already passed by the House of Commons and will avert a wilder policy.

"He would beg Your Majesty to read his letter once more in the light of this telegram, for he despairs of making his meaning plainer."

The meeting at Bradford, of which Rosebery's letter of the 24th had been the preliminary warning, was attended by 4,500 people. Rosebery spoke for an hour and a quarter, almost entirely on the House of Lords. He traced the history of Parliament from 1832 and the change in its political complexion. He was a Second Chamber man, but with the House of Lords as it was, he hesitated with regard to his principle. The present Second Chamber was a permanent party organisation. The other day a Liberal Peer had gone over and advised the Government that as he could not follow them they had better retire into obscurity. "A very strange piece of advice, because he cannot follow us, he invites us to join him." The House of Lords was a great national danger from a constitutional point of view: it was the greatest issue since the tyranny of Charles I and James II. The abolition of the veto would be a grave difficulty in practice; but he did not believe it would come to revolution, because we settle things without cataclysms. The Government could not claim a mandate, but it was for the House of Commons to pass a firm resolution, and he was sure they would. It could never be expunged from the books of the House. After that he appealed to the people of the country, to ask whether they desired a revision of the constitution or not—"We fling down the gauntlet. It is for you to back us up."

The voice of Balmoral was not likely to echo these sentiments and the Queen wrote (October 30th) that she had waited to read the speech before saying more. She complained bitterly that she had never been consulted on this policy, not to speak of her sanction being obtained. She quoted several of Rosebery's strenuous expressions, certain to arouse public passions. She admitted the necessity of reforms in the House of Lords, but the opinion of the Sovereign was ignored by this demand for a revision of the Constitution:

"The Queen is truly grieved at having had to write all this to Lord Rosebery, whose personal devotion and loyalty to herself are well known to her, and she does not doubt he is placed in a most difficult position, but she does not think he will avert the evils he dreads by the course he proposes to pursue."

Rosebery, it will be observed, altogether refused to admit the need of the Queen's sanction before submitting a question to a popular audience. His defence of his action is given in full:

10 DOWNING STREET, WHITEHALL, *November 1st*, 1894.

"Lord Rosebery with his humble duty desires to express his sense of the considerate tone of Your Majesty's letter just received, in spite of the difference of opinion which unfortunately exists between Your Majesty and himself with regard to the best course to adopt under present circumstances.

"Lord Rosebery's own view of the situation is this—that it is from the broadest point of view important to take advantage of the present opportunity. He believes that the system by which the House of Lords—now, unfortunately, owing to causes on which he will not dwell, a party organisation—controls a Liberal but not a Conservative Government is obnoxious to the conscience of the country as well as to its best interests. But he also believes that this is a moment of calm and therefore favourable to revision. What he has always dreaded, as he has stated in public, is that the question of the House of Lords should come for decision at a crisis of passion and storm. Then the Constitution would be hurriedly cast into the crucible with lamentable and incalculable results.

"The policy of the Government practically comes to this—that the Constitution cannot long stand the strain of a permanent control exercised by a Conservative branch of the Legislature on all Liberal Governments; that it is well that this question should be decided at a peaceful juncture; and that in the issue between the House of Lords and the House of Commons the Government takes the side of the House of Commons.

"Beyond this Lord Rosebery does not go.

"Your Majesty will have noticed the marked way in which he asserted himself as a Second Chamber man, as against any of his own party who, unthinkingly in his opinion, declare themselves partisans of an uncontrolled House of Commons. This point is vital to Lord Rosebery: it might not be by any means vital to other Liberal Governments, and he begs Your Majesty's serious attention to this point.

"Your Majesty notes however that expressions were used by Lord Rosebery which appear to Your Majesty too energetic. Lord Rosebery would humbly remind Your Majesty that he was speaking to a tumultuous audience of 5,000 people; that under these circumstances it is necessary to use broad popular language; and that it is impossible to argue points under such circumstances in the style appropriate to a drawing room or a library. He has not seen among hostile criticisms any that describe his language as excessive; he has seen several however that characterise it as feeble, including the 'Times.'

"To turn to another point he would never dream of proposing a constitutional resolution to the House of Commons without submitting it after mature consideration by the Cabinet to Your Majesty. But he would humbly deprecate the view that it is necessary for a minister before laying a question before a popular audience to receive the approval of the Crown. Such a principle would tend to make the Sovereign a party in all the controversies of the hour and would hazardously compromise the neutrality of the Sovereign. But should a Ministry desire to present to Parliament a resolution of this kind they would certainly be ignorant of the first elements of their duty did they neglect to obtain the sanction of the Sovereign to its being presented for the decision of Parliament.

"Your Majesty will, he is sure, do him the justice to recollect that within a month of his succeeding Mr. Gladstone in Her Councils he submitted the question of the House of Lords to Your Majesty with the reasons which made him consider it the gravest problem before the Government. He was not then animated by pique at any action of the House of Lords, for no such action had taken place during his short tenure of the Treasury. He simply felt it his duty to warn Your Majesty of what was in his mind; and he therefore believed that Your Majesty would not feel any astonishment at the intention of the Government to propose a resolution on this subject. Nothing was less in his contemplation than to take Your Majesty by surprise.

"In conclusion, he will only once more express his sorrow at finding himself in disagreement with Your Majesty. Your Majesty does him no more than justice in believing in his loyalty, devotion and honesty of aim. But he wishes that he could persuade Your Majesty that the policy which he recommends is sound in itself, essentially conservative in the best sense, and the one best calculated to avert evils which might wreck and ruin much in the Constitution which he desires to preserve."

A postscript to this letter followed on November 8th:

"Lord Rosebery with his humble duty ventures to make an addition to his last letter, for he is in truth concerned and distressed beyond measure with regard to Your Majesty's feelings on this House of Lords question. If by any conceivable means he could relieve Your Majesty he would gladly do so. Did he believe that his resignation of office would assist Your Majesty, he would ask Your Majesty's permission to retire to-morrow. But he fears that the result would be quite different. He believes that he is in fact the moderating influence in this matter. Nearly if not quite half of the Cabinet is in favour of a Single Chamber. The more prominent people in the Liberal party appear to be of the same opinion.

"Lord Rosebery is consequently between two fires; on the one side he is attacked by the Tories, and on the other (which is a greater difficulty) by his own side because he is strongly in favour of a Second Chamber.

"Had Lord Rosebery persuaded the Government to take no action whatever with regard to the House of Lords the Government would have been turned out within a week of the re-assembling of Parliament, and this too on a cause which he cannot conscientiously defend.

"He has taken the mildest and he firmly believes the wisest course in the interest of the Constitution and of all concerned. But he is aware that any dealing with the House of Lords is distasteful to Your Majesty, and he wishes with all his heart that One who has been so good to him and to whom he is so sincerely devoted should be spared all pain on this and on every other subject."

[379]

The Queen replied in a somewhat softened mood:

About November 13th, 1894.

"The Queen did not answer Lord Rosebery's letter of Novr. 1st feeling it was useless to further discuss a question in which there is, alas! such divergence of opinion between us.

"But she must thank him for his kind letter of the 8th.

"He is mistaken however in thinking that '*any dealing with the H. of L.*' is '*distasteful*' to her.

"The Queen fully recognises the necessity for its reform . . . and would be glad to know the broad outlines of Lord Rosebery's plan of reconstruction.

"The Queen cannot agree with what Lord Rosebery says, in his letter of the 1st, as to the announcement of this Policy.

"It is *not* a 'mere question of policy,' but as he himself said '*a question of enormous importance,*' a '*question of the revision of the entire constitution*' and, as such, she maintains her sanction for its public declaration should have been obtained.

"The Queen believes and appreciates what Lord R. says: that he is concerned and distressed at her feeling—and she sees that Lord Rosebery evidently thinks that the House of Lords will suffer less at his hands than at those of his followers, and she realises that his position is a difficult one.

"But the Queen would ask Lord Rosebery and his Cabinet to bear in mind that 57 years ago the Constitution was delivered into her keeping and that right or wrong she has her views as to the fulfilment of that trust.

"She cannot but think Lord Rosebery will feel that *his* position is not the only difficult one in these democratic days."

so the constitutional duel was suspended for the time.

Unfortunately there were other fences to be got over. Rosebery went to Glasgow on November 11th, and, besides refuting Lord Salisbury's description of him as a Single Chamber man, and pointing out that temperance legislation could have no chance in the present House of Lords, he proclaimed Scottish Disestablishment as a permanent part of the Liberal programme. The manses might or might not be Tory agencies, but the Established Church was in no way representative of Scotland as a whole.

The Queen called attention to her oath on accession to the Throne, and deeply deplored the speech. She would do all that lay in her power to be true to her promise.

Fortunately, this question, which aroused such bitter passions in

[380]

heavenly minds, solved itself later by happier methods than did the grant of Home Rule.

Rosebery had been for a couple of days to Balmoral early in October, when Her Majesty was in great good humour. After the above correspondence he did not in fact see the Queen during the year, not being summoned to Windsor.

At one of his earlier visits to Windsor (June 21st) :

"The Queen told me some curious things. She did not know if she was Alexandrina Victoria or *vice versâ*.[8] Quite true that George IV wished her to be Georgina, and that the Duke of Kent insisted on Alexandrina as the Russian Emperor had been so kind. William IV had wished to change her name to Charlotte, when he was King."

So the Victorians, now so sadly regarded, might have been Charlotteans, if not Alexandrinians or Georgineans.

Throughout the Session of 1894 Harcourt was conducting his Budget with extraordinary skill and with the supple discretion which he so often displayed in Parliament, though so seldom in Council. That memorable measure, which to this harassed generation of surtax payers appears so merciful, excited no little disquiet among the propertied class. Rosebery did not wish to argue points endlessly in the Cabinet, so he prepared a memorandum for Harcourt's personal consumption, no doubt stating the defendants' case more emphatically than he would to a colleague with whom he was in greater sympathy. As Lord Spencer, not entirely agreeing with Rosebery, put it to Harcourt,[9] Rosebery, by not circulating his memorandum, had desired to bow to the judgment of the author of the Budget. Looking back at all the circumstances, one may doubt whether, if Rosebery were to write a memorandum at all, it would not have been wiser to compose one for the Cabinet rather than for a critic so hostile. At any rate his paper aroused a reply which is given in full in Harcourt's *Life*.[10] Four years later (April 1898) Rosebery noted as follows :

"It is usual in Cabinets to exchange in strict confidence observations on each other's proposals. This is of the essence of a Cabinet : as their deliberations must be largely on paper, Cabinet sittings being, in proportion to the vast interests of government, brief and hurried.

"But of course if such minutes were couched in the tone of this of V. W. H., such interchange of opinion would be impossible.

[8] More probably Georgina.
[9] *Life,* vol. ii, p. 287.
[10] Vol. ii, pp. 283-6.

"I took no notice of this document except to show it to J. Morley—a judge little favourable to me—who expressed himself as full of indignation.[11]

"There was practically no opposition in the Cabinet to the Budget, except that I reduced the maximum with the aid of Fowler (so Fowler says, and I have no doubt he assisted, though not at the Cabinet) from 10 to 8 per cent. We spent dreary hours in listening to H. reading out typewritten discourses on the Budget (which was the work of Alfred Milner).

"Afterwards, when I resigned the leadership in 1896, Harcourt informed the Press that I had offered the most violent opposition to his Budget, which he had only overcome by the threat of resignation. This was in the first place untrue, and secondly, had it been true, a violation of Cabinet confidence."

It would be tedious to reproduce here the whole of the conflicting arguments. In his paper Harcourt dealt *seriatim* with Rosebery's protests. Rosebery, for his own satisfaction, made comments in pencil on some of his colleague's rejoinders: for instance, Rosebery had said that property would be arrayed against the Government as an alarmed adversary, and the last relics of their propertied followers would be alienated. Harcourt, in reply, cited his recollection of Mr. Gladstone's great battle on the Succession Duty in 1853, after which landed proprietors had hated him. Rosebery pencilled: "The Budgets may resemble each other, but there is a difference in the men."

Harcourt went on to speak of "another party which was founded 1894 years ago," and to think it likely that many young men would "go away sorrowful because they had great possessions." Against this was noted: "No, it is the young men who are to inherit great possessions who will suffer. So this refined innuendo is beside the mark."

It was hopeless, Harcourt proceeded, to avert "the horizontal division of parties" which was the outcome of Household Suffrage. Rosebery differed, because the Tories had a fair representation of all classes.

Death Duties, said Harcourt, only occur once in a generation. Rosebery observed that there had been three Dukes of Bedford in three years, to take one example.[12]

[11] Sir William Harcourt evidently put a different construction on the comment Morley made to him. *Life,* vol. ii, p. 287.

[12] As Harcourt's biographer remarks, vol. ii, p. 288: "Events were to make an ironic comment on this phase of the Budget when, ten years later, the Nuneham estates changed hands by death twice within six months."

The money was needed, Harcourt said, for the reduction of other taxes, "or what is more probable, to satisfy further Jingo panics." He himself could not be interested in the possible loss to Election Funds, for he had paid as much in purse and in person as he intended to do. Against this is noted the single word "Coriolanus!!"

In conclusion Harcourt thought it hardly fair to bury the two memoranda in their "respective bosoms," but that their colleagues should form their judgment upon them. Rosebery's pencilled comment runs: "Mine has never entered my bosom: your views not merely pervade London in a red box, but are recited to the loungers of the lobbies."

The only concession in Harcourt's paper was the desire to mitigate the scale of graduation of death duties so far as exigencies of the Revenue would permit.

At the end of the document Rosebery wrote: "Mr. Pitt said 'Patience.'"

But the immortal advice from Spain, "Patience, and shuffle the cards," comes easily to the Walpoles and Campbell-Bannermans of public life, never to a Charles Fox or a Rosebery. Still, in writing to the Queen (July 13th), he put the best face he could on the business.

"With regard to the Budget, it is practically passed, and it would be impossible now to make any change in its provisions. Lord Rosebery is himself inclined to take a somewhat gloomy view of its effects on the class to which he himself belongs. He cannot however deny that there is much to be said for it in the sense of its being logically just, and he believes that the landowning class must avert its severer effects by two courses which in themselves are good; that is, by handing over property in their lifetime to their children, and by greater simplicity of living."

The whole episode may be regarded as marking the definite separation of Rosebery from his Chancellor of the Exchequer. There had been acute divergences on foreign affairs, sometimes involving moral issues, but not accusations of personal interest. In this correspondence incautiously invited by Rosebery, Harcourt enjoyed giving rein to his powers of provocation by implying that the paper under reply merely came from a rich man who disliked being taxed. Cardinal de Retz was not far wrong when he wrote:

"On a plus de peine dans les Partis, de vivre avec ceux qui en sont, que d'agir contre ceux qui y sont opposés."

Still greater was the enjoyment of Harcourt's son. Lewis Harcourt, like Tennyson's son Hallam in a different way of life, had joyfully put aside the prospect of a brilliant personal career. It was his task to be his father's right-hand man; and to do everything to ensure his succession to the seat of power when Gladstone left it. It was an admirable renunciation; and the intense chagrin felt by the son when the father was passed over demands the sympathy of everybody. But it had its dangerous side. It is not good for anybody to live entirely in political *couloirs*, with no responsibility or public duty to keep him straight. Throughout this brief Government Lewis Harcourt's part was to glorify his father's great financial achievement. It was not his business to help the Government as a whole, in the lobbies or elsewhere—and it was tempting to dismiss with a shrug the Prime Minister and one or two of his colleagues as unworthy leaders of the party. Fifteen years had to pass before Lewis Harcourt was able to show his real quality as a capable Minister and an excellent colleague in a Liberal administration.

As Leader of the House of Lords Rosebery perforce had to intervene with a few words in many discussions. These are not worth noting separately. On the Budget, he confided himself to moving the second reading, leaving the defence of the measure to the Lord Chancellor.

With his knowledge of London needs, he spoke at some length on the Report of a Select Committee on the question of Betterment in Town Improvements. That Committee had fenced round acceptance of the principle with safeguards which made its application most difficult, as he pointed out in detail (August 16th). He also took charge of the Equalisation of Rates Bill, which obtained a modified blessing from Lord Salisbury. And he conducted a measure enabling the British Museum to buy sixty-nine houses and gardens from the Duke of Bedford.

Rosebery combined the Presidency of the Council with his office of First Lord of the Treasury, and in the former capacity attended the first Court of the new Welsh University. It was a great occasion, he said, because it would be a people's university, not "a place to which men of wealth will come to put a final polish on a leisurely course of education fastidiously gone through." Besides, it represented the spirit of nationality in its best form.

He spoke at the Royal Academy Banquet, and attended, June 4th, at Eton, where the Provost wished him success at Epsom in two days' time, and Rosebery—after deploring the fact that there were only two Etonians in his Cabinet, against three Harrovians—

Matthew Dawson   Lord Rosebery

LADAS, 1894

J. Watts up

thanked the Provost for his unprecedented good wishes, and added that, in spite of representations he received from Anti-Gamblers, he felt no vestige of shame in possessing a good horse. And a very good horse it was. Through the year Rosebery had been able to pay flying visits to Newmarket to see *Ladas* at work, and to enjoy the company of his trainer, Matthew Dawson, a man as remarkable in intellect as in character. The colt won the Two Thousand easily, and then the intermediate event of the Newmarket Stakes (May 9th). Then came the Derby. Rosebery noted (June 6th) :

"A memorable day for me. I won the Derby with *Ladas* just twenty-five years after the first *Ladas* disgraced himself and me in the same race. The scene was one of delirious enthusiasm. I scarcely know why.

"It began raining heavily after the race, but the Prince of Wales asked me as a personal favour to come to his dinner, as this was an historical occasion. So I went up and he proposed my health."

As a rule Rosebery, entertaining a party of old friends at the Durdans, was excused attendance at the Prince's Derby Dinner. To anticipate events, the hero of the Derby caused some disappointment later on, being defeated, with some ill-luck, in the three other great races he contested this year, including the St. Leger at Doncaster.

Not a few of Rosebery's political followers looked on these racing triumphs with anything but favour. It is necessary to distinguish the various notes of disapproval. To a powerful minority of keen Liberals the Turf represented open vice. Such men would no more have thought of being seen on a race-course than of frequenting a *Maison Tellier*. But others, less fanatical, disliked the thought of a Liberal Prime Minister winning the Derby. As Rosebery himself pointed out, it was absurd to overlook the possession of a few bad horses and to object to a good one. Beyond question; but if an analogy may be suggested from another kind of sport, it is safe to say that all Queen Victoria's Prime Ministers, except Disraeli, were, or had been, in the habit of going out shooting. Some, like Sir Robert Peel and Rosebery himself, were adepts. But if any one of them had earned the fame of having killed an unequalled number of grouse or partridges in a day, like a Lord de Grey or a Lord Walsingham, heads would have been shaken. To watch *Ladas* gallop was no greater distraction from serious politics than to denounce Vaticanism in a pamphlet, with Gladstone, or to work in a chemical laboratory, with Salisbury. But it was somehow felt that the ownership of a Derby favourite was too absorbing a pastime for the wearer of Gladstone's mantle.

[385]

In another *apologia* for his taste for racing he mentioned that Oliver Cromwell owned horses. This fired the inimitable invention of Frank Lockwood, who sent him a sketch of the Lord Protector, in the slouch hat and soft riding boots of the seventeenth century, but with race-glasses slung over his shoulder, gloomily regarding a string of weedy thoroughbreds, with O.C. on their quartersheets, being ridden round the ring of a race-course.

A distraction of a less invidious sort was a visit to Bristol (October 30th) to receive its Freedom—the first offered him in England—and to unveil a statue of Burke, the gift of the local magnate, Sir William Wills. He dwelt on the apparent paradox that Burke, an ardent reformer all his life, ended in a frenzy of violent Toryism. Burke dreaded Parliamentary reform, because in the circumstances of the moment it might lead to the revolution that he hated. It was a consolation to us pygmies of a later day that this great master of eloquence and political genius saw so little of success in his lifetime. His last memorable and pathetic words to Bristol—"What shadows we are, and what shadows we pursue"—sum up the life of every politician, and perhaps of every man. Burke, he concluded, looms larger and larger, while the figures of others of his day grow dimmer and dimmer, for his fame rests on the broad foundation of political wisdom.

There was some return to social life. He dined with Horace Farquhar[13]—a well-known figure in London as a close ally of Lord Fife—and noted "the first time I have dined out unofficially for years." Earlier there had been two eminently unofficial occasions. First, his old allies of Loder's Club at Christ Church celebrated their new Prime Minister by a dinner at the Grand Hotel (April 27th), one of his closest friends, Philip Wroughton, being in the chair.[14]

[13] (1844-1923.) G.C.B. *Cr.* Lord Farquhar 1898, and Earl 1923.

[14] Lord Bute.	Sir C. Boyle.
Colonel Follett.	W. W. Phipps.
Philip Wroughton.	E. W. Hamilton.
J. H. Mossop.	J. Frederick.
F. Hamlyn.	Lord Tweedmouth.
G. Duncombe.	W. G. Marshall.
A. Smith Barry.	Hon. W. V. Verney.
A. Turnor.	C. Cotes.
E. S. Hope.	Sir Frederick Milner.
F. Parker.	A. V. Pryor.
Lord Galway.	Lord Emlyn.
Lord Ilchester.	H. Evans Gordon.
Mr. Fuller Maitland.	

At the second (June 25th) the same party assembled:

"Gave dinner to twenty-five old Christ Church friends in honour of the final disappearance of *Ladas* the First. Very pleasant."

He went to see *Faust*:

"How long, I wonder, since I have been to an opera?"

And to a concert at Buckingham Palace:

"How many years since I last went to a Queen's Concert?"

Free from departmental work, he was able to spend more of the autumn in Scotland. He was twice at Dunrobin, the Highland home of his great friends the Duke and Duchess of Sutherland. There he again attempted deer-stalking, with more success, and killed his fair share of stags. There were also happily quiet days at Dalmeny for the boys' summer holidays, and again in October.

Relations with the Gladstone family were unimpaired:

April 18th.—"Drove with Neil to see Mr. G. at Dollis Hill. Mr. G. in bed. Greatly occupied by the flag on the Victoria Tower. If at all, it should be larger, and would be a great strain on the tower. He seemed doubtful about graduation. As charming as ever. Neil asked for his blessing and received it."

He went to Hawarden in November, for a family party, and found his host depressed but, as always, busily occupied:

"The pamphlet Mr. G. sat up all night writing was 'The Ministry and the Sugar Duties in 1844.'"

The happiest occasion of the year was the marriage of Henry Asquith, a colleague with whom he had become closely intimate, with Margot Tennant. Rosebery's friendship with the whole family at Glen had been affectionate for many years past.

The saddest was the hopeless illness of Blanche Lady Waterford, perhaps the figure in the London world best loved by everybody who knew her, and a very perfect character. Rosebery wrote: "I went to see Lady Waterford. A divine spectacle of resignation."

The Prince of Wales had attended the funeral of his brother-in-law the Emperor of Russia, and as usual had helped by his sympathy and clear sense to improve international relations. On his return Rosebery wrote to him:

[387]

10 DOWNING STREET, *December 6th,* 1894.

SIR,

"I am anxious to be among the first to welcome your Royal Highness home, and to express my deep sense of the good and patriotic work that you have accomplished since you left England.

"Never has Your Royal Highness stood so high in the national esteem as to-day, for never have you had such an opportunity. That at last has come, and has enabled you to justify the highest anticipations, and to render a signal service to your country, as well as to Russia and the peace of the world.

"I am, Sir,
Your obedient servant,
ROSEBERY."

In spite of freedom from departmental drudgery, and open-air weeks in Scotland, Rosebery was weakening under the mental strain of his discomfortable leadership. He was at Mentmore after the middle of December, and became decidedly unwell, with some sort of chill, as he thought. His doctor, however, sanctioned a visit to Sandringham, and Rosebery did not suffer physically at the moment.

CHAPTER XVI

The Life of Pitt and Other Literary Work, 1891-1911

A S ALL experience tells, the aimlessness, and the occasional leth-
argy which mark the reaction from an overwhelming trouble,
are best fought by physical fatigue on the one side, and by regular
or even monotonous mental employment on the other. Rosebery
was sure not to neglect exercise in the open air, but the other
remedy might have been less easy to discover. The outlines of
party politics were blurred, and his work on the County Council
was done for the time being. It was thus fortunate that an opportunity had already offered for literary work exactly suited to his
own tastes and to his special gifts. The short historical biographies
of "Twelve English Statesmen," were being published by Messrs.
Macmillan, under the general editorship of John Morley, who himself rather unexpectedly undertook the Life of Walpole. Rosebery
had been invited to take charge of William Pitt. His uncle, Lord
Stanhope, had been responsible for the principal biography of his
illustrious relative in four volumes; Macaulay had written a famous essay; and Professor Goldwin Smith an appreciation. But
Rosebery saw clearly that there was room for something different.
In an octavo volume of some 300 pages, he could present a kit-cat
portrait, set in a background adorned by other political figures.
The result was the book which establishes his claims to a high place
in the world of letters. Two of his later works, that on the last days
of Napoleon and that on Randolph Churchill, may appear even more
symmetrically perfect, but neither of these represents the same scope
of research and concentrated labour. When the book appeared, a
chorus of approval greeted it in England and America. I select the
opinions of a few who, for one reason or another, were qualified
to give them, some as adepts in the writing craft, others as political
experts. Rosebery kept these letters in a special portfolio, as he did
no others of the like kind. Mr. Gladstone's praise was unstinted,
though it was impossible for him not to add some qualifications on
matters of personal opinion. He wrote:

[389]

"My dear Rosebery,

"To-day brings with it the discharge of a very pleasant duty, for I received to-day (probably through your kindness) a copy of your Pitt, and though I am a slow, a distracted, and a laden man, I have read half of it, and have seen him launched into the War. My anticipations were high, but it has passed them. It is (in my view) the ablest monograph of the kind that I have ever read. Let me say all in one word, it is masterly work, and places you at once high on the literary ladder.

"There are of course questions of detail to remark upon. Beyond these I find one sentence only before page 123 from which I seriously differ. It is that about inner Cabinets.[1]

"At page 123 we come to the divergence of the roads on the War. My summing up of the matter is this: that it is probably at once the biggest error ever recorded in history, and the most excusable. . . . Let me end with a most hearty, most thorough-going congratulation.

"Affectly yours,

"Hawarden,   W. E. Gladstone.
November 25th, 1891."

Mary Gladstone, to whom a copy had also been sent, wrote that her father had pronounced the book to be a masterpiece, and that he seemed "Almost startled, if you understand what I mean, at the historic grip and grasp, besides at its pure literary qualities."

Sir William Harcourt was not less enthusiastically friendly:

Malwood, Lyndhurst, *November 25th*, 1891.

Dear Rosebery,

"I sat up till the small hours this morning devouring 'Pitt,' which reached me yesterday.

"It is what our favourite writers of the eighteenth century would have called 'an excellent piece.'

"I think the style admirable,—the grouping of the topics (of all arts the most difficult) as good as possible—interspersed and lighted up at sufficient intervals with flashes of wit. It is the carbon of Stanhope crystallised and cut into a brilliant. I feel certain it will be—nay is—an accomplished literary success, and everyone will say as they do of the newborn babe, 'How like its father.' . . . Everyone will feel, my dear friend, that you have wisely and bravely encountered the *annus luctus*, and produced a worthy memorial of your sorrow.

"When I have shaken off the glamour of your word-painting, I shall

---

[1] *Pitt*, Macmillan, 1891, p. 109. "An inner Cabinet, indeed, is not unfamiliar to us; and, as the numbers constituting Cabinets increase, it must become a recognised institution."

Subsequent experience has tended to enforce Rosebery's view rather than that of his chief.

one day have a Whig crow or two to pluck with you, for I am still a Whig and learned from Sir Cornewall Lewis to revere Grenville. But if there are some things which shock the Whig soul there are others which will make the Tories furious, so on the whole (as Goschen said) justice is done. To me the history of Pitt's socialistic scheme of 1796 was quite new (as it is barely discernible in Stanhope) in which he out-Josephs Joe and out-Jesses Collings. . . . Good-bye, my dear fellow. *Valete et plaudite*. It has given all a happy day."

Other colleagues presented their bouquets. Lord Ripon saying how much he admired "the excellence of its style, the vigour of its portrait, and the skill of its advocacy"; Sir Charles Dilke had been certain that he would produce a perfect book on this subject; Cardinal Manning sent a long letter, observing that to him the two greatest men in our history were William Pitt and S. Thomas of Canterbury. "In isolated grandeur they are of one heroic kind." The comparison sounds complementary to Rosebery's of Charles Fox and Martin Luther, on which the Duchess of Cleveland made amused comment in her letter of congratulation. Admiring letters poured in from French and American friends; Herbert Bismarck, fluent in English, was amazed at "the stupendous amount of knowledge embodied in this one volume . . . I think you have managed to remain wonderfully impartial, and that must not have been an easy task, as everybody who cares for his own country always must have a certain bias towards its greatest men." Lastly came the experts, pronouncing their verdict of academic approval. William Cory, since he gave up school-mastering, had immersed himself in the study of Modern History. He wrote:

PILGRIMS' LANE, N.W., *November 26th*, 1891.
"DEAR AUTHOR, GIVER OF A GOOD BOOK,
"I thank you kindly for sending me *Pitt*, and I send my notes straight off. . . . I have Everard's latest photograph on my mantelpiece. I wish he had lived to see your progress and to share your pains.
"Let me write as Pitt did,
"Yours affy.,
WILLIAM COY."

Fifteen sides of note-paper are covered with closely written notes of learned and instructive criticism, concluded thus:

"I have read the book with all my might, and I feel that I have learnt a great deal from it and it makes me wish to read a great deal more.

[391]

"It seems to me not (as I feared) too witty or smart, far above Macaulay in real generosity, far above Lecky in beauty of form, far above Froude in judicial statement.

"It seems to me a treatise that may actually do good to our people and to the candid men of other lands.

"I have been busy and anxious ever since it came here (Nov. 23), but I have enjoyed it heartily.

"Non sine lacrymis."

The Master of Balliol had not been able to add Rosebery's name to his glowing list of political *alumni*; but at any rate his triumph was a triumph for Oxford, and he wrote kindly if a shade pontifically:

BALLIOL COLLEGE, OXFORD, *November 26th*, 1891.

"The book has arrived here, and I am delighted with it. I know of no life of an English Statesman which is equal to it in justice of appreciation, or in pathetic interest. It will greatly raise your reputation, not merely as a literary man, but as a politician. The sadness, the courage, the greatness, the tragedy of Pitt's life, are given as they have never been before, because no one has been capable of feeling them in the same way. There is no one in political life, except perhaps Morley, who could have written such a book, and he would not have treated the subject with equal fairness.

"There is nothing in common between Pitt and Gladstone, a good deal between Pitt and Peel, and something between Chatham and Gladstone. But these comparisons are shadowy and hardly worth making.

"It doubles the power of the statesmen when he possesses the gift of writing as well as of speaking; there is more wisdom and also more freedom in it. If he has the gift of silence, without the appearance of excessive caution, and an insight into the natures of men, which can only be given by a silent sympathy with them, he may have a large share in the government of them.

"Believe me, dear Lord Rosebery,

Ever yours sincerely,

B. JOWETT.

"Are you not rather too hard on the Whigs, who gave us some excellent political maxims of toleration and the like? I asked the Duke of Bedford why the Whigs have always been so unpopular. He said, 'Because they were so jobbing and exclusive.' I think it was rather because they were so ignorant of the world and of mankind."

Rosebery must have valued as highly as any the opinions of James Bryce and H. D. Traill. The latter was just issuing his "Life

[392]

of Lord Salisbury," in the parallel series, *The Queen's Prime Ministers*, and spoke of his "literary twinship," and of Rosebery's "masterly picture of the man, his times, and his contemporaries. In particular such a vivid and striking little sketch as that of Fox makes one hope that you will some day give us a gallery of eighteenth-century portraits."

Bryce wrote:

54 PORTLAND PLACE, *November 24th*, 1891.

"MY DEAR ROSEBERY,

"Thank you heartily for your *Pitt*. It came last night, and getting in very tired and rather poorly, at 11.30 p.m., I was imprudent enough to glance at it and got so fascinated that I had to sit up well into the small hours. It seems to me the most vivid and telling book of the kind I have read, and able to hold its place beside Macaulay's and Goldwin Smith's biographies, and above all others that have dealt with Pitt.

"If you were to wish for any criticism with a view to the next edition, I would say that it strikes me you sometimes assume rather too much knowledge of the events of the time in the reader's mind. True, you are writing not a history but the life of Pitt: I would not ask for much to be added, but here and there, as at the coalition time, a page or so might supply a setting of facts which will make the story plainer to the less and less instructed public of our day. This is really the only fault or suggestion I have to pick or find; you do indeed seem to me somewhat too lenient to Pitt's faults, but you know the facts so much better than I that I acquiesce.

"What I do want to express is my unqualified admiration for the vigour and the brightness with which the story has been told, as well as for the penetration, the analytical power, and the political wisdom that abound throughout the book,

"Sincerely yours,

J. BRYCE."

This was the considered opinion of one master in the same craft. Another seemed to be a little more doubtful. John Morley, the editor of the series, set down a typed slip beginning:

"Nothing can be more agreeable to read, or more brightly written, in spite of a certain heaviness, due partly to excess of substantives, and partly to too great a desire to impress not only the author's meaning, but his opinion. For instance . . ."

A critical list follows, coolly but not ill-naturedly drawn. In conversation with myself Morley was not entirely favourable to the book as a whole. He seemed to look on it rather as a brilliant prize essay than as what an historical monograph should be—the overflow from a vast reservoir of learning, skilfully directed into a particular channel. This, surely, was not quite fair. Rosebery was not a Stubbs or a Maitland, but his knowledge of the eighteenth century was deep as well as wide. Perhaps, too, Morley entertained some unconscious mistrust of one who had not ground regularly at the academic mill, and had not undergone the probation of a chartered man of letters. But there should be some reciprocity in these judgments. Morley himself justly resented the slipshod opinion that ranked him as a reviewer turned politician, not as a tried official capable of firm decision and prompt action at difficult moments.

Rosebery's delighted letter to his mother from Amalfi may conclude the chapter. She must have been misled by his attachment to Lady Holland and St. Ann's Hill.

January 22nd, 1892.
"I was very glad to learn that you liked my little book. I was particularly pleased that you guessed that my sympathies were secretly with Fox against Pitt. It is the greatest tribute to my fairness that I have received, for they are wholly and entirely the other way."

In a conversation with Sir William Harcourt in 1894, John Morley spoke of Rosebery's "affectation of literature."[2] His rather grudging judgment of *Pitt* has been described above, and its probable explanation. As a matter of fact, in after years, when their intimacy had grown close, he thoroughly enjoyed long talks with Rosebery on literature, French and British, as on many other topics. He would certainly then have admitted that nobody could be freer than Rosebery from pretensions as a critic of the academic type. In the two volumes of Miscellanies brought together by Mr. John Buchan, of thirty-three pieces only the addresses on Robert Burns, Dr. Johnson, Thackeray and Robert Louis Stevenson deal directly with men of letters. And the first two of these appear on the canvas as great human figures rather than as authors. There is no detailed examination of their writings, and a palpable unwillingness to embark on such a quest.

The centenary of Burns's death was honoured on July 21st, 1896. Twelve years before (July 26th, 1884), Rosebery had unveiled the Burns statue on the Thames Embankment, the gift of Mr. John Gordon Crawford. It was not quite the same thing as a speech to

[2] *Life of Sir William Harcourt*, vol. ii, p. 269.

Scotsmen in Scotland, but it was a forecast of these two great efforts. After saying, amid applause, that too much had been made of the painful character of part of Burns's life, he concluded:

"It was not much for him to die so young: he died in noble company, for he died at the age which took away Raphael and Byron—the age which Lord Beaconsfield has called the fatal age of 37. After all, in life there is but a very limited stock of life's breath; some draw it in deep sighs and make an end; some draw it in quick draughts and have done with it; and some draw it placidly through four-score quiet years; but genius as a rule makes quick work with it. It crowds a lifetime into a few brief years, and then passes away, as if glad to be delivered of its message to the world, and glad to be delivered from an uncongenial sphere. Byron and Burns together hardly more than exceeded those three-score years and ten which are said to fulfil the life of man; but none will deny that they had lived their full life—that they had done the full work which was appointed them to do, and we have no right to repine in view of so much achievement if to the mere mortal eye they do not seem to live their full tale of years. They had exhausted human fame and human happiness, and it was time for them to be gone."

Now, on the afternoon of that July day in 1896, Rosebery addressed the burgesses of Dumfries, "surrounded by the choicest and the most sacred haunts of the poet." It was, indeed, he told them, a wider demonstration than "Scotsmen honouring the greatest of Scotsmen," for representatives had come from all quarters of the globe to pay tribute to Robert Burns. The speech as a whole is in a minor key. Burns died at Dumfries, and his last days there were spent in poverty and in deep depression. "There is nothing much more melancholy in all biography," reflected Rosebery; and it would have been happy for him to have died earlier. But Burns himself had foretold that a hundred years after his death he would be more respected than he was "at present"; and that prophecy was being incomparably fulfilled. The world-wide celebration of his birthday; the pilgrimages to his different resorts; the erection of statues, "a hardy annual"; the countless editions of his works:

"Whatever Burns may have contemplated in his prediction, whatever dream he may have fondled in the wildest moments of elation, must have fallen utterly short of the reality. And it is all spontaneous. There is no puff, no advertisement, no manipulation. . . . His true life began with his death; with the body passed all that was gross and impure; the clear spirit stood revealed, and soared at once to its accepted place among the fixed stars, in the firmament of the rare immortals."

The same evening found Rosebery at Glasgow, holding a great audience in St. Andrew's Hall. This second address is the more finished of the two, perhaps giving clearer evidence of the *limæ labor* than any that he delivered, and in sheer eloquence touching his highest level. It covers, too, a wider field than the Dumfries speech, but also called up the spirit of the man rather than that of the poet, though devoting a few pregnant sentences to his art. Shakespeare and Burns, he maintained, are the two great natural forces in British literature whose power seems sheer inspiration and nothing else; if the speaker had to prove his words by quoting the poetry of Burns he would never cease, so its incomparable excellence must be taken for granted. "But I must ask you to remember that the poetry is only a fragment of Burns." Contemporary evidence was unanimous on his amazing personal charm and the magnetism of his conversation. His prose was as surprising as his poetry. Then there was his supreme quality of universal sympathy from which "every wayfarer in the journey of life may pluck strength and courage as he passes." After touching on the misunderstood, because idealistic, part which Burns took in the political movements of his day, Rosebery boldly faced the charges based on the poet's wild love affairs and his addiction to drink. He did not greatly enforce the defence, a critic might suggest, by recalling the amours of one or two well-known historical figures; or by reminding us that Shakespeare and Ben Jonson haunted the Mermaid Tavern, and that Goethe at Weimar drank bottles of Moselle. But he reached the conclusion of the whole matter in a passage of noble rhetoric, which I cannot forbear quoting in full:

"I should like to go a step further and affirm that we have something to be grateful for even in the weaknesses of men like Burns. Mankind is helped in its progress almost as much by the study of imperfection as by the contemplation of perfection. Had we nothing before us in our futile and halting lives but saints and the ideal, we might well fail altogether. We grope blindly along the catacombs of the world, we climb the dark ladder of life, we feel our way to futurity, but we can scarcely see an inch around or before us. We stumble and falter and fall, our hands and knees are bruised and sore, and we look up for light and guidance. Could we see nothing but distant unapproachable impeccability, we might well sink prostrate in the hopelessness of emulation and the weariness of despair. Is it not then, when all seems blank and lightless and lifeless, when strength and courage flag, and when perfection seems as remote as a star, is it not then that imperfection helps us? When we see that the greatest and choicest images of God have had their weaknesses like ours, their temptations, their hours of darkness, their bloody sweat, are we not encouraged by their lapses and catastrophes to find energy for one more effort, one more struggle? Where they failed we feel it a less dishonour to fail; their errors and sorrows make, as it were, an easier ascent from infinite imperfection to infinite perfection.

"Man, after all, is not ripened by virtue alone. Were it so, this world were a paradise of angels. No! like the growth of the earth, he is the fruit of all the seasons; the accident of a thousand accidents, a living mystery, moving through the seen to the unseen. He is sown in dishonour; he is matured under all the varieties of heat and cold; in mist and wrath, in snow and vapours, in the melancholy of autumn, in the torpor of winter, as well as in the rapture and fragrance of summer, or the balmy affluence of the spring—its breath, its sunshine, its dew. And at the end he is reaped—the product, not of one climate, but of all; not of good alone, but of evil; not of joy alone, but of sorrow—perhaps mellowed and ripened, perhaps stricken and withered and sour. How, then, shall we judge anyone? How, at any rate, shall we judge a giant, great in gifts and great in temptation, great in strength and great in weakness? Let us glory in his strength and be comforted in his weakness. And when we thank heaven for the inestimable gift of Burns, we do not need to remember wherein he was imperfect, we cannot bring ourselves to regret that he was made of the same clay as ourselves."

Thirteen years later (September 15th, 1909) Rosebery journeyed to Lichfield for the celebration of the bicentenary of Dr. Johnson's birth. Most of us think of Johnson, as we do of Lamb and Dickens, as a supreme embodiment of the spirit of London; and here Rosebery, a pioneer of London government, could feel completely at home. But Johnson also implies Boswell, the "raw, uncouth young Scot"; and a most acute and sympathetic analysis of his compatriot's character and of his immortal work occupies a full two-fifths of Rosebery's address. It must be remembered, too, that of all the centuries the eighteenth was that which appealed the most to Rosebery's tastes and sympathies, so that he was well equipped for this task. It might be thought that of Johnson himself all has been said that can be said, but I venture to think that no critic, not Macaulay or another, has drawn a miniature portrait of the great moralist and humorist so just in outline, so mellow in tint as this. He pictures the tremendous intellectual supremacy of Johnson, his all-embracing humanity and generosity. "He was John Bull himself"— rough in manners, insular, prepared to counter a lampoon with an oaken cudgel. "He exalted the character, of which he may be regarded as the sublime type, but he embodied the spirit." Most of all was he the master conversationalist, having read everything, able to express himself on any subject in a singular vigour of phrase, intolerant of affectation, epigrammatic, paradoxical, sometimes overwhelming. Again Rosebery concludes on a note of high seriousness. Johnson was "the great Christian soul"; his extreme conscientiousness made him fear death more than most, though when the summons came he met it with serene composure.

"Men like this are the stay of religion in their time, and for those who come after. Laymen who hold high and pure the standard of their faith do more for Christianity, it may be averred, than a multitude of priests. To say this is not to disparage the clergy; rather the reverse, for it implies that their course is regular and habitual. But their championship is felt to be the natural result of their profession and their vows, while the conspicuous layman, who is also a conspicuous Christian, has all the honours of a volunteer. No one, I think, can doubt that Samuel Johnson and William Ewart Gladstone were priceless champions of their faith, and that their places will not easily be filled. . . .

"We leave him more reluctantly than any of the dead, for he is the only one with whom we can hold converse; and so it is with the conviction that it will not be for long, as life is insipid without him. Therefore we do not say good-bye. Rather let us think that we have only paid one more pilgrimage to his shrine; for though his dust rests with a whole Sahara of various kinds in Westminster Abbey, his memory, which lives throughout the Anglo-Saxon world, is especially green in Fleet Street and in Lichfield. We salute once more with reverence to-day the memory of that brave, manly, tender soul, and pass on with the hope that from his abundant store we may draw some measure of faith and courage to sustain our own lives."

Rosebery's nearest approach to a definite literary appreciation was made at the opening of the exhibition of Thackeray relics at the Charterhouse (June 30th, 1911). After a rapid survey of the novelist's life he discounted, no doubt unconsciously, his own treatment of Burns and of Johnson, with the words: "In the life of a man of letters his work is the one notable thing, and there is rarely much else to record." But he placed himself outside the ranks of professed critics:

"A real critic picks the plums with a knife and eats them on the blade. He has rules and a science of his own. He knows the whole business, and perhaps thinks that he could do it better. But the ordinary reader has no such pretension. He comes at last, if not at first, to be guided by the simple fact that he likes what he likes, and dislikes what he dislikes. He does not always know why; he is only conscious of pleasure or the reverse. He knows that he takes one book down a second time or a third, and leaves another to the dust.

"And so on that humble but natural footing I disclaim all pretension to discriminate except by an individual palate."

Since this particular palate is the subject of record, it must be noted that in the course of his address Rosebery illustrates his preferences and his points of criticism by touching on the works of Defoe, Fielding, Richardson, Goldsmith, "the divine Miss Austen," Dickens, Bulwer Lytton, Mrs. Gaskell, Disraeli, and Charlotte Brontë.

His uncle Lord Stanhope had observed: "Novels are read by women, even by those who read nothing else; and novels are read by men, even by those who read everything else."[3] Rosebery was not a voracious novel-reader in the sense that some statesmen have been who found in their favourite relaxation in sensational fiction of light calibre, but he had been brought up among good books of every sort, and had always been familiar with every author in the above list. He was also a devoted admirer of Anthony Trollope's art, and it is to be regretted that he did not leave any written appreciation of the Barchester novels or of the political series which opened with *Phineas Finn*. His survey of Disraeli's writings would surely have been both wide and intimate.

The speech on Robert Louis Stevenson was a much briefer affair, less than half the length of that on Thackeray. It was delivered at Edinburgh (December 10th, 1896) at a meeting called to consider the question of a Scottish memorial to the romantic figure which had passed at Samoa two years before. Rosebery had inquired in the Press whether any such tribute was contemplated, and was therefore called on to preside. It may seem strange that he had never seen Stevenson, for he seldom missed the cream of Edinburgh culture; but comparatively little of Stevenson's Bohemian youth was spent in Edinburgh; and in any case he never would have guessed how little Rosebery thought of the starched conventions of polite life in choosing his acquaintances. In later years, after some of the famous books had thrilled the world, their author passed most of

[3] *Reign of Queen Anne* (end of 1870), p. 565.

his time abroad: and after his father's death in 1887 he bade adieu to Scotland. A year later he settled in the South Seas.

It is perhaps stranger that Stevenson's father should not have made one of the Dalmeny circle of guests. In his speech Rosebery again disdains any thought of reviewing the works, but "as an outside reader" calls attention to two or three points. First an examination of the style—"something suggestive, something musical, something pregnant"—of the exquisite spirit of irony; and of the dramatic power of realistic imagination. Of these last three examples, the duel-scene of the *Master of Ballantrae*, the Italian hat of the *Pavilion on the Links*, and the "two walking-sticks that I think those who have read *Treasure Island* will never forget." It was a brilliant little address, but so cursory that Stevenson the essayist and Stevenson the verse-writer are not even mentioned. It was evidently the vivid Stevenson, shining in the flashing colour of his stories, that he wanted his fellow citizens to commemorate.

CHAPTER XVII

Randolph Churchill—Political Attacks—Sleeplessness—The Liberal Defeat—Dissociation from Harcourt— Resignation of Leadership

STILL in deep snow, Rosebery was summoned to Osborne. It was a sorrowful moment, for Sir Henry Ponsonby, the mainstay of the house, was struck down with paralysis the same day, and the Queen was deeply concerned. Rosebery's audience was not difficult, and at dinner he was placed next the Queen:

"She told me positively what I have often discussed. I was telling her that I had got the foreign diplomatists to agree to my addressing them as 'Sir,' instead of 'Monsieur le Ministre,' by telling them that we so addressed our princes and kings. 'Not the King, Lord Rosebery,' said the Queen; 'the King of England is always addressed as Sire,' and then after a pause, 'Yes, I remember it well in my young days.'"

At another audience, a month later:

"She said among other things that she thought there were too many bishops in the House of Lords. It turned out that this was because of the Deceased Wife's Sister."

Throughout the year the reconstruction of 38 Berkeley Square would have left Rosebery houseless, but for the accident of office. He was thus able to join the broken line of Prime Ministers who found a home in 10 Downing Street, and lunched there for the first time late in January. His Parliamentary Dinner was given there on February 4th. But he usually did his work in the delightful room at the Privy Council Office which is allotted to the Lord President. When Downing Street was no longer his he wrote to his mother from Dalmeny (July 11th):

"It is rapture to feel that one has no pied-à-terre in London, and so a valid excuse for remaining in the country. Were it not for my neighbours I should delay my builders."

[401]

The leaves of life kept falling. George Wyndham, the Lecon-fields' eldest son, the heir to many hopes, died in the middle of January, and Rosebery spent much time with the bereaved parents. Before the month ended, Randolph Churchill's troubled life closed. The ship that had never sought to sail on calm seas was "moored at last on the stormless shore." Few deaths could affect Rosebery more. They had been close friends at Oxford, Randolph slightly the younger of the pair, and intimacy had been continuous. The differ-ence in political outlook was sufficient to be stimulating, not of the quality that vexes or alienates.

There was nothing to disturb or distract their friendship during thirty years. The two had many of the same tastes and, up to a point, a similar outlook on life, particularly public life. Each had tensely strung nerves; each had his serious side, and his definite political convictions: each had a bubbling sense of humour. The equally obvious divergences of the two characters were not of the sort that create friction. Randolph Churchill was the origin or the victim of many disputes, but no cloud ever rose between him and Rosebery. This early letter of thanks illustrates the old-fashioned formality which adorned one facet of Randolph's complex attitude to the world:

March, 1874.

"Suffer for a moment the cynical feelings, which at times I know you are fond of giving way to, to subside, and believe that I do sin-cerely thank you for a pledge of a friendship which is as highly to be appreciated and valued, as it is I think rarely hastily bestowed, and allow me to say that the refined good taste for which you are not un-justly celebrated is easily to be discerned in the pretty old bowl which you have so kindly sent me."

Letters and notes passed continually during the following years, generally in a light vein like the following:

FOREIGN OFFICE, *June 30th*, 1886.

"MY DEAR RANDOLPH,

"Never in the annals of civilised warfare has so inhuman an outrage been perpetrated as you committed last night.

"I do not complain of your speaking of my 'enormous and unlimited wealth' though as a matter of fact it is not enormous, and I have never had any difficulty in finding its limit. But what is monstrous is this, that in consequence of what you said thousands of mendicant pens are being sharpened. The parson's widow, the bedridden Scot born at Dalmeny, the author who has long watched my career, the industrious

[402]

grocer who has been ruined by backing my horses, the poet who has composed a sonnet to the G.O.M., the family that wishes to emigrate—all these, and a myriad others are preparing for action. Not to speak of the hospital that wants a wing, the roofless church, the club of hearty Liberals in an impoverished district, the football club that wants a patron, the village band that wants instruments, all of which are preparing for the warpath. May heaven forgive you, for I cannot.

"Yrs. sincly,

AR."

2 CONNAUGHT PLACE, July 1st, 1886.

"DEAR ROSEBERY,

"Your letter is most affecting, but what can I do? You will support that old monster, and therefore you must be fleeced and fined in this world. And in the future world, well ——! ! !

"I am off to-morrow to Norway, post only twice a week, telegraph station 100 miles off. So I shall be well out of the ways of news of these damned elections. Don't punish me by repeating this bit of news, as I have concealed it from my colleagues.

"Yours ever,

"RANDOLPH S. C."

In 1887 the Roseberys were in Rome, and heard that Randolph Churchill and Harry Tyrwhitt had just arrived. The four dined together, and Rosebery made a short memorandum of some of the talk. Churchill spoke of himself with great frankness; but I can only note here such parts of the conversation as affected Rosebery. One or two of them are touched on in Rosebery's memoir of his friend.

" 'Do you know, Lady Rosebery, Rosebery prevented me from becoming a Liberal? We had a long talk when Salisbury was coming in in 1885, and I agreed to call on him the next day at 1. I called, but he was out, or I should have been a Liberal.'

" 'To begin with,' I replied, 'I was in at the right time, but you were late. You were detained too long in Portland Place (Goschen). In the next place you never had any idea of becoming a Liberal. You only wanted to gain your point with Salisbury, and when you gained that there was no question of your becoming a Liberal. You only talked about it in case you failed with Salisbury. I have never mentioned that conversation to a soul.'

" 'Oh, I have, often, once to Salisbury, I think. But I thought of it seriously then, and it is impossible now.' "

This, of course, was all banter, and the talk passed on to the circumstances of Randolph Churchill's resignation, depicted by him

[403]

in sparkling colours of indignation, contempt, and humour. He concluded his tirade with:

"There is only one place, that is Prime Minister. I like to be boss. I like to hold the reins. I told him I thought it an odious place, a sort of dunghill. Moreover a P.M. in the House of Lords was nobody. 'Perhaps that is so on the Liberal side, but not with us. Moreover if the P.M. resigns all his colleagues must go with him, but if anyone else goes (naïvely alluding to himself) he has to go alone. Then whatever you do, the P.M. gets the credit of it.'

"I said it was more a Churchill Government than a Salisbury Government, and that while he was making speeches and Dartford[1] programmes all over the country, Salisbury was playing a silent and secondary part.

"'Oh, as to the Dartford speech. Salisbury came to my room in the House of Commons: I told him the whole of what I was going to say and he approved it all.'"

On a later occasion Churchill said:

"'I would not live the last fourteen years over again for a million a year. I have been successful enough, but I would not.'
"'But you have worked very hard.'
"'No, thank God, I never have. You have. You worked hard at Oxford.'
"'I wish I had. But you used to read Gibbon there.'
"'Yes, bye the bye, so I did. After your success as Foreign Minister you should never enter the Cabinet again except as Prime Minister.'
"'But I would sooner be a Lord in Waiting.'
"He told me that I had caused the Bulgarian mess by agreeing to the term of five years.[2] I explained to him how that matter stood; but was interested to hear that his Cabinet had adopted the view the Queen took in October."

A final note of Churchill's conversation:

"'If there is one thing I hate and detest it is political intrigue.'
"I only replied by a solemn and deliberate wink."

The Roseberys were soon back in England and Rosebery wrote:

THE DURDANS, EPSOM, *April 7th*, 1887.
"MY DEAR RANDOLPH,
"You will be glad to learn that I returned in good health yesterday, unimpaired by reading through a speech of 1 hour 50 minutes delivered at Paddington.

[1] The Dartford speech was a bold exposition of Tory democracy.
[2] See p. 217.

[404]

"You will be even more glad to hear that I have brought with me three cigarette holders for you. I hope they are the right bore and shape. If so, I hope you will accept them as a slight memorial of an old friendship, not to be blown away like cigarette smoke.

"Yours sincerely,

AR"

After the appearance of Rosebery's *Pitt*, Randolph Churchill wrote to him a long and striking letter of praise and appreciation. He was particularly charmed by "the subtle delicate irony which constantly flavours the narrative," comparing it only to the irony of Motley and of Edmond About. Rosebery replied gratefully from Naples on January 20th, 1892:

"MY DEAR RANDOLPH,

"I was greatly pleased for a variety of reasons, just as I left England, to receive your letter. First and foremost that you had passed safely through all your perils and fatigues. Secondly that you liked my little book. And thirdly (for a genuine Gladstonian must have three heads) with the piquant interest of the letter itself.

"As to what you say of irony, I delight in About's. I do not know enough of Motley to say anything except that I think his letters the best since Horace Walpole's. But About is the modern French writer whom I think I like the best. All French irony is, I suppose, the offspring of Voltaire and some of his writings, such as Candide, are surely insurpassable in that respect. Heine's irony (which I know only in French) is perhaps more taking as it is mixed up with a rich vein of poetry.

"In English the irony of Gibbon always seems to me most admirable; partly, because I seem to see the smug pig face of the author winking at me through the elaborate persiflage of some of his most pompous sentences. Then there are things in Thackeray—such as the Rose and the Ring—which are surely full of sparkling irony, though not perhaps so polished and sardonic as Gibbon's. I have probably forgotten the best, though these occur to me at once. Brett's article in the *Nineteenth Century* of this month carries perhaps the use of the weapon too far.

"What you say about statesmen is, I think, true. It seems impossible for a man like Pitt or even Peel (who was modelled on Pitt) to exist now in their original forms. They would of course have adapted themselves to an altered state of things, but in doing so they would probably have lost some of their power and their charm. A statesman in 1892 must I suppose have a dash of the demagogue. He has to deal with three new conditions at least:

"A democratic constituency.

[405]

"A powerful and penetrating press.

"A web of caucus.

"It is very interesting to calculate who of the various Prime Ministers of the century would best have adapted themselves to these new conditions. Perhaps Palmerston in his prime, or Disraeli. But for all that, I am not quite convinced of the correctness of the general belief that the best and most durable ministry in our democracy will resemble a well-oiled weathercock. Many ministries however will be launched and submerged before we ascertain the exact nature of our present constitution.

"Forgive this long letter on this majestic paper—adopted for purposes of economy, as a long letter takes up about six sheets of my ordinary notepaper. But it is your letter that has made mine long.

"I dashed down here last week for a little sunshine and sleep. In my three days here I have had two of summer and one thunderstorm, so my average is good. I shall soon however have to return, when I shall hope to see you—I suppose with a lateways sort of appearance.

"Yours,

AR"

Soon afterwards Randolph was consulting Rosebery on a proposal that he should enter the London County Council, which, needless to say, came to nothing. Before the defeat of the second Home Rule measure, Rosebery listened to his friend sitting up till 1.30, "discoursing of a ministry of which Hartington was to be the head, Arthur Balfour Chancellor of the Exchequer, he India, and I F.O."

But apart from these day-dreams there was a fresh link in Randolph Churchill's accession to the Turf. His health was beginning to break down, but this new excitement seemed to add zest to his political imaginings. He wrote a long letter from Gastein on September 2nd, 1893:

"As an old and attached friend, and to a very great extent as one who finds himself in perfect agreement with you in almost every question of foreign and domestic policy——"

The Home Rule Bill had scraped through the House of Commons. Randolph Churchill searchingly compared it with the measure of 1886, greatly to its disadvantage, and urged Rosebery to use his great political power in the country by "a happy combination of party loyalty, wise independent counsel and a reasonable consideration of the arguments and views of those who dread Repeal." He was prompted, he said in conclusion, by—

"The dream which often comes upon me, that some day not very remote I may have the gratification of finding myself in the same party and holding the same opinion as you will hold. I do not even draw the line against speculations as to being, if the fates are kind, even your colleague. I send this to you with some trepidation."

Rosebery replied:

BALMORAL, *September 25th*, 1893.

"MY DEAR RANDOLPH,

"This can only be a note of apology, and thanks for your extraordinarily kind and interesting letter. I was too busy when it came to acknowledge it.

"You are quite wrong in what you say of my position—I have no position—none to speak of at all. All that I have to my credit is that people think I may be a better Foreign Minister than some other members of the present Government. But this is all—it is neutral and negative; and this I can judge and know better than you or anybody.

"As to this policy I cannot speak with perfect freedom or frankness. But my speech is supposed at least not to have erred on the side of any want of candour, and it may sufficiently answer what you have advanced.

"When you come back we will talk all this over, but I am no letter writer. Only let me say once for all how much I was taken, and indeed touched, by your letter."

When Randolph Churchill started on his last tragic voyage, Rosebery went down to Southampton for a good-bye which might easily have been the last. A letter came from Japan, as Rosebery narrates, containing great plans for travel which never could be realised. The first page of it contained lamentations over the autumn failure of *Ladas* with unsparing censure of the great master of training horses, Matthew Dawson, for having run the horse too often. He was just as ready to scarify a leading trainer as a leading Cabinet Minister. The handwriting is sadly tremulous, and there is something pathetic in the brave invalid's concern for his friend's racing stable. The end was nearing. He came home, and died in January 1895.[3]

Years passed, and Lord Randolph's son wrote his *Life* in a fashion which astonished and delighted the world. As Rosebery said of the book: "It is one to be marked among the first dozen, perhaps the first half-dozen, biographies in our language."

Rosebery felt that there remained room for something quite different—a shorter study by a contemporary friend. Some brief

[3] I am greatly indebted to the Duke of Marlborough for permission to examine Lord Randolph's correspondence preserved in the Blenheim archives.

records of this kind, for which the *Agricola* remains the shapely model, have a place in every library. They differ in origin and in aim; Cavendish's *Wolsey* is the tribute of a faithful follower: the two best-known examples from the nineteenth century, Carlyle's *Sterling* and Disraeli's *Lord George Bentinck*, owe more to the fame of the artists than to that of the sitters. Rosebery's *Randolph Churchill* is a portrait painted by a devoted friend on a level of absolute social and political equality. He never did anything better, or with a surer touch. The book is such easy reading, so fresh, and so stimulating, that it would be absurd to set down here any analysis of its contents or any portrayal of its manner and style.

In November of the previous year a conference was held in Downing Street on the co-ordination of the fighting services. Spencer from the Admiralty, Campbell-Bannerman from the War Office, and Rosebery himself introduced what he afterwards considered to have been the germ of the Committee of Imperial Defence.

It met again this year, with the addition of the Colonial Secretary, Ripon, under the name of the "Defence Committee."

A vast meeting under the auspices of the National Liberal Federation was held on January 18th, the day on which he would have wished to stand by his sister at her son's burial.

"Ten thousand people in a specially erected hall. My voice very bad. The singing simply magnificent. I never heard anything so fine."

Two-thirds of a long speech were given to the subject of Welsh Disestablishment, but he opened by thanks to his colleagues:

"Among those who have all done much strenuous and admirable work we must all enthusiastically give the first place to the Chancellor of the Exchequer."

He went on to press the campaign against the House of Lords, and to compare the difficulties of the Government with those of the Opposition. It would be tedious, now that the controversy has closed, to recapitulate his arguments, closely reasoned and illuminated by historical analogies, on the Establishment in Wales. He cited with great effect Bishop Thirlwall's speech on the Irish Church Bill when repudiating the charge of sacrilege brought against its authors.

On the following morning he talked to the Liberal Agents and Officers of the Federation. The chairman was "Tom Ellis," the Chief Liberal Whip, a Welshman of sterling quality and the utmost personal charm. His name will appear later in these pages, before the early death which robbed the Liberal party of one of its most sympathetic figures.

In the Debate on the Address (February 5th), Lord Salisbury spoke with a greater bitterness than is usual on that occasion, especially on the subject of the Reform of the House of Lords. Rosebery's reply was adequate, but rather less animated than usual. He dwelt once more, with genuine indignation, on the Conservative Leader's neglect of any measure which would make of the House of Lords a reasonable Second Chamber.

Among the interesting events of the spring were a series of deputations to the Prime Minister on the subject of London University. A fierce struggle was being waged between those who valued the University as a purely examining body, and those who desired to make it the great centre of teaching which it has since become. There are no such gladiators as educational theorists, and Rosebery had to twit one speaker with intending to enforce his views by every means short of barricades in the streets. His conclusion was that without lowering the examination standard—this being the dread of the one party—it would be possible to frame a scheme for a single University on the model of all others in the United Kingdom —with one exception in Ireland of a different character.

Physically, Rosebery was losing ground. Facing the Opposition in the House, with his depleted party, was not agreeable, but it was a natural incident of the situation. What was not natural was the declared hostility of his colleague, the Leader in the Commons, and the consequent disruption of the party. Labouchere's attacks in *Truth* were incessant. Few of the readers of that organ can have recognised a familiar Latin tag; but Labouchere quoted in the original the most final of historical condemnations, that of the Emperor Galba, who, by universal consent, would have been fitted for the highest place—if only he had never occupied it.

Travellers from the South Seas tell how the great unarmed whale, caught unawares in shallow waters, becomes the helpless victim of its savage smaller congener, *Orca Gladiator*, backed by a ravenous crowd of thresher sharks. Such a comparison might have risen to the mind when Disraeli was assailing Sir Robert Peel, or when Randolph Churchill was harrying the sedater leaders of his own front bench. But to apply it to Rosebery would have seemed absurd. He was a master of sarcasm no less than of grave argument; his private character was irreproachable; there was nothing in his political past to invite either ridicule or solemn censure. If a marine parallel were desired, he could have been likened to the formidable sperm whale, which no inhabitant of the ocean dare attack. But circumstances made him vulnerable. His home was lonely, for though his children were a solace, they were too young to be a support; he had the full affection, but could not have the companionship of his mother and sisters; nor could anybody turn the edge of trouble as his wife, with her calm and often humorous outlook, would often have done. Thus there was no screen between his sensitiveness and the east wind of Radical criticism.

He was in a poor state, then, to resist an attack of illness. This befell after a Royal dinner-party, at which at least one illustrious personage was suffering from influenza. Two days later, after he had presided at a Cabinet and given a large Parliamentary Dinner, the malady declared itself, and he was in bed for the best part of three weeks, it being a fortnight before he could look at a letter. On March 11th he was able to go to Windsor under the care of Sir George Murray, his always devoted private secretary.

"The Queen was very kind, insisted on my sitting down. I kissed her hand on entering and leaving. Nearly toppled over from weakness on rising the second time from my knees.

"She agreed with me in thinking Davidson of Rochester, with health, destined to Canterbury."

But recovery was tardy, and the curse of sleeplessness potent. More than a week later Murray wrote to Sir Arthur Bigge[4] that he could give only a poor account of the patient. He had not had a good night since he had been at Epsom. Four hours' sleep the most he ever got, and it was often not more than two or three. His appetite, his spirits, and his temper were all pretty good, but if the sleeplessness lasted he must break down. The doctor thought it the most obstinate and puzzling case he had ever come across. He put it down to long-continued derangement of the digestive organs.

The Queen suggested a sea voyage, but this could not be attempted at once. Towards the end of the month there was a shade of improvement in the matter of sleep; a Cabinet was held at 38 Berkeley Square, and John Morley paid a visit to the Durdans.

"John Morley said he had pointed out to Campbell-Bannerman what great chances he had if Harcourt disappeared. 'You might be Leader

[4] (1849-1931.) Assistant Private Secretary to the Queen, Private Secretary to King George V when Prince of Wales 1901-10, and to His Majesty from 1910. G.C.B., etc., etc. *Cr.* Lord Stamfordham 1911.

of the House of Commons, a solution I rather think the Prime Minister would prefer,'—looking hard at me. I said nothing."

March 15th.—"I took the opportunity of telling J. M. that I always thought the great mistake I had made was in not insisting on Harcourt's trying his hand at forming a Government before I tried mine, and that I had given up my view under pressure from him (J. M.)."

A day or two later:

"Campbell-Bannerman came down for the day. Delightful drive with him to Boxhill."

Other colleagues came down for an hour or two, and John Burns paid a visit, but there was now and then "an evil day after a sleepless night."

The Durdans remained his headquarters through April. A visit to Newmarket to see his colt *Sir Visto* run third for the Two Thousand was followed by a Cabinet the next day.

"At 11.30 received a note from W. V. H. to say he could not attend as he had to put the finishing touches on the Budget. However at 12.30 he bounced in, had a row about Nicaragua,[5] and bounced off again, but I, John Morley, and Acland made him come back."

He was picking up strength, and at his next audience, at Buckingham Palace, declined the favour of being seated. Nobody but a cripple must sit in the Queen's presence. But at a reception at the National Liberal Club, which most of the Cabinet, including Harcourt, attended, he lost the thread of his argument, "stuck in a sentence," but was able to conclude a firmly phrased speech with an appeal not to forget the permanent and abiding obstacle of the House of Lords. On May 13th he started with Lord Spencer for a cruise on the Admiralty yacht *Enchantress* to Plymouth, Falmouth, Scilly and its flowers, Pembroke Dock, and the wooded banks of the Dart.

Uganda and the Nile valley remained bones of contention. Rosebery wrote to Harcourt (April 5th) a mildly worded letter, pointing out that consideration by a committee of experts of the Uganda Railway pledged the Government to nothing. It was quite possible that investigation might prove the financial sacrifice too great. But Harcourt, as his biographer has stated, had the poorest opinion of the future of Uganda,[6] and he disliked even more the apparent con-

[5] The trouble over Nicaragua is described above, p. 368.
[6] *Life of Sir William Harcourt,* vol. ii, p. 322.

nection of the Nyanza area with a British claim to control the whole Nile valley. In the House of Commons on March 28th there was an important debate on the alleged French encroachments on the Niger and towards the Nile head-waters. The Conservative speakers, especially Mr. J. W. Lowther,[7] were not immoderate. Sir Edward Grey, in reply, categorically placed the entire Nile valley within the British and Egyptian spheres of influence, adding that a French advance under secret instructions into a territory in which our claims were known would be "an unfriendly act." In the technical language of diplomacy the phrase is of the strongest, and Harcourt, not without reason, complained afterwards that its use had not been sanctioned by him. Grey proceeded to say that everything would be done to maintain good relations with France, if the French Government and public would co-operate with this object.

But this was not the only point of dispute with France. A Commission had been appointed to delimit the frontiers of Siam and Burmah, the purpose being to secure a substantial buffer between British and French territory. This was a matter of much concern to Rosebery. To him the risk was far greater than any that could threaten the North-West Frontier, and later he wrote to Sir Donald Stewart, the Commander-in-Chief in India, that it was a mad policy to scatter our resources by lodging an army on the Chitral route while we have a frontier with France, a great military power at least as unscrupulous and aggressive as Russia is represented to be. The Indian Government, he thought, realised only one frontier question.

He addressed the Viceroy, Lord Elgin, in similar terms, objecting strongly to the occupation of Chitral so long as France was menacing India in strict alliance with Russia, for Russia would in time be tempted to fortify her frontier.

To return to the debate at the end of March, Rosebery wrote to the Queen on March 29th:

"We are, it is to be feared, approaching a situation of some gravity with regard to France, who, both in Siam and Africa, is behaving with a gross want of good faith and even of delicacy. Lord Rosebery would beg Your Majesty to read the admirable statement of Sir Edward Grey on this point last night. Lord Rosebery rather apprehends that the Cabinet (which meets to-morrow) may not remain unaffected by this state of things, for, as Your Majesty is aware, it contains a small but

[7] b. 1855. Speaker of the House of Commons 1905-21. Cr. Viscount Ullswater 1921.

powerful section which advocates an attitude of unbounded deference to all foreign nations, more especially to France."

He had telegraphed that morning that the Cabinet might prove critical, though he hoped the crisis might be tided over.

The Queen, pleasantly ensconced at Cimiez, naturally felt some apprehension. She telegraphed back (March 29th):

"Your telegram is rather disquieting.

"While trusting that the Government will preserve a strong attitude against French encroachments, I hope crisis may be averted on national grounds and also that personally it would be very awkward if complications arose with a country in which I am now residing and receiving marked courtesy and attention."

The alarming Cabinet passed off satisfactorily, Rosebery wrote: "for though there was some grumbling in the usual quarters, there was no attempt to disavow Sir Edward Grey's position."

He added that the small but important section of the Cabinet which he had mentioned differed so acutely with him on questions of foreign policy that they would long ago have left the Government were they not restrained by considerations of a different character dependent on other motive forces. Ultimately, at a Cabinet on May 27th, it was agreed "after a long, windy, and irrelevant discussion" on domestic slavery, that the British East Africa Company's territory from Uganda to the sea should be placed under a Protectorate. The Uganda Railway was a more difficult job. Rosebery said that its construction touched his honour and his conscience, and after a strenuous fight he carried his point.

It is necessary to dwell for a moment on Rosebery's attitude towards France. Since those days the two countries have been united by the sacred ties of joint effort and common sacrifice; but it would be useless to deny that forty years ago there was little love lost between France and ourselves. Private friendships abounded. Rosebery himself delighted in Paris and the society of French people. His wife's French relations treated him with the intimacy of cousins. He haunted the bookshops and was a member of two select Paris clubs. But the respective Foreign Offices disliked and mistrusted each other. The Quai d'Orsay might well resent the calm assumption of some Britons that, as the first civilising agent in the world, we are entitled to the prime share of all unoccupied territories. On the other hand, we had something to complain of. The French diplomacy of that day was not candid, and sometimes not straightforward; but what mattered more was the poor calibre of some of the French colonial representatives. It is only of late years that French Governments have taken pains to establish a service of really excellent colonial administrators, comparable with any other. In the days of which we are speaking it was too often the abject or dissipated failures from other careers who drifted into responsible posts in the less attractive colonies of France. Consequently I have not attempted to conceal Rosebery's bitter judgments of French diplomatic action; but it is to be noted that he was not thereby deflected towards alliance or formal understanding with any other Power. He believed that the Concert of Europe could be made to work, and that England, an active member of that Council unhampered by any formal alliances, could take a leading part in its deliberations. His Liberal critics thought differently. Sir William Harcourt, we are told, believed that England could act as a friendly policeman of a rather disorderly mob. This was all very well, but in truth it was a more arrogant attitude to take. The mob does not always obey the policeman's mandate, and it may unite and turn upon him in force. The Concert of Europe was an imperfect instrument, but surely Rosebery's ambitions for its development came nearer to the ideal towards which the League of Nations is striving than did the vague imaginings of his opponents. Europe was not prepared to accept the preachments of an isolated peacemaker who in the past had acquired, not by peace, the choicest portions of the two hemispheres.

During the remainder of the summer session little parliamentary work fell on Rosebery's shoulders. East Africa and Uganda were still in a transitional stage, and all that happened was a short and inconclusive discussion in the House of Lords.

At the beginning of June Rosebery once more triumphed in the Derby with his colt *Sir Visto*. Strange, as he said, after waiting twenty-five years to win at all, to win twice running. Refreshed by this good fortune, though still a semi-invalid, he hired a 350-ton yacht for a cruise in the Channel, going straight to Guernsey, where he visited Victor Hugo's grave, and attended a French service, which he found quite unintelligible. Then to Herm and Alderney, where he was disappointed at seeing only one inferior cow.[8] Jersey came next, and a meeting of the States, where the Constable grace-

[8] The cows spoken of in the last century as "Alderneys" were in reality Jerseys. There is no specific breed on Alderney, and any cattle on the island would be Guernseys.

fully alluded in his speech to the Liberal Government of the Queen as having done them justice. "Indeed," Rosebery noted, "I am told they find a great difference between Liberal and Tory Governments in that respect."

Rosebery's historic sense was stimulated by the traditions of the Norman Duchy, and his romantic vein once more found expression over an island scene:

"We spent a couple of hours on Burhon Island,—a rough reef close to Alderney. I never enjoyed anything more. The blue tumultuous sea dashing among the rocks, the myriads of gulls hovering like a host of angels, the dowager puffins seated with solemn perplexity, the mass of bluebells, the inspiriting air, made this a garden of Eden for fallen man."

On June 21st the end came. Rosebery had gone to the Durdans, and while enjoying dinner and the shortest night of the year under his veranda, received the news of the Government's defeat on the Cordite vote in the House of Commons. Should the Government resign or ask for a dissolution of Parliament? At the meeting next day, Rosebery, Harcourt, Ripon, and Tweedmouth[9] were the original minority in favour of the first course. After four hours' discussion they carried their point, Rosebery journeyed to Windsor at 6.30 p.m., his resignation was accepted, and before 9 p.m. the Queen's Private Secretary had gone in search of Lord Salisbury. Rosebery stayed at Windsor on Sunday morning, a day of religious observances. At the 8.30 service in St. George's Chapel he accidentally occupied his own Garter stall; at Matins in the Mausoleum Dr. Montagu Butler preached an admirable sermon, of which Rosebery wrote to him enthusiastically; at 3 Rosebery attended Eton Chapel, and then sadly visited his old room. He returned to London and—

June 23rd.—"Harcourt came to me spontaneously before dinner: the first time since I have been P.M."
June 24th.—"Harcourt came twice! . . . I called on Mr. Gladstone, old and cold. . . . Ripon, E. Grey, Fowler and Bryce lunched with me. . . . Asquith called on me. . . . I to Willesden. . . .[10] The Gladstones, Tweedmouths, Mrs. Drew and G. Murray dined with me."

Troops of friends were at 10 Downing Street during the following days, and on June 28th Rosebery went to Windsor for his

[9] Edward Marjoribanks, Rosebery's Christ Church contemporary, M.P. 1880-94. Succeeded as 2nd Lord Tweedmouth, 1894.
[10] To visit his wife's grave.

final audience. The Queen invested him with the Order of the Thistle, a rare distinction for a Knight of the Garter, and of course peculiarly acceptable to him.

"To London,—free. . . . To Willesden again this evening before dinner."

His last months of office had been undisturbed by any difficulties at Court. In May he had to tell Sir Arthur Bigge that the fatigue of writing to the Queen in a legible hand was too much for him.

"What I suggest, then, is this. Murray's handwriting is like the Chevalier Bayard, beyond reproach. But I cannot use it in writing to the Queen. So I propose that I shall sometimes dictate to him confidential letters addressed to you and signed by me and that you shall understand that these are intended to be laid before the Queen directly. Murray's letters to you signed by him will be for your own eye."

This ingenious compromise with etiquette was approved. Throughout the year the effect of Rosebery's illness on his handwriting, both in his letters and his notebooks, is painfully apparent. The change had begun to be noticeable in the previous year, and during both years the entries in his rough diaries are rarer and briefer.

Rosebery also had to take a rather painful share in the negotiations for the Duke of Cambridge's retirement from the Commandership-in-Chief, of which the full story is told in Mr. J. A. Spender's *Life of Sir Henry Campbell-Bannerman.*

His final submission to the Sovereign, on the very day of his resignation, was a protest against the conferring of the Order of the Garter on Oriental potentates. In spite of at least two unfortunate precedents—

"To do so is in effect to lower the Garter, to efface its great traditions, and to forget the object of all ancient Orders of Chivalry."

Rosebery was aware that the Queen held this view, as had the Prince Consort with conviction, and he wondered whether a separate class of the Star of India might not be instituted, limited to Sovereigns only. He hoped that Lord Salisbury would concur, and leave a written minute similar to this.

Thus Rosebery quitted office, for the last time, at the age of forty-eight. He became the trusted personal confidant of the Queen's two illustrious successors, but he served neither in political place. Our

English Horace of the early eighteenth century, himself versed in the diplomacy of Europe, at much the same stage of life anticipated his own epitaph:

"High hopes he conceived, and he smothered great fears,
In a life parti-coloured, half pleasure, half care."

Rosebery's life was indeed parti-coloured. He cherished many high hopes. He was not tormented by fears, but he perpetually had to smother doubts, for he was the head of a greatly distracted party. For the moment he was too busy to think of the future. On June 27th, in the House of Lords, he had to clear up the strange episode of Sir Henry Campbell-Bannerman's seals, due to Lord Salisbury's characteristic carelessness in all matters not intrinsically important. At the same time furniture was removed from 10 Downing Street, and he "dressed in the caverns of Berkeley Square," still not strictly habitable. Houseless, he gave a large dinner at the Reform Club to such unofficial friends as Bishop Davidson of Rochester, Dean Farrar, Lord Acton, Sir Alfred Lyall, and Mr. Lecky; and there was a smoking party at the Eighty Club. There, by his own account, he spoke poorly, but the speech had an important bearing on the future. He gave up the Liberal Unionists, finally merged in the Tory ranks, and then insisted on the need for concentration of aims in the approaching struggle. In 1868, and in 1880, he reminded his hearers, victory had followed the emphasis laid on a single political issue. In 1892 "a mountain range of policy," with illimitable peaks in the distance, had proved inadequate. Now the crucial point was the domination of the House of Lords. God forbid that such causes as Home Rule and the liquor question should be forgotten; but with the present Upper Chamber there, these could never be carried through. His words "the annihilation of the House of Lords" aroused frantic cheers.

There was also a great Liberal gathering at the Albert Hall, "where Asquith made one of the best speeches of the kind I ever heard." He himself, in an hour's effort, compared the treatment of Ireland by England with that of the Children of Israel by Pharaoh; and he did not forget to dot the "i's" once more in assailing the Upper House.

That Chamber provided the easiest field for a Tory rebutter of these indictments. Lord Salisbury took advantage of the last sitting of the Parliament, and on familiar lines delivered a Demosthenic condemnation of the audacious orator. Rosebery pointed out that the "annihilation" was to be of "the legislative preponderance" of the House, not of the House itself.

He had come up on purpose to reply:

"Basking in my hammock after breakfast, I saw that Salisbury was going to make an attack on me at noon. So hurried up to town, and we had a regular rough and tumble, he and Argyll and I for an hour and three quarters."

The "rough and tumble" was not very happy or dignified. On the previous day, on a totally different subject, the Duke of Argyll had taken occasion to drag in Rosebery's speeches in the latter's absence, and to reprove him with customary ardour. Rosebery touched on this, and made a dignified reply to Lord Salisbury. Then the Duke of Argyll rose. He and Labouchere, at the opposite poles of character and of professed Liberalism, had the common gift of exciting Rosebery to a frenzy of annoyance. Accordingly, when the Duke delivered his portentous contribution to the debate, Rosebery intervened no less than seventeen times with corrections or interpellations. At the close he made a telling rejoinder, disposing of many of the Duke's points, and asking him whether he had never heard of the suspensory veto as a half-way house between the systems of two Chambers or one; but he guarded himself against adopting that policy as his own. The squabble was pursued for some days in a series of letters to *The Times*.

The General Election brought inevitable disaster to the Liberal party. Inevitable, probably, in any case; but made more certain by the public disunion of its leaders. Rosebery, as we have seen, placed the House of Lords Question in the forefront, and this, at any rate, would have united all sections of opinion in the country. But Morley must put Home Rule first; and Harcourt, perhaps unconsciously incapable of following Rosebery's lead on any road, assumed that local option was the first and great commandment for the Liberal party. He lost his seat at Derby, and Morley went down at Newcastle. The Unionists met the new Parliament with a majority of 152.

This time there was nothing to make Midlothian a centre of quivering interest, so while the election was raging Rosebery hired a big yacht for a month. His faithful friend James Patten-Mac-Dougall, secretary of the Scottish Liberal Association, and his best informant on Scottish affairs, had toured with him on the *Christine* in 1892, and now joined him on the *Santa Cecilia*. Arran was their first landing, then Ailsa Craig, Jura, and northward along that enchanted coast, hearing at Oban of Harcourt's disaster. Still northward, and able to read till 10 p.m. by natural light, to the gloomy pile of Cape Wrath, and the Orkneys—seeing Kirkwall, "gloomily and silently enjoying its annual holiday," Scapa Bay (unwitting of its future fame) and the undecipherable Runic inscriptions of Maes Howe—"how humbling to human fame and achievement." He overwalked, doing twenty miles in one day, with consequent loss of sleep. Back to the mainland, to Loch Laxford where "the entrance is wildness itself,—a rugged hurricane of rocks,—a petrified storm at sea." From Oban he went straight to London (July 29th), where he talked confidentially to Wemyss Reid. The latter left a note of the conversation. Rosebery recapitulated the course of events since 1890—how he had resolved to quit political life after his wife's death; how, at Gladstone's persuasion, he had made three speeches before the election of 1892; how these speeches were treated as a reason for his taking office; how, without his concurrence, Gladstone had named him to the Queen for the Foreign Office. In the pressure they put on him his succession to Mr. G. was openly talked of. When Gladstone retired, Harcourt came to see Rosebery, saying, "Of course we can't go on."

"'Can't go on,' I replied. 'Here is a man of eighty-three, whose retirement has seemed imminent for years, and we are to be told that the Ministry must break up when he goes, because none of its members would serve under anybody else! That would be as bad as it was when Pitt died. For my part, if I am asked to take office under ——— [a respected but not pre-eminent Liberal] I shall do so.' Harcourt looked astonished, and went away. Then began a series of intrigues on his behalf, carried on by his son Loulou. Of course I do not blame Loulou, he was perfectly right to try to serve his father."

Rosebery went on to describe what followed, and came to the position as it stood. He had hoped to retire at the General Election, but his party had been pulverised, so how could he? But, he added with great energy:

"No earthly power will induce me to take part in the dishonest hypocrisy of the last two year or two. Nothing will lead me again to consent to anything like a dual leadership between myself and a man whom I cannot trust . . . it may not be necessary to act during this short session, but everybody must know that the thing must come to a head."

He was dead against proclaiming any policy at this moment, and said he would only make a good-tempered general speech in the House of Lords when Parliament met. "I must endeavour to conceal my indecent joy from them."

A day or two later he told Asquith and Campbell-Bannerman of his resolve. Asquith was strong against a letter from Rosebery to Harcourt:

"On account of (1) the unpleasant position of the front bench in the House of Commons; (2) it would give me the appearance of deserting the party in misfortune."

Campbell-Bannerman went off to Marienbad, with no idea of returning for the early opening of Parliament. Rosebery could not avoid this, but he snatched another ten days yachting to Skye and Eriskay, "a little rocky colony of Roman Catholics."

"We landed exactly 150 years, to a week, after Prince Charles Edward."

The party visited some other islets to Stornoway, and thence to the Ross-shire coast.

On returning to Dalmeny (August 12th) he replied to Lord Spencer, who had written forwarding Harcourt's suggestion for a meeting at Spencer House. Rosebery formally dissociated himself from Harcourt, and sent the latter a copy with a covering note. Harcourt's answer and Lord Spencer's descriptive memorandum are given in full in the *Life of Sir William Harcourt*.[11]

The simple truth was that the two men differed fundamentally on the obligations of personal and party loyalty. Harcourt had brought himself to serve under his younger colleague, and had served brilliantly. But he, and still more his son, made no pretence that the service was cheerful; and once his own great measure was through, he cared nothing for the Government, differing, as he did, from its chief on most questions of foreign policy. When the election came, he struck out on a course of his own. On the other hand, he was a convinced party man, and he believed that the interests of the Liberal party would be best served by maintaining a pretence of agreement in Opposition. How far this was feasible he does not seem to have considered.

Rosebery, on the other hand, was not a "good" party man of the type that refuses to see a beam in the eye that gazes from the same

---

[11] Vol. ii, pp. 874-7.

bench in Parliament. Perhaps he was too well able to observe a mote in it. So he scouted what he considered the hypocrisy of a patched-up unanimity when the necessity for common action had vanished. The paramount rule of absolute loyalty between members of a Government had been altogether outraged, he felt. For, though a poor partisan, he was staunch to any combination of which he was a declared unit. So the breach between him and Harcourt was never closed.

The "good-tempered" speech on the Address in reply to what Rosebery called the jejune Speech from the Throne first touched on external affairs. The late Government had decided that the occupation of Chitral would not add to the security of the Indian Empire. What was wanted for that Empire was concentration, financial and military. Was the army there to be increased? Then there was the French advance on the Mekong to enforce the need of concentration. As to the General Election, he reminded the Government that the majority of 152 was really a majority of but 14, on the proportion of votes. That was not discouraging to Liberals. Coming to Ireland, he had never thought of withdrawing his phrase about the "predominant partner," but he felt that conviction would be brought to the heart and mind of that partner, for, in Macaulay's phrase, the Union remains a union only in name. Lord Salisbury's reply was largely devoted to a vindication of the House of Lords, and, on Ireland, he merely had observed in Rosebery's speech a not indistinct indication that he projected shaking off the incumbrance of Home Rule.

Rosebery started for Scotland, and spent much of the autumn at Dalmeny, with a visit to Dunrobin, and one to Doncaster, where *Sir Visto*, after a terrible alarm of lameness from his having been cast in his box, won the St. Leger in good style. A sign of coming revolution was: "This year for the first time pot hats were generally worn,—even by the Duke of Cambridge."

These were interludes, for the Liberal camp was still agitated by the leaders' dissensions. In October Wemyss Reid was at Dalmeny, and set his impressions on paper at full length, mainly describing the place and the social existence, but recording some political talk, much on the lines of his earlier conversation.

A series of Liberal functions took Rosebery to Scarborough (October 17th). On one day they lasted without intermission from 12.30 p.m. to 1.30 a.m.—a full measure of Yorkshire enthusiasm. Here he opened up the policy which later was to get him into trouble with some of his friends, that of the need of educating and reorganising the Liberal party, and of avoiding long indigestible programmes. But he repeated his censure of the House of Lords, and his mistrust of the Government's Indian policy.

Soon afterwards, in London, he saw Lord Spencer, on the eve of departure for a tour in India.

"I am afraid I disappointed him by remaining quite clear and firm in my attitude. He seemed to go further than usual in saying that on a clear call of duty he might undertake the leadership."

He was at Hawarden in November (20th), finding his host very well, and ready to talk till midnight. Mrs. Gladstone was rather feeble, and on the morning of his departure Rosebery noted:

"Had a long talk with Mrs. G. in bed and Mr. G. . . . Both very affectionate."

There was nothing cheering in the political prospect, and it was a pleasanter occupation to preside at the annual meeting of the Scottish Historical Society (October 29th). Scottish history enthralled him; and, as will be seen later, it was the favourite fare of his book-collector's appetite. In his address he revelled in the prospect of reading the back volumes of the Society's issue, now that he was a free man; and he dwelt with delight on the number of small books of family and parochial history which were being poured out in Scotland as a mark of the spirit of the times.

November saw him starting for Paris, and thence he passed to Madrid. After two days he went on to Seville, always turning southward when he could. Ever attracted by the unusual, he was escorted more than once by his friendly host Mr. Johnson, the Vice-Consul, to watch the dance of gaily attired choirboys, "Seises," before the high altar. He brought back an oil painting of this strange survival of semi-paganism on holy ground. On one occasion the dance was diversified by the advent of a dog before the altar. On his return to Madrid he breakfasted with Senor Castelar off national dishes, meeting various deputies and Joaquin Ferrer, the host's secretary. For the last week of the year Rosebery returned to Dalmeny.

The New Year, as it happened, started on a warning note. In the previous autumn opinion had been stirred by tales of fresh outrages inflicted on Armenians in Turkey, and the Foreign Office had to admit their truth, with the utter deadlock in the matter of reforms. Rosebery was asked by correspondents the reason for his silence in face of these facts. He replied that he was haunted by the horrors of Asia Minor, which called for vengeance as loudly as those which moved Milton's great appeal. But the knowledge and the responsibility rested with the Government, who exercised a dictatorship before which he could only bow until they could be called to account in Parliament. That occasion came on February 11th, and Rosebery commented on "the curt and cold paragraph" of the Queen's Speech dealing with Armenia. He spoke bitterly of "the spirit of edifying humility, the spirit of a Christian Statesman," in which Lord Salisbury had bowed to the wishes of the Sultan. He himself was proud of the Opposition for having refrained from denouncing the Government in hopes that brave words would be followed by brave deeds. He recalled the promises of 1878, made at continual banquets, of good government for the Turkish provinces. Now we were told that the Treaty of Berlin contained no promise or guarantee. "By a strange irony of fortune it devolves on the noble Marquess, who partly blew that bubble then, to prick that bubble to-day . . . this is where we stand as the result of 'Peace with honour'—in an elaborate impotence, elaborately declared." He went on to describe the apathy and degradation which had taken the place of the age of crusades. It was perhaps the most scathing speech that he ever made in the House. Lord Salisbury had to admit that the Powers would not allow the use of any pressure but that of persuasion and influence, and tried to speak hopefully of methods of which he must have known the utter futility. But the force at the back of his weak-sounding plea was the knowledge that the country, however indignant, would not go to war alone. The Duke of Argyll twitted Rosebery with having kept silence about the Armenian troubles for eleven months of his Premiership, and with the marked coldness of feeling in dispatches while his Government was in power.

Throughout the summer the miseries of Armenia continued to excite sympathy and rage in Britain. Questions were frequent in both Houses. In May the Duke of Argyll, just recovering from a serious illness, made an indignant protest, and Rosebery seized the occasion to assure his untiring antagonist of the pleasure with which the House welcomed his return. Speaking at Newton Abbot soon afterwards, Rosebery denounced the Cyprus Convention as a fraud and a sham, and Lord Salisbury's failure to continue that concurrence with the Powers for the suppression of outrages for which Rosebery was working when he left office.

Autumn came, and nothing was done to save the Armenians. The veteran crusader of Hawarden once more buckled on his armour, and spoke at Liverpool (September 14th), in the trumpet tones of 1876. He would break off relations with Turkey, and do what we could directly to repress the local outrages. This seemed to involve armed intervention; but he added that if a European war was threatened it might be necessary for us to recede from that mode of action. The reaction on Rosebery's position of his old leader's reappearance will be noted in due course. Meanwhile there were other grave matters touching the honour of the Empire. The Jameson Raid from Bechuanaland into the Transvaal coincided with the New Year, and the German Emperor's telegram of congratulation to President Kruger helped to silence many Englishmen for whom filibustering in itself had no attraction. At Rochdale (April 29th) and at Newton Abbot (May 15th) Rosebery did not spare Chamberlain's "new diplomacy," which had invited the President here for discussion by a dispatch which unfortunately reached the newspapers before it reached Pretoria, and recommended a policy which Kruger immediately repudiated. And then—

"In the vigorous practice of the new diplomacy, the Colonial Secretary went to a public dinner, and said that the administration of President Kruger, the gentleman he had invited to England and whom he was anxious to conciliate, was eminently corrupt. That is a very new diplomacy indeed. A greater comedy of errors was never achieved by any diplomacy, either new or old."

In the second speech (May 15th) he insisted on the need for prompt and searching inquiry—for the sake of the accused themselves, and for the clearing of our national character, freely accused in Europe of complicity in the raid. He thought the appointment of a Parliamentary Committee a great mistake.

The problem of inquiry came up in Parliament (June), and the Government seemed to take it lightly. Rosebery observed that nobody who watched the course of foreign opinion could help seeing how the feeling that finds expression in the phrase *perfide Albion* had been deepened by what had taken place. The inquiry was a travesty and a mockery.

The Parliamentary Committee was appointed at the close of the session, but of course could do nothing till the following year. Its history does not greatly concern this book, but few will dispute Rosebery's condemnation of its appointment. It proved to be an admirable machine for smothering most of the relevant facts.

After Nicaragua, Venezuela. The frontier between that state and British Guiana had been a matter of contest for years, and almost at the moment of the Jameson Raid, President Cleveland, the Democratic chief, had issued a message invoking the Monroe Doctrine against this country. It included an extravagant pretension to appoint a United States Boundary Commission. This was treated as *non avenue*, and we were on the brink of war with the Union. Rosebery was anxious that nothing should be said admitting that the interests of the United States were affected, or that the prolonged occupation of part of the disputed territory should be a factor in the proposed arbitration.

Always glad to keep foreign affairs free from party, he asked Sanderson[12] to come and see him from the Foreign Office—

"and laid before him my suggestion for getting a friendly Power to offer its good offices between the U.S. and us. Both countries had got into an *impasse* like two great waggons in a deep narrow lane. I saw no other dignified way out. No one, Lord Salisbury might be assured, would know of my having made the suggestion."

The negotiations dragged on through the summer, and a satisfactory conclusion was deferred till the autumn.

Meanwhile, Rosebery continued to find his personal position less and less tolerable. His last few months of office had run more smoothly, as in February 1895 he had called a Cabinet to announce that he must resign unless he were better supported in the House of Commons. Kimberley thought this "an amazing announcement," and that his colleagues' confidence in his judgment was seriously shaken.

" 'His extreme sensitiveness to personal attacks indicates a certain weakness in his character,' his older friend noted, adding that 'Harcourt joined in deprecating Rosebery's resignation, but his talk was that the sooner we were driven out of office the better.' "

On this Rosebery commented some time later:

"His amazement shows that the device was successful. It would of course not have been possible for me to resign; but it was the only way in which I could restore any discipline, or deal with the open and insulting disloyalty of one member of the Cabinet at least. This had come to a head on, I think, the previous evening, which had been entirely

[12] Sir Thomas Sanderson. (1841-1924.) Private secretary to successive Secretaries of State for Foreign Affairs. Permanent Under-Secretary 1894-1906. *Cr.* Lord Sanderson 1905. G.C.B.

devoted to attacks on me while the Government sate silent. This shameful exhibition had excited great comment, for the silence of the Government under such circumstances was much more damaging than the attacks of my foes. So I called a Cabinet to play the last card left to me, and on the whole it succeeded."[13]

Just before the meeting of Parliament in the current year eight of Rosebery's former colleagues came to Mentmore, with Sir E. Grey and Tom Ellis. There was some useful talk after dinner about Education and about Armenia, and a few days later he held a conference in Parliament Street with the principal Party organisers. He was invited to meet the Scottish Members of Parliament at dinner, and, on another occasion, to meet leading Nonconformists, clerical and lay. They gathered to salute the Liberal leader, all unconscious of such a note as he made on June 21st at the Durdans.

"The anniversary of the late Government being beaten. Sitting under the veranda at 9 p.m., the exact time and place where I received the telegrams, we drank a joyful glass."

He spoke at the City Liberal Club (July 27th), declaring politics to be in a state of flux, and laying stress on the mutual independence of the Liberal and Irish parties. This went too far for Lord Ripon, who objected to such a categorical declaration, in a long talk at Studley: "Very friendly, sincere, and single-minded" was Rosebery's impression. Rosebery spoke briefly at the second reading of the Irish Land Bill, but took little part in its prolonged Committee stage.

Confidential.   38 BERKELEY SQUARE, *August 6th*, 1896.
"MY DEAR SPENCER,

"I have been thinking very carefully over the situation of our Party in the House of Lords with reference to the Irish Land Bill.

"As you know, my view has been that every man should be a law to himself in that matter, and that it was undesirable to take action as a Party, or to issue a whip. Under this principle I have to consider what I shall do myself, and after the best consideration I have been able to give to the matter, I have come to the strong conclusion that I should not endeavour to prevent the defeat of the Government by its own supporters, if such defeat be imminent (as it is). The Government has not deserved any such service at our hands, and they have besides the

[13] In the debate on the Address, Leonard Courtnay, Dilke, and Labouchere had assailed Rosebery in unmeasured terms, with copious citations from his speeches in the House of Lords, Campbell-Bannerman had denied any divergence between the Prime Minister and his colleagues, but Harcourt had left the attacks unnoticed.

power of reversing in the House of Commons by the enormous majority of their own supporters any votes that the House of Lords may give in antagonism to them. And, if defeated, *an object lesson of the working of the House of Lords* will be furnished infinitely more effective than any speeches that any Liberal could make.

"I know of nothing to weigh against all these considerations so therefore, as far as I am concerned, I shall make no effort to assist the Government this evening. *But I do not attempt in the slightest degree to influence you:* you occupy in regard to Irish questions a different position to mine.

"Y. sincly.,

AR"

At last the Uganda Railway was to be made. "One of the rare, but none the less grateful questions on which both sides of the House are agreed," said Rosebery. This was true of the House of Lords at any rate; and the claim advanced both by him and by Lord Salisbury that its construction would prove a death-blow to the slave trade has been abundantly vindicated. Every previous traveller in East Africa had observed, with helpless indignation, slave caravans working their way to the coast for shipment. At Dalmeny he drew up the following memorandum:

August 25th, 1896.—"There will be I suppose this autumn calls for a definite Liberal policy. Any such calls will be in my opinion premature, and, as far as I am concerned, futile.

"In the first place, any promulgation of policy is too soon after the last election and too long before the next election. This consideration is in itself conclusive to my mind.

"But, secondly, the Liberal party needs very tender handling just now. Its personal difficulties for the moment can scarcely be exaggerated. Declarations of policy from leader would *ipso facto* elicit violent contradictions. These disputes, besides having the unpleasant effect of washing dirty linen in public, would dishearten Liberals, and discourage Liberal Unionists—disgusted with the Tory party—from returning to us. But, what is most important, they would distract attention from the incredible blunders of the Government. They would, so to speak, draw a red herring across the trail of the Government—a feat useful to them and disastrous to us.

"In another respect too the Liberal party requires tender handling even more. It is impossible for the Liberal party to remain nailed to the innumerable political propositions lightly accepted by Mr. Gladstone for the promotion of his Irish Policy. The party needs to make a new start and to shed much of this—which may be desirable in the abstract or may not—but which by its bulk and multifarious aggressiveness constitutes an encumbrance—not an inspiration or assistance. The party will have, in order to be successful, to concentrate itself on one or two points—possibly of the former policy, possibly not. But this necessary reconstruction of policy and therefore of party is a delicate and gradual process, even if there were no personal difficulties beside.

"As regiments shattered in battle have to be reconstructed by some sort of screen, so our party needs something of the kind for the present. That shelter has been abundantly furnished by the present Government. Their inconceivable blunders furnish an abundant topic for Liberal concentration and attack.

"I believe that the best chance for the Liberal party lies much more in reaction from the present Government than in any gospel of its own. The present Government is the first Tory govt. since 1867: weakly and distractedly Tory no doubt, but compelled to be Tory by the brute force of its majority. Since 1867 Conservative Governments have not openly opposed Liberal policy (except in Ireland): they have competed not unsuccessfully at an auction of Liberal measures. Now their majority robs them of all excuse for not being Tory, and, reluctantly I think, Tory they are.

"This is an immense advantage to the Liberal party, because it forces real Liberals back to that party, and helps on the process which all true Liberals must have at heart—the restoration of the Liberal party to what it was in richness, variety and strength before 1886. That work would even now be in full operation but for two circumstances: the distracted condition of the Liberal front bench, and the Irish question. Neither of these fall within the scope of this memorandum, the sole moral of which is that the Liberal party should devote itself to exposing and impressing on the electorate the preposterous policy and blundering of the Tory Government—in a word to 'rubbing it in!' "

There was thus nothing definite to prepare friends or foes for the bombshell which exploded on October 8th, when this letter to Tom Ellis was issued:

DALMENY, *October 6th*, 1896.

"MY DEAR ELLIS,

"The recent course of events makes it necessary to clear the air. I find myself in apparent difference with a considerable mass of the Liberal party on the Eastern question, and in some conflict of opinion with Mr. Gladstone, who must necessarily always exercise a matchless authority in the party; while scarcely from any quarter do I receive explicit support.

"This situation, except as regards Mr. Gladstone, is not altogether new, but in saying this I complain of no one. I regret only that I should

[428]

appear to divide the energies and try the faith of Liberals. This question, however, is above and beyond personal considerations.

"When I speak, which I do this week, I must speak my mind, and speak it without reference to party. Under these circumstances it is best for the party and myself that I should speak not as a leader, but as a free man. I consequently beg to notify you that the leadership of the party, so far as I am concerned, is vacant, and that I resume my liberty of action.

"I can only feel the deepest gratitude and regret in parting from you and those who, like you, have given me such loyal co-operation under circumstances so difficult.

"Believe me, my dear Ellis,

"Yours very sincerely,

ROSEBERY."

Here is the story:

October 7th.—"I sent for the Central News man and gave him my letter for publication at 8 p.m. to avoid the evening newspapers. To bed early. At 1 William arrives like Lady Macbeth with an agonised telegram from Cook of the *Daily News* begging to be authorised to contradict the fatal rumour."

October 8th.—"A good deal of fuss about my resignation. Mr. Harmsworth[14] came to interview me. I lunched him instead. An interesting young man.

"Asquith came to luncheon. He behaved as always extremely well, but complained a little:

(1) of no one having been consulted. (I explained to him that this was of the essence of the matter.)"

October 8th.—"Fowler also arrived to stay."

October 9th.—"At 6 to the Empire Theatre to make my fateful speech. So behindhand that I was scribbling the last heads or argument as the carriage was waiting, long after the others had gone. But it went off well enough—indeed too well—as the Empire Theatre was so conversational to speak in that I lasted for nearly two hours.

"Home to supper. What a relief!"

None of the four thousand hearers of the speech could doubt the sincerity of the whole and the emotion that inspired a great part of it. His notes, more copious than usual, cover thirteen half-sheets of large notepaper. He looked tired and anxious, and the audience, warm in its greeting, showed signs of tension unlike the customary uproar of such mass meetings. Rosebery covered the whole field of the Turkish difficulty, saying, amid loud cheers, that in foreign

[14] Alfred Harmsworth, *cr.* Lord Northcliffe 1905 and Viscount Northcliffe 1918.

politics he had never known party, pointing out the essential difference between the existing position and that of 1876, and dealing with the various policies now advocated.

"I am obliged to differ from Mr. Gladstone on this question (some cheers, and a voice, 'Good old Rosebery'). But we differ as friends (loud cheers). This morning only I had a long and affectionate letter from him, in answer to the announcement of my resignation, which I shall always cherish. Whatever our differences of opinion may be, they never could alter the veneration, the unbounded respect, the deep affection with which I regard him."

When, seventeen years ago, Rosebery continued, he had spoken of the great statesman fighting the battle of liberty at an advanced age, he little thought that he would see a still nobler sight, the same statesman, fuller still of years and if possible still fuller of honour, leaving his well-earned retirement to fight one more battle for the principles for which his life had been spent.

Rosebery's "only panacea for dealing with the Eastern question is concerted action of the Powers." All the Powers, if possible, but at any rate all those directly interested. Oliver Cromwell, who had been invoked to justify isolated action, had in fact proceeded solely by diplomatic methods.

Rosebery passed on to speak of his resignation. It was not solely the result of differences on the Armenian question. That was the last of a series of incidents. A Liberal leader if a Peer could only succeed if he received very exceptional support (loud cheers, and a voice, "Which you never got"), very exceptional loyalty, and very exceptional co-operation inside and outside Parliament "to make up for his own inherent deficiencies." His resignation was for one object alone, "to promote unity." At the close of his speech he thanked his colleagues, naming those who were on the platform; and after disposing of a rumour that Asquith had not heartily supported him, went on :

"Consummate and considerable as are his powers of brain, in my opinion his head is not equal to his heart. And it is that rare combination of head and heart which in my humble judgment, if my prophecy be worth anything, will take him to the highest office of the State."

Even more affectionate was his expression of thanks to Ronald Munro Ferguson: "We have been more like elder and younger brother than like Minister and Secretary," as all who had seen them together knew to be the truth. These were the farewells of a political death-bed, "this solemn moment," as the speaker himself called it. But the party collected round the patient's couch had no intention of attending his political funeral, as the events of the next ten years were to prove.

Rosebery had written to Mr. Gladstone on the day of his resignation as follows:

Confidential.   DALMENY, *October 7th,* 1896.
"MY DEAR MR. GLADSTONE,

"I wish you to know from myself that I have resigned the leadership of the Liberal party—that is, if I ever held it, of which I am not quite sure!

"I will not disguise that you have, by again coming forward and advocating a policy which I cannot support, innocently and unconsciously dealt the *coup de grâce*; by enabling discontented Liberals to pelt me with your authority. But, as you well know, the situation has long been almost impossible and almost intolerable, and I for one am glad that it should cease.

"I hope that my retirement may at any rate produce some greater amount of unity in the distracted and honeycombed party called 'Liberal.'

"My love to Mrs. Gladstone.

"Yr. affte.
AR"

Mr. Gladstone sent a long answer by return of post, and a short one two days later. In the first he said:

"I cannot at this date regard your resignation as an accomplished fact: and you may find you have a stage yet to travel. . . . And now I turn to that with which I should perhaps have begun. Your letter is an acknowledgement of receipt for a stab under the fifth rib: and regarded in that view it is not only kind, but kindness itself. I can desire nothing more than to follow it. Our political relations have been tragical enough: but you have prevented their carrying any infection into the personal sphere. Will it surprise you when I tell you that my first knowledge of a difference between us was when I read the letter stating that sole action meant European war?"

Mr. Gladstone went on to explain that he had believed Rosebery to be not warm, but concurrent or acquiescent in his policy, and he thought that Salisbury was much in his sense, though with few or no friends in his Cabinet. The movement in the country had been all that he himself could expect or desire.

Looking back to those days, one cannot but grievingly admire

[431]

the generous faith that mistook popular indignation against the merciless Sultan for willingness to engage in a crusade of which no one could foresee the progress or the end.

In his second letter, after reading the speech, the old chief wrote:

"After what you said of me last night I would, if I could, add to the acknowledgements contained in my letter of Thursday as to our personal relations."

Both letters ended as usual, "Yours affectionately."

Other ex-colleagues wrote laments and expostulations—Ripon doubted whether, from a public point of view, the Armenian business should have been treated as the main ground for resignation, and added:

"You have handed us over to Harcourt without escape, and you are not ignorant of all which that means."

Arnold Morley looked forward to soon seeing Rosebery leader again; warm-hearted Tom Ellis wrote:

"Fourteen days have passed by since you wrote to me the two letters which filled me with pain and sadness. I have been finding it more and more difficult to give any adequate expression to the keenness of the regret I feel at the circumstances which drove you to the decision and at the momentous decision itself. I had nursed the hope that it could have been warded off. I had returned to the stillness of my home in Wales from Dalmeny, with my mind very full of the difficulties of the situation but with a new confidence that with patience the difficulties might, with Time's help, be surmounted. Those days at Dalmeny were among the very happiest of my life. I had caught a sort of infection of happiness from the children and from our candid and earnest talks. On my return I quietly thought over them and made all sorts of plans for the future.

"Your letter and your great speech seem to show that the decision was inevitable. But I cannot even now admit it, and my mind constantly rebels against the assumption that it was inevitable. But every hour's reflection upon the new situation created by the decision only serves to emphasise my regret and my sadness. The sense of desolation grows on me.

"The kindness of your personal letter to me—a kindness which I shall never forget—increases my sense of desolation. For I recall your thousand kindnesses to me, the joy of discussing with you plans and difficulties and obstacles, the inspiration which you gave me in my work and in my life, and I realise how you kindled admiration and devotion in those who came into contact with you. I recall the many plans and schemes which many of us talked over and worked at in order to help you as Leader of our Party.

"And now we have to strive to put the best face on things, to work without devotion and without much hope. We have to try to say and assume that all will go well with the Party when in our inmost hearts we are depressed and torn with doubts and misgivings.

"Let me thank you heart and soul for all your kindness to me. It will be a great joy to me if at any time I can be of any service to you.

"Believe me, dear Lord Rosebery,

Your sincere and faithful

TOM ELLIS."

Shaw Lefevre[15] was warmly sympathetic, doubting the possibility of leadership for a Liberal Peer in Opposition; Arthur Acland,[16] out of health and himself the object of many attacks in the Press, felt sure that so deliberate and grave a step must mean something very definite; Spencer, to whom Rosebery had written hoping that he would lead the Opposition in the Lords, deprecated this possibility, and assured Rosebery that he had not lost the confidence of Liberals in the country, but confessed himself puzzled by the resignation; Herschell wound up a long and friendly letter with the hope that Rosebery would still work for the party:

"If you were to withdraw yourself from politics it would be said: 'See, he cared not for Liberal principles, but only to be leader of the Liberal party; as soon as this becomes impossible his ardour cools, and he no longer cares to fight the Liberal battle.' However untrue this might be, it would have enough semblance of truth to find credit with many."

Campbell-Bannerman, returning from Australia, congratulated him on securing the sympathy and appreciation of all parties and countries, and of by far the larger number of Liberals:

"One may say *felix opportunitate demissionis;* for the prudent view of the Armenian question blends satisfactorily with the implied protest against disloyalty of the domestic kind . . . and there is some irony in the fact that the ex-Prime Minister whose main alleged fault in the eyes of some one could name was that he was too Jingo, Imperialist, and Great Englander, resigns because he cannot agree with those of his followers who are willing to plunge us in a wanton war."

[15] (1831-1928.) M.P. 1863-95. First Commissioner of Works 1880 and 1892. President Local Government Board 1894-5. *Cf.* Lord Eversley, 1906.

[16] (1847-1926.) M.P. 1885-99. Vice-President for Education 1892-5. Succeeded as thirteenth Baronet 1919.

[433]

A letter from his friend the editor of the *Westminster Gazette* gave him peculiar pleasure; he wrote in reply:

Private. Newmarket, *October 13th,* 1896.

"My dear Spender,

"I was too tired and too shy to say what I wished to say yesterday. Let me send a line of thanks to you, then, for your constant able and spirited support of me through these arduous times. I shall always think of you as a friend—whatever the future may have in store.

"Always,

Yrs. sincerely,

AR"

"Would you send me six copies of last Saturday's *Westminster*? It was the only thing that almost persuaded me that I had made a fairly good speech."

The story of this resignation has been given at length for two reasons. In the first place, it illustrates some of Rosebery's strength and a touch of his weakness—the strength, the capacity for prompt action at need and for eloquent defence of that action; the weakness, the failure to make generally clear the motives that inspired the action. Secondly, it was the outward and visible demonstration of the truth long apparent to initiates, that the gulf between the two sections of the Liberal party, roughly distinguished as Imperialists and Little Englanders, was steadily widening. As always happens in such disputes, the wildest partisan utterances were treated as confessions of faith by either hostile group. All Imperialists bore the burden of Alfred Austin's fatuous lines on the Jameson Raid; all their opponents were accused of callous indifference to the fate and fortunes of their fellow-countrymen overseas. Rosebery's Imperialism was of the sanest brand, in few ways differing from that of Kimberley, or Campbell-Bannerman, or Bryce, or Ripon, though less confident than the last in the early capacity of the coloured races for self-government. In the opposite ranks, Harcourt and John Morley were not in truth careless of the Empire, but they seemed to involve in a common condemnation the invasion of land speculators and mining syndicates with the efforts of genuine pioneers and the new consciousness of nationhood in the minds of overseas settlers. In Imperial matters they and many of their followers were strictly Conservative; there was a great deal more Radicalism and more Home Rule inherent in the Imperialist creed, when it was held by sensible men.

[434]

CHAPTER XVIII

Pressure from Political Friends. Herbert Bismarck. The South African War. The Chesterfield Speech and the Liberal League

T HE ordinary current of what should have been a placid year was ruffled by all these political emotions. At its very start it was troubled by a great personal loss in the sage friendship of William Rogers. At the New Year he was too ill to be visited, but he rallied before the end and faced it in humorous tranquillity.

January 15*th.*—"To Rogers—calm and cheerful. He had realised 'that he had not above ten years to live.' Wished to live in a flat at the West End."

Four days later Rogers died, leaving a gap in Rosebery's life that nothing could fill. In the same week he lost another good friend in Henry Calcraft. He was a good-humoured version of Charles Greville; a most capable Civil Servant,[1] well read, caustic in speech but kind of heart, and a favourite in whatever London could claim as its Faubourg Saint-Germain.

Critics thought that Rosebery's political speeches of 1896 reached a higher level than any before, and the same was true of his other addresses of the year. Those on Burns at Dumfries and Glasgow, and on Robert Louis Stevenson at Edinburgh, are separately noticed. But he also presided (November 26th) when Mr. Herbert Paul enlightened Edinburgh on Parliamentary Oratory, "in one of the most brilliant and fascinating addresses that I have ever had the fortune to hear," Rosebery said in replying to a vote of thanks. He pointed out the risk that in Parliament a fine debate, rather than agreement and persuasion, might tend to be the object aimed at.

Rosebery again took the chair (December 7th) when Sir Walter Besant lectured on the History and Greatness of London, as the moral progenitor of the People's Palace had the best right to do. Rosebery pressed the County Council to found an historical depart-

[1] He was Permanent Secretary to the Board of Trade.

ment which would commemorate the houses of famous men—a hint taken later on; and he did not forget to dilate on the problem of London administration, the greatest of all problems for statesmen, he thought, and one generally ignored.

He had been in Spain for ten days in the early summer, again basking at Madrid, Granada, and Seville. He loved nightingales, and in their season he drove out most evenings from Epsom to listen beside the Surrey copses. At Granada "the finest nightingale in Spain" was offered to him for 200 pesetas. After flatly refusing to sing when talked to by its owner's little boy, it was sent to pass the night in Rosebery's room. The next day, "Chiquito a failure, not having sung a note. He has returned home. The theory is that weather has to do with it, and that nightingales will not sing in thunder." Probably after his return he did not regret the company of the poor little captive.

Rosebery summed up his Spanish impressions in a letter to a friend:

"The more I see of Spain the more I like it—better, I think, than Italy, though the people are not so gay as the Italians. But the Spaniards are so casual, so fiery, so lazy, so cynical, and so superstitious that they have the charm of a perpetual puzzle. And then they scorn civilization as much as J. J. Rousseau!"

While he was away, the Prince of Wales's *Persimmon* won the Derby, just beating *St. Frusquin*, owned by Leopold de Rothschild, to whom the Durdans had been lent for the week.

"My Durdans party must be a sad one, and I am sad in sympathy. When I said to my servant John that I supposed everyone would believe that every horse had been stopped to enable the Prince of Wales to win the Derby, he replied, 'No doubt, but I am bound to tell your Lordship that many people thought the same thing when *Ladas* won, and you were Prime Minister!'"

At Seville there were the Corpus Christi processions. More solemn and imposing, he thought, than "the scratch collection of richly clad idols at Easter." He saw a thrilling bull-fight, and for the first time in his life a cock-fight—"a stupid, beastly sight . . . the fascination lay in the audience all standing up at once, screaming offers to bet all at once—a scene for Goya or Velasquez. I missed the central passive figure in Hogarth's print."

Most of the autumn was passed in Scotland, both before and after the political crisis. Before going north he shot grouse with Lord

Ripon. On one day the four guns killed nearly 1,200 birds, of which the amazing Lord de Grey accounted for more than half. Rosebery, excellent performer though he was, was limited to a quarter of the total, being handicapped by the break-down of his dog. He also shot grouse in Scotland, and secured two or three stags at Dunrobin. But there were many quiet weeks at Dalmeny with the children. On one Sunday he took his sons, now at Eton, to a Free Church in Edinburgh. The preacher chose the tale of Onesimus, saying that he fled to Rome, where an escaped slave might find good hiding. One of the boys very pardonably heard the phrase as "a good hiding."

Before the year closed he was in Paris for a few days, coming across John Morley and with him wandering to book-shops and harrowed by the Conciergerie. Not a word of politics.

He was invited for a night to Windsor, where the Queen said:

" 'I wanted to write to you after your speech, but I heard you were coming to Abergeldie. Then, you did not come, and I thought it perhaps better not to write. But I thought it very good and very patriotic. They treated you very badly. Sir William, and I believe Mr. Morley too.' I waved this off."

In December he attended the City Liberal Club for a presentation to an esteemed official:

"A genial gathering. My last public engagement in the world."

But many active political friends were among the guests at Mentmore, determined not to let him go.

The Address in the House of Lords was moved on January 19th. Lord Kimberley, once again leader of the Opposition, lamented Rosebery's absence, and paid the inevitable compliments. The Prime Minister was no less eulogistic:

"The noble lord is a man exceedingly popular in private life, and, I think, not less popular in public life, and the ability with which he conducted a position of exceeding difficulty won the sympathy of all. . . . He made a most patriotic and, I may say, a most useful and beneficial speech. I should be inclined to add that I do not see why that speech should involve his retirement from the leadership of his party."

In Rosebery's own judgment it also involved temporary retirement from the House of Lords, for he did not open his lips there throughout the session. Lord Salisbury's speech became famous from a sentence about Russia and Turkey in 1853, before the Crimean war:

"Many members of this House will keenly feel the nature of the mistake that we made when I say that we put all our money on the wrong horse."

The fruits of that unlucky investment remained, and one of them was served up this year, when the Cretans rose in rebellion,[2] and the Greeks sent ships and troops to help them. A Ministerial Statement (February 15th) favoured autonomy for Crete within the Turkish Empire, and the withdrawal of troops of both Greece and Turkey was to be enforced by the Powers if necessary. This declaration was discussed soon afterwards in the House. Kimberley boldly advocated the junction of the island to Greece. Lord Salisbury assured the House that Crete would in any event be withdrawn from the arbitrary power of the Sultan. No more could be done without agreement with the Powers. But some of Rosebery's henchmen felt that he ought to be in the fray. Telegrams followed him abroad, and Cook of the *Daily News* wrote strongly urging him to speak out. He had already indited a memorandum defining his position and intentions:

NAPLES, *February 26th*, 1897.

"It is time, in view of appeals that are telegraphed to me from England to declare myself on the Cretan question and to attempt to control events, that I should define my position. It is clear enough. On Oct. 9 I resigned the leadership of the Liberal party, and two days afterwards I bade it more or less formally farewell. I did not make it clear then whether I said farewell to the Liberal Party or to party politics or to public life. It is not necessary now to make that clear; at any rate for my present purpose.

"But the main point is obvious and remains in force. I resigned the leadership of the Liberal party, not to destroy that party but to promote its union. With the same object I have ever since remained persistently silent and refused all engagements.

"I could not in my judgment within six months of my resignation step forward, and, by taking an independent line, embarrass the Liberal party, which I have always sought to serve, especially by my resignation.

"This view does not necessarily imply my permanent silence or retirement. It is of course difficult to fix an arbitrary limit of time for this and I shall not attempt to do so. But six months under the circumstances would appear a decent minimum.

[2] This was the first appearance in active life of Monsieur Venizelos.

[438]

"Beyond this I am bound to say that I have had a revolting experience of the higher positions in British government, and that it will take some time to wash out of my mouth the taste of the last administration."

He now replied to Cook as follows:

"MY DEAR COOK,

"I have just received your letter of March 1. Many thanks for it, though I don't agree with it. You lay down two propositions: 1. that I am *de facto* leader of the Liberal party in the matter of foreign affairs: 2. that I am bound to utter a public opinion on the Cretan question. I deny both.

"Last October I laid down the leadership—I retained and reserved nothing. Such a course involves a sacrifice—to some men a great sacrifice. In exchange I obtained absolute liberty of action. No one has any claim now, except that of personal attachment, to press me or ask me to do anything. But, beyond that, who considers me *de facto* leader of the Liberal party in any respect, or who, for that reason or any other wishes for my opinion on the Cretan or any other question? We can easily test this. I have been away above seven weeks. Since then I have not received a single communication from any member of the late Government or from any member of the House of Lords. I have had letters from three members of the House of Commons: one from Sir Samuel Montagu forwarding an invitation from Whitechapel, and several from Munro Ferguson and another private member—both very intimate personal friends. Is this the correspondence of a 'Liberal leader' *de facto* or *de jure*? Does this represent a call from any section of the country for my opinion on any subject whatever?

"Do not think I am complaining, for my feeling is very different. I am only adducing facts to rebut your propositions. I am giving reasons for not departing from my present attitude of abstention.

"I propose to remain quiet in the country on my return, offering no opinions on any subject whatever. Some few friends like yourself have a right to ask me for my views but I recognise no public claim in any quarter."

The Cretan matter dragged its slow length along, through the summer and on into the following year, but neither on this nor on any other external question did Rosebery say a word in public during 1897.

Ronald Ferguson was untiring in keeping his former chief abreast of events. By this time the split in the ex-Cabinet was openly recognised, and some of its members classed as "Friendlies." There was increasing caution, Ferguson said, among those who could not be so

[439]

classed, in regard to attacking the Concert. But Harcourt had harassed the Government (March 24th) on Crete when he should have backed their main policy, and conferred with them on South Africa when he should have harassed. Ferguson told Rosebery candidly that in Scotland many people were thinking that either he had gone over, or that he had ceased to care for his old followers. But he loyally explained to inquisitive Members of Parliament Rosebery's objection to speech-making.

Another principal informant in his voluntary exile was Wemyss Reid. At first, Rosebery wrote (January 23rd), he saw the reward of his action in the sequence of events. He was struck by the exact, almost literal agreement between the speeches of the Liberal leaders in the two Houses.

"I always told my colleagues that that would be the precious and almost invaluable result of my withdrawal, and so it is."

The newspapers had not found him out, and he begged his correspondent not to mention that he had written, as he wished to enjoy the blessed peace of oblivion. He watched the intrigues and smallnesses of London as from another planet, and he begged his friend, imbedded in that Cloaca Maxima, not to be disturbed by the petty irritations of that position. For it was only through the annoyance and discomfort of his friends that he was capable of being vexed. He looked forward to a hearty laugh with Reid in Berkeley Square, but begged him till then to write freely.

In a later letter (March 11th) he repeated his refusal to speak on the Cretan imbroglio, with detailed reasons for keeping in retirement. The party situation was not really harmonised as it seemed to be. "So I will continue to cultivate my cabbages." His loyalty to Mr. Gladstone had evidently been cruelly strained, for he wrote:

"Talking of retirements, Mr. Gladstone's last letter on European war leaves me in doubt whether he considers me a knave or a fool; but possibly he means both."

And there was in fact an earlier grievance of 1894, for Rosebery had told his confidential correspondent:

"You are correct in saying that no one knew definitely that Mr. Gladstone was going to resign till a day or two before. In spite of remonstrance he deliberately left his successor barely a week to constitute the Government and frame a policy and a Queen's Speech before

[440]

the Opening of Parliament. This I have always thought was hardly fair play."

Again on May 7th:

"MY DEAR REID,

"A thousand thanks for your kind thought of my birthday.

"I recognise only too plainly that my friends are abused at the present moment. I comfort myself by thinking that they suffer because they are wisely opposing the worst form of Jingoism—all the more dangerous because cloaked by hysteria and the abused phrases of humanity and religion.

"You may think I take all this too seriously. If so, you are mistaken. I am only concerned for my friends, who, instead of swimming with the tide, choose to face obloquy, and suspicion on behalf of sound principle. Nevertheless I hope that all my remaining birthdays and theirs will find us ready to do the same.

"Yours sincerely,

AR"

Rosebery shared with most people mistrust of the Report issued by the South African Committee of Enquiry into the Raid, not the less, perhaps, because of Harcourt's partial responsibility for it.[3]

"I am still anxious to learn every development of this discreditable business of the S.A. Committee. Will the indignation die out, or does it spread?

"I have never read a document at once so shameful and so absurd. One would laugh, did one not cry."

It was the year of the Queen's second Jubilee, and the Colonial Premiers had collected in force to do her honour while conferring on Imperial affairs. There was a great banquet at the Imperial Institute (June 18th), with the Prince of Wales in the chair, and all the leading statesmen round the table. Rosebery had to propose "the Houses of Legislature, Home and Colonial," some thirty in number, as he reminded his hearers.

"I do not for one moment believe," he said, "that under any other form of government than a limited constitutional monarchy could the British Empire have been formed or could have continued to exist. Under either an absolute monarchy or under a republic it must have crumbled away, if it could ever have been formed."

[3] The whole story is told in the *Life of Sir William Harcourt*, vol. ii, ch. xxii, pp. 423-37.

He alluded to the famous speech of Daniel Webster about the British sentry and the British drum in every region of the globe, but there was something better than these "which is co-equal with the British flag, and that is the British sentiment of constitutional freedom." He trusted that the Prime Ministers would not separate without an effort to draw the bonds of Empire closer.

The overseas visitors were also entertained at the National Liberal Club, with Lord Carrington in the chair and Labouchere as vice-chairman. Rosebery and Harcourt headed the long list of public men. Rosebery gave the toast of the Empire. It had been claimed, he remarked, as a prerogative of Lord Beaconsfield, but his Imperialism was merely European and Asiatic, while the newer Imperialism was American, African, and Australian as well. W. E. Forster and Sir John Seeley had higher claims as pioneers in the movement. He looked forward to seeing a contented Empire of Britains, on the principle by which the Empire had been built up, the bond of Empire in the person of the Sovereign, and local self-government as the basis of it.

The everlasting duel between Protection and Free Trade had almost ceased to excite the leaders of the two parties. A few country Tories still laid wreaths on the grave of the Corn Laws. In the early 'eighties Fair Trade had flickered through its brief day of notoriety. But the policy of the country seemed to be rigidly fixed, so that Rosebery's appearance at the Free Trade Hall at Manchester, when the centenary of the Chamber of Commerce was celebrated, was no resumption of Liberal leadership. One of the Conservative members was on the platform, and Mr. A. J. Balfour had been invited. But in his long address Rosebery chanted the praises of Cobden and Bright, declared that the great military preparations of European countries had led them into fiscal errors, and asserted that although the complaints of farmers were well-founded, they were mainly due to improvements in transport. Anyhow, they were better off than they were before the repeal of the Corn Laws. To-day more interest attaches to the paragraphs on Free Trade and the Empire. Free Trade, he asserted, had produced the wealth that enabled us to sustain the burden of Empire; but also it had averted revolution after 1841, and revolution would have meant the dismemberment of the Empire. But he believed that anything in the direction of an Imperial Commercial League would weaken the Empire internally, and excite the permanent hostility of the whole world. If the free import of the food of the people were checked, it would only succeed in making the Empire odious to the working classes of this country. Again, with all our liabilities, was it not worth while to walk warily in the path of Empire? When, that very year, we had denounced our commercial treaties with Germany and Belgium in the interests of Canada, a note of alarm was sounded at what we thought simply an ordinary proceeding.

"A scattered Empire like ours, founded on commerce and cemented by commerce, an Empire also well defended so as not to invite wanton aggression, can and will make for nothing but peace. But an Empire spread all over the world, with a uniform barrier of a Customs Union presented everywhere in the face of every traveller, would be, I will not say an Empire of war, but a perpetual menace, a perpetual incentive and invitation to war."

These sentiments were vociferously applauded; and it is certain that to the end of his days Rosebery would have been prepared to repeat the speech without modifying a sentence or an epithet.

He always spoke more gladly in Scotland than elsewhere. Edinburgh, so rich in official libraries and institutional libraries, had at last seen the need for free public libraries. A public-spirited citizen, Thomas Nelson, had bequeathed money for day shelters in poor districts, where humble people could have a chance of finding books and newspapers. Thus branches of the central library were founded, and Rosebery was asked to open one of them (May 10th). He was impressed by the excellent combination of free club with a free library; but it was necessary, he said, to distinguish the two conflicting interests in reading—newspaper and book—the ephemeral and the abiding. A just proportion would obtain the best result from both.

By this time golf had begun to captivate Englishmen as well as Scotsmen, but it had not spread far inland in either country. Edinburgh, of course, teemed with experts. Had Rosebery been thirty years younger, his love of walking, his keen eye, and his firm muscles would surely have made him proficient at the game. But he never attempted to play; and when he opened the new Club House at Barnton, close to Dalmeny, he had to admit his utter ignorance of the art. But he could claim to share that ignorance with Dr. Boyd,[4] who lived at the Mecca of St. Andrews; and though now presented with a set of clubs, he expressed his dread of making a

[4] Andrew Kennedy Hutchison Boyd (1825-1899) wrote, under initials A.K.H.B., many books, including *Twenty-five Years of St. Andrews*. Principal of St. Andrews University.

[443]

start in middle life, because when a man was seriously inoculated with a love of golf he was very little use for any other purpose afterwards. Rosebery concluded with a sly allusion to "a distinguished statesman charged with giving too much time to golf, and not enough to the House of Commons."

Since 1891 there had been a choice herd of shorthorns at Dalmeny, founded on selections from famous reservoirs of the Cruikshank blood such as Upper-mill, Collynie, and Lord Lovat's at Beaufort. Its owner, rather unaccountably perhaps, never paid much attention to the science of stockbreeding; but this year there was a successful sale and a vast company at luncheon. The host, however, avoided agricultural topics in his speech of thanks. Next came a really great occasion at Stirling, the six-hundredth anniversary of Wallace's victory at Stirling Bridge. Nothing could be more skilful than Rosebery's treatment of a difficult subject, difficult because Wallace's fame is overgrown by legends veiling a very slender column of proved facts. He advanced two propositions—first, that Wallace was the first champion who asserted Scotland as an independent country, for without him Bannockburn might never have been fought; secondly, that he was the type of the man of destiny— the same type whether you call it Cæsar, or Luther, or Washington, or Mirabeau, or Cavour.

He was again at Stirling a month later (October 10th), to receive its freedom. The Provost pleased him by saying that he was thus honoured, though our most cosmopolitan public man, because he was a Scot of the Scots, and the son of their first member after the great Reform of 1832. In Rosebery's reply he ran over the astonishingly picturesque list of former burgesses, concluding with the member for the Stirling Burghs—"There is none I am prouder to be on the same list with than Sir Henry Campbell-Bannerman."

The renewed North Bridge at Edinburgh, the link between the old city and the new, was to have been opened (September 15th) by the Duke and Duchess of York. In their enforced absence Rosebery officiated. At the luncheon that followed he proposed "The City of Edinburgh." Pericles at Athens could not have been more utterly inspired by the genius of his beloved capital.

"The City of Edinburgh, in the words that were used of another city, is 'the joy of the whole earth.' There is nothing like it. Whether we remain in the incomparable street in which we are assembled this afternoon, or whether we cross to those darker recesses which embody three-quarters of the history of Scotland, we are in a city of which there is no like and no parallel, as I believe, in the whole world."

Small wonder that to the Edinburgh burgesses the Rosebery of Downing Street and the Rosebery of Epsom Downs were merged in the Rosebery who was laird of Dalmeny and their fellow-citizen.

He was not less at home in the chair of the Scottish History Society, for Scottish history was one of the veins into which he dug deepest. At the annual meeting (November 23rd) he had much to say of the exiled Stuarts, and lamented the lack of information about the dignities they conferred in their pathetic abdicated past.[5]

On the same day Professor Masson, leaving the Professorship of Rhetoric at the University, received the gift of his portrait at Rosebery's hands. This was Rosebery's tribute to the venerable scholar :

"There is more than being a great Professor or a great man of letters —there is something about the character of the man that is more eminent, to my mind, than all his works. If you will allow me, I will illustrate it by a figure. Last night in my house by the sea I[6] was gazing at the waters in front of me, and in the absolutely calm and impressive face of the Firth of Forth there were reflected the stars in the heavens, a blurred and faint reflection it may be, but at any rate a true and sincere portraiture of the eternal lights and lamps of the firmament of the heavens. And I thought that we in the course of human life meet rarely, but now and then, with some human soul that seems to have caught the reflection of the eternal verities, not by striving or by seeking to improve themselves so that they may earn that complexion, but by the simple and pure search for truth they caught that glory, and it is reflected in their lives."

[5] This was later somewhat repaired by the Marquis de Ruvigny in his book *The Jacobite Peerage*.

[6] A year or two after his marriage Rosebery was able to realise a cherished dream. He took in hand the restoration of Barnbougle. Poised on the water's edge, buffeted by gales and dashed by heavy seas, it would have been fantastic as the mansion-house of a great estate. But its capabilities as a serious toy were unlimited. The renewal was achieved with singular skill. A vast hall or picture gallery was the main feature, furnished with many bookcases, which overflowed into another large saloon adjoining. There were other smaller dwelling-rooms, but very little bedroom accommodation. Rosebery himself, however, in his widowed days, slept at the castle often than not, soothed by the rhythm of the dolorous sea. All his Scottish collections, the harvest of many years, were housed there. There were gathered the thousands of Scottish books, tracts, and pamphlets which, before his death, Rosebery presented to the National Library; there, too, were volumes of literary autographs and historical manuscripts. The castle was a fascinating re-birth, one wisely conceived and skilfully carried out.

The other Edinburgh occasion of the year was a banquet to Mr. J. B. Balfour,[7] at the Scottish Liberal Club. The guest, a great lawyer, and a man of fine courtesy, popular on all sides, had been Lord Advocate in Gladstone's and Rosebery's Governments. But he had earlier held the office when Rosebery was grappling with Scottish business at the Home Office, so their personal relations were as close as possible, and led to frequent correspondence. But Rosebery did not touch on party politics when he spoke from the chair. Much of his speech was given to recitals of the glowing tributes paid by others, by Mr. Gladstone and by Mr. Balfour's Conservative successor as Lord Advocate.

Naples the siren had sung her unrecorded song to Rosebery for thirty years, and he had not stopped his ears against it. But it was only now that he fell into her arms. He spent six weeks under the spell from late in January, seeing more of Italian society than in previous years. He had formerly visited not a few possible villas, and this time he came to a decision. Of all those he had seen, the Villa Delahante at Posilipo appealed to him most. As early as 1879 he had written to Sir James Lacaita:

"The Villa Delahante has been the dream of my life, but it does not seem easy to realise. Perhaps you could however ascertain what is the sort of price asked, as I should like to own it even if I could never see it again."

The villa had belonged to the Bourbon Count of Syracuse, the brother of "King Bomba," and had become the property of a French railway contractor, M. Delahante. Beautifully situated in a large sloping garden, with many trees, in a curve of the bay, it included four structures, the principal residence, two close by somewhat smaller, and intended to house guests, and a delicious little pavilion with a couple of rooms, poised over the blue water of a tiny private harbour. After long bargaining, in August he saw M. Delahante at Versailles, "an alert, bright-eyed old man of 81," and in October he became owner of the "Villa Rosebery." It became an intense joy to him, and he was fortunate in having an old Eton friend Rolfe, now Consul at Naples, who was glad to exercise supervision over the new purchase. Only one objection could exist, and this was swallowed up in the fascination of the spot. It was essentially a summer retreat, a villeggiatura to which the Italian flies when, in Landor's words,

[7] J. B. Balfour (1837-1905). Solicitor-General for Scotland 1880; Lord Advocate 1881, 1886, and 1892-5; Lord of Appeal 1899. *Cr.* Baron Kinross 1902.

"The piper's music fills the street,
The piper's music makes the heat
Hotter by ten degrees."

But it is not always summer in Southern Italy, and lofty ceilings, unheated rooms with tiled or marble floors, are cheerless in the winter months even there. And it is then that the Englishman or Scot in turn tries to escape his own climate, unless he hunts the fox: from May to October business or pleasure are apt to keep him at home.

Other foreign journeys were to Homburg and Gastein. Of the former he wrote to his mother (July 28th):

"It is unusually pleasant, being unusually empty. A black cloud, I fear, hangs over the place, as, I understand, the Prince of Wales is not going there this year, and that to Homburg is as if the mineral springs ceased to flow."

He enjoyed there the company of one of his most valued friends, Philip Wroughton, and walked fifteen miles a day—"the daily round, the common task," as he noted.

Rosebery's warm amity with Herbert Bismarck had been unabated during the past years. In 1892 he had hoped to attend his friend's wedding at Vienna, but it was celebrated on the very day of the dissolution of Parliament. After his arrival at the Foreign Office he wrote:

"So I am once more at the Foreign Office. Your father's absence makes a great change. I do not speak of Germany, for diplomacy is making holiday and I have no special relations with any country just now. But I feel the alteration, though I could not well explain to myself how it shows itself. It is perhaps like shooting at a place where the head gamekeeper has been changed. The pheasants are as numerous, the woods are the same, one sees no difference in the beaters; and yet one feels that the scene is different. However, your father will perhaps think this metaphor more suitable to the late Duc de Gramont."

The correspondence went on, interchanging social and political gossip, but with no tinge of backstairs politics. It was often in a light vein:

June 18th, 1893.—"That cursed name of ROSEMBERG haunts me on the Continent; and when people telegraph to me, as they sometimes do 'Earl Rosebery,' it usually comes out 'Carl Rosemberg.' London is

[447]

emptying fast, but as for me, I shall never leave it till I leave life or office.

"Future statesmen will have to be all 'blood and iron' to lead this life. Which allusion leads me to send my warm good wishes to your father, and your mother, and if she will accept them, to the Countess."

A daughter was born to the Bismarcks in 1894, and to Rosebery's pleasure was given the name of Hannah. In that year he wrote (March 25th, 1894):

"I only realise that I am no longer Foreign Secretary in the cessation of departmental work. Scarcely any boxes, but an enormous responsibility as to my sayings and doings. One is more watched, one cannot put on one's slippers, one is (or should be) always in uniform— buckled very tight. I have always preferred the Foreign Office and always shall."

At the end of the same year Princess Bismarck died.

38 BERKELEY SQUARE, December 7th, 1894.

"MY DEAR HERBERT,

"It was with unbounded grief that I learned the sad news. So noble and simple and sympathetic a nature, so much to her husband and her children. I can hardly realise the home without her.

"I do not write to your father. I write to you as I telegraphed to you, for I am loath to trouble him, and I know that you will convey to him my heartfelt sympathy better than I can myself.

"I fear the blow comes upon you with terrible suddenness and that you were not even in time to witness the end. But I am not sure that it is not best so, and that the haunting recollection of the last moments is not more of a pain than a satisfaction. I remember your mother as she looked at you and at your father—the tenderness and the pride; and that look will always abide with me till the end.

"Ever, my dear Herbert,
"Your affectionate friend in sorrow and in joy,

AR"

"Perhaps you will find a moment to tell me some details of her illness, and of your father?"

In July 1895 Rosebery wrote on leaving office:

"I accept congratulations with both hands, and rejoice in my freedom, for which I have long been pining."

That freedom enabled him to write more openly on public matters.

March 29th, 1896.—"I am seriously uneasy about Foreign Affairs. Nowhere, except in Russia, can I see any definite policy. I blame nobody in particular, I quite admit that the situation is fluctuating and difficult, but that circumstance rather increases than diminishes my apprehensions. I especially regret that we should plunge into the Soudan at this moment. For we can all see the beginning of a Soudan expedition, but who can foresee the end? Besides it is like firing all your stock of gunpowder at butterflies when you are expecting big game."

The following year Rosebery was still the looker-on. He wrote (June 13th, 1897):

"Here we are in a tempestuous madness of Jubilee, which everyone wishes to celebrate at everyone else's expense. In the mean time *delirant Achivi.* . . . It is strange how with almost all parliament at your feet how difficult it is to govern in these days. Difficulties used to arrive in old days from excitement,—the present danger is from profound apathy. The ship of the state moves heavily through the oily waters of the Dead Sea."

Not long afterwards Herbert Bismarck came to Homburg to see his friend; and in October Rosebery paid a long deferred visit to Schönhausen for the christening of the second daughter, going on for a night to Friedrichsrüh. This long friendship was indeed kept in good repair. Rosebery's humour was tickled by one racial characteristic of his comrade. He wrote from Homburg:

"Fond as I am of him, his energy is rather overpowering. He has no idea of the loudness of his voice, and though I lead him into desolate spots, he bellows secrets through the woods. It is like living with a hurricane. But there is no warmer heart or better friend."

A Teutonic Lawrence Boythorn, he might have added.[8]

The Jubilee celebrations opened with an almost private service in St. George's Chapel (June 20th). At its close all the Royal Family made obeisance to the Queen and were embraced by her.

"All were moved, the Queen, the spectators, and the actors in the ceremony,—I never saw anything more profoundly pathetic."

The procession through London two days later was

[8] Monsieur Jules Cambon, formerly French Ambassador at Berlin, tells of his observing to Herr Kiderlen Wächter how tenderly Herbert Bismarck spoke of his father, but how unlike his roughness of manner was to Prince Bülow's pleasant dealing. "Yes," said Kiderlen, "but Herbert Bismarck had one quality that Bülow had not." "What was that?" I asked. "Heart."

"perfectly successful and profoundly interesting. The most striking moment was when the crowd spontaneously sang 'God Save the Queen' before the Queen's arrival."

Rosebery's personal contribution to the celebrations is explained in this letter to the Queen:

December 6th, 1897.

". . . I think it probable that Your Majesty may have a Jubilee collection of cuttings in which it might find a place. It is a hymn which I wrote for Jubilee Sunday and for Epsom Church.[9] No one knows that I wrote it, and I am well aware that such a theme is quite outside and beyond my poor powers. Nevertheless I am sure that Your Majesty will not disdain it, as expressing the sincere and earnest aspirations of one of Your Majesty's most devoted Subjects."

The famous fancy ball at Devonshire House soon followed, and Rosebery went:

"As a gentleman of the 18th century. I was described greatly to my disgust as that effeminate gossip Horace Walpole. If challenged for a name I should have given 'The Duke of Devonshire of that time!' But I had no idea of anybody. The best dress was, I thought, Lady Algernon Lennox as Princesse de Lamballe. The Chancellor as George III unspeakable."

Friends of very different types passed with the year. In May Colonel Henry Forester, known to his contemporaries as "the Lad," was mourned by all the world of Melton and Newmarket. He was brother to the two brilliant ladies who cheered Lord Beaconsfield's old age. "A mercy," Rosebery wrote, "as he would have remained blind; so I cannot grieve, but a dear friend and a noble gentleman gone."

As the year was ending:

"Frank Lockwood died of influenza. A terrible blow."

A blow indeed it was to everybody who loved and admired that quick brain, that gifted hand never unkindly employed, that gallant humorous soul.

A humble companion died on the same day as Colonel Forester, who would have liked the joining of the horse's name with his own:

"A bad day. The death of another dear old friend, the horse I loved as some love dogs. . . . I chose a grave for *Raby*. He died standing, like an old hero as he was."

[9] See Appendix.

[450]

When the Gladstones paid their last visit to Scotland in the autumn of 1897 Rosebery had vainly tried to persuade them to pause at Dalmeny. An interchange of affectionate notes followed. Then came Mr. Gladstone's sojourn abroad, and the wearing physical distress of his last winter and spring. Early in May the end was known to be near. On the 13th Rosebery and John Morley went to Hawarden for a final farewell, and on the 19th that great life ended. On the next day in the House of Lords Lord Salisbury paid perhaps the noblest tribute ever offered to a dead statesman by a living opponent. Rosebery was able to touch a nearer chord; and in particular reminded his hearers that—

"All our thoughts must be turned, now that he has gone, to that solitary and pathetic figure, who for sixty years shared all the sorrows and all the joys of Mr. Gladstone's life; who received his every confidence and every aspiration; who shared his triumphs with him, and cheered him under his defeats; who by her tender vigilance, I firmly believe, sustained and prolonged his years."

At midnight on the 27th Rosebery went with Reginald Brett[10] to the vigil over the coffin in Westminster Hall:

"The vast Hall, the coffin with its kneeling watchers, the silence and solitude, most impressive."

At the burial next day, when he was one of the pallbearers, his thoughts were again with the one left behind:

"A noble sight and ceremony. Mrs. Gladstone a figure of indescribable pathos. Supported by her two sons she knelt at the head of the coffin, and when it was lowered seemed to wish to kiss the ground, saying 'once more, only once more' (I was close) with a dim idea, I think, that she was to kiss him, but the two sons gently raised her. . . . She was noble to-day, like the Mater Dolorosa in the old pictures,—a figure of sublime unspeakable woe."

In November Rosebery spoke in Edinburgh when the Scottish form of the Gladstone National Memorial was considered. Men of all parties were there, and he was able to point to the restored Mercat Cross, Mr. Gladstone's tribute to Edinburgh, as enduring evidence of the statesman's pride in his Scottish blood and his love for the Scottish capital.

In this narrative much space has been given to Rosebery's twenty years of close association with the mighty Liberal chief. It pervaded

[10] (1852-1930.) Succeeded as 2nd Viscount Esher 1899. G.C.B., etc.

[451]

the whole of Rosebery's brief official career, and it was one of life's ironies that the closing of that career should have been due to the last appearance on the political stage of the figure that trod it longest in our whole history.

In a recently published book of Lord Rendel's[11] Rosebery's relations with Gladstone are freely discussed, with frequent signs of the writer's animus against Rosebery as a politician. Lord Rendel was a man of marked ability, and, had his early desire for official life been fulfilled, would have been a prominent figure of the Liberal centre, and a follower of Campbell-Bannerman. As it was, he seems to have taken too seriously Mr. Gladstone's passing allusions to his differences with Rosebery on some foreign questions. And he lost his sense of perspective when he thought[12] that Gladstone never "regarded except with some scorn Lord Rosebery's boasted nostrum of 'Concert of Europe' "—Mr. Gladstone was quite prepared for isolated action on occasion, as he showed at Alexandria and on the Afghan frontier; but he never underrated the value of European agreement. The unintended effect of Lord Rendel's book, in spite of a meagre allusion to their personal friendship, is a distortion of the real relations between Rosebery and his leader, as I have attempted to describe them. Another curious blunder may also be noted,[13] where Lord Granville's supersession in 1886 is ascribed to his speech against the Royal Titles Bill. But Rosebery, who was preferred, also spoke against the Bill.[14]

Lord Rendel's own bias against the Concert of Europe is explained by his judgment of Rosebery's attitude on the Far Eastern Question in 1894. He had long been concerned with China in the business of the Armstrong firm, and in various secret negotiations carried on through the medium of Sir Robert Hart. Therefore, when China's dispute with Japan over Corea threatened war, Lord Rendel's sympathies were solely with the first. In his book (pp. 258–65) he narrates his failure to induce Rosebery to support China by single action, and Rosebery's use of the "effective but cowardly phrase 'the paramount duty of maintaining the concert of Europe.' "[15] This is not the place to discuss the value of Lord Rendel's

[11] *The Personal Papers of Lord Rendel.*
[12] *Op. cit.,* p. 130.
[13] *Op. cit.,* p. 32.
[14] See p. 78.
[15] Among the corrigenda for insertion in *The Personal Papers of Lord Rendel* appears the following: ch. vi, p. 259—The Concert of Europe. "It may be recorded here that on October 10th, 1880, Mr. Gladstone wrote to Mrs. Gladstone as follows: 'It is the working of the European Concert for purposes of justice, peace and liberty,

arguments for solitary "firm and friendly advice" to Japan, which would hardly have been taken except as veiling a threat. But years later, after the defeat of China, and the gathering of vultures round the prey, Rosebery wrote to Wemyss Reid from his retirement:

Confidential.   MENTMORE, *December 30th,* 1897.
"MY DEAR REID,

". . . As to China my main point is this: that my policy was two-fold.

"1. To have Japan on our side.

"2. To reserve strength for this question and possible occasions of a similar kind. (As it is, we are scattered in various wars, which greatly weakens our voice and action.) I would have Great Britain hanging like a thundercloud over these filibusters: not dispersed in showers all over the Empire. I constantly warned the country of this vast impending crisis, of this Greater Eastern question."

Rosebery's encomium of Gladstone was his sole contribution in Parliament during 1898; nor, until a startling occurrence abroad later in the year roused him to speak, did he utter a word on current politics. But he delivered a long address on London Government at St. James Hall (March 1st). A municipal election was impending, and Rosebery dwelt on two perils of the moment—one, the introduction of party politics into municipal life; the other, the threatened partition of London into a number of municipalities exercising most of the County Council's functions. The transformation of vestries into Borough Councils was effected on simple lines in the following year; but at that date the discrepancy between the Moderate vote for the Council and the Unionist vote for Parliament made the Council unpopular among London Conservatives.

There was a distribution of medals to the Fire Brigade in Victoria Park. Rosebery's younger daughter Margaret officiated, making her first public appearance. What Napoleon called "two o'clock in the morning courage," Rosebery said, was the courage that every fireman requires and that, he was proud to think, every London fireman possesses.

He had spoken on municipal politics earlier in the year at Glasgow (June 23rd), after the People's Palace was opened. It was a municipal foundation by that centre of collective enterprise, and Rosebery had no dread of municipal collectivism. On this occasion he went so far as to admit a case of overwhelming strength in

with efficiency and success, which is the great matter at issue. That has always been the ideal of my life in Foreign Policy.'"

favour of a man who chose to be a town councillor rather than a Member of Parliament. For a moment the Imperial stop was kept mute.

And in July he made a rattling defence of the London County Council at the Chairman's dinner, dwelling on its new responsibilities and its glorious future. But it is safe to say that the gathering which he most enjoyed was the Eton dinner to Lord Curzon, Lord Minto, and Bishop Welldon, before their departure to high posts in the distant Empire. Rosebery presided, and his gift of blending humour with real feeling just fitted the occasion. Such farewells must not be jocular, but equally they must not be tearful.

The advance into the Soudan, of which Rosebery had at first thought doubtfully, had culminated with the brilliant engagement of Omdurman, and but a few weeks later it became known that Lord Kitchener, proceeding southwards up the Nile, had encountered Major Marchand and a party from the French Congo at Fashoda, where the French flag had been hoisted. The rights of the territorial question were discussed with some temper in Paris and London, and Rosebery thought it his duty to speak out for the Government. This was not splitting the party, for Harcourt, little as he favoured the British advance, had no patience with the French pretensions. At the same time, Rosebery's awakening from a two years' slumber might seem a challenge to the leader in the Commons.

But on the peaceful ground of a ploughing match at Epsom, Rosebery, at a dinner which followed, spoke of the policy pursued by the Government at Fashoda as the policy declared by Sir Edward Grey in March 1895, for which he was personally responsible. Sir Edward's speech, it will be recalled, had nearly produced a Cabinet crisis, and its resuscitation at once put a match to the "leadership" bonfire.

And when receiving the Freedom of Perth (October 23rd), he delivered a long address on Foreign Affairs. He spoke feelingly of the rescript issued by the young Emperor Nicholas of Russia. It was a melancholy and humiliating confession that the peace of Europe mainly depended, not on the divine precepts of the Christian religion, but on the awe inspired in every nation by the existence of vast armaments. He went on to speak of the reconquest of the Soudan as a great victory for civilisation. A warm personal compliment to Major Marchand's enterprise was followed by a close examination of the French case, and friendly suggestions to France for a settlement. At the Mansion House banquet to Lord Kitchener he laid most stress on the triumph won by exterminating the menace of Dervish rule, and warding off danger not only from ourselves, but from those neighbours whose gratitude we had a right to claim.

And before the year ended he attended a meeting of City magnates (December 1st), again at the Mansion House, in support of the Gordon Memorial College. The general effect of all this was to restore him as an active force in public life. The Liberals of the Centre were not likely to ignore this, and when, early in December, Sir William Harcourt solemnly resigned his leadership, and when, at the beginning of the next year, John Morley also retired, their retreat seemed to Rosebery's eager followers to bring him nearer the footlights. For a party whose three most eminent members had all said good-bye—without quite going—was an anomaly that could not persist. Thoughtful people extended warm sympathy to Campbell-Bannerman in his succession to the leadership of his party in the House of Commons.

In most respects this year 1898 was the most uneventful that Rosebery had yet spent. He paid short visits to Naples, first in January, and again at Whitsuntide, when he slept for the first time at the villa. He had some delightful outings in the Rendels' yacht, and dined with them among the fireflies. In July he was at Vienna, and greatly interested in an hour's talk with Baron Kallay.[16] Rosebery, and his friend the ever agreeable Ralph Milbanke, so long Councillor at Vienna, dined at a small restaurant in the Exhibition:

"At one table Thun the Prime Minister, at another Franz Ferdinand the Heir Apparent. Neither, I think, destined to save Austria."

After a long fortnight at Gastein he was at Vienna again for a day, meeting Count Goluchowski:

"A pleasant Gallicised Pole, giving one the idea of a good diplomatist without much power; short, without dignity, but agreeable, unaffected, and unassuming."

His other foreign expedition was to Amsterdam, on Ferdinand Rothschild's yacht, with the two boys, for the fine celebrations of the young Queen's assumption of the throne. The Rembrandt Exhibition was a feature of the year, and except for the "Night-Watch," Rosebery thought that the best pictures came from

[16] The well-known Hungarian statesman and administrator.

England. Most of the autumn was spent in Scotland, including a visit to Mar Lodge, where Rosebery again did fairly "on the hill." The Empress Frederick spent some days at Dalmeny, and gave her host "one of the little rings that Frederick the Great gave to his friends, with a little portrait of himself. A charming gift."

The short list of contemporary close friends grew shorter at the end of the year. In September Christopher Sykes had a seizure, and after lingering on for three months he died. He had always been a favourite comrade of Rosebery's, especially in Paris, where there was unusual leisure for strolling and quiet talk of old days. "He was 'never in the way, and never out of the way,' as Charles II said of Godolphin," was Rosebery's epitaph for him. Two days later a still heavier blow fell. As Rosebery arrived at Mentmore from a very pleasant week's shooting with Lord Derby, he was handed two telegrams, "one from Ferdy, saying he was rheumatic and could not come to Mentmore to-day—the other from his butler saying he was dead."

Ferdinand Rothschild's attachment to Rosebery, and its full return, have already been noted. The fun of his frequent letters; his extraordinary judgment of works of art; his cosmopolitan knowledge combined with a complete adaptability to English life; a certain sensitiveness not unlike Rosebery's own; the memory of his warm friendship for his cousin Hannah—all these sharpened the pang of his loss.

After the refusals of Sir William Harcourt and John Morley to take an "active and responsible part in the formal counsels of the heads of the Liberal Party," Sir Henry Campbell-Bannerman was elected leader in the House of Commons. Rosebery cordially approved; and the new chief made a popular start on the green benches. But neither of his colleagues had actually retired from politics. Morley was beginning to be immersed in the *Life of Gladstone*, but he opposed the Government on the Soudan Question in February and found himself in the opposite lobby to Sir E. Grey and other Liberals. Harcourt made a successful reappearance on finance, and he too prided himself on being in direct opposition to Rosebery's followers. Rosebery himself had no more reason to maintain silence than other retired leaders, but as usual he did not entirely appreciate the colour that the public would place on his apparent resumption of activity. The City Liberal Club dined on May 5th, and Rosebery presided. He opened with a threnody over recent losses: William Rogers—"If I had to seek anywhere for an embodiment of what

THE RETURN

OF

"THE LITTLE MINISTER".

Will the Elders reinstate him.?

"PUNCH"

June 18th 1898.

By kind permission of the Proprietors of "Punch"

John Morley	Sir William Harcourt	Sir Henry Fowler	Lord Rosebery	H. H. Asquith

I think true Liberalism in mind and spirit is, I should think of Mr. Rogers"; Lord Herschell—"I have come to the deliberate conviction that he was the first public servant of his country at the time when he died"; and Thomas Ellis, a loss like that of Francis Horner or Charles Buller—"There was something in the lofty purity of that spirit which impressed everybody with whom he came into contact, every party, every class, every section of the community." He congratulated Campbell-Bannerman on the cordial spirit he had spread in the ranks, and then made tolerably direct appeal to the Liberal Unionists, and gave "advice to politicians" to constitute a new party to embody all the elements which existed in the Liberal party before 1886. He asked for combination of the old Liberal spirit with the new Imperial spirit, and for the larger patriotism which, when large issues are presented, makes all parties sink their differences.

His friends had no idea of leaving him alone. On July 26th Herbert Gladstone came to the Durdans for the night, and joined in the after-dinner drive.

"The same old story as with E. Grey and Fowler. I point out in reply:

"1. That I definitely resigned in 1896.

"2. That my resignation was sincere, solemn and not strategical.

"3. That nothing but some unsuspected crisis could bring me back.

"4. That if I came back now I should not bring peace, but a sword. Old and dominant rivalries and enmities would revive.

"5. Whereas now all is for the best in the best possible of worlds,— bye-elections going well, party united, etc."

Meanwhile, the South African trouble, the history of which is not part of this biography, was becoming more menacing. Tempers were hardening on both sides, and the protagonists, Chamberlain and Milner and Kruger, utterly different as they were, were no experts in the art of conciliatory firmness. The only inevitable wars are wars for which people prepare, and this was one of them. Rosebery's part in the drama will be set forth in a later chapter. Again in this year he was silent in the House of Lords. That House, however, took a rather comical share in a matter of direct concern to Rosebery. In the last days of his Government of 1895 a statue of Oliver Cromwell was officially promised. There were loud protests in the House of Commons, especially from Irish members mindful of Drogheda, and to avoid unseemly controversy a private person offered to bear the cost of the statue. It was an open secret that this person was Rosebery himself. Then came a battle over the site, the acceptance of the statue having been confirmed by the Conservative Government. One act of the comedy was played in the House of Lords, where a protest against the erection of the statue without the sanction of Parliament was carried by six Peers against four members of the Government. The statue was unveiled without ceremony on November 14th, and a crowd filled the Queen's Hall in the evening when Rosebery was surrounded by a band of Liberal Peers and Members of Parliament. Rosebery noted the curious paradox that Bernini's bust of Cromwell had been accepted by the present Government and placed in the very heart of the House of Commons. He went on to explain, not to defend, Cromwell's Irish policy and the King's execution. He sketched the tributes paid by many critics, some of them no sympathisers with the Protector's policy: Cromwell was a great soldier, a great ruler, and a great maintainer of British power and influence abroad. Rosebery dwelt lovingly on this last Imperial aspect of the hero. Then he passed to Cromwell's spiritual side, to the unfair charge of hypocrisy, and in conclusion to the present need of a Cromwell, who would not be the same in externals, but—

"He would be strenuous, he would be sincere. He would not compromise with principles. His faith would be in God and in freedom, and in the influence of Great Britain as promoting, as asserting both."

This was one of Rosebery's best addresses, on a level of uniform eloquence. His temporary abstention from party warfare seemed during the last year or two to give colour to his social or literary speeches, probably because he was less physically tired. And he began to be thought of as a public orator, able to speak for the nation because no longer a party chief. But it will appear later how strictly this conception of him was limited.

The Conservative Government, with one of those impulses that dignify British public life, had nominated J. B. Balfour, a Liberal ex-Minister, to the highest judicial post in Scotland, that of Lord President of the Court of Session. His farewell to politics was honoured at the Scottish Liberal Club (November 27th); and Rosebery as Chairman remarked that he would have liked, in spite of missiles that might have been thrown at him, to propose the toast of Her Majesty's Government in gratitude for their generous and wise act. He referred to the dinner of three years before, and to the universal goodwill shown to a man who, in a career of nine-and-thirty years, had never bartered or in any way compromised his opinions. No appointment of his own, Rosebery said, had ever given him the pleasure that this did.

Before this (May 17th), the Northbrook Society had entertained Lord Elgin in London, and it fell to Rosebery to propose the returned Viceroy's health. He was able to praise with justice Elgin's patient calmness in confronting the difficulties of war, plague, and famine. He described the frontier as a cactus hedge.

"Absolutely impervious to those who wish to enter it, but eminently undesirable if you wish to make it a seat to occupy."

He had also presided, at the annual dinner of the Civil Service (October 26th), and at an excursion of Caledonian Railway servants to Carlisle. He received the Freedom of Bath, where he unveiled tablets to the memory of Chatham and William Pitt, and sketched their history with his usual diligent accuracy. Chatham's connection with Bath was the closer, and Rosebery devoted to him the bulk of his speech. He concluded his eulogism with:

"I regard Mr. Pitt as the first Liberal Imperialist. . . . I venture to think,—I may be wrong,—in ten years perhaps you will remember my prophecy,—I believe the party of Liberal Imperialism is destined to control the destinies of this country."

A pleasant incident of this visit was a stay at Wells with Bishop Kennion, the appointment of Rosebery's short premiership.

The following letter has its human interest:

To Dr. Randall Davidson.

[*Copy.*]   38 BERKELEY SQUARE, *May 9th,* 1900.
"MY DEAR BISHOP,

"I am only just recovering from the stupefaction produced by yesterday's proceedings, but I must write you a line to wish you joy of your move and your speech.[17] I only heard the last half of the speech, as I had to go and see my boy's tutor at Eton, but I thought it excellent. The only criticism I would offer is one of manner—it was a little breathless and hurried: a pause or two would have been an improvement. Archbishop Tait you will remember was quite at the other extreme. Speaking in the House of Lords, where every auditor gives the impression of

[17] On May 8th, 1900, the Bishop of Winchester made a long speech urging the desirability of legislative effect being given to such of the recommendations of the final Report of the Royal Commission on Liquor Licensing Laws as were common both to the "Majority" and the "Minority" Reports.

[461]

profound weariness and boredom, one is apt to hurry in order to release a suffering audience. I know you will forgive my presumption.

"I was diverted at hearing a prime minister speak of a motion brought forward by a Bishop and amended by a Primate as a 'fraud and a wile.'

"Y. sincy,

AR"

Rosebery had hired the Duke of Sutherland's yacht *Catania* and spent a few days at Naples and more at Messina. He went on to Greece, and to Constantinople, where a curious dilemma confronted him. The Sultan, the infamous Abdul Hamid, had got wind of his arrival; carriages and aides-de-camp met the yacht. Rosebery told the Ambassador, Sir N. O'Connor, that he could accept no favours from the Sultan, and would not see him. The Ambassador was dismayed; but finally a message was sent that Rosebery begged to be allowed to remain a private tourist. A series of elaborate *pourparlers* ensued. Turkish Ministers, who could not dine out without the Sultan's leave, were forbidden to meet Rosebery unless he agreed to come to the palace; one of them, who managed to see him, pleaded that this insult would drive the Sultan into the arms of Russia. It was a painful interview, but Rosebery, asserting that he was a private individual, remained obdurate, and, merely sending a message that he was *vivement froissé* that Ministers had been refused permission to meet him at dinner, steamed out of the harbour.

Rosebery's sons were finishing their delightful Eton existence, and his younger daughter's marriage in April made the first break in the family circle.

THE SOUTH AFRICAN WAR

When President Kruger's insolent ultimatum of October 1899 made war certain, Rosebery felt himself absolved from his rule of silence. At the Pitt celebrations at Bath (October 26th, 1899) he maintained that it was no moment for criticism; time for that when the war should be over. He examined at length the incident of Majuba Hill and the "sublime experiment" of Mr. Gladstone in making peace. It was an attempt to carry into international policy the principles of the Gospel itself; but it was also due to Mr. Gladstone's conviction, only realised by his intimates, that the overpowering might of England permitted action which weaker countries could not take. But the terms had been regarded as proof of weakness, and, were their author here, he would not contemplate the

[462]

grant of such terms again. They might think this a small war, but no wars are small.

A day or two later, at Edinburgh, he bade farewell to the Scots Greys and the Gordon Highlanders, and again spoke of an inquisition after the war, but urged present support to those who had the direction of affairs.

At Chatham (January 23rd, 1900), when the eyes of the country had been partly opened to the magnitude of its task, he dwelt on its most formidable character. This was not merely because of the recent reverses, but because we had lost the sympathy of Europe and also much of our prestige. But that would be recovered, secured by our Navy and our possession of capital. But we must employ the scientific methods which we had rejected. In the House of Lords (January 30th and February 15th) he repeated his hope that investigation would be deferred; but in the debate on the Army proposals of the Government he declared that the Government had never been in time. Lincoln's first demand in the Civil War was for 5,000 men, and by the time the war was over the United States had put two-and-three-quarter millions in the field. The Government had no notion how the feeling of constant danger was present to the minds of the people.

Rosebery's view of the situation was simple, and certainly was that of many thoughtful people in Britain. One minority considered the war a sheer iniquity, an orgy of greed and violence. Another, at the opposite pole, thought nothing too bad for the Boers, a tribe of psalm-singing hypocrites who deserved to lose the gold mines they were too stupid to exploit. A third held that Chamberlain and Milner had displayed all possible skill and patience in negotiating with such an impossible opponent as President Kruger, and that the war was inevitable. Rosebery had, of course, thought the raid a senseless blunder, but he both liked and admired Cecil Rhodes, who was often his guest. He was not disposed to think hardly of such a Napoleonic Imperialist. And he resented the hue-and-cry let loose against Dr. Jameson, whose personal qualities made it difficult not to turn a half-blind eye to his solitary lapse. Years afterwards when "the Doctor" died, Rosebery wrote to his brother:

"I have known few people if any so irresistibly attractive of affection as your brother. It was I think his eyes—the eyes of an affectionate dog I used to call them and there can scarcely be higher praise—that first impressed one, combined with the good natured humour of the mouth. These lured one past the externals to know the man, and when one knew the man one realised at once the noble and generous character which has fascinated so many thousands. I was most impressed by him when I went to see him in prison and found him the same cheerful unchanged unsubdued 'doctor.' One would have trusted him readily with one's life or anything else—one could 'draw at sight' upon his face."

Rosebery was not specially bound to any of the principals in the Government camp. He had always been friendly with Chamberlain but nothing more; and though he appreciated, as everybody must, the distinction of Milner's intellect and character, he was in no way under the Balliol spell in the manner of two or three of the Liberal Imperialists. He thought that negotiations with the Transvaal Government had been sadly mismanaged, and that in a sense Milner was greatly responsible for the war. But, as has been noted, he wished to defer all criticism until victory was complete. A stricter partisan, as he recognised, would regret that roughness or clumsiness in negotiating, insensibility to the opponent's case, even neglect of military preparation, would all be forgotten when the day was won. But it would be a greater misfortune to hamper victory by untimely criticism. The only hope of discouraging future carelessness or mismanagement lay in drastic inquiry when peace was attained. From the first it was the cue of the Unionists to denounce all Liberals as enemies of their country. Even the Imperialist wing could not escape. Some of these, curiously enough, believed that annexation of the two Dutch republics would not be necessary; while most Liberals of the Centre, such as Campbell-Bannerman, and even some of the Left, like John Morley, saw from the first that it was inevitable. Rosebery himself had no doubts on this point.

The strange publication of the recriminatory Spion Kop dispatches in April was hotly debated in both Houses. Rosebery bitterly assailed the Government for washing dirty linen in the presence of the world.

"Mr. Gladstone once said to me of a statesman now dead, and whom I shall not name, that he was of a composition to which water would add strength. I am afraid that history will write that epitaph on His Majesty's Government."

The war progressed without repetition of the earlier reverses, and the spectacular occupation of the Boer capitals created the illusion that it was drawing to its close. There was a discussion in the House of Lords (July 28th) on the military strength of England in relation to the continent of Europe. The refusal to sanction the Commander-in-Chief's participation in debate was blamed by Rosebery; and a few days afterwards he put down a motion on which the question could be discussed. On the first occasion Lord Lansdowne had flouted the idea, on the obvious ground that the officer would become a political partisan, and was stung to sharp reprimand of his old friend's methods of criticism. In his second speech Rosebery carefully abstained from personalities, and made a good point by the reminder that five years ago the then Opposition had declined to take the Secretary of State for War as the mouthpiece of his experts, but had turned the Government out. There was no division, but the sense of the House was rather with Lansdowne on this single question, though the War Office was not winning many laurels just then.

Parliament was dissolved in the middle of September. The "Khaki Election" was an undisguised party manœuvre, and it met with all success. The Government, which had lost rather more than the customary number of by-elections, found itself a shade stronger than at the dissolution.

When the Address was moved in the House of Lords, "the close of the war in South Africa" was the theme of the Government representatives. Lord Kimberley disposed of that pretension, and when Rosebery's turn came he devoted himself to a fierce denunciation of "this wanton election" for which no cause or reason would ever be given. Above all, he resented the cry that every Liberal vote was a vote "sold" or "given" to the Boers. What an encouragement to them that some forty-five per cent. of the voters had taken their side. There was Mr. Charles Rose[18] at Newmarket, who had lost two sons in the war in which the third was fighting. Placards were put up all over the constituency representing him as helping Mr. Kruger to haul down the British flag, with remarks too scurrilous to mention. "That was a tragic Imperialist indeed! There is a Nemesis attending methods of that kind." He also spoke caustically of the reconstruction of the Government, and of the festival circle of its members that could assemble at Hatfield at Christmas. The Duke of Devonshire ignored the main indictments in the speech, and did little but remark that when Rosebery had reconstructed the Opposition he could judge better of the reconstruction of the Government.

This was a fair taunt enough, though it was no answer to Rosebery's charges. The fact remained, and remains, that the election of

[18] (1847-1913.) M.P. 1903-13. *Cr.* Baronet 1909.

1900, and the methods whereby it was won, mark the least creditable chapter in sixty years of British political history. Rosebery wrote to a friend in October: "I never remember dirtier work done than at this election."

But the Opposition was shattered into at least three fragments, roughly represented by Rosebery, Campbell-Bannerman, and Harcourt.

The Liberal Imperial Council was formed in 1901, with Lord Brassey as Chairman and Mr. Robert Perks[19] as one of its Vice-Chairmen. It was composed of Rosebery's followers, but he did not belong to it himself. He wrote to Perks (June 29th, 1901):

"The less your new party is tainted with Roseberyism the better. My conviction is that I had better remain as I am and take no part. Later on as an independent coadjutor I may or may not be of use."

Since Rosebery's resignation Mr. Perks had been one of his frequent correspondents, and was becoming one of his most trusted lieutenants. The blend of sturdy Nonconformity with generous Imperial sentiment appealed directly to Rosebery's heart. To his head also, because he found an ally against that large Nonconformist section to which the war meant simply unjust aggression from first to last.

The war had taken a guerilla aspect. There was no attempt to treat the Boers as *francs-tireurs* outside the conventions of warfare, but it was considered necessary to combat them by methods equally irregular according to the European standard of the day. These included the punitive burning of farms, and the massing of women and children in concentration camps. The heart-searchings of the Liberal party became deeper. On June 14th, 1901, Sir Henry Campbell-Bannerman made his famous speech at a dinner given by the National Reform Union: "When was a war not a war? When it was carried on by methods of barbarism in South Africa." This phrase was of course seized on as an attack on the humanity of our soldiers, whom the speaker should have expressly exonerated before he used it, instead of doing so later in the House of Commons. One hundred and fourteen members of the City Liberal Club asked Rosebery to address them, but he preferred to begin by a written reply, which appeared in *The Times*. In this he reiterated his determination not to return to party politics. His line of conduct

[19] *b.* 1849. Civil Engineer; M.P. 1892-1910; President of Wesleyan Conference. *Cr.* Baronet 1908.

was simple, obvious and loyal, so it had been called mysterious. There was a great Liberal force in the country, but it must make up its mind about the war. Neutrality and an open mind made up an impossible attitude. The war was either just or unjust, the methods either uncivilised or legitimate. But this was not a transient difference of opinion. It was based on a sincere fundamental and incurable antagonism of principle with regard to the Empire at large and our consequent policy. One school or the other must prevail if the Liberal party was once more to become a force. A party cannot be conducted on the principle of Issachar.

The letter was followed by a speech to the Club which developed and extended it. He spoke amiably of the trying situation of his "old friend Sir Henry Campbell-Bannerman," but ironically of the speeches at the National Reform Union. He thought that no Government had ever crowded such a frightful assembly of errors, of weaknesses, and of wholesale blunders into its history as had this Government. Two later sentences stuck in the memories of hearers and readers: "You start with a clean slate as regards those cumbersome programmes with which you were overloaded in the past," and "I must plough my furrow alone. That is my fate agreeable or the reverse; but before I get to the end of that furrow it is possible that I may find myself not alone."

There had been a party meeting at the Reform Club a week before, at which Campbell-Bannerman had lamented "personal antagonisms," and had received a vote of confidence from all sections. It was clear that Rosebery's closest allies thought his declaration of the fundamental cleavage in the Liberal party somewhat untimely.

The whole tale of the dissensions that racked the Liberal party, with the rival banquets known as "war to the knife and fork," is admirably told in Mr. Spender's *Life of Sir Henry Campbell-Bannerman*, who was the unhappy central figure in the controversy. Rosebery was not allowed to remain out of the fray, but he was no willing participant. Perhaps he erred in associating, as he did, criticism of the Government's war policy with indifference to the future of the Empire, and in not distinguishing publicly between those Liberals who thought the war and its conduct a blunder and those who thought them a heartless crime. But he felt compelled to stand by the Imperialist creed in its entirety, and on the platform it is impossible to refine indefinitely. He could not feel sure which way duty pointed. To Perks, who wrote to him at Gastein of the need of a leader, he replied (July 25th):

[467]

"You are, as I always tell you, fighting for a cause, not for a man. I, having retired, am neither in a position to come forward or to speak on behalf of the Liberal party, though this does not imply that I may not be of use."

Consequently, as the year was closing, and peace with Dutch South Africa still seemed distant, he accepted an invitation to speak at Chesterfield. The occasion was announced some time beforehand, to the annoyance of the anti-war leaders. In some respects Rosebery's task was delicate. Some of his closest friends, he thought, had gone too far in their canonisation of Milner, and their blunt determination to pursue the war to a finish at any cost. He spoke for two hours, and more than half of the speech was devoted to the war, its preliminaries, and the hopes for its conclusion. He began by blaming the Government for their heavy-handed diplomacy and their blindness over the Boer armaments. The General Election of 1900, he said, had struck deeper at the roots of political morality than anything within his political recollection. He derided Lord Halsbury's phrase of "a sort of warfare" in South Africa. He defended, on the whole, the methods of concentration camps and of martial law. He then came to peace policy. He protested to the utmost of his power against Milner's declared intentions of avoiding any settlement with the enemy. He begged the Government to recall the resistance of the United Netherlands against Spain, and the history of Lord North's administration. Rosebery proceeded to offer two suggestions to the Government. The first, of which nothing came directly, was a picturesque sketch of a fortuitous meeting between a British representative and a representative of the exiled Dutch Government. The second, of which the wisdom was proved by the event, was the negotiation of peace by Lord Kitchener, not by the present High Commissioner or by one specially sent out. There had been a fierce clamour from the Left for Milner's recall, and to this Rosebery would not assent. He was for as full an amnesty as possible, for lavish generosity in re-stocking farms, and appeasing the remains of civil rancour. We were bound, he said, to the Boers—

"for better or worse, in a permanent, inevitable and fateful marriage. . . . I want to bind, to heal, not to keep open the mortal wound which is being caused by this war."

After summarising his policy, he continued, "what I can do to further it I will do." Those on the platform sprang to their feet

By kind permission of the Proprietors of "Punch"

THE "DEUS IN MACHINA"

Lord R-s-b-ry: "H'm, I see you are in difficulties, madam. For myself, I shall not voluntarily re-enter the water; but I will give you a few elementary hints on the natatory art!"

and waved their hats, for it sounded like a resumption of leadership. He went on to remind them that his policy did not run on party lines, but he appealed not to the party but to the country.

Rosebery developed his theme of pacification at Liverpool early in the following year (February 14th). His allusion to a fortuitous meeting of negotiators had been ridiculed by people ignorant of history.[20]

A Dutch Minister had now come over unofficially, and there was a possibility of conversations with Boer delegates. Rosebery never felt certain, he observed, that a wise statesman could not have concluded peace with General Botha in March of last year.

When, in the early summer of 1902, the peace of Vereeniging was concluded by Lord Kitchener with General Botha, the settlement followed in broad outline the conditions for which Rosebery had contended.

The sensation caused by the Chesterfield speech was not only due to the South African pronouncement. The opening passages asserted the doctrine of "the clean slate" and urged that the "fly-blown phylacteries of the Liberal Party" should be put aside.[21] The general effect, however, was to induce Campbell-Bannerman to open negotiations, and he went to luncheon in Berkeley Square. His impressions of the conversation and of Rosebery's attitude are set out in his *Life*,[22] Rosebery's in a memorandum jotted down at the time:

LONDON, December 23rd, 1901.

"Yesterday when I was at the Chapel Royal C.-Bannerman called on me leaving a card followed up by a note, expressing a wish to see me. So I asked him to luncheon to-day. He struck me as much changed (I had not seen him for many months). He had lost his tranquil and portly ease, seemed aged and shrunk and irritable (for him). He began talking about substantial agreement &c. and I somehow fell at once into Irish Home Rule and stated definitely that I could have nothing further to do with Mr. Gladstone's policy, that much had happened since 1892 including the Irish Local Government Bill and my own experience at the F.O. What I had then seen of the working of the Austro-Hungarian and Swedish-Norwegian systems had made me feel

[20] The instances he had in mind were the conclusion of the Tripartite Treaty by the Abbé Dubois under Louis XV and Mr. Oswald's secret negotiations in Paris in 1783 for peace with our insurgent colonies.

[21] Campbell-Bannerman, we are told, objected to this metaphor on zoological grounds. No rational fly would lay its eggs on a phylactery.

[22] Vol. ii, pp. 16-18.

that I could never be a party to introducing anything of the kind in Great Britain.

"This rather disconcerted C.-B., as he had just declared himself at Dunfermline in favour of Irish Home Rule. He tried to soften down my declaration, but I was emphatic.

"As to the war, we dwelt chiefly on 'methods of barbarism.' He declared that the effect of this fatal phrase on foreign opinion had been recently manufactured by *The Times*. I instanced as *per contra* its effect on me when I was alone at Gastein. I took occasion to speak my regret at the Holborn restaurant dinner, the speech which he then made, and the company amid which he had deliberately placed himself. To this he said nothing and offered no explanation. He gave me the impression of not being very proud of it. He spoke however with complacency of his recent tour in Devonshire and Lancashire, and with great bitterness (quite unlike him) of the 'rebellion' attempted in Scotland which had been 'put down and squashed out by our fellows.' He named Haldane and Munro Ferguson with peculiar asperity.

"I inferred that union between his section and Asquith's was more remote than ever. (More especially as the same evening Haldane proposed himself at Mentmore and spoke with an acrimony which could scarcely be exceeded of C.-B.)

"C.-B. ended by acknowledging, in reply to my remark in justification of Asquith that he (C.-B.) had definitely thrown himself into the arms of the Pro-Boer section, that his private opinions had always been with that section. (This I had never doubted.)

"He told me that he had seen Harcourt and Morley since the Chesterfield speech. The first had been somewhat obstreperous, but had been cooled down.

"In the midst of the conversation he said that he must catch his train and hurried off."

There was a good deal of essential agreement between the two men, but neither could co-operate with the extreme followers of the other. Rosebery's Liverpool speeches, and his expressed conviction that a Parliament in Ireland could not be thought of for the time being, gave body to the metaphor of the clean slate. To say that the Newcastle programme was indigestible fare was one thing; to abandon Gladstone's Home Rule was another. Accordingly Campbell-Bannerman at Leicester asked what the Irish policy of the party was to be. Was it coercion? Rosebery promptly wrote to *The Times* that his friend's declarations, both on domestic policy and on the war, had brought about "a moment of definite separation," with a compliment to Sir Henry's devotion to "what he conceives to be the interests" of the Liberal party. Soon afterwards Asquith made a speech on Ireland, asserting that the Irish problem was neither settled nor shelved, but that British opinion must be won by "step by step" methods. Most English Liberals did not greatly differ from him in this matter. Only a few stalwarts would have engaged to make an Irish Bill on Gladstonian lines the first measure following a Liberal victory. But the immediate consequence of the public dissention was the foundation of the Liberal League. After a gathering of Liberal Imperialists in Berkeley Square the new birth was announced, and its meaning and purpose were set out at a vast meeting in Glasgow on March 10th.

Rosebery had always kept in touch with the organisers at the Liberal headquarters, especially with Charles Geake, active, genial, and clear-headed. He represented the outlook of the *Westminster Gazette*; so for the new organisation it was necessary to look elsewhere. A principal agent was therefore found in W. Allard, the extremely skilful secretary of the Home Counties Liberal Federation. No more loyal or efficient agent could have been chosen. From 1902 to 1910 many letters passed between him and Rosebery. From the start the leader announced a severe limitation of his own speeches. He was perpetually spurred to make more speeches, even after the Government of 1905 had abstracted some of the lights of the League.

Rosebery sketched the history of the political severance, disclaiming any personal division between himself and one of the oldest of his political friends. He compared the new League with the Liberation Society, whose course was still unaccomplished. The League was not to be shut out from the party, unlike Liberal Unionist leaders, who were undistinguishable from Conservatives. After repudiating the prospect of an independent Irish Parliament, and explaining the doctrine of the clean slate as the abandonment of the Newcastle programme, he named education, with praise of Haldane's activity on the subject; temperance, on which he urged them to take what they could get, proceeding in the van of popular sentiment; and above all efficiency, "a condition of national fitness equal to the demands of our Empire." The seven years of Conservative Government had been "seven years lost for all social and human causes; seven years lost for all measures which make for national health and national efficiency; seven years lost in our training and preparation for the keen race of nations, both in commerce and in dominion." He begged them to remember that at Chesterfield he spoke not to a party or a party machine, but to the nation.

The Centre of a political party and its chiefs, who always more or less speak for the Centre, resent the formation of special organisations within its ranks. Men of like minds are bound to group themselves morally, but they must not do more. Hence orthodox Liberals of the Centre were irritated by the League. The Radicals of the Left, of course, regarded it with loathing. This is not the place to write the history of the Liberal League, which was less Rosebery's creation than the creation of others to maintain him in active leadership. It was not destined, as some of its promoters hoped, and as Rosebery thought possible, to become an Aaron's rod swallowing up the other sticks in the Liberal bundle. But it served a real purpose at the time, putting heart into many of the best men in the party, and probably preventing some of them from quitting political life in disgust. And it was able to do this because it was a genuine Liberal organisation, in no way anxious to end as the Left wing of the Tory party, as the subsequent history of its field-officers shows. Nearly all of them became Liberal Ministers, and one concluded his career on the Woolsack in a Socialist Government. Rosebery, at any rate, was determined that the League should not be thought a mere appanage of himself. Some months later he wrote to Perks:

"I wish very much that it [a Glasgow paper] would cease to make adherence to me personally a condition of its support. I am sure that that does harm, and when I heard that they were making it a test, I begged them not to use my name in any way. If the League becomes a matter of a person instead of a principle, I shall leave it. But of this I hope there is no fear."

"How does fortune banter us!" In 1903 she bantered the Liberal party into an appearance of complete reunion in resistance to Josseph Chamberlain's fiscal raid. It was not all banter, because the common experiences of 1903 insensibly helped the fusion of 1905. Rosebery was a convinced Free Trader, and his dread of any attempt to frame an Imperial Zollverein has already been noted.[23] He repeated his fears in a speech at Leeds in May 1902, and at Burnley in May 1903. Campbell-Bannerman welcomed the co-operation offered in Rosebery's speech at Leicester (November 17th, 1903):

[23] See pp. 254, 442.

"In this very place, and from this very platform, an attempt was made to proscribe my policy and my friends. Why do I recall that now? Is it for purposes of recrimination? God forbid. Let bygones be bygones. I fling back the message of peace. I say this—that Liberals will be fools, and worse than fools, if they be not united, shoulder to shoulder, to resist this mad and dangerous experiment, if they do not stand close and cordial together to maintain the noble fabric of our commerce and our Empire."

But the limitations which seemed so simple to Rosebery, and to some others so puzzling, were still operative. He had set them down in a memorandum not long before:

August, 1903.

"1. In 1896 for reasons good or bad but which I thought and think more than sufficient, I severed all political connections and retired from public life for ever.

"2. In 1901 very reluctantly I returned for a time, lured by the hope of effecting something towards peace, and incidentally as it were laid down, what I believe to be the only sound policy for the Liberal Party.

"3. Not long afterwards my policy was publicly repudiated and condemned by one of the joint official leaders of the Liberal Party.

"4. In order to prevent the total proscription of that policy, of which there had been previous symptoms, I assisted in forming the Liberal League, which thus became and remains my only formal connection with public life. It is a protective and defensive body.

"5. Such then is my position succinctly stated. But I may have soon to face the not remote contingency of being asked to join a Liberal Government.

"6. My answer is unhesitatingly, No.

"Personally my wish to have done with the contentions of public life has never wavered since 1896, on the contrary it has strengthened.

"Politically it would not be possible to join a hierarchy of which the only positive or distinctive note has been proscription of my policy and a reiterated attachment to the policy of Gladstone's Home Rule.

"Moreover, for those who regard office as a crown and a reward, it is clear that it should fall to those who have borne the burden and heat of the political day since 1895.

"My associates in the Liberal League do not comprise more than a score of members of the House of Commons. That does not impose on me any obligation or responsibility with regard to administration. Quite the contrary. Several too of these associates more easily satisfied and more in the bondage of politics than I, will no doubt join such a Government and influence it soundly.

[475]

"7. There are other obvious considerations. It is the great majority of the party which should frame the policy and form the Government. With that majority I have no connection.

"AR"

Rosebery's share in the campaign for Free Trade has not been sufficiently recognised. Asquith's feat of dogging the footsteps of Joseph Chamberlain from platform to platform was supreme; but the President of the League was scarcely less busy. In 1903, at an agricultural meeting at Bishop's Stortford (June 11th), at a great Liberal League dinner in London (June 12th) and at a meeting of its Sheffield branch (October 13th) he had hammered away at the Chamberlain projects without qualification and without reserve. As he was well entitled to do, he examined most closely the Imperial aspect of the policy, his proposition being that "this proposal would tend to dislocate, and in time dissolve, the bonds of union of the Empire." The defence and the diplomacy of the Empire were at the charge of this country, and Sir Wilfred Laurier's preference in the Canadian tariff was an acknowledgment of this. There could be no fair or practicable Imperial Tariff.

This controversy is not closed to-day, but it is impossible here even to summarise the arguments, adorned by witty illustration, which he developed in this speech and in that at Leicester. He pursued the topic in South London (November 25th). Towards the close of an animated speech, he asked, "Will the Government fool these people once again?" A rhetorical pause, during which "a voice" called out, "Not if you will take the lead," and the whole audience rose, waving hats and handkerchiefs. Rosebery raised a laugh by quietly repeating his question; but such incidents, even when harmony reigned in the party, made the paradox of his position painfully obvious.

There was also a great Free Trade demonstration in Edinburgh (December 13th). The regular Association and the League had formed a United Free Trade Committee, and Rosebery had to address two large and excited gatherings (February 17th). In the following spring he spoke of the party fortunes being at the high-water mark of 1880, so that it would be fatuous not to force the Government to resign; and at a League meeting (February 28th) he considered the reunion of the party permanent. But the League should not be dissolved until the party, in office, carried its principles into effect. He again passionately urged the Imperial objections to the Chamberlain proposals.

[476]

Again at Newcastle (March 15th), and at Lincoln (September 20th), he uttered a general indictment of the Government—no high courage or high aims, and unable to deal straightforwardly with the nation. The whole series of these speeches, which was carried on at Glasgow at the City Liberal Club (December 5th), and in a most amusing speech in the House of Lords (March 19th, 1905) on fiscal policy and the Colonial Conference, up to the time (June 5th) when the Government's prolonged adhesion to Downing Street at last broke down—deserves fuller examination than it is possible to give it here.

But one or two other subjects of public importance engaged his attention. He spoke in the House (March 5th, 1901) on the unlucky squabble between Lords Lansdowne and Wolseley on War Office administration, rather taking the part of the latter, and in the painful debate which followed a few days later (March 15th). He assisted Lord Wolseley's demand for justificatory papers, which obtained good support but of course was defeated. The Government was said to have promised an inquiry into the operations in South Africa, and when the committee on the purchase of horses reported, Rosebery spoke at length on Tweedmouth's motion for an inquiry, which the Government refused.

"Lord Kitchener declared the horses were 'flatcatchers.' The Government—if I may say so unofficially—are, after their electoral campaign, good judges of what 'flatcatchers' are."

The Government was goaded by frequent questionings to the appointment of the Esher Committee on War Office Reorganisation in 1904. Rosebery, before knowing of this, had written to Lord Esher (September 4th, 1903):

"My policy is a free hand to Kitchener to organise on the basis of an Admiralty Board, to prepare the way for such a board. I would give him a limited time for this, and then make him, if possible, first Lord of the new board, with the option or reversion of being Chief of the Staff."

Both in the House of Lords and on more than one platform he had advocated the appointment of Lord Kitchener as Secretary of State for War. It needed a still greater military crisis to force this solution on Government or country.

Rosebery's judgment on a step of great moment in foreign policy for once placed him in a minority of his fellow-countrymen. In the summer of 1904 Lord Lansdowne concluded with M. Delcassé the Anglo-French Agreement. Its general effect was the recognition of our occupation of Egypt, the *quid pro quo* being admission of French interests in Morocco. A section of the coast was to be neutralised, and Spanish interests were to be borne in mind. Any causes of dispute in Siam were also to disappear. The Agreement was popular, but Rosebery saw the seeds of danger in it. He had been sent Mr. M. Affalo's book *The Truth About Morocco*, in which Ministers were arraigned. His reply ran:

August 4th, 1904.—"All criticism of the Anglo-French Agreement (though that instrument is so much worse for us than the author of the book foreboded) is lost in a generous clamour of pleasure at good relations with France. I doubt if there be any who do not share in that pleasure; no one certainly feels it more completely than I. . . . But in my judgment this unhappy Agreement is much more likely to promote than to prevent unfriendliness in the not distant future. . . . My mournful and supreme conviction in the matter is that this Agreement is much more likely to lead to complication than to peace."

At the City Liberal Club (March 9th, 1905), describing himself as "a well-known and conspicuous heretic" in the matter, he spoke of "the inestimable boon of a good understanding with France," but expressed the deepest doubt about the Treaty. He discriminated entirely between King Edward's work in founding a good understanding and this unfortunate superstructure. He was never going to refer to the subject again.

He was severely taken to task by *The Times* for this speech, and found it impossible to drop the subject altogether. At Stourbridge (October 26th), while reiterating his scepticism, he deprecated the notion that friendship with France must mean animosity to Germany. But the criticisms still went on, and at Bodmin he felt obliged to recur to the Agreement. He had never recanted his view of the complications which were likely to result, and in effect, he said, have resulted.

"I see that in the press I am called a Germanophil, because I am not friendly to this particular treaty. I am a friend of Germany just as I am a friend of France and of every civilised and Christian country in Europe. But when it comes to a conflict of interests, I repeat that I am the friend of no Power but Great Britain. If, perhaps, I had any natural predisposition to any special friendship with any foreign country, it would be with France. I scarcely know a word of German, I have scarcely any German friends. But I love French literature, I love many French people; I am a great deal in France, and I have given a practical proof of my friendship in a way which, perhaps, may not be agreeable to everybody here. In writing a book about Napoleon, I took the French as against the English view. It would not be pleasant for me when I next visit France to find that owing to misrepresentation I was considered an enemy of that country."

It must be noted that Rosebery's objections were solely based on the likelihood of our being involved in Moroccan complications, a thing which did in fact occur. His remarks have no bearing on the later developments of the *entente*.

CHAPTER XIX

The New Century and Reign—More Pressure from Liberals.
Reasons for Abstention. Misunderstandings. The
New Liberal Government. Rectorial Addresses

THE death of Queen Victoria in January 1901 had closed a
chapter of history. The new century opened out a vista of
great possibilities for a Sovereign in the prime of his powers. King
Edward had long admitted Rosebery to his close confidence, and he
was now consulted on a variety of matters, great and small, either
directly or through Francis Knollys. As the infant century progressed it seemed likely that the next Government would be of
Liberal complexion; for Leaguers and anti-Leaguers alike lent
willing hands against the Education Bill of 1902 and in support of
Free Trade from 1903. In past years the King had treated Gladstone with the utmost consideration, and he had no prejudice against
Liberals as such. Indeed, he had always known intimately some of
the leaders and some of the rank and file; while several of the
gentlemen of his Household had made no secret of their progressive
opinions. It seemed likely, then, that Rosebery might before long
be dragged from his retirement to advise the Crown. Campbell-
Bannerman had long been liked at Court; but the accident of Lady
Campbell-Bannerman's annual cure at Marienbad did not bring her
husband into close contact with the Sovereign until 1904.

Meanwhile, not only Rosebery's former Imperialist colleagues but
some who were not Liberal Leaguers, such as Lord Spencer, declined to treat his retirement as definite. So, and with still greater
enthusiasm, did a cluster of younger Liberals who had imbibed the
pure milk of the League. They were all good Imperialists, and mostly
lukewarm Home Rulers. Headed by Ronald Ferguson, the group
included Freeman Thomas,[1] destined to climb the highest peaks of
national service; the two sons of Sir Charles Tennant; Rowland
Barran of Leeds; James Mellor Paulton ("Harry" Paulton to his

---

[1] Created Baron Willingdon 1910 and Viscount 1924; Governor-General of
Canada 1926-31; Viceroy of India and Earl of Willingdon 1931.

many friends), son of a notable Lancashire Liberal; and other Members of Parliament.

Since the disruption of 1896 the Liberal Press had found three journalists of the first rank in capacity and character—to represent the three sections of the party—E. T. Cook, a convinced Imperialist, in Rosebery's inner confidence; J. A. Spender, bringing the culture of Balliol into Fleet Street, and making the *Westminster Gazette* the voice of the Liberal Centre; and H. W. Massingham, whose pungent and accomplished pen set forth the moral greatness of Little England. There was some pretty ringcraft over the capture and recapture of the *Daily News* and the *Daily Chronicle*, in which Rosebery acted as "judicious bottle-holder" to the Imperialist champion.

During these years of mingled suspense and activity, when, as somebody said at the time, Arthur Balfour was obstructing the King's Highway, and Joseph Chamberlain was driving to the public danger, Rosebery employed his leisure in jotting down a number of memoranda on the situation as he saw it. He also wrote drafts of letters destined never to be sent. In one (September 1903), "suppressed for indiscretion," he replied to the League Secretaries, who had sent a formal letter urging him to make more speeches.

"As for the 'call of the country,' 'the desire of the Liberal party,' those are empty phrases of which I know the flatulence. Had the Liberal party entertained the 'desire' you speak of it would have joined the League. As it is, one or both of the leaders of the Liberal party is engaged in hypothetically forming a Government which will succeed this one, and which will be enthusiastically supported and betrayed by the leaders of Radical opinion. On the other hand, the 'call of the country' is expressed in such a whisper that I having a shocking ear have not caught it. My duty and sole duty is to the Liberal League."

Certainly this was not exactly "discreet"; but about the same time (September 30th, 1903) he drew up a serious statement of his position:

"Why do I say that it is impossible for me to form a Government?
"The physical and personal causes I record elsewhere. The political are equally serious.
"1. I should not bring harmony to the Liberal party. I shall always be (and justly) an object of suspicion to the Radical party or rather to the pro-Boer, pro-Armenian, pro-Macedonian and generally hysterical section of it. A less obnoxious person might be able to work with them. I do not blame these people, nor do I blame myself. I simply record a natural antipathy. Were I more of a humbug I might surmount it. I

[481]

should also be specially repugnant to the Irish party, where others might not.

"2. As I have stated in public a Liberal Prime Minister who is a peer must possess the signal confidence and indeed enthusiasm of the Liberal party. This I do not and perhaps could never possess. But it is a matter of vital necessity, I could not be a Minister on sufferance. Nor will I return to 1894-5.

"3. There are certain persons—two I think—with whom I could not sit in Cabinet with honour. Now my personal feelings should not prevent the strongest possible Cabinet being formed. Personally, I think that either of these two men, given fair play and no favour, would wreck any Government. But that is no reason why those who trust them (if there be such) or believe in their powers should not employ them. I could not, and so, again, I should be a cause of division.

"4. I have only indeed a score of followers in the House of Commons, and so it may seem absurd to discuss the question. It is possible and even probable, however, that were I invited to form a Government a large mass of M.P.s would gravitate towards me. But they would equally gravitate towards anyone else in the same position. And as I count only on my score, I could not attempt to form a Government with dignity or propriety. A man in the House of Commons might succeed under these circumstances, but not a peer.

"5. As to the physical and personal causes referred to in the beginning, they may be summed up by saying that I should not be efficient.

"6. I am not and cannot make myself enough of a party man. Since 1896 I seem to myself to have shed party feeling.

"7. And the people who should form a party Ministry are its appointed leaders who have borne the burden and heat of the day; not I who long ago severed myself from party connection.

"These reasons are very familiar to me. They were familiar to me before Chesterfield, and nothing since has occurred to alter them. I have never had news of office since 1896. And now the only new question that occurs is whether my presence in politics as I am, is not a hindrance rather than a help to those I wish to serve? It seemed to me that an independent voice in politics might sometimes be of service. But I am quite prepared for the opinion that such a voice is an embarrassment, and should be silenced.

Personal Disqualifications.

"1. My memory, my power of application, my hearing, and my general vigour are all impaired. I especially complain, as a disability, of my loss of recollection of faces and names, so that I enter every room as a stranger, unable almost to greet anyone who does not first greet me, and even then unable to recall their names. This is fatal for a political leader, or even a member of society.

"2. In the last seven years, since I left party politics, I have fallen into a solitary habit of life which I should now find it impossible altogether to abandon.

"3. But, mainly and principally, I have an absolute conviction that were I to return to office I should once more be sleepless. My occasional speaking experiences make this evident. Now there would be no harm in this if it only meant death, for there could be no better death. But the horror is that it means life and office and total incapacity in both. I cannot forget 1895. To lie night after night, staring wide awake, hopeless of sleep, tormented in nerves, and to realise all that was going on, at which I was present, so to speak, like a disembodied spirit, to watch one's own corpse as it were, day after day, is an experience which no sane man with a conscience would repeat; or the repetition of which he could offer as service to his country.

"In fine, my belief is that while urging efficiency I should present in my own person the signal model of inefficiency."

It is a tragic picture to be painted of a man of fifty-six, the idol of a devoted band girded up to follow his lead to any heights that he would scale, free from any apparent ailment that could cripple his energies, and in the plenitude of his powers of speech and command. To examine its content for a moment—of the two impossible colleagues, Harcourt was obviously one; the other could only be Campbell-Bannerman. The reunion of November 1903 had not in truth cancelled the sentence of "definite separation" pronounced in February 1902; and of this separation the Liberal League was the living witness.

The other reference to be noted is that of "an independent voice in politics" that might sometimes be of service. Later he realised more completely that in our party system no such voice, however eloquent, could be raised to guide public opinion at difficult moments. None in fact ever has been. A man who had gained a name for great public services outside party might conceivably fill such a place. If the Duke of Wellington had not joined the straitest sect of the Tories, perhaps he might; and even as it was, once or twice he tried to advise his friends to set aside party feeling for the sake of the country. A Wilberforce or a Shaftesbury, sacrificing further philanthropic laurels for high politics, might have won the nation's heart as a constitutional adviser. Not so the retired leader of a party. Men of long political experience, such as the 3rd Lord Grey, Lord Russell, the Duke of Argyll, *rude donati*, from time to time gave the world the benefit of their reflections in letters to *The Times*, or in short pamphlets. These were read with interest and respect : but the surface of the political lake was scarcely rippled. Rosebery at this time was far from falling into this category. But all the fascination of his personality could not prevent people from seeing in him a party politician, only differing from others by the fact that he could not quite agree with either party as it stood at the moment.

In October 1904 Sir William Harcourt died. He and Rosebery had seldom met of late, but they were on terms of courtesy, and when Harcourt had a sharp operation early in 1903, Rosebery made a sympathetic and complimentary reference to him in public. In the previous year there had been an amusing experience at the Guildhall banquet to the new Sovereigns (October 25th, 1902) :

"Sate between the Italian Ambassador, Pansa, and Harcourt, exactly opposite C.-B. Harcourt very pleasant. He said, 'I wonder if I took one of those orchids and put it in my buttonhole I should be taken for Joe?' . . . The Queen lovely in white with the Garter riband and diamond insignia. She and the King much amused at my environment."

Lord Kimberley had also gone, and Lord Spencer's health foreboded the calamitous illness that attacked him a year later. Reginald Brett, now succeeding as Lord Esher, was at Balmoral, and sent a long letter to Rosebery in which some inspiration from the writer's illustrious host was suspected. After recounting the party's losses, he maintained that the position was changed by Rosebery's decided lead against the *whole* policy of the Government. "How can you reconcile it to your conscience to turn out the Government unless you are ready to form another?" Esher proceeded to a shrewd analysis of the leaders remaining—"C.-B.—Asquith—E. Grey," and concluded with an appeal almost *verbatim* the same as those which had succeeded in 1892. There was no such success now. Rosebery answered curtly :

DALMENY, *October 6th*, 1904.
"MY DEAR R.,

"Many thanks for your letter. But for the life of me I can see no change in the political situation which affects me in the slightest degree. Certainly the removal of an old man who had retired from politics does not.

"Yours,

AR"

[484]

But once more he wrote (October 14th, 1904) a long memorandum on his position. After sketching the earlier history of his resignation, the Chesterfield speech, his breach with Campbell-Bannerman, and the formation of the Liberal League, he observed:

"It is said in one striking letter to *The Times*, and by many others in private, notably Mr. Lloyd George, that I should undertake a campaign, like Mr. Gladstone's in Midlothian, and so to speak—though it is not so expressed—force myself on the country and the Liberal party.

"Putting all disparities between Mr. Gladstone and myself on one side, there is an obvious answer to this—that I should only be the cat pulling the chestnuts out of the fire for others with whom I should not agree . . . moreover my hostility to Home Rule and to the Anglo-French Convention, both expressed with extreme emphasis, would act as considerable bars if not total disqualifications.

"I have in fact at this juncture the confidence of neither the Crown, the House of Commons, either party, or the public at large. Those are strange foundations on which to rear political ambitions, had I any desire that way. . . .

"But it is urged on me if you cannot be the head of a Government, ought you not to undertake the Foreign Office (were it offered) from a sense of public duty? Those who talk like this are ignorant of the interior of the last two Liberal Governments. I carried on foreign policy in those Cabinets in a minority of one. In the Cabinet of 1886 the absorption in Home Rule enabled me to do this. In 1892-5 it was one long battle, carried on in silence in 1893 after fierce combats in 1892, and again with daily contest in 1894-5. Such a condition of things is not fair either to the Minister or the Government. The strain on the Minister is excessive, while it is not fair to the Government that he should carry on a policy which is not theirs. . . .

"My conclusion is clear—that the next Liberal Government should represent the official and dominant forces of Liberalism and be as homogeneous as possible. That would exclude me, even if I had a wish instead of an aversion for office.

"Oh, but, say others, Mr. Gladstone in 1880 swept down on official Liberalism, and dominated it, and formed his own Government. My answer is simple:

"1. I am not Mr. Gladstone.

"2. I am not in the House of Commons.

"To which I would add:

"3. That the Government was a failure.

"4. That I always thought, even in 1880, and think now, that Mr. Gladstone should not have taken office."

[485]

This final judgment is striking, and it is right to add that it is surprising to anybody who had studied Rosebery's correspondence of 1879 and 1880. Nor is it easy to conjecture what would have been the fate of a Hartington or Granville administration in the latter year. It is reasonable to surmise that Rosebery, when writing "failure," had in his mind Mr. Gladstone's Irish policy, and to some extent his foreign policy so far as it differed from Rosebery's own.

He recapitulated many of the same arguments in a letter to Mr. J. A. Spender at almost the same time, adding, for the benefit of that trusted journalist:

"I never was so unsupported in the party or the country. The Press except the *Leeds Mercury* were unanimously hostile, putting on one side the neutrality of the cold-blooded *Westminster Gazette*."

He felt it impossible to make any announcement such as was suggested, but would continue to hold his peace. When the next spring came he drew a modest picture of himself:

May 2nd, 1905.

"From my own point of view (which seems however to be imperfectly understood, or rather not understood at all) I am not dissatisfied with the last three years.

"I have striven for the public good without even the remotest personal interest. I am not a candidate for any office, even the humblest. There is no merit in that, for after ten years of comparative freedom I should ill accommodate myself to official bonds. Nor am I any longer fit for it, according to the high standard which I conceive to be necessary. I have not sought popularity—maybe I have sought unpopularity. I have said the things which it was necessary to say, and yet which no one who aimed at popularity or even acceptability could say. They have, however, been said, and I believe that my sacrifice—for in a sense it is a sacrifice—has not been fruitless.

"I have made moreover an even greater sacrifice than popularity. I have left the life I love and engaged in the life I hate. I have done this for two reasons:

"1. To save what I believe to be the sound core or group of the Liberal party from extinction. Ever since Sir H. Campbell-Bannerman spoke to me of Asquith's movement as a 'rebellion' which 'had been crushed,' I saw that close union and effort was necessary to avert the blighting effects of official proscription. This I think has been effected; and the official Liberal chiefs find that before taking office they have as their first and most formidable task to reckon with the Liberal League; an organisation in no way hostile to them, but determined to

[486]

maintain a certain tone and spirit in politics, which it is the object of the Extreme Left to extinguish.

"2. To further a Liberal victory. Ever since the great smash of 1895, when I was nominally leader, followed by the still greater smash of 1900, I have been anxious to do what I honestly could to further the return of the Liberals to power, on a sound basis. Here too I think that I have not been useless, by retaining and perhaps attracting men of moderate views, as well as by attacking the Government. Men of extreme views will probably say that I have done more harm than good, but they are not sound or cool judges. I do not think that I have been of much use, but still not without use.

"There is no doubt that I could have done much more, had I thrown myself headlong into the fray, and conducted a strenuous political campaign, as my friends, and even Lloyd George last year, have constantly urged. This however was not possible, for two if not three reasons. For had I been successful I—

"1. Should have been compelled to take office, which has never been in my contemplation:

"2. Might have displaced the two official leaders of the Liberal party, which I had no wish to do. It would have annoyed them and me almost equally. And—

"3. There might have been caused a schism in the Liberal party, which, though it may and perhaps must come, I should not like to be caused by me."

But he was not allowed to hold his peace for good. The Liberal League was there, as keen as any other Liberal organisation to defeat the Government, and when its annual meeting came round in the following spring he was expected to utter a political pronouncement. This he did with fullness, dealing with foreign and colonial policy, education, housing, preaching progress in domestic reforms in the general terms usual to a speaker in Opposition. On Ireland he merely begged for a general statement of their main policy from the party leaders. But he soon became more explicit. In his speeches at Stourbridge and in Cornwall, already mentioned in another connection, he spoke out. At Stourbridge (October 25th, 1905) he presented the dilemma that the Liberal chiefs must either make Home Rule the first measure in a new Parliament, or drop it altogether for the time being:

"Any middle policy, that of placing Home Rule in the position of a reliquary, and only exhibiting it at great moments of public stress, as Roman Catholics are accustomed to exhibit relics of a saint—is not one which will earn sympathy or success in this country."

[487]

He was in Cornwall a month later. On November 23rd Campbell-Bannerman spoke at Stirling. He advised the Irish to accept any instalment of representative control "provided it was consistent with, and led up to, the larger policy." At Bodmin Rosebery fastened on this expression. Free Trade was the dominant issue, and the party unity must be maintained. But he objected to the raising of the banner of Home Rule, and said "emphatically and explicitly and once for all, I cannot serve under that banner." The speech was delivered under an unlucky misapprehension, as the following note of Rosebery's makes clear. But the divergence went deeper. Rosebery had ceased to be a Home Ruler in the strict sense, but some of his Liberal League colleagues had not. The wording of the note is singularly restrained. It was written after the four League Vice-Presidents had joined Campbell-Bannerman's Government.

"On Friday, November 24th, I read the abstract of C.-Bannerman's speech at Stirling in the Western newspapers, and, in a speech at Truro that evening, I gave fair warning that that speech had filled me with some misgivings, but that I should await a fuller report before pronouncing a definite opinion. On the next day I received a fuller report, and pronounced, at Bodmin, my definite opinion that that speech raised the Home Rule question in a pronounced form.

"I may mention, though I attach no importance to the fact, that all the M.P.s staying in the house with me shared that judgment; only that some, notably Mr. Fletcher Moulton, were much more violent.

"I arrived in London on November 28th, and there found—from a note written by Edward Grey—that Asquith, and through him Haldane and Grey, had arrived at an understanding some time before with C.-Bannermann, who had assured them that his Irish policy was identical with that declared recently by Asquith, and that the Stirling speech was the outcome of this concordat between the Vice-Presidents of the League and C.-Bannerman.

"It was an oversight that I was not told of this; an unfortunate oversight, in view of the fact that I was speaking daily in Cornwall and that I had given fair warning on November 24th of the line I was likely to take on November 25th. It was also lamentable, because I was quite ready to ignore the Stirling speech; for, as under no circumstances did I propose to take office in C.-Bannerman's Government, I was not anxious to challenge any part of the policy of the imminent Government; and yet, owing to the oversight, I said what I did, and caused some friction in the Free Trade party, which I had been trying so hard to consolidate.

"However, I may fairly hope that no harm was done. The Stirling speech will probably have lost my interpretation before the General Election, and the vice-presidents were able to join the Government at once, under their private understanding; except I believe Edward Grey, who showed reluctance to serve under C.-Bannerman as leader of the House of Commons. None of them embarrassed me by consulting or communicating with me, which was considerate on their part. They were well aware that I was not prepared to accept office in any shape, and so communication with me would only have compromised them needlessly, and possibly me, too. The oversight was due no doubt to the fact that as they knew that I would not take office, communication had naturally become slack, and that in fact from October 22nd, when I left him at Dalmeny, till December 11th, when I shook hands with him at my large reception, I had no communication, direct or indirect with Asquith, though he was carrying on negotiations with C.-Bannerman. It was I think natural that he should not reveal these to one who was not going to be a colleague, but it is none the less a pity that he forgot to inform me of the pact relating to Ireland, which would have prevented what seemed like a schism; more especially as I had given fair warning on November 24th of my first impressions. A telegram then would have stopped my saying anything. That he should forget, in view of the large calls on his time, is easily to be understood."

Sir Henry Campbell-Bannerman became Prime Minister on December 5th, and the hopes which almost to the last Rosebery's friends had cherished, that he would add strength to another Liberal Cabinet were finally shattered. In his solitude at Naples in the early summer he had made a cool estimate of the probable situation:

"I am beginning to be perplexed as to what I shall do when the new Liberal Government is safely installed. It seems to me plain that my best course would be total and final retirement.

"But I have not found total and final retirement easy in the past.

"It would however be much easier in the future, unless I am much mistaken; for I cannot see who would wish to draw me from it. Formerly, there were only too many. But hereafter there will I think be none.

"What alternative indeed is there? I could speak as now independently. But defence may not be easy, and criticism would be open to hopeless misconstruction. Even as small a detail as to the side of the table I should speak from presents difficulty. The only argument that I can see against retirement is the future of Liberal Imperialism. The next Government will be radical, perhaps extremely radical; it will at any rate not be Liberal Imperialist. It will contain a notable nucleus indeed of that description, but this will tend to drift away; and will be impelled by the forces behind it in a very different direction.

"I may note that I have done my best for the cause, but have been baffled by the party machine. I acknowledge that I did not realise the strength of the machine—the *ingens Machina*. But the machine is a permanent force; it will retain its jealousy of and enmity to whatever is extraneous to it. And I should be infinitely weaker than now in opposition to it.

"I am indeed beginning to doubt if the fierce play of party admits of an independent political position. It is little to say this, for everybody has long been convinced of it. I am not quite but nearly convinced.

"Is it then worth while to spend the few remaining years of one's life in embarrassing one's friends in office by maintaining an independent political position, and raising the voice of one crying in the wilderness? The question answers itself.

"True, the ideas may permeate and leaven. But is even that limited effect worth the continued maintenance of an attitude of virtue between two opposing lines of battle, exposed to the fire of both? That is my present condition; it cannot be permanently prolonged.

"There is no doubt the Liberal League. Will the League continue to exist? On that I cannot pronounce with certainty, but I should say not. Politicians do not care to preach and parade in a wilderness. The fruitful oasis of bounty and patronage will be elsewhere.

"Seeing then no other considerations of public welfare I think I see clear and near the time at which I shall bid a final farewell to the political scene.

AR"

It will be seen that there was no formal farewell until the moment came when all controversial politics withered before the blast of war. But during the intervening years he took his own line, heading no group, sitting on the cross-benches in the House of Lords, as powerful as ever in speech, but without the backing with which even the very strongest cannot dispense.

The Liberal League continued to attract Rosebery's personal supporters, though its special purpose no longer existed. It had not entirely succeeded in this; but it had by no means failed in its appeal to one type of genuine Liberalism. Rosebery presided at the Annual Meeting in December 1905, and made a reasoned defence of his speech at Bodmin.

The League remained dormant in 1906; but he spoke again at a Council Meeting in 1907, showing marked mistrust of the Government, especially as being too prone to make large promises. He was moved to one prophecy:

"The Liberal party may through some of its members find itself permanently connected with hostility to property in all its forms. If so, I venture to predict that, at no distant time, it will find itself squeezed out between Socialism and Conservatism. Socialism can promise much more to the predatory elements in politics; Conservatism can afford much more confidence to those who wish to keep things as they are."

The following year (March 12th, 1908) there was another great meeting, when Rosebery spoke with more favour of the Liberal Government as a bulwark against Socialism. This time he discussed the future of the League. He had doubted whether it should be continued, "having amply achieved its purpose, but had been over-ridden by active members of the Association." At the end of the year (December 26th, 1907) he wrote to Mr. Perks:

". . . I am inclined to allow events to develop themselves before coming to a decision. We are between two difficulties: our nominally League M.P.s, who are a sort of quicksand, and the provisional stalwarts (who are not a few), who form a rock full of sharp points. I think it probable that we should arouse as much resentment among the latter as gratitude among the former if we dissolved, i.e. we should displease our real friends and please those who wish to leave us. And yet *cui bono*? At present I see no answer to this; while you and I are, more or less, in bonds. This is not a perfect survey, but it is not far from the mark.

"Yrs.,

AR"

It will be recalled that the Lord Rectorship of Glasgow University had been snatched from Rosebery by an untoward chance. Some years later (November 16th, 1900) he was elected and delivered his Rectorial Address. For once he did not choose a Scottish subject, but he turned to one very near his heart—the British Empire. From a general sketch of our inheritance and our obligations he passed to one of the fascinating might-have-beens of history:

"Had the elder Pitt, when he became First Minister, not left the House of Commons, he would probably have retained his sanity and his authority. He would have prevented, or suppressed, the reckless budget of Charles Townshend, have induced George III to listen to reason, have introduced representatives from America into the Imperial Parliament, and preserved the thirteen American colonies to the British Crown. Is it fanciful to dwell for a moment on what might have happened? The Reform Bill which was passed in 1832 would probably have been passed much earlier; for the new blood of America would have burst the old vessels of the Constitution. It would have provided for some self-adjusting system of representation, such as now prevails in the United States, by which increasing population is proportionately represented. And at last, when the Americans became the majority, the seat of Empire would perhaps have been moved solemnly across the Atlantic, and Britain have become the historical shrine and the European outpost of the world empire. . . . It would have been the most sublime transference of power known to mankind. Our conceptions can scarcely picture the procession across the Atlantic, the greatest sovereign in the greatest fleet in the universe, Ministers, Government, Parliament, departing solemnly for the other hemisphere, not, as in the case of the Portuguese sovereigns emigrating to Brazil, under the spur of necessity, but under the vigorous embrace of the younger world . . . above all, had there been no separation there would have been no War of Independence, no War of 1812, with all the bitter memories that these have left on American soil. To secure that priceless boon I could have been satisfied to see the British Federal Parliament sitting in Columbia Territory."

Setting aside this wondrous day-dream, he noted the changed relation of Britain to the world. The colonial passion of other powers was not of direct importance to us, who do not desire to increase our territories, but indirectly it raises delicate and disputable points. "Are we," he asked, "too complacent?" The example of Prussia's recovery after the Napoleonic wars has a lesson for us. Are we training enough first-rate men for our developed responsibilities? Should Greek be any longer a compulsory subject? And is not an insidious luxury becoming prevalent? He asked, "whether our land is not becoming the playground and pleasance of the plutocrats of all nations?" Even healthy sport, like other good things, can be overdone. In a word, are we thorough enough? And again he referred to Germany and the United States, their commerce and industry. Rosebery waved no flags in the address.

"From my point of view," he said, "there is not a close in the darkest quarters of Glasgow, or a crofter's cabin in the Hebrides, which is not a matter of imperial concern; quite as truly, in its proportion and degree, as those more glowing topics to which that adjective is too often limited. And mark this, in all that I have said there is no word of war, not even the beat of a drum or the distant singing of a bullet. To some the Empire is little else, and that makes many hate the word. That is not my view. Our Empire is not founded on the precedents associated with that name, it is not the realm of conquest which that term has been wont to imply. It has often used the sword, it could not exist without the sword, but it does not live by the sword. Defence and readiness to fight are vital enough in their way, but not less vital is the civil and domestic side; the commerce, the education, the intelligence, the unceasing leaven of a high and sour decadence of a low ideal. War and conquest can fill the lives of but a part of the nation: a sane and simple duty to the Empire may well inspire the whole."

Setting aside this wondrous day-dream, he noted the changed quence in a like vein.

Eight years afterwards (June 12th, 1908) Rosebery spoke again at Glasgow, this time as Chancellor of the University. The veteran Lord Stair had died at the end of 1903, and was succeeded in his office by Lord Kelvin, a son of Glasgow, whose great career was bound up with the Scottish city, but bequeathed a world-wide inheritance of applied science. This time Rosebery recurred to his home-land, and in a most scholarly address traced the influence of the national Universities on the Scottish character. It does not lend itself greatly to verbal quotation, but on the text that the modern tendency was to swamp self-reliance, he spoke of it as the—

"Scottish characteristic, the heart of Scottish independence and Scottish success. That is the stamp that I would fain see the University of Glasgow affix to her teaching and to the graduates whom she sends into the world."

It has been mentioned that St. Andrews, the senior University, had long declined to nominate a Liberal Lord Rector. By 1910 any partisan tint of Rosebery's had become extremely faint; and in the following year (September 14th, 1911), the Five Hundredth Anniversary of its foundation, the University welcomed the delivery of his Rectorial Address. He appreciated the signal honour of being chosen for this occasion. The result was one of his most exquisite utterances, equally marked by historical research and by the play of romantic fancy. The central conception was that of the first Lord Rector of 1411 as a Struldbrug. Dean Swift, as everybody knows, imagined these unhappy beings as doomed to immortality, while subject to all the infirmities of old age. In the Greek legend Zeus showed more mercy to the aspiring mortal. Rosebery, with a quite unerring touch, pictured the veteran watching the tragedies of Scottish annals, the bloodshed, the martyrdoms, the final freedom from religious intolerance, the universal sway of justice in later days. He would hear the shriek of despair that greeted the Union, and then

[493]

see how Scotland rose and throve by neglect. He would sum up with the words:

"Be of good cheer. . . . I have seen life and death and glory chasing each other like shadows on a summer sea, and all has seemed to be vanity. But I remain in the conviction that, though individuals may suffer, when we take stock of a century at its end, we shall find that the world is better and happier than it was at the beginning. *Sursum corda*. Lift up your hearts, for the world is moving onward. It is guided from above, and guided we may be sure with wisdom and goodness which will not abandon us. That is the comfort which even in blackest darkness must afford light."

NAPOLEON

Rosebery's judgment of mankind, in the pages of history, and under his own eyes, was always biased by his estimate of the strength of an individual character or intellect. He was not harsh to amiable weakness, but it repelled him. In public life he had little toleration for the class which John Morley, with almost affectionate derision, loved to describe as "the simpletons." Perhaps too little; for, after all, every noble cause and movement, from the early Christian Church down to the Abolition of Slavery and the Prevention of Cruelty to Animals, has owed much to the enthusiasm of "simpletons." Be that as it may, it was the strong fibre of Cromwell and the Pitts, father and son, that won his historical loyalty, the intellectual power of Gladstone, and the supple vigour of Disraeli, that awakened his young ambition; the massive power of Bismarck and Cavour, the soaring energy of Cecil Rhodes, that fascinated him in his active years. So that it was not surprising that he made a special study of Napoleon. And with his diligent collector's *flair* he brought together a remarkable series of portraits and autographs of the Emperor, besides a mass of State papers of his time. It at last became almost a joke that friends, hunting for an appropriate birthday gift, filled his rooms with Napoleonic relics of genuine or dubious authenticity. It is safe to say that no historical figure has inspired the production of a mass of literature approaching that in which Napoleon's fame is smothered. Napoleon as a youth in Corsica, Napoleon as a soldier, Napoleon as a statesman, Napoleon and the Church, Napoleon and women—the volumes would overcrowd any average library. Rosebery sat down to write a monograph on the phase in which the credit of Britain is especially at stake, that of Napoleon's exile to St. Helena. He applied himself to the task with the closest diligence, and the result was *Napoleon, the Last Phase,* first published in 1908. He had studied all the narratives of the Emperor's companions, and practically all the commentaries on them by French and other writers. The book is a large quarto of some 250 pages on the sombre episode of St. Helena, as he calls it—"not a bright page for either Great Britain or Napoleon; it consorts with the dignity of neither." It was an attempt to penetrate the darkness which surrounds the last act of the Napoleonic drama, and thus Rosebery justifies it.

He could not help asking, "Why collect these morbid, sordid, insincere chronicles? Does not history tell us that there is nothing so melancholy as the aspect of great men in retirement?" He wrote his book, he explained, partly to lay a literary ghost, dormant for years and only quickened by stimulating leisure. Again, because the final judgment of History had not yet been recorded, and lastly because Napoleon the *man* appeared then as he never had before.

The book cannot be other than melancholy reading, but nobody can fail to admire its thoroughness and genuine impartiality. If, as he told an English audience[2] he seemed to have taken the French side, it was because the facts as he saw them led him there. The book has not the charm of the *Churchill* monograph; but it is bound to survive as the best documented and most sympathetic narration of those six heart-breaking years. A great deal still remains unrecorded and mysterious about them.

The other important outcome of Rosebery's leisure was *Chatham, his Early Life and Connections,* published in 1910. He had full access to the family papers at Dropmore and to others at Holland House. Chatham's Life has never been written at full length, and Rosebery decided that, strictly speaking, it never can be. His book gives a delightful picture of William Pitt's youth, with copious extracts from the Dropmore correspondence with his sisters, and it tells of the amazing rise to wealth and power of the Temple-Grenville stock. The story goes on with a sketch of the leading actors then on the political stage, and of continental affairs. It carries through the complicated tale of European warfare till Pitt's accession to office in 1746, right up to the formation of the Duke of Devonshire's administration in 1756, in which Pitt was the leading figure.

The book is eminently readable, with many of the happy touches that were Rosebery's own, reminiscent of Macaulay's, but generally

[2] See p. 478.

with a lighter hand. He was dissatisfied with it himself, and it never attained the popularity of his *Pitt*. Perhaps he tried to do rather too much, or too little. He found himself swimming *in gurgite vasto* of European politics, and there was no apparent reason why the book should close just before the most glorious act of the Chatham drama. The conclusion, therefore, seems to be more abrupt and artificial than that of Trevelyan's fascinating *Early Life of Charles James Fox*.

Rosebery's comparative desertion from political platforms, except on the Free Trade issue, set him free on more of the uncontroversial occasions when his speeches sounded with the happiest ring. In 1901, first in Edinburgh (January 31st), and then in the shadow of the ruined Palace of Linlithgow (February 7th), he moved Addresses of condolence and welcome on the King's accession. His knowledge of history and of contemporary Europe, and his deep personal devotion to both Sovereigns, enabled him to pay tributes to Queen Victoria and King Edward with a felicity which no speaker of his time could have emulated. Just before, at the meeting of the Scottish History Society, he had lamented the death of Lord Bute, one of his oldest friends and a man of most original character, living in research of the remote past, and so not receiving the credit which his attainments merited.

Rosebery was not much of a practical gardener; but he was a practical reader, and at the Royal Caledonian Horticultural Show (September 13th, 1901) he was able to please his hearers with excerpts from Bacon's Essays and from John Reid's *"Scots' Gardener"* of Charles II's day. When Scottish Home Industries called him to Glasgow (October 23rd), he complained amid laughter that these, too, were "a little out of my ordinary line of business," but he took occasion to defend Harris tweed from attacks made on it by a correspondent of *The Times* as the den in which countless bacilli lurked. It was not difficult, in that company, to make a case for the work done in Highland shielings.

The 220th Anniversary Dinner of the Company of Merchants of Edinburgh (November 14th) was a graver occasion. But the fiscal controversy was not yet alive, and all that Rosebery did was to express preference for a business Administration in which party machinery would be both useless and forgotten. On the next day, at the Philosophical Institution, Henry Asquith delivered an admirable address on Biography, which is fortunately included in his published works. Rosebery, when thanked for presiding, complained that he had never been told what the subject of the address would be. However, he named Purcell's *Manning* as one of the great books of biography in the language. In his own Utopia, he proceeded, he would appoint a Board of Censors to decide whose biographies might be written, and whose not. Licensed biographies might be divided into three classes; three volumes, two, or one being permitted to each class. On the other hand, the class permitted to write autobiographies should be infinitely extended, because every truthful autobiography must be interesting.

Everybody must wish that Rosebery had joined that goodly fellowship of autobiographers. But his present biographer may congratulate himself that the skeleton of an autobiography can be articulated from the candid memoranda and notes of which there are so many.

In the winter of that year and in 1902 he was immersed in the political whirlpool, but he came to Glasgow (October 12th, 1902) to unveil Gladstone's statue. It was a non-party occasion, and he delivered a non-party speech, touching in turn on Gladstone's many-sidedness, "to those who were privileged to know him, his politics seemed but the least part of him"; his faith, not only in religion, but in great causes, inspiring him with deep-seated and impervious certainty; his industry, to which an eight-hour day would have been a holiday; his courage, physical no less than moral—"brave among the brave":

"Such lives speak for themselves. They need no statues. They face the future with the confidence of high purpose and endeavour. The statues are not for them, but for us, to bid us be conscious of our trust, mindful of our duty, scornful of opposition to principle and faith."

The Scottish History Society again claimed him for its annual meeting (November 29th, 1903)—when a presentation was made to the indefatigable secretary, Mr. Thomas Law. Rosebery pleaded for the preservation of the family papers, diaries, account-books, and what not of the past, too often neglected or thrown away. Charters were the affairs of special societies; but these humbler records should be the peculiar care of this Society.

Two very different occasions fell on the same snowy day (December 2nd). In the forenoon a tablet was unveiled in St. Giles' to the memory of the 1st Battalion the Royal Scots fallen in the war.

Rosebery traced the history of the regiment, and did honour to the glorious dead. In the evening he attended the dinner of the National Fat Stock Club, at whose show he had won a series of prizes. Prizes or no prizes, the fattening industry was vastly expensive to an amateur; but Rosebery, who knew little about it, looked on it as part of his duty to the neighbourhood. So he delighted his professional audience by observing:

"It is by personal, careful, and daily attention to the beasts on my part—by wakeful nights devoted to the corpulence of a particular animal—by handing to every beast his appointed oil-cake from my own hand—it is only by these means that I have been able to obtain success."

Rosebery unveiled the Stevenson Memorial in St. Giles' (June 27th, 1904), of which, eight years before, he had been the true begetter. The best intellect of Edinburgh assembled round the powerful work of the American sculptor St. Gaudens. Rosebery spoke simply, with no further critical estimate of the beloved writer.

He touched on Scottish history again when the Royal Scottish Corporation dined in London (November 30th, 1904), dwelling on the impression of extreme savagery that Scotland produced on strangers even to the end of the eighteenth century: "Is it not a noble and inspiring thought for all of us that it is from that foundation that springs the Scotland of to-day?" He ended by a thought of the Scotsmen scattered all over the Empire, quoting the exquisite stanza—"from the lone shieling of the misty island"—that would make the fortune of any poem enshrining it.[3]

The Scottish branch of the Associated Booksellers gave him another opportunity of showing his love of letters (June 9th, 1905). Mr. John Murray gave the toast of Literature in a capital speech. Rosebery in his reply took up the proposer's points, denied his own competence to reply to the health of Homer, Dante, and Voltaire, but claimed that Literature and Education are Edinburgh's staple products:

"There is no author bred under the shade of Edinburgh town, no publisher who has learned his business there, who does not feel that *genius loci,* that immemorial tradition, that splendour of historical association, which has made Edinburgh what she is, which has made you happy to come here, and us proud to welcome you."

[3] Rosebery, who at the time disclaimed knowledge of its authorship, afterwards made a learned examination of the different claims that have been made in its regard.

The Auld Brig of Ayr was threatened with demolition, unless ample funds could be collected to restore it. Rosebery had vowed, he said at a great Ayr meeting (September 25th), never to utter another word about Burns in public. But Burns glorified the Auld Brig, so it was for the poet's sake that Rosebery had to plead in a forty-minute speech:

"If every man who has attended a Burns Dinner and shed tears for the memory of Burns, and made speeches about Burns, and recited poems about Burns, and drunk whisky in honour of Burns, if every one of them now living in the world were to send a shilling or even sixpence, why, your coffers would be overflowing, and you would have to gild the Auld Brig in order to expend your funds."

As Lord-Lieutenant Rosebery had to open the vast Asylum at Bangour. His County Council experience made him familiar with his distressing subject, and while praising the accommodation provided, he said that the full blossom of municipal work would not be reached until the worthy workman be provided with the comforts extended to the intellectually ill.

Sir James Gibson Craig had just ceased to be Convener of Midlothian, and was presented (October 18th, 1906) with his portrait after life-long service to the county. Rosebery was able to assert with conviction that Sir James had chosen the wiser part by abstaining from political life:

"All his work has been tangible and useful. Do you think he could have said that if he had gone to the House of Commons?"

The year after (July 14th, 1907) Rosebery again laid stress on the paramount interest and importance of local affairs when a still older County Convener, Sir Robert Dundas of Arniston, one of the chiefs of that historic family, in turn presented his portrait to the county: "A great Scottish gentleman, and a great Scottish worthy," said Rosebery.

But the most memorable appearance of Rosebery in Edinburgh during these years was the parade of the Scots Greys (November 16th, 1906). The occasion was the unveiling of the Memorial to fallen officers and men; but it was rendered more acute by a recent order depriving the Scottish garrison of cavalry. At the open-air ceremony, in pouring rain, Rosebery delivered a perfect little discourse. He spoke of the laurels won under Marlborough, at Waterloo, in the Crimea, and now in South Africa:

"Honour to the brave who will return no more. We shall not see their faces again. In the service of their Sovereign and their country they have undergone the sharpness of death, and sleep their eternal sleep, thousands of miles away in the green solitudes of Africa. Their places, their comrades, their saddles will know them no more, for they will never return to us as we knew them. But in a nobler and a higher sense, have they not returned to us to-day? They return to us with a message of duty, of courage, of patriotism. They return to us with a memory of high duty faithfully performed; they return to us with the inspiration of their example. Peace, then, to their dust, honour to their memory. Scotland for ever!"

At the luncheon afterwards he lamented that a Scottish Secretary of War and a Scottish Prime Minister had brought about the removal of cavalry. What were Scottish Liberal members for? It was a delicate position for Rosebery, whose active lieutenant Haldane had been, but he skated skilfully on the thin ice.

At a great public meeting on the same question (December 3rd) he ridiculed the alleged cost of £200,000 for retaining the regiment: "Scotland, if she asks for ever so little, is always stinted and always starved." And when he distributed prizes to the Midlothian Garrison Artillery Volunteers he returned more hopefully to the same question. In this latter speech (December 9th, 1906) he spoke strongly against any form of obligatory service.

The Ayr Brig appeal came up again. Rosebery was once more summoned to Glasgow. He was able to invent a speech of winning freshness on the old theme: what Burns did for Scotland; what he did for the Church "by dissociating religion from the outward husk of cant in which it was enveloped and withered." And for once he quoted freely from the poet. The Auld Brig was saved, and in July 1910 Rosebery presided at its re-opening.

As a matter of course Rosebery was summoned to the inauguration of Queen Victoria's statue at Leith (October 15th, 1907). The Provost called on him as the orator and mouthpiece of Scotland whenever a great occasion arose. Rosebery's encomium pointed to the conclusion of the whole matter:

"The test of a reign must be the condition of the nation itself—its moral, physical, intellectual welfare; and what reign will better bear that test than the long years of Queen Victoria? . . . In due course Edward the Pacificator follows Victoria the Good. Long may we look to a succession of monarchs deriving their ideas of duty and ambition from this august source."

Soon afterwards there was a series of engagements at Glasgow. Rosebery became a Bonnet-maker and Dyer; and the remarkable Provands Lordship Club, boasting their headquarters at the oldest inhabited house in Scotland, entertained him at dinner—old Scots fare served on pewter, and rum punch, at plain deal tables lit by candles in brass candlesticks. This was delightful, but more serious affairs took him to Glasgow. In August he had spoken strongly in the House of Lords against the Scottish Landholders' Bill, largely because it seemed to burden Scotland with the Irish system of fair rents and fixity of tenure. Now in Glasgow he denounced the measure with great vigour, explaining how it had caused him to break eighteen months of silence on political questions. Mr. Gladstone, he said, would have approached the case with laborious investigation. The crofter system was unsuited to Scotland as a whole; the bill introduced dual ownership, however much that might be denied; and it initiated in Scotland the fatal Irish system of landholding.

There was plenty to be said both for and against the measure. The significance of Rosebery's attitude lies in the fact that since 1905 he had become a critic pure and simple of the Government. When he agreed with them he did not think it necessary to say so; they were the party in power. But when he differed, as he often did, duty obliged him to protest. He thus gave the impression of being more perpetually hostile to his Liberal friends than he actually was. He was an authentic occupant of the cross-benches, on which formerly he must always have cast a somewhat envious eye.

Yachting had become a regular custom with Rosebery since he was again master of his own time. He became owner of a fine vessel, the *Zaida*, and was elected to the Royal Yacht Squadron. Naples was one principal element in determining his choice, for Posilipo was an admirable base for any Mediterranean tour. One or other member of his family often joined in a cruise, he usually slept well at sea, and altogether life on board his yacht afforded the chief fruition of his later years now that he seldom was seen on a race-course. When England was plunged in mourning in 1901, after Rosebery had attended King Edward's first Council—"A confused and undignified ceremony; except for the new King, who was perfection" —he soon started for Rome, where his son Neil joined him at the beginning of April. The elder, Dalmeny, was now at Sandhurst, after making the most of his Eton years. Rosebery lingered longer than usual at Rome, seeing much of the diplomatic world. One evening (March 27th) he was inspired to a "purple" reflection, such as he seldom noted now:

"After dinner to the Coliseum—a band playing, then a rocket or two, then Bengal lights—these last vulgar. But before they began I was profoundly impressed with the scene—this great gaunt skeleton of time in which there once throbbed so full and tumultuous a life, where the dusty Pagan crowd thronged, as to a bull-fight, to see the torn Christians furnish sport; this imperishable monument which defies time, and watches impassively the vicissitudes of Rome, now containing a small crowd of tourists, listening to an Italian military band and waiting for the paltry fireworks, with the cold moon looking cynically down."

After the Palm Sunday celebrations they passed on to Naples and the Villa Rosebery, with a new steam launch for excursions to the town and beyond. But for a longer distance greater tonnage was needed, and they were given berths in H.M.S. *Cæsar* to Malta, saw the British Fleet in its splendour, drove four-in-hand with Lord Charles Beresford; Rosebery had a very interesting two hours with Admiral Fisher; and so back to Naples in H.M.S. *Surprise*.

The Duchess of Cleveland died at Wiesbaden on May 18th, 1901, and another chapter was closed. She had shown amazing energy in travel—visiting Spain, Egypt, Constantinople (where she was decorated by the Sultan), and then India (where she went alone and unattended, by her own wish). At past eighty she had preserved all the wit and spirits of her girlhood. She and her son had always kept up a correspondence of warm affection, and in the previous year they had joined in a common sorrow, the loss of Lord Leconfield and his chivalrous friendship for his mother-in-law and brother-in-law. Some months before Rosebery had written (June 1st, 1900):

"I send you my most heartfelt and affectionate wishes for your health and happiness. You always have them, but never more than on your birthday."

Rosebery now hastened to Wiesbaden. His mother had been under the care of Dr. Pagenstecker, the world-famous oculist; in his friendly company Rosebery found "Wiesbaden more glorious with blossom than any place I ever saw." A simple funeral (May 24th) at Raby was the last scene.

A quiet summer followed. "I have not spent Derby Day in London since I was at school." Then a visit to Geneva where Neil Primrose was studying, and excursions to Coppet and Prangins. He went on to Gastein, "lonelier than ever," and read enormously in French, including little pocket volumes of Musset which he read out of doors. And not French books exclusively: "Took Plutarch's *Demosthenes* out with me. What good reading it is." When June 21st came:

"A glorious unspeakable day, rewarding one for the past and obliterating it. Sate out all day. I love this longest day, not least because it is the anniversary of the fall of the last Government. And to-night how I enjoyed my after-dinner walk on the Kaiser promenade; the dark bulk of the mountains, the pure air of heaven itself, the great black chine of the opposite mass that girds in Gastein, with a divine moon— new not perhaps the newest."

In October Rosebery engaged in a new enterprise. He joined the Board of the Great Northern Railway. The autumn months in Scotland passed as usual.

Rosebery's Scottish activities during the first decade of the century are touched on elsewhere. But he was also busy in England from time to time. It was a compliment to him as a public orator to be asked to lead the Winchester celebration of King Alfred's Millenary (September 19th, 1901), for mediæval history had never been his playground as modern history was, and in his dedicatory speech he said:

"In him we venerate not so much the striking actor in our history as an ideal Englishman, the perfect sovereign, the pioneer of England's greatness."

A Service followed—"The Cathedral stunned me by its magnificence."

Rosebery became Chancellor of the University of London in 1902. He was the first to be elected by Convocation. It was the tradition to appoint a Liberal Chancellor. At his first Presentation Day he honoured the memory of the four personal friends who had preceded him, Lords Granville, Derby, Herschell, and Kimberley. Later in the year he formally visited the new physical laboratories, and was surrounded by a galaxy of men of science.

At the opening of the Goldsmiths' College (September 29th, 1905), one of the germs of the Imperial College of Science and Technology, Rosebery praised the munificence of the Great City Company and the co-operation of the local authorities, but he was happiest in foretelling the priceless work to be done by the newer Universities with London at their head.

Two years later (May 8th, 1907) a somewhat delicate situation arose. The Chancellorship of Oxford fell vacant, and in response to a requisition Rosebery allowed his name to be put forward, well knowing that tradition would enforce the choice of a Conservative candidate. On Presentation Day the Chancellor explained his position to a sympathetic audience: his election to Oxford was impossible and his devotion to London could not be excelled.

He opened the London Day Training College in Southampton Row, and thought that the education of examiners might be as important as that of teachers.

One pleasant educational episode fell in this period. Rosebery had always remained a pugnacious Etonian, and had never even seen Harrow. Recently a lamentable fire at Eton had cost the lives of two boys. The Head of the School at Harrow had been deputed to take a wreath to the funeral. Rosebery—now to his great pleasure a "Fellow of Eton,"[4] spontaneously attended Speech Day at Harrow, and told how deeply this act had gone to the hearts of Etonians.

One further London interlude can be mentioned here. At the 10th Annual Meeting of the London Topographical Society Rosebery spoke of the fascinating subject of Whitehall Palace.

It was one of the best of his short addresses, for he was in his element in telling how the home of thirty Archbishops of York, seized by Henry VIII, the favourite palace of Stuart Kings and stained with the blood of one of them, was deserted and in the main destroyed at the close of the seventeenth century. He revelled, too, in telling of the "splendid dream" of the plan that Inigo Jones drew for James I for a palace far larger than the Escorial, far grander than the Louvre or Versailles, with its huge central court and six great side courts.

"One may look back with regret," said Rosebery, "if it be ever worth while to look back with regret, to the opportunity lost by Barry when the new Houses of Parliament were erected. . . .

"Had the Stuarts spent the money they squandered otherwise in realising the plan of Inigo Jones, it would have stood in mitigation of the judgment of history. The recording angel of architecture would have blotted out many of their misdeeds with a grateful tear; and we, as we passed by the stately façade of the palace, would have said, 'They were bad Kings, but after all they left us that.' "

Oxford was not to lose Rosebery altogether, for when Cecil Rhodes died and created his famous foundation, a Trust was formed

---

[4] This old title had recently been revived for the Governing Body of Eton.

of which Rosebery was the senior member. His friendship with Rhodes was of long standing, and the two had many talks and walks together at the Durdans. When Rosebery was in office correspondence passed freely on South and East African questions. Rhodes, full of his spinal railway system northwards, was lukewarm about the Uganda railway; but of course favoured expansion towards the Lakes. In April 1895 he wrote:

"I am getting on well, but Africa is changing, and I know there are many breakers ahead. Still, if you have personally gained all that can be personally won, I think it makes you very much stronger to do your best to carry out your fixed ideas.

"I have been touched to hear that you have been ill, but as an outsider I believe if you have patience you will win. I feel mental worry has helped your sleeplessness."

In 1899 Rhodes had sent a hundred guineas to the Methodist Million Fund, and had received cordial thanks from Mr. Robert Perks. Telling Rosebery of this letter Rhodes wrote:

"I am going to face the music. You must remember my little troubles are nothing to yours."

It was fitting that the statesman to whom the Empire meant most should be one to hold in trust the benefaction left by the greatest dreamer of Imperial dreams. A tablet was erected in the Examination Schools at Oxford to Commemorate the foundation of the Scholarships. It happened that the scholarly and eloquent President of Magdalen[5] was vice-Chancellor. He reminded the hearers that Rosebery was the only living Oxonian Prime Minister, an historian, statesman, and orator, through whom Cecil Rhodes had been admitted to the Privy Council. Rosebery dwelt on Rhodes's devotion to Oxford, and on the way in which his last years were solaced by his inspiration of combining service to the University with his Imperial ideas. Nobody had ever been more slandered in his lifetime than Rhodes, whose life was simplicity itself. Rosebery recalled two conversations, one showing Rhodes with a strong desire for posthumous fame; the other when the hand of death was nearly on him, in a different mood—"life and fame and achievement, everything is too short." But Rosebery believed that in South Africa, in the whole Empire, and perhaps not least at Oxford his fame is still secure.

[5] Mr. (afterwards Sir Herbert) Warren.

"In this ancient University his surest and noblest monument will be the career, the merits, and the reputation of the scholars whom he has summoned within these walls."

The Rhodes Trust was fortunate in securing as its first secretary Mr. Francis Wylie.[6] An accomplished son of Oxford, he was for a time tutor to Rosebery's sons, to their great advantage. This enabled their father to estimate the qualities which made him a valued official of the Trust long after Rosebery himself had been unable to help in its active conduct. The noble Rhodes House now stands as an embodiment of its founder's vision.

Epsom always kept a strong hold on Rosebery's affections. He liked the historical associations, not merely those of the most famous racecourse in the world, but of the town where Pepys and Nell Gwyn had visited, where fashion has thronged to the Wells, where "the bad Lord Lyttelton" had been haunted. It had a pleasant flavour of his own more reckless days, when the fascination had beguiled him into the imprudent purchase of an extra home. That house, Durdans, or The Durdans, had a chequered history. The original dwelling was believed to have been built from the materials of Henry VIII's gorgeous palace of Nonsuch, which fell into the rapacious hands of Barbara Palmer, Duchess of Cleveland, became derelict, and was pulled down. The Durdans belonged to that Earl of Berkeley whose daughter Henrietta became the heroine of a notorious family scandal. In the eighteenth century it passed to the Earl of Guilford, and was afterwards inhabited by Frederick Prince of Wales, who enjoyed the hawking for which Epsom Downs were famous. Before long the fine house was stripped and demolished. Another was being erected on the same site when it was entirely destroyed by fire in 1764. Soon a smaller building took its place, the property changed hands more than once, and ultimately belonged to Mr. Arthur Heathcote, locally known as "Squire Heathcote," an offshoot of the family of which Lord Ancaster is the head. He seems to have been something of a Squire Western, and is chiefly remembered from his ownership of the Derby winner *Amato*, singular as having run in that race and that alone. The horse is buried in the grounds of the Durdans, side by side with a favourite staghound, and his memory is kept green by the Amato Inn, just below the Durdans and a popular resort of tipsters of the humbler class. When Rosebery bought the estate it was a small affair, with a few

[6] Sir Francis Wylie resigned his post in 1930.

paddocks belonging to it. As years went on he added to it considerably, and divided his stud of mares and yearlings between it and Mentmore. He also greatly improved the house and gardens, adding a delightful library and other rooms. There, too, was housed the wonderful collection of sporting pictures, headed by Stubbs' *Eclipse*, which he began to form in the days when they could be bought for comparatively little, before American taste had swept these open-air products of British art into the net that has captured so many bigger fish. Rosebery was fond of telling how, when he was Foreign Secretary, it now and then happened that some solemn diplomatist from abroad came down on solemn business, and stared in amazement at the spectacle of the Minister surrounded by effigies of race-horses, jockeys, and fighting-cocks.[7]

Certainly there could be no pleasanter parties than those at the Durdans, serious or gay. Nothing could oust his Scottish homes from his affections; but in his later years there was little to choose between them and the Durdans. He was on the pleasantest terms with his Epsom neighbours, notably Mr. and Mrs. Northey of Woodcote Place, whose family had been conspicuous there for two hundred years; and Mr. and Mrs. Aston of Woodcote Grove. Mr. Aston was a keen Liberal Leaguer, and Rosebery's frequent companion in long walks. One day—

"On the way back past Epsom Common, I saw a huge blaze! ''Tis Durdans,' I said. Aston tried to reassure me, but in vain. What an agony it was till I got home and saw that it was the lower yard on fire—fine flames they were. But what a reaction of joy and gratitude. I realised what it would be to lose my beloved nest. Thanks be to God."

Sir Rowland Blades[8] and his family, close by at Leatherhead, were frequent visitors and valued friends.

But Epsom was not only a *Sans Souci* for a weary statesman. Rosebery meant to be a good townsman, and he became an active member of the Urban District Council, scrupulously attending its meetings. He also zealously supported the renovation of the two churches which he and his family attended. Epsom College was

[7] There is a parallel story of a bishop, one of the most famous scholars of his day, who received a peculiarly pompous clergyman on business. The visitor began, "I find Your Lordship in your study, immersed, no doubt, in the researches that have made your name so famous." "As a matter of fact," replied the bishop, "I was looking at the *Sporting Times*." And it was true, for one of the sons of the palace took in the pink periodical.

[8] Lord Mayor of London 1926-7; *cr.* Lord Ebbisham 1928.

founded in 1855, and soon became noted for its science teaching—when science teaching was generally kept in the background. It then became a recognised portal to the profession of medicine. Rosebery was its President, and maintained friendship with the successive headmasters, all men of mark in the educational world. He was conspicuous at the Jubilee festival in 1905. Soon afterwards his devotion to the Epsom ratepayers brought him into conflict with a still older love, the London County Council. London had to house its lunatics somewhere, and it acquired the large estate of Horton Manor, on which vast buildings began to rise. Rosebery wrote a piteous letter to *The Times* (March 4th, 1907), detailing the circumstances, and making appeal for mercy to the new Council. He quoted an earlier letter from the leading residents of Epsom to the L.C.C., of which it may be concluded he was the author. Did it not strike the Council as hard, it had then been asked, that the little community of Epsom should be selected as the dumping-ground for so great a proportion of the mental disease of the County of London? In his present letter, his blood boiled, he declared, at the injustice of the infliction, and he dwelt on the prospect of escaped lunatics penetrating into the houses of nervous residents. In fact, from time to time a few patients, happily of the milder variety, did escape; and Rosebery wrote further indignant letters to the Press. In his many walks and drives he encountered parties of these poor people oftener than his fellow townsmen had the chance of doing; but in his protests he was certainly the mouthpiece of local sentiment. However, the mass of practical considerations prevailed; and nothing happened until the world-wide lunacy of the war distracted the ordinary existence of peace-time lunatics, as of everybody else. They were carted off to distant establishments, and Horton, for the time being, overflowed with wounded soldiers.

Rosebery was at any rate safe from strange incursions in his smaller home of Rosebery, in the hills on the Peebleshire border. Before the days of motorcars it was something of an expedition to get to it, but during these years he spent many autumn days there, with his sons or a neighbour or two. There was a small grouse-moor, with a converted farm-house as a shooting-box; and a good stretch of coverts and low-ground shooting, with the singular variety of game in limited quantities which makes that form of sport so pleasant in Scotland. There were friendly houses within easy reach, and places of interest, like Cockpen famed in verse, and the soft beauty of Hawthornden. For a moment Rosebery contemplated considerable additions to the simple house, which he had made agreeably habitable but nothing more. Plans were prepared by a distinguished architect of Edinburgh, not on the scale of Inigo Jones and Whitehall, but such as would have turned Rosebery into a regular country house. The shifting events of his later years made its owner abandon them, not without regret.

CHAPTER XX

The Closing Years

COMPLETE good humour reigned when, in 1907, the Prime Minister was granted the Freedom of Edinburgh. Rosebery made a point of being present, and, in the course of a brief speech, said:

"What we recognise most in Sir Henry Campbell-Bannerman, besides the great qualities which have brought him to his high office, are those Scottish qualities of humour, geniality, courtesy, and if I may add the most distinctive and Scottish word of all, pawkiness, that have marked his career. Let me also say this on my own behalf, that I should have travelled far, even if I had not been near, to come to-day to pay honour to one for whom, though I may be sometimes separated on questions of public policy, I have long learned to honour and regard as a colleague in many Governments, and a friend whose regard I have never forfeited, as he has preserved mine. It is only people of little faith and thin convictions who never differ from each other on public policy. This at least we have always cherished in our public life as our guiding principle, that these differences of opinion, where they do not touch personal honour, should never in the slightest degree affect personal friendship."

This Scottish tribute from an old friend gave particular pleasure to the Scottish Prime Minister. It was one of the last he was to enjoy, for he was struck down by illness on November 13th. He recovered slightly in the New Year, but died on April 22nd, 1908.

The succession of a Liberal League Prime Minister did not soften Rosebery towards the new Government. He recognised two bugbears—Protection and Socialism. The first seemed to have been definitely quelled; but the second was becoming formidable. The Treasury policy, especially in its treatment of land, seemed to him to violate the canons of Gladstonian Liberalism; and he definitely ranged himself in the opposing camp.

The Budget of 1909–10 brought his discontent to a head. Its whole story does not concern this book; but Rosebery's share in the

fierce struggle must be recorded. In a letter to the Press he wrote
(June 21st, 1909) :

"This is not a Budget but a revolution, a social and political revolution of the first magnitude. . . . It will be carried over the heads of the people by a majority in the House of Commons without the faintest desire or attempt to ascertain the views of the people on the vast changes projected . . . there is no referendum here. A powerful Government does not, naturally, seek a general election. . . . So that the boasted freedom of our Constitution has really come to this—that the most sweeping changes may be carried out by a Ministry of great numerical backing in the House of Commons, without the nation having, or ever having had, or hoping to have, a voice in the matter before it is decided. . . . Surely the country must see that there are vast flaws in the Constitution, and that the absolute rule of a party in power differs very little from the absolute rule of an individual, which is what we used to call despotism?"

There is nothing in this letter about the merits of the financial proposals themselves. Rosebery hammered out his opinion of these in a very long address delivered (September 10th, 1909) in response to a requisition from the business community in Glasgow. It was a painful task in many respects, he said, but duty forbade him to remain absolutely silent. He proceeded to a root-and-branch condemnation of the measure, with scarcely a word of qualification. Its features, he said, were a want of adequate preparation, a violent onslaught on the ownership of land, and the creation of a general feeling of insecurity. With great skill, with few rhetorical adornments, and with complete abstention from humorous comments, he marshalled all the well-known arguments against the new principles of taxation. It was a departure, he maintained, from the sound rule of not taking more in a single year than is necessary for the service of that year. Then, he continued:

"The most suspicious part of the Budget is that relating to land . . . the source is suspicious, because in the main it is that of our old friends of the Land Nationalisation League. . . . Mr. Lloyd George, in October 1906, said 'Nationalisation of the Land must come, but it must come by easy stages.' . . . The Land Nationalisation League were extremely jubilant over the Budget."

Rosebery went on to examine the familiar contention that land should be placed in a special category for taxation. He would have none of it, saying that all the arguments were equally applicable to

[511]

railway stocks. If unearned increment were taxed in the case of land, the same would soon happen to all securities.

"When did landowners become part of the criminal class? . . . Do these taxes only touch the rich? . . . the figures of the Budget introduced total uncertainty into an important trade; they select one kind of property for exceptional dealing on grounds which may easily be extended to all property, and they must immediately result in a considerable increase in unemployment."

Death duties, he went on, as introduced by Sir William Harcourt in his Government, were regarded as a sort of deferred income-tax on unearned incomes. Now earned and unearned incomes were differentiated, and the maximum figure was almost doubled. Death duties were a capital tax, popular with Chancellors of the Exchequer who spend them as income. It sounded very pleasant to tax the rich to give to the poor, but that is an operation which very soon percolates to the poor. He would ask the Government, several of whose members had served under Mr. Gladstone, with what feelings they would approach him, were he alive, with such a Budget. They would soon find themselves on the stairs, if not in the street.

"Because in his eyes, and in my eyes, too, his humble disciple, Liberalism and Liberty were cognate terms; they were twin sisters."

In concluding the speech he declared:

"In my opinion, the deep, subtle, insidious danger which underlies it all is the danger of Socialism. . . . I cannot help feeling that the Government is dallying with Socialism . . . how far they are advanced on that path I will not say, but on that path I, at any rate, cannot follow them an inch. I may think Tariff Reform or Protection an evil, but Socialism is the end of all, the negation of faith, of family, of property, of monarchy, of Empire."

Such was the outline of the address, eagerly anticipated, and enthusiastically greeted by the Opposition. Two other passages must be cited, from their bearing on the subsequent fortunes of the Budget. Quite early in the speech he declared:

"It is my duty to-day to show why I believe it not to be in the best interests of the nation that this financial measure should become law."

And before dilating on the Socialist danger he said:

"The peers should see this constantly drifting and changing Budget in a definite shape before they venture to pronounce any opinion on it.

. . . I hear a great many people in easy chairs say, 'Why trouble about the Budget when the House of Lords is sure to throw it out?' If the House of Lords relies on the support of the people in the easy chairs, the House of Lords is not likely to do that which they expect. . . . I have come to the deliberate conclusion that the Government wishes the House of Lords to throw out the Finance Bill. It believes, I imagine, that it will be a taking cry in the country. In no other way can I explain the prodding and taunting of the House of Lords which is so considerable a feature in the speeches of some members of the Government towards the House of Lords—not all of them."

The Finance Bill plodded its way through the House of Commons, much modified and amended, as such a colossal measure was bound to be. It reached the House of Lords on November 23rd, and received the unusual compliment of six full days' debate, before and after dinner. When the second reading was moved, Lord Lansdowne countered it with the Resolution, "That this House is not justified in giving its consent to this Bill until it has been submitted to the judgment of the country." Rosebery spoke early on the third day. He expressed his sense of the awful gravity of the situation, the most serious since 1832. On the merits of the Bill, he recurred to his Glasgow speech, and had never thought of reversing or recalling one single syllable of it. The Bill had at any rate the aspect of being both crude and vindictive. But he was not willing to link the fortunes of the Second Chamber with opposition to the Budget. If we had the Referendum it would be an occasion for its use. But he did apprehend the result of an appeal to the country on an unreformed hereditary Second Chamber, mixed up with the promises of the Budget. The House was playing for too heavy a stake on this occasion.

"I think that you are risking in your opposition to what I agree with you in thinking is an iniquitous and dangerous measure, the very existence of a Second Chamber. . . . I am sorry—with all my heart I am sorry—that I cannot give a vote against the Budget on this occasion."

Several peers commented on the speech; but it was not until the last day of the debate that Lord Curzon set himself to dissect it.

The Glasgow speech, he observed, had been the first blow, as many thought a smashing blow in the campaign. He wondered if Rosebery had quite realised the responsibility which he had assumed by the speech. He was not a recluse thinking aloud in his study, but an ex-Prime Minister speaking aloud to his countrymen. No speech in Lord Curzon's time had anything like the instantaneous and overwhelming effect upon the people; and when Rosebery said the future of Great Britain was being put in the melting-pot, and it was not in the best interests of the nation that the measure should become law, the average reader, particularly if he happened to be a legislator, might be pardoned for thinking that it was his duty to do what he could to prevent it. There was a sting in Curzon's conclusion, though he did not dispute the purity of Rosebery's motives:

"The impression produced on us was as though some great and famous commander had left us in the breach after he himself had taken us up to the walls and had fired the powder in the train."

Rosebery said no more in public, but he was wounded by this interpretation of his speeches. He wrote to Sir R. Perks on November 26th, 1909:

"I see the air darkened by brick-bats, and though I foresaw it, it seems to me very absurd. If you turn to my Glasgow speech, you will see that my language was as distinct on this point as it could be. I never said privately or publicly that I could support the House of Lords in rejecting the Budget. Indeed, what I said as Prime Minister (July 19th, 1894) made that impossible, in my judgment. I should have wished to remain silent, but that was impossible."

He opened his heart again to the same trusted friend on December 5th:

"My last speech I knew must make me odious to both sides. The flesh therefore would have inclined me to silence; but the spirit made me feel that that course would be ignominious. So I faced the music. But I scarcely anticipated that I should be taunted by the Anti-budgeteers with perfidy and cowardice (for that is what the charges amount to), bolstered up by snippets from my Glasgow speech, when the whole passage would be conclusive. This is what Curzon does, an honourable man and a friend of my own; and I do not complain, for it is what all the professional politicians would do. But it brings home to me once more the dirt and squalor of party politics. I am glad that you are out of them for the present, and I for ever.

"I view this situation with good humour, but it makes me feel how difficult it is for me to speak on behalf of such men, who use independent utterances for their own purposes, and stone the speaker when he differs from them on a question of policy.

"The situation is the gravest in my lifetime, but at this moment I do not see how I, distrusted and detested by both parties, can usefully intervene. Perhaps the situation may clear in this respect, but it threatens to become murkier.

"The decision will be fought at this Election: the House of Lords, the Budget, and Tariff Reform, and there will be a decisive voice on none of them. Eventually we shall, I think, as usual 'muddle through.'"

Rosebery tells his own story of this transaction. The harshest critic could only say that once more he failed to realise that his past history made it impossible for the public to regard him as an outsider bringing an independent judgment to bear on a novel situation. To the commercial audience at Glasgow he had not thought it necessary to foretell the probable reaction on the House of Lords of rejection of the Bill; consequently his speech there was almost entirely devoted to the iniquities of the measure. Here he seemed to be in line with the regular Opposition; and when in the House of Lords he warned them of the deeper considerations that could not be escaped, they looked on him as a backslider.

REFORM OF THE HOUSE OF LORDS

The well-worn subject of House of Lords reform was pushed into the foreground by the rejection of the Budget and the consequent General Election.

On December 22nd Rosebery wrote to *The Times* that in the polemics of the General Election there was danger that the reform of the House of Lords would be disregarded. The Government desired to turn the House into a pliant phantom. On the other hand, Mr. Balfour had given no pledge of Reform. "Have we not then to ask for definite declarations of policy from both sides?"

In another letter, to the *Glasgow Daily Record and Mail*, he pointed out that the situation had changed since 1894-5, when he had attacked the House of Lords. There was now a danger that a chance Socialist majority might wreck the nation by measures, nominally financial, which it would claim to exclude from any modification.

As a matter of fact, the subject had not been allowed to sleep since the Liberal Government came into power. In 1907 Lord Newton, whose drily humorous and independent speeches always gave Rosebery pleasure, introduced a Bill with extensive proposals for reforming the composition of the House. Rosebery spoke on the second day of the debate. The first day had made two things clear— that the regular Conservative Opposition preferred a renewed enquiry by a Committee rather than a Bill, and that the Liberal Government were convinced that the urgent question was not the composition of the House of Lords but its relation to the House of Commons. Rosebery unhesitatingly preferred the device of a Select Committee on the lines which he had fruitlessly advocated twenty-three years before. A Bill, he thought, had no chance of acceptance by the House of Commons, and, on the other hand, he refused to admit that all reform of the House must wait until the relations between the two Houses had been adjusted. He had come to three fundamental conclusions, first, that the mainly hereditary constitution of the House cannot logically be defended; secondly, that the thinking part of the country would prefer a House of Lords unreformed to no Second Chamber at all; and thirdly, that there can be no reform of the House except with a Conservative Government in power. The only hope was to keep, so far as possible, the party element out of the discussion.

The result was the nomination of a Committee, from which the Government stood aloof, though three Liberals, Lord Selby, the former Speaker, Lord Courtney, and Lord Ribblesdale joined it with their approval. Its principal outcome was the general acceptance of the principle that for English Peers, as for Scottish and Irish, the possession of a peerage should not *ipso facto* involve a place in Parliament.

After the General Election at the opening of the year 1910, Parliament met on February 21st. For once the King's Speech contained no programme of general legislation; but it foreshadowed proposals to define the relations between the two Houses, and to secure to the House of Commons undivided control over finance, and predominance in legislation.

After the customary speeches Rosebery rose, and having made some general observations, of course hostile to the Government, he indicated a point of difference from the Leader of the Opposition. Lord Lansdowne, in speaking of reform of the House, had not condemned an attempt to effect it, but treated it as primarily the business of the Government, who should lay proposals on the table. Rosebery thought otherwise. He maintained that there was a golden opportunity, which might not recur, for putting themselves right with the public: Unionist candidates had broken their shins against the hereditary character of the House of Lords; the country should be allowed to judge between the plan of the House of Commons and that of the House of Lords; more important than the House of

THE PROBLEM PICTURE

Lord Rosebery: "That's mine, pretty good, eh?"
Lord Lansdowne: "H'm, I can't say I quite ——"
Lord Curzon: "I'm sure I could improve it."
Lord Halsbury: "Take it away!"

Lords or any of its principles was the existence of a strong and efficient Second Chamber.

This debate then closed; but three days later Rosebery gave notice of a motion. Accordingly, on March 14th, he brought up three Resolutions. The first declared the necessity of a strong and efficient Second Chamber; the second, that this could best be obtained by the reform and reconstitution of the House of Lords; the last, that the possession of a peerage should not of itself give the right to sit and vote. He called attention to the postponement by the Government of a scheme of reform, while the powers of the House were to be limited at once:

"If the proposals are not to be parallel, if they are not to be *pari passu*, the Government must know perfectly well that they will never come to fruition."

He thought the proposal to deprive the House of all its powers and then to reconstitute it on a democratic basis a remarkable instance of an illogical proposition. He went on to describe a sham Second Chamber system as worse than that of a Single Chamber. Rosebery devoted much of his speech to an examination of the Third Resolution, and came into collision with Lord Halsbury, the standard-bearer of ancient Toryism, who later on in the debate asserted uncompromising opposition to any plan of reform that had been suggested by anybody.

The debates continued until March 22nd, punctuated by many excellent speeches, Rosebery throughout being careful to explain that these were only broad Resolutions of principle, on which a Bill could be founded later. The Third Resolution was the only one on which a division was taken (March 22nd), only 16 peers being found to follow Lord Halsbury into the lobby. The 175 who supported Rosebery belonged to both parties, and included all the Ministers present.

Rosebery had hoped to drive his nail in a little deeper when the House reassembled after the Easter recess. But on May 6th the whole nation was plunged into mourning by the King's death, and he felt that although his Resolutions were not controversial in the sense that the Government Resolutions were, their discussion ought to be postponed. It was further deferred by the appointment of the small Conference, representing both Houses, at which an attempt was made to define the lines on which their future relations should be drawn. The attempt failed, and the Conference closed early in

November. Rosebery's hands were again freed, and he urged strongly (November 15th) that his Resolutions should not be ignored in spite of Lansdowne's demand for the prompt consideration of the Government's Parliament Bill. On the very next day Lord Lansdowne formally repeated this demand, with which the Government spokesman complied. Rosebery announced that he would proceed next day with his new Resolutions. This he did, the first Resolution enacting a tripartite Chamber consisting:

A. Of hereditary peers chosen from among themselves and by the Crown.

B. Of Lords sitting by virtue of offices and qualifications.

C. Chosen from outside.

Rosebery defended his scheme from the charge of vagueness, and explained the absence of any provision for dealing with differences between the two Houses. Lord Curzon, however, in a long speech, attempted to dot some of the i's, declaring, for instance, that the hereditary element should not be predominant, and discussing possible methods of election. Rosebery replied at the close of a friendly debate, and this Resolution, the only one that was moved, was carried *nem. con.*

The second reading of the Parliament Bill was moved on the 21st; and was countered by Lansdowne with a fresh set of Resolutions covering the relations between the two Houses. The debate was to be adjourned in order that these might be considered. Rosebery naturally supported this, commenting severely on the Prime Minister's speech implying that the House of Lords was under sentence of death. The Lord Chancellor, Loreburn, while admitting Rosebery's lifelong lead in this business, maintained that the House had neglected the whole question for years.

The Lansdowne Resolutions (November 23rd and 24th) for the settlement of differences by a Joint Committee, by Joint Sittings, or in the last resort by Referendum, were discussed for two days. Rosebery spoke on the second day. His old friend John Morley, now Lord President, had appealed to him to divulge his whole plan, and repeated a witticism which years before Sir William Harcourt had thought particularly brilliant, describing Rosebery as "a dark horse in a loose box," and begging him to come out of his box. If he would produce a plan to constitute a real revising body, he would do a useful work.

In a very short reply Rosebery said that his friend's parallel about the horse was only too congenial. But nobody except the Government could lay a detailed scheme on the Table of the House.

The Resolutions were of course carried, like Rosebery's own. Parliament was prorogued on November 28th.

So ended Rosebery's persistent and consistent campaign for Reform of the House of Lords. More than twenty years have passed, and the composition of the House remains practically as it was. The combined wisdom of two, or of three, parties in the State has not produced any modification. This may prove the hopelessness of Rosebery's task. But it does not detract from the credit due to his laborious devotion to the job he had undertaken almost as a boy.

Since death had so early claimed Hannah Rosebery, her husband had done all he could, in the spirit of one of the most gracious poems that Roman genius has bequeathed to us:

> "Thou must be father and mother too:
>   No neck but thine
> The arms of all my merry crew
>   Can now entwine.

> "Whene'er thou kiss their tears away
>   Kiss too for me:
> All our home's burden from today
>   Must fall on thee."[1]

The four children had now grown up; the younger daughter had married. The elder was not long in following her example: the bridegroom was Charles Grant of the Coldstream Guards, son of General Sir Robert Grant, and presumptive successor to the ancient Shropshire family of Cotes of Woodcote.

The two boys said good-bye to Eton, after happy and prosperous schooldays. One passed through Sandhurst, the other studied abroad. Their father wrote at Dalmeny:

"Walked with the boys and read sermon with them,—for the last time as boys here with me. When they are next here Harry will be an officer and Neil an Oxford man."

At the beginning of 1903, Dalmeny, now in the Grenadiers and a county cricketer, came of age. At Dalmeny congratulations poured in from Scottish and English public bodies. The Duke of Buccleuch

[1] I have ventured to quote Mr. S. G. Tremenheere's excellent rendering of *Propertius* iv, 11. (London, 1931.)

proposed the toast of the evening. When Rosebery's turn came, he re-echoed for his son the hope expressed at his own coming of age by the father of one of the guests, that "wherever his fortune or his fate may carry him he must always remember the land to which he belongs, the people among whom he was bred, his kindred, his traditions." But he could not help *in ipsis floribus* from striking a note in a minor key. The occasion, he said, marked a milestone on the way of life; and he raised a smile by admitting to "something of a dowager feeling for the first time in his life." There were similar celebrations after the move to Mentmore.

Many parents, perhaps most, when their children grow up, look longingly back to the days of the united household of which they were the central luminaries. A man in whom the sense of proprietorship was so strongly developed as it was in Rosebery is specially susceptible to such reflections. As time went on and the family scattered, his love for his children never weakened or wavered, but the memory of the holidays at Mentmore or Dalmeny remained most precious to him. Perhaps he never experienced the positive pleasure which it is given to some to feel when they see the new generation stripped for the race and awaiting its turn. But he was all that a father-in-law could be to the wives and husbands of his sons and daughters. His affectionate regard for them was amply returned.

And there were compensations, such as a stay at Oxford with Neil. "We dined at the Bullingdon dinner in the barn. I sat next Agar-Robartes the president, with Neil next me." Thomas Robartes, a picture of energy and the joy of life, became the closest friend of the young generation at Mentmore. Later he made a definite mark in the House of Commons, before the war came to blight the unusual promise of his days. He sometimes joined the yachting expeditions, as did other friends of an older generation, somewhat younger than Rosebery's own, such as Luke White, Lord Annaly, a popular social figure and successor to his relative Lord Spencer as Master of the Pytchley—Rosebery maintained a close friendship with him and Lady Annaly. Others were Lord and Lady Arran, he a staunch supporter of the Liberal League, and Evan Charteris, who carried on the old amity between the houses of Gosford and Dalmeny and was able to discuss Scottish history and culture on even terms with his host. Throughout this period Rosebery depended much on the friendship and service of his personal private secretary, Neville Waterfield, his perpetual companion and the re-

cipient of greater confidence than as a rule he found it easy to give
to his nearest belongings.

For Rosebery the neighbourliness of the Lowlands overstepped
the limits of political agreement. The Duke and Duchess of Buccleuch and their children, Lord and Lady Wemyss (he "The
Brigadier" as Rosebery liked to style the veteran of the Royal Company of Archers), with the whole of the Charteris family, and
Lord and Lady Elphinstone, were close friends but not political
allies. The nearest great house of all was Hopetoun. There three
generations kept up close friendship with Dalmeny. The 7th Earl
of Hopetoun, created Marquess of Linlithgow 1902, made an honoured name as the first Governor-General of the Australian Commonwealth. His son and successor and his wife, the daughter of
Rosebery's Christ Church contemporary Sir Frederick Milner, carried on the friendly tradition to the last. On the other hand Sir
Thomas[2] and Lady Carmichael were ardent supporters, as were Sir
Edward[3] and Lady Colebrooke.

Looking northwards, the Duke[4] and Duchess of Montrose were
intimate friends, as were the Duke's sister, Lady Breadalbane and
her husband,[5] and the kindred families of Stirling-Maxwell and
Stirling of Keir. Lord and Lady Mar and Kellie,[6] inheritors of that
great Scottish name, were also of the inner circle of Rosebery's
friendship. But as has been shown by his frequent visits to Dunrobin, by far his closest intimacy was with the Duke[7] and Duchess
of Sutherland. Of the other ladies with whom he maintained cordial
friendship, some have flitted through these pages; but special mention must be made of the Duchess of Abercorn,[8] of Lady de Grey,[9]
and of Georgiana Lady Dudley.[10]

There was a long yachting cruise in the Mediterranean in the
spring of 1902, with a son and a daughter, starting from Cannes
to Corsica. As they approached in the evening, "there was the

[2] (1859-1926.) Governor of Victoria 1908-11, of Madras 1911-12, and of Bengal
1912-17. *Cr.* Lord Carmichael 1912.
[3] 5th Baronet. *Cr.* Lord Colebrooke 1906.
[4] 5th Duke of Montrose (1852-1925). Lord Clerk Register of Scotland.
[5] 7th Earl of Breadalbane (1851-1922) ; *cr.* Marquess 1885.
[6] 12th Earl of Mar and 14th Earl of Kellie, *b.* 1865.
[7] (1851-1913.) Succeeded as 4th Duke 1892. *m.* Lady Millicent, daughter of the
4th Earl of Rosslyn.
[8] Lady Mary Curzon, wife of the 2nd Duke of Abercorn.
[9] Lady Gladys Herbert, wife of the 4th Earl of Lonsdale, and secondly of Lord de
Grey, afterwards 2nd Marquess of Ripon.
[10] Daughter of Sir Thomas Moncrieffe and widow of the first Earl of Dudley.

strong scent of the island of which Napoleon spoke so much." At Ajaccio "the population is handsome: the males are so largely dressed in brown velveteen that one feels that some enterprising draper must have made a fortunate investment in that material." Naples sweltered in a sirocco, so Rosebery and Neil went on to Sicily, Girgente and its temples carpeted with more abundant and brilliant flowers than he had ever seen, Syracuse, back to Naples, and on to Villefranche. At Paris it was the day of elections, "as dull as a Scots Sunday in a country town." There was not much more foreign travel that year. He took Neil to Paris in August, and on to Tunis and Courmayeur. There he out-walked his son; got nearly to the end of his books, but found *"Whitaker's Almanack* a great resource." Neil also accompanied him to Balmoral for "an easy and pleasant man party," where cigars in the drawing-room betokened a revolution in the new reign.

The Adriatic coast was new ground the next year. Starting from Venice (April 1903), again with Neil as companion, he paused at Miramar, with its wonderful gardens and its tawdry relics of the hapless Emperor Maximilian; was amazed by the amphitheatre at Pola; dined with the Herbert Bismarcks at Fiume; was attracted by the churches of Zara, in spite of a bitter north-east wind—"the Venetian lions are everywhere, they should be the emblems of Great Britain"; was somewhat disappointed by the ruined palace at Spalato; but was deeply impressed by Ragusa, its suburbs and its church relics of ancient silver. To Corfu and then to Sicily and Naples, where King Edward arrived with the Mediterranean Fleet. But for this, the life at the villa was as usual. This year Gastein was the customary scene of Rosebery's August abroad.

The same pair were at Seville in the yacht for the following Easter (April 1904), with Evan Charteris as a third. Rosebery enjoyed the matchless Cathedral organ as much as ever, but after dinner he "walked back to the yacht, while the others went to that tedious imposture the dancing." Evidently he found that repetition stales a spectacle interesting only from its strangeness. They went on to Algiers and Biserta, and for a short stay at Naples.

The summer yachting tour (August 1904) was from Holyhead to the West Coast of Scotland, picking up Evan Charteris at Oban, and along the countless lochs of the west coast.

During these years Rosebery was always reading, but rarely noted the name of a book. But he liked keeping in touch with the lettered

[524]

world. I recall a dinner at Berkeley Square at which he received Acton, W. Courtney, G. Prothero, Spender, Welby, Godley, and myself. He described it—"Literary dinner at home. Very pleasant. Some stayed till 1."

His character as a writer was now fairly established:

January 23rd, 1902.—"Rowton dined with us. Long talk with him. He told me that he and Natty Rothschild had come to the conclusion that they might publish the first part of Dizzy's life, and that there was only one person they wished to write it (myself), but they feared it was impossible for me to give the time. I said 'Quite.' But it is strange to have been asked to write the authoritative lives of both Gladstone and Dizzy."

This, it will be remembered, was but a month after the Chesterfield speech, and all the political world was bubbling with rumours of Rosebery's political intentions.

Rosebery's share in the preliminaries to the General Election of January 1906 has been described above. His principal satisfaction with it was the return of Dalmeny for Midlothian by upwards of 3,000 votes. The unlucky misunderstanding with his Liberal League colleagues had in no way poisoned personal relations. Sir Edward and Lady Grey spent Christmas at the Durdans, meeting Jameson, and sedulously "walking the course." But after Parliament met there was nothing to keep him in London. His leading comrades had joined the Government, bound up with those who were by no means his comrades. They must have their fair chance, and for the moment he was really "out of politics." A long stay abroad was the obvious consequence, and early in March he started for Paris, and remained away for nearly three months. In the first weeks his companion was the ever congenial "Peter" Wroughton. They joined the yacht at Genoa. At Leghorn:

"A pathetic sight, a whole community there to see emigrants off: slipping bottles of wine into their hands—men, women, and children. The emigrants trying to be brave, and looking their last at the old home."

At Palermo Rosebery had to say good-bye to his old friend, and a pencil note in his diary shows how painfully solitude beckoned to him:

"Much as I loved him, I was mad to be alone."

[525]

As he explored Sicily the weather was bad and he became seriously unwell. He was little better when he returned to Naples, and matters were not improved by a violent eruption of Vesuvius, which rained black ash all over the country. During the next days the mountain thundered from behind a canopy of cloud and smoke, until the cone cracked "like the end of the world," and an earthquake drove the Neapolitans into the streets. Life in the choking dust was not agreeable, until the south-west breeze freed the villa. Rosebery's cough persisted, but he hung on, and enjoyed the amazing sunsets which the cataclysm had helped to paint. King Edward and Queen Alexandra arrived, and various expeditions did not improve Rosebery's persistent cough. It grew worse; he retired to bed with a temperature of over 103 degrees; got up in three days with his "legs very volatile"; gazed at Vesuvius knocked out of shape "like a prize-fighter's nose" by the eruption, and stayed on in convalescence till late in May. He was back in England on the 28th, still much below the mark, and sleeping badly. He was not abroad again during the year, but the following spring (May 1907) found him again at Naples for three weeks, with the yacht, and with Annaly as a companion. He thought Vesuvius dwarfed, "but his glow of purple and green is more splendid than ever." He once more noted what he was reading:

"I wish I could enjoy Pascal as, say, Macaulay did. I almost wish I did not enjoy Retz so much; but his acid flavour is so refreshing after the insipid graces and maternal flutterings of Madame de Sévigné."

They sauntered back to Marseilles in wonderful weather.

"Cleopatra on the Cydnus was not a patch on our delightful progress to-day."

In April next year (1908) he was again at the Villa Rosebery, both his sons sailing with him from Marseilles, and his younger daughter joining him at Naples. He sought peace there again in October. The weather was perfect: "nothing to record except pure enjoyment."

Italy called him again in the following spring (April 1909), but this time to Venice, crowded with strangers for a great Exhibition. He saw something of Horatio Brown, one of the Englishmen whom Italy had captured as a lifelong resident. He was for some time one of Rosebery's regular correspondents, and under his care Rosebery made acquaintance with several palaces that tourists do not see. It was all unusually pleasant, and so was Ravenna, where it appeared that the *Zaida* was the first yacht that had ever reached the ancient city.

"The population stands day and night on the quay to which we are moored, breathlessly interested, and chattering."

Neil Primrose and Lord and Lady Arran had joined him at Venice.

For once he was able to stay at the Villa Rosebery at the proper season of the year. After the Derby (June 7th), there was now nothing to keep him in London, and he sailed from Marseilles in the following week. He led his usual life through June, but out of spirits, for he had determined to give up the villa. It was a rather surprising resolution, for, as will appear directly, he was dropping some of his usual pursuits, and might well have given more time to Naples. One local change had some minor influence on him. His old school friend Rolfe, the Consul, had gone, and his capable successor was a stranger. Rolfe had looked after Rosebery and the villa as a brother might. But its owner had come to the conclusion that the time for departure had arrived. His children were amused by a ten days' visit, but none of them would have wished for the villa, even if they could have afforded its expense. He himself may have begun to fear the new Liberal theories of taxation; but if he could save by abandoning the villa, he did not wish to recoup himself by selling it. He therefore handed it over to the Foreign Office as a summer retreat for the Embassy at Rome, a gift for which, so far as I know, there is no precedent. So on June 28th, 1909, starting for the Balearic Islands, he noted in his diary:

"Left at 2.30 in yacht. Good-bye, Naples."

And in London, on November 1st:

"The Treasury Solicitor and the Notary and I finally signed away the beloved Villa at Naples. *Sic transit gloria.*"

As has been said, there was a gradual renunciation of some active pursuits. At Sandringham in 1907 he wrote:

"I must give up shooting in public. I have no legs and no arms, and my gun weighs a ton. This I suppose is my illness in the spring, and I am not young enough to recuperate. So let us make our bow gracefully."

His eyesight also was interfering with his shooting in a way which he hardly realised at the time; and a year later, again at Sandringham:

"I am giving up shooting here this year—a pang, but probably necessary."

But he still got plenty of enjoyment from sport at his English and Scottish homes, where, though there was plenty to shoot, he had not to lift his ton-weight gun to his shoulder four or five hundred times a day.

And the customary visits to Sandringham and Windsor continued.

A certain increase of deafness began to hamper Rosebery in listening to a speech or a play, but did not sensibly interfere with conversation; and King Edward found him as amusing as ever, and as acute a critic of European politics. One day at Castle Rising in Norfolk:

"Strolled about with the King in the morning to the church and almshouses. The King said he likes nothing so much as seeing churches."

Once (November 1904) there was a terrific wardrobe contretemps. Rosebery was talking to a friend at Berkeley Square at 7.5 p.m.:

"I uttered a piercing shriek. 'What is it?' 'The special train for the Windsor banquet leaves at 7.30!' Tore into breeches, &c., ran into the station as the train was moving out, jumped into a carriage with the Methuens—only to find out I was in wrong costume—I should have been in uniform. Banquet gloriously beautiful; 150 people or so in Waterloo gallery—plate and orchids illimitable. The Queen of Portugal noble and gracious. As our King came out after dinner—'I see you belong to the American Embassy.' "[11]

Through the succeeding year Rosebery's happy relations with the Sovereigns were unchanged. Once the Queen and the Empress Marie of Russia spent the day at Mentmore.

"Very easy and pleasant. The Queen seized upon and copied a letter of Uncle Sam dropped out of my Webster's dictionary. How pleased he would have been."

In 1909 Rosebery was at Balmoral in the autumn, and at Sandringham in November for the King's Birthday. A real tragedy

[11] No uniform is worn by civilians in the service of the United States.

broke up the gaiety of the visit: Montague Guest,[12] a popular figure at club and country house, dropped dead out shooting.

"I had to propose the King's health—always difficult, but more so than usual to-night because of poor Monty's death. However, the King was pleased, and came up to thank me and say how much he had been touched."

This was to be the last visit to King Edward, and the forecast of a deeper grief.

On May 6th, 1910, Rosebery was at the Durdans, and heard in the morning how grave the King's state was:

"I spent the afternoon in deep sorrow."

From the first the new Sovereigns extended to him the same gracious friendship of which he had had many proofs while they were Prince and Princess of Wales.

The accession of King George V concerned Rosebery in two respects that must be noted. He went on a mission to Vienna to announce the new reign, carried it out with dignity, and was graciously welcomed by the Emperor Francis Joseph, who conferred on him the Order of St. Stephen of Hungary, the most distinguished that a Protestant could receive. This was accepted after some demur on the side of our Foreign Office, on the ground that a dangerous precedent would be created. Events have made this fear groundless. This was Rosebery's last official appearance.

The other event caused general surprise. He was created Earl of Midlothian, an unexpected addition to his ancient Scottish titles and his more modern Barony of the United Kingdom. The explanation was this. On two or three recent occasions Scottish territorial titles had been assumed not for ancestral or proprietary reasons, but by peers promoted on general grounds of public service. This offended Rosebery's historical sense; and he was determined to anticipate the possible capture of the Midlothian name by some gifted outsider. But he never attempted to combine it with his older title.

PARLIAMENT BILL, 1910-11

The second General Election of 1910 brought to a head the proposals for limiting the veto of the House of Lords by the Parliament Bill. Rosebery, who had fought so long for reform of the House by the modification of the hereditary principle, saw his hopes shat-

[12] (1839-1909.) M.P. 1869-74 and 1880-85, brother of first Lord Wimborne.

[529]

tered. He had warned his brother peers in the spring (March 14th) that the choice lay between immediate bold reform and ultimate loss of powers. Now that the battle was engaged he declared unreservedly against the Government. He spoke at Manchester on the last day of November, asserting that the Liberal proposals amounted to the creation of a Single Chamber; that a great constitutional change was advocated with a levity which would have been impossible in the United States; that the House of Lords "with great calmness and deliberation set to work to proceed with their own reforms"; that the failure of the Conference of eight should have been followed by the assembling of a larger Conference; that the Irish contingent had prevented this from being done; that the hope expressed in the preamble of the Bill for the formation of a democratic Chamber would never be realised.

The next week (December 4th) he obeyed a requisition from citizens of Edinburgh, and repeated his denunciation of the Bill. He dotted the I on Ireland, saying that Britain had to toe the line at the dictation of the Irish leader. He rebutted the charge of inconsistency which Haldane had brought against him, based on his hostile attitude to the Peers in 1895, and argued with much force that it was incongruous to define relations between two Houses when the composition of one of them was unknown. The House of Commons, he proceeded, would be subject to no control but that of physical force. He then turned to the Referendum, giving qualified approval to it as a means of deciding great constitutional questions. In a second speech he described the meeting as the greatest since the Midlothian campaign in 1879, and professed himself as "desperately in earnest in this matter."

Rosebery issued a Message to the People of Scotland, beginning: "The present Dissolution is the most wanton and reckless that the country has known," and depicting the iniquity of the Government in four more brief sentences.

When the Bill reached the House of Lords the question had narrowed itself to a single issue. Would the Bill be passed substantially unamended, or if not, would a sufficient creation of peers take place in order to carry it?

Rosebery wrote to *The Times* (July 26th, 1911) deprecating insistence on amendments moved by the "die-hard" Conservative Peers, which might mitigate the operation of the measure, but would not prevent it from being destructive of the existing Second Cham-

LORD ROSEBERY, ABOUT 1911

ber without replacing it by anything. To protest as strongly as possible was the only course open to them.

When the two feverish nights of debate came on and the critical division was called (August 11th), on the question of insistence on the Lords' amendment, Rosebery rose and said:

"I am going to make the last, the shortest, and perhaps the most painful speech of my life."

He had never supported the amendments, he went on, but he could not conceive a more painful position than having to vote apparently in favour of a Bill which was abhorrent to him. But he had in his letter to the Press urged the Peers to abstain from voting; and as things were, it was his duty to follow the Government into the Division Lobby.

In the critical division only 243 peers voted, most Unionists abstaining. The Government won by 17.

Rosebery's attitude provoked some comments, on the lines of those which flamed out when the Budget of 1909-10 was rejected. One fell from Lord Selborne in the debate, and was answered by Rosebery in *The Times*:

"I cannot but think," [he wrote,] "that the position would be rendered even more intolerable by the introduction of hundreds of peers. . . . I should, of course, have preferred to abstain. But I should never have forgiven myself if the creation of a brigade of peers had taken place when my vote might have averted it."

His old Christ Church ally, the Duke of Northumberland, replied, by a letter to the same journal, that Rosebery by his own showing had *pro tanto* made himself responsible for the House of Lords being a sham for all effective purposes, and so his countrymen would be apt to hold him.

In his rejoinder Rosebery made an admission which he naturally had not let drop before—that the "subordinate and limited capacity for delay might under some circumstances be of some importance."

If the large creation of peers had taken place the House would have been "deprived of even this meagre resource."

By old custom a Protest Book is kept in the House of Lords, but it is not often adorned with signatures. Rosebery drew up and signed a solemn Protest against the Parliament Bill. Four bishops, and ten lay peers, mostly not of conspicuous distinction, appended their signatures.

Thus closed Rosebery's active share in the proceedings of the House of Lords.

Rosebery was casting politics to the winds at an age that for some men has marked the noontide of their public life. At sixty-three Gladstone was conducting his great administration of 1868–74; at sixty-three Disraeli had just "dished the Whigs" with his fine conjuring trick of Parliamentary reform. But Rosebery at any rate handed on the torch which he did not care himself to keep alight. Neil Primrose was elected for the Wisbech Division in January 1910. His father did not allow his disgust with politics to cool his other enthusiasms. At the Old Edinburgh Club he made a delightful speech on one of his favourite subjects, the many-coloured past of the city; he impressed on a London audience the charm of Harris tweeds and their peat reek; he gave the members of the Eton Society at their banquet (July 1911) historical and personal reminiscences of "Pop"; and he delivered (September 1911) at St. Andrews the Rectorial Address which is separately noted.

At the opening of the Mitchell Library in Glasgow he praised Mr. Carnegie for his endowment of a number of district libraries radiating the light and warmth of the central institution, and lamented the absence of a Scottish National Library; and he celebrated the memory of William Rogers—"the most true and broad-minded Christian I have ever known"—at the opening of the Library at Bishopsgate. There he made a confession of faith:

"There is no excuse for any man who has not his own private collection of books, and I appeal to every person in this assembly to say whether his own little shelf of books, even if it be merely a shelf, is not infinitely dearer to him than the whole collection of the British Museum."

The Advocates' Library in Edinburgh belonged to the Scottish Bar. For years Rosebery urged the creation of a National Library of which this was the obvious nucleus. On one occasion he urged it as the appropriate memorial of Queen Victoria's Jubilee. The project found favour, but was checked by the Great War, like so many others. It matured in 1922, when an appeal was issued signed by the Lord Provosts, the principals of the four Universities, and some representative Scots, headed by Rosebery. Sir Alexander Grant came forward with £100,000, and in 1925 a Bill passed through Parliament. Rosebery gave £5,000 for the Manuscript Department, and in 1927 made the presentation described in the Report of that year:

"In July 1927 Lord Rosebery presented to the National Library of Scotland his collection of Scottish books at Barnbougle Castle, and they were received in November. The collection was in three sections:

"1. Pamphlets. 120 volumes and over 2,000 single pamphlets all finely bound, published mainly between 1585 and 1903. Particularly original pamphlets dealing with the religious troubles of the 17th century, the Darien scheme, the Union, and Jacobitism.

"2. Early printed and rare books, including a series of broadsides and proclamations. Of the 700 items in this section many are unique.

"3. Books relating to Mary Queen of Scots. 300 volumes, the largest collection known."

He was again to the front (December 1911) at the meeting of the Scottish History Society, speaking of the interest of old household records. One of the speakers remarked that he had acquired a new reputation as a formidable, drastic, and one might almost say incendiary critic of books.

And in the following year he returned to his old topic of Scottish education, reverting to his lively contest with the Duke of Argyll over Lord Young's Act of forty years back. He wondered whether better men had been produced under the old system than before.

"It was an education of poverty and oatmeal and the classics, but on the whole it did not turn out bad men. And now we are rearing a generation on tea and football—spectators of football—the success of the Scottish nation has always been based on character, and if the schools of the country fail to produce the character they did in old times, they have something yet wanting in their sphere of operations."

These were questions not unnatural from one who saw little to cheer him in the vista of the future. In two-and-a-half years the youth of Scotland was ready with its answer.

What that answer might have to be was the subject of Rosebery's address at Glasgow when he opened the University O.T.C. headquarters. Haldane had lately made a speech of some depression on the condition of the Territorial Army, and Lord Roberts was pressing for universal military training. Rosebery told his hearers that for good or evil we were now embraced in the middle of the Continental system. We had certain vague liabilities—he would rather they were definite alliances—which might lead us into a war greater

[533]

than any since the fall of Napoleon. We must be prepared at the proper time to make good that liability.

He spoke to the Midlothian Boy Scouts (July 21st) with no war-like note; and of a battle long ago when in June 1913 a memorial was unveiled at Selkirk of a fine local tradition concerning Flodden Field. The tragic tale was one for Rosebery's happiest eloquence, and he did not omit to point a moral for the twentieth century. The King of Scots had involved the honour and safety of every man over whom he reigned. "That moral is not dead yet . . . let us at least take this lesson to heart, to be vigilant as to the wars in which we engage, and hold our statesmen responsible for their part."

At the beginning of 1914 Rosebery underwent an operation of some severity, but he recovered quickly, and in June was able, at a London County Council meeting, to compliment Sir John Benn on his new dignity, and to protest against the new duty thrust upon the Council as education authority.

He also was at Glasgow for a memorial to Lord Lister, and he gave away prizes at Epsom College, where Mr. Smith-Pearse re-signed the headmastership after twenty-five years' service.

Then came the outbreak of war. Rosebery, as has been seen, deprecated the policy which brought us directly into the Continental system; but he never, in public or private, let fall a word of blame for our entrance into the struggle.

He made a series of speeches in Scotland. We first came in for Peace—he said at Broxburn—for which Sir Edward Grey strove, and for Honour, because we had guaranteed the independence of Belgium. At a great gathering in Edinburgh (September 18th), Asquith made a stirring speech, and Rosebery, dragged forward though unwilling, said that the war must be fought out to the bitter end, with no patched-up truce. He spoke again at Juniper Green; at the Scottish Corporation in London (November 30th), where he was flanked by two Scottish colleagues, Lord Balfour of Burleigh and Lord Kinnaird, each of whom had lost his eldest son; and at a vast Glasgow call to arms (December 9th). He read to a hushed audience the news of the Falkland Islands engagement, and the whole crowd rose cheering to its feet. Other speeches followed—to railway workers at Edinburgh, where the stupidity of war was his main theme, and at Dalkeith, where he celebrated the prowess of the Royal Scots. The call for recruits was becoming urgent, and at Edinburgh (December 31st, 1915) Rosebery pleaded earnestly for Bantam battalions, having discovered a pamphlet of 1733, styled

"The Humble Remonstrance of the Five Foot Hughians," against a standard of height for the Army. He wrote to his old American friend Chauncey Depew:

August 28th, 1917.

"MY DEAR DEPEW,

"Your valued volume has reached me safely, as racy as ever, and I am reading it with keen enjoyment. I need not say that I began with the 'Art of public speaking,' from which I derived much pleasure, and should have obtained profit, were I going to make any more speeches. I am a full decade younger than you in years and a full decade older in fact.

"Well, we are in the war up to our necks together, heart in heart and hand in hand. If the war makes our two nations brothers in fact and sympathy for all time to come it will almost be worth what it has cost. By Jove, Uncle Sam is shelling out his dollars! So are we our pounds sterling. I hope rather than think that all the security is good in both cases.

"I am a shy prophet, but have arrived at a conviction that the Huns are not prepared to face a fourth winter of war. But I am appalled at the thoughts of the peace congress, when all Europe will be grabbing for all it is worth, irrespective of the exertions or the feelings of the other allies.

"It is heartbreaking to think that had Russia played up the war might well have been over by now. And we all congratulate Russia on becoming a Red anarchical Republic and a bloody chaos—perforce no doubt, but I would as soon congratulate a man on having the smallpox.

"I hope you are as young as ever and as well as I wish you; and that this letter may escape a U boat.

"Y. sincerely,

AR"

At this distance of time, when international hatreds are silenced, if not all dead, it would be an ill deed to reproduce the denunciations of German statesmen and German methods of warfare profusely scattered through his speeches, as through most others of those years. Through 1915, 1916, and 1917 this note inevitably sounded louder; and when the *Lusitania* was sunk Rosebery wrote to *The Times* in terms of concentrated bitterness. Almost at the same time, at London University, he offered sympathy to the Vice-Chancellor, whose only son had fallen.

"Well, we shall have losses and we shall meet them. We shall have gaps in the ranks, and we shall fill them up, whether in the University or out of it."

[535]

His own home was not to escape. Reginald Wyndham,[13] as popular in the Life Guards as with the Balvoir hounds, fell in November 1914. Dalmeny, who had left the Guards soon after his marriage in 1909, rejoined the Army, and in due course became Military Secretary to General Allenby. Neil Primrose, after some service in France, became Under-Secretary for Foreign Affairs, joint Parliamentary Secretary to the Treasury, and a Privy Councillor. He married in 1915 Victoria Stanley, the only daughter of the 17th Lord Derby. He was not content with the prizes of the political arena when his friends were risking their lives abroad, so he rejoined the Bucks Yeomanry, did excellent service in Egypt, and met a soldier's end at Gaza in Palestine in November 1917. He was buried there, and Memorial Services were held in England and Scotland. Rosebery wrote to the Archbishop of Canterbury:

November 29th, 1917.

"My dear Archbishop,

"I thank you warmly for your kind words, and for giving your blessing to the service on Monday.

"I cannot complain. I had enjoyed all Neil's life and could not have enjoyed much more. Indeed, I never expected to see him again. The bitterness of death was almost over when I parted with him. It is the poor little widow who is to be pitied.

"Once more accept my gratitude for this last proof of your true friendship.

"Very sincerely yours,

AR"

This stunning calamity, added to the daily and nightly strain of wartime, plunged Rosebery into an old age which nature, left to herself, would have deferred. Circumstances had enabled Neil to be the most frequent companion of his father's travel abroad, and the understanding between the two was perfect. Neil's popularity in the House of Commons was unbounded, he was much favoured by Mr. Lloyd George, and struck up a close friendship with Mr. Timothy Healy. He spoke well, with modest coolness, and something of his father's charm of expression. Rosebery, curiously enough, used to doubt whether Neil would have acquired that faculty of clear judgment in public life which only experience can give. It can simply be said that many tried men, of different parties, foretold a very brilliant future for him. One episode must be mentioned, touching both father and son. When the second Coalition Government was

[13] William Reginald (1876-1914), second son of 2nd Lord Leconfield.

formed in December 1916 the new Prime Minister naturally desired to strengthen his administration to the utmost. Rosebery was offered a high post not involving departmental labour. One argument was subtly pressed—that acceptance would help Neil in his career. This Rosebery by no means credited; he had several reasons for declining the offer, and declined it was. Had he been able to admit the plea he would certainly have accepted, at any cost to himself. Indeed, there was no willingness anywhere to admit failure of his powers. When, in June 1916, Lord Kitchener went down in the *Hampshire* to find his "vast and wandering grave," Rosebery was asked by the family to write the great soldier's Life, but thought it impossible to agree.

Through 1916 and 1917 he had carried on a series of war speeches, principally in Scotland, lauding the extent of overseas patriotism, smiling at the Ford peace-ship, urging drastic national retrenchment, and proclaiming confidence in final victory. Once his burning indignation goaded him to write to *The Times* calling for reprisals in kind directed against the authors of Zeppelin raids and the destruction of unoffending civilians. This earned him sharp reproof from two opposite quarters—from Sir Evelyn Wood, who described himself as "the oldest midshipman, Field-Marshal, and student of war," and quoted Marshal Marmont's saying, *"les représailles sont toujours inutiles"*; and from Professor Sanday of Oxford, who protested that we should be beaten at the game of driving up the standard of ruthlessness in war. Rosebery replied that reprisal is a choice among evils, but might be the least of them. After the blow had fallen he did not slacken in his public work. There were many other ruined homes of rich and poor; and in the terrible stress of 1918 he felt he must work with the rest. Just as the sky was clearing for the nation he was struck down. He was busy in Scotland, with Rosebery as his headquarters, for Dalmeny had been handed over for a war hospital. He also occupied a small house in Edinburgh as a *point d'appui*. His younger daughter was his companion at Rosebery, and after a busy day he collapsed and lost consciousness from the circulation of an embolism, which produced an almost paralytic effect. He was removed to Edinburgh, under the care of Dr. Rainy, the eminent son of an eminent father, and slowly recovered strength. But there were intervals of grave anxiety. He was sometimes delirious; and his sister and daughter recall the night of November 11th, when he was lying unconscious. The Edinburgh crowd filled Randolph Crescent, calling for a speech from their beloved orator on the great occasion.

[537]

One of his first impulses was to ask for Boswell's *Life of Johnson*. He wished to see what in his address at Lichfield he had called the most striking of all Johnson's letters. His own words of it had been these:

"When the shadow was finally on him, he was able to recognise that what was coming was divine, an angel, though formidable and obscure; and so he passed with serene composure beyond mankind."

But he himself was to wait for many weary years before the shadow came close. It would be as painful to read as to write in these pages their detailed story.

He rallied considerably in some respects, and though even at first he moved with difficulty, and eyesight and hearing became feebler, he was able in a degree to enjoy books, and far more the company of old friends. Some of these had gone. Lord Rothschild, a staunch friend and the head of Hannah Rosebery's family, died in 1915; his brother Leopold, whose son Evelyn, a gallant and gentle figure, fell when Neil Primrose did—in May 1917.

Rosebery wrote of Leopold in terms which all who knew him would re-echo.

"I know of no death of a private individual which will be followed by more general sorrow, for all his life he was encompassed by love and gratitude, the universal tribute to his great heart."

His brother-in-law, Arthur Sassoon, shrewd, hospitable, and genial, also a valued friend, had died some time before. "Peter" Wroughton too had gone. Rosebery had drawn a fine portrait of him:

"One of the best and noblest Christian gentlemen. I have known and loved him for 44 years, and never knew him fail for a moment or descend a degree below his high level. He was the most natural man I ever knew, and always revealing a nature superior to others, but quite unconscious in his simplicity of what a splendid fellow he was."

Luis de Soveral, so long Portuguese Minister in London, died in 1922 after a long and painful illness. Rosebery wrote to King Manuel, who had lost the most faithful of servants and friends:

DALMENY HOUSE, EDINBURGH, *October 7th, 1922.*
"SIRE,
"I hope Your Majesty will excuse my dictating this letter, but I can scarcely write with my own hand, and then only in pencil. I cannot refrain from intruding on you with regard to the death of our dear

[538]

BARNBOUGLE

ROSEBERY HOUSE, GOREBRIDGE

friend Soveral. No Sovereign ever had a truer servant or friend than Your Majesty had in him, and I feel most deeply for your loss, which is exceptional. To all of us he was the most charming of companions and the truest of friends. Indeed, I doubt if any death since that of King Edward will leave so large a gap in society. He was, moreover, a consummate diplomatist, perhaps the best in my circle of knowledge.

"I trust that Your Majesty will be able to bear up under this heavy affliction, and remain,

"Your Majesty's devoted servant,
ROSEBERY."

But through the years of the war, and after Rosebery's illness, a band of loyal friends, old and young, did what they could for him.

It has been a faithfully observed tradition that nobody who has loyally served the Royal Family, or has won the confidence of any of its members, is ever forgotten or neglected in days of adversity. Rosebery, strictly speaking, had only served Queen Victoria; but he was honoured by the friendship and trust of four generations of the Royal House. So now that he was disabled the King and Queen often paid gracious visits to him who could no longer be their guest. Queen Alexandra and Princess Victoria and others of the Royal Family never allowed him to think himself forgotten.

From the political world Asquith, John Morley, and Haldane, with their refreshingly diverse minds, were often with him; Lord and Lady Lansdowne, mourning a bereavement like his, not less often. Wemyss Reid, sagacious observer and loyal friend, had died too early; but Alfred Spender, equally trusted and equally informed in public affairs, never omitted to keep Rosebery abreast of the world's news. Nobody was more affectionately attentive than Sir George Murray, who had become the most conspicuous pillar of the Civil Service, and who enjoyed Rosebery's personal confidence to an extent to which no one else had attained since the death of Edward Hamilton.

During these agitated years, perhaps his greatest stand-by was Frederic Harrison. He and Rosebery had first made friends on the London County Council in 1889, and the intimacy grew until circumstances made it closer still. There is nothing like a "cure" for cementing friendships, and at Whitsuntide in 1915 the two passed three weeks together at Bath. Motoring was still permitted, and they explored the beauties of Bradford-on-Avon and Castle Combe, of Longleat and Bowood. After this, correspondence became regular. Rosebery—who did not think very much of the Government that was driven to declare war in 1914, or of its successor the first Coalition, and was suspicious of the second Coalition, though on the whole he welcomed its formation—was glad to open his mind to a deep political thinker like Frederic Harrison, detached like himself from any party allegiance. After his illness he dictated frequent short notes to Harrison, starting two months after the attack, and continuing without intermission till 1922. They also met often, and their common friendship with John Morley was another link. When they were apart, Rosebery was perpetually on the look-out for Harrison's delightful replies.

Sir George Trevelyan, a still older friend, was another steady correspondent of these years. They had long written to each other about each other's books, and other people's books. Rosebery's letter of July 13th, 1911, about Macaulay, has been quoted above, and he welcomed Trevelyan's praise of his *Early Life of Chatham* and of his little brochure on the *Love Episode of William Pitt*. After Rosebery's attack the interchange went freely on. In one dictated letter he wished that Lord Brougham, much as he disliked him, could reappear "to deliver one of his huge seven-hour speeches crushing the Treaty of Versailles in gross and in detail. There is no one capable of doing it now. He might have done it, and I could have forgiven him much." But most of the notes were on books, the last in 1927, a cutting dismissal of three recently published volumes of memoirs as "arrant rubbish."

These friends belonged to the attenuated band of Rosebery's "playfellows"—to use a phrase of which my father was fond. But the younger contingent were equally faithful. Baron Edmond de Rothschild's son James had come to live in England, and had made the choicest of happy marriages here. He was Neil's closest friend; and he and his wife stepped into the position of much-liked nephew and niece at Berkeley Square and the Durdans. Annaly, Lord and Lady Arran, and Evan Charteris were assiduous visitors; John Buchan often came and often wrote; Ronald Ferguson remained an unbreakable pillar of support and friendship. Count Albert Mensdorff, the popular and hospitable Australian Ambassador of happier days, was able to return as a frequent guest, always received with pleasure.

Hew Dalrymple, younger son of the Lord Stair whose name occurs earlier in these pages, was a most regular and welcome visitor. The two had become more and more intimate; and when Rosebery was no longer active, Dalrymple, with his close knowledge of every phase of Edinburgh life, social, artistic, and literary, and of Scottish life generally, brought the fresh air of the Lothians into the solitary house as scarcely any other could.

During these lingering years Rosebery's three remaining children did what was possible to ease his burden, as did his sisters. Lady Leconfield, in particular, was able to devote many hours to him, to his great comfort. Most of all, there was the solace of his half-dozen grandchildren. One year some of them enjoyed the moorland air of Toxside, the Rosebery shooting-lodge, when he visited them most days. The spring of 1922 brought a new sorrow to his home. His younger daughter's only son, Jack Madeley, a boy singularly perfect in character and in bearing, died after a wearing illness on the last day of March. For us, his parents, it was the tale told in the grave unadorned lines of Callimachus:

δωδεκατῆ τὸν παῖδα . . .

. . . τὴν πολλὴν ἐλπίδα . . .;

for his grandfather, it shut out much of such sunshine as was left. He wrote to Frederic Harrison:

April 9th, 1922.

"My dear friend,

"Many thanks for your kind note. The blow is indeed a heavy one; heaviest of course for my daughter and son-in-law, but scarcely less heavy for me who adored the child."

Still, a precious treasure was left to him in Ruth Primrose, Neil's only child, fated soon to be motherless as well. She spent much time with her grandfather at the Durdans—a fairy presence brightening gloomy days. And the other grandchildren helped from time to time to make the house less silent. Its owner's reserve made him unwilling to see new faces. So that some of those who were pressing to the front on the political field, and would gladly have made their bow to a Prime Minister of twenty-five years back, never had the chance of seeing him. Infirmities increased, but he was able to enjoy drives over the downs and by the copses where, in past years, he had waited on many May nights for the song of the nightingale. By the happiest fortune, two personal servants[14] of long standing remained to tend him with such understanding and devotion as earned the gratitude of the whole family.

The end came in the early morning of May 21st, 1929. He had

[14] His valet William Titley, who was in his service for forty-five years, from 1884; and Joseph Liddle, an admirable butler. Both of them were valued friends.

always prepared himself for the passage to another world. One of his last farewells to this was to ask for the music of his Eton tutor's famous "Boating Song." Its lilt was one of the last sounds to reach his ears.

He was buried in the little church at Dalmeny, a noble relic of the Middle Ages. Earlier in the day there was a service at St. Giles' Cathedral. The Duke of York and many of Rosebery's brother Knights of the Thistle were there, and Dr. Warr[15] pronounced a fine eulogy on—

"the most representative Scotsman of his times, raised to an unchallenged supremacy in this people's affection; for two generations he reigned among us as the recognised spokesman of our brave and rugged land, the alert and jealous guardian of its traditions, the indomitable champion of its interests. . . . In death he comes back to his own people."

These words went straight to the heart of everybody in the church, for they were exactly what Rosebery himself would have wished said.

Conclusion (Political Career)

Several biographies of contemporary statesmen include estimates of Rosebery's character and gifts, in their bearing on the career of the hero of each memoir. A reader from a far land would derive the impression of a man of exceptional ability and personal charm; an eloquent speaker with a theatrical tinge; but wayward in opinion, easily swayed by prejudice, somewhat deficient in moral courage, not too industrious, and enjoying too many sides of life to take any of them quite seriously.

I hope that in some material respects this study has served to correct this impression. In the first place, I have tried to show that, far from taking life easily, he erred from time to time by being too much in earnest about too many things. The statesman of the Second Empire, best remembered from his luckless profession that he entered on war with *un cœur léger*, years afterwards assured an incredulous world that the phrase really meant "an unburdened conscience." Rosebery's story tells how he never undertook any enterprise with a light heart; but how conscience perpetually troubled his

[15] The Very Rev. Charles Warr, Dean of the Order of the Thistle.

search for the path of duty. He was, indeed, something of a political Hamlet—

"thinking too precisely in the event";

but nobody save Hamlet himself called Hamlet a coward. Rosebery was not spared the imputation. Mr. Timothy Healy, for instance, once declared that Lord Rosebery was not a man to go tiger-hunting with. If he thought that timidity was the reason, he was altogether wrong. But there are people who do not go tiger-hunting, not because they dread the tiger, but because they are afraid of looking foolish if they come back without the skin. There Healy would have been nearer the mark. Rosebery himself in his last days wrote on a half-sheet of paper that from the first his main fault had been Pride. One sees what he meant; but after all, pride is one of the richer virtues, and goes happily in the yoke with humility, of which it is the near kinsman. It might have been safer to fix on self-consciousness as his bane. He found it hardly possible to get outside his own personality, to look at himself as one of the outside crowd might; or to look at contemporary movements without wondering whether he ought, or ought not, to take a part in them.

It was this that made almost pathetic his reiterated declarations that he was "out of politics" after 1896. In the years of his retirement he jotted down many passing thoughts about public men—including himself: here is one:

"The secret of my life, which seems to me sufficiently obvious, is that I always detested politics. I had been landed in them accidentally by the Midlothian Election, which was nothing but a chivalrous adventure. When I found myself in this evil-smelling bog I was always trying to extricate myself.

"That is the secret of what people used to call my lost opportunities, and so forth. If you will look over my life you will see that it is quite obvious. But nothing is so obvious as the thing which one does not wish to see."

Again, he wrote at greater length:

"I saw in some book the other day that I was described as a failure, and this led me into a train of thought which whirled me from myself. But let me at once say that according to the usual apprehension of the word the description is sufficiently accurate. What! a man who has been more or less in public life for a quarter of a century, who has been Foreign Secretary and First Minister, but who has never enjoyed an instant in power, and has now been long in seclusion without a follower and almost forgotten, what can be a greater failure?"

He goes on to examine examples of failure, according to the standards of the world. The greatest, as he remembers from a sermon of Professor Drummond's, the career of Christ. But leaving this sublime example, no parallel but a striking illustration—even such renunciations as those of Charles V and Philip V are not the cases on which he would chiefly rely. The just conclusion he thinks is this:

"We must realise a man's conception of life before condemning his life as a failure.

"Failure is a term easily and often wrongly applied to a career because people do not understand what was aimed at, and judge it by their own objects. But it is impossible to say that a life is a failure without knowing its aim. The ordinary aims are easily realised: honours, power, wealth, fame, social distinction.

"But the wise man, I think, does not consider these as the best purpose of life. What he wishes to achieve is happiness in the large sense of the word, a well-ordered life of work, friendship, family affection and, if possible, religious faith; congenial work, a healthy existence, pleasant relations of family and friendship, and reverent loyalty to God. These objects constitute the ambitions of the wise."

Those who read this book must judge how far Rosebery had in fact realised this practical and not ignoble philosophy of life. On the political side Mr. George Trevelyan draws a striking parallel between him and the Duke of Shrewsbury, so conspicuous at the junction of the seventeenth and eighteenth centuries. Our vivid historian could have added that the six years that Shrewsbury spent at Rome might well have been copied by Rosebery with six years at Naples, but for his thought for his children.[16]

The curious might also hit on points of similarity with a later statesman, Charles Earl Grey, the hero of the Reform Bill, as por-

[16] "The character and career of Charles Talbot, Duke of Shrewsbury, bear some resemblance to those of Lord Rosebery two centuries later. A cultured, super-sensitive nobleman, self-indulgent but no libertine, a wit in whose brilliant but weighty conversation everyone delighted, he was known to all ranks and both sexes as 'The King of Hearts,' 'The only man the Whigs and Tories both spoke well of.' Called upon to lead a party, he saw too clearly the faults of both parties."—*Blenheim* (1930), p. 201."

trayed by Professor Carless Davis. But Grey would never have tackled the County Council as Rosebery did.[17]

In 1895 Mr. Gladstone summed up Rosebery's character:

"I can say three things of him:
"1. He is one of the very ablest men I have known.
"2. He is of the highest honour and probity.
"3. I do not know whether he really has common sense."

The veteran leader, it will be noted, did not fall into the common error of doubting Rosebery's serious purpose. Nor did he mistrust Rosebery for being one of the epigrammatic, who, as John Morley observes in his *Rousseau*, "have by no means a monopoly of shallow thinking." But doubtless many people besides Queen Victoria were made uneasy by his flashes of humour and wit. None would have applied to him the whole of Pope's flagellation of Wharton; but not a few may have quoted against him:

> "Though wondering senates hung on all he spoke,
> The club must hail him master of the joke.
> Shall parts so various aim at nothing new?
> He'd shine a Tully and a Wilmot too."

This is ill-natured, but I have heard a kinder lover of Pope, asked if he had seen Rosebery, cite with a laugh the still more famous couplet about Walpole:

> "Seen him I have, but in his happier hour
> Of social pleasure, ill-exchanged for power"—

the power which Rosebery truly said he never possessed, even as Prime Minister.

Every treatise on oratory tells how evanescent is the orator's art.

[17] "He loved seclusion for its own sake. 'How I long,' he wrote as a young man, 'to return to Tacitus and our own comfortable fire.'

"Charles was in fact by temperament unfitted for the daily round. He hated the business of pelting Ministers with small charges and innuendoes wrapped up in small questions. He hated still more the sepulchral atmosphere of the House of Lords. When he was in the Commons he loved to sally forth from Howick, like another Chatham, for an operation of war; to defend the liberties of British subjects, or the rights of oppressed peoples; to expatiate on the first principles of the constitution or of international law. On such a subject he was graceful, incisive, even eloquent, his gestures and his delivery were consummate . . . the opinion of his Whig admirers was tersely summarised by Mr. Creevey, 'There is nothing approaching this damned fellow in the Kingdom when he mounts his best horse. . . .'

"Burdett, though a dull man, put his finger on a deep-seated defect: 'Lord Grey is always thinking of himself and of his failures in life.' . . ."—*The Age of Grey and Peel,* pp. 201-3. (Clarendon Press, 1929.)

Nobody reads old speeches; they bloomed for a day, and in the evening they were cut down, dried up, and withered. Yet the names of the great orators stand out as sharply as any on the roll of fame. Rosebery's place on that roll is assured. His successor as President of the Scottish History Society, Mr. John Buchan, acutely pointed out that Rosebery, unlike some orators who were also writers, showed rare skill in discriminating between the demands of the ear and the eye—the spoken and the written word. Enough has been said of Rosebery's polished prose; but his speeches require a sentence or two of notice. His oratory was sometimes considered too theatrical. Perhaps the utterances that have moved the world most deeply have been of another type. Bright denouncing the Crimean war, Lincoln at Gettysburg, in no way bring the stage to mind. But much of the noblest oratory has been histrionic. Cicero uses the phrase "a great orator, and so to speak a great tragedian."[18] The majestic French preachers of the seventeenth century, Chatham, Sheridan, Grattan, even Burke on occasion seemed to be pacing the boards rather than standing firm on the rostra. In one of those Dialogues of the Dead which for eighteen hundred years have attracted imaginative writers, Fénelon, himself a master, conceives a conversation between Demosthenes and Cicero.[19] The Greek explains to his Roman follower the superiority claimed by the unconscious orator, whose personality is swallowed up by concern for his subject. Cicero, he says, is never the perfect orator when he is only Cicero, gifted with wit, and art, and turn of phrase, but not the austere and apparently artless Demosthenes.

On this showing Rosebery was more of a Cicero than a Demosthenes, and even so not to be altogether despised as an orator. In truth, nobody who ever heard one of Rosebery's great platform speeches can forget the experience. The earnestness, the humour, the inflexions of voice, most of all, perhaps, the answering thrill running through the audience like an electric current, must remain a clear memory even to those who have listened to all the best speakers on platform or in pulpit of the last fifty years. In the House of Lords, it seemed to me, he never reached the same level. The

[18] *Brutus,* 205.
[19] "Tu occupais l'assemblée de toi-même; et moi je ne l'occupais, je ne l'occupais jamais, que de l'affaire dont je parlais . . . tu a été un orateur parfait quand tu a été, comme moi, simple, grave, austère, sans art apparent, en un mot quand tu a été Démosthène; mais lorsqu'on a senti en tes discours l'esprit, le tour, et l'art, alors tu n'as pas plus été que Cicéron, t'éloignant de la perfection autant que tu t'éloignais de mon caractère." (*30ième Dialogue des Morts.*)

gifts and graces were all there; but the touch of theatricality was more obvious to that chill audience, and the atmosphere was visibly depressing to the speaker. On minor occasions, when a tart reply was needed, or when a matter of policy had to be discussed or explained, Rosebery showed, in the House as elsewhere, the easy mastery that everybody expected from him.

Few outside his home circle knew how religiously-minded Rosebery was. Without ever attaching himself to any one school of thought in the Church, or to one category of observances, he was disappointed when circumstances kept him away from Sunday service. He was a regular communicant of the Church of England; but in Scotland he most often attended Kirk, and in Roman Catholic countries often went to Mass. It was a custom with him, when they were unable to go to church, to read prayers and a sermon to his children from their quite early years, the sermon being eclectically picked from Chalmers, or Newman, or from some other favourite. Rosebery enjoyed many friendships with churchmen—most of all with wise old William Rogers from early days; in later days most with Randall Davidson, whose steady and unquestioned progress to the highest place he took as a matter of course. There was a near local connection: Davidson's Mains, the cradle of the Archbishop's family, is close to Dalmeny. His balanced judgment and tolerant sympathy which never sank to compromise between right and wrong, represented for Rosebery the sound ecclesiastical temper in a world where the Christian ideal is in peril of being obscured by the dust of warring faiths. During his crippled years no friendship, and no ministrations, made him happier than did those of the Archbishop of Canterbury.

The Durdans, Epsom, *March 21st,* 1922.
"My dear Lord Archbishop,

"Let me thank you once more for your visit. You come to my solitude like a being from another world. Let me say once for all that I love you as much as I honour you, and therefore your visits either in Scotland or here are doubly welcome.

"Yours very sincerely,

AR"

There has been no attempt to collect for this book the reminiscences or the formal appreciations of the few survivors from Rosebery's active days. It would have been agreeable to revive memories of some of those *symposia* in which he delighted. His fidelity to

[547]

Loder's Club of Christ Church days has been described. Political affinities gave birth to the "Articles," inspired originally by Arthur Acland as a dining-club of carefully chosen Liberals. The members entertained the club in turn, Rosebery himself, Herbert Gardner,[20] and Carrington being frequent hosts, Haldane and Asquith active members. To the champagne that sparkled in the glasses was added the conversational champagne of Frank Lockwood and Birrell, for whose contributions to the gaiety of evenings Rosebery was duly grateful. He was also the founder of a cheerful Scottish institution, the Loco Club, which held its amusing gatherings at the New Club, Edinburgh.

His serious reading has been touched on in the course of the narrative; but he had strong likes and dislikes on the lighter side. Mr. Edward Cooper's racing stories seemed to him to be the best of their kind, but he did not care much for sensational fiction. Good comedy always appealed to him. He read *Happy Thoughts* aloud to his children, and the *Diary of a Nobody* was his favourite bedside companion.

His life, however, has to tell its own story. Still, in another vein, I am allowed to quote from some sheets of notes left by Mrs. Drew, who, as Mary Gladstone, had more chances than most of seeing him without his mask of reticence and reserve. Their friendly relations, diversified by some sparring, lasted after the death of Mrs. Drew's parents and her own widowhood. They often met, and the charities in which Mrs. Drew was interested profited by their meetings. In her note she says:

"Very few people have had the nous, or had the privilege of seeing the heart of gold that is in him. It is a curiously cold, impassive face, but surely his smile is the most irradiating that has ever been seen. He is absolutely transformed by it. It reminded me of the scene from the Righi—the cold snow-clad mountains lying like death upon the horizon, and suddenly in one flush they become alive, glorious, radiant, the most wonderful transformation scene in the world. . . . He has a remarkable capacity for entering into the feelings of others, especially those who are poor or unhappy, and he has an extraordinary aptitude for getting his neighbours out of a tight place. At a tenants' dinner an old farmer, not wishing his host to be shown up, turned to Lord Rosebery and whispered to him, 'There is something gone wrong with the pudding, my Lord, it has got frozen by mistake.' Lord Rosebery

[20] (1846-1921.) M.P. 1885-95. President of Board of Agriculture 1892-5. *Cr.* Lord Burghdere 1895.

beckoned to a footman, and after a colloquy with him, he turned to his guest: 'Oh, I find it is all right; it is a new kind of pudding, and it is frozen on purpose.' "

Mrs. Drew goes on to compare the understanding and regard which united the household at Dalmeny, owner and servants, with the attitude of those who looked on their household simply as part of the machinery of life. This showed her quick perception, for this human interest in his surroundings was a marked feature in Rosebery's character. It was notable in friendships which he established in the racing world.[21] Matthew Dawson was an exceptional character, a man who would have made his mark anywhere, and a most interesting companion. But Rosebery was prodigal with help and advice to weaker figures in that exciting arena. Two jockeys who rode for him, at a long interval of time, Harry Constable and Danny Maher, were his particular care. Both were exceptional horsemen; both were happily married; both broke down physically; and one of them dissipated health and fortune by wild extravagance. Rosebery lavished time and trouble on both invalids and their families, in a way that more ostentatious philanthropists might envy.

When all is said and done, Rosebery remains something of an enigma to those who knew him best. Sometimes a character may be illustrated on the negative side: what a man dislikes or ignores may be as focal as the list of his tastes and pursuits. There were some notable gaps in Rosebery's well-furnished intellect. Like many men of letters, perhaps like most, he was without any mathematical faculty; but in addition he never at any age made a study of philosophy, or of any branch of science. It is strangest, perhaps, that, with his devotion to an open-air life, zoology, botany, and geology remained sealed books to him. The love of nature which was so strong in him was that of an artist or a bookman, rather than that of a Gilbert White or a Hugh Miller. But few men spent more hours in the open air, when he was not enslaved by office. His long walks have been mentioned, but he loved dining out of doors, even when the days were growing shorter, and when the chillier guests begged for rugs over their knees. His after-dinner drives remain in the memory of those who shared them; he never talked better than then, or more openly. It is a hopeless task to fix in cold print any impression of his personal charm. "You have not been under the

[21] Mr. John Corlett was a frequent correspondent, and on one occasion he and his merry Corpus band of the *Sporting Times* lunched together at the Durdans.

wand of the magician," said Pitt to somebody who had not heard his great rival speak; and so it must be for those who did not know Rosebery. Though the Fairy Queens beside his cradle, unlike those in Macaulay's poem of which he was so fond, lavished many various gifts upon him, it would be untrue to call it a very happy life. But he warmed both hands before its fire, and he did not fear death. *Ave atque vale.*

CHAPTER XXI

The Turf. Later Years

SOME of the Mentmore yearlings were once more trained in 1890. The colts were sold, amongst them *Bonavista* by *Bend Or—Vista*, who had already produced two fillies of no racing merit. *Bonavista* won the Two Thousand and other races for Sir Charles Rose before being exported, leaving behind him *Cyllene*, the most successful transmitter of the *Stockwell* line. The Duke of Westminster, than whom there was no sounder judge of bloodstock, had always tried to buy *Vista*, her owner told me. He realised the value of a *Doncaster—Macaroni* cross. Two two-year-old fillies won in 1890, *Corstorphine*, a daughter of *Foxhall*, whom Rosebery bought as a stallion, and *Keroual* by *Foxhall—Kermesse*.

Next year *Corstorphine* ran second for the Oaks.

Eighteen ninety-two was a lean year. *Accumulator,* by *Dutch Skater—Illuminata*, ran five times without winning. *Amaze* won one race. Meanwhile the discarded *Bonavista* carried off the Two Thousand.

But in the following year the sun shone. The two-year-old *Ladas*, by *Hampton—Illuminata*, ran four times, winning the Woodcote, Coventry, and Champagne Stakes and the Middle Park Plate. Gamblers shook their heads at the audacious naming of this beautiful brown colt, who recalled to old race-goers the perfect shape of his grandsire *Rosicrucian*. Years afterwards Rosebery wrote to Mr. Somerville Tattersall, with whom he carried on an hereditary friendship:

"I agree with you that the bravest thing ever done was to name the horse *Ladas*, and I thought so at the time. . . ."

The filly *Tressure*, by *Bend Or—Bonny Jean*, ran third for the One Thousand.

Eighteen ninety-four blazed more brilliantly still. *Ladas* ran away with the Two Thousand, the Newmarket Stakes, and the Derby. Nobody had seen a Prime Minister leading in a winner at Epsom.

[551]

Later in the year a cloud came over the sun. The colt was third in the Princess of Wales Stakes, second in the Eclipse Stakes and in the St. Leger. He was unlucky, but had trained off somewhat. *Sir Visto,* two-year-old by *Barcaldine—Vista,* made some amends in October by winning the Imperial Produce Stakes at Kempton. *Sir Visto,* a far less attractive colt than *Ladas,* after being twice beaten at Newmarket, duly won the Derby of 1895, and surpassed his stable companion by carrying off the St. Leger as well. His half-brother by *Donovan, Velasquez,* made his debut in the following season and showed marvellous promise, winning four of the principal two-year-old races, at Ascot, Newmarket, Goodwood, and Doncaster. Rosebery believed him to be the best colt he ever bred or owned. He was somewhat amiss in the autumn, and as a three-year-old in 1897, and as a four-year-old, did not show the same astonishing form, running second to formidable rivals in *Galtee More, Persimmon, Love Wisely,* and *Cyllene,* all first-class animals. However, a winner of the Princess of Wales Stakes, the Eclipse Stakes, of the Champion Stakes twice, and a total of over £26,000 in stakes, cannot be called a failure, though he was certainly a disappointment.

Illuminata had bred very regularly, producing in 1892 *Gas,* who did not win though very speedy, and in 1894 *Chelandry* by *Goldfinch,* who added to the gains of 1896 by carrying off four races, including the National Breeders' Produce Stakes at Sandown and the Imperial Produce Stakes at Kempton. In 1897 she compensated for the Classic failures of *Velasquez* by taking the One Thousand. Another *Illuminata* filly, *Corposant,* ran third for the Oaks of 1899.

There was a momentary lull in Rosebery's racing. *Gas* went early to the stud and her second foal was *Valve* (1901). She was leased for her racing career, and won several times as a two-year-old. She became a valuable addition to the Mentmore paddocks. The next year *Cicero,* by *Cyllene,* was foaled. He was a rather small yearling, chestnut, with the exquisite quality of his sire, recalling their Arab ancestry. He won the Coventry Stakes and the National Breeders' Produce Stakes in 1904. In that year a formidable French contingent was in evidence, offspring of *Flying Fox,* who had been bought by Monsieur Edmond Blanc. *Jardy* was a colt of very high class, and won the Middle Park Plate; but he was amiss the next year, and *Cicero,* who had given his trainer some anxiety, beat him for the Derby of 1905. *Cicero* was defeated for the Eclipse Stakes by another of Monsieur Blanc's colts, *Val d'Or.* Meanwhile *Chelan-*

Lord Rosebery and his Sons, Ascot, 1910

dry was taking the place of her dam and of *Vista* as a breeder of winners. Between 1900 and 1907 she produced six, including *Chelys*, by *Sir Visto*; *Traquair*, by *Ayrshire*, who carried on the National Breeders' Produce Stakes tradition in 1906; *Popinjay*, by *St. Frusquin*; and in 1907 *Neil Gow*, by *Marco*. This last also won the great two-year-old race at Sandown, beat *Lemberg* by a short head in the Two Thousand, was fourth in the Derby of 1910, and ran a dead heat with *Lemberg* in the Eclipse Stakes. He broke down before the St. Leger.

The older generation of present race-goers will recall the later successes of the Mentmore stud, Percy Peck and George Blackwell sharing the trainers' duties. *Prue* once more won for him the National Breeders' Produce Stakes in 1912, and the Coronation Stakes the next year. *Vaucluse,* a daughter of *Valve*, took the One Thousand in 1915. *Prue* is from *Prune*, by *Persimmon—Tressure*, and so goes back to *Bonnie Jean*. In 1924 *Plack*[1] seemed likely to satisfy Rosebery's ambition of winning the Gold Cup at Ascot, one of the few great races that evaded him.

One singular fact remains to be noted. None of the four remarkable colts that Rosebery owned, *Ladas, Sir Visto, Velasquez,* and *Cicero*, achieved much success as a sire of winners. The last did most, but he was never in the first rank of stallions. The highly descended brood mares, on the other hand, have gone producing generations of good horses.

[1] By Hurry On—Groat, won the One Thousand, and many other races.

APPENDIX I

Two Visits to Prince Bismarck

September 27th, 1890.—"H. Bismarck and I, after having passed two nights at Ostend and one at Berlin, arrived at Hammermükle, the station for Varzin at 5.30 to-day (Saturday). The old Prince was at the station on horseback waiting for us, and greeted us warmly, thanking me for coming into so remote a province to see him. He then sent his horses away and got into a victoria with me.

"He talked about his trees as we drove along. I incidentally alluded to H. B.'s settling at Schönhausen. The Prince said he was glad of it, but feared the solitude would be too much for him. I replied that I thought he liked solitude, that this year he had spent a solitary two months at Konigstein and Ostend. 'Ah, he liked solitude this year because he is very much out of temper. He took my removal much more to heart than I did. I was glad that an opportunity was offered me of getting out before I died. I feared I was condemned to servitude for life.' 'So did all the world,' said I.

"We drove through a great farm. All the farms here seem enormous owing to the severity of the winter which requires that everything shall be housed, and then we drove up to a three-sided quadrangle consisting of a plain country-house centre with two long low wings of a farmhouse character. There is besides a new wing, very comfortable but of a villa character externally and quite uncongenial to the rest of the house. This the Prince wished to continue but fortunately found it too expensive. . . .

"The Prince at once took me to my rooms, a vast bedroom and a vast sitting-room, the latter filled with presentation books, some English, notably some crazy books by Mrs. Bernal Osborne and a volume of the immortal speeches of Sir H. Parkes. . . .

"After dinner, on returning to the drawing-room, where he has his four pipes on a sofa, he showed me a cuckoo clock which he had procured for his room at Berlin, hoping that the loudness with which it proclaimed the hour would be a hint to ambassadors not to prolong their stay; but unfortunately they only saw in it a topic for further conversation. . . ."

[554]

September 28th, 1890.—"H.B. came to fetch me at 10.30 to walk with his father, whom he had left discussing a pint of hock. We three took a pleasant walk through the beeches. . . . He spoke of the young Emperor, said that he was full of vanity, that he lives only for applause, that he does not work, he does not even read what he ought. He is very extravagant, is making debts, and his butcher's bills are not paid.

"'You are overthrown, Prince,' I said, 'with the power you created —hoist with your own petard as Shakespeare says.'

"'Quite true. In 1862 my old Emperor met me with his abdication ready written in his hand. But he was willing to fight and he fought.' . . .

"He spoke much of his own fall. The principal passion among Germans, he said, was envy. In England happily patriotism comes before party, but not in Germany. . . .

"After luncheon we drove for 3 or 4 hours in a victoria across the country and through the woods in break-neck fashion.

"'The intrigues began by ministers wanting my place and even more by their wives wanting my precedence; and then the Grand Duke of Baden took an active part, for he had been offended by my refusing him some audience. The young Emperor went on so that I at last asked outright, "Does Your Majesty wish to get rid of me?" No answer. "In that case it is easily done. I can resign my Prime Ministership of Prussia and retain the Chancellorship." The Emperor eagerly embraced this proposal, but said, "You will support the army proposals." I said, "Yes, but if I support the whole proposal it must be as Prime Minister." And so it was settled that the resignation of the Prime Ministership should take place in June. But then came the Socialist question. I said that if I remained I must fight. He agreed entirely for three weeks. Then supervened the Grand Duke of Baden and turned him round like paper. I drafted the rescript according to the Emperor's orders, but said to him, "I strongly advise Your Majesty to throw this into the fire." However, he seized it and signed it in a great hurry. Then I kept it back for some days, still hoping that he might change his mind; but at dinner at my house he asked for it, and desired it to be promulgated. Had he said to me, "I wish to govern alone" nothing would have been easier; but he tried to get rid of me by ill-treatment. He did business in a way which hurt my dignity, saying his nerves would stand it better than mine. When I saw that the Emperor wished to get rid of me I thought deeply as to whether I should be justified in making such a "hole" as I should cause after being for 28 years in affairs.

"'The old Emperor was good-tempered. The Emperor Frederick was polite; this young man is neither good-tempered nor polite. I always got on very well with Empress Frederick: it is a mistake to think otherwise; though I opposed her in the Battenberg affair. When Miss

Dörnberg returned after a year in Japan the Empress said to her, "You have heard of the terrible upset in our lives," meaning my dismissal.

"'I do not know on what terms I am with the young Emperor. Since my dismissal the only communication I have received from him is a copy of a letter he wrote to Schweringer to take care of my health. As he had done this for some years without the imperial orders, Schweringer was inclined not to answer it; but I urged him to do so, and he sent a somewhat ironical reply.'

"'P. Bismarck thinks that Trochu was a traitor to the Empress. But that if the Empress had shown more courage and shown herself to the army and in Paris he thinks she might have maintained herself. He thinks that the Empire might have continued had it not gone to war in 1870; though the Emperor was of a contrary opinion. I had a curious interview of two hours with the Emperor Napoleon in 1867. He wished to ask me my opinion as to the expediency of giving France liberal institutions. I said that as long as he kept the gardes du corps— as long as he had 50,000 picked men in Paris on whom he could rely, he could afford himself the luxury of liberal institutions: I even advised some concessions. But he distrusted the disinterestedness of my advice; whereas I was quite loyal in the matter.

"'It was subject of consideration with me whether we should not restore the Empire and negotiate with it, giving it 100,000 picked men from the 3 or 400,000 prisoners we had in Germany. It would have suited us, for it would have been a very weak government, restored by the foreigner and minus two provinces. I told Thiers that we might do this. "You would not commit such a crime," cried the little man. I replied that we should act just as suited our interests.'

"He talks a great deal of his trees and estate as we drive along. He has some 20,000 acres half wood, half arable. He has no tenants—all is in his own hand—with a very capable manager. He has also built three large mills for making paper out of wood. To-day we drove to a harvest home on one of his farms, but being rainy we did not get out. A woman presented flowers on a plate, reciting some German verses, and the Prince thanked her; then the dancers came out of the barn headed by a band of music and gave hearty cheers for the Prince and his family. 'The only good I have done in my life of which I do not regret is my wells. I have six wells for villages here at a cost of £100 apiece.'

"'Are not people in Germany as afraid of buying estates as they are in England?'

"'Yes, and if I had foreseen ten years ago what would happen I would not have bought either: I would rather have sold.'

"'I suppose every year that rolls over the Balkan peninsula strengthens these little states against Russia?'

" 'Yes, and time is on the side of Austria.'

" 'In one sense,' I replied, 'but not in another, if in that time Austria goes to pieces.'

" 'Yes, it is extraordinary—the Austrian Empire has lasted four centuries, with nothing to hold it together but the memory of four centuries of misgovernment.' "

September 29th, 1890.—"Lotar Bucher writes shorthand, and sits in the morning pencil and paper in hand looking in mute appeal to the Prince to dictate something; but he won't. The Prince's memory is by no means so good as it was, H. B. tells me: H. B.'s own is excellent.

"Talking of *cabinets noirs* at luncheon Prince B. mentioned that the Emperor Alexander told him in Russia that the German princes had been so hostile to Russia during the Crimean war. 'They wrote to friends in Russia "horrible things *by the post*—so of course one saw them." '

"While on our long drive in the afternoon we talked much about his memoirs, which he *will* not write. 'I do not care to dictate my memoirs because I am too lazy. The only consolation of my present position is that I have nothing to do. Formerly, when I woke I had to think of all I had to do. Now I have only to wind up my watch or take a walk. Moreover if I write memoirs I must either tell lies or reveal the character of my old master in all its nakedness. For he was always wrong. He was always being worked upon by his wife the Empress Augusta, the granddaughter of the Emperor Paul, a wild character constantly conspiring. At last I knew so many of her conspiracies that that kept her quiet. For instance in 1848 she had a conspiracy to set her husband on one side (on his accession to the throne I suppose) and make herself regent. He sometimes said to me, "I know I am henpecked."

" 'He was always wrong. In 1868 he wanted to go to Frankfort and humiliate us before Austria. In 1864 he wanted more Danish territory, when I thought we had already too much, and would not speak to me for three days when I refused to agree with him. Then again, he was in favour of Augustenburg's claims, and wanted another Grand Duke to vote against us at Frankfort. In 1866 he did not want to go to war with Austria, but I told him it was absolutely necessary: it was like two bulls in a herd of cows, they must fight in order to decide who is to be possessor. Then when he did fight he wanted to march on. He wished to advance into Hungary with no provisions or water, with cholera and other diseases among our troops with 200,000 of the former Confederation army ready to fall on us—105,000 Bavarians alone—and the French Emperor with 60 or 100,000. It would have been madness. I said to him that it might be advisable if he wished to reconstitute the

[557]

Eastern Empire at Constantinople, but not otherwise! He appealed to the Crown Prince who sided with me. So he wrote on the foot of my report, "Deserted by my minister in the face of the enemy and unable under the circumstances to obtain another I appeal to my son to help me, as he also turns against me, I must submit." This is among my family papers.

" 'Again in 1870 he resisted violently becoming Emperor. That was dynastic pride. He wanted all Germany to bow before the King of Prussia. He said he would not accept the position of "honorary major." I explained that the German princes would not allow the necessary power to one who was not Emperor—they would only consider him their equal. There the Crown Prince did not help me. He sate agitated and silent, not daring to look his father in the face. When at last he gave way he would be Emperor of Germany and nothing else: a title to which the Princes would not submit. At last, on the day of the proclamation of the Empire he was so angry with me that he walked off the dais and greeted Moltke and the others, treating me as if I did not exist, as if I was air.

" 'Nor did the Crown Prince help me when in 1866 the King wanted to put down the Parliament and proclaim a new constitution. In vain I pointed out that after all it was not a difficult parliament, that I had carried on government with a party of 11 out of 500 members, that it would never do to show ourselves before Germany as less liberal than the other States, &c. The Crown Prince sate during the long discussion in the railway carriage from Prague, hot and red, but saying nothing.

" 'The reasons I give for not writing memoirs may be mere excuses for my laziness; but for one thing, I could not write my views of the last three years without writing a book which would not be allowed to be published in Prussia, for it would be high treason.'

"Prince B. told me a little later the story of how he persuaded the King to ride off the field of Sadowa. 'The King went slowly and reluctantly' (after the well-known conversation), 'so I took my foot out of the stirrup and gave the King's horse a good kick with my toe in the flank—and off he went at a gallop. The King looked round and asked, "What is that?" I replied that his horse had probably been frightened by the firing. I don't know if he believed me or not, but he said nothing.' (This incident seems to me a good parable of their relations.)

" 'The relation between King and vassal implies mutual confidence. That existed between me and the old King, and I had a warm affection for him. But not between this young King and me.' I reminded him that in 1887 Prince Wilhelm had seemed his pupil, his disciple. 'Yes, too much so:

> Souvent Prince varie
> Follet (sic) qui s'y fie.

In our last week he hurt my dignity.'

[558]

"I told him what I knew he was aware of—the Kaiser's supposed fear of his inkstand. 'Yes, that was one of the lies told. I said nothing but what was respectful—my eyes may have spoken, but I cannot control them so well. But I am accustomed to be treated like a gentleman —to live in better company. The young Emperor said, "I hear Bleich-röder has brought Windhorst here—so it seems you are living with Jews and Jesuits." I said that it was necessary for my business—that was a matter for myself. "No," he said, "you should not have seen them without informing (or consulting) me." I replied that I could not allow anyone to interfere with my household arrangements or as to the people I chose to receive at my house.

" 'At our last interview the Emperor kissed me on both cheeks, and said that he was only parting with me out of regard for my health. "But," I said, "I have not enjoyed such good health for years past as now—apart from the worry of the last few weeks."

" 'Instead of ministers advising the Sovereign, you now have a Sovereign advising the ministers. Caprivi is determined to have no will of his own. Marschall thinks he is clever, which he is not. The Emperor has most experience of foreign affairs of the three—which does not prevent his being very foolish.'

"At this juncture Prince B. summoned a woman whom he saw, one of his tenants, to ask her about the potato harvest. She told a long story complaining of the depredations of the wild boars among her potatoes. His demeanour with the peasantry is very genial.

" 'The Emperor's jealousy is most extraordinary. He cannot bear this subscription for a monument to me. In order to hinder it as much as he could he took the presidency: then he tried to prevent officers in the army subscribing and failed; then he declared that anything over 500,000 marks should not go to the monument—which he had no earthly right to do—and now it is between 7 and 800,000 marks and not yet closed. He reminds me of a landlord who cannot bear rich peasants. He cannot bear anyone to be distinguished but himself. The old King understood our positions. He was never jealous, he knew there could be no jealousy between us. He knew I was his servant and was glad I was a strong one.

" 'I see the Emperor is reported to have said to Count Moltke the other day that he was sorry he could not pay a similar visit at Friedrichs-rühe. But how is he so sure that he would be welcome at Friedrichsrühe? I do not wish to see him there, because I cannot lie or dissemble; I cannot pretend to approve his conduct, so his visit would only be an embarrassment to me.'

"He talks much in these drives of his trees, which are a passion with him. He told me that jays are constantly employed burying acorns, as dogs bury bones, with the object of retrieving and eating them (in winter). The consequence is that they are invaluable planters of oaks.

[559]

" 'After leaving office this year I was at a loss for something to do, so I took to reading the classics again, Shakespeare and Schiller, which I had not read for years, with the greatest enjoyment.

" 'William I did not so much oppose universal suffrage. I did not foresee in establishing it that the particularism of the different Sovereigns would be so little powerful. Universal suffrage loses half its danger, if it is exercised openly and not by ballot.' . . .

"After luncheon to-day he said as he rose, 'How I should like to get drunk to-day. Not for years have I felt that wish so strongly as during the last few days.' (Does my society depress him?)—all this in high good humour. I said, 'They tell of many of your drinking exploits—there was one of your drinking off a bottle of champagne at a draught and frightening the King.'

" 'Ah, that was with King Frederick Wilhelm IV at Lessling (?). There was a great stag's horn that held a bottle—one had to drink between two tines of the antlers—and if one tipped it too much the wine came with a rush all over one. I said, "We will see what diplomacy can do," and drank it off without spilling a drop. I then said to the servant who came to take it, "Fill that again." "No, no," said the King in alarm, "Bismarck, that is enough." There was skill as well as power in my drinking. Poor Frederick Wilhelm IV, so often represented with a bottle of Clicquot, was never drunk in his life.'

"He dilated at length on the dynasties holding Germany together, even the bad ones. 'The German always likes to draw closer the connection of their own community. They would like their own government in every village. After all that has been done in Hanover, and after 24 years half the nation remains devoted to the old dynasty.'

"In the victoria he said: 'James Rothschild died worth 1,700 millions of francs. The old King would not allow us to shoot anything at Ferrières. "There must be nothing taken," he said, "in a house I inhabit." But I got hold of the butler, who was giving us wretched wine, and asked if he had ever been put on a pallet and flogged with a stirrup leather? After that we got good wine. We only shot one day when the King was away, and they gave us bad cartridges.'

"Passing a prosperous village of peasant freeholders he talked about the Stein legislation. 'It had not helped to unite the nation for the war of independence. On the contrary both parties were dissatisfied with it. So late as 1840, when I was a sort of magistrate, a peasant before me, referring to the year of Stein's legislation, said, "That was the year in which half our property was given to the landlords!" It was very unfair, but on the whole I approve of it, as it weakened many small freeholders.'

"Talking as usual about trees I asked him if he cut down trees himself 'like Mr. Gladstone'? He replied with a laugh, 'No—what I envy Mr. Gladstone for is his eloquence—he can speak for ever about nothing. I can only speak when I have something to say, and, as for eloquence, I am only eloquent when I am attacked—when I am in a passion.

" 'Busch used to sit at table with a notebook in his lap and take notes. But he was a long way off me at table and made many mistakes.' . . ."

October 1st, 1890.—"At luncheon Prince B. talked with great pleasure of Walter Scott's novels, and of Dugald Dalgetty, Caleb Balderstone, Meg Merrilies, &c. As a young man, when he had lived much alone, one of the few English books he had was the *Bride of Lammermoor*, 'which I read often and even studied.'

"I have forgotten all my Russian. I learned it when I was 44; and one remembers what one learns according to the time at which one learns it, and all that one learns in childhood. I used to talk for hours to the Russian peasants who drove me about their condition. . . .

"The Prince of Hohenzollern's estate had been offered to him for a million of thalers, but the cost was too great, as it was, he said about the sums he had spent on the agricultural estate near Friedrichsrüh. The present owner is the candidate for the Spanish throne of 1870. I quoted Plon Plon's wise remark on that candidature: that it was not worth while to go to war to get rid of the Prince of Hohenzollern, as the Spaniards would soon do it of their own accord. Prince B. agreed. He said: 'I remember the evening of Sedan when I was riding back with some princes and they were talking about the war. I said that I thought the Prince would have made a very good neighbour for France, that he was closely related to the Bonapartes, and I always took it for granted that he would go to Paris on his way to Spain and come to an understanding with the Emperor. A voice behind exclaimed, "Not a bit of it!" I turned round and saw the Prince himself!'

"I said, 'The sun shines on the Socialists to-day,' as it is the day on which the anti-Socialist law expires. 'Yes, it is a serious day, one cannot meet them with smiles.' I spoke of the internal differences which divided them, but he said that in Germany they had hitherto kept well together.

" 'But you have done a little socialism.' 'No, I do not acknowledge that—what I did I did for the relief of the poor, not to secure their domination.'

"The State Insurance scheme, he told me, was not yet in operation and many wish to drop it.

"His favourite charger he had for 19 years. He rode her once for 18 hours without food or water. On her return she pricked her ears on getting into the stable, buried her nose in the manger and fed heartily. I told him of Copenhagen giving a kick after Waterloo day.

[561]

"His agent has told him that the peasantry around are full of vague hopes excited by the Emperor; while many wish to emigrate, which Prince B. has always considered a sign of prosperity in Germany.

"Prince B. well satisfied with his interview with the Queen. She pressed him strongly to promise her that there should be no regency during the life of the Emperor Frederick—a pledge he had no difficulty in giving. She speaks German absolutely like a native—much better than her daughter, Empress Frederick."

On October 16th, 1897, Rosebery started for Schönhausen, the old home of the Bismarck family, for the christening of Herbert Bismarck's eldest son,[1] of whom he was one of the godfathers. It was an interesting old place, with many family traditions. On the day after the friendly ceremony Herbert Bismarck and he set out for Friedrichsrüh, on a visit to the old Prince. He met Rosebery at the door, and expressed great pleasure at seeing him again.

"The Prince ate and drank much less than he did when I saw him last—perhaps two glasses of wine, and after dinner nothing but a glass of water instead of the old tankard of beer. He also only smoked one pipe after dinner, though two were put out for him. I never saw him look better, though he is a little thinner, and is a trifle deaf. But he declines to take exercise, which annoys Schweringer, who says that if he would take ordinary precautions he might live to an unlimited age, as all his organs are perfectly sound. He told us an anecdote of when he went with his King, in 1873 he thought, to Petersburg, and the King asked him to find out what present he could make to Gortchakoff, as he had already given him his portrait and his highest order in diamonds. Should he give a snuff box? Bismarck repudiated the suggestion, but when he went to sound Gortchakoff, the old fellow promptly replied, 'A good solid gold box with diamonds,'—an answer which Prince Bismarck said he was ashamed to take to his own master. But it would be impossible to repeat or remember all his conversation, which was as witty and ready as ever. He talked from seven till past eleven thus, his present hour for retiring to bed—a circumstance which is very rare with him, for he usually utters but few words, and buried himself in his newspaper. At only rare moments in the evening did his brow cloud for a moment, and that was when he was brought back to the contemplation of the present, by being shown some telegram about current politics in the evening newspaper. . . . When he sat down to dinner he turned to me and said, 'Among the many friends who have deserted me since I left office, the one I regret most is my old friend and companion my stomach, which is by no means so true to me as he was.'

[1] Otto, 3rd Prince von Bismarck, born September 27th, 1897, succeeded his father 1904.

[562]

This led me to speak of someone who sat through long dinners without eating a morsel, and I asked him if that was not the case with Victor Emmanuel. He replied that it was, and that he well remembered watching him at dinner presiding in this fasting fashion, but at midnight he would become clamorous for an enormous meal. . . .

"He talked of having been in Glasgow, and of having gone thence to a place which was pronounced 'Curcoobree' and spelled Kirkcudbright, and which he pronounced and spelled quite correctly, for the purpose he thought of visiting the scene of one of Scott's novels. . . .

"He talked about the Hohenzollern candidature for the throne of Spain. Prince Hohenzollern, the former candidate, had been writing to the papers to say that his candidature was entirely Bismarck's affair and plan. 'For the sake of my game,' said the Prince, 'I do not care to contradict him; for we have eight miles of frontier together at Varzin, and he could therefore be a disagreeable neighbour. But, as a matter of fact, it was his father who pushed the affair. He was devoured with the idea, after his son had become Prince of Roumania, that he was destined to have two sons, one King of Spain, and the other Emperor of Constantinople.' He, Prince Bismarck, had thought that the Prince, as a descendant of Murat, would have been rather agreeable to the French than otherwise, that he would pass through Paris to Madrid, and would then arrange things with the Emperor. He never thought that a German King in Spain would be of any use to Prussia, and did not dream that it would cause much offence to France. . . .

"I asked him if Thiers was clever. He said very clever and very business-like, and repeated what he had once told me before, about his speaking German to them, and Favre going off into theatrical despair, while little Thiers went and wrote on a piece of paper in the corner, and handed it to him saying, '*Est-ce que cela fait votre affaire?*' and it was quite satisfactory.

"But Thiers, however, made one great mistake. He was filled with the Napoleonic ideas of making war, and asked Bismarck not to fix the ransom of Paris at too high a figure. Bismarck had never had the slightest idea of asking any ransom for Paris, as he considered that included in the indemnity. He at once asked for (I think) a milliard, and Thiers was delighted when he had beaten him down to two hundred millions. This money the old King sorely wanted to take for his army, whether as a military fund, or for distribution, I did not clearly understand. Bismarck told him to take it if he chose, and no one would say anything—certainly he would not. But the King wanted Bismarck's signature, and that, Bismarck said, was impossible. For the moment *he* took it, he should have to account for it, and then it would no longer be available for the King's purposes. There was a long struggle of this kind, and eventually the King did not dare take it, and so lost it.

[563]

"I was always under the impression that the choice before the French was either to give up Belfort, or to receive the Prussian troops in Paris. But to-night it appeared that it was a choice between taking Belfort or Metz, but Belfort would have required ten thousand men to hold it, and Thiers got it back by representing that he could not get the Treaty through the Assembly without it. As it was, the Treaty was signed much more promptly than Bismarck expected (at least, so I understood), which was managed by special trains to Bordeaux. At this stage he spoke of his great anxiety to conclude peace promptly, being in hourly dread of the intervention of some third power—England, or Russia.

"At the beginning of the Campaign some Italian revolutionaries waited upon him to offer, if he provided some money, five millions of francs I think, and some arms, to dethrone the King if he took arms for France. Crispi was among them, or at least his representative. However, the matter fell through, as the Italians remained quiescent.

"Presently Bismarck remarked to me, 'There is one calamity which Providence has spared me, that of being King of Italy.' I told him that even that would be preferable to being King of Greece, which he admitted.

"I recommended him to read Le Brun's *Memoirs*, giving an account of Le Brun's negotiations with the Archduke Albert before the war. As to that, he said he had heard, or he believed, that the Russians had threatened to march three hundred thousand men into Austria, if she moved. And so heartily was the Emperor of Russia with the Germans that, on receiving the telegram announcing the first German victory, he had shouted out with regard to the King—'After all, he is a fine old fellow,' and drinking his health had thrown the glass over his shoulder to break it against the wall.

" 'Well,' said Prince Bismarck, 'I am glad it is all over. I should not like to have to do it again. I feel like the man who rode through the snow, always afraid of riding into the Lake of Constance, which was on his way, and when he met a man and asked him where it was, found that he had ridden across it without knowing it, in the snow, and was so struck with horror at what he had done that he fell down dead. But,' said the Prince, 'it was not so bad to deal with the old King. He was not always easy, but he was at any rate a gentleman, and one could trust him.'

"As to life, since the death of his wife he was weary of it. He had nothing to live for. I said he had his children. 'No,' he said, 'They are all happily settled; they would shed a tear or two, and then it would be over.' It is curious, by the by, that, within a few weeks, I should have found both Bismarck and Gladstone weary of life. . . .

"All this time we had been seated in a sort of circle round the Prince.

[564]

The conversation was entirely confined to him and to me, unless Herbert interposed to assist in a reminiscence. At last they told him that it was half-past eleven o'clock, which was his bed-time, and he took leave of us. The evening had been a great treat, because he seldom speaks a word at night, but buries himself in his newspapers. They deceived him purposely as to the time at which I was leaving, so that he should not get up to see me off."

A Jubilee Hymn

King of Kings and Lord of Lords
  Hear a kneeling nation's prayers;
For this happy day affords
  Gratitude for sixty years.
Hear our voice of thankfulness
  Rising to thy face unseen;
Bless our Sovereign Mother, bless
  Thy chosen Servant, bless our Queen.

Bless her children, bless her race,
  So may, when the time arrives,
Those who never saw her face
  Bless her living in their lives.
Bless the memories of the dead
  That o'ershade her lonely throne;
Bless the tears that she has shed
  For sorrows other than her own.

Bless her subjects, bless our land,
  Church and Senate, home and mart,
Bind her people hand to hand,
  Close and closer, heart to heart.
Bless her empire, where 'tis written
  Land with sea for once agrees,
Lands of Britain, seas of Britain,
  British lands athwart the seas.

King of Kings and Lord of Lords,
  Hush the angry nations' rage,
Still the clamour, sheathe the swords,
  And the wrath of man assuage.
Let the archangels of peace
  Compass us with guardian wings,
Unity and faith increase,
  Lord of Lords and King of Kings.

And when to the trumpet's peal,
   At thy seat of judgment dread,
Sovereigns and subjects kneel,
   Pale battalions of the dead,
Lord, have mercy, purge our taint,
   Sin and wrath, in love divine:
Kingdoms here are shadows faint;
   May we reign with Thee in Thine.

II

Lord, our only help and stay,
   Through this life to that unseen,
Suppliant we bring our thanks,
   Lord, we bless Thee for our Queen.
Cherish and prolong her years,
   Guide her with Thy sovereign grace,
Grant she may, when Thou shalt call,
   See Thy glory, face to face.

Frankincense let others bring,
   Wealth of spikenard, stores of myrrh;
Our oblation is a Life,
   Many a long and toilsome year.
Fourscore years of light and cloud,
   Carked with care but pure of stain,
Scarred with sorrow, bright with faith,
   Lord, we bring Victoria's reign.

Glories gild our Empire here,
   Spacious rule on earth and sea,
Glories dim, and futile rule,
   If not consecrate to Thee.
Rushlights in Thy shadeless sun,
   Transient our splendour vain.
Power and wisdom only rest
   With the Lamb for mortals slain.

Living streams of crystal pure,
   From Thy throne, O Lord, proceed;
Let them cleanse our life below,
   Sanctify each word and deed,
Cast we down our crowns of gold,
   Seek we crowns of thorns like thine;

[567]

Let us lose this world for Thee,
  Mortal glories for divine.

Yet, O Lord, we fain would ask
  Blessings for one earthly crown;
Grant that it may represent
  Living faith and pure renown.
Bless the Queen and bless the realm;
  So may Queen and Kingdom own
Duty gives the crown on earth,
  Glory is with God alone.

Index

Germany, relations with England, 187-189, 213, 276-279, 366
  Rosebery in, 192, 195
Gibbon, Edward, cited, 41
  Rosebery's reading of, 304
Gibraltar, 227
Giers, Nikolai de, Russian Chancellor, 218
Gimcrack Stakes, races, 283
Girard, William, 96, 97
Gladiateur Stakes, races, 283
Gladstone, Herbert, 459
  as Junior Lord of the Treasury, 185, 186
  Irish problems attitude, 202
Gladstone, Mary (see Drew, Mary Gladstone), 548
Gladstone, William Ewart, 8, 37, 89, 155, 215, 235, 302
  at Dalmeny, 199
  comments on Rosebery, 223, 389, 545
  correspondence, 173, 321, 339, 431
  death, 451
  Egyptian problems, 129, 338
  fissure in Liberal Party, 239
  foreign interests, 222
  House of Lords reform, 164, 278
  illness, 319
  Irish problems, 75, 117, 120, 180, 200, 203-206, 274-276
  Labouchere episode, 331
  Midlothian campaign of 1879-80, 102-106
  navy problems, 356
  offers to Rosebery, 67-70, 107, 137, 139, 157, 168, 171, 173, 207, 317-326, 332
  opinion of Rosebery, 112
  political reverses, 316
  quoted in defense of racing, 75
  reading, 207
  retirement, 359
  Rosebery's friendship with, 97, 100, 137, 152, 206, 266, 295, 303, 343, 387, 430, 440, 451, 497
  Scottish question attitude, 122-129, 131
  second government, 99
  speeches, 103, 223
  talks with Rosebery, 182, 191, 304, 316, 326, 329
  Turkish problem, 79, 80, 424
Gladstone, Mrs. William Ewart, 37
  political interests, 132, 169
  Rosebery's friendship with, 206, 422

Gladstone Club, Glasgow University, 103, 112
Glasgow, Rosebery's speeches in, 134, 196, 199, 224, 241, 250, 291, 294, 332, 380, 396, 453, 477, 492, 493, 496, 497, 500, 501, 511, 532, 534
Glasgow Public School Union, Rosebery's speech at inaugural gathering of, 52
Glasgow Trades House, 294
Glasgow University, 103, 533
  Rosebery as Chancellor of, 493
  Rosebery as Lord Rector of, 91, 296, 491
Globe, London, 82
Goa, India, 235
Godley, Arthur, 115
Gold Cup, race, 553
Goldfinch, horse, 552
Goldsmiths' College, Rosebery's speech at, 503
Goluchowski, Count, 455
Goodwood, race meeting, 282, 552
Gordon, Sir Arthur, 154
  of Colombo, 151
Gordon, Charles, Egyptian command, 168, 173
Gordon Memorial College, Rosebery's support of, 455
Goschen, George J., Viscount, 237, 239
  as guest of Rosebery, 195
  Rosebery's talk with, 156
Gough, Alexander, 6
Gough, Catherine Canham, 6
Graham, Sir James, 100
Granada, 314, 436
Grangemouth, Rosebery's speech at, 199
Grant, Charles, 521
Grant, Sir Alexander, 532
Grant, Sir Robert, 521
Grant, Ulysses S., 58
Granville, George, Earl, 38, 45, 46, 67, 84, 98, 452
  Alabama Claims debates, 71
  as Foreign Secretary, 209
  Australian-French issue, 165
  congratulated by Rosebery, 114
  correspondence, 33, 169, 192
  death, 305
  horse supply investigation, 75
  House of Lords reform, 166, 257, 259
  Irish problems attitude, 180
  oratory, 72
  political influence, 69

Marischal, Earls, 3
Marjoribanks, Edward (*see* Tweed-mouth, E d w a r d Marjoribanks, Lord)
Marjoribanks, Fanny, Lady (*see* Tweedmouth, Fanny, Lady)
Marlborough House, frequenters of, 95
Marriage of Peleus and Thetis, The, Rosebery, 16
Marschall von Bieberstein, Baron, 293
Marseilles, Rosebery in, 526
Mary, Queen, 539
Mary, Queen of Scots, Rosebery's speech on, 18
Massingham, H. W., 481
Masson, David, Rosebery's tribute to, 445
Maxwell, Sir William Stirling, 48
Mecca, Richard Burton, 229
Melbourne, Roseberys in, 141, 143, 145
Melville, Whyte, quoted, 38
"Memoirs of His Own Time," Rose-bery, 16
"Mendacious Club," 54, 140
Mensdorff, Count Albert, 540
Mentmore, improvements at, 506
  racing stable, 551, 552, 553
  Rosebery's life at, 172, 193, 195, 206, 301, 388, 426
  the Rothschild estate, 92
Merchants of Edinburgh, Company of, Rosebery's speech at, 496
Mercury, Leeds, 99; 329, *note*; 486
Meredith, George, 280
Messina, 462
Michelangelo, 40, 42
Middle Park Plate, race, 285, 551, 552
Middleton, Earl of, 2
Midlothian, county election campaign of 1879-80, 100-106
  Dalmeny (Harry) returned for, 525
  Gladstone's victory at the poll, 199
  Rosebery as Lord Lieutenant of, 157
  Rosebery created Earl of, 529
Midlothian Boy Scouts, Rosebery's speech to, 534
Midlothian Garrison Artillery Volun-teers, Rosebery's speech to, 500
Midlothian Liberal Association, 182
Milan, 264, 304
Milner, Alfred, Viscount, 172, 176
  in the South African War, 468
  in the South African problem, 463
Milner, Sir Frederick, 523

Milton, John, 16
  quoted, 14
Miner, The, horse, 284
Minto, Gilbert John, Earl of, 454
Miramar, Italy, 524
Miscellanies, John Buchan, x
Miss Agnes, horse, 283
Mr. Smith, Mrs. Walford, 235
Mr. Sponge's Sporting Tour, Surtees, 38, *note*
Molyneux Stakes, race, 284
Monarch, boat, 13
Monasteries of the Levant, Robert Curzon, 21
Monroe Doctrine, 425
Monson, Sir Edmund, 345
Montalembert, Comte de, 43
Montrose, 5th Duke of, 523
Montrose, Duchess of, 523
Morier, Sir Robert, 215
  Rosebery's communications with, 218
Morley, Albert, 3rd Earl of, 37
  foreign attitude, 84
  on English government, 112
Morley, Arnold, letter to Rosebery, 432
Morley, John, ix, 169, 280, 360, 451; 262, *note*
  congratulations to Rosebery, 169
  defense of Rosebery, 365
  friendship with Rosebery, 115, 264, 306, 321, 327, 334, 437, 539, 540
  friction with Rosebery, 363
  House of Lords reform, 257, 520
  in the South African trouble, 464
  Labouchere episode, 329
  later political interests, 456
  literary work, 389
  London interests, 311
  meeting at Leeds, 239
  opinion of Rosebery's writings, 393
  quoted, 95, 494, 545
  retirement, 455
  speeches, 364
  talks with Rosebery, 243, 303, 410
Mormons, Rosebery's notes on, 55
Mossop, J. H., 40
Moukhtar, Pasha, 238
Mundig, horse, 35
Murray, Sir George, x, 410, 539
Murray, John, speech of, 498

Nairne, Carolina, 4
Napier, John, 4

[583]

Rosebery, Archibald Philip, 5th Earl of
—(*Continued*)
Confirmation, 12
deafness, 528
death, 541
democracy theories, 114
early life of, 8-19
education, 9-20, 26-29, 31, 32, 35, 294
Egypt problems, attitude, 219-221,
  236, 338-343, 366
employment reform attitude, 196
financial difficulties, 312
foreign interests, 80, 82-86, 165, 187,
  242, 253, 276, 290, 328, 365-369, 422-
  425, 429, 438-440, 449, 452, 454, 459,
  462-471, 472, 477
friends, 15, 27, 37, 40, 41, 52-66, 91-
  97, 106, 280, 300, 304, 356, 402, 411,
  417, 426, 450, 456, 480, 507, 522,
  539-545, 547
grandchildren, 541
handwriting, 36, 339, 416
House of Lords reform attitude, 279,
  369-380, 408
hunting, 20, 28, 34, 437
illnesses, 97, 103, 108-110, 167, 358,
  410, 526
Imperial creed, 149, 166, 224, 249-253
impression of a political torchlight
  procession in New York City, 61
Irish problems attitude, 120, 155, 179-
  186, 198, 221, 224, 241-244, 261, 269,
  274-276, 289, 349, 364, 487
landholdings, 196
last illness, 537
letters (*see* individual correspondents)
literary interests, 14, 16, 235, 312,
  389-400, 408, 495, 525, 540
London interests, 263, 266-273, 279,
  290, 310-312, 332, 384, 410, 435, 453
Lord Rectorships, 87-91, 112, 297, 491,
  493, 532
marriage, 92
Napoleon collection, 494
oratory, 72, 73, 101-139, 200, 546
Order of St. Stephen of Hungary
  conferred on, 529
Order of the Garter conferred on, 332
Order of the Thistle conferred on,
  416
pastimes, 13, 34, 443
personality, 15, 35, 47, 54, 77, 101,
  267, 294, 425, 434, 542-547, 549
political life, 30, 33, 44-46, 67-86, 101-
  139, 155-178, 179-186, 194-226, 256-

Rosebery, Archibald Philip, 5th Earl of
—(*Continued*)
  281, 302-304, 315-332, 419-434, 481-
  494, 501, 510-521, 529-532, 542
racing interests, 34, 37, 73, 282-286,
  385, 549, 551-553
reading, 26, 151, 153, 229, 235, 301,
  399, 503, 526, 548
religious attitude, 51, 61, 94, 547
resignation of Liberal Party leadership, 429
royal title dispute, 78
Scottish interests, 50, 113, 122-129,
  131, 134, 137-139, 194, 262, 265
social life, 137, 165, 245, 386, 507
speeches (*see* separate occasions *and*
  places)
travels, 29, 32, 40-44, 52-66, 130, 140-
  155, 192, 195, 237-239, 264, 281, 287,
  293, 304, 306, 310, 313, 318, 418,
  422, 437, 446, 501, 525-528
Turkish dispute, 81
yachting, 501, 525
Rosebery, Dorothea, Lady, 5
Rosebery, Hannah, Lady (wife of Rosebery), death, 298, 521
early life of, 92
illnesses, 281, 294-298
letters, 108
on Gladstone, 97
political interests, 97, 103, 132, 169
religious nature, 93
Rosebery's affection for, 300
travels, 130, 140-155, 227-239, 281,
  287
Rosebery, James, 2nd Earl of, 5
Rosebery, Neil, 3rd Earl of, 6
Rosebery, Villa, 310, 502, 526
Rosebery's parting with, 527
Rosebery's purchase of, 446
Rosebery Club, Edinburgh University,
  112, 199
Rosebery house, 508, 537
Rosicrucian, horse, 284, 551
Rosslyn, Robert, 4th Earl of, 39
Scottish church patronage stand, 77
Rothschild, Adolph, Baron, villa at
  Pregny, 288
Rothschild, Alphonse, Baron de, 306
Rothschild, Edmond, Baron, de, 540
Rothschild, Evelina, Baroness, de, 94
Rothschild, Evelyn de, 538
Rothschild, Ferdinand, Baron, 66, 92, 94
death, 456
Rosebery entertained by, 455